THE
Penguin History
of
AMERICAN
LIFE

PENGUIN BOOKS

MIDDLE PASSAGES

James T. Campbell is an associate professor of American Civilization, Africana Studies and History at Brown University. He is the author of *Songs of Zion: The African Methodist Episcopal Church in the United States and South Africa* (1995), which was awarded the Organization of American Historians' Frederick Jackson Turner Prize and the Carl Sandburg Literary Award for Non-Fiction. A graduate of Yale and Stanford, he lives with his family in Barrington, Rhode Island.

M·i·d·d·l·e PASSAGES

*African American
Journeys to Africa,
1787 - 2005*

JAMES T. CAMPBELL

PENGUIN BOOKS

PENGUIN BOOKS

Published by the Penguin Group

Penguin Group (USA) Inc., 375 Hudson Street, New York, New York 10014, U.S.A. • Penguin
Group (Canada), 90 Eglinton Avenue East, Suite 700, Toronto, Ontario, Canada M4P 2Y3
(a division of Pearson Penguin Canada Inc.) • Penguin Books Ltd, 80 Strand, London
WC2R 0RL, England • Penguin Ireland, 25 St Stephen's Green, Dublin 2, Ireland (a division of
Penguin Books Ltd) • Penguin Group (Australia), 250 Camberwell Road, Camberwell, Victoria
3124, Australia (a division of Pearson Australia Group Pty Ltd) • Penguin Books India Pvt Ltd,
11 Community Centre, Panchsheel Park, New Delhi – 110 017, India • Penguin Group (NZ),
67 Apollo Drive, Mairangi Bay, Auckland 1311, New Zealand (a division of Pearson New
Zealand Ltd) • Penguin Books (South Africa) (Pty) Ltd, 24 Sturdee Avenue,
Rosebank, Johannesburg 2196, South Africa

Penguin Books Ltd, Registered Offices:
80 Strand, London WC2R 0RL, England

First published in the United States of America by The Penguin Press,
a member of Penguin Group (USA) Inc. 2006
Published in Penguin Books 2007

1   3   5   7   9   10   8   6   4   2

Grateful acknowledgment is made for permission to reprint "The Negro Speaks of Rivers,"
"Poem (1)," "Afro-American Fragment," and excerpts from "Negro," "Aunt Sue's Stories,"
"Danse Africaine," "Johannesburg Mines," and "Advertisement for the Waldorf Astoria" from
The Collected Poems of Langston Hughes. Copyright © 1994 by The Estate of Langston Hughes.
Used by permission of Alfred A. Knopf, a division of Random House, Inc.

Illustration credits appear on page 514.

THE LIBRARY OF CONGRESS HAS CATALOGED THE HARDCOVER EDITION AS FOLLOWS:
Campbell, James T.
Middle passages : African American journeys to Africa, 1787–2005 / James Campbell.
p. cm.
Includes bibliographical references and index.
ISBN 1-59420-083-1 (hc.)
ISBN 978-0-14-311198-6 (pbk.)
1. Africa—Description and travel. 2. African Americans—Travel—Africa—History
I. Title.
DT12.25.C36   2006
005058672

Printed in the United States of America
Designed by Marysarah Quinn

For my parents,
Ralph E. Campbell and
Patricia Tierney Campbell,
with love and gratitude

Preface

DAVID LEVERING LEWIS

When Ludwig Max Goldberger's *Land of Unlimited Possibilities* was published in 1903, nearly three hundred years of American history were said to attest to the admiring German economist's thesis. Scholarship then and since, notwithstanding occasional dissents in recent days, has certified the national gospel of material and social progress. America was unique, the place where people disencumbered themselves from their pasts, where they lived in a perpetual state of renewal and reinvention. America was the past transcended and forgotten; it was history's tabula rasa.

By striking coincidence, *Land of Unlimited Possibilities* appeared in the same year as W. E. B. Du Bois's *The Souls of Black Folk*, a book bearing an equally iconic title, but a book unveiling American experiences that were practically the antitheses of the possibilities lauded by the former as virtual birthrights. Not only was the rags-to-riches world of mainstream popular imagination absent from *The Souls of Black Folk*, poverty was revealed as a constituent of color in America. No limitless possibilities existed for those racially exempted from the miraculous agency of laisser faire. Du Bois described a condition in which the active citizenship of an entire racial group had been nullified in law, politics, and practice—a people reduced to the status of outsiders in their own country. "It is a peculiar sensation, this double-consciousness," he wrote in this Ur-text of the African American's three hundred-year quest for definition and identity. "One ever feels his two-ness—an American, a Negro; two souls, two thoughts, two unreconciled strivings. . . ."

In this first book in the Penguin History of American Life series, James Campbell chooses the wide Atlantic world as the theater in which to address this tortured quest of the African American personality for self-definition over against the limited possibilities of a racially constricted universe. The focus and scope of this book, as with those soon to come from the Penguin History of American Life series, embody the interdisciplinary and integrationist ambitions of a twelve-member editorial board that seeks projects that engage history vertically as well as horizontally. We are committed to historical writing that demonstrates the permeability of traditional boundaries, whether geographical, ethnic, or cultural, and the value of blurring conventional categories of historical writing.

Middle Passages: African American Journeys to Africa, 1787–2005 is destined to claim a place in the forefront of the new history that calls itself, variously, Global, Diasporic, and Atlantic because it achieves in reality what has been in large measure an aspiration. A growing academic chorus rightly insists that the imbrication of the particular and the general requires ambitious conceptual parameters in which the local must be understood globally and vice versa. But as a number of recent titles signifying a new interpretive catholicity reveals, writing the new history is inordinately demanding and also noticeably deficient in results. Considerations of language fluency and disciplinary dexterity aside, the problem is that macro-history too often swallows up what is discrete or unique in a mass of thesis-driven generalities (a besetting aspect of the old annales school); or, conversely, that history in microcosm or as sub-field parochializes the global. As Campbell's achievement demonstrates, the trick is to discern in a given historical exploration what is complementarily illustrative and explanatory.

Campbell's book poses a bedrock question about a perennial. The question was implicit from the day in May 1787 when three English ships out of Plymouth deposited 411 bewildered souls at the mouth of the Sierra Leone

River on Africa's Windward Coast. The West African colony was the philanthropic solution conceived by Sir Granville Sharpe (famous for his defense in the *Somerset* case effectively ending slavery in Great Britain) and the Committee for the Black Poor to the problem of destitute black people, whose numbers had increased tenfold in England with the arrival of former American slaves at the end of the War of Independence. Two years later, the Sierra Leone colony lay moribund, its Granville Town settlement torched by the local African potentate, many settlers dead of malaria or hiring themselves to the British slave fort up the Sierra Leone River. The obvious question is, what did these transplanted American Negroes make of a British experiment in West Africa that would be replicated a few decades later by powerful white interests in the United States? What did Africa mean to them?

Africans on the North American continent have asked that question in various ways for more than three centuries. The author's remarkable narrative tunes in with virtually perfect fidelity on some two hundred years of this interrogative wave band, from the first organized efforts at return at the beginning of the nineteenth century to the expectations and recriminations of the ambivalent sojourners of recent years. Harlem Renaissance poet Countee Cullen's well known "Heritage" serves as an epigraph establishing one of *Middle Passages*'s two leitmotifs: "What is Africa to me: . . . *One three centuries removed / From the scenes his father loved / Spicy groves, cinnamon tree / What is Africa to me?*"

James Campbell's second leitmotif echoes Du Bois's famous interrogation in *Souls:* "How does it feel to be a problem?" From the record of black Americans' presumptuous equivocations toward Africa on the one hand, and their everlasting war of identity in America on the other (Cullen twinned with Du Bois), Campbell fashions a one-of-a-kind book, wherein the cross-pollination of biography and history transports the reader almost seamlessly into and out of eras and cultures and between continents and personalities. As the author propounds, "strange as it may sound, Africa has served historically as one of the chief terrains on which Americans have negotiated their relationship to American society. To put the matter more simply, when an African American asks, 'What is Africa to me?' he or she is also asking 'What is America to me?'"

But before the questions and the answers are addressed, readers encounter in the "curious story" of one Ayuba Sulieman Diallo a complicated truth still too often absent from the literature, the scholarship of Ira Berlin or John Thornton notwithstanding. Ayuba, son of a Fula Muslim notable engaged in the slave trade, falls into bondage himself in the early eighteenth century. He survives the lethal "middle passage," his left shoulder branded with the Royal Africa Company's RAC, impresses his Maryland masters and eventually the British philanthropist James Oglethorpe with his Arabic literacy, enjoys a season of celebrity among the English upper crust who finance Ayuba's return to his Gambia home in the summer of 1734. As the British slave traffic's earliest African returnee, Ayuba was proof positive to the Fulani that those who vanished into the Atlantic slave trade were not "generally either eaten or murdered, since none ever returned." Ayuba promptly returned to the family business of human commerce. "Most obviously," Campbell writes, "his experience highlights African participation in the transatlantic slave trade, an issue of considerable controversy in the eighteenth century, as it remains today." While the institution of West African slavery is not the major concern, *Middle Passages* leaves this fraught topic with the crucial reminder that, as Robin Blackburn's *The Making of New World Slavery* has shown with definitive clarity, the scale, inhumanity, and ideology of African slavery were radically exacerbated in the vortex of transatlantic commerce.

No such experience as Ayuba Sulieman Diallo's is readily imaginable in the American South of a century later. While Ayuba's benefactors had still seen him as a sable gentleman, James Campbell's early-nineteenth-century subjects living in the wake of the Haitian Revolution, Eli Whitney's cotton gin, and South Carolina's Stono Rebellion were seen, North as well as South, as members of a race whose subjugation made it virtually impossible for whites to acknowledge individual promise or achievement. The Sierra Leone colony of Granville Sharpe's initiative having survived through an infusion of Jamaican Maroons and Nova Scotian blacks (more American slaves manumitted for British military service during the Revolution), its formal establishment in 1807 heartened American free people of color. A literate handful, like Baltimorean Daniel Coker, first bishop of the new African Methodist

Episcopal Church (AME), and Paul Cuffee, remarkable Newport, Rhode Island, merchant and sea captain who actually financed and led two exploratory voyages to Sierra Leone between 1810 and 1815, began contemplating the ancestral homeland as their Zion. Emigrationist fever spread among the free populations of Baltimore, Philadelphia, Boston, and Newport. America had come to seem a dead end to these men and women—" strangers and outcasts in a strange land," said one Newporter.

Africa beckoned them as a field for redemption where their superior knowledge and divine guidance could "improve the condition of the degraded inhabitants of the land of [my] ancestors," as Cuffe is quoted as saying. None questioned the regnant European gospel of African moral and material backwardness or, indeed, the truth, as Booker T. Washington would be wont to say, that the school of American Negro slavery had been strangely providential in delivering them from their ancestors' savagery and ignorance. Indeed, when early-nineteenth-century Africans in America began leaving for Africa they brought along their own version of racial superiority: Ethiopianism. If Wilson Moses retrieved its historical importance in his classic, *The Golden Age of Black Nationalism*, the characters in *Middle Passages* are walking elucidations of the Ethiopianist gospel—"Princes shall come out of Egypt; Ethiopia shall soon stretch forth her hands unto God."

African American notables conceived of themselves as forming the vanguard of an African "race" rising to greatness under Negro American tutelage. "This land only wants industrious, informed, and Christian people to make it one of the greatest nations in the world," Bishop Daniel Coker preached, and thereby expressed an Ethiopianist constant embraced down the decades past Martin Delany, Henry McNeal Turner, W. E. B. Du Bois, and George Schuyler to Era Bell Thompson, Richard Wright, and Keith Richburg, mutatis mutandis the Civil War, two World Wars, the cold war, the civil rights revolution, and the New World Order. Using Africa to prove a point about African America was, far more often than not, what Africa meant to African Americans.

And yet, *Middle Passages* shows that things weren't always that simple. For many blacks in antebellum America, emigrationism lost its appeal after Speaker of the House of Representatives Henry Clay publicly revealed that the new American Colonization Society's Jeffersonian repatriationists, Federalist evangelicals, and calculating Upper South slaveholders were plotting the removal to Liberia of what they deemed to be the anomalous presence of a free black population in the United States. In heated public assemblies in Philadelphia, Newport, and elsewhere, black people united in declaring, in effect, that "we won't go to Africa if white folk want to send us there." From that time until now, as the perusal of Campbell reveals, African Americans have adamantly insisted on being quintessentially American whenever others hint that they might be better off elsewhere.

But go they did, even so, and their significance in Africa as Protestant missionaries has, until *Middle Passages* (and *Songs of Zion,* James Campbell's pathbreaking first book), been much underappreciated. On the dubious proposition of "sympathy of blood," white missionary organizations dispatched black missionaries in the years from the Berlin Conference of 1884 to World War I to Angola, Cameroon, the Congo Free State, Mozambique, Nyasaland, Rhodesia, and South Africa. A.M.E. missionaries likewise carried the gospel to Liberia, South Africa, and the Congo with as much or as little "sympathy of blood." A.M.E. Bishop Henry McNeal Turner, a leonine race man as eloquent as Frederick Douglass and perhaps the leading emigrationist voice in the late nineteenth century, traveled four times to Africa and established missions in Liberia and South Africa. Turner was the Ethiopian gospeler par excellence: Campbell reminds us that he once made the shockingly preposterous proposal that slavery be reinstituted in Africa so that African Americans could hold the Africans in bondage for seven uplifting years. The black nationalist Martin Delany's quixotic engagement with Africa, egotistically related in his *Official Report of the Niger Valley Explorer Party* (1861), has drawn a fair share of scholarly attention elsewhere as another of those who were, writes the author, "alienated from the land of his birth, yet steeped in its fundamental values."

Ethiopianist gospelers to a man, a few were simply sui generis. None of the author's pre–World War I figures, however, surpassed in adventurousness and achievement the missionary superstar William Henry Sheppard, rescued by *Middle Passages* from historical limbo. A character out of Somerset Maugham's *Rain* and Joseph Conrad's *Heart of Darkness,* Sheppard arrived in Africa in 1890 as the subaltern of Reverend Samuel Lapsley, an aristocratic white southern Presbyterian missionary. A young man whose meek demeanor belied his fine physique, Sheppard coped so competently with disease, death, cannibalism, and the near genocidal mayhem racking King Leopold's Congo that the relationship with his white superior was quickly reversed as the delicate Lapsley faded. The moment related in this book where the two missionaries encounter George Washington Williams, father of Negro History, at Stanley Pool (today's Kinshasa) as he exits the Congo for the United States bent on exposing the horror of Leopold's stygian enterprise is grippingly symbolic. Campbell trumps that moment with the disclosure that after meeting Conrad at Stanley Pool, Sheppard and Lapsley embarked on the very steamer described by the Polish novelist in *Heart of Darkness* as he chugged slowly upriver and beyond civilization.

Sheppard stayed in the Congo more than twenty years, planting a Presbyterian mission station among people who soon sought his protection if not his god. He mastered the languages, photographed sites and peoples, and studied the customs with an anthropological eye so precise that his notebooks served as models for the field. His writings, speeches, and honorary membership in Britain's Royal Geographical Society enabled Sheppard to speak with powerful authority about Leopold's atrocities in the Congo after his return to the United States. But status as an honorary white man was at a discount in Virginia where Sheppard returned to live with his wife and children.

Langston Hughes's debut in *Middle Passages* signals the advent of a new wrinkle in the Ethiopianist creed. The existential question had been altered by Freud, the Great War, and the Great Black Migration out of the South. "Civilization has met its Waterloo," Hughes's distinguished mentor, Du Bois, announced, in keeping with the Spenglerian ethos of the period. The new question, then, wasn't what America could mean to Africa but what Africa could mean to America, rich, materialistic, and soulless? In the famous passage in *I Wonder as I Wander,* the Harlem Renaissance's future bard tosses his books overboard from his freighter as he sails away from Columbia College, his demanding Negrophobic father, and the quotidian humiliations of America under *Plessy v. Ferguson* to West Africa. Hughes's jettisoned library symbolized the poet's zestful disdain for the Eurocentric learning that a later generation of blacks and women would disparage as the canon of Dead White Males. Bishop Turner had wanted to shape up the Africans with Christianity, commerce, and civilization. Hughes's generation, Campbell stresses, wanted Africa to reveal profound truths that could shape the spirit and aesthetic of the West. But if one of Langston Hughes's most famous poems sang that his soul had grown "deep like the rivers" of the Nile and the Congo, he was flustered to find that all the Africans he met believed him to be a white man. Hughes was at the head of a long twentieth-century line of seemingly deracinated blacks on the rebound from Mother Africa who discovered just how much America was in their bones.

After his first experience in Africa, Hughes looked for Africa mostly in Harlem. Jazz Age America (that false dawn of cultural diversity) followed him there. The trope of the era was that America desperately needed the vital artistic and musical energies of Africa and that black Americans were uniquely endowed to mediate them. In this flipped perspective, African Americans were much less inclined to think of themselves as saviors of the "Dark Continent." Rather, Africa was expected to save them. In Du Bois's grand Pan-African schemes, the Continent would gradually shake off the fetters of colonialism to emerge united and powerful, a model of humanity and a living reproach to five hundred years of European exploitation. Marcus Garvey never saw Africa, but his plans for what the Continent was to do for the diaspora's black people were as ambitious as Du Bois's—only, as Campbell's engrossing chapter makes clear, Garvey's designs were antithetical to Du Bois because they were Garvey's and vice versa.

When Africa's long awaited postcolonial era arrived, African Americans watched with exhilaration as Ghana, Nigeria, the Congo, and the Francophone belt of nations achieved independence. By the mid-1960s, though, exhilaration had dissipated in the face of army coups d'etat, grandiose economic projects, the rigged international market, and cold war intrusions, as *Middle Passages'* excellent reckoning makes depressingly clear. As African politics and economics began to perform embarrassingly, moreover, the civil rights revolution in the United States seemed to foretell a "Second Reconstruction." Until then, the Continent had been seen by growing numbers of black

Americans as the lodestar of a planetary future in which proud people of color would enjoy a decision-making majority. "Black Star," the author's eighth chapter captures that period of almost conveyor-belt black American expatriation to Ghana, Nigeria, Tanganyika, and Senegal, of slave-fort tourism and celebrity sojourns. *Ebony* magazine discovered the sub-Sahara for the black bourgeoisie in a series of articles and photos by their analytically innocent correspondent, Era Bell Thompson. Honesty requires the disclosure that one David Levering Lewis has a reference among the tribe of Ph.D.s hired by the University of Ghana.

Finally, then, 218 years after those three ships out of Plymouth deposited a group of former American slaves at the mouth of the Sierra Leone River, what has Africa come to mean to the Africans in America who populate James Campbell's intellectually capacious book? One line of mid- to late-twentieth-century thought seems to descend from George Schuyler's *Slaves Today: A Story of Liberia* (1930) through Richard Wright's *Black Power: A Record of Reactions in a Land of Pathos* (1954) to *Washington Post* Africa correspondent Keith Richburg's *Out of America: A Black Man Confronts Africa* (1997). Theirs might be described as vintage Ethiopianism updated: Africa is about where Joseph Conrad left it, an atavistic universe in which the commerce, culture, and values of the Occident are horribly deformed, and God bless the United States of America. The second line of thought, more or less descending from Du Bois's *The World and Africa* (1947) through Walter Rodney's *How Europe Underdeveloped Africa* (1972) to *New York Times* Africa correspondent Howard French's *A Continent for the Taking: The Tragedy and Hope of Africa* (2004), makes its bias equally evident by such titles.

A generation ago, Theodore Draper suggested in *The Rediscovery of Black Nationalism* (1970) that African American political culture has adhered to a dialectic in which alienation and militancy historically alternate with optimism and accommodation in reactive response to the perceived degree to which the American social contract is genuinely inclusive. One answer to Countee Cullen's poetic question might come from asking what Americans of African descent think of a book like Ludwig Goldberger's *Land of Unlimited Possibilities* were it to appear in 2005. James Campbell's superlative appreciation of the long, rich, yet fraught, interrogative relationship of one of the oldest American peoples to their imagined place of origin may well prove definitive. Certainly, after *Middle Passages,* we will begin to understand the many meanings of the question.

What Is Africa to Me?

IN 1923, a then little-known twenty-one year old poet named Langston Hughes set sail for Africa. Two years before, Hughes had written "The Negro Speaks of Rivers," in which he traced a continuous river of black history from the Nile and the Congo to the "muddy bosom" of the Mississippi. Determined to trace that river to its source, he signed on as a messmate on a steamer, the *West Hesseltine,* bound from Brooklyn to West Africa. As the ship cleared Sandy Hook, he went belowdecks and collected the crate of books that he had brought along for the voyage. Standing alone on the fantail, he tossed the books, one by one, into the sea, symbolically jettisoning his book-bound Western identity.

The voyage left an enduring imprint on Hughes's poetry, but at the cost of certain preconceptions. In his autobiography, *The Big Sea,* the poet recalled one of his first encounters with Africans, a group of Kru men who had signed on as deckhands when the ship reached the Windward Coast. Expounding on the shared predicament of black people across the globe, he was dismayed to discover that the Africans regarded him as "a white man." This assessment, he learned, had only partly to do with his wavy hair and copper skin.

One of the Kru men from Liberia, working on our ship, who had seen many American Negroes, of various shades and colors, and knew much about America, explained to me.

"Here," he said, "on the West Coast, there are not many colored people—people of mixed blood—and those foreign colored men who are here come mostly as missionaries, to teach us something, since they think we know nothing. Or they come from the West Indies, as clerks and administrators in the colonial governments, to help carry out the white man's laws. So the Africans call them all white men."

"But I am not white," I said.

"You are not black either," the Kru man said simply. "There is a man of my color." And he pointed to George, the pantryman, who protested loudly.

"Don't point at me," George said. "I'm from Lexington, Kentucky, U.S.A. And no African blood, nowhere."

"You black," said the Kru man.

"I can't part my hair," said George, "and it ain't nappy."

But to tell the truth, George shaved a part in his hair every other week, since the comb wouldn't work. The Kru man knew this, so they both laughed loudly, for George's face was as African as Africa.

This "comedy of misrecognition" contains a host of lessons. Hughes's voyage, indeed his entire career, attests to Africa's persistent hold on the African American imagination. George's anxious disavowal reminds us that, historically, the majority of black Americans have not shared the poet's Pan-African sensibility. And the Kru man's matter-of-fact explanation provides perhaps the most important lesson of all: that Africans have ideas and experiences of their own, which sometimes have little to do with the preconceptions of western visitors, white or black.

HUGHES WAS NEITHER the first nor the last person to learn these lessons. Since the last years of the eighteenth century, thousands of African Americans have traveled to Africa, retracing the passage of millions of African captives. The scope of African American history is revealed in the sheer variety of those who have made the journey, from manumitted slaves and missionaries to poets and Peace Corps volunteers. The roster includes many of black America's most eminent political leaders, intellectuals, and artists—Alexander Crummell, Martin Delany, W. E. B. Du Bois, George Schuyler, Ralph Bunche, Richard Wright, Louis Armstrong, Maya Angelou, Martin Luther King, Jr., Malcolm X, Muhammad Ali, and Alice Walker, to name only a few—as well as men and women whose names and struggles have been lost to history. Some settled permanently in Africa, while others, like Hughes, passed through only fleetingly. The most common destination in the nineteenth century was Liberia, an African American colony established on the Windward Coast of West Africa in 1820, but over the years black travelers have found their way to every corner of the continent. Hundreds have produced memoirs of their journeys. In at least one case, members of the same family left accounts more than a century apart: Harry Dean, a swashbuckling ship's captain who set out in the early twentieth century on a self-proclaimed quest to "found an Ethiopian Empire," was (or at least purported to be) the great grandson of Paul Cuffe, who transported a group of settlers from the United States to Sierra Leone in 1816.

The book that follows examines a series of African journeys undertaken by African Americans over the last 220 years. These journeys illuminate African American history in two seemingly contradictory ways. Most obviously, they highlight Africa's abiding presence in black political, intellectual, and imaginative life. Even as direct memories of the continent faded—by the Civil War, only about one percent of black people in the United States were African-born—African Americans continued to look to Africa, seeking in its dim outlines a clue to the meaning of their own bitter, bewildering history. Needless to say, they discerned different things. Where Hughes imagined an idyllic homeland, adherents of the contemporaneous Garvey movement saw the continent as the future seat of a great black empire. Others, traveling at different times and under different auspices, have cast Africa as a "Dark Continent" crying out for Christian civilization, a headquarters for global anticolonial revolution, or a field of opportunity for entrepreneurs. Still others have denied any connection to the continent, the better to advance their claim to full citizenship in the United States. Yet whatever the individual motives and aspirations, every African American has confronted the question that Hughes's contemporary, Countee Cullen, posed so eloquently in his 1925 poem "Heritage": "What is Africa to me?"

If the journeys in this book illuminate African Americans' ties to Africa, they also cast fresh and unexpected light on their relationship to the United States. Langston Hughes's desire to go to Africa (and his impulsive decision to jettison his books along the way) bespoke a deep alienation from the land of his birth, but it also ironically testified to his immersion in a post–World War I American culture consumed by fears of "overcivilization" and a yearning for authentic experience. The particulars differ, but the same kind of entanglement can be seen in the antebellum struggles over African emigration and colonization, in the rise of an African mission movement in the late nineteenth century, in the Black Arts debates of the 1920s and 1960s, and in the emergence, in our own time, of an African heritage tourist industry. As paradoxical as it may sound, Africa has served historically as one of the chief terrains on which African Americans have negotiated their relationship to American society. To put the matter more poetically, when an African American asks "What is Africa to me?" he or she is also asking "What is America to me?"

What is Africa to me? What is America to me? Most of African American history—and much of the history of the United States as a whole—is encompassed by these two intertwined questions. This book examines how different people tried to answer them.

THIS STUDY SPANS more than two centuries and sometimes it feels like it took that long to write. There is no way that I can properly acknowledge all the people who helped me along the way, but let me offer a brief and inadequate thank you to some of them.

While I have relied chiefly on published accounts, I was able to interview a few of the individuals whose journeys are recounted in the book. I am grateful to Ray Kea, Lynne Duke, Bill Sutherland, and the late St. Clair Drake for their generosity and candor. I do not know how to express my gratitude to Robert Lee except to say that speaking with him changed my life. I once asked him how I could ever possibly repay him for the stories he shared. "Just tell the truth," he said. I have tried to honor that injunction.

I have spent most of my adult life working in universities, and one thing about academia: you learn who your friends are. I would like to thank my friends from Northwestern University, especially James Oakes, T.W. Heyck, Peter Hayes, Josef Barton, Ed Muir, the late Robert Wiebe, and the late Leon Forrest. At Brown University, I have been blessed with wonderful colleagues and students, whom I would like to thank collectively. (It would take pages to thank them all.) The years between Northwestern and Brown were spent at the University of the Witwatersrand in Johannesburg, South Africa, where I had the finest colleagues and friends imaginable. If I lived to be a thousand I could not return everything that I owe to Bruce Murray and Charles van Onselen. I hope that they will accept this book as a token of good faith.

I am pleased to acknowledge the support of several research institutions, without which this book would never have been completed. The germ of this study first emerged during a short stay at the W.E.B. Du Bois Center for Pan-African Studies in Accra, Ghana. I began writing in earnest during a year's fellowship at the Charles Warren Center for Studies in American History at Harvard University. The writing was completed during a sabbatical at the Research Institute of Comparative Studies in Race and Ethnicity at Stanford University. It is impossible to imagine more congenial places to work than these. My deepest thanks to the administrators, staff, and affiliated faculty of all three centers, and especially to my fellow fellows for their generosity, humor, and wisdom.

Several individuals read and commented on draft chapters, enriching the book with their insight and saving me from several embarrassing errors. Thank you, David Armitage, Clare Corbould, Annette Counts, Paul Davis, David Engerman, Matthew Guterl, Jonathan Hansen, Christopher Jones, Bruce Schulman (my truest bluest friend), and Glenda Sluga. Needless to say, none of these people is responsible for the errors and misinterpretations that surely remain.

Several scholars graciously shared unpublished work, including James Sidbury, whose fine forthcoming book examines African American ideas about Africa in the colonial and early national period, and Kevin Gaines, who granted me permission to quote and cite his superb study of African American expatriates in Ghana while it was still in manuscript.

Several other people offered essential support. Thank you, Colleen Sullivan, John Hinshaw, Joe Opala, Brianna Larkin, Michael Goldberger, Brett Shadle, Wallace Best, Steven Chanan, Paul la Hausse, Patrick Pearson, Steve Vandermyde, Phil Mancini, and Stephen Greener Davis (who should start charging me rent).

Working with Penguin Press has been a delight. I am especially indebted to my editor, Scott Moyers, and to Janie Fleming, Beena Kamlani, and David Levering Lewis, who first nominated this project for inclusion in Penguin's History of American Life series. Thanks also to Susan Oba for the photographs and to Chelsea Shriver and Kathryn de Boer for the map.

My greatest debts are, as always, to my family. Thanks to Jodi and Kirby, Jack and Lisa, Andy and Breina, Tony and Jib, and, above all, to Chris, who put me up (and put up with me) during my sabbatical year in California. Andrea van Niekerk is the love of my life. Our children, Thomas, Daniel, and Leah, are the proof of God's grace.

The book is dedicated to my parents, who taught me to see.

CONTENTS

Africa, 2006

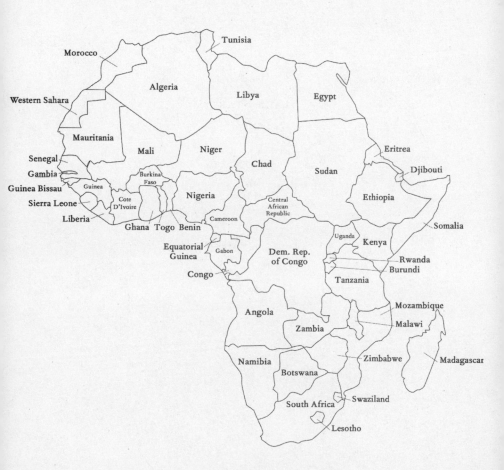

M·i·d·d·l·e
PASSAGES

Ayuba's Journey

IN THE FOUR HUNDRED YEARS after Columbus touched ground at San Salvador, more than twelve million Africans were loaded into ships and borne into the maelstrom of New World slavery.

About five hundred thousand Africans were imported into the territory of what is today the United States. The first recorded arrivals came in 1619, when colonists at Jamestown purchased "twenty Negars" from a "Dutch manne o war," apparently a privateer out of Flanders, which had pirated the cargo of a Portuguese slave ship bound for Vera Cruz. The last enslaved Africans to arrive in the United States sailed into Mobile Bay on the good ship *Clotilde* on a moonless night in 1859, 240 years later. If the first slaves at Jamestown were the offspring of opportunism, the 103 men, women, and children offloaded in the Alabama darkness on the eve of the Civil War were the products of a prank, a wager between local planters to see whether it was still possible, more than a half century after the U.S. Congress had outlawed the transatlantic slave trade, to land a slave ship directly from Africa.

For most, transportation across the Atlantic was a journey of no return.

Yet from the earliest days of the trade, a few captives found their way back to Africa. We will likely never know who these first returnees were, but something of the character of their journeys can be gleaned from the unlikely tale of Ayuba Suleiman Diallo.

Ayuba—appropriately called Job by English contemporaries—was born in 1703 among the Fula (or Fulani) people in an area called Bondou, between the Senegal and Gambia rivers. As his name suggests, he was a Muslim, as were perhaps 10 percent of the Africans imported to the Americas. Sources from the period describe him as a "prince," son of the "king" of Bondou, but he was actually the son of a Marabout, a member of an elite, hereditary class of Muslim clerics. Ayuba was literate, pious, and wealthy. His household included two wives, three children, a substantial herd of cattle, and a large retinue of slaves. Ayuba was no stranger to slavery, but he was certainly not a man who expected to find himself enslaved.

Through the sixteenth and early seventeenth centuries, Ayuba's home region played only a peripheral role in the transatlantic slave trade. While the British and French maintained rival "factories" in the area—the French along the Senegal River, the British along the Gambia—they were chiefly interested in gum, a by-product of the sap of acacia trees, used in the manufacture of everything from candy to paint to medicine. European traders certainly had no qualms about purchasing such captives as were available, but in a region characterized by relative peace and stability the supply was initially too small to sustain a regular trade. The prospects for slaving improved in the 1720s, as the upheaval generated by the emergence of the Bambara empire in the interior unleashed a flow of captives and war prisoners to the coast. By the early 1730s, upward of three thousand people per year were shipped from the region, most of them on British ships bound for the West Indies or mainland North America.

Ayuba's journey into slavery commenced in 1730, when his father dispatched him on a trading mission to Joar, a village along the Gambia, where an English ship, the *Arabella*, had recently anchored. He set out with a small entourage, including two slaves, whom he hoped to trade for paper. Paper was precious to Marabouts, whose income chiefly derived from the sale of *gris gris*, tiny slips of paper inscribed with Koranic verses, which were packed in leather pouches and worn as talismans. Ayuba had previously undertaken several such missions and he completed the two-hundred-mile overland journey without incident, but he and the English ship's captain, a man named Pike, were unable to agree on a price for the captives. With negotiations at an impasse, Ayuba sent his retainers back to Bondou to report to his father, while he and an interpreter, a Fula man named Loumein Yoai, continued south with their captives, across the Gambia, into the country of the "Mandingoes."

The denouement was predictable. The men succeeded in dealing the slaves, whom they exchanged for twenty-eight head of cattle, and set out for home, unaware that they were being followed by a group of Mandinke men. Stopping to rest one hot afternoon, they made the mistake of removing their swords and pistols, and were promptly waylaid. A few days later, Ayuba and Yoai found themselves back in Joar, now as the bartered rather than barterers. In a gesture to fast-eroding traditions of legitimate enslavement, their abductors shaved their heads and beards before selling them—"to make them appear like Slaves taken in war"—but they need not have bothered. Though he recognized the men, Pike had no qualms about buying them. His sole concession was to give Ayuba "leave to redeem himself and his man." A desperate Ayuba sent a message to his father, who immediately dispatched another shipment of slaves to ransom his son. But slave-ship captains were loath to linger with a cargo of fresh captives, and by the time the caravan arrived, the *Arabella* had already sailed.

Sources from the period say nothing about the next chapter of Ayuba's life, during which he endured what historians call the middle passage. If his experience was a typical one, he and Yoai would first have had the initials RAC branded onto their left shoulders, marking them as the property of the Royal Africa Company, the chartered corporation that enjoyed a monopoly on the British slave trade. They would then have been chained together at wrist and ankle and loaded into a low compartment, perhaps three feet high, crammed with hundreds of other men. (Women and children were generally housed in separate compartments from men.) Aside from periods of enforced exercise on deck, they would have spent the next six to eight weeks in the hold, rank with the smell of seasickness and the overflowing "necessary tubs," subsisting on rice and thin gruel, unappetizing fare but adequate to sustain life. Slave-ship captains well appreciated the value of their involuntary passengers, and made every effort to keep them alive. They installed netting along the rails to prevent captives from hurling themselves overboard. Those who refused to eat were force-fed, often using a *speculum oris,* a mechanical device invented for patients with lockjaw but quickly adapted for use on slave ships. Despite such precautions, somewhere between 10 and 20 percent of the captives on a typical voyage perished before reaching the Americas. If a ship were stricken with disease—smallpox, cholera, amoebic dysentery ("bloody flux," in the parlance of the time)—mortality was much higher.

Ayuba survived the middle passage. He found himself in Annapolis, Maryland, where he was auctioned to a Kent Island planter named Tolsey. (Yoai also survived the passage and was sold to a different planter.) Ayuba was initially put to work in a tobacco field, but the shock of capture and transportation had taken a toll, and his health deteriorated. Tolsey assigned him the less arduous task of tending cattle, but still he languished. Awash in despair, frustrated by his inability to communicate with anyone around him, he ran away. But where could he go? Apprehended after a few days, he was consigned to the county jail, while authorities tried to determine the identity of his owner.

The jail in which Ayuba was held was actually the back room of a neighborhood tavern, which ensured that he became something of a local curiosity. Among the curious was an attorney named Thomas Bluett. Bluett, who would later pen a widely circulated biography of "Job Ben Solomon" discerned that this "was no common slave." Doubtless he was reacting in part to Ayuba's appearance—centuries of mixing with Berbers from the north had left Fula people with tawny skin and curly hair rather than the dark skin and crinkly hair of most enslaved Africans—but he was also struck by his "affable carriage and the easy composure of his countenance," suggestive of a man of breeding. The impression was confirmed when Ayuba seized a pen and wrote several lines of what proved to be Arabic. Eventually authorities located an old African in the neighborhood who spoke Joloff, one of the main languages of the Senegambia region, and through him discovered the mysterious captive's identity and heard his tale of woe.

The encounter marked the beginning of Ayuba's return to Africa, a tale of reversal and restoration worthy of a Dickens novel. Indeed, his story bore a curious resemblance to a popular novel of the era, Aphra Behn's *Oronooko; or, the Royal Slave*. The first female-authored novel in the English language, Behn's 1678 romance recounted the story of a Coramantee prince, Oronooko, who was wrongfully enslaved and carried to the West Indies. The prototypical "noble savage," Oronooko was educated, loyal, courageous—in every way the superior of the men who held him bound. After losing his love to a rapacious planter, he orchestrated a massive slave revolt, but was ultimately defeated, captured, and tortured to death. Despite its unsettling subject, Behn's novel proved fabulously popular among contemporaries, going through multiple editions in England and North America. It also became the basis for a perennially popular play, versions of which were staged throughout Europe and the Americas. Bluett was certainly familiar with the story, which may suggest one more reason for his fascination with Ayuba, as well as for his misleading characterization of him as a "prince."

With Bluett's help (and with the consent of Tolsey, who had given up any hope of extracting labor from his captive), Ayuba wrote a letter to his father, "acquainting him with his misfortunes, hoping he might yet find means to redeem him." The letter never reached Africa but it did find its way to London, where it passed through various hands, eventually settling on the desk of James Oglethorpe, a prominent philanthropist, best known to history as the founder of the Georgia colony. Oglethorpe recognized the script as Arabic, and passed the letter on to an Oxford professor for translation. So moved was he by the contents that he immediately posted a bond for Ayuba's purchase price. In March 1733, two years after his arrival in Maryland, the newly redeemed captive found himself back on a ship, bound for London, accompanied by Thomas Bluett, now cast in the role of English tutor.

If Ayuba's voyage to England was unlikely, his reception in the country was utterly unbelievable. Though he did not meet Oglethorpe, who had left for Georgia, he was quickly adopted by the English gentry, who vied to receive this real live Oronooko. Leading merchants "strove who should oftenest invite him to their tables"; scholars probed him for information about his homeland and the finer points of Koranic law. The Gentlemen's Society of

Spalding, England's premier assembly of scholars, extended him an honorary membership, inscribing his name on its rolls alongside such luminaries as Isaac Newton and Alexander Pope. When rumors surfaced of a plot to reenslave Ayuba, his new English friends quickly raised a subscription, redeeming Oglethorpe's bond and dispelling the last shadows of slavery. At Ayuba's request, they also redeemed his old companion, Loumein Yoai, and he too was soon traveling back across the Atlantic.

Ayuba's most influential patron was Sir Hans Sloane, president of the Royal Society and personal physician to the royal family. Sloane was intimately familiar with slavery, having begun his career as a physician in Jamaica, where he acquired his fortune (he married the widow of a wealthy planter) and a treasure trove of botanical and animal specimens. When Ayuba met him in the 1730s, he was England's most distinguished naturalist and "antiquary," famous for his unrivaled collection of "curiosities"—everything from rare gems to West Indian butterflies to Egyptian mummies. (Bequeathed to the state after his death, Sloane's collections became the basis of the new British Museum.) Whether Sloane regarded Ayuba as a friend or just another curiosity is hard to know, but the two men, born on different continents but both touched by American slavery, spent days in each other's company, discussing their respective homes and poring over some of the Arabic manuscripts in Sloane's forty-thousand-volume library. When his companion expressed an interest in meeting the British royal family, Sloane pledged to arrange it, but only after ensuring that "he had proper clothes to go in." A few days later, Ayuba, adorned in a turban and a long silk garment contrived by Sloane's tailor to look like the traditional garb of Bondou, was graciously received by the royal family, including Queen Caroline, who presented him with a gold watch.

Ayuba's reception in Britain, which anticipated the treatment of other African and African American notables in the eighteenth and nineteenth centuries, flowed from a variety of sources, including sincere philanthropy, scholarly curiosity, and rank exoticism. But there were also practical motives at work. With the continuing upheaval in the Senegambia, Ayuba's natal region had acquired considerable strategic significance, bestriding as it did the main overland route into the interior. The presence of a friendly regime in

Bondou promised not only to facilitate the gum trade, but also to ensure that the slaves flowing down to the coast would find their way into holds of British rather than French ships. And what better way to secure the friendship of Bondou than by restoring its long-lost prince?

After a memorable year in England, Ayuba boarded another Royal Africa Company slave ship, and sailed, this time as a passenger rather than cargo, back to the Senegambia. In his first journey, he had traveled with nothing besides the clothes on his back. Now he carried crates of presents, including lamps and looking glasses, agricultural implements (a gift from the Duke of Montague), candles, and reams of writing paper, the commodity he had sought on his initial ill-fated journey to the Gambia. He also carried a "handsomely engrossed" certificate from the Royal Africa Company attesting to his freedom, as well as a letter of introduction to the company's local factors, enjoining them to treat him "with the greatest Respect, and all the Civility you possibly can." As a further concession to their new ally, the company announced a new policy on the acquisition of Muslim slaves, who would henceforth be given an opportunity to redeem themselves "upon paying two other good Slaves for one."

Ayuba arrived in Africa in August 1734. After two weeks at James Fort, the British fortress at the mouth of the Gambia, he proceeded upriver to Joar. He was accompanied by Francis Moore, a company factor who would later earn distinction as the author of the first great African travel account in the English language. (The book, *Travels into the Inland Parts of Africa*, published in 1738, included a chapter about "Job.") As fate would have it, among the first people Ayuba encountered near Joar were the Mandinke men who had enslaved him three years before. According to Moore, his normally placid companion flew into a rage and was only with difficulty restrained from killing them. Oblivious to their peril, the men fell into conversation with their erstwhile captive, in the course of which they described how their chief had recently been killed when his pistol—the same pistol stolen from Ayuba—had accidentally discharged. Ayuba collapsed to his knees at the news, offering praise to a righteous God.

Reports of renewed fighting and slave raiding in the interior convinced Ayuba that traveling to Bondou was too risky, so he returned with Moore to

James Fort. He spent the next six months traveling along the Gambia, promoting the fortunes of the Royal Africa Company, endeavoring to "make so
good an understanding between the Company and his country people, that
the English nation should reap the benefits of the gum trade." As officials
had hoped, his appearance also improved Britain's slaving prospects in the
area, alleviating "a great deal of the horror of the Pholeys [Fula] for the state
of slavery amongst the English." (Prior to Ayuba's return, the Fula "imagined that all who were sold for slaves, were generally either eaten or murdered, since none ever returned," a company official explained.) If Ayuba
felt any reservations about facilitating the slave trade, he never expressed
them publicly. On the contrary, one of his first actions on returning to Africa
was purchasing "a woman-slave and two horses" to assist him in his travels,
using some of the presents he had received in England.

Unlike millions of other captives, Ayuba Suleiman Diallo made it home.
He entered his village in style, galloping on the back of a charger, clad in the
silk robes fashioned for him by Hans Sloane's London tailor. His father had
died, though not before learning of his son's redemption. His wives and children all survived to welcome him. (In a departure from an otherwise
Odyssean script, one of his wives had remarried, but the rival prudently
stepped aside.) In the years that followed, Ayuba continued to work as an
agent for the Royal Africa Company, from which he apparently received a
small retainer. He corresponded occasionally with the friends he had made—
he sent Sloane a set of poison-tipped arrows for his collection—but he never
returned to England. With the dissolution of the Royal Africa Company in
the early 1750s, Ayuba Suleiman Diallo disappears from the archival record,
save for a single notation in the membership book of the Gentlemen's Society
of Spalding recording his death in 1773.

THOUGH AYUBA'S STORY is obviously unique, it illuminates several important historical themes. Most obviously, his experience highlights African
participation in the transatlantic slave trade, an issue of considerable controversy in the eighteenth century, as it remains today. As unpalatable as it may
be to some, the plain fact is that Africans were not universally victims of the

slave trade. Some, at least, participated willingly; a few profited handsomely. With rare exceptions, the European presence in Africa during the centuries of the slave trade was confined to coastal forts and factories, leaving the actual business of procuring captives and marching them to the coast to African trading partners. The Senegambia was in fact the only region of West Africa in which it was possible for European ships to navigate deep into the interior, a circumstance that at least spared Ayuba the horror of a long overland journey in a slave coffle. The popular image of Europeans on horseback sweeping into unsuspecting villages may express a symbolic truth, but it is not historically accurate. The vast majority of African captives would never have seen a white man until they reached the coast or even until they were loaded aboard ship; indeed, this is part of what made the experience of loading so disorienting and terrifying.

Like many hard historical truths, African participation in the slave trade is susceptible to misunderstanding and abuse. Defenders of the trade, facing rising opposition in the late-eighteenth and early-nineteenth centuries, would place great stress on African complicity. Their arguments quickly assumed the quality of a catechism: slavery was endemic to Africa, a land wracked by perpetual war and unspeakable savagery; those imported to America were in fact the lucky ones, for their labor was light and they enjoyed the blessings of Christianity and "civilization." Even at the time, such rationalizations could not stand close scrutiny. While slavery certainly existed in Africa prior to the Europeans' arrival (as it did in virtually every other civilization known to history), the opening of the transatlantic trade radically transformed the institution's scale and character, sparking a vast new demand for slaves and precipitating centuries of war and political upheaval. European traders actively fomented conflict, most notably by offering guns and powder in exchange for slaves. The pistol that figured so prominently in Ayuba's story was not manufactured in Africa; it was one of the nearly twenty million guns exported to Africa by Europeans during the centuries of the slave trade. Great Britain alone, in a single decade at the peak of the traffic, exported more than one and a half million small arms to West Africa. In such circumstances, Africans who declined to trade with Europeans could quickly find themselves among the traded.

Ayuba's experience also helps to dispel one of the enduring misconceptions about the slave trade: the idea that Africans sold "their own people." In Africa (as in North and South America, ancient Greece and Rome, and virtually every other known slave society), slaves tended to be culturally and ethnically alien to those who enslaved them. Africa was and is a dizzyingly diverse continent, with more than two thousand mutually unintelligible languages and a virtually infinite array of ethnic, political, and religious identities and rivalries. The men who sold Ayuba were not Fula but Mandinke. The identity of the slaves trafficked by Ayuba is unclear, but they were almost certainly neither Fula nor Muslim. Today, of course, most Americans imagine Africa as a single place, inhabited by a single race of people, but that conception is itself an outgrowth of the slave trade, an artifact of the centuries-long encounter between Africa and the West. Such a conception would have made little sense to Ayuba.

This theme points to another. The decades of Ayuba's life coincide with the birth of race, the idea, still prevalent today, that the human species is divided by nature into a small number of distinct groups or races, each identifiable through phenotypic signatures (chiefly skin color and hair texture) and each endowed with distinct capacities and traits. The roots of this perdurable (and deeply misleading) notion are not easily disentangled. Clearly they reach far back in time, to the earliest European encounters with sub-Saharan Africans in the middle of the fifteenth century. Yet they also reflect a series of specifically eighteenth-century intellectual and cultural developments, most notably the rise of natural science, which was fast displacing religion as the primary idiom for describing human nature and variety. In an era in which all of the world's flora and fauna was being sorted into an elaborate classificatory scheme, it was perhaps inevitable that human beings too would be sorted and classified. Whatever the precise sources, the end result was a recognizably modern conception of biological race, complete with an insistence on the innate, ineradicable inferiority of people of African descent. In the nineteenth century, this belief would become the standard justification for slavery, and it remains the institution's most enduring legacy.

Ayuba's life straddled this process. The readiness with which Captain Pike acquired him from his captors suggests just how powerful the association of Africans with slavery had become. Having negotiated with Ayuba only days before, Pike knew perfectly well that he was no war prisoner, but he bought him nonetheless. At the same time, however, Ayuba had the good fortune to be enslaved at a time when ideas about race and slavery were still sufficiently inchoate so as to leave some uncertainty about his status. His personal attributes—not only his tawny skin, but also his literacy and piety, the carriage and composure that marked him as a man of breeding—were not sufficient to spare him enslavement, but they clearly troubled contemporaries who, simply put, wondered whether they had enslaved the wrong man. By the time of Ayuba's death in 1773, no such doubts would have been possible. The simple fact that he was an African, a Negro, was proof that he was properly a slave.

While Ayuba's fitness for enslavement was a source of debate, the institution of slavery itself was apparently not. This is perhaps the most important moral to be gleaned from this strange tale. Ayuba was captured while on a slave-trading expedition. He attempted to redeem himself by having his father send other captives in his place. One of his first acts on returning to Africa was to acquire a slave for his personal use. Ayuba made no effort to conceal these facts, nor did his early biographers, who clearly did not imagine that such revelations would reduce readers' sympathy for their subject. At least some of Ayuba's new British sponsors cultivated his friendship in hopes that it would increase the flow of slaves into British ships. What evidence there is suggests that he fulfilled that mandate. In his final appearance in the records of the Royal Africa Company, Ayuba was seeking compensation for a lost watch—presumably the watch he had received from Queen Caroline—and two slaves.

VIEWED THROUGH THE MORAL LENSES of our own time, Ayuba seems guilty of the most appalling hypocrisy, but he would not have seemed so to contemporaries. To enter Ayuba's world is to enter a place in which the peculiar institution was not peculiar at all, where slavery was not only almost universally practiced but also almost universally accepted. To be sure, it was a fate to be avoided, but the institution itself was generally regarded as part of the natural order of things, a fact of life, much as we today might think of homelessness, hunger, or other lamentable but seemingly "inevitable" realities. A generation later, the picture would look very different. By the time of the American Revolution, slavery had blossomed into one of the central political, philosophical, and moral problems of the age.

As with the roots of race, the origins of antislavery sentiment are complex. Clearly the process had something to do with capitalism: as "free" labor became more widespread and seemingly natural, other labor relations—indentured servitude, debt bondage, slavery—came increasingly to appear antiquated and anomalous. Enlightenment ideas of human equality and shared human nature surely contributed to growing doubts about the institution, as did the rapid spread of evangelical religion. The deepening imperial crisis was also an important catalyst. As American colonists railed against the British plot to "enslave" them, they could scarcely help but reflect on the existence of slavery in their own midst, on the fate of those for whom unalienable rights to life, liberty, and the pursuit of happiness did not exist. As historian David B. Davis has written, "By the eve of the American Revolution there was a remarkable convergence of cultural and intellectual developments which at once undercut traditional rationalizations for slavery and offered new modes of sensibility for identifying with its victims."

The result was a paradox of truly historic proportions: at the very moment at which ideas about black people's fitness for slavery were solidifying, the institution of slavery itself came in for unprecedented criticism. A new transatlantic movement emerged, dedicated to abolishing the institution, or at least to ending the "monstrous" traffic that carried fresh captives to the Americas. Slavery within Britain was effectively ended by the *Somerset* decision in 1772, a year before Ayuba's death. Five years later, Vermont became the first American territory to prohibit slavery. In the years that followed, courts and legislatures in all the northern states proceeded to abolish the institution, though they typically did so grudgingly and gradually. Even in states that did not abolish slavery—predictably those states where it remained most profitable—thousands of masters manumitted their slaves by private means. To be sure, slavery had its vocal defenders, and not all of them in the South, but the very fact that they felt compelled to defend the practice revealed how this once seemingly inevitable institution, a ubiquitous feature of human life since the very dawn of civilization, had come to seem not just unjust but unnatural, an offense against the fundamental principles of man and God.

Much of African American history—indeed, much of American history as a whole—was encapsulated in this paradox, in the simultaneous, seemingly contradictory emergence of antiblack racism and antislavery. Leaders of the revolutionary generation grappled with the contradiction, struggling to reconcile their beliefs about human equality and freedom with their fast solidifying conviction that all human beings were not equal, that not everyone possessed the capacity for responsible freedom. The problem bore even harder on African Americans, not only on the enslaved but also on the growing population of free people of color, who found their freedom circumscribed by segregation, disfranchisement, and a thousand daily affronts. The first initiatives to repatriate African Americans to Africa—to reproduce, in an organized way, the experience of individuals like Ayuba Suleiman Diallo—emerged from this climate of conflicted belief.

ONE

Windward Coast

ON JULY 4, 1826, the United States celebrated the fiftieth anniversary of the Declaration of Independence. By an extraordinary coincidence, the two most revered signers of the Declaration, Thomas Jefferson and John Adams, died on that very day, one in Virginia and one in Massachusetts. At the same time, in a village called Caldwell, in what would later become the independent nation of Liberia, an eighty-year-old African died of fever. His name was Occramar Marycoo, but most knew him as Newport Gardner, an appellation compounded of the city in which he spent most of his life and the surname of the slave-ship captain who once owned him. Unlike Adams and Jefferson, Marycoo does not appear in any history textbook. No monuments honor his memory. Yet the story of his life and death, of the forces that took him from Africa as a boy and took him back as an old man, is, in its way, as much the history of America's founding as the stories of his more celebrated contemporaries.

When Ayuba Suleiman Diallo died in 1773, the notion of a captive returning to Africa was still an utter novelty. By the time of Newport Gardner's death, African colonization was one of the central issues in American politics. The intervening half century produced a raft of African repatriation schemes, some authored by black people themselves, some by whites (including both opponents and proponents of slavery), some by whites and blacks working uneasily together. Ultimately, none of these ventures fulfilled the hopes of promoters (or the fears of critics), but they did lead to the creation of two colonies on the Windward Coast of West Africa: Sierra Leone, established in 1787, and Liberia, settled in 1820. Less concrete though no less important, they established the terms of debates for future generations of African Americans struggling to make sense of their relationship to Africa—terms that would prevail through the nineteenth century and in certain ways into our own time.

To reconstruct this tangled history requires tarrying at sites not included in the standard tour of American history, from the stony coast of Nova Scotia to the broad estuary of the Sierra Leone River, where a tiny settlement, hopefully dubbed Freetown by its founders, clung to life in the shadow of one of the largest British slave fortresses on the continent. It also requires introducing a motley cast of characters, most of them little known today, including not only Newport Gardner but also Samuel Hopkins, the astringent Puritan who introduced him to the gospel; Paul Cuffe, the African and Native American mariner who carried the first shipload of emigrants from the United States to Sierra Leone in 1815; Robert Finley, an erratic New Jersey minister who founded the American Colonization Society; and Daniel Coker, the escaped slave who led the society's first expedition to what would become Liberia. To confront this history is to enter foreign territory, a world where men and women routinely invoked Providence and anxiously scrutinized events for intimations of God's purposes. Yet it is also a curiously modern tale, a story of what we today would call globalization, of the accelerating movement of people, ideas, and goods, all unfolding within and against the first truly global industry: the transatlantic slave trade.

In April 1773, officials in Massachusetts received a petition from four Negroes, Peter Bestes, Sambo Freeman, Felix Holbrook, and Chester Joie. The men requested that slaves in the colony be given one day a week to work on their own behalf in order to raise money to purchase their freedom. Once free, they proposed to "leave the province ... from our joynt labours procur[ing] money to transport ourselves to some part of the *Coast* of Africa, where we propose a settlement." Though the battles of Lexington and Concord lay two years in the future (almost to the day), Massachusetts was already ablaze with revolutionary fervor, with "Sons of Liberty" offering paeans to freedom and warning of a sinister British plot to "enslave" them. The petitioners were only too happy to harness such rhetoric to their own purposes. "The efforts by the legislature of this province in their last session to free themselves from slavery, gave us, who are in that deplorable state, a high degree of satisfaction," they wrote. "We expect great things from men who have made such a noble stand against the designs of their *fellow-men* to enslave them." Though the tone is ironical, the petitioners clearly hoped to chafe white Americans' consciences by exposing the gulf between their professions and their practice, an early example of an enduring tradition in African American politics, one that Martin Luther King, Jr., would bring to a kind of perfection nearly two hundred years later. The difference, of course, was that the authors did not dream of winning their rights as American citizens. They simply wanted the right to leave.

Little else is known about the petition. Officials apparently ignored the appeal, and the four men retreated back into historical obscurity. A second scheme, launched the same year from neighboring Rhode Island, produced a fuller historical record, though no better immediate results. The author of the venture was a white minister, Samuel Hopkins, pastor of Newport's First Congregational Church. Hopkins was a leader of the New Divinity movement, an attempt to restore to American Christianity the severity and theological rigor of New England's Puritan founders. Like his mentor, the great Jonathan Edwards, Hopkins believed that Americans were a covenanted people, pledged to God and ordained to play a signal role in the unfolding design of Providence. He also believed that the colonists—being, like all humans, inherently sinful and depraved—had betrayed their covenant, sinking into sloth, lust, and greed. And nothing better symbolized their apostasy than slavery and the infernal trade that sustained it.

Confirmation for such convictions was easily found in Newport, where Hopkins settled in 1770. Not only was Newport a major point of entry for slaves—nearly 10 percent of the city was enslaved—but it was also headquarters of the North American slave-trading fleet. In all, more than 60 percent of slaving voyages from North America, more than a thousand expeditions in all, embarked from tiny Rhode Island, most from Newport. Some two dozen distilleries lined the city's waterfront, transforming West Indian sugar and molasses into rum, which was then carried to West Africa to trade for more slaves, who were carried to the West Indies to produce more sugar, thus completing the notorious triangle. "The inhabitants of Rhode Island, especially those of Newport, have had by far the greater share of this traffic of all these United States," Hopkins declared. "This trade in the human species has been the first wheel of commerce in Newport, on which every other movement in business has chiefly depended. That town has been built up, and flourished in times past, at the expense of the blood, the liberty, and the happiness of the poor Africans; and the inhabitants have lived on this, and by it have gotten most of their wealth and riches."

For Hopkins, the British assault on American liberties was a sign of divine chastisement, which would lift only when Americans had repented the sin of slavery and restored the covenant. Fortunately, the means of atonement were conveniently at hand. Returning black people to Africa promised not only to remove the stigma of slavery and sin from America but also to "spread the light of the gospel in that now dark part of the world." The idea accorded well with Hopkins's Old Testament theology, which stressed God's capacity to turn man's sinful gropings to his own purposes. Just as "in the case of Joseph being sold a slave into Egypt," the suffering of Africans within the slave trade "may be the occasion of an overbalancing good," he wrote. "We may hope that all this dark and dreadful scene will not only have an end, but is designed by the Most High to be the means of introducing the gospel among the nations of Africa."

For readers today, steeped in a thoroughly unprovidential understanding of history, Hopkins's ideas about sin, atonement, and the capacity of God to wring good from evil may appear quaint. But they were coin of the realm among eighteenth-century Americans, not only among whites, who viewed the "calamity" of the imperial crisis as a divine rebuke for their sins, but also among blacks, who found in such ideas an explanation for their own bitter, bewildering history. Probably the best example is Phillis Wheatley, the celebrated "sable muse," whose *Poems on Various Subjects, Religious and Moral* was the first book ever published by a black person in America. Wheatley had no illusions about slavery's cruelty—she owed her first name to the slave ship that brought her to Boston in 1761, when she was just eight years old—yet she could still declare in her poem "On being brought from Africa to America": " 'Twas mercy brought me from my Pagan land, / Taught my benighted soul to understand / That there's a God, that there's a Saviour too. . . ." Whatever one thinks of that sentiment—and many modern readers will doubtless find it lamentable, or worse—it reflected a profound faith in Providence, in an overruling God orchestrating the affairs of man for His own inscrutable but benign ends. Indeed, Wheatley's very first poem, published in the *Newport Mercury* in 1767 when she was only fourteen, offered a meditation on precisely this theme. Entitled "On Messrs. Hussey and Coffin," the poem told of two local men who had survived a storm at sea, but it was redolent of the poet's own passage across the stormy Atlantic just six years before: "Did Fear and Danger so perplex your Mind, / As made you fearful of the whistling Wind?" she asked. "Regard them not;—the Great Supreme, the Wise, / Intends for something hidden from our Eyes."

Wheatley's book was published in 1773, the same year Hopkins announced his scheme to return Christian Africans to their homeland as missionaries. Recognizing a kindred spirit, he immediately wrote to her, requesting twenty copies of her book and outlining his plan. Though not all the correspondence survives, it appears that he also invited her to join the venture. Wheatley declined the offer, citing the deteriorating health of her mistress, but she did pledge to do all she could "to promote this laudable design." The letter included several scriptural warrants for the venture, including the prophecy of African redemption in Psalms ("Ethiopia shall soon stretch forth her hands unto God") and the story of Christ's encounter with the Canaanite woman in the Gospel of Matthew. "Europe and America have long been fed with the heavenly provision, and I fear they loathe it, while Africa is perishing with a spiritual famine," Wheatley wrote. "O that they could partake of the crumbs, the precious crumbs, which fall from the table of these distinguished children of the kingdom."

Newport offered a uniquely fertile field for such ideas. With its bustling wharfs and workshops, the city possessed the most cosmopolitan black community in North America, composed of slaves and free people of color, many

African born, most of them Christian, all immersed in the wider Atlantic world of commerce and ideas. In contrast to the plantation South, blacks in Newport typically lived in close proximity to Europeans, worshipping in white churches (usually in segregated galleries), working alongside whites in shops and sail lofts, distilleries and ropewalks, sleeping in the back rooms and garrets of white homes. To borrow a phrase from Langston Hughes, black Newporters understood "the ways of white folks." At the same time, however, they shared a strong sense of racial solidarity, rooted in the common experience of discrimination and still vital memories of Africa. While it was the custom of masters to confer names on new slaves—place names such as Bristol and Newport were common, as were classical names such as Scipio and Caesar—many black Newporters chose to retain their African names (or reverted to them after obtaining freedom) and they conferred African names on their children. The peculiar character of the community was exemplified by the city's Free African Union Society, America's first black mutual aid society, established in 1780. On the one hand, the society endeavored to "elevate" black people in the United States, through the creation of a school for black children; a night school for adults; a temperance society; and a registry of births, marriages, and deaths (a simple but profound acknowledgment of black humanity, neglected by white officials and owners). On the other hand, the society bespoke a still vital sense of connection with Africa, expressed both in its name and in its founding documents, in which members professed their "earnest desire of returning to Affrica."

Among the Africans to rally to Hopkins's message was the young Occramar Marycoo or, as he was known at the time, Newport Gardner. Like Phillis Wheatley, Marycoo was carried from Africa in the early 1760s, in his case to Newport. He was about fourteen years old at the time. Judging from his name, which appears to have Akan roots, he probably hailed from the area of the Gold Coast. His English name derived from his master, Caleb Gardner, one of Newport's leading citizens, as well as one of the city's most successful slaveship captains. The circumstances of Marycoo's enslavement remain unclear. According to a persistent local tradition, he was voluntarily surrendered by his parents to a ship's captain, who pledged to take the boy to America for education and then treacherously sold him into slavery. The story, one of several such in Newport lore, is almost certainly apocryphal. A more likely scenario is that Marycoo was purchased in the customary way by Gardner himself, who is known to have made several voyages to the Gold Coast in the early 1760s. It was not unusual for slave-ship captains, who customarily received a "privilege," or commission, of 4 Africans for every 104 they delivered, to retain children as cabin boys or personal servants. What little is known about the circumstances of Marycoo's enslavement suggests such a scenario.

While the story of Marycoo being inveigled into slavery with promises of education is probably apocryphal, he did in fact receive a first-rate education through the good offices of Gardner's wife, who permitted him to attend lessons along with her own children. He proved a brilliant student, quickly mastering English and French. He also proved a gifted singer. Treated by Mrs. Gardner to a few lessons from an itinerant musician, Marycoo blossomed into the city's premier vocal teacher, training generations of students in a rented attic studio. He also wrote several original songs, the first compositions published by a black person in American history. The compositions were mostly hymns and anthems, for Marycoo by this time was a devout Christian. Details of his conversion are unknown, but by the late 1760s he was attending prayer meetings at the home of Sarah Osborn, a white woman of modest means, who had taken it upon herself to provide religious instruction to Newport's African population. After Osborn's death, the work was carried on by the newly arrived Samuel Hopkins. Gardner began attending worship at his church, eventually rising to the office of sexton.

Hopkins recognized Marycoo as a perfect candidate for his African venture. "He is a discerning, judicious, steady, good man, and feels greatly interested in promoting a Christian settlement in Africa," he wrote. Unfortunately, he was also a slave. While the details are obscure, it appears that Caleb Gardner refused to release his claim on him, at least not on acceptable terms. With Marycoo temporarily out of the picture, Hopkins turned to two other Africans who worshipped in his church, John Quamino and Bristol Yamma. Both were pious men, with good "natural abilities," though of relatively "slender acquaintance as to letters." Most important, both were free. In 1774, the pair traveled to Princeton, where they began their training as missionaries, under the tutelage of the Reverend John Witherspoon, president of the college there. But that was as far as the plan got. With the outbreak of the Revolutionary War in 1775, the scheme was suspended, and the two men returned to Rhode Island. Quamino signed on to a privateer, hoping to earn money to purchase the freedom of his wife. He was killed in a naval engagement in 1779. Yamma survived until 1793, but he too died without ever returning to his native land. Only Occramar Marycoo would survive to see the shores of Africa, though he would be an old man by the time he did so.

FOCUSED AS HE WAS on God's Providence, Samuel Hopkins seems not to have asked some obvious practical questions. Where would his returning missionaries settle? Would they return to their original homes, or would they establish a distinct settlement? How would they sustain themselves? How would they be received by Africans? For Hopkins, if not for the Africans he recruited, the whole enterprise seems to have existed as much in the realm of scriptural speculation as of human history. But with the establishment of the Sierra Leone colony in 1787, the idea of returning Africans and African Americans to their ancestral continent became a realistic possibility.

Though its sponsors were based in London, Sierra Leone was the offspring of the American Revolution. During the war, thousands of African American slaves escaped their American masters and fled to the British lines, drawn by the promise of freedom. At the war's end, more than ten thousand black loyalists remained with the British, most of them in New York City and Charleston. The fate of these people, in fact, was a major point of contention in the negotiations to end the war, with American officials (including George Washington, who had seen several of his own slaves run away to the British) insisting that they be returned to their rightful owners. The British acceded to the demand in the Treaty of Paris, but then reneged on their pledge; when the last British troops left the United States in 1783, thousands of black loyalists went with them. While some were betrayed—carried to the West Indies and sold back into slavery—the lion's share, about three thousand in all, were settled in Nova Scotia, where they lived free, if impecunious, lives. Still others found their way to Britain, the majority to London, which by the 1780s boasted a black population of more than five thousand.

Like the much larger population of free people of color in the United States, black Britons lived in a kind of social limbo, no longer enslaved (the

1772 *Somerset* decision, while not formally abolishing slavery in Britain, had knocked the legal props out from under the institution) yet less than fully free. Denied the compensation available to other displaced loyalists, excluded from all but the most menial employment, many black Britons were reduced to begging or living by their wits. As in the United States, the emergence of a conspicuous black underclass provoked contradictory responses from whites. A charitable organization, The Committee for the Relief of the Black Poor of London, was chartered in 1786 and began dispensing sixpence per person per day from two London public houses. Within six months, the committee, which included the leading lights of Britain's nascent antislavery movement, was supporting more than a thousand people with daily doles. In other quarters, however, the proliferation of the black poor produced not charity but fear and loathing. Newspapers warned of increased crime, vice and, worst of all, of the "stain and contamination" of English blood, of the birth of "a little race of mulattoes, mischievous as monkeys and infinitely more dangerous." As in the United States a generation later, the union of philanthropy and fear issued in an organized movement to remove black people from Britain's shores.

But where to send them? Attention quickly came to focus on a broad river mouth on Africa's Windward Coast, known to the Portuguese as Sierra Leone, or Lion Mountain, after the massif rearing abruptly up from the narrow coastal plain. The chief promoter of Sierra Leone was a man named Henry Smeathman, an eccentric English entomologist, known to contemporaries as the flycatcher. Smeathman had spent three years on Africa's Windward Coast in the 1770s, collecting specimens near the Sierra Leone River, and ever since had been touting the site as an ideal place for a colony. He seems initially to have been thinking of a penal colony—Australia had yet to be founded—but the agitation over the black poor caused him to recast his plans. In 1786, he published a book, the argument of which was apparent from its lengthy title: *Plan of a Settlement to be made near Sierra Leone, on the Grain Coast of Africa: Intended more particularly for the service and happy establishment of Blacks and People of Colour, to be shipped as freemen under the direction of the Committee for Relieving the Black Poor, and under the Protection of the British Government.*

Smeathman died of a fever a short time later, but not before sharing his vision with Sir Granville Sharpe, a leader of the Committee for the Black Poor and Britain's most celebrated antislavery crusader. By trade a musician and linen draper, Sharpe first won national acclaim in 1772, when he successfully argued the *Somerset* case, effectively ending slavery within Britain—a singular achievement, given his lack of any formal legal training. For Sharpe, the proposed Sierra Leone colony offered a solution to a host of problems. Not only would it relieve Britain of the burden of the black poor, but it would also benefit black people themselves, giving them an opportunity for self-government in a nation of their own. (Sharpe even drafted a constitution for the colony, modeled on ancient Anglo-Saxon usages.) The colony also promised significant economic benefits to Britain, including new markets for manufactures and new sources of valuable products such as cotton, sugar, and indigo, all of which (if Smeathman could be believed) grew luxuriantly in Sierra Leone. One can discern here the origins of one of the great shibboleths of the anti–slave trade movement, what would come to be called the legitimate commerce policy. By encouraging legitimate commerce in Africa, the argument ran, Britain could free itself of its dependence on the fruits of New World slavery, while at the same time providing Africans with legitimate means to obtain the European commodities they had come to covet, thus alleviating their need to sell their brethren.

Sharpe and his colleagues had no trouble enlisting the support of the British government, which was only too happy to underwrite a scheme that promised to expand commerce while ridding the nation of an impoverished, unsettling population. But black people themselves proved more skeptical. Many feared that Sierra Leone was intended as a convict colony or, worse, that settlers would simply be recaptured and shipped back to the Americas as slaves. When few recruits came forward, the Committee for the Black Poor resorted to virtual bribery, limiting the daily sixpence dole to individuals who agreed to settle in Sierra Leone. The committee eventually secured more than four hundred "volunteers," but as the day of sailing approached, many abandoned the venture. Ultimately, promoters turned to the time-honored tradition of the press gang, rounding up indigent black people off the streets, throwing in nearly a hundred white prostitutes for good measure. In April 1787, three ships and 411 souls set sail from Plymouth to establish what Granville Sharpe had already dubbed The Province of Freedom. After a brutal month-long passage, which claimed the lives of more than thirty of the party, the flotilla arrived at the broad mouth of the Sierra Leone River, where it established a settlement called Granville Town.

From the outset, the colony was beset by difficulties. In his promotional writings, Smeathman had described Sierra Leone as a "terrestrial Elysium," a land of "vernal beauty [and] tropic luxuriance, where fruit and flowers lavish their fragrance on the same bough," a place of such "mildness and fertility . . . that a man possessed of a change of clothing, an axe, a hoe, and a pocket knife may soon place himself in an easy and comfortable situation." The reality could scarcely have been more different. With an average annual rainfall of 180 inches per year, the country was indeed prolific of vegetation, but also completely inhospitable to most of the food crops that settlers were accustomed to growing and eating. Malaria and yellow fever were endemic. In the first four months of the settlement, 122 people, nearly a third of the colonists, died. The colony also had the ironic distinction of being sited in the middle of one of the most active slaving grounds in Africa. Bunce Island, the main British slave fort on the Windward Coast, lay just a few miles up the Sierra Leone River, disgorging a steady stream of captives into the Atlantic— some fifty thousand over the course of the eighteenth century. Colonists became accustomed to the sight of slave ships sailing by, traveling upriver loaded in ballast and returning laden with bodies.

The coup de grace to the struggling colony was delivered by King Tom, the Temne chief who controlled the south shore of the river. The king initially welcomed the settlers, but he came to rue the decision, especially after a British ship fired on one of his villages. In 1789, he gave the colonists three days to gather their belongings, and then burned Granville Town to the ground. By that time, many of the surviving settlers had already drifted away. A few found refuge in local villages, while others moved to Bunce Island, which offered abundant employment for clerks, shipwrights, and the like. In fairness, the only other alternative for many was starvation, but there is still something shocking in the spectacle of the settlers, refugees from American slavery, working at a slave-trading fort. It certainly shocked Sharpe, who penned a bitter letter to the colonists. "I could not have conceived that men who were well aware of the wickedness of slave-dealing, and had themselves been sufferers . . . under the galling yoke of bondage . . . should become so basely depraved as to yield themselves instruments to promote and extend the same detestable oppression over their brethren," he wrote.

Salvation for Sierra Leone came from an unexpected direction: Nova Scotia. The years had not been kind to the black Loyalists settled in the province after the American Revolution. Many never received the land they were promised; others struggled to scratch out a living on small, stony farms. Though taxed as freemen, they were denied access to the vote and to decent paying work. But when they accepted lower paying jobs, they found themselves targeted by white mobs, who accused them of driving down wages. In 1790, the Nova Scotians dispatched a representative, Thomas Peters, an escaped slave who had served as a sergeant in the British army, to London to inquire of Sharpe and his colleagues about the possibility of resettlement in Sierra Leone. Presumably they were unaware of the colony's moribund state, and presumably Sharpe, who was trying to revive Sierra Leone under the auspices of a private chartered company, did not enlighten them. Sharpe and his colleagues pledged twenty acres of land to each male settler that Peters could recruit. The English government once again agreed to supply free passage and initial provisions. In January 1792, a flotilla of fifteen ships set out from Halifax, bearing some twelve hundred emigrants. Though scattered by a winter storm, all fifteen ships eventually arrived safely, and the colonists established a settlement not far from the ruins of Granville Town, which they called Freetown.

In contrast to the original colonists, the Nova Scotians were a tightly knit group, many of whom had worked and worshipped together; in many cases, members of religious congregations traveled together. Perhaps a third had been born in Africa, several from the area around Sierra Leone, setting the stage for some extraordinary reunions. Frank Peters, who had been carried to South Carolina as a child, was approached by an aged woman, exhibiting "very peculiar emotions." Only when she embraced him did he recognize his mother. Martha Webb had an even more providential reunion with her mother, whom she recognized in a coffle of slaves being prepared for sale. She managed to redeem her from the local chief. John Gordon, a Methodist lay preacher and one of the leaders of the settlers, had an even stranger reunion. Gordon had grown up among the Koranko people, a hundred miles inland from Freetown. Captured as a young man, he was sold to English traders at Bunce Island and carried to Maryland. A few years after his return to Africa, Gordon chanced to be trading near his old home, where he met the Mandinke man who had originally enslaved him. When Ayuba Suleiman Diallo encountered his kidnappers sixty years before, his first reaction was homicidal. Gordon, steeped in a Christian, providential understanding of black history, offered his captor a gift: "Your thoughts were evil, but God meant it for good," he said. "I now know God and Christ."

Such optimism was difficult to maintain as time passed and troubles mounted. A French fleet sacked and burned the settlement in 1794. Relations between settlers and the indigenous inhabitants spiraled downward, culminating in two major assaults on the colony by a confederation of local African tribes. The slave trade from the region continued unabated. Most ominously, tensions mounted between the colony's black settlers and its white sponsors. After his experience with the original settlement, Granville Sharpe had more or less given up his dream of a self-governing colony. While emigrants still enjoyed full civil rights, political authority was vested in a council of eight white men, all appointed by directors of the Sierra Leone Company. Not surprisingly, the settlers bitterly resented the arrangement; for many, the whole purpose of resettling in Africa had been to escape white authority. Conflict came to focus on land. Colonists believed they had been promised freehold title, but company officials insisted on the payment of quitrents, a system that asserted the sovereignty of the company while raising revenue for English investors. By 1800, things had reached such a pass that the settlers rose in armed rebellion. Among the rebels was Henry Washington, whose one-time master, George Washington, had led an earlier rebellion against the British.

The rebellion might have succeeded but for the timely arrival of a British squadron, transporting another group of settlers, some five hundred Jamaican "Maroons." A community of rebels and fugitives, the Maroons had survived for sixty years in the mountain fastnesses of the Jamaican interior, repelling every British attempt to conquer them. After a series of battles in the 1790s, they had been persuaded to lay down their arms in exchange for promises of amnesty and continued independence, only to be betrayed, chained, and transported to Sierra Leone. In yet another bitter irony in an already bitter history, the Maroons' first action in their new home was to assist their captors in suppressing the rebellion of the Nova Scotians. The rebellion—and the public executions that followed—eliminated the last vestiges of Granville Sharpe's Province of Freedom. In 1807, with the chartered company on the edge of bankruptcy, Sierra Leone became a British crown colony, the first in West Africa.

Ironically, Sierra Leone's failure as a settler refuge cleared the way for it to play a different, but equally important, role in the global antislavery movement. The same year that brought formal colonial rule to Sierra Leone also saw the British Parliament pass William Wilberforce's momentous bill abolishing the transatlantic slave trade. In contrast to the United States, which passed a similar bill a few months later, the British actually proposed to enforce the ban, dispatching a naval squadron to the African coast. Suspicious ships were boarded and those found to be carrying slaves were condemned. But what to do with the ships' human cargoes? Sierra Leone provided the answer. Over the course of the next half century, tens of thousands of recaptives, Africans redeemed from the holds of slave ships, were carried to Freetown, where they mingled, sometimes uneasily, with English officials, African American settlers, and other recaptives from virtually every corner of Africa. Freetown earned its name, but not in the way that its founders had expected.

THOUGH SIERRA LEONE realized few of its sponsors' hopes, news of its founding galvanized the black community in the United States. Even before the first colonists left England, a group of seventy-five black Bostonians petitioned the Massachusetts General Court, seeking assistance to help them "to return to Africa, our native country . . . where we shall live among our equals and be more comfortable and happy, than we can be in our present situation." Though they conveyed few other details, the petitioners apparently hoped to sustain themselves through trade, establishing a "mutual intercourse and profitable commerce" between West Africa and the United States. Similar resolutions emanated from Newport's Free African Union Society, whose leaders had somehow obtained a copy of Henry Smeathman's book. "We are waiting and longing to hear what has been the issue and success of the attempt made in England to make a settlement of Blacks in Affrica, hopeing this will open the way for us," they declared in a 1787 circular letter, addressed to black communities all along the eastern seaboard. In the early 1790s, the Newporters voted to send an advance party to Africa to locate "lands proper and sufficient to settle upon," to be led by Newport Gardner. The party never sailed—it appears that Caleb Gardner once again refused to release his valuable slave—but blacks in neighboring Providence did send an emissary, John McKenzie, secretary of the city's African Society, to Sierra Leone in 1795.

Nothing ultimately came of McKenzie's visit or of any of these early ventures, but they were not insignificant. Not only did they keep the dream of African repatriation alive, but they also crystallized enduring tensions in African Americans' attitudes toward both Africa and the United States. Obviously, the emigration movement expressed and encouraged a strong sense of identification with Africa and its people. Africa was black people's "native country"; its "warm climate" was much "more agreeable and natural" to people of color than the chill air of New England. Yet these early back-to-Africa efforts also rested on the idea that black people in the United States were no longer like other Africans, that they had graduated to a higher civil and religious status, which equipped them for the task of redeeming their benighted brethren. Returning to Africa, the Boston petitioners explained, offered a providential means of "inlightening and civilizing those nations, which are now sunk in ignorance and barbarism." The Newporters likewise portrayed emigration as a means to alleviate not only their own "calamitous state" but also "the unhappy state and circumstances of our brethren, the Natives in Affrica, from whom we spring, being in heathenish darkness and sunk down in barbarity . . . so foolish and wicked as to sell one another."

As the final comment suggests, emigration posed the question of African complicity in the slave trade. The same developing sense of racial identity that impelled some African Americans to seek to "redeem" their African brethren also compelled them to face the fact that some of these same brethren had, literally or figuratively, sold them into slavery. In the eighteenth century as in our own, this was a sensitive subject, and different people resolved it in different ways. Olaudah Equiano, the famous slave narrator and an early supporter of the Sierra Leone colony, offered a scriptural explanation, portraying Africans as descendants of the biblical Israelites, still living under an Old Testament dispensation in which slavery was not yet regarded as sinful. The implication, of course, was that the spread of Christianity would toll the end of slavery and the slave trade on the continent. Others, less steeped in Scripture, blamed Europeans. Africans, they argued, had lived in "simplicity, innocence, and contentment" until European slave traders had corrupted them, enticing them with liquor, lucre, and guns to enslave one another. Many laid the onus on African chiefs, accusing them of betraying their public trust by peddling their own people. One of the primary benefits of emigration, according to this argument, was that it would liberate Africans from the thrall of these "imposters and bloodsuckers."

Emigrants' ambivalence toward Africa was mirrored in their ambivalence toward America. Obviously the desire to emigrate bespoke profound estrangement from the United States. As the Newporters put it, they were "strangers and outcasts in a strange land, attended with many disadvantages and evils, with respect to living, which are like to continue on us and our children while [we] live in this Country." Yet there was a decidedly American quality to their aspirations. While advocates spoke of "returning" to their home, the object was not to return to some prelapsarian African past, but to create a distinct colony, where black people could enjoy all the privileges that they were promised but denied in the United States. Thus the Newporters stressed the importance of securing "a good and proper title" to lands on which they settled, including the right to bequeath it "to our Heirs or children," two fundamental American rights routinely denied to African Americans, slave and free. The Bostonians went still further, proposing to ground their rights in a new "civil society united by a political constitution in which they shall agree." In the very act of fleeing America, these early proponents of African emigration revealed just how profoundly American they were.

This paradox provides the backdrop to the story of Captain Paul Cuffe, the pioneering emigrationist and author of the first African American travel account of Africa. Like many "black" New Englanders, Cuffe was of mixed Native American and African descent. His father, known to whites as Cuffe Slocum, was carried from West Africa as a child in 1728, presumably from the Gold Coast, where Kofi was a common name. He was taken to Newport, where he was sold to a Quaker ship captain, Ebenezer Slocum, whom he served for seventeen years before receiving a grant of freedom. Cuffe's mother, Ruth, was a full-blooded Wampanoag Indian from Cuttyhunk, a tiny island off Nantucket. Paul, sixth of the couple's ten children, was born in 1759. Cuffe grew up among Native Americans on Cuttyhunk, before moving in his early teens to the mainland, to a farm his father had purchased in Dartmouth, Massachusetts. Befitting his origins, Cuffe appears to have had a flexible sense of identity. In early documents, he characterized himself as Musta, or Mustee, a term for people of mixed black and native descent. He married a Native American woman, Alice Pequit. Yet in the 1770s he and his brothers relinquished the surname of Slocum, by which they had been known, and adopted Cuffe, the African name of their father.

While most of his siblings remained farmers, Paul took to the sea. He crewed on coastal traders and whalers, and made several voyages to the Caribbean. During the American Revolution, he served on blockade runners, an experience that led to a short stint as a prisoner of war. Released by the British, he returned to Massachusetts, where he built a small open boat and went to work in the coastal trade with his older brother John. After twice being divested of boat and cargo by pirates, John returned to the family farm, but Paul persisted and, in time, prospered. By the early nineteenth century, he had sailed all over the Atlantic world, from the whaling grounds off South Africa to Sweden. Some of his most profitable voyages were to the American South, where his humility and scrupulously correct conduct allayed the suspicions of people who had never before seen a black captain and crew. The owner of a fleet of ships and his own trading house, Cuffe may have been the wealthiest man of color in the United States.

Cuffe's first appearance in the public record came in 1778, when he and brother John launched a tax revolt. Though the new Massachusetts constitution was ostensibly color blind, individual towns exercised considerable discretion on racial matters. In Dartmouth, people of color were not permitted to participate in town meetings or to vote in elections for the state legislature. The town also refused to grant the Cuffe children a clear title to the family farm after their father's death, even as it continued to assess taxes on the property. The Cuffes refused to pay. In a widely publicized petition, signed by several of their black neighbors, the brothers stood on the revolutionary principle of "no taxation without representation," but they also noted the cruelty of extracting taxes from "poor Dispised miserable" people, who "by Reason of Long Bondag and hard Slavery [had] been deprived of Injoying the Profits of our Labourer or the advantage of Inheriting Estates from our Parents as our Neighbouers the white peopel do." The dispute dragged on for three years, and included a stint in jail for the brothers. The Cuffes eventually made a token payment to settle their account, but the struggle was not unavailing. In 1783, the state of Massachusetts, prompted in part by the protest in Dartmouth, guaranteed the franchise to black citizens.

Traveling along the eastern seaboard, Cuffe was doubtless exposed to contemporary debates over African emigration, but the first evidence of his taking any interest in the issue came in 1807, when he was nearly fifty years old. From that moment until his death nine years later, Africa consumed his thoughts and prayers. What prompted his conversion is unclear, but the timing is suggestive. The year 1807 marked Cuffe's acceptance into full membership of the Society of Friends, or Quakers, an affiliation that gave him access to a rich tradition of antislavery writing, as well as to a transatlantic network of merchants and philanthropists with interests in the Sierra Leone colony. The same year saw the passage of bills in the British Parliament and U.S. Congress abolishing the transatlantic slave trade, a momentous development in the history of the Atlantic world and one that Cuffe, who made his living on the Atlantic, watched with keen interest. A correspondent from *The Times* of London who interviewed Cuffe during a visit to Britain traced his interest in African regeneration to a book, *The History of the Rise, Progress and Accomplishment of the Abolition of the African Slave-Trade by the British Parliament*, written in 1807 by Thomas Clarkson, the man who spearheaded the movement. "[W]hen Mr. Clarkson's History of the Abolition of the Slave Trade fell into his hands," the correspondent wrote, "it awakened all the powers of his mind to a consideration of his origin, and the duties he owed to his people." While that account is surely oversimplified, Cuffe did read Clarkson's book, and later carried a copy of it with him to Africa. Significantly, the book included a long and sympathetic discussion of the Sierra Leone colony, with which Clarkson and his brother John were both deeply involved. For Clarkson, the colony was the key to Africa's future, the flower "from which may issue the seeds of reformation to this injured continent."

Cuffe's growing interest in African emigration also doubtless reflected his dimming hopes for black life in America. The years around the turn of the century were a grim time for people of color, both slave and free. With the invention of the cotton gin in the 1790s, the southern economy boomed, driving up the value of slave labor and dashing hopes that the institution would die out naturally. The period also saw a mounting assault on free Negroes. Free people of color had long been stigmatized as idle, vicious, and disorderly, but in the wake of the Haitian revolution and the abortive Gabriel Prosser rebellion in Virginia, they were increasingly perceived as a menace, a walking incitement to slave revolt. Virtually all the southern states enacted new restrictions on private manumissions, requiring masters who desired to free their slaves to transport them out of state. In several states, free people of color were given a stark choice between leaving or accepting reenslavement. Thousands of free blacks in the South simply pulled up stakes and headed north, but in truth their prospects in northern states were not much better. Looking at this baleful scene, Cuffe had good reason to think that the only chance for black elevation lay outside the United States, that African Americans would never "rise to be a people" until they had a nation of their own.

It was at this moment that Cuffe was invited to visit Sierra Leone. The invitation came from James Pemberton, a Quaker merchant from Philadelphia and president of the Pennsylvania Abolition Society. Pemberton, whom Cuffe first met in 1808, was the American correspondent of the London-based African Institution, an organization founded by Clarkson, William Wilberforce, and other British antislavery leaders to promote the economic development of the struggling Sierra Leone colony. Still chasing the will-o'-the-wisp of legitimate commerce, the directors of the institution had recently written to Pemberton, requesting his help in recruiting a contingent of African Americans to come to Sierra Leone to teach agriculture and other "useful arts" to the inhabitants. The goal was not mass emigration but rather to transport a small number of instructors trained in the production and processing of "tropical produce" such as "Rice, Indigo, Cotton or Tobacco," crops traditionally produced by New World slaves, which might now become the staples of Sierra Leone. Cuffe seemed heaven-sent for the purpose, and Pemberton asked him to organize and lead the expedition.

Cuffe spent several months pondering the opportunity, corresponding with prominent Quakers in England and the United States, as well as with various African American leaders. In late 1808, he traveled to Newport to discuss the possibilities with both black and white leaders there. Samuel Hopkins had died a few years before, but Cuffe did meet Newport Gardner, who remained dedicated to the emigrationist cause, despite having passed his sixtieth birthday. Cuffe himself was nearly fifty and in increasingly fragile health, but he decided to heed Providence's call. "As to Poor me i feel very feeble and almost Worn out in hard Service and incapable of doing much for my Brethren, the African Race," he wrote to Pemberton, "but blessed be god i am What I am and all that I can conceive that god please to Lay upon me, to make an instrument of me for that Service."

By early 1809, Cuffe had committed to undertake an "exploratory" mission to Sierra Leone. The trip was delayed by the deepening conflict between the United States and Great Britain, which led to an embargo on all foreign trade, but a brief diplomatic thaw in 1810 enabled him to resume preparations. On January 2, 1811, this son of an African slave embarked for Africa's Windward Coast on his ship *Traveller*, a stout brig of seventy tons burden. In addition to his cargo of meat, flour, tobacco, and other trading staples, he carried a sheaf of testimonials from prominent whites, useful insurance for a black captain and crew in seas frequented by illegal slave traders. After a stormy two-month passage, the "dust of Africa" darkened *Traveller*'s rigging. A few days later Cuffe anchored his ship in Freetown Roads, near a trio of condemned slave ships, early prizes in the British navy's campaign against the trade and a vivid reminder of the high stakes of his venture.

Cuffe spent the next two months in Sierra Leone, recording his daily activities in a logbook in his distinctive unpunctuated prose. As an American, he encountered considerable hostility from British officials and merchants, but he was eventually permitted to offload most of his cargo, and to take on a cargo of African products, chiefly "elephant's teeth"—ivory—and camwood, an African hardwood used to make red dye. Cuffe also purchased an assortment of local crafts, which he hoped to use to demonstrate the colony's commercial possibilities, as well as the "mental endowments" of its inhabitants.

Though he spoke of "the African Race" in his writings, Cuffe had little actual contact with indigenous Africans during his stay. Like most nineteenth-century African American visitors to West Africa, he spent virtually all his time in the settler enclave around Freetown, a western beachhead occupied by some fifteen hundred African American emigrants, most from Nova Scotia. Interspersed among the settlers were a few dozen British officials and merchants, about six hundred Kru men (migrants from farther up the coast, who dominated the maritime trades on the coast), and a small but growing number of recaptives liberated from slave ships. Perhaps not surprisingly, Cuffe spent most of his time with the Nova Scotians, whose culture and values were much like his own. His chief contact among the settlers was John Kizell, a man whose personal history encapsulated the history of the Sierra Leone colony. As a child, Kizell was kidnapped from the area around Sherbro Island, a hundred miles south of Freetown, and carried to a plantation in South Carolina, from which he escaped during the Revolution. He served in the British army, and after the war emigrated to Nova Scotia, and thence to Sierra Leone. Twenty years later, he was one of the leaders of the colony, a lay minister and merchant with businesses in Freetown and on Sherbro Island. With his knowledge of local languages and customs, Kizell was an indispensable mediator between British officials and local chiefs, and he quickly positioned himself to play the same role for Cuffe. Cuffe regarded him as an ideal partner, though later colonists would question where Kizell's real loyalties lay.

Cuffe's encounters with the indigenous inhabitants of Sierra Leone were less encouraging. Shortly after his arrival, he and his crew entertained King Tom, the Temne chief who was the colony's nominal landlord. The meeting got off to an awkward beginning, when Cuffe, a teetotaler, refused Tom and his entourage the customary gift of rum. Instead, he presented the bemused king with a collection of books, including a Bible, a history of Quakerism, and various edifying tracts and pamphlets, as well as "a letter of advice from myself . . . for the use and encouragement of the nations of Africa." A few days later, Cuffe paid a call to King George, Tom's counterpart among the Bullom people, who controlled the territory on the opposite shore of the Sierra Leone River. The conversation was a bit easier, thanks to the presence of the king's interpreter, who had spent several years in England, but the result was much the same. Again, the captain refused to provide rum, and instead, "gave the king a Testament and several other books, and let him know by the interpreter the useful records contained in those books, and the great fountain they pointed unto." The response of the king to the books is un-

recorded, but Cuffe left the encounter with mixed feelings. Though the Bullom people "acknowledge by words the existence of a Deity"—in fact, they
were Muslims—they exhibited no interest in Christianity. Nor did the king
evince any enthusiasm for abolishing the slave trade, telling the captain that
such a course would make "them poor and they could not git things as they
used to git when they traded in slaves." "So accustomed are they to wars and
slavery," Cuffe reported, "that I apprehend it would be a difficult task to convince them of the impropriety of these pernicious practices."

In April 1811, Cuffe set sail for Britain, to meet with Sierra Leone's promoters there. His arrival in Liverpool, until recently the headquarters of the
British slave-trading fleet, caused a sensation among the British press and
public. *The Times* of London, the *Edinburgh Review,* and the Liverpool *Mercury* all ran profiles. "It must have been a strange and animating spectacle to
see this free and enlightened African entering, as an independent trader, with
his black crew, into that port which was so lately that *nidus* of the Slave trade,"
the *Review* reported. A short biography, published in pamphlet form, quickly
went through two editions. For the next four months, the humble, plainspoken
captain was feted by leaders of the British antislavery movement, including
Wilberforce, Clarkson, and the Duke of Gloucester, nephew of the king and
honorary chair of the African Institution. In July, the institution convened in
special session to hear Cuffe and give him its blessing. "Clarkson and I are
both of the mind that the present opportunity for promoting the civilization
of Africa, through the means of Paul Cuffe, should not be lost," wrote indus-
trialist William Allen, who attended the meeting. "He seems like a man made
on purpose for the business; he has great experience as well as integrity."

In September, Cuffe sailed back to Sierra Leone. In addition to the usual
cargo—tea and tobacco, beef and butter—he carried a large crate of donated books, as well as an assortment of seeds, collected by the African Institution to test the colony's suitability for various crops. On this second visit to
Africa, Cuffe remained for three months, arranging the planned emigration
of African American settlers. He distributed the seeds—"few knew what to
do with them," he lamented—and surveyed local waterways for mill sites.
He also leased a large warehouse, with an eye to opening a branch of his
business in Freetown. He then set sail for home.

The voyage began inauspiciously. Four days out of Freetown, *Traveller* was detained by a British frigate on suspicion of slave trading. On reaching Newport, the ship was detained again, this time by a U.S. revenue cruiser. In the time Cuffe had been away, relations between Britain and the United States had soured again, and Congress had enacted a new nonintercourse act. In trading with a British port, he had unwittingly violated American law and stood to lose his ship and cargo. Facing ruin, Cuffe immediately embarked for Washington, D.C., armed with letters of introduction from his many prominent white patrons. Such was the influence of his patrons that he was granted an audience with President James Madison, becoming the first African American to be received officially at the White House. After leaving the president, Cuffe had a long interview with Secretary of the Treasury Albert Gallatin, who quizzed him about his plans and, to the captain's surprise, pledged all possible federal assistance to his efforts. Cuffe's property was restored to him, though the combination of heavy duties and "dull" markets rendered the trip a net loss.

On his return journey from Washington, Cuffe stopped in Baltimore, Philadelphia, and New York to promote his venture. He found enthusiasm for emigration at a fever pitch. African institutions were chartered in all three cities, to coordinate efforts with one another and with partners in London and Freetown. In New York, the captain's supporters underwrote publication of a short pamphlet, "A Brief Account of the Settlement and Present Situation of the Colony of Sierra Leone, in Africa," which included an account of his recent visit, as well as an open letter to African Americans from colonists in Freetown, enjoining them to follow their "forefathers out of the Egyptian bondage" and return to Africa. Hundreds of volunteers came forward. But politics once again intruded. In July 1812, the long-simmering conflict between the United States and Great Britain boiled over into war. For the next three years, commerce across the Atlantic was at a standstill.

At the outset of the war, Cuffe hoped that he might be exempted from the normal restrictions on trading with the enemy. While his allies in London petitioned the Privy Council for a special waiver, he returned to Washington, where he submitted a memorial to the U.S. Congress. In the memorial, he outlined his plan to carry a shipload of emigrants to Freetown, along with their provisions and implements, returning with "such of the native productions of that country" as were necessary to offset the cost of the venture. Disavowing any hopes of "pecuniary profit," Cuffe stressed that he was motivated solely by "Christian benevolence," a determination "to improve the condition of the degraded inhabitants of the land of [my] ancestors," most notably by diverting them from the sinful practice of "selling their fellow creatures into a state of slavery." Reprinted in papers across the United States, the petition attracted broad support in the Senate, which granted the waiver. In the House of Representatives, however, the bill became ensnared in partisan conflict, with southern Democrats rallying against what they saw as Federalist favoritism to a New Englander. In desperation, supporters of the bill reminded their southern opponents that Sierra Leone's success would "invite the emigration of free blacks, a part of our population which we could well spare," offering a preview of what would soon become the standard argument of the African Colonization Society. But Democrats were unmoved, and the bill was narrowly defeated.

Cuffe was finally able to sail for Africa in December 1815. He carried with him a company of thirty-eight settlers. By his own admission, the group bore little resemblance to the emigrants envisioned by his allies in London. Leaders of the African Institution had imagined transporting a small number of skilled pioneers, men who could teach the inhabitants of Sierra Leone how to grow staples like indigo and cotton. Cuffe's colonists, in contrast, consisted of nine families, including twenty children. All of the men were "common laborers," drawn from the free black communities of Boston and Philadelphia. At least two were native Africans, who were intent on returning home rather than remaining in Sierra Leone. Cuffe acknowledged the problem in a letter to William Allen, noting that the emigrants were poor and not "so much acquainted with treatment of tropical produce as would be desirable." Nonetheless, he hoped that they could make a useful contribution to Sierra Leone.

The families reached Freetown safely and, after some haggling, were granted the standard allotment of land provided to settlers. For Cuffe himself, however, the voyage was a financial disaster. Not only did he bear the brunt of the voyage's costs—few of the emigrants were able to pay for their passage—but he was also required to advance a year's provisions for the families, to ensure they did not become a burden on the colony. Duties were high, prices were low, and little was available in exchange besides camwood, with which the American market was already glutted. In the end, Cuffe lost more than $4,000 on the voyage, a severe setback, especially on the heels of three lean years of war.

While Cuffe strove to remain hopeful, he clearly felt the burden of many years of fruitless labor. Despite British naval patrols, the slave trade in the region continued to flourish, with the enthusiastic participation of local chiefs. "[I]t is to be lamented to see & hear with what rigor these [sic] slave trade is prosecuted," he confided to William Allen. Even with the influx of African recaptives into Freetown, the number of Africans carried away from Sierra Leone was still "far greater than the number taken in." Cuffe continued to hope that an enlarged commerce with America might "wean" Africans from the trade, but his efforts to promote it were stymied by "the many obstructions thrown in the way by government as well as by individuals." Such was his frustration that he was increasingly willing to look beyond Freetown. "[S]hould it appear that there could be no more view at Sierra Leone, could not there be a settlement made at some other place or port with prudence and equal safety," he asked in a letter to John Kizell. Though Kizell's reply does not survive, it is clear from other letters that he and Cuffe had begun to think of a new colony down the coast at Sherbro Island, where they might avoid British authority and commercial restrictions. In that suggestion lay the seeds of Liberia.

Paul Cuffe died in 1817, without ever returning to Africa. His final letters betray an uncharacteristic sense of desperation. Each passing month brought fresh reports of "motions of insurrection in the Southern states" and of the preparations taken by whites to meet violence with violence. With grim prescience, Cuffe warned that Americans were "preparing instruments for their own execution." The only way to forestall the impending cataclysm was for whites to rid themselves of slavery, but few masters were willing to manumit their slaves until they had some "safe ground" to which they could be sent. The very "peace and tranquility of the world" hinged on finding some place to resettle black Americans.

FOR THE BETTER PART of a decade, a man of color stood as the public face of African emigration. But as Paul Cuffe passed on to his reward, the torch of African repatriation passed into white hands. In December 1816, the

Society for the Colonization of the Free People of Color in the United States (later renamed the American Colonization Society) was established in Washington, D.C. In 1819, the society planted a second colony on Africa's Windward Coast, immediately south of Sierra Leone; the colony was dubbed Liberia, from the Latin word for freedom.

On the surface, Liberia represented the fulfillment of Cuffe's dream, an African refuge where black people could escape the shadow of bondage and "rise to be a people." But where Cuffe saw emigration as a way to stem the slave trade, the colonization movement was at best equivocal on the slavery question. Much of the new society's support, in fact, came from southern whites, who hoped to strengthen slavery by ridding the nation of free people of color.

As with the black emigration movement, the roots of the American Colonization Society reached back to American Revolution. Indeed, it was Thomas Jefferson who first advocated colonization. Jefferson's racial beliefs have lately become a subject of considerable popular interest, in the wake of DNA tests of descendants that appear to confirm (as some of his political opponents alleged at the time) that he fathered children by an enslaved woman, Sally Hemings. Even without this evidence, it is clear that the nation's third president was tortured by questions of race and slavery. Though a substantial slave owner himself, he genuinely abhorred the institution, as much for what it did to whites as to blacks. For Jefferson, the success of the new government depended on the virtue of its citizenry, on nurturing habits of reason and self-reliance, temperateness and democratic equality—precisely the qualities that slavery extinguished. "The whole commerce between master and slave is an exercise of the most boisterous passions, the most unremitting despotism on the one part and degrading submissions on the other," he wrote in *Notes on the State of Virginia*, published in 1780. "Our children see this and learn to imitate it." Slavery endangered the whole republican experiment.

Yet Jefferson could never countenance the logical implication of his abhorrence of black slavery: black freedom. An early proponent of what would later be called "scientific racism," he believed that nature had fashioned white and black people in fundamentally different ways. Though endowed with stout hearts and strong bodies, black people were "inferior in the faculties of reason and imagination." They lacked forethought. While imitative and capable of performing tasks by rote, they lacked originality and insight. They had no gift for oratory, and none had yet been born capable of comprehending Euclid's geometry. In short, they had none of the requisites of responsible republican citizenship. Jefferson also noted the painful history of relations between blacks and whites, which he believed precluded their ever living as equals within a common society. "Deep rooted prejudices entertained by the whites; ten thousand recollections, by the blacks, of the injuries they have sustained; new provocations; the real distinctions which nature has made; and many other circumstances, will divide us into parties, and produce convulsions, which will probably never end but in the extermination of the one race or of the other," he warned. For Jefferson, the dilemma seemed insoluble. "[W]e have a wolf by the ear," he declared, "and we can neither hold him nor safely let him go."

The only hope was that the problem would go away, that somehow both slavery and black people could be swept from the republic—in a word, colonization. Jefferson first advocated the idea in 1776, the year he authored the Declaration of Independence, when he chaired a committee on colonization in Virginia. He returned to it in *Notes on the State of Virginia*, offering a plan in which young blacks would be trained at public expense in "tillage" and other useful arts and transported outside of the United States. He returned to the issue in 1801, his first year in the White House, following the abortive Gabriel Prosser rebellion in Virginia. Warning of future bloodbaths, he urged the governor and legislature of Virginia to arrange for the removal of black people with all possible speed. His suggested destination was the West Indies, but he also dispatched an envoy to London to inquire whether the British would accept African Americans in Sierra Leone. He offered his most cold-blooded proposal in a private letter in 1824, two years before his death and four years after the Missouri crisis, the first in a series of sectional crises that would eventually culminate in secession. While conceding the impracticality of colonizing all slaves, Jefferson suggested that it might be possible to eliminate future "breeders," by forcibly separating infants from their mothers and deporting them. Such a scheme had the advantage of being far cheaper than competing plans, entailing "only the expense of nourishment . . . and of transportation." Admittedly, such a policy might occasion "scruples," but to Jefferson these were insignificant compared to the survival of the republic—akin, in biblical parlance, to "straining at a gnat, and swallowing a camel."

The challenge of fulfilling Jefferson's vision would fall to Robert Finley, a Presbyterian minister from New Jersey. With New Jersey's passage of a gradual abolition bill in 1804, the state's free black population soared. The increase continued in the 1810s, as thousands of free blacks from southern states entered the state, borne north by violent harassment and threats of reenslavement. The appearance of these ill-educated, ill-clad refugees provoked a sharp reaction from northern whites. Like the so-called urban underclass of our own time, free people of color were stigmatized as idle and ignorant, as dangerously disorderly people, whose penchant for vice and violent crime menaced social order. Northern states passed laws requiring free blacks to post good conduct bonds and bind their children to mandatory apprenticeships. A few passed laws preventing them from taking up residence at all.

Finley was more sympathetic than most, believing that black people's degradation was as much a product of blighting circumstance as of any inherent incapacity. Yet he could envision no way in which African Americans could ever achieve full American citizenship. His solution was colonization. For Finley, sending black Americans back to their ancestral continent promised all manner of blessings. An African American colony in Africa would encourage commerce, providing "a powerful means of putting an end to the slave trade." It would diffuse the blessings of "civilization and Christianity to Africa." It would benefit African Americans, who, once free of the shadow of slavery and prejudice, could "rise to that condition to which they are entitled by the laws of God and nature." Slave masters would feel free to manumit their slaves, now that they no longer faced the prospect of having to live alongside them. For Finley, the very alignment of so many interests was proof that "this scheme is from God."

Finley was not some isolated visionary but a prominent member of what contemporaries called the Benevolent Empire, an interwoven fabric of religious and reform organizations spun out of the great evangelical revivals of the early nineteenth century. His father-in-law, Elias Boudinot, was a Federalist congressman and president of the American Bible Society, an organization dedicated to placing a Bible in every American home. Finley found an even more valuable ally in Samuel Mills, an officer of the Bible Society and the dynamo of the Benevolent Empire. Though only thirty-three years old, Mills had already played a central role in establishing and sustaining a dozen benevolent organizations, including the nation's first overseas mission society, the American Board of Commissioners of Foreign Missions. Like Finley, Mills believed that African Americans had no future living among white people, and that they and the nation would be best served by colonization.

With their political connections, energy, and unshakable faith in their own rectitude, Finley and Mills possessed several of the requisites of a successful movement. What they lacked was any knowledge of Africa. To remedy the deficiency, they turned to Paul Cuffe, peppering the ailing captain with letters and questions. What could he tell them about Africa's climate, soil, and produce? Was Sierra Leone a viable destination, or was there some "other situation in Africa where the contemplated settlement or settlements could be formed with greater advantage"? When was the best season to embark? The letters leave no doubt that the men saw their efforts as a continuation of Cuffe's work. Indeed, they hoped that he might lead the first colonization expedition himself. Cuffe, for his part, welcomed their support and endeavored to answer their questions. He also urged them to collaborate with the various emigration organizations that had sprung up among African Americans, who would naturally be skeptical of a white-led colonization movement.

Experience would show the wisdom of Cuffe's advice, but Finley and Mills chose to ignore it. Instead, they devoted their energies to winning the support of the federal government. Spurning Philadelphia, the long-time capital of American benevolence and locus of Cuffe's greatest support, they headquartered the new society in Washington, D.C. Capitalizing on the political connections of Finley's father-in-law, they assembled a board of directors that read like a who's who of the nation's leaders. Supreme Court justice Bushrod Washington, George Washington's nephew and heir, was the society's president. The roster of vice presidents included Speaker of the House Henry Clay, General Andrew Jackson, Secretary of the Treasury William Crawford, and a raft of other political leaders. Day-to-day affairs of the society were overseen by Francis Scott Key, an aristocratic lawyer best known to history as the author of "The Star Spangled Banner." But one consorts with politicians at one's peril. While Finley had facilely assumed that colonization would promote abolition, the leaders who gathered at the inaugural meeting formally repudiated that linkage. On the contrary, Virginia Congressman John Randolph argued, colonization would "materially tend to secure" slavery, by eliminating free blacks, a population whose very existence was an incitement to "mischief" and "discontent" among slaves. Henry Clay agreed, insisting that the society avoid the "delicate question" of abolition altogether and emphasize instead the deportation of free people of color. In a final peroration, clearly aimed at southern slaveowners, he asked: "Can there be a nobler cause than that which, whilst it proposed to rid our country of a useless and pernicious, if not dangerous portion of its population, contemplates the spreading of the arts of civilized life, and the possible redemption from ignorance and barbarism of a benighted quarter of the globe?"

Clay's speech, reprinted in newspapers all around the country, may have reassured slaveowners but it enraged free people of color. Virtually overnight, African American support for African repatriation evaporated. In Philadelphia, some three thousand people crowded into a protest meeting at Bethel African Methodist Church. Denouncing the "unmerited stigma" that Clay had "cast upon the reputation of the free people of color," the Philadelphians asserted their determination to remain in the United States, fighting for their full rights as American citizens. America, not Africa, was "the land of our nativity," a land that had been "manured" by the "blood and sweat" of black people. They further stated their determination to continue fighting for the freedom of their brethren still in bondage. "We will never separate ourselves voluntarily from the slave population of the country," they declared. "[T]hey are our brethren by ties of consanguinity, of suffering, and of wrong." Significantly, the leaders who convened the meeting were all members of the local African institution and supporters of Paul Cuffe, and included Bishop Richard Allen, founder of the A.M.E. Church, and James Forten, a wealthy sailmaker who had outfitted Cuffe's *Traveller* for its inaugural visit to Sierra Leone. Forten had been particularly keen about emigration, quizzing Cuffe about the prospects for relocating his business to Freetown. But the appearance of the Society for the Colonization of the Free People of Color had altered his perspective. Though he remained convinced that blacks "will never become a people until they come out from amongst the white people," he was unwilling to endorse a scheme launched by slaveholders "to make their property more secure."

The response from Philadelphia clearly startled supporters of colonization. Robert Finley rushed to Philadelphia to meet with black community
leaders, assuring them that colonization would remain strictly voluntary. He
came away from the meeting confident that he had converted the men—"the
more enlightened they were, the more decisively they expressed themselves
on the desirableness of becoming a separate people," he reported—but he
badly misjudged the group's temper. A few weeks after his visit, a second,
even larger protest meeting convened at Bethel Church. Participants sharpened the attack on the society, arguing that colonization would remove the
only population genuinely committed to abolition. "Let no purpose be assisted which will stay the course of the entire abolition of slavery," they resolved. Hoping to alleviate such concerns, colonizationists elimated any
reference to free people of color in the name of the organization, which was
ever after known as the American Colonization Society. But nothing could
remove the onus of suspicion that Henry Clay's inaugural speech had laid on
colonization, and indeed on Africa itself.

The fact that free people of color had expressed themselves virtually
unanimously against colonization did not prevent A.C.S. leaders from proceeding. In late 1817, Samuel Mills and a companion, Ebenezer Burgess, embarked for Africa to find a location for the proposed colony. After a stopover
in England, where they met with leaders of London's African Institution,
they proceeded to Sierra Leone. Stricken with fever, Mills died on the return
voyage, but not before writing an account of his voyage, which Burgess edited and delivered to the society for publication. Predictably, the report was
positively rapturous about the prospects of colonization. Far from the howling waste imagined by most Americans, Africa was a veritable cornucopia,
with rich, fertile soil, innumerable navigable rivers, and limitless commercial
possibilities. All that the continent lacked was population; because of the
ravages of the slave trade, there were too few people to cultivate crops, or
even to pluck the fruit dangling from untended groves of "banana, orange,
lime, and plantain trees." The agents were particularly enthusiastic about
Sherbro Island, south of Freetown, which they had visited on the advice of
Paul Cuffe. Sherbro was "a land stored with the choicest minerals, bearing
the richest fruits," ideal for the intended colony. As for John Kizell, the Nova
Scotian settler who hosted them on the island, he was "a second Paul Cuffe,"

a man of Christian piety and native sympathy, ideally positioned to mediate between settlers and the indigenous people of the area. The travelers' own encounters with the locals were less satisfactory. Like many Western visitors to Africa, they grew exasperated with the endless "palavers," with chiefs' incessant demands for rum, with Africans' apparent inability to grasp the significance of the enterprise in which they were offered a part. But Mills and Burgess were not men to let a few Africans stand in the way of Africa's redemption. "If the people [prove] troublesome," Mills wrote dismissively, "fire a big gun out in the bay, and they will all fly to the bush."

Buoyed by the report, a congressman sympathetic to the colonization society introduced a bill amending the 1807 antislave trade act. Following the example of Britain, the bill proposed sending a U.S. Navy cruiser to West Africa to arrest ships illegally trading in slaves and to create a colony on the coast for the Africans redeemed from their holds, akin to the British colony at Sierra Leone. The proposal was obviously a stalking horse, intended to get the government to underwrite the colonization of African Americans. After vigorous debate about the legality of establishing an American colony overseas, President James Monroe (who was himself a member of the Virginia chapter of the colonization society) agreed to support the venture, as long as no federal money was expended. After further lobbying by colonizationists, Monroe agreed to pay for one shipload of colonists, ostensibly to build housing for the African recaptives to come. In recognition of the president's support, the capital of Liberia was called Monrovia.

ALL THAT THE PROPOSED colony lacked was colonists. Recruiting them would prove difficult. To most African Americans, the A.C.S. was nothing more or less than a state-sponsored deportation scheme, designed to rid the United States of its free black population in order to bolster the institution of slavery. Yet despite such suspicions, a small number of individuals volunteered for the inaugural expedition. One of them was Daniel Coker.

Daniel Coker's life reminds us of just how peculiar America's "Peculiar Institution" really was. He was born in 1780 on a Maryland plantation, the son of a white woman and her black slave. His given name was Isaac. While details of his early life are sparse, it appears that he was registered at birth as the child of a mulatto slave woman, sparing the community an unpleasant scandal at the cost of consigning a freeborn American to slavery. (Even without the ruse, Coker's propects would have been bleak, since Maryland law at the time stipulated that any child born of a white mother by a black father, whether slave or free, be bound over for labor until the age of thirty-one.) Despite his unfree status, Coker received a good education, thanks to his white half brother, Daniel, who refused to attend school without his playmate. When Coker escaped to New York in the 1790s, he adopted Daniel's name as his own, apparently to throw off his pursuers. In New York, Coker completed his education and began to preach in the Methodist Church, in which he was eventually ordained a deacon.

In 1807, a group of black leaders in Baltimore invited Coker to return to Maryland to open a school. As a fugitive, he was initially reluctant to accept, but the men prevailed on a local Quaker abolitionist to buy his freedom. Coker opened Baltimore's first school for black children, as well as its first black Methodist church, established after white Methodists in the city had attempted to introduce segregated seating at Sunday services. In 1816, Coker's church united with other black Methodist congregations along the eastern seaboard to create the African Methodist Episcopal Church, the country's first independent black denomination. Coker also earned distinction as an antislavery pamphleteer, most notably for his "Dialogue Between a Virginian and an African Minister," published in 1810. One of the first antislavery tracts published by an African American, the dialogue used an imagined conversation between a plodding white slaveholder and a brilliant black minister to assert and rebut a series of proslavery arguments.

Perhaps because of the strange turnings in his own life, Coker was a man preternaturally attentive to the "interpositions of providence" in human affairs. Blending his observations of American society with his reading of the Old Testament, particularly the story of the Exodus, Coker came to be persuaded that African Americans were destined to return to Africa, to carry back to Canaan the culture and religion that they had acquired in the providential school of slavery. He was an enthusiastic supporter of Paul Cuffe, hosting the captain during his visits to Baltimore and helping to establish the local branch of the African Institution. He continued to believe in African repatriation even after the rise of the American Colonization Society had cast the idea into disrepute among other black leaders. His persistence may have had something to do with his location: perched on the border of North and South, Maryland was a hotbed of colonizationist sentiment. There is also evidence to suggest a falling-out between Coker and the black Philadelphians who spearheaded the anticolonization movement. In early 1817, as the controversy over colonization exploded across black America, Coker attended the first conference of the newly established A.M.E. Church. Delegates at the conference initially elected him bishop, but then changed their minds and elevated Philadelphia's Richard Allen in his stead. "He being nearly white, the people said that they could not have an African Connection with a man as light as Daniel Coker as its head," one delegate recalled. There are also suggestions of a conflict or scandal, which led to Coker's temporary suspension from the A.M.E. ministry in 1818, a year in which he was also declared insolvent. Whatever his motives may have been, Coker defied other black leaders and cast his lot with the colonizationists.

In early February 1820, two Africa-bound ships embarked from New York. The *Cyane* was an American warship, sent to patrol the African coast for illegal slave traders. The *Elizabeth* carried a contingent of black colonists, eighty-eight in all, led by Coker and accompanied by three white agents representing the U.S. government and the colonization society. Nominally, the expedition was a laboring party, assigned the task of "clearing and cultivating the land, and building small houses for the accommodation of the recaptured Africans." In fact, they were settlers, recruited from free black communities along the eastern seaboard, as well as from an all-black settlement in the Illinois Territory. Nearly two thirds of them were children. One of the children, a two-year-old, died the evening before the *Elizabeth* embarked, a portent of things to come.

As the ship sailed, Coker began a journal, in which he described the voyage and his initial impressions of Africa. The journal was carried back to the United States on the *Elizabeth* and rushed into publication by the colonization society. In contrast to Paul Cuffe's logbook, which focused on business matters, Coker's journal was a spiritual autobiography, full of biblical references and meditations on the role of Providence in human affairs. Not surprisingly, he drew most of his daily devotions from the Old Testament, whose tales of captivity, dispersal, and return offered obvious parallels to African Americans' experience. An encounter with a wreck, its passengers and crew all apparently drowned, provoked thoughts of Moses and the Exodus, when God divided the sea and "led his chosen armies through." After one long evening spent "poring over our plan of a town" with the white agents, Coker turned to Isaiah 18, in which a people from "the land shadowing with wings, which is beyond the rivers of Ethiopia," a people "scattered and peeled . . . meted out and trodden under foot," would be gathered again by God at the foot of Mount Zion. "Oh my God, what is God about to do for Africa?" he wrote. "Surely something great."

When not writing in his journal, Coker engaged in discussions with the white agents, who, in a gesture of goodwill, had invited him to share their cabin. He was pleased to discover that all three were devout Christians, and together they offered "fervent prayer" for the success of their colony. Beyond the confines of the cabin, however, goodwill was in dwindling supply. Given their experiences, the settlers were naturally suspicious of white people, and they were surprised and chagrined to find themselves subordinate to white agents. Efforts by the agents to quell this "mutinous spirit" succeeded only in inflaming the situation. Coker tried to act "as a kind of middle link between the white and the colored," but his ties to the agents (as well as his very fair skin) rendered him suspect. By the time the *Elizabeth* reached Africa, the company had divided into rival camps, with many colonists refusing to take orders from either the white agents or the "mulatto" Coker.

The *Elizabeth* landed first in Freetown, where Coker and the agents sought the advice and assistance of local officials. None was forthcoming— the last thing British officials wanted to do was to encourage the founding of an American colony—but the visit did afford Coker his first glimpse of African life. His initial impression was shock at the people's ignorance of religious truth. "Oh! My dears, what darkness has covered the minds of this people," he wrote after a visit to a Kru village. "None but those who come and see, can judge. You would be astonished to see me traveling in the wilderness, guided by a little foot path, until, coming suddenly upon a little town of huts in the thickets; and there, to behold hundreds of men, women and children, naked, sitting on the ground or on mats, living on the natural productions of the earth, as ignorant of God as the brutes that perish." Yet the people were also gentle and kind, extending their hands and such food as they had. While some Africans had been corrupted "from intercourse with the slave-traders," most seemed to Coker like innocent children. "Such is their conduct that any one who loves souls would weep over them, and be willing to suffer and die with them," he wrote. "I can say, that my soul cleaves to Africa."

Coker's reference to his host's nakedness is especially noteworthy. Like generations of Western travelers, black and white, he was obviously shaken by the sight of exposed bodies: by the "natives sit[ting] naked on the shore" as the ship approached; the naked "children of nature" who came on board to offload the ship; the men and women, "all nearly naked," trading at Freetown's teeming market. Different travelers have interpreted African nudity differently; the sights that shocked Coker in the 1820s would be cited by Western visitors in the 1920s as an emblem of innocence, proof of Africans' freedom from Western repression. To Coker, however, nakedness was symbolic of the "gross darkness" that pervaded the land. In one journal entry, Coker cited Isaiah 20, an obscure passage, in which the prophet goes naked, in the manner of "Ethiopian" slaves, to alert the Jews to the "humiliation" awaiting them should they fail to uphold God's covenant.

After a fruitless week in Freetown, the colonists proceeded south to Sherbro Island, to a place called Campellar, where Paul Cuffe's old associate, John Kizell, had built a rudimentary settlement. If the voyage across the Atlantic had been disillusioning to some colonists, the sight of their new home must have been utterly demoralizing. Campellar was anything but the verdant Eden described by Mills and Burgess. Located on the eastern edge of the island, it was a low, muddy place, pocked by mangrove trees and a handful of ramshackle huts. Fresh water was in short supply. "The water at the place is not good or plenty," Coker wrote, "and it is too near the river, which is salt, to admit of a well." The arrival of the rains a few weeks later solved that problem, but brought new ones. During its four-month rainy season, Sherbro Island received nearly two hundred inches of rain, most of it in torrential downpours that washed away crops and turned the low-lying settlement into a quagmire.

Relations between the colonists and the indigenous people of the area began badly and deteriorated from there. Local chiefs, led by the Sherbro king, proved quite ready to accept tribute and engage in long palavers, but they refused to cede the land necessary for a settlement, much to the frustration of Coker and the A.C.S. agents. As with Paul Cuffe, the difficulties revolved in part around rum. From the chiefs' point of view, rum was the essential lubricant of all political and commercial transactions, but Coker refused to provide it. (The "first impressions on heathens are to be made by example," he wrote, quoting one of the books he had been reading.) Beneath that bit of cultural miscommunication was the hard rock of the slave trade. The area around Sherbro Island was one of the liveliest slaving grounds on the west coast, and all the local chiefs were deeply implicated in the traffic. As Coker observed, "They well know, if we get foot hold, it will be against the slave trade." The difference in interests was underscored when Coker and his party, returning from a long, fruitless palaver with the Sherbro king, came upon a hundred Africans in irons, waiting to be loaded onto a Spanish schooner. While the evidence is unclear, it appears that the colonists attempted to liberate the captives, an act that certainly did not endear them to local authorities.

Coker strove to stay hopeful. "I have no doubt that we shall succeed in getting lands," he wrote in his journal. "We must not get discouraged because these things do not go as fast as we could wish. These people are very slow in doing business." Unfortunately, time was not a resource the colonists enjoyed. The same attributes that made Campellar inhospitable to humans made it an ideal breeding ground for malaria and a variety of water-borne pathogens. Within three weeks of their arrival, many of the settlers had debilitating fevers. Soon they began to die. By July, three months after the *Elizabeth*'s arrival, a quarter of the settlers were dead, including all three white agents, leaving the embattled Coker in command of the colony.

As the colony struggled, smoldering racial animosities burst back into flame. Colonists initially blamed the white agents for the failure of negotiations. The problem, one settler declared, was that "the King & the head men . . . will not let a *white* man have the land." After the agents' deaths, the same charge was leveled at Coker. The allegation was apparently fanned by Kizell, who had fallen out with Coker, after a dispute over control of colony stores. "White blood is good, and black blood is good," Kizell is alleged to have said, "but [Africans] know that mulattoes are bastards, and will have no dealings with them." The charge was patently untrue; after centuries of the transatlantic trade, mixed-race people were ubiquitous on the coast, and chiefs routinely treated with them. Nonetheless, the statement speaks volumes about the state of affairs in the colony.

Coker succeeded in moving the suffering colonists to higher ground, to a place called Yonie, but his position had become untenable. African chiefs disdained him. Colonists ignored his orders. By early October, just six months after arriving in Africa, the situation had become so enflamed that he was forced to flee for his life to Freetown, accompanied by only a dozen loyalists. He made one attempt to reclaim his authority, traveling back to Yonie on a U.S. naval ship, but his appearance with a white escort only confirmed colonists' suspicions of him. After a brief standoff, Coker retreated back to Freetown, to await the arrival of the next contingent of A.C.S. agents and colonists, a group that included his wife and children.

The ship, the *Nautilus*, finally arrived in March 1821, a year to the day after the *Elizabeth*. For Coker, the arrival was bittersweet. While he was reunited with his wife and two sons, a third child, just a year old, had died in the passage. Hopes that he might be restored to his position were dashed. Like their predecessors on the *Elizabeth*, the colonists on the *Nautilus*, most of them recruited from the free black community of Richmond, Virginia, had quickly fallen out with the white agents sent out by the colonization society. Once again, Coker found himself caught in the crossfire. The conflict was exacerbated by religious differences, with the Virginians, staunch Baptists, refusing to "converse" or "commune" with either Methodists or Anglicans. "O Bigotry, thou art no friend to religion or colonizing," a discouraged Coker wrote.

Throughout his travails, Coker continued to keep a journal. Never published, the manuscript has a far more somber tone than the initial journal published by the colonization society. Coker recorded the extremes of weather, the ravages of fever on his children, the ever-growing roster of the dead. Mostly he communed with his own spirit, searching for meaning in his "late trials." Under the circumstances, he remained remarkably free of rancor or self-pity, but something of his state of mind can be gleaned from the biblical lessons he chose for his daily devotions: the book of Job ("well suited to my case"); Paul's letter to the Romans ("Lord, they have killed thy prophets, and digged down thine altars; and I am left alone, and they seek my life."); and, inevitably, the Exodus. "Moses was I think permitted to see the promised land but not to enter in," he wrote. "I think it likely that I shall not be permitted to see our expected earthly canaan. But this will be of but small moment so that some thousand of Africa's Children are safely landed."

Coker's prophecy proved correct. Though he survived long enough to witness the establishment of Liberia, he never saw the colony himself. Instead he remained in Sierra Leone, where he served as teacher and headman in a recaptive village called Hastings, outside Freetown. There he raised his family and presided over a small, nondenominational church. And there he died, fulfilling his pledge to give his life to "bleeding, groaning, dark, benighted Africa."

AS COKER RETIRED to Freetown, colonization society leaders sought a viable site for their colony. With the *Nautilus* émigrés settled in temporary quarters in Sierra Leone, the white agents proceeded down the coast. They negotiated a grant of land with a chief at Grand Bassa, but the treaty was contingent on the colonists' agreeing not to interfere with the slave trade. A.C.S. officials in the United States, struggling to rebut charges that colonization was a proslavery plot, rejected the treaty, and the search began anew. Eventually the agents settled on a strip of land around Cape Mesurado, some 250 miles south of Freetown. As at Sherbro, the local chief, King Peter, temporized, dragging out negotiations and then refusing to consent to a treaty. But his reluctance evaporated when an American naval officer, accompanying the agents, drew a pistol, cocked it, and held it to his temple. In the version of the story published by the colonization society, a shaft of golden sunlight burst through a gloomy sky at that exact moment, offering proof of providential approval. Whether the sun shone or not, the king signed the treaty, ceding control of a hundred miles of coastline in exchange for three hundred dollars' worth of rum, tobacco, and trinkets. The birth of nations is rarely a pretty process, but Liberia's birth was seedier than most.

Because most of the *Nautilus* emigrants were Virginians, it became the custom of A.C.S. promoters to characterize the settlement of Liberia as the Jamestown of Africa. The analogy was more apt than they knew. Like the Jamestown colonists two centuries before, the founders of Liberia struggled to find safe drinking water and to identify crops they could grow in the unfamiliar climate. They were ravaged by disease, strange fevers that attacked settlers within weeks of their arrival, killing scores. And like their predecessors in Jamestown, the settlers were quickly locked in mortal struggle with the indigenous population. While African American settlers continued to purvey the rhetoric of redeeming their benighted brethren, Liberia's history offered little in the way of either Christian brotherhood or racial solidarity. Conflict came to a head in late 1822, after the colonists had raided a slave factory on the coast, liberating the captives awaiting shipment and burning the holding pens to the ground. In the wake of the raid, King Peter, like Virginia's Powhatan two hundred years before, assembled a confederation of all the local tribes and attempted to destroy the colony. Eight hundred Africans swept into the settlement, but they were cut down by the superior firepower of the colonists. Peter launched a second unsuccessful assault in 1823. The years that followed would see sporadic raids and counterraids, but the military balance had shifted decisively in favor of the settlers.

Back in the United States, A.C.S. officials struggled to recruit colonists and to raise the funds to support them. In good years, one or two ships were dispatched, carrying food, trade goods, and fresh settlers to replace those carried away by fever. In early 1826, two ships arrived, one from North Carolina, the other from Boston. Among the passengers on the latter was an elderly African man named Occramar Marycoo, or, as he was known to most contemporaries, Newport Gardner. More than half a century after the Reverend Samuel Hopkins had hatched his scheme to atone for the sin of slavery by sending educated, Christian Africans to their ancestral continent, Gardner had finally returned to Africa.

By the standards of most African captives, the years had been kind to Gardner. In the early 1790s, he used the proceeds from a winning lottery ticket to purchase freedom for himself, his wife, Limas, and their first four children. (The couple's other children—they had thirteen in all—were all born after

passage of Rhode Island's gradual emancipation act and thus free at birth.)
The family lived comfortably enough on the money that Gardner made teaching music, supplemented by the small royalties he earned from his compositions. He continued to devote himself to the cause of racial elevation, teaching
in Newport's Free African School and serving for more than thirty years as an
officer in the Free African Union Society and its successor, the African Benevolent Society. He also served as sexton of Samuel Hopkins's First Congregational Church, right up until Hopkins's death in 1803. Townspeople became
accustomed to the sight of the two men, one black and one white, both gray-
ing, walking along the street arm in arm, deep in conversation.

Yet the years had not blinded Gardner to the hard lot of living as an
African in America, nor dimmed his desire to vindicate this history of suffering by carrying the gospel of Christ back to his natal continent. For all the
blessings of his own life, Gardner remained an outcast, a stranger in a
strange land. Thus in 1826, at the age of eighty, he boarded the *Vine*, a brig
out of Boston, and embarked for Liberia, accompanied by two dozen black
Newporters, including one of his own sons. "I go to set an example to the
youth of my race, I go to encourage the young," he declared as he boarded.
"They can never be elevated here. I have tried for sixty years—it is vain."

A few days after the *Vine* sailed, the *Boston Recorder and Telegraph* carried
an advertisement for a newly published anthem, "composed by Dea[con]
Newport Gardner, a native of Africa." The anthem drew on the story of the
Canaanite woman in the Gospel of Matthew—the same story that Phillis
Wheatley had referenced when Samuel Hopkins had written to her of his
African repatriation scheme more than half a century before. In the story, a
Canaanite woman begs Jesus to heal her daughter, but he rebuffs her, telling
her that the Son of Man had come to save the Jews, not to feed the dogs. "And
she said, 'Truth, Lord: yet the dogs eat of the crumbs which fall from their
masters' table.' Then Jesus answered and said unto her, 'O woman, great is
thy faith: be it unto thee even as thou wilt.' And her daughter was made whole
from that very hour." It is a curious story, as discomfiting today as when it
was written, but it marks a pivotal moment in the New Testament. Through
the simple piety of a member of a despised race, the gospel of salvation intended for the House of Israel becomes the birthright of all humankind.

Something in the story touched an eighty-year-old Canaanite in America—a man who had tasted the terror of capture as a child, who had encountered the gospel as a slave, who had heard the words of the Declaration of Independence read from the balcony of Newport's Colony House in July 1776, and then seen those soaring professions mocked and betrayed. Out of that experience came "Promise Anthem": "Hear the words of the Lord, O ye African race; hear the words of Promise. But it is not meet to take the children's bread and cast it to the dogs. Truth, Lord, yet the dogs eat of the crumbs that fall from their master's table. O, African, trust in the Lord: Amen. Hallelujah. Praise the Lord. Praise ye the Lord. Hallelujah. Amen."

On July 4, 1826, a few months after the *Vine*'s arrival in Liberia, Americans celebrated the fiftieth anniversary of the Declaration of Independence, and mourned the passing of its two greatest signers, Thomas Jefferson and John Adams. The two men had been adversaries for much of their careers, divided by philosophy, partisan affiliation, and attitudes toward slavery, but they had reconciled late in life, united by the second sight of those who live beyond their time. Their passing together, on the golden anniversary of the country they had brought into being, conferred a seemingly providential endorsement to the national celebration.

At virtually the same time, an old, fever-ridden African died in a rude hut in Liberia. Few noted his passing or pondered the strange Providence of his life. Fewer still wondered what the death of Newport Gardner might say about America's democratic promise.

· TWO ·

Representing the Race

HAD MARTIN DELANY had his way, December 27 would stand in history alongside the Fourth of July or Bastille Day as the birthday of a mighty nation. On that day in 1859, Delany and his fellow "commissioner," Robert Campbell, signed a treaty with Okukeno, the *alake*, or king, of Abeokuta, an Egba settlement in what is today Nigeria. Seven other chiefs placed their marks beside Okukeno's, conferring upon "the said Commissioners, on behalf of the African race in America, the right and privilege of settling in common with the Egba people." For Delany, the treaty represented the culmination of a dual quest to forge a future for the Negro race and to assert his own position as the race's representative leader. Standing in Abeokuta, he foresaw a proud and independent nation, exhibiting for all the world to see the capacity of black people to rule themselves.

History had other plans. By the time Delany returned home, the *alake*, facing British colonial pressure and a mounting backlash within Abeokuta itself, had abrogated the treaty. In America, the escalating sectional crisis exploded into civil war, making possible the abolition of slavery and temporarily foreclosing African American interest in African emigration. Delany himself marched south as a major in the Union army, the first black man ever to hold field rank in the U.S. military. In his authorized biography, published in 1868, the Abeokuta colony was not even mentioned. Yet the story of the abortive colony represents, in its own peculiar way, one of the epics of the nineteenth century, as a series of sweeping changes on three continents all came to a point at a single place and time. At the center of that convergence stood Martin Robison Delany, one of African American history's most curious and compelling characters.

DELANY WAS BORN in 1812 in western Virginia, the child of a freeborn mother and an enslaved father. He was, by his own account, of "unadulterated" African blood, with piercing dark eyes and a skin that contemporary William Lloyd Garrison described as "black as jet." When he was ten, his mother carried him and his siblings to Chambersburg, Pennsylvania, apparently to escape the harassment of local officials, who objected to her teaching her children to read. At the age of nineteen, Delany moved to Pittsburgh, where he completed his education under the tutelage of Louis Woodson, minister of the local A.M.E. church and a pioneering black nationalist. If his later writing is any guide, he received an exceptionally thorough education, embracing theology, political economy, classical and modern literature, law, geography, and the physical sciences. Over the course of his life, Delany would put most of these subjects to use, working variously as a barber, journalist, novelist, medical doctor, inventor, antislavery lecturer, astronomer, pharmacist, politician, explorer, soldier, and jurist. William Herndon's famous description of Abraham Lincoln—"His ambition was a little engine that knew no rest"—might be applied equally to his African American contemporary, Martin Delany.

To understand Delany's extraordinary career it is necessary to understand the circumstances of the free black community into which he was born. By the time he came of age, every northern state had abolished slavery. (The last to act was New York, which abolished the institution on July 4, 1827.) Yet in none of these states did African Americans enjoy full citizenship. Free people of color were excluded from skilled trades, mocked in minstrel shows (fast emerging as the nation's premier form of popular entertainment), and consigned to segregated schools, churches, even cemeteries. The basic privileges of citizenship—the right to bequeath and inherit property, to testify in court, to sit on juries, and, most important, to vote—were sharply circumscribed. In New York, for example, the state constitution of 1821 imposed new franchise restrictions on free people of color even as it extended universal suffrage to white men; by 1825, only sixteen African Americans remained on the voters' rolls of New York City, out of a total black population of more than twelve thousand. Discrimination was worse in the Midwest, where so-called black codes worked to exclude all African Americans, slave or free. Free blacks wishing to settle in Ohio, for example, were legally required to provide good conduct bonds of $500, as well as testimonials from two white citizens.

The legislative assault on people of color reached its logical conclusion in the era's frequent "race riots," essentially pogroms, in which white mobs rampaged through black neighborhoods, beating residents and looting and burning property. One historian has counted forty-one significant riots in the United States in the quarter century between 1824 and 1849. If one includes the work of antiabolitionist mobs, the number of episodes is well over one hundred. Providence endured race riots in 1824 and 1831. Philadelphia experienced the first of five major riots in 1829. Cincinnati was engulfed the same year, prompting an exodus of the city's black population.

The situation was equally bleak at the level of national politics. The rapid expansion of upland cotton cultivation following the invention of the cotton gin had long since eliminated any hopes that slavery would die a natural death. The southern antislavery movement, always feeble, was all but extinct, and slaveholders exercised unchallenged sway over every southern state and, increasingly, over the federal government as well. By the 1830s, the U.S. Congress, including both the House of Representatives and the Senate, included just one man who was avowedly opposed to slavery—former president John Quincy Adams. The awkward diffidence with which southerners had defended their peculiar institution had been replaced by an unapologetic proslavery ideology, which represented Negro slavery not as a necessary evil but as "a good, a positive good," the cornerstone of white freedom and a blessing to the slaves themselves, whose retarded intellectual development rendered them incapable of freedom. "We see [slavery] now in its true light," South Carolina senator John C. Calhoun declared, "and regard it as the most stable and safe basis for free institutions in the world."

As the horrors multiplied, some free people of color sought asylum outside the United States. An invitation from Jean-Pierre Boyer, president of Haiti, prompted a short-lived emigration movement to the black republic in the 1820s. Others looked to Canada. Following the Cincinnati riot, more than two thousand black Ohioans embarked for Ontario, where they established several all-black settlements, settlements that would later become a refuge for southern slaves fleeing north on the Underground Railroad. Yet even in these grim times, the vast majority of free people of color opposed emigration, evincing a determination to stay and fight for their full portion as American citizens. As for colonization to Liberia, free people of color remained almost unanimously opposed, disdaining a scheme that most continued to see as a proslavery plot. "I have for several years been striving to reconcile my mind to the colonization of Africans in Liberia," wrote Richard Allen, founder of the A.M.E. Church and an early supporter of Paul Cuffe, but after long reflection he had concluded that the scheme profited no one but the slaveholder. "This land which we watered with our tears and our blood is now our mother country," Allen declared.

Allen's letter appeared in an early issue of *Freedom's Journal,* black America's first newspaper and an important venue for the roiling national debate over colonization. A four-page weekly, the journal was the work of two free New Yorkers, Samuel Cornish and John Russwurm. "We wish to plead our own cause," the editors announced in the inaugural issue, which appeared in March 1827. "Too long have others spoken for us. Too long has the publick been deceived by misrepresentations in things which concern us deeply." Though welcoming diverse viewpoints, Cornish and Russwurm left no doubt where they stood on the issue of African Americans' future. "In the discussion of political subjects, we shall ever regard the constitution of the United States as our polar star," they wrote. "Born in this Republican country; constituting one of its constituent parts; attuned to its climate and soil," black Americans were entitled to full civil equality, including the right to vote. The task of responsible leaders was not to conjure false dreams of paradise across the sea but to prepare African Americans for the responsibilities of citizenship, which *Freedom's Journal* sought to do through the inclusion of edifying articles on education, temperance, history, and other topics calculated to promote "moral, religious, civil and literary improvement." "We are unvarying in our opinion that the time is coming (though it may be distant) in which our posterity will enjoy equal rights," the editors wrote.

Yet even as they renounced colonization and pledged allegiance to the United States, Cornish and Russwurm remained keenly interested in Africa. "[E]verything that relates to Africa shall find a ready admission into our columns," they announced, adding that "as that vast continent becomes daily more known, we trust that many things will come to light, proving that the natives of it are neither so ignorant nor stupid as they have generally been supposed to be." Implicit in that statement was an acknowledgment of an enduring fact of African American life: that in a world bewitched by the idea of race, the status and reputation of African Americans was inextricably bound up with the status of Africans. In addition to arguments about colonization, *Freedom's Journal* carried articles on African geography and climate, essays on the accomplishments of ancient Egypt and Ethiopia, even the occasional African-themed poem. The editors were particularly interested in the reports of contemporary explorers, from Paul Cuffe (whose account of his first voyage to Sierra Leone was serialized in the inaugural issues) to English travelers such as Mungo Park, Dixon Denham, and Hugh Clapperton. Over the course of the nineteenth century, the tradition of Dark Continent reportage pioneered by Park and his successors would become more flagrantly racist, providing much of the intellectual justification for European colonialism, but in 1827 Cornish and Russwurm remained hopeful that the "progress of geographic discovery" in Africa would help to dispel the fog of myth and misrepresentation that pervaded the continent, making possible a proper appreciation of black people everywhere.

Undeterred by African American opposition, white officials of the American Colonization Society continued to promote colonization as the last best hope of the black race. *The African Repository,* the society's monthly

journal, published a steady stream of letters from Liberian settlers, all painting the colony in roseate hues. "We are all going on with some elegant improvements to our farms," ran a typical letter. "Monrovia now looks like
many little towns in America, with nice stone or frame buildings . . . [and] is
as happy a little community as any . . . you will find of its size in America."
The A.C.S. scored a major coup in 1829, when John Russwurm, in a stun-
ning reversal, resigned from *Freedom's Journal* and announced his intention
to go to Liberia to edit its first newspaper, the *Liberia Herald*. Word of Russwurm's apostasy raced through the black American community—the editor
received death threats—but if A.C.S. officials imagined that others would
follow his example they were disappointed. In most years, the society struggled to recruit enough colonists to fill a single ship, too few even to replenish
those settlers claimed annually by fever.

The colonization society received a fillip in 1831, following the Nat
Turner revolt in Southampton County, Virginia. The revolt, which claimed
more than sixty lives, was the southern nightmare brought to life: a black
army, led by a messianic slave, putting white men, women, and even children
to the sword. Echoing the dark forebodings of Thomas Jefferson, A.C.S. officials offered colonization as the only way to avoid a future bloodbath. Between December 1831 and December 1832, the society dispatched six ships
for Liberia, carrying more than a thousand colonists, including more than
three hundred from Southampton County. In one case, A.C.S. officials
cleared a ship, the *Ajax*, in full knowledge that some of the emigrants were
carrying cholera. In a grim reenactment of the middle passage, the entire
complement was soon infected and most of the passengers perished, including thirty children. Undeterred by that horror, state colonization societies
in Maryland, Pennsylvania, New York, Mississippi, and Louisiana all announced the creation of new Liberian settlements, in some cases with the
support of state legislatures.

The idea that colonization would somehow resolve the slavery problem
was, of course, chimerical, as it had been during Jefferson's day. Even as the
A.C.S. struggled to ship a few hundred settlers per year to Liberia, the
African American population was growing by more than sixty thousand per
year through natural increase. But the spike in colonization after the Nat

Turner uprising wrought a dramatic change in the character of Liberian society. While most early colonists had been free people of color, those arriving after 1831 were chiefly southern slaves, manumitted on condition that they accept colonization to Africa. The most dramatic example was the new settlement at the mouth of the Sinoe River, which was populated by residents of a single Mississippi plantation, whose owner, Isaac Ross, had stipulated in his will that his slaves be freed and shipped to Liberia. Most of these settlers were penniless when they arrived. Few had ever seen the inside of the school. Many lacked even basic agricultural experience, having worked as house servants. These were hardly the settlers one might have chosen to make their way in a difficult frontier environment. Given Liberia's subsequent history, one might also question the wisdom of populating a country with settlers whose primary social model was the southern plantation.

For black leaders, the increase in conditional manumissions after the Nat Turner uprising confirmed what they had always alleged: that colonization would not be voluntary; that underlying the mushy rhetoric about African redemption lay the hard rock of American racism. The result was another round of mass meetings and resolutions, in which free people of color across the North reiterated their opposition to colonization and their determination to continue fighting for freedom and full citizenship in the United States. The most notable outcome of this revived anticolonization movement was a change in nomenclature, from "African" to "Negro" or "Colored." Since colonial days, "African" had remained the accepted term of address for black people in North America. For some at least, it was a term of great pride, as the various "African" institutions chartered in the late-eighteenth and early-nineteenth centuries attested. But by the early 1830s, many black leaders had concluded that the term was an unaffordable luxury, that in calling themselves Africans they lent credence to colonizationists' claims that they rightly "belonged" in Africa rather than the United States. "Let us and our friends unite, in baptizing the term *'Colored American,'* and henceforth let us be written of, preached of, and prayed of as such," wrote Samuel Cornish, founder of *Freedom's Journal* and a leader of the recently established Colored Convention Movement. "It is the true term, and one which is above reproach." Others nominated "Negro," a term previously eschewed because of its connotations of enslavement. In 1835, leaders of the new National Negro Convention movement called upon black Americans "to remove the title of African from their institutions, the marbles of their churches, and etc." and to replace it with Negro. While some institutions elected to keep their historical names (most notably the African Methodist Episcopal Church), many complied, and "African" was literally effaced from the dedicatory plaques and escutcheons of hundreds of churches, schools, and benevolent societies.

REMOVING "AFRICAN" FROM CHURCH cornerstones was one thing; removing the continent from the imaginations of black Americans was quite another. In a nation ruled by descendants of Europe, Africa has long been and remains the touchstone of black difference, the point of departure for any discussion of African American history, identity, and destiny. So it was in the antebellum years. Even as the generations of men and women born in Africa passed away and direct memories of the continent faded, Africa remained a palpable presence in African American life, a subject of allegiance and anxiety, of theological speculation and political debate. And nowhere did Africa bulk larger than in the mind of Martin Delany.

Delany spent the 1830s in Pittsburgh, working as a barber while apprenticing as a medical doctor. Though still a young man, he became one of the leaders of the black community in the city, helping to found two literary societies, a temperance union, a Masonic lodge, and a Young Men's Moral Reform Society. In 1843, he launched *The Mystery,* one of the first black periodicals in the United States. Judging from the few surviving issues, he produced the bulk of the copy himself, interspersing hortatory essays and editorials with advertisements and reports of local events. The paper, which ran for four years, provided an early glimpse of what would become his signature themes, including an emphasis on black "self elevation" and a determination to overthrow slavery by any means necessary. Both commitments were apparent in the paper's masthead, which featured an epigram from Byron: HEREDITARY BONDSMEN! KNOW YE NOT WHO WOULD BE FREE, THEMSELVES MUST STRIKE THE FIRST BLOW?

Even at this early stage of his career, Delany defied easy classification.

Viewed from one perspective, he was the archetypal antebellum reformer, invoking the virtues of industry, thrift, and self-reliance while inveighing against idleness, intemperance, and vice. Though keenly aware of the burden of racism, he insisted that free people of color had both the opportunity and the obligation to live dignified, respectable lives, and that by doing so, they could conquer white prejudice and claim their full portion in American social, economic, and political life. Yet Delany was also a thoroughgoing black nationalist. While leaders such as Frederick Douglass and William Whipper advocated the "abolition of complexional distinctions," he championed race pride and the power of his own undiluted black blood. (Delany, Douglass once complained, "has gone about the same length in favor of black, as the whites have in favor of the doctrine of white supremacy.") Black people's survival, he argued, hinged on cultivating "national feeling," a phrase that for Delany connoted not only unity of purpose but also genuine self-determination. But he was not yet an advocate of emigration, still focusing his energies on achieving freedom and full citizenship in the United States.

If one idea distinguished Delany's thinking it was his abhorrence of black dependency, in all its forms. Such a sentiment was hardly unusual in the antebellum era, but it was sharpened in Delany's case by his training in biology, which warned that characteristics of temperament acquired in one generation were transmitted to the next. Thus the servility and dependency instilled in African Americans, both slave and free, would become part of their "physiological condition," which would be "transmitted to the offspring," making black degradation perpetual. Subsequent research on biological inheritance would debunk this idea, but it was a cornerstone of Delany's thought, undergirding not only his opposition to slavery but also his suspicions of white philanthropy, his contempt for domestic service, and his oft-expressed reservations about black religion, which he believed reinforced fatal habits of submission and passivity. Most important, it helps to explain his disdain for the American Colonization Society and its misbegotten stepchild, Liberia. To expect "a conclave of upstart colored hirelings of the slave power," men who had tamely submitted to their own expatriation, to raise up a proud black nation was, for Delany, about as sensible as expecting a lamb to birth a lion.

Unlike many contemporaries, however, Delany did not allow his feelings about Liberia to color his attitude toward the rest of Africa; on the contrary, he stood second to none in his reverence for the continent. Rejecting portrayals of African history as a record of unrelieved savagery, he argued that Africans had raised great civilizations in the past, indeed that many of the West's most vaunted achievements—its science, art, and philosophy—were African in origin. In an 1853 address to Pittsburgh's St. Cyprian Masonic Lodge, an institution he had helped to found, Delany posited the basic syllogism of what later generations would call "Afrocentrism": Egypt was an African society, an offshoot of the great empire of Ethiopia; Greece and Rome imported their civilization from Egypt; therefore, the West owed its civilization to Africa. According to Delany, religious revelation itself came from Africa, having originated with the "erudite" Ethiopians and Egyptians, who passed it on to the slave Moses, a man described in the Bible as "learned in all the ways of the Egyptians." This Afrocentric sensibility was enshrined even in the names Delany gave his children, including Ethiopia and Rameses.

Delany first stepped onto the national stage in 1847, when he met Frederick Douglass and William Lloyd Garrison, who had come to Pittsburgh on an antislavery speaking tour. Impressed by his "energy and spirit," the two men invited him to accompany them. By the end of the tour, Delany and Douglass had agreed to collaborate on a national black newspaper, to be published independently of Garrison's *Liberator*. The inaugural issue of the paper, the *North Star*, rolled off the presses in December 1847, with Douglass and Delany as coeditors.

The partnership lasted eighteen months. Delany spent most of that time on the road, setting up a distribution network for the *North Star* and penning essays on diverse subjects, from the problem of color prejudice among fair-skinned African Americans to the proslavery plot to annex Cuba. His main contribution, however, was a series of some twenty letters in which he described his travels through the northern free black community. Like their author, the letters defy easy characterization, mixing irony and indignation, lyricism and censoriousness. In one letter, Delany recounted having rocks thrown at him as he traveled the National Road; in another, he described an encounter with an Ohio mob intent on tarring and feathering him. Yet the overall tone was hopeful. Despite the innumerable barriers they faced, free people of color were rising—opening schools, creating businesses, sustaining themselves in trades. "This is what I desire to see—our people coming out of old employments of domestic servitude and menial occupations," he wrote. "This must be done if we expect ever to be elevated to an equality with the dominant class."

The letters also provide a record of Delany and Douglass's estrangement. By the end of 1848, the two men were openly squabbling in the pages of the paper. In June 1849, Delany resigned from the *North Star*, inaugurating a rivalry that would persist for the next thirty-six years, until Delany's 1886 death. While waged over issues of political strategy, the conflict was fundamentally a struggle for dominance between two brilliant, proud, sensitive men, each of whom regarded himself as the authentic leader of the black race. For all their differences in background and temperament, Delany and Douglass shared an almost mystical sense of leadership, of having been anointed by history to speak on behalf of a silent, suffering race. Significantly, they based their claims on different grounds. Douglass rested his case on his experience as a slave, which he recounted in no fewer than three published autobiographies. He had been beaten, seen loved ones sold away, known the pangs of hunger and hopelessness, and yet risen from the darkness into the light of freedom, manhood, and self-knowledge. Delany, who had never been a slave, predicated his claim not on personal history but on his pure, "unadulterated" black blood. A mulatto leader could never adequately represent the race, he warned, since whites would simply "say that his talents emanate from the preponderance of white blood in him." (Douglass, of course, was a mulatto.) Not coincidentally, the two men adopted very different postures toward Africa. While both opposed Liberian colonization, Delany self-consciously draped himself in the mantle of his ancestral continent, sometimes literally donning African garb for public appearances. As he himself once boasted, he was "the *most* African of all the black men now in this country." For Douglass, Africa was an irrelevancy, a distraction from the struggle for full equality in the United States.

Understanding the rivalry with Douglass and the terms in which it was waged helps to explain many aspects of Delany's character and career, including the sense of ceremony with which he went about his business. Author Anna Julia Cooper, who knew him in his later years, recalled: "The late Martin R. Delany, who was an unadulterated black man, used to say when honors fell upon him, that when he entered the council of kings, the black race entered with him." At the same time, this context casts fresh light on some of Delany's less savory characteristics, including his gift for self-aggrandizement and his penchant for abrupt, often opportunistic, shifts in political allegiance. Conceiving himself as the virtual embodiment of "the African race," Delany sometimes failed to see any distinction between his own interests and those of black people as a whole. This quality was perhaps most obvious during the Reconstruction era, when Delany found himself in an unlikely alliance with some of the South's most notorious white supremacists, but it also shaped his antebellum career as an African emigrationist.

DELANY ENTERED NATIONAL POLITICS at a pivotal moment. In 1848, Liberia became a self-governing republic, joining Haiti in the ranks of independent black nations. In contrast to Haiti, which achieved nationhood through revolution, Liberia was granted independence by its white sponsors, who hoped that nationhood would increase the colony's diplomatic standing, especially with France and Britain, both of which had flatly refused to acknowledge the sovereignty of a private corporation, disputing Liberia's territorial claims and refusing to pay its customs and duties. In practice, Liberia remained a ward of the A.C.S., which continued to recruit colonists and to underwrite the costs of their transportation and resettlement. Yet however qualified Liberia's independence, the sheer fact of nationhood dramatically elevated its status among African Americans.

As Liberia became independent, the predicament of black people in the United States grew ever more precarious. The annexation of Texas by the United States in 1845 opened a vast new field for slavery, while foreclosing an important asylum for fugitive slaves. The onset of the Mexican War one year later, and the massive cession of territory that followed, further emboldened southern slaveowners, who insisted, under threat of secession, on their right to carry slaves into the new territories. The Compromise of 1850 forestalled secession, but at the cost of a draconian new Fugitive Slave Act, which required all able-bodied citizens to participate actively in the apprehension of escaped slaves. Black people claimed as fugitives bore the burden of proving their free status, but they were denied any practical means to do so, including the right to testify in their own defense. As Delany observed, the act virtually licensed kidnapping. "We are slaves in the midst of freedom," he wrote, "waiting patiently . . . for masters to come and lay claim to us."

Viewed from the perspective of today, the crises over slave extension in the 1850s appear as steps on the road to the Civil War and eventual abolition. But to free people of color at the time, they seemed steps on the road to perdition, elements in a southern plot to nationalize slavery. Such fears were seemingly confirmed by the Kansas-Nebraska Act of 1854, which opened the door to slavery in territories from which it had previously been excluded, and the Supreme Court's notorious 1857 *Dred Scott* decision, which established the sanctity of slave property even in (to use Delany's phrase) "the nominally free states." As Chief Justice Roger Taney explained, the Founding Fathers had never contemplated members of the "African race" as "people" within the meaning of the Constitution; thus Negroes were not citizens, whether slave or free. Black people, he added in a chilling obiter dictum, were "beings of an inferior order, and altogether unfit to associate with the white race, either in social or political relations; and so inferior that they had no rights which the white man was bound to respect."

The combination of Liberian independence and dwindling hopes in the United States produced another surge in colonizationist activity. Between 1848 and 1854, more than forty ships embarked for Liberia, carrying more than four thousand colonists; virtually overnight, the republic's settler population increased threefold. Included in the roster of new colonists were Edward Blyden and Alexander Crummell, two of the towering figures in the history of Pan-Africanism, who emigrated in 1851 and 1853, respectively. Even long-time critics of Liberia reconsidered their opposition, including the Reverend Henry Highland Garnet, whose calls for violent resistance to slavery had marked him as one of black America's most militant leaders. Through the 1840s, Garnet had steadfastly opposed colonization, pledging to ignore "the harp-like strains that whisper freedom among the groves of

Africa . . . while three millions of my country are wailing in the dark prison-house of oppression." But by the early 1850s, he had reconsidered. "My mind of late has greatly changed in regard to the American Colonization scheme," he declared. "I would rather see a man free in Liberia, than a slave in the United States."

While some African Americans made their peace with Liberia, many others did not. The 1850s witnessed a ferocious debate over colonization, which continued even as the country careered into a war that would render the whole question moot. The character of the debate was neatly captured in rival accounts written by two men who had the distinction of having sailed to Liberia on the same ship, the *Isla de Cuba*, in 1853. Daniel Peterson's *The Looking-Glass* was a veritable testimonial for the colonization society. As if to confirm the allegations of Martin Delany, Peterson was a former domestic servant, whose experience working in the homes of some of the most "eminent" families in Baltimore and Philadelphia had given him a rare appreciation of white people's innate kindness and generosity. "I have found all my best friends among the white people," he boasted. His description of Liberia, written after less than a month in the republic, was rapturous. "I must say that I never saw a more attractive place," he gushed. The climate was salubrious, the soil was rich, the settlers were healthy and prosperous. Peterson was less impressed with the indigenous population, whom he described as filthy, naked, and idolatrous, but he was confident that once exposed to the blessings of Christianity and sustained labor, they could be rendered useful. Just as the "lands want ploughing up and sowing," so the "minds of the natives must be broken up with the ploughshare of the gospel."

If Peterson offered a caricature of colonizationism, William Nesbit's *Four Months in Liberia: or, African Colonization Exposed* made the anticolonization case with equal starkness. Nesbit hailed from Pittsburgh, and appears to have worked for a time with Delany, who contributed a preface to the book. His motives for emigration remain unclear: in his book, he alternately described himself as a dupe of colonizationists and as an undercover agent working to expose their lies. But there was no mistaking his reaction to Liberia. "On stepping ashore, I found that we had been completely gulled and done for," he wrote. "The whole country presents the most woe begone and hopeless aspect which it is possible for a man to conceive of." Where Peterson saw a veritable "Garden of Eden," Nesbit saw a rancid backwater, a land of "violent and appalling storms," "loathsome" diseases, "wild beasts of prey, obnoxious and poisonous reptiles, and destroying insects." Where Peterson described enterprising settlers ruling themselves with intelligence and the "utmost decorum," Nesbit saw a "cod-fish aristocracy," loading themselves with empty titles while their society sank back into the swamp from which it had emerged. Perhaps the only thing the two men shared was a disdain for the "naked natives," whom Nesbit also regarded as "filthy and disgusting . . . lazy, rude, and ignorant." But while Peterson had proffered this portrait as proof of African Americans' providential calling, Nesbit offered it as a warning of the condition to which settlers in Liberia were "fast retrograding."

Nesbit had one more bombshell to drop: African American settlers, he alleged, were guilty of enslaving indigenous Africans. "Let the colonist himself be barefoot, and three parts naked, let him feel the gnawings of want ever so keenly, still he is never too poor to own slaves and to have a hut for them a short distance from his own," he wrote. Like so many of the book's claims, the charge was at once simplistic and broadly true. As early as the 1820s, recaptive Africans deposited at Monrovia by U.S. Navy patrols were distributed as "apprentices" on settler farms. Soon thereafter the settlers began recruiting indigenous Africans, chiefly children, as domestic laborers, using a system that combined African practices of pawnship with elements of indentured servitude. As the republic's defenders were quick to point out, such practices were a far cry from slavery, which the Liberian Constitution strictly forbade. "Servants" and "apprentices" were contracted for a fixed numbers of years; they enjoyed access to courts and a variety of other rights and privileges. But both systems were subject to widespread abuse and could all too easily devolve into slavery, pure and simple. With the beginnings of sugar and coffee production in the 1850s, the Liberian countryside bore a more than passing resemblance to the Old South, complete with porticoed plantation homes, widespread concubinage, and physical abuse of African workers, many of whom served for life. As in the South, the system was rationalized with bromides about Christianity, civilization, and the importance of instilling habits of industry in indolent people.

Delany played a conspicuous role in the debates of the 1850s. But his positions were not always consistent, reflecting the desperation of the times and his own changing circumstances. He continued to sound the call for self-elevation in the United States, even as he conceded that laws such as the Fugitive Slave Act had made black people "aliens to the laws and political privileges of the country." He remained an "inveterate hater" of colonization. In the wake of independence, he briefly held out hope that Liberia might slip the leading strings of the A.C.S. and "become a place of note and interest," but he soon concluded that independence was a sham, just another wrinkle in colonizationists' "degrading, expatriating, insolent, slaveholding scheme." Yet when the Massachusetts Colonization Society offered him and two other African Americans an opportunity to enroll at Harvard Medical School in 1850, he leaped at the chance. While his intentions remain unclear, officials of the colonization society clearly expected him to move to Liberia upon finishing him studies. Delany was spared the decision. In 1851, he and his two classmates were expelled, following protests by other students, who argued that "the admission of blacks to the medical Lectures" undermined the "reputation" of Harvard and hence lessened "the value of a degree from it."

The expulsion was devastating to Delany, and doubtless encouraged his dawning interest in emigration. Yet he continued to vacillate. A few months after leaving Harvard, he attended a black emigration convention in Toronto, but ended up voting against the final resolution, arguing that free people of color had an obligation to remain in the United States fighting for the freedom of their brethren still in bondage. At the same time, he lent his name and support to a new black settlement in Greytown, Nicaragua. In 1852, Greytown residents elected him mayor in abstentia, an office he accepted despite never having set foot in the settlement.

The year 1852 also saw the publication of Delany's first book, *The Condition, Elevation, Emigration, and Destiny of the Colored People of the United States,* a wide-ranging tract that encapsulated all the uncertainties and tensions in his thought. Written in a white heat of indignation—he claimed to have composed the entire manuscript in a month—the book is both brilliant and bewildering. The first two thirds included a ringing defense of African Americans' claim to full American citizenship. In the balance of the book, however, Delany reversed field, endorsing emigration. Black Americans, he argued, were trapped as a "nation within a nation," an anomalous position akin to the historical predicament of the Jews. Despised and dependent, they would never command respect until they had created a nation of their own, a place where they constituted "the ruling element." Anticipating charges that emigration meant abandoning southern slaves to their plight, Delany argued that the rise of an independent nation would, through a kind of "reflex influence," elevate the status of black people everywhere and thus strike a powerful blow against slavery.

Having "incontrovertibly shown" the necessity of emigration, Delany turned to the real question: "Where shall we go?" The answer, needless to say, was not Liberia. "Liberia is not an Independent Republic," he wrote; "in fact, *it is not* an independent nation at all; but a poor *miserable mockery*—a *burlesque* on government—a pitiful dependency on the American Colonizationists." Canada offered a temporary refuge, but Delany saw little logic in settling in a country where black people would constitute an even tinier minority than they did in the United States. The best option, he concluded, was "Central America," a region embracing in his mind everything from Mexico to Brazil, including the islands of the Caribbean. This vast swath of territory had few white settlers and, in Delany's curious rendering, no tradition of racial discrimination. Its climate suited people of color, while its soil was perfect for the kind of staple crops—cotton, rice, indigo—that black people were expert at growing. In language suffused with the contemporary rhetoric of Manifest Destiny, he called upon African Americans to claim Central and South America as their providential "asylum," just as Europeans had done in North America.

As if to make the book even more confusing, Delany attached an appendix, "A Project for an Expedition of Adventure, to the Eastern Coast of Africa," in which he appeared to endorse African emigration. The proposal, which he claimed to have drafted in 1838, called for the creation of a "Board of Commissioners," trained scientists embodying "the qualifications of physician, botanist, chemist, geologist, geographer and surveyor," to undertake a three-year exploration of East Africa, there to locate land for an African American colony. The colony would become the starting point for a transcontinental railway line, which, when linked with a black transatlantic shipping line, would ignite a commercial revolution throughout Africa and its diaspora. The appendix closed with more Manifest Destiny brio: "The land is ours; there it lies with inexhaustible resources; let us go and possess it."

Why include an East African scheme in a book that discountenanced African emigration? Delany claimed to have included it for purely historical purposes, to establish blacks' priority against whites who might in the future claim credit for conceiving such an enterprise. (As we shall see, the proposal was virtually identical to the 1841 British Niger expedition, which may account for his claim to have drafted the plan in 1838.) Whatever the appendix's rationale, Delany at the time clearly saw the Americas rather than Africa as the future site of black nationality. "We must not leave this continent," he wrote, treating North and South America as a single body. "America is our destination and our home." In his 1853 call for a National Emigration Convention, he explicitly excluded from participation anyone "who would introduce the subject of emigration to the Eastern Hemisphere"—that is, to Africa. "[O]ur object and determination are to consider our claims to the West Indies, Central and South America, and the Canadas," he wrote. Years later, having become an advocate of African emigration, Delany would claim that the convention included "Secret Sessions" devoted to Africa, but there was no suggestion of this at the time.

For better or worse, nothing came of Delany's Central American proposal. The only notable product of the inaugural National Emigration Convention, which assembled in Cleveland in 1854, was Delany's own "Political Destiny of the Colored Race on the American Continent," a sprawling seven-hour lecture that ranged from the burning of the library of Alexandria (the beginning of a white conspiracy to erase Africa's accomplishments from history) to the recent passage of the "nefarious" Kansas-Nebraska Act. From the outset, the convention was dogged by disputes over direction and leadership, with most delegates rejecting Delany's Central America scheme in favor of Haiti or Canada. Delany himself joined the black expatriate community in Canada in 1855, notwithstanding his oft-repeated doubts about the settlement's long-term viability. By the time a second, smaller convention convened in 1856, the movement was virtually moribund.

Delany's activities during the 1850s betrayed a distinctly erratic quality, as he struggled to create some movement that would serve the needs of the race for self-determination and his own needs for authority and control. "We must have a position, independently of anything pertaining to white men," he raged. "I weary of our miserable condition, and [am] heartily sick of whimpering, whining and sniveling at the feet of white men, begging for their refuse and offals." This aversion to white authority may explain his refusal to join John Brown, who came to Canada in hopes of enlisting Delany in his planned attack on Harper's Ferry, an event that Brown intended as the trigger for a violent slave insurrection across the South. Delany was also doubtless put off by Brown's alliance with Frederick Douglass, his perennial bête noire. It was Douglass who had usurped Delany's rightful role as race leader, making it impossible for his emigration proposals to get a fair hearing. Too many black leaders "seemed to know no other purpose for living, than to move, say and do, as Frederick Douglass moved, said, or did, or bade them do," he complained.

Stymied in the political realm, Delany pursued his dream of racial regeneration in the realm of the imagination. Sometime in about 1853, he began work on a novel, *Blake; or, the Huts of America,* which appeared in serialized form in the *Anglo-African Magazine* between 1859 and 1862. The first black-authored novel to be published in the United States—William Wells Brown's *Clotel,* generally credited as the first African American novel, was published in London in 1853—Blake apparently began as Delany's answer to Harriet Beecher Stowe's *Uncle Tom's Cabin.* First published in 1852, Stowe's best-selling novel caused an immediate sensation in antislavery circles; it was championed by no less a figure that Frederick Douglass, who saw the book's popularity as evidence that the torpid consciences of white Americans might yet be awakened. Delany, on the other hand, hated everything about it, from its saintly, long-suffering protagonist to its tidy colonizationist conclusion. (The novel ends with Uncle Tom's survivors happily embarking for Liberia.) Through the spring of 1853, the two men debated the novel's merits in a series of letters reprinted in *Frederick Douglass' Paper.* One might imagine that Delany was at something of a disadvantage in the exchange, having confessed in one letter to "not having as yet *read* Uncle Tom's Cabin, *my wife* having *told* me the most I know about it," but he gave as good as he got. Stowe *"knows nothing about us,"* he wrote, "neither does any other white person—and consequently, can contrive no successful scheme for our elevation; it must be done by ourselves."

In *Blake,* Delany answered his own challenge, offering a very different vision of black character and destiny from that offered by Stowe. The protagonist, Henry Blake or Henrico Blacus, a thinly veiled alter ego of the author, was an educated, far-seeing revolutionary, who traveled the world organizing a massive slave insurrection. Even by Delany's formidable standards, the novel was a confusing work. In form, it uneasily combined aspects of different literary genres: the stark brutality of slave narratives; the mobility and fluid identities of picaresque literature; the melodramatic flourishes and unlikely reunions of sentimental fiction. While some of the text appears to have been written in 1853, other episodes were added later, including a discussion of the 1857 *Dred Scott* decision and a detailed description of slave trading on the African coast, clearly based on Delany's 1859 visit to the continent. To complicate matters further, the final installment of the novel has been lost, leaving readers uncertain of the fate of Blake's planned insurrection. Yet for all its difficulties, the novel was quintessential Delany, revealing not only his characteristic ideas about racial leadership but also his sense of himself as a Mosaic figure, leading a scattered people out of bondage to a promised land—a promised land that clearly lay in the Americas. Though the novel's protagonist makes one voyage to Africa (having been pressed into service on a Spanish slave ship), the bulk of his travels are in the Americas, particularly in the U.S. South and in Cuba, which Henry Blake identified as the future home of a great black nation. The book's subtitle—"The Huts of America"—was itself evidence of Delany's belief that America had displaced Africa as the authentic home of the race.

By THE TIME *BLAKE* appeared, Delany had reversed himself again, turning away from the Americas and embracing the cause of African emigration. Ironically, his reversal appears to have been prompted by two books about Africa written by white missionaries. The first, *Seventeen Years Explorations*

and *Adventures in the Wilds of Africa,* introduced the world to David Livingstone, a man whose name would become a byword for white intrepidity in the
"Dark Continent." A Scottish missionary of humble origins, Livingstone
epitomized the white naturalist explorer, a role created in the last years of the
eighteenth century by Mungo Park and carried down through the nineteenth
century by such adventurers as Denham and Clapperton, the swashbuckling
Richard Burton, and the rapacious Henry Morton Stanley. Though he failed
in his quest to locate the source of the Nile, the grail of African exploration,
Livingstone did accumulate an impressive résumé of "discoveries," including
Lake Ngami, Lake Nyasa, and the Zambezi River, whose towering falls he
named for Britain's Queen Victoria. Lost and presumed dead, he returned to
Britain in 1856, receiving a hero's welcome. His book, published a year later,
became an immediate best seller on both sides of the Atlantic.

It is difficult today to appreciate the influence of Livingstone's book or of
the Dark Continent literary tradition of which it was so important a part. The
books churned out by Livingstone, Burton, Stanley, and other Victorian-era
explorers were not simply best-selling adventure tales; they were the intellectual foundations of empire, posing a stark opposition between an "enlightened" West, imagined as rational, progressive, and white, and a "benighted"
Africa, imagined as irrational, backward, and black. While Livingstone was
more sympathetic to Africans than most, his book still brimmed with savage
cannibals and backbent slaves. Such a work would seem an unlikely inspiration for a black nationalist, but the book clearly struck a chord with Delany,
appealing both to his scientific sensibility and to his conception of himself as
a heroic figure. When Delany embarked for Africa in 1859, he would style
himself as a scientific explorer, in the mold of Livingstone.

The second book that Delany credited, Thomas Bowen's *Central Africa:
Adventures and Missionary Labors in Several Countries in the Interior of Africa,*
also published in 1857, represented an even less likely source. Bowen's book
described the establishment of an American Southern Baptist mission in
Abeokuta, a settlement in Yorubaland, in what is today Nigeria. Not only
was Bowen a representative of a proslavery church, but he was also an ardent
colonizationist, who would capitalize on the success of his book to launch a
new scheme for deporting free people of color. With the support of the

A.C.S. and a racist southern senator, Bowen succeeded in persuading the U.S. Senate to appropriate a quarter million dollars to remove free African Americans to the Niger Valley. (The bill failed to win approval in the northern-dominated House of Representatives.) Yet Bowen's book also held much interest for Delany, most notably its account of the region's fledgling cotton industry. When Delany embarked for Africa in 1859, Abeokuta would be his destination.

The first indication of Delany's new course came in early 1858, when he and Jonathan Myers, a black merchant from Wisconsin, announced plans to create the Mercantile Line of the Free Colored People of North America, a transatlantic shipping line to be owned and operated by black people. Hearkening back to Paul Cuffe (and forward to Marcus Garvey's Black Star Line), the proposed enterprise combined emigration and commerce, with ships transporting settlers to Africa and returning with holds filled with African commodities. In keeping with Delany's earlier East African proposal, the scheme included an exploration component. The inaugural voyage was slated to carry "an efficient corps of scientific men of color, numbering 150 to 200," to survey local conditions and resources and select the proper site for the proposed colony. Delany himself would lead the expedition.

Delany and Myers corresponded with various interested parties through 1858, soliciting advice on possible destinations, but they clearly had their sights on the Niger Valley. While details of their plans remain sketchy, they apparently hoped to establish an "industrial colony" to stimulate the local production of staple crops, particularly of cotton, a crop that (according to Bowen) grew prolifically in the area. Like most of his contemporaries, Delany believed that black people had a special fitness for producing cotton. He also believed, again like his contemporaries, that free labor was invariably more productive than slave labor. Putting these ideas together, he imagined African American colonists and their African hosts inaugurating a new cotton kingdom in the Niger Valley, displacing the American South as the chief supplier of raw cotton to the British textile industry. In one fell swoop, African American emigrants could regenerate themselves, redeem their wounded ancestral continent, and deal a mortal blow to the slave power in the United States.

Hoping to secure broad support for his venture, Delany convened a third National Emigration Convention. The convention, which assembled in Canada in mid-1858, did not go according to plan. While acknowledging the need for further information about Africa, the assembled delegates declared themselves "entirely opposed" to the Niger Valley scheme. Rehearsing arguments Delany himself had long advanced, they insisted that the race's destiny lay not in Africa but in the Americas, with different speakers pressing the advantages of Canada, Haiti, or various sites in Central and South America. The most that Delany could extract was authorization for a five-man "Scientific Corps," to undertake a "Topographical, Geological and Geographical Examination of the [Niger] Valley." Even then, delegates disavowed any "pecuniary responsibility" for the venture or for any agreements that Delany might enter.

With no money and only the flimsiest of mandates, Delany set out to organize the expedition. Even with the size of the proposed party sliced from two hundred to five, he was unable to fill his complement. In the end, only one other man, Robert Campbell, agreed to accompany him. Born in Jamaica of mixed African, English, and Scottish descent, Campbell was head of the science department at Philadelphia's Institute for Colored Youth. In training and temperament, he was much like Delany, a man of letters and of science, who fell easily in Africa into the role of naturalist-explorer. In contrast to the dark-skinned Delany, however, he was exceedingly fair skinned, virtually white. Perhaps not surprisingly, the two men proved to be as much competitors as partners, and they would ultimately publish rival accounts of their journey.

The first hurdle that Delany and Campbell faced was simply getting to Africa. When early fund-raising efforts failed, Campbell turned to colonizationists for support. While he did not directly ally himself with the colonization society, he did accept the support of its newly established black auxiliary, the African Civilization Society, which also had designs on the Niger Valley. (Chartered in 1858 with the eminent Henry Highland Garnet in the leading role, the civilization society was an attempt to capitalize on the interest in Africa sparked by Bowen's book, without introducing the stigma of colonization.) Campbell also placed a solicitation for funds in a white newspaper, including testimonials from several prominent white colonizationists. With the funds he obtained, he sailed for London, where he published another financial appeal. He reached Nigeria in July 1859, several months before Delany.

Delany railed against Campbell's decision to seek white support, which seemingly confirmed all his allegations about dependent, white-loving mulattoes. Yet he too was forced to beg money from whites. When the National Emigration Convention refused to support the venture, he appealed for support from the American Missionary Society—specifically from Henry Ward Beecher, a prominent cleric and brother of novelist Harriet Beecher Stowe. In an obvious bit of pandering, he told Beecher of his dream of planting "an Enlightened and Christian Nationality" among the "tractable and docile people" of Africa. Abolitionist William Lloyd Garrison received a similarly ingratiating letter. But neither Beecher nor Garrison offered support. In the end, Delany, like Campbell, was forced to make his peace with colonizationists. In early 1859, he met with leaders of both the American Colonization Society and the African Civilization Society, coming away with a small grant and an offer of free passage on a Liberian ship. In exchange, he agreed to visit Liberia before proceeding to the Niger Valley and to report impartially on both places.

In May 1859, Delany joined a contingent of Liberian colonists on the barque *Mendi* and embarked for Monrovia. The situation was rife with irony. After decades excoriating colonization—"that most pernicious and impudent of all schemes for the perpetuity of the degradation of our race"—he sailed for Africa on an A.C.S. ship. His relationship with the National Emigration Convention, which he had founded and which he claimed as his sponsor, was virtually nonexistent. (Leaders of the convention, now renamed the Association for the Promotion of the Interests of the Colored People of Canada and the United States, formally repudiated Delany shortly after his departure, stripping away the last vestige of popular mandate.) His co-commissioner, Campbell, had sailed for Africa without him. These were hardly propitious circumstances for undertaking what Delany called "the grandest prospect for the regeneration of a people, that was ever presented in the history of the world."

. . .

DELANY AND CAMPBELL were not the only people casting their eyes on the Niger Valley in the 1850s. A magnet for generations of European explorers—Mungo Park met his death trying to trace the Niger's course—the region emerged in midcentury as the linchpin of British imperial policy in West Africa. It was also the site of a remarkable return migration of Yoruba-speaking Africans, initially recaptives from Sierra Leone and later newly manumitted slaves from Cuba and Brazil. These developments occurred against the backdrop of the Yoruba wars, a bloody half century of forced migration, slave raiding, and intermittent civil war. In short, the place to which the two African American explorers were bound was not some pristine, precolonial Africa, but a complex, conflict-ridden region, scored by slavery, war, and a long history of transatlantic encounters.

At the center of this extraordinary convergence lay Abeokuta, the place described by Bowen and site of Delany's proposed colony. Scarcely twenty-five years old, Abeokuta had arisen from the ashes of Oyo, one of the great precolonial kingdoms of the African savannah. With its fearsome cavalry, Oyo had emerged in the early seventeenth century as the most powerful polity in Yorubaland. For two hundred years, the empire dominated the slave trade through the Bight of Benin, but in the early nineteenth century it went into rapid decline, a victim of internal rebellion and external pressure from Fulani raiders in the north. It was Oyo's collapse that precipitated the Yoruba wars.

The predicament of the Egba, a Yoruba-speaking people on the southern fringes of the old Oyo empire, was particularly dire. As raiders and refugees pushed southward, thousands of Egba were killed and tens of thousands more were left homeless, a prey for slavers. In 1830, a group of these refugees, led by their chief, Sodeke, established a settlement in the forest belt called Abeokuta—literally Under-Stone, a reference to the city's fortified position. As word of the new settlement spread, refugees poured in. Recognizing the safety of numbers, Sodeke welcomed each new contingent, assigning each an area within the city's walled perimeter. By 1840, Abeokuta boasted a population of nearly forty thousand, mostly Egba, living in distinct villages under their individual chiefs and headmen.

The reverberations of the Yoruba wars rippled out into the Atlantic world. As war engulfed the region, European slave ships descended on Lagos and Badagri to meet the coffles coming down from the interior. Most of these captives ended up in Cuba and Brazil, but many were recaptured by British antislavery patrols and deposited at Freetown. By the 1830s, Yoruba speakers, known locally as the Aku, after the traditional Yoruba greeting, constituted the single largest stratum in Sierra Leone's recaptive community. They also became perhaps the best-educated population in Africa, thanks to the mission schools that the British built in each recaptive village. Fluent in English yet retaining a strong sense of Yoruba identity, the Aku emerged as a kind of local elite, working in missions, the colonial administration, and Freetown's numerous merchant houses. Some acquired their own trading vessels, usually condemned slave ships, with which they were able to establish commercial links with their former homeland.

The upheavals in Yorubaland coincided with and contributed to a shift in British African policy. Through most of the slave-trade era, the British presence was confined to a few coastal outposts, a reflection both of the parsimony of imperial officials and the power of coastal chiefs, who jealously guarded their position as middlemen between Europeans and the slaving grounds in the interior. In the 1840s, however, Britain began to adopt a more assertive policy. The chief architect of the change was Thomas Buxton, a leader of the British evangelical and antislavery movements. In *The African Slave Trade and Its Remedy,* published in 1840, Buxton argued that coastal patrols alone would never stem the slave trade. His solution was "legitimate commerce," a phrase that would remain a slogan of British philanthropy for the rest of the century. By encouraging Africans in the interior to produce legitimate commodities for exchange, Buxton hoped to wean them away from the existing commerce in people, bringing the slave trade to a natural, nonviolent end. In the process, Britain could secure new markets for its manufactures and new sources of products such as cotton and indigo, currently produced by New World slaves.

Buxton's book was the inspiration for the ill-fated Niger expedition, undertaken by the British government as the first in a series of pioneer columns marching into Africa's interior along its great waterways. Launched amid great patriotic fanfare, the Niger expedition proved an utter failure: nearly half of the expedition's legion of botanists, geologists, and commissioners died of fever, while the planned model communities of repatriated former slaves never took root. In years to come, the expedition would serve as a byword for the excesses of sentimental philanthropy. (Mrs. Jellyby's scheme to uplift the natives of Borrioboola-Gha in Dickens's *Bleak House* was clearly modeled on the venture.) Yet even as the expedition ground to its ignominious end, the legitimate commerce policy received support from an unexpected quarter. In the early 1840s, reports began to arrive from Sierra Leone of a spontaneous movement of Aku recaptives back to their former homes in Yorubaland. At least two contingents embarked in early 1840 and hundreds of other individuals had reportedly applied for passports. Initially nonplussed by the migration, British officials soon embraced it as an opportunity to salvage Buxton's vision.

What prompted the Aku migration is not entirely clear. The first parties appear to have been organized by merchants, who hoped to encourage the budding interregional trade. Some emigrants professed missionary motives, the desire to spread "the light of the Gospel" among "their country people who are now living in darkness." Others simply dreamed of being reunited with loved ones. Doubtless the publicity surrounding the Niger expedition encouraged the enthusiasm. Whatever the range of motives, by 1844, upwards of eight hundred Sierra Leoneans had resettled in Yorubaland and many more were on the way. (Known as the Aku in Sierra Leone, these emigrants would become known as Saros in Yorubaland, a term derived from "sierra.") Word of the exodus even reached across the Atlantic, to Brazil and Cuba, where Yoruba-speaking Africans organized mutual aid societies to arrange self-purchase and transportation back to Africa. While the return migration from the New World was smaller than the one from Sierra Leone, hundreds of former slaves found their way home from Brazil and Cuba, adding yet another layer of social complexity to the region.

While returnees dispersed themselves throughout the region, many headed for Abeokuta, which enjoyed a reputation for welcoming outsiders. A British official visiting the settlement in the early 1850s estimated the Saro population at nearly three thousand. Even that number understates the impact of the settlers, whose distinctive attributes—Christianity, command of English, commercial expertise—enabled them to play a disproportionate role in local affairs. White missionaries came on the emigrants' heels. By 1850, when American Thomas Bowen arrived, seven different denominations were operating in Abeokuta; the Anglican Church Mission Society (C.M.S.) alone supported five churches, each with its own school. A book on the C.M.S. mission, *Sunrise Within the Tropics,* quickly ran through four editions. Abeokuta became "a household word among the readers of missionary magazines," a beacon of light in the dark jungles of heathenism and slavery.

If one man's experience could encapsulate the history of Abeokuta it would be the life of Samuel Crowther, a one-time slave who rose to become the Anglican Church's first black bishop. Crowther, whose given name was Ajayi, was fifteen years old in 1821 when his Yorubaland village was attacked. Loaded onto a Portuguese slave ship bound for Brazil, he was rescued by a British cruiser and taken to Sierra Leone, where he acquired a new religion and a new name. (It was C.M.S. custom to name converts after the mission's English benefactors—a Newgate vicar in Crowther's case.) A brilliant student, Crowther was the first person to graduate from Freetown's new Fourah Bay College; he later continued his education in England. He participated in the 1841 Niger expedition, surviving to become one of the official chroniclers of the ill-fated venture. Two years later he was ordained an Anglican minister. When the C.M.S. first opened work in Abeokuta in 1846, it dispatched Crowther, along with a white missionary named Henry Townshend. A short time after his arrival, Crowther had the singular experience of baptizing his own mother, from whom he had been separated for a quarter century.

In *The African Slave Trade and Its Remedy,* Buxton had enumerated a dozen objectives for his pioneer columns—not just spreading Christianity and ending the slave trade but also reducing local languages to written form, eradicating disease, building roads and canals (to facilitate commerce), and improving the production and marketing of agricultural products. In almost every particular, the work of Samuel Crowther and his family conformed to this vision. In addition to his evangelical work, Crowther produced the first dictionaries and grammars of the Yoruba language. His son Samuel Jr. studied medicine at King's College, London, and returned to open the settlement's first Western medical clinic. Another son, Josiah, and son-in-law Henry Robbins spearheaded the settlement's most ambitious economic initiative, a scheme to cultivate indigenous cotton for export. In the early 1850s, the pair apprenticed at a Manchester textile mill, where they learned the latest techniques for processing, packing, and shipping raw cotton.

Abeokuta's fledgling cotton industry was the brainchild of Thomas Clegg, a wealthy British millowner and prominent Anglican layman. Clegg had long warned of the evils of British dependence on American cotton, which not only underwrote slavery but also left the country vulnerable to the vagaries of American politics. With the mixture of philanthropy and commercial calculation so characteristic of his class, Clegg saw in Abeokuta's cotton industry an opportunity to advance Christian civilization, attack slavery, and serve the interests of British manufacturers and merchants. In addition to providing apprenticeships for African students at his Manchester mill, he financed an industrial school at Abeokuta, where students could learn techniques for cultivating and processing cotton. When Delany began to consider African emigration, Clegg was one of the people to whom he wrote for advice. Clegg advised him to proceed forthwith to the Niger Valley, where African American settlers could "benefit your countrymen whilest you make a profitable trade."

The purpose of this background is not to question Delany's priority (though some of his ideas were less original than he claimed) but simply to illuminate some of the conflicts and competing agendas that surrounded Abeokuta. Delany and Thomas Clegg may have shared an interest in cotton cultivation, but their broader visions of Africa's future were profoundly different. Conflict between rival Yoruba city-states remained endemic, erupting into renewed war in early 1860. Relations between the C.M.S. and the Saro community were less harmonious than they appeared, as Samuel Crowther and Reverend Townshend, his nominal supervisor, jockeyed for influence. Relations between the Saros and the indigenous community of Abeokuta were likewise strained. While local chiefs valued the distinctive skills the Saros brought, the emigrants' domination of local commerce generated growing resentment. Delany and Campbell would find themselves, wittingly and unwittingly, entangled in all these disputes.

DELANY WAS AWAY from the United States for eighteen months, from May 1859 until Christmas Day 1860. He spent four months in Liberia, where, with charm and a convenient case of historical amnesia, he won the esteem of Americo-Liberian leaders. His hosts included ex-president Henry Roberts (whom he once memorably described as "a fawning servilian of the negro-hating Colonizationists") and pioneering Pan-Africanists, Edward Blyden and Alexander Crummell. (Crummell's famous essay, "The Duty of Colored Americans to Africa," was written in response to Delany's visit.) In September, Delany proceeded on to Lagos, where he was reunited with Campbell. For the next seven months, the pair traveled in Yorubaland. Though they never reached the Niger River itself, they did venture as far north as Ilorin, a Muslim settlement where they saw a slave market in operation. The bulk of their time was spent at Abeokuta, where, in December 1859, they signed a treaty with the *alake*, securing a grant of land for the planned African American colony. In April 1860, they set sail for England, where they hoped to rally support for their venture.

The books that Delany and Campbell wrote about their travels differed markedly. Campbell's book, *A Pilgrimage to My Motherland*, appeared first. Mindful of the many misrepresentations of Africa "propagated in consequence of writers not confining the subject of their books to their own observations," he related only things he had seen. An astute observer, he discussed African food and fashion, religion, marriage, even childhood games. He also offered candid commentary on more troubling subjects, such as domestic slavery and warfare—topics that Delany, anxious to make the best possible case for emigration, would contrive to avoid. Though generally dispassionate, Campbell's account included moments of self-deprecating comedy—the travelers getting lost or swindled—and others of great poignance, as when he and Delany entered a deserted village in the aftermath of a slave raid.

Delany's *Official Report of the Niger Valley Exploring Party* was at once less personal and vastly more ambitious. As its title suggests, the book was cast as a report to the defunct National Emigration Convention; it was also the "official" report, presumably to distinguish it from Campbell's account. A full third of the text was consumed by the preliminary "history of the project" and by Delany's subsequent seven-month sojourn in Great Britain, with Africa sandwiched in the middle. Throughout the book, Delany laid great stress on the honors and courtesies extended to him by his various hosts, from the chief at Ilorin, who, against all precedent, revealed his face, to the scientists and statesmen at the International Statistical Congress in London, who invited him to deliver an address. Characteristically, Delany interpreted such distinctions not only as confirmations of his status as race leader but also as tokens of respect for the race that he represented. The end result is a penetrating but frequently self-aggrandizing book, with Delany alternately styling himself as an ambassador negotiating "on behalf of the African race in America" and as a Moses, leading his wayward people to the promised land.

For all the differences in scope and tone, the books also bore significant similarities, most notably in their debts to the Dark Continent tradition of African travel writing. In Campbell's case, the debt was apparent as early as the frontispiece, which featured an image of the author in a kind of turban, a sartorial flourish appropriated not from Africa—the people of the Niger Valley wore nothing remotely similar—but from the frontispiece of explorer Richard Burton's most recent book, which showed the celebrated author in identical garb and pose. Both Campbell and Delany cast their journeys as "explorations," representing Africa and Africans in the language of natural science. Delany's text, in particular, conformed to the conventions of contemporary European travel writing, with long discussions of climate, the prevalence and prevention of disease, mineral resources, fertility of the soil (which, needless to say, he judged ideal for cotton cultivation), commercial opportunities, flora and fauna, animal husbandry, and personal hygiene for the traveler. In keeping with their "naturalist" callings, both men carried "scientific instruments"—microscopes, barometers, and the like—as well as a rifle, which they used liberally to collect "specimens." They also carried some kind of camera or daguerreotype machine. Indeed, Delany and Campbell were among the first people to introduce photography to Africa, an ironic distinction given the role that the medium would come to play in Western racial thought. (Sadly, none of the images they made appear to survive.)

The travel accounts produced by Delany and Campbell reveal the close relationship between African American representations of Africa and those prevailing in the wider Western world. But Delany and Campbell were not simply white travelers in blackface. Nor were they the unwitting captives of a hegemonic "white" discourse, certainly not in any easy or unproblematic way. On several occasions, in fact, they took direct issue with contemporary representations of Africa, slating white writers who they believed had unfairly disparaged the continent and its people.

Delany's discussion of insect life offers an apt example. Nineteenth-century travel accounts of Africa were replete with tales of Africa's voracious bugs—of termites, or white ants, capable of leveling forests, and black driver ants, traveling in endless columns, consuming insect, animal, and even human flesh. Given his interest in attracting emigrants, Delany dismissed such reports as exaggerations, arguing, in a neat bit of proto-ecology, that African ants served as a "sanitary means," and were in any case no more destructive than the London moths that had destroyed his woolen suit. He took special aim at David Livingstone, who had recounted how driver ants—"black rascals," he called them—would "stand deliberately and watch for the whites, which, on coming out of their holes, they instantly seize, putting them to death." Delany offered an ironic riposte: perhaps the whites were attempting to enslave the black ants, he wrote, "in which case they served the white rascals right. . . . Though I have never seen an encounter, it is nevertheless true, that the blacks do subdue the whites whenever they meet."

In effect, Delany was beating Livingstone at his own game, turning his assumptions and modes of representation back against him. But this kind of appropriation is not without hazards, particularly when one is dealing with a narrative form as suffused with racial and imperial authority as African travel writing. Consider Delany's discussion of "tropical fevers." Fever was a concern of virtually every nineteenth-century African traveler, black as well as white. (Known colloquially as the white man's graveyard, West

Africa also claimed the lives of thousands of black settlers.) Having endured several bouts of what was probably malaria, Delany did not deny the problem, but he sought to minimize it. He argued—correctly—that fever was far less prevalent in Yorubaland than in Liberia. He further suggested that the incidence and severity of fever could be moderated by temperance, proper dress and hygiene, as well as by prophylactic drugs, for which he provided several prescriptions of his own devising. He went on to explain how fever was often accompanied by a "morbid affliction of the mind," expressed in temporary "despondency" and "an almost frantic desire" to return home. "It is generally while laboring under this last described symptom," he continued, "that persons send from Africa such despairing accounts of their disappointments and sufferings, with horrible feelings of dread for the worst to come." Fortunately, "an entire recovery" normally ensued, after which "the love of country is most ardent and abiding."

Delany had naturalized the naturalizers: those who criticized Africa were sick; they only needed to remain longer to become well. The problem arose in the ensuing pages, when Delany set out to explain the etiology of African fevers. One of the basic tenets of medical science, from Hippocrates right through the nineteenth century, was that fevers were products of miasmas, mysterious vapors rising from decaying vegetation. Delany accepted the paradigm, which explained for him why the problem was worst in Liberia, a country draped in "a dense, heavy-wooded, primitive forest, rank with the growth and putrefied vegetation of a thousand ages." Fortunately the solution was at hand. The "natural remedy for the permanent decrease of the native fever, is the clearing up and cultivation of the land," he wrote, a process that was itself part of "a general improvement of the country, brought about by a populating and civilizing progress." As proof of the theory, he offered the Yoruba, who, in their enthusiasm for cultivation and commerce, had already "improved" considerable land, producing a substantial drop in the incidence of fever.

The point is not to question Delany's scientific credentials—it would be another forty years before scientists distinguished malaria from other native fevers, or recognized the *Anopheles* mosquito as its vector—but to highlight again the relationship between African American representations of Africa and those prevailing in the wider society. Of all the ideas about landscape embedded in Western travel writing, none played a more central role in the construction of colonial authority than the idea of improvement. In European encounters with indigenous people in North and South America, and later with Africans and Asians, the idea of improving the land legitimized and naturalized certain ways of being on the earth, while providing a justification for extinguishing the claims of others, who, through want of industry or imagination, had failed to heed this supposedly natural imperative. It is hard to imagine a better example of this logic than Delany's *Official Report*, in which the terms "improve" and "improvement" appeared more than twenty times. For Delany, as for generations of Western travelers, Africa was at once primordial and pestilential, superabundant and stagnant. Nature itself decreed that the continent be reclaimed, cultivated, improved.

Compared to Campbell, Delany had little to say about African people, confining his remarks largely to the "leaders" and "civilized" Africans with whom he interacted—Americo-Liberian politicians, Saro merchants, and the occasional chief. But what comments he made were often distinctly condescending, revealing the same improvement ethic evident in his discussion of the land. For all his expostulations on Africa's past glories, Delany exhibited little respect for African culture in the present, sketching instead a prospect of a continent remade by commerce, industry, and civilization. Africans would never acquire "the well-regulated pursuits of civilized life," he warned, until their whole way of life, their "habits, manners, and customs," had been uprooted. What ultimately distinguished Delany's vision from that of Livingstone or his ilk was not so much his vision of Africa's future, but his insistence that white people could never bring it to fruition. The continent's regeneration could only be stimulated by the *"descendants of Africa,"* people endowed with "all the *natural* characteristics, claims, sentiments, and sympathies" of the African race yet possessing all the knowledge and technique of modern civilization—in short, by African Americans. When Delany uttered his most famous aphorism—*"Africa for the African race, and black men to rule them"*—he was not calling for African self-government but for a kind of racial trusteeship by a "carefully selected" cadre of "progressive" African Americans.

. . .

THE TREATY THAT DELANY and Campbell signed with the *alake* of Abeokuta granted "the Commissioners, on behalf of the African race in America" the right to introduce and settle African American colonists "on any part of the territory belonging to Abeokuta, not otherwise occupied." For their part, Delany and Campbell pledged to introduce only "select and intelligent people of high moral as well as religious character"—people who would enrich Abeokuta with their "Intelligence, Education, a Knowledge of the Arts and Sciences, Agriculture, and other Mechanical and Industrial Occupations, which they shall put into immediate operation, by improving the land and in other useful vocations."

Though nothing ultimately came of it, the treaty gave Delany new credibility, offering an irrefutable answer to all those who had dismissed African emigration as idle fancy. It certainly elevated his standing in England, where he arrived in May 1860, just weeks after Frederick Douglass had completed a celebrated tour. Like Douglass (and Paul Cuffe before him), Delany was warmly embraced by the English elite. A new organization, the African Aid Society, was chartered to assist in the development of the Niger Valley venture. The society was chaired by Lord Alfred Churchill, "the learned Oriental traveler and Christian philanthropist," and, not coincidentally, a leader of Britain's Cotton Supply Association, an organization founded a few years before to reduce British dependence on slave-produced U.S. cotton. The society's thirty-member board represented a virtual who's who of Britain's missionary, mercantile, and manufacturing establishment, including the leaders of all the major mission societies, eight fellows of the Royal Geographic Society, a brace of parliamentarians, and two mill owners, Thomas Clegg and Henry Dunlop, who together pledged to purchase as much cotton as Delany and his colonists could supply.

Delany had always been quick to condemn black leaders who trafficked with white philanthropy, but if he felt any qualms about his own position he never acknowledged them. On the contrary, he gloried in his newfound visibility, accepting each new courtesy as a token of respect not only for himself but also for the race he represented. As for his patrons, they clearly glimpsed in his scheme an opportunity to realize that great philanthropic desideratum: to do well while doing good. The proposed colony, according to the prospectus of the African Aid Society, would not only strike a blow against slavery in both Africa and the Americas, but it would also "open new cotton fields for the supply of British industry, and new markets for our commerce, realizing the sublime promise of the Scripture, 'Cast thy bread upon the waters, and after many days it shall return unto thee.'" Indeed, the prospectus went further, extolling African American emigration as a solution to the chronic labor problems that had dogged British plantation colonies since the abolition of slavery in the empire two decades before. Thus the society's charter endorsed African American emigration not only to the Niger Valley but also to other "countries that may offer a suitable field of labor," including the West Indies and Natal, South Africa, which were both starving for workers in their sugar fields. Revealingly, the emigrant application form that the African Aid Society had printed included a question about plantation work experience.

The climax of Delany's time in England came in July, when he was invited to address the International Statistical Congress in London, a gathering that included many of the leading scientists of Europe, Asia, and the United States, as well as His Royal Highness Prince Albert. For the rest of his days, Delany would regard the address not only as a highlight of his own life but also as a watershed moment in the black struggle for respect and recognition. The fact that several southerners in the American delegation walked out in protest only made the occasion sweeter.

Yet even as Delany enchanted the English, developments in Africa doomed his planned colony. In March 1860, war broke out between Ijaye and Ibadan, two of the principal chiefdoms of Yorubaland, quickly engulfing the whole region. A major battle was fought on the very day that Delany and Campbell sailed from Lagos. For the next four years, Yorubaland was convulsed by war and renewed slave raiding, hardly a prospect to entice potential immigrants. At the same time, political tensions within Abeokuta reached a breaking point. Like most Western travelers, Delany and Campbell tended to see Africans in fairly undifferentiated ways; they certainly never appreciated the divisions within Abeokuta, or the way in which their presence exacerbated them. Given affinities of language and culture, the travelers had naturally gravitated toward the Saro community, especially to Samuel Crowther, Jr., who served as their guide during their tour. It was Crowther who pressed on the *alake* the advantages of the treaty, to which he and his father served as the sole witnesses. Yet in aligning themselves with the Crowthers, they invited opposition from many in the non-Saro population, who resented the influence these outsiders wielded over local affairs. They also faced opposition from white missionaries, who were naturally uneasy with the idea of introducing a population of African American settlers disdainful of both African and British authority. "The Americans Mr Campbell and Dr Delany go ahead without us," one missionary wrote to his superiors in London. "They are indeed not the white man's friends though they will take his money." Reverend Townshend, superintendent of the C.M.S. mission and the Crowthers' chief rival for the ear of the *alake*, was particularly hostile, seeing the whole venture as one more attempt to usurp his authority.

Townshend continued to campaign against the treaty after Delany's and Campbell's departure. Skillfully exploiting local resentment of Sierra Leonean emigrants, he portrayed the treaty as a Saro swindle, designed to steal Egba land. Townshend's cause was aided by flaws in the treaty itself, which rested on erroneous ideas about local land-holding practices, a common problem in encounters between colonizers and indigenous peoples. As Delany and Campbell understood it, Yoruba land was "common property; every individual enjoys the right of taking unoccupied land, as much as he can use, wherever and whenever he pleases." In fact, control of land was vested in kinship groups, which allocated it among members. Technically, there was no unoccupied land in Abeokuta, and what was currently unused the *alake* certainly had no right to allocate. With popular opposition swelling, the *alake* chose the better side of valor and abrogated the treaty, putting paid to dreams of an African American colony in the Niger Valley.

None of this was known to Delany and Campbell when they first returned to America. Both rushed into print with accounts of their travels, in which they declared their intentions to resettle permanently in Africa with their families. Only Campbell honored the pledge, returning with his family in 1862. They settled in Lagos, where in 1863 he established Nigeria's first newspaper, the *Anglo-African*.

Delany did not return. Arriving back in Canada in late 1860, he set about recruiting a party of Niger colonists, but his chronic shortage of funds forced a series of postponements. In desperation, he turned again to the colonizationists, agreeing to merge his venture with Henry Highland Garnet's African Civilization Society, but significant financial support remained elusive. A petition for funds from the British Foreign Office proved unavailing, as did appeals to his erstwhile patrons in England, who, having been informed of the abrogation of the Abeokuta treaty, were now touting Cameroon as the site for their cotton and colonization scheme.

On top of these obstacles, Delany faced the uncertainties unleashed by the American Civil War, which commenced a few months after his return. In the short run, the war spurred interest in colonization, as white Americans confronted the prospect of a vastly enlarged free black population. President Lincoln flirted with a variety of schemes in the early days of the war, most focused on Central America. In 1862 a Congressional Select Committee on Emancipation and Colonization advocated a $20-million appropriation to facilitate the removal of "free persons of African descent." The committee's report included a copy of Delany's 1852 speech, "The Political Destiny of the Colored Race on the American Continent," apparently as a way to show black support for emigration. But such support was fast ebbing. With the promulgation of the preliminary Emancipation Proclamation in late 1862, and Lincoln's subsequent call for black volunteers for the Union army, abolition was recognized as all but inevitable. And with the promise of full American citizenship at last in reach, few African Americans were interested in emigrating to Africa.

Delany upheld the banner of Africa longer than most. In an open letter written in September 1861, after learning of the abrogation of the Abeokuta treaty, he reiterated his determination to emigrate: "[M]y destiny is fixed in Africa, where my family and myself, by God's providence, will soon be happily situated." In March 1862, he regaled an audience in Providence, Rhode Island, with reports of the seven hundred acre farm awaiting him in the fertile Niger Valley. A few months later, he took his campaign to Rochester,

New York, the home of Frederick Douglass, prompting a furious retort from his old rival. By the end of 1862, however, Delany had come to recognize the logic of events. Though he continued to lecture on Africa—he delivered an address in Chicago in March 1863, in an African ceremonial robe—he no longer announced his intention to settle there. By that time, he had already begun recruiting troops for the all-black Fifty-fourth Massachusetts Regiment; his son Toussaint served in the famous unit, alongside two of Douglass's sons.

In the days that followed, Delany threw himself into the struggle to secure full American citizenship for African Americans, more or less turning his back on his decade-long career as an emigrationist. In February 1865, he emerged from a White House meeting with Abraham Lincoln with a commission as a major in the Union army, making him the first African American to hold field rank in U.S. history. Following the war, Delany worked for the Bureau of Refugees, Freedmen, and Abandoned Lands, a federal agency designed, at least in theory, to prepare freed slaves for the rights and responsibilities of citizenship. *Life and Public Services of Martin R. Delany*, a hagiographic biography published with Delany's cooperation in 1868, completely ignored his emigration efforts, referring only to his role in advancing "explorations in certain portions of Africa." The only other reference to Africa in the text occurs in the opening pages, in which Delany traced his lineage to African royalty—to a Golah chief on his father's side and a Mandingo prince on his mother's side. The claim, which appeared in none of Delany's previous speeches and writings, is impossible to verify. But at the very least it suggests how important Africa remained to his sense of individual and racial identity, even as he turned away from emigration and committed himself to an American future.

Delany spent the Reconstruction years in South Carolina, where he charted a characteristically iconoclastic course. Despite an unprepossessing title—he served as assistant subassistant commissioner of the Freedmen's Bureau at Hilton Head—he emerged as a major political force in the Low Country, overseeing contracts between white landowners and black tenants and exercising personal control over the local constabulary. He helped to draft a new state constitution for South Carolina in 1868, and two years later was appointed commander in chief of the state militia. Having finally attained real political power, he acted in surprisingly conciliatory ways. Though he continued to stress the need for black people to acquire land and an independent subsistence, he rejected calls for outright confiscation and redistribution, touting instead a "triple alliance" in which black workers, white landowners, and northern capital would work together to develop the South, sharing the profits equally. When Frederick Douglass published a letter castigating President Andrew Johnson for his betrayal of the freed people, Delany replied with an open letter urging African Americans to be "neither disheartened nor impatient," but to exercise meekness, forbearance, and faith in God—precisely the kind of admonition that he had long ridiculed. "God is just," he concluded. "Stand still and see his salvation."

Though his politics exhibited unwonted moderation, Delany remained combative and sensitive to racial slight. By the end of the 1860s, he was at loggerheads with the white leaders of the Republican Party, whom he accused (as he had once accused white abolitionists) of reserving leadership positions for themselves and their mulatto allies. (Delany had tried and failed to secure a federal patronage position for himself, lending a personal edge to the allegation.) In another open letter to Douglass, published in 1871, he complained: "Under the rallying-cry of acting for and representing the 'negro,' men of every shade of complexion have attained to places of honor, profit, trust, and power in the party, except the real negro himself . . . who remains to-day as before emancipation, a political nonentity before the governments of the country."

In 1874, a frustrated Delany left the mainstream Republican Party and cast his lot with the so-called Independent Republicans, a breakaway party pledged to rooting out corruption and restoring political comity. The independents rewarded his defection by nominating him for the office of lieutenant governor. Delany acquitted himself well in the general election—he lost by only fifteen thousand votes—but the episode cost him whatever remained of his political credibility. As an alarmed Frederick Douglass warned at the time, the independent movement was a tool of white supremacists, who used concerns about conflict and corruption to drive a wedge between the Republican Party's white northern and black southern wings. Subsequent events would bear out Douglass's warning, but Delany remained oblivious to the threat. In 1875, he gave a major speech in New York City in which he denounced "carpet-baggers" and told surprised listeners that "Southern men" would no longer tolerate rule by outsiders.

There was worse to come. In 1876, Delany broke with the Republicans entirely and stumped for the Democratic candidate for governor, Wade Hampton, a former Confederate general and an avowed white supremacist. His appearance at a Hampton rally at Edisto Island prompted an angry walk-out by black voters, who refused (in the mocking words of the local newspaper) to listen to "de dam nigger dimocrat." Two days later, a black speaker thought to be Delany was fired on, prompting a pitched battle between the local black militia and white members of a Charleston rifle club supporting Hampton. Seven people died in the melee. The chaos continued past the November election, which produced charges and countercharges of fraud and no clear winner in either the gubernatorial or presidential races. Eventually a compromise was struck, in which the Republicans were allowed to retain control of the White House in exchange for withdrawing federal troops from the South, ending the Reconstruction experiment. Wade Hampton was installed as governor and Delany was rewarded with appointment as a trial judge, though two years later, with Democratic rule consolidated, he was dismissed from his position.

As the wages of southern Redemption became apparent, Delany turned his eyes back to Africa. In his final book, *Principia of Ethnology*, published in 1879, he cited the biblical story of Ham, long beloved of slavery's defenders, as proof of the divine injunction for racial separation. In time, he argued, each of humanity's original three races would revert to its pure form in a land of its own—Africa, in the case of black people. With dreams of a colony in the Niger Valley a distant memory, Delany pinned his hopes on Liberia, the very society he had once denounced as a "burlesque." In the late 1870s, he served on the board of the Liberian Exodus Joint Stock Steamship Company, a South Carolina–based cooperative that succeeded in transporting one contingent of settlers to Liberia before sinking into a sea of debt. After the company collapsed, he unsuccessfully sought appointment as U.S. minister to Liberia. In 1880, he wrote to William Coppinger, secretary of the

American Colonization Society, another long-time nemesis, seeking help in securing appointment as doorkeeper to the U.S. Senate, a federal patronage position typically reserved for a black man. All he needed was a few "government favors" to accumulate the resources that he needed to embark for Africa, "the field of my destined labor." The favors never came, and Martin Robison Delany never returned to Africa.

· THREE ·

Emigration or Extermination

In late February 1892, in the last days of a bitter northern winter, a curious story appeared in New York City newspapers. In the preceding weeks, several parties of African Americans from the South, mostly from Arkansas and the Oklahoma Territory, had arrived in the city, bound for Africa. Some had been in contact with the American Colonization Society, the wizened antebellum organization that still worked to resettle African Americans in Liberia. Others had simply arrived unannounced. In either case, there were no ships awaiting them. Some three hundred people were left stranded, most with little more than the clothes on their backs.

As embarrassed colonization society officials scrambled to charter a ship, newspapers carried sympathetic, if patronizing, accounts of the would-be colonists' plight. Reporters focused on a group from McCrory, Arkansas. Desperate to leave the South, the McCrorians had formed an emigration club, pooling their resources to buy train tickets to Savannah, Georgia, and steamship tickets from there to New York, where they expected to board a Liberia-bound ship. To learn about their destination, they had also purchased a copy of *In Darkest Africa*, the latest two-volume best seller by the celebrated "Dark Continent" explorer Henry Morton Stanley. The group's leader, an aging minister named Thornton, had carried the book with him from Arkansas, along with an old stable lantern. Noting the lantern, a waggish reporter from *The New York Times* asked the minister whether he, like Diogenes, had gone abroad in search of an honest man. The question was more apt than the reporter knew, but the joke was lost on Thornton. The lantern was for Africa, the minister explained. It was a dark place.

TO UNDERSTAND THE PREDICAMENT of Reverend Thornton and his companions it is necessary to go back to the decades after the Civil War, to the period of Reconstruction and so-called Redemption. Probably no other period in American history has given rise to such contradictory interpretations. The once conventional interpretation, enshrined in generations of textbooks, scholarly monographs, novels, and films, told of a "tragic era," a period of bitter conflict and unbridled corruption, all brought about by a misguided attempt by Yankee "carpetbaggers" and southern "scalawags" to confer on former slaves civil and political rights that they were not equipped to bear. This interpretation was vividly displayed in D.W. Griffith's classic 1915 film, *The Birth of a Nation*. Griffith began his portrayal of Reconstruction with an intertitle—the film was silent—featuring excerpts from a recent textbook, *A History of the American People,* published by a prominent Princeton University professor. While the sentiments were commonplace, the passage is of more than passing interest, given that the professor in question, Woodrow Wilson, was by 1915 sitting in the White House. "Adventurers swarmed out of the north, as much the enemies of one race as of the other, to cozen, beguile and use the negroes. In the villages the negroes were the office holders, men who knew none of the uses of authority, except its insolences. . . . The policy of the congresional leaders wrought . . . a veritable overthrow of civilization in the South . . . in the determination to put the white South under the heel of the black South." According to this interpretation, proud white southerners eventually rose up in righteous indignation and drove out the usurpers. "The white men were roused by a mere instinct of self preservation," Wilson's *History* continued, "until at last there sprung into existence a great Ku Klux Klan, a veritable empire of the South, to protect the Southern Country." *The Birth of a Nation*, with its cast of blackface thugs and rapists and noble white Klansmen, was the first film ever shown at the White House, in a special screening for Wilson and his cabinet, as well as the nine justices of the U.S. Supreme Court, all of whom gave it an enthusiastic thumbs-up. "History writ with lightning," the president called it.

The conventional understanding of Reconstruction and Redemption endured in American history textbooks until the late 1950s and early 1960s, when the swelling civil rights movement compelled a reinterpretation of the period. Cast against the backdrop of violent struggles in Montgomery, Little Rock, and Birmingham, Reconstruction appeared not as a mad experiment but as a missed opportunity, a first, faltering attempt to make America (in Martin Luther King, Jr.'s, words) "live up to the true meaning of its creed." Within this revisionist tradition, the era was marked less by its excesses than by its limitations, particularly the failure to redistribute land, which ensured that erstwhile slaves would remain economically dependent on whites. Southern Redemption, in this version, stood out not as a return to political sanity but as a colossal betrayal, a violent counterrevolution undertaken in the name of white supremacy. The civil rights movement itself was cast as a "Second Reconstruction," an attempt to restore to African Americans the basic rights of citizenship that they had briefly enjoyed after the Civil War.

However one represents the period, the collapse of Reconstruction inaugurated a bleak and violent time in African American life—the nadir of American race relations, in historian Rayford Logan's oft-quoted phrase. One by one, southern state governments were reclaimed by white supremacists, whose victory was sealed in the presidential election of 1876, when disputed ballots in three southern states (including, inevitably, Florida) prevented the determination of a clear winner. In the compromise that followed, northern Republicans retained the White House but agreed to withdraw federal troops from the southern states, leaving black and white southerners to work out their affairs without outside meddling. The process reached a climax in the 1890s, as the unsettled conditions created by economic depression and the rise of populism ignited a racist firestorm. As the last few black elected officials were hounded from office, state legislatures passed disfranchisement laws, stripping more than 90 percent of black southerners of the defense of the ballot. Segregation, long a matter of custom, was systematized and enshrined in law. By 1900, virtually every corner of southern life—schools, cemeteries, park benches, railroad cars, drinking fountains, hotels, restaurants, theaters, even the Bibles on which court witnesses swore to tell the truth—had been Jim Crowed.

The retreat from Reconstruction was abetted by northern Republicans, whose commitment to racial equality, qualified at the best of times, was fast flagging. While the U.S. Congress refused to intervene in defense of freedpeople's rights, a conservative Supreme Court struck down civil rights legislation and narrowed constitutional guarantees of equal protection and the franchise to a virtual nullity. Fourteenth Amendment guarantees of equal protection of the laws, the court ruled, only pertained to state enactments, leaving private actors—hotels, railroads, restaurants, theaters—free to discriminate as they saw fit. As for the Fifteenth Amendment, the court held that states were prohibited only from denying the franchise "on account of race, color or previous condition of servitude," leaving them perfectly free to restrict voting through other means, including such patently discriminatory devices as poll taxes, literacy tests, grandfather clauses, and closed primaries. Ultimately, it would take the 1964 Voting Rights Act and the 1965 Civil Rights Act to restore the rights enshrined in the constitution nearly a century before.

The regime of the Redeemers was consolidated not only in federal courts but also in the courtroom of Judge Lynch. By the early 1890s, more than two hundred African Americans per year—about twenty people per month— died at the hands of mobs. Contrary to Hollywood history, these murders were not all the work of a few hooded men with ropes. Often they were public carnivals, in which black bodies were hanged, shot, burned, flayed, dismembered, and, in many cases, literally parceled out as souvenirs. Most lynchings were enacted with the connivance, even active participation, of local politicians and law enforcement officials. Newspapers sometimes advertised "lynching bees" in advance; in a few cases, special trains were laid on, to enable spectators to attend the festivities. In New Orleans, a mob appropriated a local music hall and sold tickets entitling patrons to shoot the victim, who was bound on the stage. (Seats closer to the stage sold for higher prices.) In all, at least three thousand black people—men, women, and children—were lynched in the decades after southern Redemption. In not one single case were the murderers brought to justice.

Black people did not meekly submit to the new regime. In state legislatures, newspapers, churches, and a hundred other venues, African American men and women vigorously defended their prerogatives as American citizens. They also armed themselves, creating Union clubs and local militias to combat the night riders and White Leaguers. Long before the rise of the Black Power movement in the 1960s, black southerners understood the value of a loaded shotgun by the door. But with whites wielding the power of state governments and federal authorities turning a blind eye, the balance of power had shifted decisively against the freedpeople.

As the hopes of Reconstruction gave way to the violence and terror of Jim Crow, a new back-to-Africa movement sprouted across the South. In the months following final withdrawal of federal troops from the South in 1877, at least four parties of colonists embarked for Liberia, one independently and three on ships chartered by the American Colonization Society. In the years that followed, back-to-Africa sentiment continued to grow, reaching its historical peak in the grim days of the early 1890s. In terms of numbers of emigrants, the late-nineteenth-century back-to-Africa movement remained small. In all, some twenty-five hundred African Americans settled in Africa in the forty years after the Civil War, less than a quarter of the number that the colonization society had transported to Liberia in the forty years before the war. But numbers alone do not reveal the movement's full significance. Like its antebellum predecessor, the postwar back-to-Africa movement provoked a searching debate among African Americans, posing fundamental questions about black identity, history, and destiny. In a paradoxical but by now familiar process, Africa became one of the chief terrains on which African Americans debated their position and prospects in the United States.

IN THE EARLY YEARS of the nineteenth century, the African emigration movement was inextricably bound up with the career of one individual, Paul Cuffe. Martin Delany played a similar role in the years before the Civil War.

In the grim aftermath of Reconstruction, the back-to-Africa movement came to focus on Bishop Henry McNeil Turner. For forty years, this controversial, charismatic, exuberantly combative man held aloft the banner of emigration, alternately extolling the glories of Africa and deriding the timorous "Negro dirt-eaters" and "scullions" who preferred "extermination" in the American South to manly independence in their fatherland. Though he never emigrated himself, Turner made four journeys to Africa, producing in the process some of the most remarkable texts in the canon of African American writing about the continent.

Henry Turner was born in 1834 near Abbeville, South Carolina, the oldest child of free parents. According to family tradition, he owed his freeborn status to his grandfather, an enslaved African prince who was freed after his arrival in North America, "owing to some British statute or law which forbade the enslavement of royal blood." While Turner's grandfather may indeed have been of chiefly descent—thousands of such people were enslaved during the centuries of the transatlantic trade—there was no such law in British North America; and slave status was in any case determined by maternal rather than paternal descent. It is more likely that he inherited his free status (and his very fair complexion) from a white ancestor. Still, Turner's account of his royal lineage—a claim repeated by his early biographers—is noteworthy. Obviously it suggests the value that Turner and his family placed on African heritage, but it also reveals how the specific details of African Americans' African heritage were (in the manner of all things in time) growing dim, becoming not less important but less concrete, more mythic. When Paul Cuffe embarked for Africa in the 1810s, the passengers on his ship included many who could trace specific lines of descent back to Africa; a few had been born in Africa themselves. The individuals who sailed in the late nineteenth century under the auspices of Henry Turner's back-to-Africa movement were separated from the continent by another two or three generations.

Whatever the circumstances of his birth, Turner certainly chose an unpropitious moment to be born. Still reeling from the shock of the 1831 Nat Turner rebellion, white southerners directed much of their fear and rage at free people of color, whose very existence seemed a threat to social order. Free black families were hounded from their homes. Freeborn children were forcibly "apprenticed," lest their idleness infect the enslaved population. (Henry Turner himself was declared a ward of the state, which hired him out to a cotton planter.) Several southern states passed laws making it a crime to teach a black person to read or write. "We have, as far as possible, closed every avenue by which light can enter," a member of Virginia's House of Delegates declared in 1832. "If we could extinguish the capacity to see the light, our work would be completed; they would then be on a level with the beasts of the field, and we should be safe."

Like so many celebrated black writers, from Frederick Douglass to Richard Wright, Turner acquired his education through a combination of determination, guile, and luck. He learned the alphabet from a playmate and was taught to read by a local white woman, hired for the purpose by his mother. (The lessons stopped after local authorities discovered the arrangement.) When he was about fifteen, Turner took a job as a janitor at a local law firm. For whatever reason, attorneys at the firm took a shine to him. They gave him the run of their substantial library, and tutored him on a range of subjects, including science, mathematics, history, and law. This instruction, later supplemented with a year at a clandestine school in Savannah, Georgia, represented the extent of Turner's formal education. But his appetite for books had been whetted, and he remained a voracious reader for the rest of his life. Like many autodidacts, he was prone to ostentation and to the occasional malapropism, but there is no questioning the power of his mind or the breadth of his knowledge.

Inevitably, Turner gravitated to the ministry, which represented the one tenuous possibility of professional distinction for a black man in the slave South. Converted to Christianity at a Methodist camp meeting in the late 1840s, he was licensed to preach in 1853, and spent the next five years as an itinerant evangelist of the Methodist Episcopal Church, South. (The church, which had hived off from the northern Methodist church in a dispute over slavery, did not ordain black ministers at the time.) During a visit to New Orleans in 1858, he joined the African Methodist Episcopal Church, where he was immediately ordained a deacon. He would remain in the A.M.E. ministry for the rest of his life, rising through the ranks to become an elder, presiding elder and, in 1880, a bishop.

When the Civil War began in 1861, Turner was pastoring a church in Washington, D.C. He was in the city when the preliminary Emancipation Proclamation was promulgated; he would later recall racing through the streets to share the news with his congregants. When Abraham Lincoln issued the call for black volunteers, Turner converted his churchyard into a recruiting center, enlisting hundreds of soldiers for the Union army. His service was rewarded with a commission as chaplain in the First Colored Regiment, in which capacity he participated in many of the decisive battles of the war. When Turner insisted that African Americans had earned the right to full citizenship in the United States—that black people had "fought, bled and died here and have a thousand times more right than the hundreds of thousands of those who help to snub, proscribe and persecute us"—he spoke from personal experience.

During the war, Turner sent a series of long dispatches to the A.M.E. *Christian Recorder*, providing a virtually unique account of the African American experience in the Union army, as well as an early statement of some of the signature themes of his subsequent career as an emigrationist. Of these themes, none bulked larger than racial manhood. As numerous scholars have shown, manhood was a central preoccupation of African American life in the Civil War era. Striking a note that would resound a century later in the Black Power movement, black leaders worried that the experience of enslavement had emasculated black men, that the humiliations of bondage—whipping, enforced dependency, having to stand helplessly by while children were sold and wives ravished—had robbed them of those qualities of enterprise, independence, and manly self-assertion that were the foundations of any self-respecting individual or group. The best-known proponent of the theory was Frederick Douglass, whose widely read narrative portrayed a brutal fight with an overseer as the turning point of his life, the moment in which "a slave became a man." But the argument was also ubiquitous in the writing of Martin Delany, who gave it an evolutionary twist, warning that the qualities of passivity and submission instilled by slavery would, unless vigorously resisted, soon become part of African Americans' "physiological condition."

Henry Turner took the concern with racial manhood even further than

Douglass or Delany. Throughout his career as an emigrationist, he argued that erecting a powerful, independent nation in Africa was the only way to rehabilitate black manhood, to restore African Americans' self-respect and secure the respect of other races and nations. At the time of the Civil War, however, he still clung to the hope that the same result could be achieved within the United States, through exhibitions of martial valor. In one *Christian Recorder* letter, written in May 1865, he described just such an exhibition, one that vindicated black manhood in the most literal way. Marching through North Carolina, Turner's regiment encountered a burned-out bridge, forcing the soldiers to remove their uniforms and ford a "chin deep" river. "I was much amused to see the secesh women, watching with the utmost intensity, thousands of our soldiers, in a state of nudity," he wrote. "I suppose they desired to see whether these audacious Yankees were really men, made like other men, or if they were a set of varmints." Rife with sexual suggestiveness, the account clearly violated all contemporary proprieties, but Turner was not finished, larding on additional details as if to confirm every Southern nightmare. The townswomen, he reported, "thronged the windows, porticos and yards, in the finest attire imaginable," while the regiment's "brave boys would disrobe themselves, hang their garments upon their bayonets and through the water they would come, walk up the street, and seem to say to the feminine gazers, 'Yes, though naked, we are your masters.'"

After Appomattox, Turner worked (as Delany had) as an agent of the Freedmen's Bureau, a federal agency ostensibly intended to facilitate former slaves' transition to full citizenship. He soon resigned from the bureau in frustration, but he remained in the South as a missionary of the A.M.E. Church. He spent the last half of the 1860s crisscrossing Georgia and South Carolina, preaching at camp meetings, gathering in scattered congregations, helping to draw nearly a quarter of a million freedmen and women into the folds of African Methodism. The proliferation of black independent churches in the South represents one of the fundamental transformations of the Reconstruction era, and no individual did more to accomplish it than Henry Turner.

Turner's commitment to African emigration is difficult to date. In most accounts of his life, he traced his conversion to an encounter with Alexander Crummell, who preached at his Washington church in 1862. But as the war to preserve the Union evolved into a war to end slavery, he seems to have put Africa aside, committing himself to the struggle for full black citizenship in the United States. In the early, uncertain days of Reconstruction, he vacillated on the issue. In a January 1866, oration commemorating the third anniversary of the Emancipation Proclamation, he rehearsed the providential theory of black history, but said nothing about black people returning to Africa. On the contrary, he prophesied a time when "old things will be forgotten" and "the Southern people will take us by the hand and welcome us to their respect and regard." Yet just six months later, he wrote to William Coppinger, secretary of the American Colonization Society, offering his services. "I became a convert to emigration five weeks ago while riding the cars," he explained, presumably referring to some humiliation on a segregated railcar. Though he preferred the word "emigration" to "colonization"—the latter term having "become somewhat odious among our people"—he was prepared to promote the colonization society in exchange for "some inducement." "I know I have as much influence as any man South of color," he added.

With the onset of Radical Reconstruction in 1867, Turner threw himself back into American politics. He served in the Georgia constitutional convention and helped to organize the state Republican Party, under whose banner he was elected to the state legislature in 1868. When white legislators refused to seat the new black representatives, Turner took his leave with a furious attack on white "cowardice" and "pusillanimity," but at no point in the eloquent, hour-long address did he mention Africa or emigration. He continued to steer to an American star for the next three years, despite the launching of a veritable reign of terror in Georgia, much of it orchestrated by the newly created Ku Klux Klan. In the middle six months of 1868 alone, some thirty black political leaders were assassinated in Georgia—one just hours after sharing a podium with Turner—and at least two hundred others were violently assaulted. Turner received innumerable Klan threats, but he made no concessions, aside from stationing armed guards around his house. His determination was seemingly rewarded in 1870, when the U.S. Congress belatedly ordered the seating of Georgia's black representatives, but a few months later he was thwarted in his bid for reelection, after Democratic opponents engineered a fraudulent recount. That experience appears to have extinguished his last, sputtering hopes for an American future.

Though his commitment to emigration never again wavered, Turner still exhibited some uncertainty about the proper destination. In an 1871 letter to Charles Sumner, he suggested Haiti as a fit "resting place for the Negro's feet." A few years later, he proposed the creation of an autonomous black colony in New Mexico. At the same time, he was sufficiently associated with Africa to warrant a rebuke from Frederick Douglass, who accused him of working "clandestinely" for the colonization society, a charge that Turner denied. In 1875, Turner finally committed himself unequivocally to Africa. "There is no more doubt in my mind that we have ultimately to return to Africa than there is of the existence of God," he declared in a letter to William Coppinger. Having learned "the doctrines of Christianity and the elements of civil government" in the "school" of slavery, African Americans were now called to return to their ancestral continent, where "two hundred millions of our kindred" languished in "moral and spiritual blindness." A grateful Coppinger, struggling to sustain the colonization society in the face of declining interest and subscriptions, reprinted the letter in the *African Repository* and appointed Turner an honorary vice president.

Turner's association with the A.C.S. would provide rich fodder for his critics, but it had little practical effect on his activities. Far more important was his association with the A.M.E. Church, which gave him an institutional network reaching into every corner of the South. As a presiding elder, head of the church's publishing concern, and eventually as a bishop, Turner traveled incessantly, convening annual conferences, preaching at churches and camp meetings, cultivating a crop of young back-to-Africa protégés. Everywhere, he preached the gospel of Africa, urging African Americans to flee to their "fatherland" while there was yet time. By all accounts, he was a riveting speaker, occasionally orotund but also blunt and fearless, with a rare rapport with plain southern folk. When Turner had described himself as the most influential black man in the South in 1866, he was indulging in fantasy. A decade later, the claim was not so far-fetched.

THE MOVEMENT THAT TURNER was building first burst into national prominence in 1877, following the withdrawal of federal troops from the South. In South Carolina, one of the most violent battlegrounds of the Reconstruction era, black leaders convened a mass meeting at Charleston's Morris Brown A.M.E. Church to discuss emigration to Liberia. Though the American Colonization Society had survived the war and emancipation, the South Carolinians elected to proceed independently. Pursuing an idea first proposed by Paul Cuffe (and later revived by Marcus Garvey), they chartered a shipping line, the Liberian Exodus Joint Stock Steamship Company. For ten dollars subscribers received a share in the company, entitling them to a proportion of any profits, as well as the promise of a future passage to Africa. With the money thus raised—some $6,000—the company purchased the *Azor*, a steam-powered barque out of Boston, and began to fit it out for an African journey.

The Liberian Exodus Company's debt to previous back-to-Africa efforts was embodied in the person of its financial secretary, Martin Delany, who, a generation after his own journey to Africa, had returned to the emigrationist fold. In other ways, however, the company was distinctly a product of the postwar period. In contrast to the antebellum emigrationist movement, which first took root among free people of color in northern cities, the postbellum movement sprouted in the rural South, among people with direct experience of slavery, Reconstruction, and Redemption. Many of the Liberian Exodus Company's officers were themselves former slaves. And many were protégés of Henry Turner's, including at least three men he had recruited into the A.M.E. ministry: B. F. Porter, the president of the company; Samuel Flegler, who led the first group of emigrants to sail on the *Azor;* and R. H. Cain, who had represented Charleston in the U.S. House of Representatives during Reconstruction and who would soon join Turner in the A.M.E. House of Bishops.

In the spring of 1878, 206 men, women, and children boarded the *Azor* for its inaugural journey to Liberia. A throng of ten thousand people gathered to see the ship off. The *Azor*, Turner declared in his dedication speech, bore more than "a load of humanity"; it carried the race's collective future. After centuries in captivity, African Americans had been called by Providence to return to Canaan, to "take back the culture, education and religion acquired here . . . until the blaze of Gospel truth should glitter over the whole broad African continent." Looking out over Charleston harbor, where tens of thousands of Africans had first arrived in the Americas and where the first volleys of the Civil War had been fired, it was easy to believe that another transforming moment in black history was at hand.

As the *Azor* made ready in Charleston, emigration fever was also breaking out in Arkansas. Like its sister organization in South Carolina, the Liberian Exodus Arkansas Colony had roots in the A.M.E. Church, specifically in the work of the Reverend Anthony Stanford, another Turner protégé. A minister, medical doctor, and state senator—he had the dubious distinction of being the last black man driven from the Arkansas legislature—Stanford joined the emigrationist ranks in early 1877, following the collapse of Reconstruction. Six months later he reported to Turner that he had recruited five thousand prospective settlers for Liberia. While the claim was probably exaggerated, Arkansas would prove a fertile field for emigrationism. By the standards of the South, the state was something of a black stronghold, with relatively high rates of land ownership and a tradition of effective political organization. Not coincidentally, it was a site of considerable bloodshed during Redemption. Put differently, Arkansas was a place where black people had something to lose, as well as the financial and institutional resources to make emigration a realistic possibility. Roughly a third of the African Americans who settled in Africa in the last quarter of the nineteenth century— more than seven hundred people in all—hailed from this single state.

Unlike their counterparts in South Carolina, the members of the Liberian Exodus Arkansas Colony were content to travel under the auspices of the American Colonization Society. Nonetheless, they were an independent lot, as their founding charter revealed. The charter, written by Reverend Stanford and adopted at a mass meeting in Helena in November 1877, is worth quoting at length, for it expressed at once the group's deep disillusionment with the United States and its profound, paradoxical allegiance to its fundamental values and aspirations. "We hold these truths to be self-evident, that all men are created equal; that they are endowed by their creator with certain unalienable rights, that among these are life, liberty and the pursuit of happiness," the charter began, quoting the preamble of the Declaration of Independence verbatim. "And WHEREAS, In the United States of North America many of our people have been debarred by law from the rights and privileges of freemen . . . Therefore, Resolved, That we continue to seek an asylum from this deep degradation by going to Liberia, on the western coast of Africa, where we will be permitted to more fully exercise and improve those faculties which impart to man his dignity, and to evince to all who despise, ridicule and oppress our race, that we possess with them a common nature, and are susceptible of equal refinement and equal advancement that dignifies man, and that we are capable of self-government."

The Arkansas emigrants were confident that in improving their own condition, they would also uplift Africans. African Americans would bring "wealth and refinement, a higher and nobler christian manhood to develop the resources of that country," thus helping "to redeem its tens of millions to Christ." The group's constitution even listed the specific supplies that emigrants should bring to aid in Africa's redemption, including "pianos and organs, carpets, pictures, and everything that conduces to refinement and education, with books in vast number and variety." If books alone were to be used as a barometer of African Americans' changing ideas about Africa, the Arkansas colonists stood far closer to Paul Cuffe, who had sown books like seeds of civilization during his visit to Sierra Leone in 1816, than to Langston Hughes, who commenced his journey to Africa a century later by hurling his books into the sea.

In the end, neither the South Carolina nor the Arkansas Liberian Exodus companies fulfilled the expectations of promoters. In the days before the *Azor*'s departure, some of the passengers contracted measles. In the close confines of the ship, the disease ran rampant, claiming twenty-three lives before the ship had even reached Liberia. Dozens more died in the months that followed, victims of the tropical fevers—chiefly malaria—endemic to West Africa. Many of those that survived immediately began searching for ways to return to the United States. The *Azor* was consigned to the auction block after a single voyage, as the Liberian Exodus Joint Stock Steamship Company foundered in a sea of red ink. The Arkansans fared little better. In late 1877, Reverend Stanford and a companion embarked for Liberia as an advance party, returning with positive, if somewhat sobering, reports on the prospects for settlement. In the months that followed, a few hundred black Arkansans set out for New York City, in some cases selling their land, stock, and implements at a severe loss. While the number was far smaller than Stanford had originally suggested, it still overwhelmed the limited resources of the American Colonization Society, which took the better part of two years to raise the funds required to charter the necessary ships. By that time, many of the would-be colonists had returned home, while others had melted into the black population of New York City. Presumably some were still there in the winter of 1891–92, when another group of Arkansas travelers met a similar fate.

THOUGH DISAPPOINTED with the outcomes of the South Carolina and Arkansas exoduses, Turner was buoyed by both movements, which suggested that a growing number of African Americans had finally recognized the necessity of emigration. But other black leaders were aghast. Even as the hopes of Reconstruction withered, most African American leaders remained committed to winning full equality in the United States. Anxious to demonstrate blacks' qualifications for citizenship to skeptical whites, they preferred to highlight not the hopelessness of African Americans' predicament but rather their "remarkable achievements" and "unprecedented advance" in the short period since emancipation. The rise of a back-to-Africa movement obviously mocked such claims. Worse, it lent aid and comfort to the race's enemies, by suggesting that black people had never been and could never be fully American. The most vocal critic of emigration, not surprisingly, was Frederick Douglass, who denounced the postbellum movement with the same cold contempt that he had once directed at the ventures of Martin Delany. "All this native land talk . . . is nonsense," Douglass declared in one of his final public speeches. "The native land of the American Negro is America. His bones, his muscles, his sinews, are all American. His ancestors for two hundred and seventy years have lived and labored and died, on American soil, and millions of his posterity have inherited Caucasian blood." To suggest that some glorious future awaited African Americans outside the United States was "simply trifling with an afflicted people," while diverting the race from the "fight on our hands right here."

Some of the fiercest opposition to emigration came from within Turner's own church, particularly from northern church leaders, most of whom were older and of a considerably more conservative political stripe than he. While a growing number of churchmen were willing to concede that African Americans had a special calling for African mission work, they dismissed emigration as lunacy and Turner and his southern followers as a rabble. When Turner ran for election to the A.M.E. bishopric in 1880, northern church leaders united in a vicious though ultimately unsuccessful campaign to block him, and in the years that followed, they did everything in their power to mute and marginalize him. Philadelphia's Benjamin Tanner, a future A.M.E. bishop and editor of the church's flagship paper, the *Christian Recorder*, led the campaign, dismissing Turner as just the latest in a line of irresponsible black demagogues playing to the passions and credulity of the ignorant. "What one thoughtful man among us writes outweighs in value the whole Niagara of eloquence common to our people," Tanner sneered.

Turner gave as good as he got. In sermons, speeches, and newspaper articles, he ridiculed his critics as "coons" and "kitchen pimps," members of a "fungus class" of Negro leadership clinging to life in the shadow of white power. Fortunately, Africa's redemption did not depend on such "aimless, objectless, selfless, little-souled, and would-be-white negroes," but on the stout few who preferred manly independence in Africa to "scullionism" in the United States. "I would like to take yearly those who are sent to the penitentiary, hung and lynched for nothing," he once wrote, in a boast calculated to outrage his elite critics. "With them alone I could establish a government, build a country and raise a national symbol that would give character to our people everywhere." (More than a century later, Nation of Islam leader Louis Farrakhan would make an almost identical proposal.)

Charges that Turner was irresponsible and even dangerous received seeming confirmation in 1883, following the Supreme Court's invalidation of the 1875 Civil Rights Act. In an interview with the *St. Louis Globe-Democrat*, a white newspaper, the bishop denounced the "barbarous decision," declaring that the court's action "absolves the negro's allegiance to the general government, [and] makes the American flag to him a rag of contempt instead of a symbol of liberty." The comments were reprinted in papers all over the country, including the *Christian Recorder*, which demanded a retraction. Several black leaders suggested that the bishop be tried for treason. An unrepentant Turner responded by broadening his attack to embrace the one item more sacrosanct than the flag: the Constitution. "If the decision is correct, the United States Constitution is a dirty rag, a cheat, a libel, and ought to be spit on by every negro in the land," he declared. "More, if the decision is correct and is accepted by the country, then prepare to return to Africa, or get ready for extermination."

Reading Turner's writings today, one is struck primarily by their tone. But beneath the mockery and maledictions lay a coherent and consistent analysis. The keystone of Turner's thought, from the 1870s right through the end of his life, was the idea of nationality, which he saw as the essential precondition for the reclamation of black pride and manhood. Like so many other nineteenth-century political leaders, Turner assumed that people would forever remain stunted and despised until they commanded a nation of their own. "But just so long as we are a people within a people vastly our superiors in numbers, wealth, etc., having no government of our own, we shall be nothing and be so treated by the civilized world," he wrote in 1876. "The negro may wax as eloquent as Demosthenes . . . still he will be considered a cipher. . . . Nothing less than nationality will bring large prosperity and acknowledged manhood to us as a people." Thirty years later, he made the same point more pungently, in an attack on the great apostle of racial accommodation, Booker T. Washington. "Washington's policy is not worth a cent," he wrote. "Nothing less than a nation owned and controlled by the Negro will amount to a hill of beans."

Nationhood promised to do more than uplift the race in world esteem; it also promised to restore blacks' individual and collective self-respect. Anticipating an argument offered by twentieth-century black nationalists, Turner argued that centuries of oppression had damaged black people psychologically, sapping initiative, draining pride, breeding self-loathing. Even their "standard of beauty" had been corrupted by "enforced subserviency to another race." Long before "Black is beautiful" had been coined as a slogan, Turner wondered why black children played with white dolls, or why their parents debased themselves with "hair-straighteners and skin-bleachers." Worst of all, slavery and Jim Crow had undermined African Americans' faith in one another, impeding collective action. "The whole tendency of our ignoble status in this country is to develop in the negro mean, sordid, selfish, treacherous, deceitful and cranksided characteristics," he wrote. The solution, once again, lay in nationality. In erecting a proud black nation in the land of their ancestors, African Americans would redeem not only Africans but also themselves.

Turner's statements about black pride and his relentless promotion of nationhood have ensured his place in the pantheon of black nationalism, a tradition stretching from Martin Delany through twentieth-century nationalists such as Marcus Garvey and Malcolm X. Clearly he belongs in this company. Yet there is a danger, as there always is in such acts of canonization, of losing historical specificity. For all his obvious iconoclasm, Turner was emphatically a product of his times, of a late-nineteenth-century United States just beginning to flex its muscles on a world stage. Though he harnessed them to different ends, Turner subscribed to most of the core beliefs of the American Gilded Age: the boundless faith in progress and technological mastery; the cult of masculinity and manly competition; the belief in race as a fundamental determinant of individual and collective destiny. Indeed, he stands as a preeminent example of one of history's most curious axioms: that cultures create their rebels just as surely as they create their conformists.

Turner's status as a man of his times was nowhere more apparent than in his reflections on contemporary racial science. The late nineteenth century represented something of a golden age in the history of scientific racism, producing a raft of new theories to explain and confirm African Americans' innate inferiority and incapacity for responsible citizenship. Scientists measured "facial angles"—the relationship of chin, lips, and forehead—creating an index of intellect and civilization descending from the nearly vertical faces of the ancient Greeks (who were assessed using classical statuary) to the "prognathous" Negro, who stood just one step above the ape. Others examined "brain weights" and "cephalic indexes" (a measurement of a skull's volume) to prove that black people had smaller brains than white people and thus less native intelligence. An article in *Medicine*, one of the premier medical journals of the turn-of-the-century United States, traced black inferiority not to small brains but to "the large size of the negro's penis," which allegedly lacked "the sensitiveness of the terminal fibers which exists in the Caucasian." The result was a propensity to "sexual madness and excess," a biological inheritance that explained black men's propensity to rape "defenseless white women"—a propensity, the author added archly, "about as amenable to ethical culture as is the inherent odor of the race."

The late nineteenth century also marked the high tide of Social Darwinism. A misbegotten child of Darwin's theory of natural selection, Social Darwinism rendered human life as a perpetual struggle, in which the fit survived and the unfit languished and died. Everything from laissez-faire economics to the supposed "vanishing" of Native Americans was cast in terms of these supposedly inescapable "natural" laws. Not surprisingly, African Americans became the object of Social Darwinist speculation, especially after the 1880 U.S. census reported an apparent decline in their numbers. The census data was later revealed to be erroneous, but it had a dramatic impact on contemporary debates about black people's character and progress. Here was seeming proof that proslavery writers had been right, that Negroes were a naturally dependent race, able to survive in the protective custody of whites, but doomed to extinction (as Native Americans were allegedly doomed) once forced to survive on their own in a competitive, Darwinian world. Such ideas, it should be emphasized, were not the property of racial extremists but fundamental axioms of late-nineteenth-century American thought, and they had immediate, real-world consequences. White life insurance companies, for example, almost universally refused to sell policies to African Americans on the grounds that they were bad risks, a practice that continued well into the twentieth century.

Given the character of contemporary racial science, one might expect African Americans to give it a wide berth. Most did. As the new racial orthodoxy settled over the land, Frederick Douglass continued to sound the themes he had pressed for a half century: black people possessed the same intellectual and moral capacities as other human beings; claims of racial superiority and inferiority were nonsense; black people's degradation was a consequence of the prejudicial circumstances in which they were forced to live rather than of any inferior endowment. As if to underscore his beliefs, the widowed Douglass took as his second wife a white woman, Helen Pitts, his former secretary, scandalizing many of his contemporaries, black and white. (Douglass, himself the product of a mixed union, brushed the controversy aside: having honored his mother's race in his first marriage, he said, he chose to honor his father's in his second.)

While Douglass rejected the tenets of scientific racism, Turner battled the racists on their own terrain. In his writings, he discoursed freely on the size of cranial pans, the verticality of faces, and other such topics, finding in all abundant proof not of Negroes' inferiority but of their genius and distinction. He was also an avid student of phrenology, an antebellum vogue that sought to map the propensities of individuals and groups through the shape and contours of their skulls. By the late nineteenth century, phrenology was generally dismissed as quaint and unscientific, but Turner remained committed, perhaps because he himself had once been the subject of a flattering analysis in the *American Phrenological Journal*. Perhaps most surprisingly, the bishop was a confirmed Social Darwinist, though he obviously shaped the theory to his own purposes. Black people, he insisted, faced a stark choice: emigration or extermination. There was simply no way that black people, living as a dependent race in the United States, could ever develop those qualities—initiative, self-assertion, aggression, mastery of the physical environment—that races needed to survive in a remorseless, competitive world. Nature and God alike commanded African Americans to return to the land of their fathers and "begin the ground work" of a great black nation.

Turner's vision of that great black nation offers a final testament to his immersion in the culture of Gilded Age America. In contrast to most twentieth-century renderings, Turner's African utopia was not to be some kind of neoromantic idyll, where black people would live "traditional" lives, sheltered from the clatter and hum of the modern world. Rather, it would be a dynamic, modern nation-state, with all the appropriate accoutrements, including "high offices, dignitaries, artisans, mechanics, corporations, railroads, telegraph, commerce, colleges, churches, &c.,&c." He even proposed a name: the United States of Africa.

THE PROBLEM, OF COURSE, was that Turner had never been to Africa himself, a fact that his many critics were quick to note. His opportunity finally came in the early 1890s, ironically at the instigation of his fellow bish-ops of the A.M.E. Church. After decades of emigration and colonization, the church had a handful of ministers and several hundred members in Liberia and Sierra Leone, but the work had been poorly supported and ill supervised. Mindful of the work being done in Africa by rival denominations, black and white, the A.M.E. House of Bishops voted to send a bishop to West Africa to organize the church's work. Against the better judgment of some, they tapped Turner for the assignment.

Turner embarked for Africa, "the world's future paradise," in October 1891. He spent just over a month on the continent, half in Sierra Leone and half in Liberia. Like generations of African travelers, he recorded his obser-vations in a journal, though in his hands the journal form served less as a vehicle of self-reflection than as one more opportunity to promote the back-to-Africa cause. At each stop, he posted the most recent entries back to the United States for publication. The "Letters of Bishop Henry M. Turner," fourteen in all, appeared in the *A.M.E. Church Review* in early 1892 and were widely reprinted and discussed in the African American press. Though the bishop would make three more trips to the continent, his letters of 1891 offer the fullest exposition of his ideas about Africa and Africans.

In the absence of regular African steam service from the United States, Turner sailed first to Liverpool, where he boarded a ship bound for West Africa. Several Africans boarded the ship in Liverpool, providing Turner with his first opportunity to observe the people about whom he had written and argued for so long. Characteristically, he cast his assessment in racial terms, probing face and physiognomy for evidence of character and capac-ity. "The Crew tribe seems to be a superior class of men," he wrote of a group of deckhands. "Their heads are round, symmetrical and frontly high; only one cephalic cranium of the six, and not a receder in the number." He was even more impressed by his dark-skinned cabinmate, Matthew Thomas, who was bound for Lagos. Judging from his name and other aspects of his biography, Thomas was almost certainly Aku, a descendant of the recaptive Africans deposited at Sierra Leone by the Royal Navy in its campaign against the slave trade, many of whom later migrated back to their homes in Nige-ria. But to Turner, he was "a regular African." He was also "one of the most learned" men that the bishop had ever met, fluent in a bevy of modern and ancient languages. "Talk about the African being ignorant," Turner mocked, "here is one who has no superior for book learning in our country, yet he is only 37 years of age." Clearly Africa had a bright future.

A few days later, the ship anchored off Freetown. Turner's first sight was of naked African oarsmen rowing out in the pilot boat. His hopes momentarily flagged. "Things are gloomy here," he said to a companion. But as the ship began to disgorge its cargo, his spirits revived. Everywhere, he saw black men in positions of authority—piloting vessels, operating steam machinery, giving "intelligent orders" and "managing affairs." A dispute between "a half nude African" and a white clerk was cut short when the African corrected the clerk's arithmetic. "These Africans are men, naked or clothed," Turner raved in an entry later that night. "I am crazy with delight so far."

As such comments suggest, Turner's descriptions of Africa were powerfully shaped by the exigencies of the emigration debate in the United States. "Great heavens, how white people on the one hand and scullion Negroes upon the other, have misrepresented Africa!" he began. Far from the pestilential wilderness depicted by his opponents, Africa was a "paradisical spot," the "easiest place to make a living on earth." Food grew in such abundance and variety that a man "could hibernate six months annually" and still comfortably survive. The natural resources beggared description, with iron ore "in mountain heaps" and forests of "the finest wood on earth." Any emigrant with a bit of pluck and capital "would be worth millions in a few years." As for Africa's fearsome climate, it was no hotter or more dangerous than that of Houston or Memphis. "True, there is an acclimating change most people have to pass through," he conceded, but anyone in "reasonable health" had little to fear.

On the subject of Liberia, the presumed destination of returning African Americans, Turner was positively rapturous. "I thought it was a second class portion of Africa," he confessed, "but it is the richest region of the world I ever saw." Vast deposits of coal, gold, silver, diamonds, and tin sat ready for the taking. Water power was "inestimable—enough to run the machinery of the world." Best of all, Liberia offered a limitless reservoir of native labor, available for wages that were just a fraction of going rates in the United

States. Scullions who preferred menial jobs had best stay at home, Turner advised, because in Liberia native Africans did "all the mere common labor. . . ." They tilled fields, minded children, quarried stone, and bore the hammocks and sedan chairs in which Americo-Liberian settlers (and visiting dignitaries like Turner) traveled, all for just "twenty-five cents per day or five dollars per month." "I never wanted to be a young man so badly in my life," Turner concluded. "I would come here, and, if I had half as much sense as I have now, I would be worth a fortune in ten years." Such rhetoric was obviously intended to entice potential immigrants, yet there is still something jarring in hearing one of history's premier black nationalists discoursing on the virtues of cheap African labor.

Significantly, Turner seems to have had little personal contact with the "native Africans" he described. Like most Western visitors to Sierra Leone and Liberia, he spent virtually all of his time in the settler enclave on the coast, and many of his "impressions" of Africans were in fact digests of conversations with the people he met there—the British governor of Sierra Leone, a white missionary from Iowa, a general of the Liberian army, and so forth. A meeting with the great-granddaughters of Daniel Coker linked the bishop to the early days of the back-to-Africa movement. (Turner was particularly taken with ten-year-old Susan Coker, a "beautiful ginger-cake-colored" child with a "bright intellect and a fine head phrenologically.") He also spent a week in the company of the eminent scholar Edward Blyden, with whom he made his one venture out of the settler enclave, a two-day steamboat journey up the Sherbro River. But even after a month in Africa, indigenous Africans seem to have remained largely an abstraction for Turner.

Lack of contact with Africans did not prevent the bishop from expatiating on their character and prospects. Not surprisingly, his assessments were positive, though they led to some curious conclusions. According to Turner, reports of African "laziness, stupidity and worthlessness" could not have been more erroneous. On the contrary, Africans were honest, industrious, intelligent, and blessed with rare tact and taste. Living in a country of their own, they exhibited none of the cringing servility so common among blacks in the United States, but felt themselves "the equal of any man on earth." In a word, Africans had retained their manhood.

In some passages, Turner went further, arguing that Africans were actually superior to African Americans, having sprung from a "higher grade" racial stock. As evidence, he offered the testimony of an ancient African man, "said to be 108 years old," who told him that "during the times of the slave trade there were no 'big blood' first-class Africans sold to the white man," unless they had been captured in war. "I have found that we poor American Negroes were the tail-end of the African races," Turner reported. "We were slaves over here, and had been for a thousand years or more before we were sold to America." (Though he used the first person, the bishop clearly regarded himself as an exception, having descended from a captive African prince.) Turner supplemented his informant's claim with his own scientific observations. "Those who think the receding forehead, the flat nose, the proboscidated mouth and the big flat-bottom foot are natural to the African are mistaken," he wrote. "There are heads here by the millions, as vertical or perpendicular as any white man's head God ever made. A straight rule laid upon the face of three-fourths of us in America will touch the nose and mouth only; here are native Africans, without number, whose nose and chin the rule would touch without touching the mouth, which is always indicative of the highest type of intellectuality." Having examined "specimens of 19 tribes," the bishop reported seeing only a handful of people "constructed on as low [a] scale as I have seen in America."

The idea that African Americans represented the tail-end of the race obviously appealed to Turner, providing him a means simultaneously to vindicate African capacity and to mock his critics at home, whose opposition to emigration just proved their own innate slavishness. But it also posed a problem. The whole logic of African "redemption," after all, was that African Americans were the vanguard of the race, ordained by God to carry the blessings of civilization and Christianity back to their benighted ancestral continent. In Turner's words, African Americans had been prepared by God to "take intelligent possession" of their "fatherland." But did they really have the capacity? More to the point, did they have the right? If Africans were indeed as proud and self-possessed as Turner suggested, then why should they submit to the tutelage of deracinated African Americans?

Such questions had already begun to preoccupy Turner's traveling companion, Edward Blyden, who a few years later would formally renounce his half century commitment to African emigration. But Turner never pursued the problem, if indeed he even recognized it. Insofar as his encounter with Africans prompted him to amend his views at all, it did so chiefly by persuading him that the continent's redemption would unfold far more quickly and easily than he had dared imagine. The native African "is the most susceptible heathen upon the face of the globe," he raved, being ready "to lay down any habit, custom or sentiment" when presented with a superior alternative. While prone to superstition, Africans had no real religion of their own, making their conversion to Christianity "an easy matter." Contrary to stereotypes, they were also an extremely industrious people, each native doing the work of two or three civilized men at a tiny fraction of the cost. "There is no reason under heaven," Turner concluded, "that this Continent should not or cannot be redeemed and brought to God in twenty-five years—say thirty at most."

In his efforts to encourage emigration and defend Africa from its detractors, Turner managed to recapitulate virtually the entire catalogue of rationalizations for contemporary European imperialism. Africa possessed vast stores of valuable natural resources, which Africans were incapable of exploiting efficiently. It offered lucrative investment opportunities, as well as a limitless supply of cheap, pliant labor. The inhabitants themselves were "heathens," crying out for the blessings of "Christianity and civilization." The distinction, of course, was that Turner's imagined colonizers were themselves descendants of Africa, coming not to exploit the continent but to redeem it, to inaugurate a new era of manhood, equality, and proud black nationality for the entire Negro race. For Henry Turner, that distinction meant everything. It probably meant less to the indigenous people of Liberia, as the country's subsequent history would show.

TURNER'S TRIP COINCIDED WITH, and surely contributed to, a new bout of emigration fever in the American South. With disfranchisement and Jim Crow sweeping the region, with lynching an almost daily occurrence, southern blacks cast their eyes again to Africa, seeking, if not a land of milk and honey, then at least a refuge from the horrors of the United States. Emigration clubs sprouted all across the South, with members meeting in secret to conceal their purposes from local whites. Inquiries poured into the Washington headquarters of the American Colonization Society. The temper of the time was poignantly expressed in a sermon by an Atlanta minister. Incensed by a new Jim Crow ordinance on the city's streetcar system, the minister called on his congregants "to leave Georgia and go to their own country, Africa, where they would have equal rights and help govern and have streetcars of their own."

As much as any single utterance, the minister's comments exposed the historical roots of the late nineteenth-century back-to-Africa movement—frustration, despair, and desperate need, all mixed with large doses of credulity and projection. There were no streetcars in Africa in the 1890s, but what mattered to the minister and his congregants was less the reality of the continent than the idea, the vision of another place, beyond the borders of Georgia, where black men and women enjoyed dignity and respect. Yet these very circumstances created a ripe field for charlatans and confidence men, who descended on the South like crows on a carcass. In Arkansas, a man purporting to be Edward Blyden, the eminent scholar and emigrationist advocate, defrauded hundreds of people. (The real Blyden was in Africa with Turner at the time.) Another grifter, J. P. F. Lightfoot, sold hundreds of desperate black farmers special three-dollar steamship tickets. Unlike "Blyden," who evaporated after a month or two, Lightfoot was exposed, apprehended, and lynched by his enraged victims.

Not all the schemers and opportunists were black. In the late 1880s, a group of white businessmen chartered the United States and Congo National Emigration Company. Though they portrayed themselves as philanthropists, hoping to assist in the development of the newly created Congo Free State, the founders' hope for profit flowed from their rediscovery of an 1862 federal law. Passed in the early days of the Civil War and promptly forgotten, the law reserved one quarter of all revenues from the sale of abandoned lands in the South for use in assisting the removal of African Americans from the United States. By their calculation, the founders of the Congo Company were entitled to a $500,000 federal subsidy. When the U.S. Congress demurred, the men sold their interests to a group of black shareholders, who continued for the next several years to promote the venture, offering southern blacks "preferred" tickets to Africa for just one dollar—pending the federal subsidy. Hopes that the federal government would underwrite African emigration were inflamed still further by the introduction of the so-called Butler Bill in the U.S. Congress, proposing an appropriation of five million dollars to begin the systematic removal of African Americans from the South. Authored by one of the Senate's most notorious racists, the bill had no hope of passage, but its much-publicized path through Congress helped sustain the emigrationist enthusiasm. (Henry Turner publicly endorsed Butler's bill in 1890, igniting a firestorm very similar to the one that Marcus Garvey touched off a few decades later with his brief, ill-considered alliance with the Ku Klux Klan.)

Emigration fever reached a tragic climax in the winter of 1891–92, when several parties of southerners, including Reverend Thornton and the would-be emigrants from McCrory, Arkansas, arrived in New York City to meet nonexistent Liberia-bound ships. The episode drove a final nail in the coffin of the American Colonization Society, which was already reeling from the death, a few weeks before, of its longtime executive secretary, William Coppinger. Embarrassed directors of the society managed to charter a ship to carry some of the stranded colonists to Liberia but disclaimed all responsibility for the rest. A short time later, the society announced that it would no longer transport groups of colonists to Liberia, discontinuing a policy that reached back more than seventy years, to the voyage of Daniel Coker and the *Elizabeth*. Henceforth the A.C.S. would only underwrite the emigration of select individuals with essential skills. Even that commitment soon petered out, and the A.C.S. was formally disbanded.

The plight of the stranded emigrants ignited a furious debate among black Americans. Much of the anger was directed at Bishop Turner, whom critics accused of humiliating himself and the race. T. Thomas Fortune, editor of the influential *New York Age*, led the charge, deriding the bishop as "the oiled advocate of a white man's corporation, the American Colonization Society, that for the past fifty years has thrived more or less on the gullibility of simple-minded, irresponsible Negroes." Turner, needless to say, fired back, insisting that he had no more responsibility for the stranded emigrants than "the man in the moon." The real hypocrites, he declared, were comfortable northern leaders like Fortune, who, without having spent a day in the "devil-ridden" South themselves, were prepared to cast the migrants back to that land "of slaughter and death." As his opponents bayed for blood, Turner embarked on a second voyage to Sierra Leone and Liberia. In the course of the trip, he produced another dozen letters to black America, reiterating his earlier claims and warning of the growing white presence on the continent. If African Americans did not wake up soon, he warned, Europeans would secure "possession of the gold, silver, tin, lead, iron and diamond mines which God gave to the Negro," and "the black race will have no home on the face of the globe."

Though Turner waxed defiant, the debacle of 1892 had badly damaged his credibility. Just how badly became clear a year later, when the bishop, just back from his second visit to Africa, convened a national convention of black leaders in Cincinnati. Modeled on the conventions called by Martin Delany before the Civil War, the gathering was intended to forge a national consensus on emigration. It also marked Turner's not-so-subtle attempt to establish himself as heir apparent to the aged Frederick Douglass, to claim the mantle of "representative" race leader that Delany had tried to wrest from Douglass forty years before. It failed on both counts. While delegates sat patiently through the bishop's two-hour opening address, they refused to endorse anything smacking of emigration. Turner was eventually forced to refer his centerpiece resolution back to committee to spare himself a humiliating floor vote. When Douglass died a year later, his mantle fell not on Turner but on Booker T. Washington, whose bromides about submission and casting down one's bucket in the South represented everything that the bishop despised.

KARL MARX ONCE WRYLY suggested that history repeats itself, the first time as tragedy, the second as farce. If Henry Turner's vain struggle to build a proud black nation in Africa had the elements of classical tragedy, of a great man undone by fate and by aspects of his own character, the travails of some of his followers offered more farcical fare. During his travels through the South, Turner accumulated numerous protégés, many of whom followed their mentor to Africa. The range of their experiences was captured in the cases of Edward Ridgel and Charles Spencer Smith.

Edward Ridgel was born in Arkansas in 1861. He was just twenty-three years old when he was ordained into the A.M.E. ministry by Turner. He served several parishes in his home state in the 1880s, ending up in Forrest City, where he ministered to a large congregation and edited a small newspaper, the *Enterprise*. He was there during the Forrest City "riot" of 1889, one of the bloodiest in a series of racist pogroms intended to drive black Arkansans out of politics. Like Turner, Ridgel was outspoken and combative, and he played a central role in the emigration fever that swept eastern Arkansas in the early 1890s. In 1892, he announced his intention to resettle in Africa himself. Rather than seek support from the A.M.E. Church's Mission Department, an organization controlled by northern churchmen, he embarked on a national speaking tour, raising the money for his trip himself. By the time he reached New York, he had accumulated $500 and the hostility of many of the church's leading divines.

When Bishop Turner embarked on his second trip to Africa in early 1893, Ridgel went with him. They were accompanied by another A.M.E. minister, Reverend Vreeland, as well as by Vreeland's wife and Ridgel's new bride, the former Fannie Worthington. Though she too hailed from Arkansas, Fannie Worthington Ridgel had charted a rather different path through life than her husband. Her grandfather was a white man, one of Arkansas' wealthiest planters, who had scandalized local society by acknowledging and caring for his brown children. Fannie's father, James, was educated in Paris, returning to Arkansas during Reconstruction to serve two terms in the state senate. When James died, Fannie and her mother left Arkansas, settling eventually in Washington, D.C., where Fannie's fine education and fair skin ensured her membership in the city's exclusive brown elite. Whether she and Ridgel knew one another from Arkansas or whether they met during his lecture tour is not clear, but in either case they were married in 1893, two weeks before embarking for Africa.

Ridgel was initially assigned to an A.M.E. congregation in Freetown. He wrote incessantly, producing literally hundreds of letters to correspondents and newspapers in the United States, as well as a short book, *Africa and African Methodism*. Though he had come to Africa as a missionary, Ridgel had relatively little to say on the subject of missions, focusing instead on the necessity of emigration. Not surprisingly, his sentiments closely paralleled Turner's. "When Providence opens to us a door, we must not be too cowardly to enter," he wrote. "Israel was not freed in Egypt, but was commanded to cross the Red Sea . . . and find freedom in Canaan." The time had come, he continued, for African Americans "to leave the haunts of American slavery and pitch their tents on the free and sacred soil of Africa, and assist in the establishment of a mighty Negro empire." Ridgel's comments on his anti-emigration adversaries were, if anything, more derisive than Turner's. Among slavery's baleful effects, he argued, were "powerful tendencies toward white men absorbtion [sic], in principle, habit, etc." The result was a pathetic species of so-called race leaders who "despise Africa" and "extol negro-hating America. . . . [T]o my mind the negro in foreign lands must return home and become renegroized, if you please, before he can fully appreciate himself and his people."

While much of Ridgel's writing focused on the situation of black Americans, he did offer numerous observations on Africa and Africans. His comments, like Turner's, were at once enthusiastic and contradictory. Contrary to claims by black and white slanderers, Africa had a glorious history, having given the world art, science, and philosophy. Rehearsing a syllogism advanced a generation before by Martin Delany (and reiterated a generation later by W. E. B. Du Bois), Ridgel argued that Egypt was an African culture and that Egypt was the seedbed of Greek culture, thus demonstrating the African origins of so-called Western civilization. Yet Ridgel's comments about contemporary Africans fell comfortably within the confines of colonial ideology. His first reaction on arriving in Sierra Leone was horror at the sight of the naked boatmen who came out to greet the ship. "Awful! Awful! Awful!" he wrote. "The gospel is needed here." Later, he offered a ringing endorsement of British colonialism. "We regard the British government a godsend in Africa," he wrote. "Thousand of the people who are now educated and in easy circumstance would have been savage heathens."

Ridgel was particularly outspoken on the subject of "Mahometism." Islam was a recurring theme in nineteenth-century African American writing about the continent. Most authors disparaged it, presenting it both as a rival to Christianity and as one of the chief sources of the slave trade. In the late nineteenth century, however, a countertradition emerged, thanks chiefly to the work of Edward Blyden. While Blyden never equated Islam with Christianity, he praised it for its emphasis on education, piety, and temperance, all of which helped to shelter Africans from the rain of rum and cultural dissolution that Europeans had unleashed on the continent. Henry Turner had offered a similar account, portraying Islam as "the morning-star to the pure sun of Christianity." Ridgel, however, would have none of it. Mahometism was a blight on Africa, and promoters like Blyden were cranks who had "laid down the Bible for the Koran." Aside from its relative freedom from "color-phobia," there was "nothing in it worthy of commendation." Everywhere Islam spread it brought "blood, death and ruin," but it was particularly dangerous in Africa, where it functioned as a kind of "paganism in disguise," welcoming members without demanding "the complete surrender and entire change of life" required by Christianity. Ridgel found Islam's tolerance of polygamy especially detestable. Such a practice licensed "sexual passions," completely overwhelming the "higher senses."

Whatever the merits of the sentiments, they were somewhat ironic coming from Ridgel, who appears himself to have been a bigamist. It soon emerged that Ridgel had left a family behind in Arkansas in 1892, and that he was still married when he met and married Fannie Worthington. The discovery played into the hands of anti-emigrationists in the A.M.E. hierarchy, who demanded that he return to the United States for a hearing. When he refused, they released the information to the Indianapolis *Freeman*, one of the nation's largest circulating black newspapers. Bishop Turner, interpreting the campaign against Ridgel as a personal attack on him, stood by his protégé. When he made a third visit to Africa in 1895, he formally dismissed the charges and promoted him to the office of presiding elder of the Liberian church. But the controversy took a toll on Ridgel, who collapsed into depression. In late 1896, the young missionary hurled himself from a steamer into the St. Paul River and drowned.

Reverend Charles Spencer Smith, another Turner protégé, had an equally unlikely African career. Born in the African American expatriate community in Canada, Smith went South after the Civil War to work as a teacher and later as a minister of the A.M.E. Church. He served in the Alabama state legislature during Reconstruction, and embraced the cause of emigration following Redemption. By the early 1890s, Smith had established himself as one of the A.M.E. Church's leading authorities on Africa, lecturing on the subject at Wilberforce University, the church's educational flagship. As Turner and Ridgel embarked for Africa in 1893, Smith was busy making preparations to travel to Africa himself. His object was to identify "opportunities" and "inducements" for returning African Americans, but he also professed his intention to emigrate himself. "Africa doesn't need me one-thousandth part as much as I need Africa," he declared.

Smith embarked in the fall of 1894. Over the course of three months, he traveled down the West African coast, from Sierra Leone to Luanda in Angola. In the process, he underwent a kind of conversion experience, emerging not only as an opponent of African American emigration but also as a champion of European colonialism. Smith's account of his journey, published in 1895 under the title *Glimpses of Africa*, offered a bizarre coda to the nineteenth-century back-to-Africa movement.

Smith's reversal perplexed his contemporaries, but in retrospect it seems almost preordained. Though widely acknowledged as an expert on Africa, Smith had no direct knowledge of the continent, depending instead on published texts, most of them written by white missionaries and explorers. In preparing for his trip, for example, he read the collected works of H. M. Stanley, the maps of which he had embossed and hung in his office. He also acquired a set of "scientific instruments"—barometer, hygrometer, thermometer, and compass—which he would later use to record the temperature, humidity, pressure, and location of a series of well-trod West African ports. As if to complete the picture, he purchased a complete "tropical outfit" during a stopover in Liverpool, including three white flannel suits, a white pith helmet, a white sun umbrella, white canvas shoes and a "red silk cummer-band." Though an avowed black nationalist, Smith had costumed himself as a Dark Continent explorer.

In his memoir, Smith proudly claimed to have seen more of Africa than any previous African American explorer. Yet in the entire three months traveling along the African coast, he never once slept off his ship, save for a week's sojourn in Liberia. At each port, he recorded his scientific observations, occasionally venturing ashore to take photographs. While on shore, he discussed Africa's prospects with many people, but his interlocutors tended not to be Africans but English-speaking white men, chiefly missionaries, merchants, and colonial officials. With each conversation, he became more and more dubious about the wisdom of African American emigration. By the time the book appeared, all that remained of his initial convictions was an incongruous introduction by Henry Turner, obviously written without benefit of having read the book.

Though Smith pledged to confine himself to "personal observations," his book was a stew of colonial platitudes, flavored with a dash of Social Darwinism. Africans, in Smith's view, came in three varieties: civilized, semicivilized, and uncivilized. (Judging from the book's conveniently labeled photographs, the distinction between civilized and semicivilized was chiefly a function of Western-style dress, while the uncivilized were invariably distinguished by the exposed breasts of the women.) Africans were further differentiated by tribes, some of which Smith found physically attractive, others of which repulsed him. The Dwalla people of Cameroon, for example, tattooed themselves, a practice he found "very unattractive," while the natives of Fernando Po rendered "their persons disgustingly filthy by besmearing themselves with oil." Depending on their particular endowments, different tribes had different prospects in the unforgiving, Darwinian struggle for survival. The natives of Fernando Po were among the foredoomed. "They were never enslaved," Smith explained, "and are evidently too weak to survive the attrition of civilizing processes, and therefore will ultimately disappear." Fortunately, other Africans seemed to be adapting well to the new regime in Africa, exhibiting the appropriate balance between resilience and "tractability." Smith ended his discussion of the subject by approvingly quoting a British colonial official, who claimed that the African "surpasses all other low-grade varieties of man in the facility with which in one generation, in the one individual, he can skip two or three thousand years and transform himself from a naked, brutish savage, into a shorthand clerk . . . or an irreproachable butler."

By the end of his journey, the one-time emigrationist had emerged as an enthusiastic supporter of European colonialism. Africa, he opined, "would be a wilderness were it not for European capital and energy." While a "degenerate and retrogressive" people like the Portuguese had no business in Africa, the other European powers were doing everything they could "to redeem West Africa from the grasp of barbarism and to lift the long-benighted masses into the light of civilization and progress." All across the continent, "savages" who had known only "indolence" and "immediate gratification" were discovering the blessings of civilization and sustained industry. Revealingly, Smith's favorite spot in his entire journey was Matadi, the starting point of the Congo railroad and a place prominently featured in the writings of Henry Morton Stanley. Calculated on a corpses-per-mile basis, the Congo railroad may have been the deadliest construction project in human history, with literally thousands of people perishing to complete a portage around the falls of the Congo River. But Smith found it thrilling. Seeing "the bright flames of the heated furnace," hearing the "shrill notes" of a locomotive and the "busy hum of revolving machinery," he was transported into rapturous reflections on the grand "future of Africa." Needless to say, this future did not include African American emigration.

Having seen the light himself, Smith was determined to illuminate others. From the moment of his return to the United States, he waged an anti-emigration crusade, stumping the country to expose what he saw as the lies and distortions of the back-to-Africa movement. He pursued his erstwhile mentor, Henry Turner, like an avenging angel. When an International Migration Society with which Turner was associated succeeded in chartering a ship to carry a group of emigrants to Liberia in 1895, Smith appeared at the dockside with a government inspector, hoping to prevent the ship from sailing. When Turner succeeded in organizing a new A.M.E. Church mission in South Africa, Smith set out systematically to destroy it, collaborating in the work with the South African government. African Americans, he insisted, simply had no business anywhere in Africa, let alone in a progressive country like South Africa. As for the black South Africans who had invited the

A.M.E. Church into the field, they were ingrates, who should return to the European mission societies from which they had seceded. Before "the advent of Europeans," he archly reminded one African minister, Africa had no railroads or banks, no telegraphs or laws, "nothing but wild barbarism accentuated by the fierce growl of untamed beasts." It was an extraordinary statement, especially coming from a man who a few years before had been a leading spokesman of the back-to-Africa movement.

AS FOR TURNER, he continued to advocate African emigration, undeterred by the setbacks of the early 1890s or the betrayal of his one-time comrade. By the end of the century, he had made four trips to Africa, the last one, in 1898, to South Africa. He also founded and edited an emigrationist newspaper, *The Voice of Missions*. Though nominally the organ of the Sixth Episcopal District of the A.M.E. Church, the paper was Turner's personal broadsheet, and he filled its columns with reports of Africa's dazzling mineral wealth and of the fortune to be made developing commercial links between the continent and the United States. The paper's editorials made it clear that Turner, now in his sixties, had lost neither his fire nor his ability to provoke controversy. He continued to rage against "scullions" and "mushroom pimps," denouncing the "leading men" of the race as a bunch of "leading asses." His suggestion that black South Africans should drive the British "back to the Thames" prompted an official inquiry in London and Pretoria and a formal disavowal from his fellow A.M.E. bishops. Probably his most famous editorial was "God Is a Negro," which argued exactly what its title suggested. When several white newspapers decried the editorial, Turner had a ready reply: "We have as much right biblically and otherwise to believe that God is a Negro, as you buckra, or white, people have to believe that God is a fine looking, symmetrical and ornamented white man."

Turner had a more difficult time explaining away an ill-advised 1895 editorial, in which he advocated the temporary resumption of the African slave trade. His argument, in a nutshell, was that if Africans were not going to receive the blessings of Christianity and civilization from returning African Americans, then they would have to acquire them in the same way that

African Americans had, in the providential school of slavery. In contrast to the experience of African Americans, these slaves would be held by black masters and liberated after seven years, in keeping with the Old Testament injunction of Jubilee. The plan had the virtue of a certain intellectual consistency, but it appalled even Turner's supporters and he wisely said no more on the subject.

The comment that caused Turner the most trouble, however, was his suggestion that black people should arm themselves. Given his experiences and his knowledge of southern life, it was not an unreasonable suggestion. But it came back to haunt him in 1900, when an agent of *The Voice of Missions* in New Orleans killed a half dozen white people, including three policemen, igniting a riot that left more than two dozen people dead. Turner bore the brunt of blame, and his fellow bishops stripped him of the editorship of *The Voice of Missions*. Yet even then, he remained defiant, immediately launching another newspaper, *The Voice of the People*. In the columns of the new paper, Turner continued to sound the back-to-Africa tocsin, juxtaposing accounts of Africa's untapped wealth with reports of the most recent atrocities in the United States. The paper's masthead conveyed the same message graphically. On the left side of the page was a map of the United States, with an image of a lynched black man and words like "disenfranchisement," "degradation," and "oppression." On the right side of the page lay a half-illuminated Africa, characterized by "liberty," "Christianity," "self-reliance," and "manhood." A ship floated in mid-ocean above the legend: EMIGRATION OR EXTERMINATION AWAITS THE BLACK MAN.

Henry McNeil Turner died in 1915. If he never succeeded in inducing African Americans to leave the United States, he at least achieved his stated goal of dying outside the country's borders, passing away in Toronto, Canada. By the standards of his tumultuous career, his final years were peaceful. Most of his old allies and adversaries had passed on, and the back-to-Africa issue had gradually lost its political salience (though it would soon gain a new lease on life under the leadership of Marcus Garvey, who arrived in the United States in the year of Turner's death). An exodus of African Americans out of the South had indeed begun, but the migrants' destination was not Africa but the promised land of northern cities like Chicago, New York, and Cleveland.

Like so many of those who achieve the dubious label of "elder states-men," Turner was sent to his reward with a chorus of encomiums. The words he would most have appreciated came from W. E. B. Du Bois, editor of *The Crisis,* the monthly journal of the N.A.A.C.P., and a man who would himself soon undertake a memorable trip to Africa. Turner, Du Bois wrote, was "the last of his clan: mighty men, physically and mentally . . . the spiritual progeny of African chieftains." Perhaps. But he was also a nineteenth-century African American, alienated from the land of his birth yet steeped in its fundamental values.

FOUR

Mundele Ndom

IN THE COURSE OF his journey down the coast of West Africa in 1894, Charles Spencer Smith spent a day at Boma, eighty miles up the Congo River. On his way from ship to town, he passed "one of those African trees famous for their short but exceedingly thick bodies," a tree whose circumference exceeded "the outstretched arms of fourteen men." "The bark is very thick," Smith wrote, "and I notice that quite a number of persons have taken advantage of the opportunity to carve their names thereon. Among the hundreds of names that I see is that of Reverend S. P. Shephard, a colored man from America, who is laboring as a missionary among the Kassia people in the Upper Congo, under the auspices of the Board of Missions of the Southern Presbyterian Church. He has outstripped many others in the height of the point where he carved his name, and I found myself humorously ejaculating, 'Well, old fellow, if you never write your name anywhere else, you certainly have written it here. Bravo!'"

William Henry Sheppard—Smith misspelled the surname and gave the wrong initials—had passed through Boma four years before, en route to

Luebo, on the Kasai River, a further thousand miles into the interior. The carving in the bark of that great tree represented a physical trace of one of the most extraordinary journeys in African American history, an epic voyage that would carry Sheppard from a Virginia stable to a stinking stockade in the Congo, where he carefully counted eighty-one severed human hands drying over a low fire. In the course of his travels, Sheppard crossed paths with an unlikely collection of historical characters, including four American presidents and four BaKuba kings, Queen Victoria, Booker T. Washington, Mark Twain, and a Polish steamship captain named Korzeniowski, soon to announce himself to the English-speaking world as Joseph Conrad.

BY THE LATE NINETEENTH CENTURY, Europeans had been present in sub-Saharan Africa for more than four hundred years. Decades before Columbus's voyages to the New World, Portuguese and Spanish ships plied the west coast of the continent, trading for gold and slaves. In the centuries that followed, European ships carried millions of captives away from Africa, along with a cornucopia of commodities, from copper and copra to ebony and ivory. For the most part, however, Europeans pursued their ends without the assertion of formal political control, and indeed with a very limited physical presence. This situation changed abruptly in the closing decades of the nineteenth century, as European powers, vying with one another for prestige and strategic advantage, as well as for investment outlets and new sources of raw materials to fuel burgeoning industrial economies, carved out formal African empires.

The Scramble for Africa climaxed at the Berlin Conference of 1884–85. Publicly proclaiming their desire to redeem Africa from the grip of nefarious Arab slave traders, representatives of fourteen European countries etched a series of arbitrary lines on a map of the continent, establishing the borders that continue to define (and deform) African political life. Britain emerged from the conference with a dozen colonies in East, West and southern Africa. France acquired a vast swath of territory in West and North Africa. Upstart Germany secured a handful of territories, of which it would be divested after the First World War; while Portugal, an empire in dotage, obtained

Mozambique and Angola, to which it would cling until the late 1970s. The single greatest victor at the conference, however, was Belgium's King Leopold, who succeeded, through crafty diplomacy, paeans to free trade, and soaring humanitarian appeals, to claim for himself a thick "slice of this magnificent African cake." Leopold was made sole custodian of the Congo Free State, a million square miles of territory, comparable in size to all of western Europe, with some twenty million inhabitants. Over the next thirty years, half of those people would die.

Colonialism wrought dramatic changes in Africa. With the onset of formal colonial rule, white settler societies sprouted all over the continent, in Kenya and the Rhodesias, French Algeria, German Southwest Africa, and Portuguese Mozambique. Thanks to the continuing threat of malaria and other tropical fevers, West and Central Africa were generally spared large-scale settlement, and the processes of economic and cultural dispossession that it inevitably brought in train. Yet even in areas without large settler populations, colonial rule brought new taxes and regulations, and a retinue of district commissioners, judges, soldiers, and vastly expanded police forces— all the appurtenances of empire.

The onset of colonialism spurred a new burst of African exploration, as state-sponsored expeditions set out to explore the hinterlands of their new possessions. Such expeditions served a variety of practical purposes: identifying commercial opportunities; advancing scientific knowledge; demonstrating the "effective sovereignty" that delegates at the Berlin conference had established as a prerequisite for recognition of colonial claims. But they also served a more metaphorical purpose, limning the image of whites as agents of progress, carrying light and civilization into a benighted continent. Metropolitan audiences traced the progress of expeditions in newspapers, magazines (the first issue of *National Geographic* appeared in 1888), and in the signature literary genre of the era, the "Dark Continent" travelogue. Fittingly, it was Belgium's King Leopold, the most rapacious of the new colonial overlords, who sponsored the travels of the era's most robustious explorer, Henry Morton Stanley.

John Rowlands, the man known to history as H. M. Stanley, was born in Wales in 1841, the illegitimate son of a charwoman. He spent much of his childhood in a workhouse, before escaping to sea on an American merchant ship, from whose captain, Henry Stanley, he appropriated a new name. His arrival in the United States coincided with the onset of the Civil War, in which he had the rare distinction of fighting on both sides. After the war, he commenced a career as a journalist, reporting on the U.S. Army's campaign against Native Americans in the West. In 1869, he set out for Africa on behalf of the *New York Herald* to locate the "lost" missionary-explorer, David Livingstone. *How I Found Livingstone,* Stanley's first international best seller, appeared in 1872. Over the next eighteen years, he published three more travelogues, each running to two volumes and a thousand pages. *Through the Dark Continent* recounted an epic journey across the waist of Africa in search of the sources of the Nile. *The Congo and the Founding of Its Free State: A Story of Work and Exploration* was a paid testimonial to the Congo's new ruler, King Leopold. *In Darkest Africa* told the story of Stanley's "relief" of Emin Pasha, a colonial functionary in the Sudan allegedly besieged by Arab slave traders. (*In Darkest Africa* was the book that Reverend Thornton and the party of would-be African emigrants from Arkansas carried with them to New York City in 1892.)

With his grandiosity and genius for self-promotion, Stanley stands alongside P. T. Barnum (with whom he shared a publicist) as the epitome of American popular culture in the Gilded Age. From the African perspective, however, he epitomized European colonialism, in all its vainglory and casual brutality. Everywhere Stanley traveled, he left a literal trail of corpses in his wake. For each of his expeditions, he conscripted hundreds of African porters to bear him and his baggage, mere dozens of whom survived. The people through whose territory he passed fared even worse. "We have attacked and destroyed 28 large towns and three or four score villages," he noted matter-of-factly in his journal from his first cross-continental trek. Stanley initially relied on a favorite Winchester repeating rifle, but during the Emin Pasha expedition, he set out with a Maxim gun donated by inventor Hiram Maxim, an early example of celebrity product endorsement. (In a letter of thanks, Stanley predicted that the gun, which was capable of firing six hundred rounds per minute, would be "of valuable service in helping civilisation to overcome barbarism.") At the time, however, few recognized

Stanley's brutality, which remained obscured within a fog of philanthropic rhetoric and scientific rodomontade. For a generation of Americans, Stanley was the quintessential Dark Continent explorer, the embodiment of white enterprise in a benighted land.

The influence of Dark Continent travel writing was on display at the 1893 World's Columbian Exposition in Chicago, with its fabled White City. The massive American pavilion included no references to American Negroes, on the grounds that they had contributed nothing to America's four hundred years of upward progress. Yet the fair's famed Midway included a special African exhibition, where a group of exemplary "savages," specially imported from Dahomey, danced and drummed in a mock native village. The combination enraged the aged Frederick Douglass, who pointedly asked why his countrymen flocked to see "African savages brought to act the monkey" while ignoring the achievements of black people in the United States. But Douglass was in a tiny minority. The Dahomean village became one of the fair's sensations, attracting literally millions of visitors, black as well as white, anxious to see in the flesh the people of whom they had read in the works of Stanley and other explorers. (Among the visitors was the great star of blackface minstrelsy, Bert Williams, who used the experience as the basis for a musical comedy, "In Old Dahomey," the first black-authored, black-cast production to appear on Broadway.)

Following the success of the Dahomey exhibition, displays of live Africans became de rigueur at international fairs and expositions. En route to Africa in 1894, Charles Spencer Smith made a special pilgrimage to the Universal Exposition in Antwerp to view the Congo enclosure. The 1895 Cotton States Exposition in Atlanta, where Booker T. Washington delivered his famous "Atlanta Compromise" speech, included an exhibition of African "cannibals." The practice reached a climax of sorts at the 1904 St. Louis World's Fair, which included an entire anthropological hall, a veritable parliament of primitives. The stars of the show were Geronimo, the legendary Apache chief, and Ota Benga, one of a dozen Batwa men—pygmies— brought from the Congo. At the conclusion of the fair, the Batwa were transported back to their forest home, but Benga was induced to return to the United States, where he soon found himself on display in the monkey house at the Bronx Zoo, living alongside chimpanzees and orangutans in a tableau intended to illustrate the process of evolution. He died of a self-inflicted gunshot wound to the heart.

IF THE MAXIM GUN was one of the handmaids of "civilization" in Africa, then the Bible was the other. Over the first half of the nineteenth century, Christian missionaries began to arrive in Africa. The best known was David Livingstone, Stanley's quarry, who first traveled to the continent in the 1840s under the auspices of the London Missionary Society. With the onset of formal colonialism, the trickle became a torrent, as thousands of missionaries, representing a score of nations and more than a hundred societies and denominations, embarked for the continent. To understand the journey of William Sheppard, it is necessary first to understand the sources and character of this movement.

The late-nineteenth-century African mission movement poses a delicate problem of historical judgment. In their own time, missionaries were widely regarded as heroes, sharing the blessings of salvation with benighted "natives"; today they are often cast as villains, cultural imperialists imposing alien beliefs and values on captive people. Ultimately neither of these generalizations does missionaries justice, either individually or as a group. Some missionaries were indeed paragons of selfless service and others were self-satisfied fools. Some were avid supporters of European conquest while others had a distinctly ambivalent relationship with colonial authority. A few became champions of African rights. Yet whatever their individual or institutional characters, Christian missionaries were inevitably entangled in the colonial project.

To use their own terminology, missionaries sought to "convert" Africans, a simple word for a complex process. Conversion referred not only to the embrace of Christianity but to the adoption of a whole universe of practices and signs. Converts wore Western clothing and lived in square houses rather than round huts; they cultivated with ploughs and participated in the market economy; they practiced monogamy and trusted their health to Western medicine rather than to "witch doctors." As preachers of a written gospel, missionaries everywhere emphasized the importance of literacy, and many set out to reduce local languages to written form, an innovation that would fundamentally reshape African conceptions of history, identity, and authority. Many mission stations boasted their own steam presses, from which emerged a steady stream of vernacular Bibles, hymnals, and schoolbooks, as well as the first dictionaries and grammars of African languages.

Though the United States had no formal colonial presence in Africa, American churches played a central role in evangelizing the continent. By the 1890s, virtually all of the major American denominations boasted African missions. Not surprisingly, enthusiasm for African mission work was especially pronounced in black churches. The A.M.E. Church, which had long maintained a presence in the African American expatriate communities in Liberia and Sierra Leone, began work in South Africa in 1895. The National Baptist Convention was established the same year to coordinate mission activity among black Baptists. A rival Baptist society, the Lott Carey Foreign Mission Convention, named for a pioneering Liberian emigrant, was founded in 1897. The A.M.E. Zion Church opened its new mission in the Gold Coast a year later.

In terms of broad objectives, American missionaries differed little from their European counterparts: they preached the gospel, baptized converts, opened schools, and otherwise strove to divest Africans of their "heathenish" ways. Yet they differed from European missionaries in one significant respect: many were themselves of African descent. This was hardly surprising in the case of black denominations, but it was also true of white churches, many of which made it a policy to send black missionaries to Africa. To some extent, this policy reflected prevailing theories of race and disease, which ascribed to Negroes a special "adaptation" for African mission work, a "tropical fitness" enabling them to survive in regions where whites would perish. Black missionaries were also reputed to have a psychological or spiritual bond with Africans. The African "will hearken to your message where the white messengers have failed," declared H. B. Parks, secretary of missions in the A.M.E. Church. "You can understand his nature and he can understand you. It is not the spiritual love of the white missionary, but the sympathy of blood."

The ironies are palpable. At the bleakest moment in American race relations, an era of Jim Crow, disfranchisement, and lynching, a movement emerged that ascribed to African Americans a unique capacity to spread the blessings of Christian civilization. Even such overtly white supremacist denominations as the Southern Baptist Convention and the Presbyterian Church (U.S.), both of which had broken from their northern counterparts on the slavery question, recruited African Americans for the African field. William Sheppard, for example, studied for the ministry at the Tuscaloosa Theological Institute, established by southern Presbyterians in the 1880s to train black missionaries for a mission they hoped to open in "the great valley of the Congo." Methodists, not to be outdone, established the Stewart Missionary Foundation at Atlanta's Gammon Theological Seminary. In addition to its role in training missionaries, Stewart sponsored annual hymn- and essay-writing contests and a major Congress on Africa, all intended to highlight "the obligation of the American Negro to missionary work in Africa." By the end of the century, more than two dozen of Stewart's graduates had embarked for the continent.

The enthusiasm would prove fleeting. While black denominations continued to send African American missionaries to Africa, all the major white churches retreated from the policy in the early 1900s, largely in response to protests from European colonial officials, who feared that the presence of African Americans was instilling unhealthy aspirations among "impressionable" natives. At the same time, advances in tropical medicine brought a sharp reduction in mortality rates and a corresponding increase in white volunteers. Yet if the mission movement was shortlived, its impact was not. In the three decades between the Berlin Conference and the outbreak of World War I, African American missionaries found their way to every corner of the African continent—not only to the familiar terrains of Liberia and Sierra Leone, but to Portuguese Angola and Mozambique, Nyasaland, German Togo, Southern Rhodesia and South Africa, Cameroon and the Congo. Black Christians at home avidly followed their adventures, which were recounted in magazines, pamphlets, and published memoirs and autobiographies. Missionaries such as William Sheppard became celebrities, drawing packed houses during their periodic visits back to the United States. Their accounts became yet another source of information for African Americans anxious to know more about their ancestral continent.

what reports is no simple task, because missionaries conveyed no simple message. The idea that African Americans had a providential calling to redeem their ancestral land, for example, hearkened back to early debates over emigration and colonization. In the case of the mission movement, however, this venerable idea had been divorced from what had always been its corollary: the idea of a large-scale exodus back to Africa. The vast majority of black missionaries who went to Africa had no intention of settling there permanently. On the contrary, many saw uplifting their benighted brethren as an opportunity for African Americans to demonstrate their own relative progress and thereby advance their claim to full American citizenship. The result was a curious kind of ambivalence, with missionaries identifying at once with Africans and with the "civilizing" agencies that purported to save them. This ambivalence was lyrically displayed in Alexander Camphor's "Hymn of Sympathy and Prayer for Africa," which won the Stewart Missionary Foundation's hymn-writing contest in 1894: "How can we remain contented / in illuminated homes, / While our brother gropes in darkness, / and in heathenism roams?" Camphor answered his own question a few years later, when he volunteered for mission service in the Congo.

African American ideas about Africa have always been complex and conflicted, but rarely were the tensions so apparent. Was Africa a refuge from racist America or a field of service on which African Americans could prove their mettle and win full inclusion in American society? Were Africans brethren, "kindred o'er the sea," or savage heathens, entombed in the darkness of sin and superstition? How would black missionaries, cast into the far corners of colonial Africa, reconcile the competing claims of race and culture, religion and nationality? Was the advance of "civilization" bringing light to a benighted continent or ushering in a new, more terrible darkness? All these questions and more would come together in the extraordinary journey of William Henry Sheppard.

LOOKING BACK A HALF CENTURY LATER, William Sheppard would paint his childhood in roseate hues. "The white people were always very kind to us," he recalled, "as they were to all the colored people." It seems an unlikely claim, coming from a black man born in Waynesboro, Virginia, in the final days of the American Civil War, a man whose passage to manhood coincided with the political upheaval and violence of Reconstruction, Redemption, and the rise of Jim Crow. Yet it was a characteristic statement for Sheppard, who in the course of his sixty-two years was never heard to utter a critical word about white Americans.

Reflecting on the Old South in his classic 1903 book, *The Souls of Black Folk*, W. E. B. Du Bois wrote: "Before and directly after the war, when all the best of the Negroes were domestic servants in the best of the white families, there were bonds of intimacy, affection, and sometimes blood relationship, between the races." Leaving aside the question of what exactly he meant by the "best" Negroes and whites, Du Bois might well have been referring to the Sheppard family. William Sheppard, Sr., was the village barber in Waynesboro, a former slave whose wit and wisdom made him a favorite of his white customers, few of whom ever realized that he was illiterate. (The elder Sheppard obtained his knowledge of current events by having a friend read him the morning newspaper.) Sheppard's mother, Sarah, a freeborn mulatto, also moved in the most intimate circles of white life, working as the women's pool attendant at Warm Baths, a nearby spa. Revealingly, the Sheppards were members of the Presbyterian Church (U.S.), better known as the Presbyterian Church, South. Originally called the Presbyterian Church of the Confederate States of America, the church had been founded in 1860 on the principle that slavery was the "normal condition" of the "African race," and it remained, on racial issues, the most reactionary denomination in the United States. Not surprisingly, virtually all of its black adherents abandoned it after the Civil War, leaving (in the words of one historian) only the "hard core remnant of old family retainers," perhaps a thousand souls in all. The Sheppards were numbered among that group.

At the age of ten, young William left home to work as a stable and office boy for a local dentist, an experience that reaffirmed his faith in the essential decency of white people. "I loved my new home, for Dr. Henkel and his wife were so kind to me," he later wrote. "They spent much time in instructing me in my books at night." With the Henkel's encouragement, he saved his wages and proceeded, at the age of fifteen, to Hampton Institute, Virginia's premier school for African Americans.

Founded by Samuel Chapman Armstrong, a former Union general, Hampton was the wellspring of industrial education, a pedagogy that would dominate the field of black education for more than half a century. Education, Armstrong believed, needed to be practical, reflecting the particular needs of a primitive race just emerging from slavery. Rather than focusing on the abstract, academic subjects taught in white schools—mathematics, Latin, and so forth—students at Hampton studied agriculture, carpentry, bricklaying, and other industrial occupations. Such instruction, the argument went, would equip the freedpeople with marketable skills, thus enhancing their "usefulness" to the wider community, while instilling those habits of industry and self-direction that backward races were presumed to lack. Thus equipped, southern blacks would lift themselves from poverty, gradually acquiring property and earning the respect of their southern white neighbors, without any unpleasant agitation or "artificial forcing." Booker T. Washington, Hampton's most illustrious graduate, distilled the theory into a metaphor for the age: If a man is worth a dollar, he will be treated as a dollar.

As Washington's aphorism suggests, industrial education was as much a political formula as a pedagogical one. For both Armstrong and Washington, the attempt to confer civil and political equality on African Americans following the Civil War had been folly, enflaming white opposition and awakening unrealistic expectations among black people. One of Armstrong's first acts on arriving at Hampton in 1866 as an agent of the Freedmen's Bureau was to restore land to white owners, divesting former slaves of farms they had been granted by his predecessor. Armstrong admitted some discomfort in dispossessing the freedpeople, but concluded that "it was on the whole better for them." "It put them at the bottom of the ladder," he wrote, employing another of the era's signature metaphors; "it is not a bad thing for anyone to touch bottom early, if there is a good solid foundation under him and then climb from that."

By the early 1880s, Hampton Institute had grown into one of the most successful schools in the South. The student body, nearly a thousand strong, included not only African Americans but also Native Americans, Hawaiians

(Armstrong had grown up on a Hawaiian mission station, where his parents were teachers), and even a few Africans. Given the paucity of opportunities in the South, a steady stream of penniless black youths arrived at the institute seeking education. Armstrong and his colleagues debated how to winnow the wheat from the chaff, how to distinguish those truly dedicated to lives of labor and service from those who saw education as a ticket to an easier life. When Booker T. Washington arrived in the 1870s his entrance examination consisted of cleaning and dusting a room. In 1880, the year Sheppard arrived, the institute introduced a night school, under Washington's direction, offering any interested student two hours of free instruction. In exchange, students were required to perform ten hours of work, six days a week, in the institute's fields and brickyard. Those who survived a year were admitted to regular classes. Not surprisingly, most students gave up, but a few—what Washington dubbed "The Plucky Class"—finished the year, Sheppard among them. If Sheppard resented the ordeal, he never said so publicly. Writing in his autobiography decades later, he would describe his first year at Hampton as a boyhood idyll, in which he was afforded "every advantage," including ample time to swim and fish. Curiously, he did not mention Washington in the account, a striking omission given the similarities in their public personae, but he described Armstrong in rapturous terms: "General Armstrong was my ideal of manhood," he wrote. "He was a great, tender-hearted father to us all."

Few would deny that education should equip students to survive in the world, but when industrial education is viewed in its historical context—in the light of southern Redemption and the violent expulsion of black people from civic life—it is hard to see it as anything other than a reactionary doctrine, a pedagogical prop for white supremacy. The speed with which the Hampton formula spread through the Jim Crow South (not to mention its enthusiastic embrace by colonial officials in places like Rhodesia and South Africa) lends credence to that interpretation. But Hampton clearly meant something more to William Sheppard. Obviously his years there confirmed his respect for white people, but they also affirmed his faith in himself and his race. One of Sheppard's favorite places at Hampton was Armstrong's Curiosity Room, a small anthropological museum featuring the arts and artifacts of the world's darker people. During his years in the Congo, Sheppard would collect many items for the Curiosity Room, eventually bequeathing to Hampton one of the premier African art collections in the world.

After completing his studies at Hampton, Sheppard enrolled at the Tuscaloosa Theological Institute, where he trained for service as a missionary in Africa. Upon graduation, he volunteered for the Congo field, but no appointment came. Though committed in theory to the use of black missionaries, officials of the Presbyterian Church (U.S.) were not prepared to entrust the entire business of opening and running a mission to a black man, proposing instead to send black and white missionaries out in pairs. Unfortunately, no white volunteers had come forward. Sheppard spent the next three years ministering to black congregations in the South, but he continued to pester church leaders for an African appointment. During that time, he received offers from at least two other mission societies, including the northern Presbyterians, but he declined them, insisting that he would go to Africa under the auspices of his own church or not at all. His patience was finally rewarded in 1890, when a newly ordained white minister, Samuel Lapsley, volunteered for service in the Congo.

Lapsley was as unusual a figure in his way as Sheppard was in his. Born and raised on a plantation outside Selma, he was the scion of one of Alabama's first families. His father, James, was the moderator of the General Assembly of the Presbyterian Church (U.S.) and a law partner of U.S. senator John Morgan. As chair of the Senate Foreign Relations Committee, Morgan had sponsored the 1883 bill recognizing King Leopold's claim to the Congo Free State, and he remained one of the king's most avid supporters. His interests in the Congo were less than philanthropic: an avowed racist, Morgan hoped that the Congo might serve as a colony for repatriated African Americans. Whether it was Morgan who inspired young Lapsley's interest in the Congo is not clear, but he fully supported his decision to go there, and even arranged for him to meet King Leopold en route.

But Samuel Lapsley was a more complex figure than Morgan knew. A brilliant scholar, he graduated from the University of Alabama at eighteen, by which time he had already been awarded the rank of assistant professor. He was also something of a racial maverick, with a heartfelt, if paternalistic, regard for "the darkies." As a child, he had opened a Sunday school for the black workers on his family's plantation. Later, he took the highly unorthodox step of completing his theological training in the North, at a seminary in Chicago, apparently to escape the racial bigotry of the Virginia seminary where he first enrolled. Ordained in 1889, Lapsley immediately volunteered for service in the Congo.

In February 1890, Sheppard and Lapsley embarked for Africa. They sailed first to Liverpool, one-time headquarters of the British slave-trading fleet, where they laid in the stores they would need to trade with the Congo's indigenous population, including salt, beads, brass wire, bolts of calico, and a large supply of cowrie shells, which served, in the absence of specie, as a kind of currency. They also purchased clothes for themselves, in Sheppard's case an ensemble of white linen suits, puttees, and a pith helmet. That costume, the uniform of a Dark Continent explorer, would remain his trademark for the next twenty years, prompting his Congolese nickname, Mundele Ndom, essentially "black man in white man's clothing." As if to confirm the mantle, the two men made a pilgrimage to Westminster Cathedral, to view David Livingstone's tomb. They also may have attended a lecture by H. M. Stanley, who was in the city on a speaking tour.

From London, they proceeded to Rotterdam to await their Congo-bound ship. Lapsley used the interval to visit Brussels, where he had a personal interview with King Leopold. By the early twentieth century, Leopold would stand as the single most reviled figure in the world, but in 1890 he was one of the most revered. Lapsley was literally awestruck, marveling at the "kind" voice and "bright and gentle" manner of the "great and good king." What Leopold made of the missionary is not recorded, but he suggested that the Americans commence their mission work in the Kasai region, more than a thousand miles into the interior. What he did not say was that the state had recently opened a trading post on the upper Kasai River, in hopes of exploiting the region's untapped riches. Lapsley fairly floated out of the palace, little suspecting that he and Sheppard had just been invited to a holocaust.

AFTER THREE WEEKS AT SEA, the steamship *Afrikaan* dropped anchor in the Congo River, an astonishing fifteen miles wide at the mouth. The shore was "thronged with half clad natives," an unsettling spectacle to most arriving missionaries but one that Lapsley found oddly comforting. "[J]ust like our own darkies," he wrote in a letter home; "it made me feel quite at home to see them." After a brief stay at the aptly named Banana Point, the pair proceeded upriver to Boma, capital of the Congo Free State, and thence to Matadi, 180 miles from the coast, the farthest navigable point on the lower Congo. Counting the English Baptist missionaries with whom they stayed, Matadi and its environs boasted about two dozen Europeans, most of whom, Sheppard noted, had a yellow pallor from frequent bouts of fever. While staying at the mission, both men experienced attacks of fever, the first of more than sixty episodes in Sheppard's case. Ominously, they were stricken with the severest variety, hermaturic, or blackwater, fever, so called because of the red blood cells discoloring the urine of the afflicted. Associated with malaria (though apparently caused by a different parasite), hermaturia attacked the kidneys, producing rigor, vomiting, and soaring fever. In most cases, the disease was fatal, as the graves in the missionary cemetery showed. Both men recovered, but neither had seen the last of the disease.

Upstream from Matadi, the Congo River was a tumult of whirlpools and cataracts until Stanley Pool, 250 miles farther into the interior, from which point it was navigable for another 1,000 miles. The only way forward was overland, along a narrow road hacked through the jungle by an army of African laborers, working under the whip of H. M. Stanley. Construction of a railroad around the cataracts had begun, but it would be another eight years before it was opened. In the meantime, goods were borne along the road by African forced laborers, some forty thousand of them in 1890, recruited from all over West and Central Africa. Like human ants, African porters carried supplies and machinery up to Stanley Pool (including a half dozen disassembled steamships), returning with ivory, camwood, rubber, and other tropical commodities.

Still weak from the effects of fever, the missionaries set out on the road, accompanied by twenty-five porters. Sheppard's autobiography suggests that they walked, though it appears from other sources that they were borne in hammocks by African carriers, the customary form of travel for Europeans in the Congo. They traveled mostly in the early morning or late afternoon, avoiding the middle of the day, when temperatures soared above one hundred degrees. On the fifth day, they came to an American mission station. After days of seeing only African faces, both Sheppard and Lapsley were relieved to meet fellow "foreigners," and they talked late into the night, listening avidly to their hosts' "trials and triumphs." The next morning, they attended their first Sunday service in Africa, in a large galvanized-iron church that had been shipped from Boston and carried up from Matadi in pieces.

Already, the men had begun to realize that not all was well in the Congo, that tales of selfless whites bringing Christianity and civilization to a benighted continent obscured a more sordid reality. "No good here for Sierra Leone man," a group of Kru men working in Matadi reported; "plenty sick, too much flog." Sheppard, characteristically, said nothing about the conversation, but Lapsley pondered it, in terms eerily echoing antebellum debate in his native Alabama. "These imported workmen raise a question which is a 'live issue' among Christian men out here," he wrote in a letter home. "If [Africans] won't work, or are insolent, shall they be coerced with the lash?" The question continued to reverberate on the march to Stanley Pool, as the men passed endless "sun-bleached skeletons of native carriers," men who had literally been worked to death and left where they fell. Everywhere, they heard stories of Henry Morton Stanley—not of the intrepid explorer they had met in books but of the man Africans called Bula Matari, the breaker of stones. The term, which referred as much to Stanley's character as to his role in building the road to Stanley Pool, had by 1890 become a label for all state officials in the region. "If a party of white men approaches a lower Congo village the cry goes round: 'Who is coming?'" Lapsley explained. When the answer was "'Bula Matari' . . . *whiz they all go to hide in the long grass.*"

After two weeks, the missionaries reached Stanley Pool, what is today Kinshasa. By a remarkable coincidence, their stay at the settlement intersected with visits by two other men destined to play important roles in the unfolding drama of the Congo. The first was another African American, George Washington Williams, who passed through Stanley Pool, bound for the coast, just as Lapsley and Sheppard arrived. Best remembered today as the author of *History of the Negro Race in America from 1619 to 1880*, a pioneering work in African American history, Williams was something between a Renaissance man and a confidence man, who, in a short, forty-one-year life, carved out careers for himself as a soldier, preacher, journalist, and entrepreneur. Williams had come to the Congo in hopes of earning his fortune, but he left in disgust after a few months. His "Open Letter to His Serene Majesty Leopold II," written at Stanley Pool and published after his return to the United States, gave the Western world its first intimation of realities in the vaunted Free State. "Your Majesty's Government is engaged in the slave-trade, wholesale and retail," he wrote. "It buys and sells and steals slaves." Unfortunately, Williams died a few months later, before he had time to publicize his charges.

The other visitor at Stanley Pool was equally noteworthy. Stricken anew with fever, Lapsley visited the clinic of the local missionary doctor, where he met another patient, a "Russian," sick with dysentery and despair. A "gentlemanly fellow," the Russian had come out to command a steamship, but had been so horrified by what he saw that he resigned after a single voyage. He was now headed home. Lapsley noticed that he kept an English Bible on his bedside table, which "furnishes a handle I hope to use on him." Nine years later, the captain—he was actually Polish—published *Heart of Darkness* under the pen name Joseph Conrad.

While Leopold had recommended the Kasai region as a mission site, Lapsley and Sheppard initially set their sights on the valley of the Kwango, a tributary of the Kasai. Just as Western explorers garnered their reputations by "discovering" previously uncharted lakes and landmarks, missionaries earned status by evangelizing people who had never before heard the gospel, and the Kwango region was virgin territory. Unable to recruit enough porters for an overland journey, they set out in native canoes, vessels hewn from enormous logs, capable of carrying a dozen paddlers and tons of supplies. Over the next two months, they paddled hundreds of miles, searching for a likely mission site. Some river villages welcomed the travelers, offering food and hospitality, but others drove them off. "I found many of them afraid that I was a State man, come to tie somebody up," Lapsley wrote. A friendly Bateke chief offered land at the junction of the Kasai and Kwango rivers, but when the missionaries returned to claim it some weeks later they found the village in ashes and the people hostile. The village had been attacked in the interim by a contingent of the Force Publique, under a Belgian officer named Van Kerckhoven, a notorious figure even by the standards of the Congo. Van Kerckhoven paid the black soldiers under his command five brass rods for every "human head they brought him during the course of any military operations," a practice that surely provided the inspiration for the palisade of human skulls guarding Kurtz's compound in *Heart of Darkness*. Not surprisingly, the encounter had dimmed the Bateke's interest in white civilization.

Weary and discouraged, the missionaries returned to Stanley Pool to regroup. They now turned their eyes to the upper Kasai, the area recommended by King Leopold. The region was connected to Stanley Pool by a single, rusting steamship, the *Florida*. The captain professed not to have room for the missionaries' party, but he eventually consented to take Lapsley and Sheppard, a few of their porters, and half their baggage. Conrad had taken the same voyage a few months before and he memorably described it in *Heart of Darkness*: "Going up that river was like traveling back to the earliest beginnings of the world, when vegetation rioted on the earth and the big trees were king. An empty stream, a great silence, an impenetrable forest. The air was warm, thick, heavy, sluggish . . . You lost your way on that river . . . till you thought yourself bewitched and cut off for ever from everything you had known." Yet even Conrad could not capture the surreality of Sheppard and Lapsley's fever-ridden trip. With its aging boilers, the *Florida* flailed against the current, often managing only a few miles a day. Snags and sandbars, whirlpools and freak storms conspired to impede the ship's progress. Food supplies ran out after the first week; the captain had counted on trading for fresh rations along the way, but villagers fled at the sound of the approaching ship. When hungry African crew members refused to collect wood for the boiler, the captain became unhinged, tearing into them with a chicot, the stiff, hippo-hide whip that served, like the bullwhips of the Old South, as the instrument and emblem of white authority. "It makes a terrible mark where it strikes, at first a white streak, then a long welt," Lapsley wrote in his diary. "The culprit, if he happens to deserve the name, seldom shrieks, but writhes and gasps piteously after the tenth or fifteenth blow." After days of horror, Lapsley could stand it no more, and ordered the captain to desist. The captain blustered, but the floggings stopped.

A full month after leaving Stanley Pool, the *Florida* tied up at Luebo, the head of navigation on the Kasai River. With the help of their native "boys," the missionaries offloaded their supplies and set up a makeshift camp, across the river from the trading post, a few hundred yards from a native village. They were twelve hundred miles from the coast, and eight hundred miles from the nearest medical doctor. Aside from a handful of Belgian traders and administrators and one or two Catholic missionaries, they were the only Westerners in the upper Kasai, an area roughly the size of Sheppard's Virginia. The captain bid them a curt adieu, promising to return in nine months' time. With jackals howling in the distance, Lapsley and Sheppard sobbed themselves to sleep.

GROWING UP A BLACK MAN in the Redeemed South, William Sheppard learned the art of self-effacement, and he carried that art with him to Africa. In his various renderings of his African adventures, he invariably cast himself in the role of the faithful retainer, following in the footsteps of the great-souled Lapsley. It was a characteristic pose and one that naturally appealed to the southern whites who were the mission's patrons. Sheppard is a "sensible" man, with a constructive "attitude toward the white people," a white missionary visiting the Congo would later write. "[T]he people of the South may be sure that he will conduct himself entirely in accord with their traditions and sentiments." Yet the long journey to Luebo had changed Sheppard, opening fields for enterprise and self-assertion that would have been inconceivable in his native South. When the *Florida*'s rudder chain snapped in a rapids, it was Sheppard who seized hold of the heavy iron tiller and steered the vessel to safety. When a chief near Stanley Pool complained that his people were starving, Sheppard set off with his Martini Henry rifle and bagged several hippopotami, feeding the multitude. Lapsley watched the transformation in his companion with pleasure and admiration. "Sheppard is a most handy fellow and is now a thorough river man," he gushed in a letter home. "His temper is bright and even—really a man of unusual graces and strong points of character." "Brother Sheppard," he reported in another letter, "has the constitution needed, and the gift of getting on in Africa."

As Lapsley's letter suggests, shared travail had forged a rare bond between the two men. For fifteen months, these unlikely companions, raised on opposite sides of the Jim Crow divide, had lived as brothers, collecting the same salary, intoning the same prayers, enduring the same afflictions. They nursed one another "carefully and tenderly" through fever and delirium, massaging cramped muscles and swabbing sweaty faces. They picked jiggers from each other's feet and shared the dubious pleasures of python steak and roasted monkey.

The first days and weeks at Luebo were typical of new missions everywhere. Donning their "broadest and best smiles," the missionaries set out to introduce themselves to their new neighbors, no easy task in the absence of any common language. Though occasionally comic, these first encounters were fraught with significance, as Lapsley and Sheppard endeavored to demonstrate the superiority of their civilization and, by implication, of their God. They dispensed medicines from their small pharmacopia. They exhibited the inner workings of Lapsley's pocket watch and shared the wonders of matches and a handheld mirror. (The mirror was a standard weapon in the missionary arsenal, prized both for its novelty and for its alleged ability to stimulate self-reflection in "primitive" peoples.) Armed with pencil and paper, they set out to reduce the local language to written form, quizzing people on the names of objects and rendering their responses phonetically. To demonstrate the power of this unfamiliar medium, they passed sealed notes between themselves, astonishing their hosts with their ability to communicate without speaking.

Sheppard and Lapsley gradually identified the different people inhabiting the region. The local villagers were BaKete. The most numerous group in the area, though the weakest politically, was the BaLuba. The region was also home to various Songye settlements, as well as to the BaLulua, who had given their name to the Belgian administrative capital of the district, Luluabourg, seventy miles to the south. Unfortunately, Luluabourg was also home to the so-called Zappo Zaps. An offshoot of the Songye, the Zappo Zaps came from the area around the Eki River, where they had worked as mercenaries in the service of Arab slave traders. Free State authorities were quick to appreciate their potential usefulness, and in the late 1880s resettled them en masse in Luluabourg. From the missionary point of view, the Zappo Zaps were perplexing. On one hand, they were the most "civilized" of African tribes, wearing Western clothing, living in square houses, communicating in both French and English. On the other hand, they seemed to embody every Western stereotype about African savagery, with fearsome visages (Zappo Zap men filed their teeth and plucked their eyebrows and eyelashes) and a tradition of violent slave raiding, now enhanced by Belgian-supplied firearms. The Zappo Zaps were also among the small number of groups in history to indulge freely in cannibalism, consuming human flesh not simply for ritual purposes but routinely and with relish. Both Sheppard and Lapsley became quite familiar with the Zappo Zaps, who passed periodically through Luebo, often with coffles of bound slaves in tow. Though they left the missionaries in peace, Sheppard had no doubts about their character. "You can trust them as far as you can see them," he once remarked, "and the further off you see them the better you can trust them."

The dominant people in the area, however, were not the Zappo Zaps but the BaKuba. Though Lapsley and Sheppard did not yet know it, they had settled on the southern frontier of the last great precolonial kingdom in equatorial Africa. A confederation of some eighteen tribes, the BaKuba exercised suzerainity over the Kasai region, controlling trade and extracting tribute, including ivory and slaves, from their less powerful neighbors. Parties of BaKuba traders periodically appeared at the trading post at Luebo, bearing massive tusks of ivory and baskets of raw rubber, woven into small, tight balls. From the very first meeting, Sheppard was entranced by these tall, brown-skinned people, whose regal bearing, exquisitely crafted accoutrements, and general "superiority in physique, manners, dress and dialect" marked them as unlike any other Africans he had seen. Encouraged by Lapsley, who shared his admiration, Sheppard set out to learn more about the BaKuba, offering hospitality to traders and studying their language, which no Westerner had yet mastered. But when he expressed an interest in visiting the BaKuba capital himself, he was politely but firmly rebuffed. The *lukengu*, or king, not only barred strangers from his capital, but also pledged to be-head anyone who showed them the road. Belgian traders at Luebo confirmed the account. Since their arrival, they had heard tales of a fabulously wealthy city hidden in the jungle to the north, but efforts to locate it had failed. Lavish gifts sent to the *lukengu* in hopes of encouraging a wider commerce had been returned. The BaKuba traded with Europeans, but they did so on their own terms.

As the commercial hub of the region, Luebo seemed to Lapsley and Sheppard to be the perfect spot to begin their work. After a lengthy palaver, they obtained a mission site from the BaKete chief, exchanging twelve yards of cloth for a nine-acre plot of land. Aided by their hosts, they proceeded to hack a mission station out of the jungle. They laid out rectangular streets (whimsically dubbed Pennsylvania Avenue and Boulevard de Paris) and chose a site for a chapel. Their first house was a reed hut, purchased from the locals for another piece of cloth and transformed, with a coat of white clay and the addition of a verandah, into a reasonable facsimile of Lapsley's Alabama homestead. This plantation style of architecture would remain the hallmark of the mission, with each new house, workshop, or outbuilding constructed in the southern style and dressed in white, with green or red trim. A missionary arriving at Luebo in 1896 was startled to find Sheppard living in a white house, "with low verandah and large white pillars." "My first impression was how faithfully the place and surroundings reflected [an] old Southern home," he reported. "[O]ne could almost imagine himself, save for a few details, in old Virginia again."

All the mission lacked was converts. The BaKete marveled at the missionaries' appliances and appreciated their medicines, but they exhibited virtually no interest in Christianity. In the first three years of the enterprise, not a single villager came forward for baptism. What adherents the mission did attract were BaLuba and BaLulua from the surrounding area, chiefly widows and children, fugitive slaves, refugees, and others who, having no standing in traditional society, had little to lose by converting. In late 1891, a feverish Lapsley arrived back at Luebo after an exhausting overland trip to Luluabourg with twenty-one such people in tow, including three slaves he had been given as gifts by the prince of the Zappo Zaps. The mission's numbers were supplemented by so-called libres, former slaves that the missionaries purchased from their captors. Lapsley and Sheppard naturally had qualms about participating, however indirectly, in slave trading, but the alternative was to abandon slaves to their fate. Among those they redeemed was a six-year-old girl, N'tumba, whose family had been murdered by the Zappo Zaps, who then forced her to partake of the flesh of her mother. Yet even with such additions, the population at the mission totaled fewer than a hundred.

Lapsley and Sheppard anguished over the lack of converts, but their experience was typical of new missions. In Africa, as in other parts of the globe, large-scale religious conversion was always less likely in conditions of relative social stability than in contexts of upheaval. As a contemporary British missionary put it, Christianity fared poorly when traditional societies were still in their "aboriginal vigor," but "where there is a measure of disorganization . . . so there is preparation for the seed of the Word." His words would prove prophetic for the Kasai region, which stood on the brink of a cataclysm.

LAPSLEY WOULD NOT LIVE to see the full horror of Leopold's Congo. In early 1892, he traveled downriver to Boma to meet with Belgian officials, who had refused to register the mission's claim to the land at Luebo. He succeeded in securing the title, but on his return journey he was stricken anew with blackwater fever. He died at the Baptist mission outside Matadi, adding to the "mounds of triumphant martyrs" at the local cemetery. When Sheppard met the steamer from Stanley Pool a few months later, he was greeted not by his friend but by a terse note informing him of Lapsley's passing. As "weeping and wailing" spread through the settlement, he "sought a quiet spot in the forest to pour out my soul's great grief to Almighty God." He felt utterly alone.

Sheppard's role in founding the Congo mission had already earned him renown in Presbyterian circles in the United States. What he did in the wake of Lapsley's death made him an international celebrity. Gathering a small contingent of men from the mission, he set out to find the BaKuba. The impulse was clearly his own, but he portrayed it, characteristically, as a tribute to Lapsley, the "Pathfinder," who had "desired so much to journey into that land." For three months, he and his companions searched for the Kuba capital, using a variety of stratagems to find their way through the maze of forest footpaths and game trails. They measured their proximity to the capital by the mounting anxiety of the people they met along the way. "If the king hears you are here all our heads will come off," one village headman told Sheppard. Even his companions urged him to turn back. "We may possibly escape the King's wrath, but these people cannot," they warned. But Sheppard pushed forward.

Word of the party's approach eventually reached the *lukengu*, who dispatched a troop of soldiers, under command of one of his sons, to arrest the intruders and all who had aided them. Sheppard was sitting in a small village, reading a year-old newspaper, when the soldiers arrived. Affecting a calm he certainly did not feel, he addressed the commander in his own language. "These people are not to blame," he declared. "I have had no guide; no one showed me the way. Last night the chief begged me to go, but I did not go. I am the only one that is guilty." The speech startled the king's son, who had never met a foreigner who could speak the Kuba language, let alone one who could navigate through the jungle. "Well, that is very strange," he said. "I would like to speak to my father about this." With that, the soldiers departed. They returned three days later with unexpected news. After studying the matter, the tribal counselors had identified Sheppard as the reincarnated spirit of one of the *lukengu*'s ancestors, Bo Pe Mekabe. Sheppard strenuously denied the claim (to the alarm of his traveling companions), but his denials were brushed aside. "They knew me better than I knew myself," he wryly observed in his autobiography. Rather than beheadings, Sheppard and his party received a royal escort to the Kuba capital.

The story of "How Sheppard Made His Way into Lukenga's Kingdom" would be retailed endlessly in years to come, becoming one of the classic tales of nineteenth-century mission Christianity. Not surprisingly, the story invariably turned on Sheppard's being mistaken for Bo Pe Mekabe, an episode confirming stereotypes about African superstition and credulity. (Tales of Westerners embraced as kings or returning ancestors by ignorant natives were fast becoming a standard trope in imperial literature; Rudyard Kipling's "The Man Who Would Be King," the classic example of the genre, had been published just four years before.) But the episode can be read in different ways. While the BaKuba believed in the transmigration of souls, they were hardly credulous primitives. The *lukengu* and his counselors had good, pragmatic reasons to be interested in Sheppard, this black man in white clothes who was steeped in the ways of white men yet spoke their language and knew the pathways of their forest. Such a man could be very valuable, particularly at a time when the BaKuba were first beginning to feel the pressure of colonial authority. Casting Sheppard as one of their own may simply have provided a culturally legitimate rationale for admitting him to the capital. And casting him as a member of the king's own lineage ensured that whatever power he brought with him would be at the disposal of the king rather than any of his rivals.

Thus did William Sheppard become the first Westerner to enter Mushenge, the Kuba capital. Nothing in his experience prepared him for what he saw. As he and his escort neared the city, they passed groves of banana trees and raffia palms, neatly tilled fields of maize (a New World crop first introduced to the Congo by the Portuguese), and festoons of rubber vines that "made the forest look like a beautifully painted theatre or an enormous swinging garden." The city itself was a revelation, with broad avenues, tidy houses and neatly swept yards, all laid out in "perfect blocks," like a "checker board." The population numbered between four and five thousand, though it doubled in the daytime, as traders poured in from the countryside to participate in a half dozen thriving markets. Signs of industry abounded, with smiths, carvers, and weavers turning out products of exquisite craftsmanship.

After a few days exploring the city, Sheppard was introduced to the *lukengu*, Kot aMweeky, who arrived on a litter borne by sixteen men, accompanied by several hundred of his wives. In an odd role reversal, Sheppard felt the absurdity of his own dress. His threadbare suit of "what had once been white linen" and battered sun helmet were no match for Kot aMweeky's cowrie-bedecked blue cloth and eagle feather crown. After sitting with the aged king for an hour, silently watching a troupe of dancers, Sheppard again broached the question of his identity. "I want to acknowledge to you," he said, "that I am not a Makuba and I have never been here before." But the king just smiled: "You don't know it, but you are 'muana mi' (one of the family)." To seal Sheppard's new identity, the king presented him with an ornate ceremonial knife that had been in his family for seven generations.

Sheppard remained at Mushenge for four months. While his evangelical efforts proved futile—he failed to win a single convert during his stay—he proved an astute cultural observer. Two years traveling through the interior of the Congo had disabused him of much of the colonial cant about civilization and savagery, while sharpening his natural curiosity and sympathy. He recognized that Africans "had their judges, jurors, lawyers and officers of the town," even if they did not obviously conform to Western models. He also recognized that Africans knew things that he did not. "Many times in Central Africa foreigners get into serious difficulties from which they cannot extricate themselves by disregarding the advice of natives," he wrote. To be sure, this dawning cultural relativism was bounded by Sheppard's own religious convictions: he was, after all, a Christian missionary, who had come to redeem Africans from "sin" and "superstition." Nonetheless, Sheppard understood that Africans were not the simpleminded savages that most Western visitors supposed.

This open-mindedness served him well in Mushenge. Notebook in hand, he set about "prying into the king's customs," producing a priceless record of a precolonial African kingdom on the eve of its violent subsumption into the modern world. Though he had no academic training, his approach anticipated many of the methods soon to be enshrined in the new discipline of anthropology. He interacted with people of all social ranks, visiting their homes, sharing their food, exploring their courtship customs, their mode of raising children, their way of death. He studied local crafts, marveling at the BaKuba's unrivaled "knowledge of weaving, embroidery, wood carving and smelting." He spent hours with children, recording their games and "trying to find out what they were thinking about." While frustrated by his hosts' lack of receptivity to the gospel, he never doubted that he was in the presence of a "highly civilized" people, who had created a culture of great sophistication and beauty without the aid of whites. As he put it, the BaKuba were "enlightened but in darkness."

On two issues Sheppard proved unbending. The first was what he called "the poisonous cup." Like premodern people the world over, the BaKuba had radically different understandings of causality than those prevailing in the modern West. Misfortunes that we today might ascribe to disease, accident, or simple bad luck symbolized something more profound to the BaKuba, a rupture in social order brought about by the operation of malevolent forces. As Sheppard put it, "In the native mind no one dies a natural death." The primary role of the so-called witch doctor was to identify the culprit, to locate and root out the source of disorder, thus restoring the health of the social body. Once identified, the accused witch was forced to ingest a poison produced from the bark of a local tree. As in the various trials by ordeal devised by Europeans, death was taken as proof of guilt, while those who survived (in this case, by vomiting up the poison) were acquitted. Sheppard, who witnessed the poison ordeal on several occasions, found it horrifying and senseless. He railed against the "wicked custom" during his stay at the capital, and was pleased to note a decrease in public trials, though he feared that he had only driven the practice underground. On one occasion he confronted the king himself. "I tried to prove to him that the poisonous cup was a very cruel and unjust practice and there were no witches," he recalled. "And if they gave the poison to anyone whose stomach was not easily moved they would die." But such logic cut little ice with Kot aMweeky, who "thought me very foolish." "If a person is innocent he can never die," he replied.

Even more appalling for Sheppard was the BaKuba practice of human sacrifice. When a prominent individual died, it was customary to bury slaves along with the body, usually while the slaves were still alive. "They serve us here and then go with us on the journey to wait on us there," the *lukengu* explained matter-of-factly. In the case of an ordinary citizen, a single slave might suffice, but when a member of the royal family died as many as a thousand might be sacrificed. When the *lukengu* himself died, the grave was lined with the bodies of slaves to ensure that, in death as in life, his body never touched the earth. Determining the origins of this practice is virtually impossible, but it appears to have reached a peak at the very moment that Sheppard arrived in the Congo, thanks to an infusion of fresh supplies of slaves from Portuguese Angola. With labor plentiful, it became a form of "conspicuous consumption" for elite BaKuba, enabling them to express their wealth and status, both to other BaKuba and to tributary populations such as the BaKete.

For us today, as for Sheppard in 1892, human sacrifice seems uniquely barbarous. In fact, there are abundant examples of the practice in human history, both inside and outside Africa. Paradoxically, it may testify as much to a culture's vitality as to its decadence; it is hard to imagine a more powerful expression of faith in the legitimacy of an existing social order than the BaKuba's blithe assumption that the hierarchies of this world were reproduced in the next. But whatever the practice signified to the BaKuba, Sheppard found it utterly abhorrent. Once again, he confronted the king, arguing "in the strongest language I could command that it was wrong without the least shadow of justification." But on this issue too, the king was unconvinced. It was precisely the practice of "burying the living with the dead," he explained patiently, that distinguished the BaKuba from inferior groups such as "the Bakete, who only bury goats with their dead." On at least one occasion, Sheppard attempted to rescue a female slave who was being led to her death, but he was overpowered. "Seeing these awful customs practiced by these people for ages makes you indignant and depressed and also fills you with pity," he wrote. "Only by preaching God's word, having faith, patience and love will we eradicate the deep rooted evil."

As such statements suggest, Sheppard was no unalloyed admirer of the BaKuba. In matters of religion, the BaKuba were an "indifferent, stony-hearted, and superstitious people," in desperate need of the healing balm of Christian civilization. But they were not savages. On the contrary, they were a "well organized, independent and exceedingly industrious people," whose "culture, mode of living, and intelligence" refuted any notion of black inferiority.

IN 1893, a few months after leaving Mushenge, Sheppard returned to the United States for a much-deserved furlough. Word of his discovery preceded him. Newspapers in London, where he stopped on his way home, were abuzz were the achievements of this Black Livingstone, latest in the line of celebrated Dark Continent explorers. The Royal Geographic Society elected him a fellow, a distinction never before conferred on a black man (and one that the gentlemen of the society had ostentatiously withheld from the vulgar H. M. Stanley). At the society's behest, a lake in the Kasai region was formally christened Lake Sheppard. Three years before, Sheppard and Lapsley had been pleased to catch a glimpse of Queen Victoria during her morning carriage ride; now Sheppard was invited to Buckingham Palace to receive a medal from the queen's hand.

The accolades continued in the United States, where Sheppard found himself cast not only as the nation's premier missionary, but also as a spokesman for the black race. He was received at the White House by President Grover Cleveland, to whom he presented an intricately woven Kuba mat. Students at Hampton Institute, his alma mater, gave him a rapturous welcome, as did the white ministers of the Virginia Synod of the Presbyterian Church (U.S.). "A Virginia Negro, through the power of Almighty Grace, is our hero," one minister declared. For nine months, Sheppard traveled continuously, raising money for the Congo mission. Sheppard "has been speaking to crowded houses," a missionary periodical reported, "capturing all by his eloquence, fund of humor, and histrionic qualities." A natural showman, he took full advantage of the artifacts he had acquired in the Congo, underscoring his claims about the BaKuba's craftsmanship with exquisite works of art, punctuating a lurid description of their method of beheading by whipping out the blade he had received from the *lukengu*. The end of the speech was always the same: "Will you lend a helping hand to carry the light of the gospel to Africa?"

Sheppard's success as a fund-raiser was matched by his ability to inspire missionary vocations. When he returned to Africa in May 1894, he was accompanied by four new volunteers, all African Americans, the first in a stream of fresh recruits for the Congo mission. Henry Hawkins, a Mississippian, had studied with Sheppard at Tuscaloosa Theological Institute. The other three were women. The youngest was Lillian Thomas, who was just finishing her senior year at Talladega College when Sheppard came to the campus to speak. The oldest was Maria Fearing, a fifty-three-year-old former slave, who worked as matron in Talladega's boarding department. Presbyterian officials initially rejected her application on account of her age, but she traveled at her own expense and was eventually taken on as a paid missionary. Last but not least was Lucy Gantt, soon to become Mrs. Lucy Sheppard. The child of a single mother, Lucy had come to Talladega while still a child and been raised by Maria Fearing. She had seen a bit of the world since graduating from Talladega in 1886, working as a schoolteacher and also spending a year touring with the Loudin Jubilee Singers, an offshoot of the famous Fisk Jubilee Singers. She and Sheppard met while he was a student at Tuscaloosa, and they were probably engaged before he first left for Africa. The couple was married in early 1894. By the time they sailed for the Congo in May, Lucy was pregnant.

Presbyterian officials welcomed the surge of missionary vocations, but it also presented a problem, given their determination to maintain a rough parity between black and white missionaries. White volunteers remained hard to recruit and harder to retain. Of the first six whites posted to Luebo after Lapsley's death, two quickly died and two others returned home. The church's difficulties were revealed in the strange career of Samuel Verner, who arrived in the Congo in 1896. The scion of a wealthy South Carolina family, Verner had already suffered one nervous breakdown, during which he imagined himself to be a member of the Hapsburg royal family. During his convalescence, he read the works of David Livingstone, and turned his ambitions to the Dark Continent. Africa, he declared, "has thrown open its doors, given up the keys of its treasure house, and over the crumbling dust of the heroes who died that it might live, the invincible Caucasian is marching on." As such a statement suggests, Verner was less interested in redeeming Africans than in enriching himself, but Presbyterian officials were sufficiently desperate that they offered him an appointment, waiving the required three-year theological training course. Verner would devote most of his time in the Congo to various money-making schemes, eventually leaving the mission altogether to work for King Leopold. Later he would accept a commission from the organizers of the St. Louis World's Fair to collect pygmies, including the ill-fated Ota Benga, for display in the Anthropological Hall.

The Congo mission was better served by William Morrison, who arrived a year behind Verner. Morrison too came of a wealthy southern family, and he exhibited many of the signature attributes of his class, including imperiousness, impetuosity, and a firm belief in white (and specifically Anglo-Saxon) racial superiority. The chief objects of Morrison's racism, however, were not black people, whom he viewed with a certain paternal fondness, but

Belgians, whom he regarded as utterly unworthy of the great charge they had been given in the Congo. A few days in Antwerp during his initial voyage was all Morrison needed to convince him that the Belgians were "a howling mob of jabbering idiots," and nothing he saw in Africa compelled him to amend his opinion. In years to come, he would lead the international movement against King Leopold. William Sheppard would play a key role in Morrison's campaign, serving as something between reluctant ally and cat's-paw.

Together, this motley group of missionaries oversaw a dramatic expansion in the Luebo mission. Mobilizing the labor of the mission's growing number of adherents, they carved fields from the forest, erected a new chapel, and built new classrooms and workshops. (In keeping with the Hampton method, all students at the mission received instruction in a trade.) By all appearances, the mission was a model of interracial cooperation, but significant disagreements lurked beneath the surface. Though his own initial efforts had been unsuccessful, Sheppard remained convinced that the mission should focus its evangelical energies on the BaKuba. His argument was simple: if the dominant group in the region converted, subordinate groups would follow. Yet there were deeper motives here. Though separated by gulfs of religion and culture, Sheppard clearly felt a great affinity for the BaKuba, who "never were enslaved" and whose conspicuous civilization gave the lie to every stereotype about black inferiority. Unfortunately, the very qualities that recommended the BaKuba to Sheppard made them anathema to his white colleagues, who found them proud and haughty. The mission's proper target, they insisted, were the humble BaLuba. "The Baluba are by far the most numerous people in all this country, and they are universally the object of slave raids," Samuel Verner wrote. "They are a simple, laboring, inoffensive people, very susceptible to Gospel influence, and the white man's best friends."

The argument, so redolent of contemporary debates about "uppity" Negroes in the American South, rumbled on until 1897, when Sheppard won approval to open a mission to the BaKuba. What prompted the decision is unclear; the domineering Morrison, who had arrived a few months before, may simply have concluded that Luebo was not big enough for both of them. Whatever the case might be, the two men set out together for Mushenge, the

BaKuba capital. By the time they did so, however, Sheppard's old patron, Kot aMweeky, had died, unleashing a violent succession dispute. A new *lukengu*, Mishaape, eventually acceded to the throne, consolidating his position by killing or exiling the old king's family and friends. As an honorary member of the old royal family, Sheppard himself was vulnerable. Choosing the better side of valor, he and Morrison abandoned their dream of reaching the capital and decided to plant the new mission where they were, in a village called Ibaanche, midway between Luebo and Mushenge. In the months that followed, a second "white city"—Sheppard's term—emerged in the jungle.

At one level, Luebo and Ibaanche were conventional African mission stations, beacons of "Christian civilization" in a dark land. But they were much else besides: outposts of Protestantism in a Catholic-dominated colony; vehicles for the introduction of Hampton-style industrial education into Africa; laboratories for an unlikely experiment in southern interracialism. From the perspective of African residents, they were something else again. Though leaders of the mission rarely admitted it, many of those who settled at Luebo and later at Ibaanche were less interested in Christianity than in finding some place where they could live in peace, free from the exactions of a violent colonial state. This fact was not lost on Belgian officials, who increasingly regarded the Presbyterian mission as an affront to constituted authority, a refuge for fugitives and loafers and others trying to avoid the state's legitimate demand for labor.

Determining who actually governed the mission is no easy task. The Belgians and the BaKuba both regarded the mission's residents as rightfully their subjects; the missionaries regarded them as their children. Africans at the mission had their own systems of authority. As new contingents of Africans arrived at Luebo and later at Ibaanche, they settled in distinct wards or subvillages, each under the authority of a local headman. The most influential figure in the American Presbyterian Congo Mission, however, was William Sheppard. With his gift for languages and his rare tact and diplomacy, Shepete (as he was universally known by Africans) operated as a kind of paramount chief, adjudicating disputes and organizing public works, mediating between missionaries and converts. Even Morrison, who often addressed him as a subordinate, acknowledged that the mission could not have functioned without Sheppard. "There is no man in all this country who has the influence over this people that Sheppard has," he wrote.

ON ONE ISSUE, black and white missionaries were of a single mind: they needed to uplift African women. Assumptions about the appropriate relationship between men and women are a cornerstone of every culture, and they were an essential part of the nineteenth-century missionary enterprise. Missionaries took it for granted that any civilized society would have gender relations like their own, with nuclear families and sharply demarcated roles for men and women, reflecting their distinctive natures. Needless to say, they were horrified by what they found in Africa.

Precisely because they purport to be natural—ordinances of God or nature rather than mere social arrangements—gender ideologies can be difficult to trace historically. But the specific beliefs that missionaries of the Presbyterian Congo Mission carried to Africa trace back to the early nineteenth century, to what historians call domestic ideology. Within this paradigm, women were at once a subordinate sex and a superior one. While lacking the "masculine" qualities of aggression and competitiveness necessary for success in the worlds of work and politics, women were endowed with a superior moral nature, with qualities of empathy, chastity, and compassion befitting their roles as wives and mothers. Much of the history of American women's movement, from the Seneca Falls declaration of 1848 to the struggle for the Equal Rights Amendment, has been a story of women's efforts to overturn these perdurable assumptions, to assert their equality and the full civil and political rights that flow from it. At other times, however, activists have worked within domestic ideology, capitalizing on prevailing assumptions about their distinct nature and sphere to claim new prerogatives. American women first gained access to common schools, for example, not by challenging domestic ideology but by exploiting it, arguing that they needed education if they were to meet the task of raising the next generation of responsible republican citizens. Similar arguments were made to claim a place in antebellum social reform movements, including the campaigns against liquor and slavery, both of which were cast as evils threatening the sanctity of the home. In the late nineteenth century, this same logic would propel women into the mission field. For who better to uplift the "children" of Africa than women?

Domestic ideology had a profound, if paradoxical, impact on African American women. At one level, the ideology simply did not apply to them. Centuries of slavery had made a mockery of the separation of work and home, the sanctity of the family, female chastity, and other domestic ideals. Yet this ugly history only made the ideology's prescriptions more compelling. Postbellum reformers, black and white, agreed that African Americans would never rise from their degraded state until their family life had been reformed and women had been restored to their proper position. During Reconstruction, a legion of missionaries, black and white, fanned out across the South, sanctifying marriages and rooting out "irregular" unions. Southern schools instituted distinct curricula for female students, with courses in needlecraft, cooking, and other skills essential to enlightened home life. As one black woman reformer put it, women were "both the lever and the fulcrum for uplifting the race."

All of which is to say that the missionaries who came to the Congo in the 1890s, black and white, male and female, arrived with powerful assumptions about gender—assumptions that their host society violated in every particular. African women routinely worked outside the home, toiling in fields and haggling in markets. They exposed their breasts, and covered buttocks and genitals with only the tiniest strips of cloth. They were afforded no education (that missionaries could see), no training for their vital roles as wives and mothers. The horror reached a climax in the practice of polygamy, through which a teenage girl might find herself becoming the third or fourth wife of a much older man. The response of Lucy Gantt Sheppard on her arrival in the Congo was typical: "When I saw the first native woman in her strip of cloth, her face daubed with paint, her body smeared with grease, and her mind filled with sin and superstition, I could not help but wonder if she could be changed."

In the years that followed, Lucy Sheppard and her female colleagues would set out to prove that it was possible to change African women and, through them, to uplift an entire society. They established schools, sewing circles, domestic science classes, women's prayer circles—a whole host of institutions intended to instill "Christian ideals of womanhood" in their "heathen sisters." Within the conventional mission hierarchy, such work was secondary to the work of men, who, as ordained ministers, had the sole authority to baptize converts, administer communion, conduct marriages, and so forth. Within the framework of domestic ideology, however, the work of women among women was the linchpin of the enterprise. The women and girls who attended Lillian Thomas's school or who learned to sing spirituals under the baton of Lucy Sheppard were more than simple converts. They were future "Christian mothers of Christian families," "little home missionaries," whose influence would illuminate the darkness.

Considerations of gender sharpened the ambivalence toward African culture that was inherent in the mission enterprise. Lucy Sheppard and her comrades obviously identified strongly with African women, whose sexual vulnerability and ceaseless toil evoked the experience of African American women during slavery. Yet this very sense of solidarity could give rise to a fierce contempt for African traditional culture, which had seemingly reduced women to a "totally depraved and degraded state," virtually to the level of beasts. Sheppard and her colleagues quickly concluded that the only way to make progress was by removing African girls from their homes at an early age. The result was Pantops Home for Girls, which Maria Fearing opened at Luebo in late 1894. Like contemporary boarding schools for Native Americans (including William Sheppard's alma mater, Hampton Institute), Pantops served as a kind of cultural reorientation center, where young indigenes could be rescued from the baleful effects of traditional life. Girls at Pantops (and at a similar girl's home established at Ibaanche a few years later) learned proper dress and deportment. They imbibed new ideas about courtship, marriage, and motherhood. Perhaps most important, they received instruction in those occupations regarded as essential to the maintenance of a proper home—cooking, cleaning, ironing, sewing, and so forth. The Sheppards' own home became a "demonstration and practice center," where "girls took their turns, by twos, working . . . [and] learning new methods of more abundant living."

As the only married woman among the missionaries, Lucy Sheppard had a particularly important role to play as mentor and model. The "making of a

Christian home was part of my missionary task," she later recalled and she labored diligently to fulfill it. She fashioned chairs and tables from packing crates and colored cloth; somewhere, she found muslin for curtains. "I called it my *Ladies' Home Journal* home," she later explained, since most of her ideas had been culled from that magazine. When her husband decided to open the second mission at Ibaanche, she dutifully followed and began the arduous process all over again.

All that the Sheppard household needed to make a proper home was a child. But fate treated them cruelly. Lucy conceived almost immediately after the couple's marriage, and was heavily pregnant by the time she reached the Congo. In early 1895, she bore a daughter, Miriam, but the baby was two months premature and died after a few weeks. Lucy buried her at the mission cemetery at Luebo, lining the tiny coffin with her wedding dress. In 1896, she bore a second child, Lucille, who lived eight months before fever claimed her. By that time, Lucy was again pregnant, with her third child, Wilhelmina, who was born in early 1897. Desperate that her daughter might live, she and her husband made the wrenching decision to give the child up to be raised by relatives in the United States. As soon as mother and daughter were strong enough, the family embarked for the coast. Sheppard saw his wife and child onto a ship at Boma, and returned to the mission alone. It would be eighteen months before he saw Lucy again, and more than six years before he saw his daughter.

How the loss of his children and the departure of his wife affected Sheppard is difficult to say; in this regard, as in so many others, he kept his own counsel. But sometime in about 1898, he took an African mistress, who bore him a son. The episode, in the most private of realms, would eventually undo the celebrated missionary, but not before he took one more turn on the public stage.

ON HIS INITIAL JOURNEY to the BaKuba capital, Sheppard reported passing through a kind of enchanted forest, festooned with vines as long as two hundred feet. The vines, he reported, "made the forest look like a beautifully painted theatre or an enormous swinging garden." Unfortunately, he was not alone in his interest. The vines, a species of the *Landolphia* genus, represented one of two sources of natural rubber in the world. In the context of King Leopold's Congo, this was an incitement to murder.

Of all the commodities uncovered in the West's centuries-long ransacking of the tropical world, few were destined to have as profound an effect on modern life as rubber. Europeans initially encountered this remarkable material in 1735, during the first scientific expedition into the interior of South America. A shallow incision in the bark of *Hevea brasiliensis,* a tree native to the Amazonian rain forest, yielded a white latex, which, when rendered and dried, produced an elastic but strangely resilient substance. First used in pencil erasers, rubber remained a curiosity until 1835, when Charles Goodyear patented a vulcanizing technique, dramatically increasing its strength and durability. Like the plastics of our own time, rubber was a veritable invitation to invention, a miracle product that was at once pliant and tough, waterproof, and impervious to heat and electrical current. By the late nineteenth century, it had acquired a host of commercial applications, and international demand was surging. Initially, Brazil remained the sole supplier, but researchers in the 1880s discovered that a high quality latex could also be collected from the *Landolphia* vines of the Congo Free State.

Sheppard's early years in Africa coincided with an explosion in international demand for rubber, triggered by John Dunlop's invention of the pneumatic tube. If the transportation revolution of the nineteenth century ran on rails of steel, the transportation revolution of the twentieth century rolled on wheels of rubber. While American engineers set out to develop a reliable synthetic—a quest that only bore fruit in the 1940s—European governments and corporations invested millions in the creation of rubber plantations, transplanting seedlings from the Amazon to Malaysia, Indonesia, Thailand, China, India, even Liberia. But until those trees had matured, a process requiring upward of fifteen years, the global economy continued to depend on Brazil and the Congo, of each which supplied about half of the world's supply of rubber.

King Leopold and his minions were naturally anxious to capitalize on the rubber bonanza. The profits to be made were spectacular: with raw rubber trading for thirty or forty cents per pound in Europe and the United States, chartered companies operating in the Congo routinely generated returns on investment of more than 1,000 percent. Erstwhile missionary Samuel Verner did not exaggerate when he declared, "A small forest is as profitable as a gold mine, and surer of returns upon the capital invested." Unfortunately, collecting rubber was dangerous and time-consuming work, requiring tappers to climb high into the forest canopy. The latex then had to be processed— boiled, dried, kneaded, rolled, sliced, and woven. As vines were overtapped or cut down entirely, harvesters were forced to travel deeper into the forest, often leaving their villages for weeks at a time. Small wonder that Africans sought to avoid rubber collecting. As a Force Publique officer candidly put it, "The native doesn't like making rubber. He must be compelled to do it."

And compelled he was. All the techniques that Free State authorities had used to deplete the Congo's seemingly inexhaustible supplies of ivory were now directed to producing rubber, including onerous quotas, forced labor, and wholesale murder. If anything, authorities were even more heavy-handed in their pursuit of rubber, recognizing that the Congo's privileged position on the international market would last only a few more years. Should residents of a particular village "refuse obstinately to work"— should they, in other words, fail to deliver their required quota—officers of the Force Publique were ordered, according to an 1897 memo, to "take hostages." (Because men were needed to make rubber, standard practice was to make hostages of women, countless of whom were raped and murdered.) An 1898 memo to district administrators was blunter still: "I have the honour to inform you that from 1 January 1899 you must succeed in furnishing four thousand kilos of rubber every month. To effect this, I give you carte blanche . . . Employ gentleness first, and if they persist in not accepting the imposition of the state, employ the force of arms."

The communities at Luebo and Ibaanche were to some extent sheltered from the storm. As hard as it is to imagine today, King Leopold enjoyed a reputation as a philanthropist, and Free State officials were chary of jeopardizing that image by attacking an American mission station. State officials sought to circumvent the problem in late 1898 by ordering the wholesale removal of all the BaLuba around Luebo to Luluabourg, the district administrative center, but they retreated after vigorous protests by Reverend Morrison. Officials also took aim at the BaKuba, whose continued autonomy had become an affront to Free State authority. In early 1899, a contingent of the Force Publique, under a Belgian officer, attacked Mushenge, the capital, leaving fourteen people dead. The raid ended as quickly as it began, but Mishaape, the king, feared—correctly—that the soldiers would soon return and kill him.

The terror was only beginning. Determined to subdue the upper Kasai once and for all, Free State officials unleashed the Zappo Zaps. Seven hundred heavily armed men under the command of a notoriously violent chief named Malumba descended on the region, burning villages, seizing hostages, demanding impossible quantities of rubber and slaves. In early September, representatives of a nearby village came to Sheppard at Ibaanche, bringing tribute and begging him to intercede on their behalf, but he refused. "If Malumba N'kusa is leading them there is no use of my going," he told the petitioners. "It is just as if I were to take a rope and go out behind the house and hang myself to that tree." A few days later, however, a messenger arrived from Luebo with a note signed by Morrison and two other white missionaries. They too had received reports of the raids, and though they were unwilling to risk their own lives, they were willing to risk Sheppard's. "We hear of atrocities being committed in the Pianga country by the Zappo-Zaps," the note read. "We commission you immediately on receipt of this letter to go over and stop the raid."

In recounting his experience later, Sheppard would make much of the note, as if to reassure his listeners that he himself had not set out to challenge white colonial authority but was merely following the instructions of his white superiors. "These were orders," he explained. "I had to go; there was nothing else to do." Whether he was sincere or simply acting his accustomed role of faithful black servant is, as with so many of Sheppard's public pronouncements, impossible to say. But he marched out to confront the Zappo Zaps, accompanied by a handful of terrified mission residents. For two days the small party traversed a deserted land, passing a dozen smoldering villages. Leaving one village, they were suddenly attacked by a group of Zappo Zap men. With no time to flee, Sheppard loudly identified himself—"Sheppard! Sheppard!" Fortunately, the group's leader recognized him, having once come to the mission for medical treatment. He ordered his men to lower their weapons, and agreed to conduct Sheppard to Malumba N'kusa.

After a few hours' march, the party came to a clearing in the forest, in which stood a crude stockade. The scene inside was something from the seventh circle of hell. Corpses littered the ground, in various stages of slaughter. Hunks of human flesh roasted on skewers over a fire. Many of the bodies had been beheaded, it being the custom of the Zappo Zaps to use the skulls of their victims as bowls to "rub up" their favored blend of tobacco and hemp. The body of a chief who had once extended hospitality to Sheppard had been eviscerated; his blackened heart, dusted with some traditional medicine, was displayed on a spear. In a far corner of the compound, some sixty living hostages, all women, huddled in silence, while their husbands, fathers, and sons rotted before their eyes. A Free State flag fluttered serenely above.

Sheppard spent two days in the stockade, talking to the murderers, recording every detail of the scene in a notebook. As a recent biographer has suggested, his long experience at masking his own feelings, at assuming whatever role circumstances demanded, prepared him well for the task. Malumba N'kusa's initial wariness quickly evaporated in the face of Sheppard's geniality and apparent solicitude. Indeed, he became positively expansive. He recounted how he had entered villages, demanding slaves and thousands of balls of rubber; how he had herded hostages into his hastily built fort; and how, when his demands for tribute were unmet, he had ordered his men to shoot. "I don't like to fight," Malumba assured his guest, "but the state told me if the villages refused to pay to make fire." He proudly displayed the small arsenal that the state had given to him and his men, with which he now intended to storm the BaKuba capital. "We are going to kill them all," several warriors told Sheppard, "for they don't want the white men to come to their village."

The sight that most arrested Sheppard was a collection of severed human hands drying over a fire. Malumba N'kusa "conducted us to a framework of sticks, under which was burning a slow fire, and there they were, the right hands, I counted them eighty-one in all." Hand chopping, which would become a synecdoche for all the horrors of Leopold's Congo, had an eminently economic logic: in a region where bullets were scarce and expensive, collecting hands offered authorities proof that the mercenaries in their employ were using ammunition wisely, not simply squandering it on hunting or horseplay. The practice probably began with Arab slave traders, but the combination of frugality and terror also appealed to Belgian officials, who made it their own. How rigorously authorities enforced their one-hand-one-bullet policy is not clear, but soldiers of the Force Publique and the Zappo Zaps made at least a token effort to honor it. They accounted for bullets and hands, though they sometimes used unorthodox methods to balance the ledger, killing victims with rifle butts or simply harvesting the hands of the living.

After two grisly days in the stockade, Sheppard bid Malumba N'kusa a polite goodbye and raced back to Ibaanche, where he prepared a detailed report on what he had seen and heard. Staggered by the report, Morrison dispatched a second party to the area, this one led by a white man, Lachlan Vass, who had come to the Congo a few months before to command the mission's new steamboat, the S.S. *Lapsley*. Vass confirmed Sheppard's account. "The whole country is pillaged and not a village is left standing," he wrote; "in a radius of about seventy-five miles, there are probably 50,000 people sleeping in the bush, unsheltered and in the midst of the rainy season."

Armed with this confirmation, Morrison sent a vigorous protest to Belgian officials at Luluabourg, enclosing Sheppard's report. They responded with practiced duplicity. Professing shock at a raid he himself had ordered, the district adminstrator dispatched a contingent of Force Publique officers to free the surviving hostages and to arrest Malumba N'kusa. (The chief, who was quietly released a few weeks later, was understandably confused. "You have sent me to do this and yet you have put me in chains," he complained.) An official inquiry managed simultaneously to exonerate the state and to accuse Morrison and his colleagues of trying to inflate a minor skirmish into a cause célèbre. The depredations continued. A few months after the episode in the stockade, soldiers of the Force Publique attacked the Kuba capital, murdering hundreds, including Mishaape and his family, and making off with countless priceless artifacts. Morrison would later meet the Belgian commander of the force, who, unaware of the missionary's identity, laughingly recounted how the BaKuba had scurried about yelling "Shepete! Shepete!" as they were shot, as if the legendary Sheppard could somehow save them.

Free State authorities had engaged in atrocities for years with nary a peep of protest from missionaries. But they had not reckoned on Morrison, a man whose propensity for righteous indignation was matched only by his contempt for Belgians. When it became clear that the local inquiry would offer no satisfaction, he took his case to the world. Leopold's vaunted Free State, he declared in a letter to a leading missionary magazine, had "turned out to be a gigantic slave and trade company, whose philanthropy had been turned into greed." He also forwarded a copy of Sheppard's report to a correspondent in England. A few weeks later, an account of the Zappo Zap raid appeared in *The Times* of London. "We have heard reports for years past of the terrible affairs in the Congo, yet, as they have often been based on secondhand native stories, they have been difficult to verify," the paper reported. "Now the case is different." The article noted details of Sheppard's career, including his election as a fellow of the Royal Geographic Society, to underscore the report's reliability.

Morrison's actions unnerved his superiors in the Presbyterian Church (U.S.), a denomination that had long prided itself on its sensibly conservative approach to questions of race and politics. "We can hardly think it necessary to remind the Mission as to the necessity of the utmost caution, in making representations regarding these matters to those in authority, or in publishing them to the world," the Foreign Mission Executive Committee wrote in early 1900. While acknowledging the "courageous and prudent conduct" of the missionaries in uncovering the outrages, the committee reminded them "to observe all proper deference to 'the powers that be,' and to avoid anything that might give any color to a charge of doing or saying things inconsistent with [the mission's] purely spiritual and non-political character." But Morrison refused to be silenced. As the atrocities continued, he sent a stream of increasingly impertinent protests to Belgian authorities, including an open letter to Leopold himself. At the same time, he began to assemble an international network of supporters and correspondents, from the venerable Aborigines Protection Society, a vestige of the British antislavery movement, to U.S. president Theodore Roosevelt, who would later entertain both Morrison and Sheppard at the White House.

Morrison found his most valuable ally in Edmund Morel, a young British radical who had launched his own lonely campaign against Leopold a few years before. As historian Adam Hochschild has shown, Morel first became aware of what was happening in the Free State while working as a clerk for a British shipping company in Antwerp, where he saw an endless procession of ships sailing out to Africa with empty holds and returning laden with riches. He quit his job and went to work full time "to expose and destroy what I knew then to be a legalized infamy." In the newspaper he founded, *The West African Mail*, as well as in books such as *Red Rubber!* and *The Black Man's Burden*, Morel tirelessly exposed the atrocities being perpetrated in the Congo, and ultimately in all of colonial Africa. Whenever possible, he supplemented his words with photographs, including some that appear to have been taken by William Sheppard who, during his first furlough in the United States, had acquired one of the small, handheld cameras recently introduced by the Eastman Kodak Company. Confronted by "the incorruptible Kodak," by photographs of yoked slaves and severed hands, Free State officials could no longer airily dismiss critics' charges as "highly improbable" and "grossly overstated."

Morrison's and Morel's efforts began to bear fruit in 1903, during the missionary's visit to London. Following a mass meeting at Whitehall, the British Parliament passed a resolution condemning the atrocities in the Congo. The statement Morrison delivered to the British government was also introduced to the U.S. Congress, which began an investigation of its own. The ferment on both sides of the Atlantic issued in the creation of the Congo Reform Association. Like the Anglo-American anti–slave trade movement of a century before, the Congo movement was an international network of reformers who tried, through public exposés and political lobbying, to compel governments to act against what we today would call "crimes against humanity." The roster of the movement's supporters reads like a veritable who's who of Anglo-American public life, including everyone from Arthur Conan Doyle and Mark Twain (who quoted Sheppard's 1899 report in his satirical *King Leopold's Soliloquy*) to Sheppard's old teacher, Booker T. Washington. That Washington, the arch-accommodator, would publicly speak out against Leopold was testimony to just how dramatically international opinion on the Congo had swung.

Congo reformers lionized William Sheppard. His 1899 report acquired an almost scriptural status in the movement, so frequently was it quoted and glossed. Supporters talked of his "tact and heroism," his courage and unquestioned integrity. Sheppard, one newspaper declared, was the "the greatest Negro of his generation." Yet Sheppard spoke few words on his own account, and played little if any direct role in the development of the Congo Reform Association. Such was his reticence that the Belgian ambassador to the United States, who interviewed him in early 1904, came away convinced that he was merely a "tool in the hands of Morrison." He further speculated that most of the statements attributed to Sheppard had actually been written by Morrison, who signed his colleague's name to capitalize on his greater credibility.

The ambassador's claims were largely, if not completely, untrue, but they highlight a real problem. Even as he became the symbol of an international anticolonial movement, Sheppard remained very much a product of the Jim Crow South, where one lesson trumped all: black men did not challenge white authority. The anomalies of his position were vividly illustrated during his 1904–5 American lecture tour, a tour that carried him from Hampton to Princeton; Wyoming to the White House. From the perspective of church leaders, the tour was a ringing success. Audiences, white and black, packed churches and lecture halls, lavishing donations on the Congo mission. Congo reformers, however, were initially let down. "When Sheppard arrived, things were at top notch in the Congo agitation, the press was full of reports and people were anxious to hear," wrote Lachlan Vass, his colleague from Luebo. But instead of fanning the flames, Sheppard seems to have been content to reprise the role of Black Livingstone, regaling audiences with tales of adventure and exploration "even more thrilling" than those of H. M. Stanley but avoiding commentary on the political situation in the Congo.

In a later letter to a black colleague, Henry Hawkins, Sheppard addressed the criticisms against him, offering an uncharacteristically explicit acknowledgment of his predicament. "Being a colored man, I would not be understood criticizing a white government before white people," he wrote. But he also appears to have taken the criticism to heart, for he began to offer more political commentary in his lectures. A defining moment came during a visit to Warm Springs, Virginia, the resort where his mother had worked and where he himself had once waited tables. Invited to speak at the local Presbyterian church, Sheppard addressed a capacity crowd, including many people, black and white, who had known him since childhood. The audience also included the Belgian ambassador, who was vacationing nearby. Anticipating the same reticent, deferential man he had met earlier in the year, he was stunned instead to see a compelling, charismatic public speaker, who carried his audience with him into the blood-soaked stockade in the Congo jungle. The ambassador left in a lather, the episode was picked up by the national and international press, and Sheppard was once again a hero. The local Presbyterian minister was so moved by the event that he risked scandal by inviting Sheppard back to his home to dine with him and his white guests. But this breach of southern propriety had its limits: the women ate in a separate room.

LEOPOLD AND HIS supporters defended themselves against the burgeoning reform movement as they always had, using bribery, intimidation, phony commissions of inquiry, and planted stories in pet newspapers. But with continuing revelations of atrocities in the Congo—and with the *New York American*'s exposure of the monarch's systematic campaign to buy American journalists and politicians—the game was up. In 1906, the king began negotiations to surrender title of the Congo Free State to the Belgian government. The transfer was completed in 1908.

As Hochschild has argued, the victory of the Congo Reform Association marked a historic watershed, while offering a still precious precedent. Like the triumph of the Anglo-American movement to abolish the transatlantic slave trade exactly a hundred years earlier, the Congo movement showed how much could be done by a small group of determined individuals—men and women with the vision to see what others choose to ignore, and the courage to act on their convictions. And yet the victory was a curiously circumscribed one. American reformers' sincere concern for the suffering of the Congolese did not provoke any sustained reflection about injustice and racial terror at home; if anything, the movement helped to deflect concerns about American racial offenses, which seemed trivial by comparison. Though disgraced, Leopold earned a tidy profit, extorting a fifty-million-franc buy-out for a colony that he had been given for free. And just as the institution of slavery survived the abolition of the transatlantic slave trade, so did the atrocities perpetrated in the Congo survive the transfer of sovereignty from Leopold to the Belgian state. Laws were simply carried over, as were the men administering them.

Thus the battle continued, with Morrison and Sheppard, who returned to the Congo in 1906, still in the van. Rubber, which now accounted for nearly 90 percent of revenues from the colony, remained the prize. The villain was no longer Leopold but the Compagnie du Kasai, a chartered corporation that had been given a monopoly on all products of the soil in the region, including rubber. The C.K. paid for the rubber it took, but the price it offered was derisory, less than a fifth of what had been offered just a few years before. To ensure that natives collected rubber anyway, the Belgian government (which owned half the shares in the company) ordered that all African taxes be paid in *croisettes*, small copper coins that could be obtained only from the C.K. in exchange for rubber. When that system provoked protest, authorities introduced a labor tax, requiring every male resident of the Kasai to devote forty hours per month to collecting rubber. In the absence of any time-keeping system, villages were required to supply a specified quota of rubber every twenty days, a quantity so great that both men and women were forced to spend virtually all their time in the forest. The taxes were backed by the Force Publique and by the company's own soldiers, but it was increasingly unnecessary to deploy them, so beaten and terrified were the people. "We are not now suffering from the old forms of outrage so much—hand-cutting, slave-raiding, murdering, etc.—but I am sorry to say that I believe the sum total of suffering is much more than it was formerly," Morrison reported in 1908. "Now the people are thoroughly cowed; they know from bitter experience that there is no escaping from the State."

The Presbyterian Congo mission remained a haven. Having taken more than five years to gather its first hundred converts, it now attracted more than a hundred new adherents per month, as refugees poured into Luebo and Ibaanche. By 1909, the mission had grown into one of the largest in Africa, with more than twenty thousand adherents, spread between the two stations and a growing network of outstations, serviced by a corps of native evangelists. Even the BaKuba now seemed receptive to Christianity. The new *lukengu* welcomed the Presbyterian Congo mission into his realm and announced an end to mortuary killing. His own grave, he told Sheppard, would be lined with camwood rather than the broken bodies of slaves.

For the missionaries, the flood of converts was a sign of God's grace. For the historian, it is evidence of profound social and cultural dislocation. For officers of the colonial administration and of the Compagnie du Kasai, it was further proof that the mission was a blot on the landscape, a refuge for slackers fleeing the legitimate demands of the state. Yet such was the prominence of the mission, and of Morrison and Sheppard in particular, that the authorities could not risk a direct confrontation. Appreciating his position, Morrison directed a withering fire at state and company. Sheppard was, as always, more circumspect. But after a disheartening visit to the Kuba capital he too weighed in. In an article in the *Kasai Herald,* a monthly newspaper produced on the mission's new press, he described how "one of the most prosperous and intelligent of all the African tribes" had been reduced to vassalage. "Why this change?" he asked. "You have it in a few words. There are armed sentries of chartered trading companies who force the men and women to spend most of their days and nights in the forests making rubber, and the price they receive is so meager that they cannot live upon it."

Observers at the time and since have speculated whether the normally cautious Sheppard published the article of his own volition or whether he was prompted to do so by Morrison, who was clearly spoiling for a confrontation. When company officials demanded a retraction, Morrison challenged them to institute libel charges. Given the recent passage of a law mandating a five-year jail term for anyone expressing "any calumny against a Congo state official," the challenge was more than a little reckless, especially since it was Sheppard's neck in the noose. Morrison got his confrontation a few months later, following the visit of a British consular official, dispatched by his government to investigate the missionaries' allegations. The consul spent several months in the Congo, most of it with Sheppard, who served as his translator and guide. His report not only confirmed the missionaries' charges against C.K. but also rejected the possibility of reform, calling instead for "the entire abolition of the Company." When the report was published in Europe in 1909, company share prices plummeted. C.K. officials responded by instituting legal proceedings. Because the consul was immune to prosecution, they charged Morrison and Sheppard with libel, focusing their case on Sheppard's article in the *Kasai Herald*.

If their goal was to restore their reputation, state and company officials had badly miscalculated. Rather than intimidating opponents into silence, the case rekindled the Congo reform movement. Supporters in the United States organized protest meetings and prayer vigils. President Taft discussed the case with his cabinet, and dispatched an observer to the trial, as did the British government. The case also energized Belgium's opposition socialist party, whose leader, Émile Vandervelde, traveled to the Congo to lead the defense. Morrison gloried in the visibility and was devastated when the judge in the case, citing a technical error in the filing, dismissed the charges against him, leaving Sheppard alone in the dock. The case against Sheppard collapsed almost as quickly. Mixing "invincible logic" and "burning sarcasm," Vandervelde cast Sheppard not as an enemy of the state but as a sincere humanitarian, who had come to care so passionately about the BaKuba that he was virtually one of them. Whatever the merits of that last claim, the presiding judge had no doubts of Sheppard's innocence, and dismissed the case with costs. "Throw up your hat! Sheppard & I are acquitted!" Morrison wrote to Edmund Morel, annexing Sheppard's achievement as his own for a final time.

THE TRIAL BROUGHT Sheppard a last taste of international celebrity. AMERICAN NEGRO HERO OF CONGO, declared a headline in the *Boston Herald*. "Dr. Sheppard has not only stood before kings, but he has also stood against them," the author wrote. "[T]his son of a slave . . . has dared to withstand all the power of Leopold." Yet just two months later, Sheppard and his wife, Lucy, announced their intention to leave the Congo mission permanently. The reason offered was persistent ill health, along with "some family matters which I believe need my attention." That explanation, as scholars have recently shown, was at best a partial truth. In fact, Sheppard was recalled for sexual misconduct.

The episode that undid Sheppard had occurred a decade before, when

Lucy traveled to the United States with her infant daughter. During her absence, Sheppard "was guilty of the sin of adultery" with an African woman at the Ibaanche station, who bore him a son named Shepete. As the name suggests, the child's paternity was common knowledge at the mission. From the African point of view, there was nothing untoward about the child; men, particularly high-status men like Sheppard, routinely had children by more than one woman. Presumably Lucy had a different reaction when she learned of the child, but whatever it was, she kept it to herself. She continued to live with her husband, and soon bore a son of her own, Max. The two half brothers grew up together on the station, one as an African, the other as an American. Like his father, Max was identifiable by his white suits and ever-present sun helmet, by which his terrified mother hoped to ward off the lethal effects of the African sun.

What is most surprising about the business is the long silence of Sheppard's American colleagues, who surely knew about the child. Liaisons with African women were ubiquitous in colonial Africa, where a dearth of European women and great disparities of power created a perfect breeding ground for a culture of concubinage. But when the offender was a missionary, charged with preaching principles of chastity and monogamy, scandal was inescapable. At a minimum, offenders were recalled; many were defrocked. Yet Sheppard went unpunished for more than a decade. One can only speculate that leaders of the mission calculated that the costs of exposure were simply too great. Sheppard was not only the church's premier fund-raiser, he was also the Congo mission's public face. To destroy him was to risk everything.

If there was indeed a conspiracy of silence about Sheppard's misconduct, the obvious question is why it ended in 1909. One recent biographer lays the blame on Morrison: with the trial won, she suggests, Sheppard's usefulness to Morrison was at an end. But in this instance, Morrison appears to have been blameless. A more likely culprit is Lachlan Vass, master of the mission's steamboat and a man who had publicly criticized Sheppard on previous occasions. In 1909, Vass was involved in an acrimonious dispute with leaders of the mission over what he regarded as the second-class status of nonpastoral staff; he was particularly aggrieved that he, a white man, received a lower salary than the mission's African evangelists. His response, it appears, was to threaten to expose Sheppard. "I am sorry you feel that I have talked too freely concerning our African mission and regarding Sheppard in particular," he wrote in a 1910 letter to the head of the church's foreign mission committee. "But I am right about this Sheppard affair. Things have been hushed up too much in our Congo mission along certain lines." He was no longer prepared "to deceive to save Sheppard's most undeserved exalted position."

With the cat nearly out of the bag, church authorities finally acted. They summoned Sheppard, who tearfully confessed his transgression. In a supplementary statement a year later, he acknowledged three more episodes of adultery, though none appears to have produced a child. Similar charges were brought against Sheppard's colleague, Henry Hawkins, who was also recalled, ostensibly for reasons of health. Though at least one white missionary, Samuel Verner, had also sired an African child during his time in the Congo, church leaders interpreted the problem racially and responded with a new whites-only policy. "In view of all the experiences of the past few years, I am confident our Committee will deem it wise to send out only white reinforcements to Africa for the present," the chair of the church's mission committee wrote in 1910. "We do not think it necessary or wise to make any public proclamation of this policy, but we think it will probably be necessary to act upon it until we receive further light in a quiet and unostentatious way." With the exception of one woman, dispatched as a replacement wife for a recently widowed missionary, the Presbyterian Church (U.S.) ceased sending African Americans to Africa.

After enduring a period of suspension, Sheppard continued his ministry, first in Staunton, Virginia, and later in Louisville, Kentucky. The man who had stood before rulers on three continents was once again just a southern Negro. In keeping with southern custom, his salary was slashed. His starting salary at Staunton was $120 per year, only a quarter of what he and Lapsley had received twenty years before, and only a tenth of the salary earned by white ministers. The decline in wealth and status was hard on Lucy, who, as one family member later put it, had grown accustomed to "being waited on." William appears to have had an easier time, adapting seamlessly to life in the

Jim Crow South, whose rituals of deference and self-effacement he knew in his bones. A white woman from Waynesboro, who knew him before and after his two decades in Africa, praised his good grace. "He was such a good darky," she recalled. "When he returned from Africa, he remembered his place and always came to the back door."

Whatever his private feelings may have been, Sheppard threw himself into his new work. Drawing on his experience in the Congo, he saw himself not simply as a minister, responsible for Sunday service, but as a missionary, offering a fuller life to people ensnared in the coils of ignorance and poverty. In addition to his pastoral work, he devoted hours to Louisville's Presbyterian Colored Mission, a social settlement house in Smoketown, Louisville's poorest slum. The mission offered not only religious services but also a free medical clinic, gymnasium, employment bureau, and school, complete with industrial courses in carpentry, cobbling, and the like, taught by Sheppard himself. Lucy taught sewing and cooking, and also organized a chorus, teaching the children of Louisville the spirituals that she had once performed as a Jubilee Singer and later taught to the children of the Congo.

Sheppard remained a popular speaker. The years and ravages of fever had not dimmed his flair for the dramatic or rare rapport with both white and black audiences. He supplemented lectures with an "extravaganza of African artifacts, curios and impedimenta," most of them souvenirs of his sojourns among the BaKuba. In 1917, he donated four hundred of his finest pieces to Hampton Institute, each accompanied by a notecard detailing its provenance and purpose. He also turned his hand to writing, publishing through Hampton a series of ten-cent *True African Stories* for children, each describing an African child's passage from sin and ignorance to the light of Christian salvation. (Perhaps the strangest of the volumes was *The Girl Who Ate Her Mother,* recounting the story of N'tumba, one of the Luebo mission's earliest converts.) In 1917, Sheppard published an autobiography, *Presbyterian Pioneers in Congo.* Cobbled together from lectures and an African diary, the book offered a curiously foreshortened view of his life, ending in 1893 with Sheppard's discovery of the Kuba capital. The book made no reference to Belgian atrocities, nor to the author's harrowing days in the Zappo Zap stockade. Lucy Sheppard went unmentioned, as did all of Sheppard's missionary colleagues, save for Samuel Lapsley. At least half of the book was devoted to Lapsley's heroism, and it is his portrait, not Sheppard's, that adorns the frontispiece. At the end of his career, as at the beginning, Sheppard cast himself as faithful retainer to the great white "pathfinder."

In 1926, at the age of sixty-one, Sheppard was incapacitated by a stroke. He died a year later. His funeral attracted more than a thousand mourners. To accommodate the crowd, the service was held at Louisville's Second Presbyterian Church, a white church. It was a final affront to the racial order that Sheppard's life had both honored and mocked. Following the service, the mourners followed the cortege to the city's black cemetery, where they committed his body to segregated ground.

· FIVE ·

So Long, So Far Away

IT WAS A JOURNEY undertaken reluctantly. He scarcely knew his father. James Hughes was always away—chasing fortunes in Cuba, in Mexico, anywhere but "the States, where you have to live like a nigger with niggers." Writing decades later, the son would ponder his father's attitude. "My father hated Negroes. I think he hated himself, too, for being a Negro. He disliked all his family because they were Negroes and remained in the United States, where none of them had a chance to be much of anything but servants."

In the spring of 1919, after nearly a decade's absence, James Hughes appeared in Cleveland and announced that his son would be spending the summer with him at his ranch in Mexico. From the start, the trip went badly. As the train rolled through an Arkansas hamlet, the boy peered curiously out the window of his compartment at a knot of black men on a street corner, only to have his father cut short the reverie: "Look at the niggers." Things spiraled down from there. Mexico offered a respite from American racism, but there was no refuge from his father's badgering or the monotony of book-keeping lessons. Eventually the boy did what he would do on a few other occasions in his life, when placed in situations of intense emotional stress: he suffered a complete physical breakdown. After three weeks in the local American hospital—a stay, he noted happily, that cost his penny-pinching father twenty dollars a day—he returned to Cleveland, determined that he would never again speak to his father.

And yet here he was, a year later, on another train bound for Mexico. He had graduated from high school and wanted to attend college, and with his mother living on a waitress's wages, he had no choice but to turn to his father. As the train rattled southwest, he thought about his life, and about the strange counterpoint between his father's contempt for black people and his own dawning feelings of racial kinship. At sunset, as the train rolled across a long bridge spanning the Mississippi River, he fished a pen from his pocket and jotted a poem on an envelope:

> I've known rivers:
> I've known rivers ancient as the world and older than the
>   Flow of human blood in human veins.
>
> My soul has grown deep like the rivers.
>
> I bathed in the Euphrates when dawns were young.
> I built my hut near the Congo and it lulled me to sleep.
> I looked upon the Nile and raised the pyramids above it.
> I heard the singing of the Mississippi when Abe Lincoln
>   went down to New Orleans, and I've seen its muddy
>   bosom turn all golden in the sunset.
> I've known rivers:
> Ancient, dusky rivers.
>
> My soul has grown deep like the rivers.

After an agonizing year in Mexico, the budding poet persuaded his father to pay for him to attend Columbia, ostensibly to study mining engineering.

By the time he arrived in New York in September 1921, he was already some-thing of a local celebrity. "The Negro Speaks of Rivers" had appeared in July in *The Crisis*, the organ of the National Association for the Advance-ment of Colored People, and been immediately reprinted in *Literary Digest*, a prestigious white journal. A second poem, "Aunt Sue's Stories," was pub-lished a month later. Editors and critics queued to meet this latest star in the New Negro firmament. There was a renaissance in Harlem, and Langston Hughes would be its bard.

HUGHES WAS NOT the only African American to find his way to Harlem in the wake of World War I. Between 1915 and 1920, more than five hundred thousand black Americans abandoned the states of the old Confederacy and headed north, drawn chiefly by the promise of well-paying jobs in northern industry. Surprised white southerners tried various devices to prevent the loss of their labor force, but once the migration had begun there was no stop-ping it. Over a million and a half black southerners moved north in the 1920s, doubling and tripling the black populations of cities like Chicago, Cleveland, Detroit, Pittsburgh, and New York. The migration slowed dur-ing the Great Depression, but it swelled anew during the 1940s. By 1965, a half century after the onset of the exodus, more than ten million African Americans had relocated from the rural South to the urban North.

Needless to say, life in the promised land of the North rarely matched migrants' exaggerated expectations. Last hired and first fired, black workers were confined to the least skilled, lowest paying, most dangerous industrial jobs. While freed from the scourge of legal Jim Crow, most found them-selves confined to segregated ghettoes, where they paid exorbitant rents for overcrowded, decaying apartments and "kitchenettes." While lynchings were rare in the North, violence remained a central feature of black life, with the day-to-day violence of living in blighted, impoverished circumstances punctuated by bloody riots. In 1919 alone, more than two dozen northern cities were convulsed by race riots, the bloodiest of which, in Chicago, left thirty-eight people dead and more than five hundred injured.

Yet even admitting all the violence, drudgery, and disappointment, most black southerners experienced northern migration as a dramatic improvement in their fortunes. Black people in the North voted. They sat where they chose on trains and streetcars. They sent their children to decent public schools. Working in steel mills and stockyards, railyards and factories, they earned more in a month than most black southerners could hope to earn in a year. Perhaps most important, they no longer had to endure the petty rituals of deference and degradation that defined daily life in the South. "I just begun to feel like a man," a migrant in Chicago wrote to family members back in Hattiesburg, Mississippi. "It's a great deal of pleasure in knowing that you got some privilege. My children are going to the same school with the whites and I don't have to umble to no one. I have registered—will vote the next election and there isn't any 'yes sir' and 'no sir'—it's all yes and no and Sam and Bill."

Commentators at the time recognized the significance of the migration and speculated on its long-term consequences. "The intricate social and political problems occasioned by two dissimilar races in the United States have heretofore been deemed purely sectional matters," a writer in *The Atlantic Monthly* observed in 1923. "The Negro race was found almost entirely within the Southern states, and it was always assumed that it would probably always remain there. Now suddenly the race, moved by some widespread impulse, begins of its own volition a migration northward which may alter the entire aspect of the racial question in America." What the writer could not have foreseen is how contradictory the consequences would be. On the one hand, the appearance of black faces in previously white spaces fueled racist fears of "mongrelization." Best sellers like Madison Grant's *The Passing of the Great Race* and Lothrop Stoddard's *The Rising Tide of Color* warned that the once superior Nordic races were in danger of being swamped by inferior breeds—not only by African Americans but by hordes of swarthy immigrants from southern and eastern Europe. The reach of such ideas can be measured in a variety of ways, from the rise of a powerful eugenics movement to the rebirth of the Ku Klux Klan, a Reconstruction-era secret society that had been effectively suppressed by the federal government in the 1870s. In the realm of formal politics, concern with preserving the white character of American life expressed itself in two signature pieces of legislation, both passed in 1924: the Virginia Racial Integrity Act, which instituted the so-called one-drop rule of racial classification; and the Johnson-Reed Immigration Act, which slammed shut the "golden door" into the United States for all but a relative handful of immigrants from northern and western Europe.

On the other hand, the 1920s was a period of unprecedented racial exchange and cross-pollination. The same decade that produced "100 percent Americanism" and the one-drop rule also spawned the Charleston, *Shuffle Along* (a black musical revue that took Broadway by storm), and the new fashion of suntanning. The years of Madison Grant and the second Klan were also the years of Josephine Baker and Bill "Bojangles" Robinson, of Al Jolson and George Gershwin. It was the Jazz Age, the era of Louis Armstrong's Hot Five and the Duke Ellington Orchestra, house band at Harlem's fabled Cotton Club, where white patrons—the club did not serve black people—could watch black musicians and dancers disport themselves in a jungle decor. In the realm of literature, the decade saw the publication of a slew of white-authored books and plays on black themes: Sherwood Anderson's *Dark Laughter*, Eugene O'Neill's *Emperor Jones* and *All God's Chillun Got Wings*, Du Bose Heyward's *Porgy*, Clement Wood's *Nigger*, Ronald Firbank's *Prancing Nigger*, and Carl Van Vechten's *Nigger Heaven*, to name only a few. Most important, the 1920s spawned the Harlem Renaissance, an unprecedented outpouring of black art and literature. As Langston Hughes, one of the brightest stars of the renaissance, put it, this was "the period when the Negro was in vogue."

How are we to account for the Negro "vogue," especially in such a seemingly unpropitious time? Any answer must begin with World War I, which dealt a shattering blow to Western complacency. All of the modern West's values and achievements—science and rationality, efficiency, industrial technique, faith in progress—had seemingly reached their logical conclusion in the absurdity of trench warfare, a vast machine for slaughtering human beings. The war provoked a visceral response in the cultural realm, with writers, artists, and musicians all reacting against a civilization that had apparently mortgaged its soul in pursuit of material gain. This revulsion, in turn, sparked new interest in those "primitive" folk who had allegedly avoided modernity's spiritual blighting. In the backwash of the war, the very allegations that had long been used to demean people of color—claims about their irrationality, impulsiveness, emotionalism, passion—took on a positive hue. In historian David Lewis's words, a stigma became a state of grace.

The war's impact was amplified by deeper changes in Western, and specifically American, intellectual life, changes that recast popular understandings of race, setting the stage for the New Negro's entrance. Perhaps most important was a broad rethinking of the nature and meaning of human variety, a movement away from biological explanations of human difference toward understandings grounded in culture and environment. The change began in the discipline of anthropology and was most closely associated with Columbia University anthropologist Franz Boas and his remarkable collection of students, including Margaret Mead, Ruth Benedict, Melville Herskovits, and Zora Neale Hurston. From his earliest research among "Eskimos" in the 1880s until his death a half century later, Boas challenged prevailing ideas of fixed racial inheritance—the so-called natural limits of the racial mind. In a germinal 1894 essay, "Human Faculty as Determined by Race," Boas denied that African Americans were a "lower type" of human, arguing that observed differences in accomplishment were best explained not by biology but in terms of social and cultural factors, including the extremely prejudicial circumstances in which black people were forced to live. Needless to say, a single scholarly paper did not sweep away racial prejudice or usher in a golden age of cultural relativism. It took years for Boas's contentions to gain currency among his professional colleagues, and even longer for his insights to percolate into popular thought. (Ultimately it would take the horror of Nazism to discredit scientific racism fully.) Yet there is no denying the importance of Boas's intervention. If we today discuss human variety primarily in terms of culture rather than race, and if we evaluate different cultures in relative rather than fixed or hierarchical ways, it is in large measure due to the intellectual transformation that Boas and his students wrought.

Thanks in part to W. E. B. Du Bois, who featured Boas's work in the pages of *The Crisis*, the new anthropology was well known to the postwar generation of black writers and artists, as well as to the white publishers, patrons, and critics who promoted and reviewed their work. Its contribution to the New Negro movement can scarcely be overstated. Emerging ideas of cultural relativism legitimized difference, making it possible for black writers and artists to explore distinctive aspects of black life without apologetics or implications of inferiority. People who might previously have been dismissed as inferior or backward could now be valued on their own terms, as possessors of distinct cultures, with their own norms, values, and notions of beauty. This new impulse was institutionalized in the discipline of folklore studies, which emerged in the 1910s and 1920s, complete with its own professional society and journal, which Boas edited. Much of the material in the journal was collected by Boas's own students, who embarked to the four corners of the world—Mead to Samoa, Benedict to Japan and the American Southwest, Zora Neale Hurston to Eatonville, Florida, the all-black town in which she grew up—to catalogue the cultures of premodern folk before they were lost in modernity's relentless forward march.

The Boasian revolution was closely related to another momentous, if elusive, transformation in Western culture. If the 1893 World's Columbian Exposition marked the high tide of nineteenth-century beliefs in progress and material mastery, the years that followed brought a rising countercurrent, a growing awareness of the spiritual costs of progress, of the aridity and soullessness of the burgeoning industrial order. One of the signature attributes of this sensibility was a feeling of inauthenticity, of experiencing life at a remove, of having (as we still say today) lost touch with oneself amid the demands of daily life. Even before the coming of the Great War, Western writers and artists spoke of overcivilization, of life so constrained by culture and convention as to be sterile, decadent. There were echoes here of earlier movements, of European romanticism and American transcendentalism, yet the sheer pervasiveness of such ideas marked the early twentieth century as a cultural watershed.

Nowhere were fears of overcivilization more pronounced than in the arts. Chafing against what they saw as an exhausted, inbred tradition, a generation of writers, artists, and musicians cast about for fresh sources of inspiration. And where better to look than to those people who were ostensibly less civilized and constrained, those blessed primitives who still lived near to nature's heart? The classic example is Pablo Picasso, whose encounter with African sculpture at a 1907 exhibition in Paris revolutionized twentieth-

Job, Son of Solliman Dgiallo, High Priest of Benda in the Country of Foota, Africa.

The Redeemed Captive: Ayuba
Suleiman Diallo in London, ca. 1732.

Reverend Daniel Coker,
leader of the first American
Colonization Society
settlement in West Africa.

Engraving, published in
London, commemorating
Paul Cuffe's first voyage
to Africa. Based on a
drawing by John Pole, the
engraving shows Cuffe
and his ship *Traveller*
suspended between the
coasts of Africa and
New England.

M. R. DELANEY.

Martin Robison Delany following his commissioning as a major in the Union Army, 1865.

Robert Campbell, Delany's companion in the Niger Valley Exploring Party, 1859–60.

Bishop Henry McNeil Turner, leader of the late nineteenth-century back-to-Africa movement.

Reverend Charles Spencer Smith, in full colonial regalia, with "his adopted family of Dwalla children," Cameroon, 1895.

Mundele Ndom: William Sheppard—"the black man in white clothes"—poses with BaKuba men.

"The incorruptible Kodak": Photographs like this one, taken by an employee of the American Presbyterian Congo Mission, confirmed allegations of atrocities in King Leopold's Congo Free State.

Langston Hughes as a child.

The Big Sea: Hughes
in Senegal, 1966.

The busboy poet: Hughes following his "discovery" by Vachel Lindsay
in the Wardman Park Hotel, Washington, D.C., 1925.

Portrait of George Schuyler
by Carl Van Vechten

"In the Bush": A pith-helmeted
W.E.B. Du Bois in a Liberian village, 1924.

Du Bois receiving an honorary degree from the
University of Ghana on his ninety-fifth birthday, February, 1963.
He accepted Ghanaian citizenship the same day.

Richard Wright, left, sharing a laugh with George and Dorothy Padmore.

The Outsider:
Richard Wright in 1953.

"American Daughter": Era Bell
Thompson on her graduation from
high school in Bismarck, North
Dakota, 1924.

W. Alphaeus Hunton remanded to
custody after refusing to name donors
to the Civil Rights Congress' Bail
Fund, 1951. His companion is novelist
Dashiell Hammett, the Fund's
chairman.

Maya Angelou, ca. 1970,
following her return from Ghana.

Prime Minister Kwame Nkrumah and Shirley Graham Du Bois at the state
funeral of W.E.B. Du Bois, Accra, Ghana, August, 1963.

Muhammad Ali and Malcolm X at the United Nations in early March, 1964, just a few days before Malcolm broke with the Nation of Islam. They are accompanied by Nigerian Ambassador S.O. Adebo and Ali's brother, Rudolph Clay.

Ghanaian children play on a toppled statue of Nkrumah a few days after the 1966 coup.

Howard French in Kinshasa, 1997

"Unaccompanied" children at a UNICEF refugee camp at Tingi Tingi, Zaire, 1997, a few days before the camp was overrun by advancing rebels. International investigators later uncovered mass graves in the area.

The original home of Fourah Bay College, Freetown, Sierra Leone.
The building, with roof beams hewn from the timbers of captured slave ships,
was burned and gutted during the civil war.

The slave fortress on Bunce Island today.

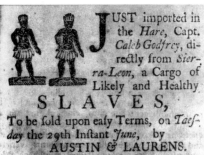

JUST imported in the *Hare*, Capt. *Caleb Godfrey*, directly from *Sierra-Leon*, a Cargo of Likely and Healthy SLAVES, To be fold upon eafy Terms, on *Tuefday* the 29th Inftant *June*, by AUSTIN & LAURENS.

Notice of a slave auction, *South Carolina Gazette*, June 17, 1756. The sale included the child Priscilla.

Thomalind Martin Polite, Priscilla's great-great-great-great-great granddaughter, Sierra Leone, 2005.

century painting and plastic arts. The same quest for authenticity and immediacy propelled Paul Gauguin's flight to Tahiti and Antonín Dvořák's appropriation of African American spirituals in his luminous New World Symphony. Just as scientists today search the world's shrinking rain forests for unknown plants from which to produce new drugs to cure disease, European artists a century ago turned to "primitive" people in search of balm for a diseased soul.

Americans also looked to the folk as the remedy to a rootless, atomized age. In the years before the New Negro's arrival, the U.S. literary scene experienced enthusiasms for Irish, Russian, even Bengali writing, all of which purportedly possessed an earthiness and soul lacking in Anglo-American letters. The early twentieth century also marked a pivotal chapter in America's strange romance with Native Americans, who, having been conquered and dispossessed, could now safely be embraced as spiritual mentors. Charlotte Osgood Mason, the Park Avenue heiress who later served as a patron to Langston Hughes and Zora Neale Hurston, spent the 1910s pursuing Native Americans' "intuitive" spirit. Mabel Dodge Luhan, hostess of New York's most celebrated literary salon, actually moved to New Mexico, the better to connect with the "tribal oversoul."

Set against this backdrop, the Harlem Renaissance seems not just predictable but well-nigh inevitable. For who was more earthy, more irrepressible, more natural than the Negro? "What American literature decidedly needs at this moment is color, music, gusto, the free expression of gay or desperate moods," declared Carl Van Doren, literary editor of *Century* magazine and one of the first to herald what would become the New Negro movement. "If the Negroes are not in a position to contribute these items, I do not know what Americans are." A critic for *The Nation*, discussing a performance by Bill "Bojangles" Robinson, made the same claim about dance. Bojangles, the reviewer opined, offered Americans "the great desideratum of modern art, a clean shortcut to areas of enjoyment long closed to us by the accumulated rubbish of the culture route." Philanthropist and art collector Albert C. Barnes, a patron of the New Negro movement, offered perhaps the fullest statement of the argument. "The white man in the mass cannot compete with the Negro in spiritual endowment," he wrote. "Many centuries have attenuated his original gifts and have made his mind dominate his spirit. . . . The requirements for practical efficiency in a world alien to his spirit have worn thin his religion and devitalized his art. His art and his life are no longer one and the same as they were in primitive man." What was needed, Barnes concluded, was a kind of "working alliance" between whites and blacks, reuniting mind and body, reason and soul, in a new America.

Today, more than eighty years later, black music, art, and literature are so integral to our understanding of American culture that it takes an effort of imagination to understand just how revolutionary these ideas were in their time. The vast American exhibition at the 1893 World's Columbian Exposition had not included a single African American product or artifact; it simply never occurred to organizers that black people had contributed meaningfully to American civilization. For them, as for most white Americans, the Negro was a cultural foundling, a figure devoid of accomplishment or civilization beyond what had rubbed off from whites. A generation later, the Negro was embraced, at least in artistic and literary circles, as an evangel, whose message would heal a wounded world.

As if all this were not precondition enough, the period around the First World War was also the moment when Americans discovered Sigmund Freud. Freud only visited the United States one time and he loathed it, but Americans loved him. His understanding of personality as a continuous struggle between id (representing the primal and instinctual) and superego (representing culture and repression) dovetailed perfectly with the era's fears about overcivilization. To Freud's chagrin, it was in the United States that his books sold best and his influence was greatest, nowhere more than in New York City, which by 1929 boasted more than five hundred Freudian analysts. (Freud even had a dramatic impact on the embryonic advertising profession, that quintessentially American industry, where the economy of desire met the marketplace: Edward Bernays, whose 1928 book, *Propaganda*, was the bible of the American advertising profession, was the doctor's nephew.) While Freud had very little to say on the subject of race—his patients, after all, were chiefly bourgeois women from Vienna—his theory was quickly racialized by Americans, with Negroes, inevitably, cast in the role of the id. Mapped onto American society, Freudian theory lent a scientific imprimatur to what artists and critics were already saying: that white civilization had been crippled by repression; that black people retained some privileged access to the primal, instinctive sources of behavior; that the psychic balance of society could somehow be restored by tapping back into blacks' spiritual and emotional vitality.

Historians today no longer believe in Clio, the muse whom the Greeks believed directed the course of history. But there are moments in human experience at which the convergence of historical forces seems so orchestrated as to appear almost purposeful. The Harlem Renaissance offers a case in point. A multitude of circumstances converged in the first decades of the twentieth century: revolutions in literature, art, and the social sciences; a calamitous war; a mass migration of African Americans from the rural South to the urban North. And all these developments came to a point in a single place. New York City was headquarters of the new anthropology and of Freudian psychology. It was home to the nation's leading publishing houses and to a dizzying array of literary journals. It was the theatrical and artistic capital of the nation, and increasingly of the world. Most important, New York was home to Harlem, the "Mecca of the New Negro." A product of historical accident, of a real-estate slump that compelled developers to sell to blacks housing built for whites, Harlem attracted migrants from every corner of the black world. By the end of the 1920s, this city within a city boasted nearly a quarter of a million inhabitants, making it not simply the largest black settlement in the United States but the largest black settlement in human history up to that time. Harlem was something new under the sun, a fit birthplace for a New Negro.

THE ARTISTS AND WRITERS associated with the New Negro movement came to Harlem by many pathways. Countee Cullen was a New Yorker, but Claude McKay hailed from Jamaica, where he had worked as a police constable. Nella Larsen came from Chicago by way of Denmark. Wallace Thurman had worked as a postal clerk in Los Angeles alongside Arna Bontemps. Zora Neale Hurston came from Florida, shaving a decade off her age en route, the better to capitalize on the enthusiasm for young black artists.

Richard Bruce Nugent and Rudolph Fisher both came from Washington, D.C.; Nugent attended art school, while Fisher graduated from Brown. Jesse Fausset came from a blue-blooded family in Philadelphia, whose members spoke French at dinner. Aaron Douglas hailed from Kansas. Yet no one followed a more circuitous course than James Langston Hughes.

Hughes was born in Joplin, Missouri, in February 1902. Like the subjects of so many of his later poems, he was of mixed racial origin. On his maternal side, he traced his descent to a white Virginia planter, who had scandalized slaveholding society by living as man and wife with a former slave of African and Indian descent. The couple's children, who carried their mother's surname, all grew up to be prominent political leaders, including the poet's namesake, John Mercer Langston, who served in the U.S. House of Representatives. John's older brother, Charles, Hughes's grandfather, never held political office, but he was one of the most prominent black men in Kansas, serving as a newspaper editor and grand master of the state's black Masonic fraternity. In the 1860s, Charles, whose first wife had died, married Mary Leary, a freeborn woman of African and Indian descent, whose first husband had died with John Brown at Harper's Ferry. The couple's political convictions were reflected in the names they gave their children, including Nat Turner, after the slave revolutionary, and Dessalines, after the great Haitian general. Carrie, Langston's mother, was the youngest.

Hughes inherited a proud pedigree from his maternal forebears, but little else. When Charles Langston died in 1892, he left no estate. Carrie, who had just completed high school, had to relinquish her dream of attending college, a setback that doubtless contributed to her perpetual sense of grievance. Her disposition was not improved by her 1898 marriage to James Hughes. Like the Langstons, Hughes was a product of sexual transgression: both his grandfathers were southern white men, one of them a slave trader. In his case, however, the alchemy of black and white produced a very different temperament. The noblesse oblige and threadbare respectability that prevailed in the Langston household had been replaced in James Hughes's case by restless ambition, crass materialism and, if his son is to be believed, a frank contempt for black people. By the time he married Carrie he had already pursued a half dozen professions, including teacher, surveyor, law clerk, homesteader, store owner, and stenographer. By the time Langston was born he was on the move again, heading first to Cuba and then to Mexico, leaving wife and child behind.

Though he rarely spoke of it, Hughes had a lonely and impoverished childhood, made all the more confusing by his parents' periodic, always abortive, reunions. For the most part, he was raised by his maternal grandmother, Mary Leary Langston, in Lawrence, Kansas, with his increasingly self-absorbed mother occasionally reappearing to reclaim him. In addition to Joplin and Lawrence, Hughes spent parts of his childhood in Buffalo, Colorado Springs, Mexico City (during one of his parents' reunions), rural Indiana, Kansas City, and Topeka, where his mother, in an odd prequel to the *Brown v. the Board of Education of Topeka* case of 1954, successfully fought to enroll him at the local white school. When his grandmother died in 1914, Hughes went to live with his mother in Lincoln, Illinois. They later moved to Cleveland, where he attended high school.

Like so many other lonely children, Hughes found a refuge in books; as he put it, he "believed in books more than in people." His "earliest memories of written words" were of the Bible and of the work of W. E. B. Du Bois, whose sonorous evocations of black "soul" echoed through several of his early poems. By his teenage years, Hughes's tastes had gravitated in more democratic directions. He was well versed in the poetry of Paul Lawrence Dunbar, whose use of Negro dialect had ignited a debate that would flare anew in the 1920s. He devoured the work of Carl Sandburg, bard of the common man, and Vachel Lindsay, whose epic poem, "The Congo: A Study of the Negro Race," a blackface performance piece full of drums and bellowing and severed hands, had shocked American audiences in the last days before World War I. (Lindsay would later claim to have "discovered" Hughes, based on a 1924 encounter in a restaurant, where Langston was working as a busboy.) He admired Mark Twain, whose penchant for sly satire and comic reversal would resurface in some of his own fiction. His most enduring loyalty was probably to Walt Whitman, that most American of American poets, a man who glimpsed beauty in the same humble places where Hughes would find it.

All the pain and perplexity of Hughes's childhood was registered in the personality of the adult, producing the strange antinomies of his character: his legendary bonhomie and his abiding loneliness, his desperate need to belong and his extraordinary emotional reserve. Though he had sexual encounters with both men and women, he seems never to have had a sustained romantic relationship. While openness and accessibility are the hallmarks of his poetry, Hughes himself remained an enigma, even to those who knew him best. Wallace Thurman, his close friend and collaborator, despaired of ever understanding him. "You are in the final analysis the most consarned and diabolical creature, to say nothing of being either the most egregiously simple or excessively complex person I know," he complained in 1929. In his novel *Infants of the Spring*, published three years later, Thurman created a "close-mouthed and cagey" character, Tony Crews, modeled on Hughes, of whom he wrote: "He fended off every attempt to probe into his inner self and did this with such an unconscious and naïve air that the prober soon came to one of two conclusions: Either he had no depth whatsoever, or else he was too deep for plumbing by ordinary mortals."

The peculiarities of his upbringing also left a deep, if paradoxical imprint on Hughes's racial identity. While his father despised black people, his grandmother was a race woman, who cherished her membership in one of black America's most celebrated families. Yet her race pride was of a distinctly aristocratic stripe, which became more pronounced as the family's fortunes declined. She refused to allow her grandson to play with other children, and strictly forbade the singing of spirituals, which she regarded as common. Denied membership in the local white Presbyterian church, she chose not to attend church at all rather than to join a black church. Hughes's first brushes with the lower-class folk that he would celebrate in his poetry were fleeting, stolen affairs. He heard snatches of the blues during a childhood visit to Kansas City. He first heard black preaching while lodged with neighbors following his grandmother's death. During his high school years in Cleveland, he worked as a soda jerk, rubbing elbows with migrants fresh from the South. While his mother bemoaned the migrants' arrival, Langston thrilled to their music, their verbal jousting, "the thunderclaps of their laughter."

It is difficult to psychoanalyze the living, let alone the dead, but it seems reasonable to suppose that Hughes's reverence for common black folk first surfaced as a kind of adolescent rebellion against his own family, against both his father's contempt and his grandmother and mother's sniffing superiority. The people whom they had rejected would become the cornerstone of his art. He would celebrate the majesty of Negroes' music, the curious power of their speech, the lyric grace of their bodies, forging through words the sense of identity and kinship that he had never found in his own family. While obviously a product of unique circumstances, this sensibility would prove a perfect qualification for membership in the New Negro movement, many of whose adherents were self-consciously rebelling against the artistic inhibitions and crabbed respectability of their older, more bourgeois forebears. In his work in *Fire!*, a short-lived journal for the "younger generation" of black writers, and his germinal 1925 essay "The Negro Artist and the Racial Mountain," Hughes would lash out at black elders who had so internalized white cultural and aesthetic judgments that they were no longer able "to catch a glimmer of their own beauty."

Yet however heartfelt his identification with the Negro, Hughes's perspective remained peculiarly that of an outsider. In contrast to Zora Neale Hurston, his one-time collaborator and a woman who seemingly embodied all the attributes of the "low-down folk" she described in her work, Hughes remained acutely conscious of the distance between himself and his subjects. The author of "Jazzonia," the man who so brilliantly captured the rhythms and sensibility of jazz in words, was embarrassingly unmusical himself. The poet who painted the "Night-dark girl of the swaying hips" in "Nude Young Dancer" was so physically self-conscious that he rarely stepped onto a dance floor. Even as critics hailed him as the poet laureate of the Negro race—or "poet low-rate," as one black critic huffed—Hughes remained the outsider looking in.

In his early poems like "Negro," Hughes endeavored to close the gulf, using first-person voice and present tense to assert his racial membership.

> I am a Negro:
>> Black as the night is black,
>> Black like the depths of my Africa. . . .
>> I am a Negro. . . .

In "Aunt Sue's Stories" he went even further, creating an alternate racial family for himself. Written during that grim year in Mexico, the poem conjured an aging black woman, clutching a "brown faced child to her bosom." Aunt Sue, he began, "has a head full of stories. / Aunt Sue has a whole heart full of stories."

> And the dark-faced child, listening,
> Knows that Aunt Sue's stories are real stories.
> He knows that Aunt Sue
> Never got her stories out of any book at all,
> But that they came
> Right out of her own life.

The irony, of course, is that Hughes had no Aunt Sue. This paean to family and folk was written by a man who possessed no such roots himself, a man who acquired his own childhood stories from books.

Had Hughes simply continued to mine this vein, his literary reputation would be secure. But he did much more. Perhaps it was moving to New York, or perhaps just escaping the shadow of his family, but the insistence on racial identity in his early poems was soon replaced by something richer and more ambiguous, an appreciation, even embrace, of his status as both insider and outsider. In poems like "Nude Young Dancer" or "The Weary Blues" (also the title of his first book), the voice is not that of the lithe dancer or of the drowsy pianist but of the poet himself, confronting a beauty that he recognizes but can never fully comprehend or possess. The keynote of such works is not celebration but poignancy, the sweet sadness of unconsummated desire. They are marvelous creations, these poems, suggestive at once of the wry wisdom of an old man and of a wounded, wondrous child, gazing out at black life from the window of a train.

BY THE TIME Hughes arrived, the Harlem Renaissance had already commenced. Claude McKay's defiant sonnet, "If We Must Die," cited by most historians as the opening salvo of the movement, was published in the Red

Summer of 1919. The years that followed brought Eugene O'Neill's *Emperor Jones* and the fabulous success of *Shuffle Along.* As Hughes packed for Columbia, novelist Jean Toomer was teaching school on a plantation outside Sparta, Georgia, from which experience would come *Cane,* his lyrical "swansong" to a "song-lit race of slaves." As Alain Locke, self-proclaimed majordomo of the movement, put it, a new race was entering modernity, singing as it came.

Reflecting back on the renaissance in his 1940 autobiography, *The Big Sea,* Hughes would deliberately distance himself from the era's enthusiasm, posing instead as the bemused bystander. "I had a swell time while it lasted," he declared in an oft-quoted passage. "But I thought it wouldn't last long. For how could a large and enthusiastic number of people be crazy about Negroes forever? But some Harlemites thought the millennium had come. They thought the race problem had at last been solved through Art plus Gladys Bentley. They were sure the New Negro would lead a new life from then on in green pastures of tolerance. . . . I don't know what made any Negroes think that, except that they were mostly intellectuals doing the thinking. The ordinary Negroes hadn't heard of the Negro Renaissance. And if they had, it hadn't raised their wages any."

It was a characteristic pose, but it was also disingenuous. Looking back from the perspective of 1940, after a decade of depression and political upheaval, Hughes (and many other black writers and artists) could scarcely help but feel sheepish about the excesses and exaggerated expectations of the New Negro movement. At the time, however, he was a fully paid-up member. Indeed, one would be hard pressed to find any individual whose work better captured the spirit of the age: the yearning for authentic experience; the contempt for civilized hypocrisy; the valorization of black soul.

Hughes also fully partook of the age's fascination with Africa. In an era in which black people were supposed to possess a depth and vitality lacking in whites, it was inevitable that Africa would attract new interest. Africa was the taproot, the source of the Negroes' distinct racial gifts. Evidence of this enthusiasm was everywhere in the 1920s, from the mounting of major exhibitions of African art in European and American museums to the career of Josephine Baker, whose bare-breasted "danse sauvage" made her the toast of

Paris. For the better part of a century, the United States and Europe had sent missionaries to Africa to save the benighted primitives. In the artistic and literary climate of the postwar world, it increasingly seemed that Africans might save the United States and Europe.

The change in Western imaginings of Africa was neatly encapsulated in the history of a book that proved a best seller on both sides of the Atlantic, *Anthologie Nègre*, published in France in 1921 and later translated and published in the United States as *The African Saga*. A collection of African stories and folktales, the book was compiled by Blaise Cendrars, a Swiss-French avante-garde poet and novelist and prominent member of the Lost Generation of writers gathered in postwar Paris. Cendrars presented the stories as a compendium of traditional wisdom, to redeem an exhausted, soulless Western civilization. (Cendrars had seen the horrors of modern civilization close up, having lost his right arm in the trenches of the western front.) The most striking feature of the stories, however, is their origin. Cendrars did not collect them himself—sub-Saharan Africa was one of the few places in the world to which he did not travel—nor were they drawn from black-authored texts. Instead, they were culled from European travel accounts, most of them by missionaries. It is hard to imagine a clearer example of what historians of science call a paradigm shift, the process by which the same data comes to be interpreted in radically new ways. The same stories that had been offered in the late nineteenth century as proof of Africans' ignorance and quaint superstition were adduced a generation later as proof of their insight and profound wisdom.

Inevitably, Africa became a touchstone of the black arts movement of the 1920s. The most obvious example is Countee Cullen's poem "Heritage," with its poignant, double-edged interrogatory: "What is Africa to me?" But Africa also suffused the critical essays of Alain Locke, the graphic art of Aaron Douglas, the furious debate on the possibilities and perils of jazz music. ("Does Jazz Put the Sin in Syncopation?," an essay published in *The Ladies' Home Journal*, offers a classic example of the latter debate.) Jean Toomer's *Cane* was set in Georgia, but Africa suffused the book; as Toomer put it, "The Dixie Pike has grown from a goat path in Africa." In "Black Death," one of Zora Neale Hurston's first short stories, the sight of a jack-o'-lantern was enough to send a character careening back to Africa:

" . . . [T]hree hundred years of America passed like the mist of morning. Africa reached out its dark hand and claimed its own. Drums. Tom, Tom, Tom, Tom, Tom, Tom beat in her ears. Strange demons seized her. Witch doctors danced before her . . ."

Needless to say, different individuals conceived of African Americans' relationship to Africa in different ways. Though haunted by the continent, Cullen explicitly rejected it as an artistic source, staking his lineage on language rather than race. African American poets, he wrote, "had more to gain from the rich background of English and American poetry than from any nebulous atavistic yearnings toward an African heritage." Critic Alain Locke developed an elaborate theory of African classicism, a tradition of discipline and control that contrasted with the spontaneity and exuberance of African American art. (Locke tried to convert Langston Hughes to his view, but Hughes was having none of it; if it was "so complex" to be primitive, he quipped, "one had almost as well be civilized.") Suggestions that African traditions might be mined as a source of inspiration and fresh motifs for classical art and music were dismissed with contempt by Zora Neale Hurston, who argued that such refinement simply killed the original, like pouring hot water on flowers. What African Americans really needed to do, she said, was to import some untutored Africans to remind them how to sing and dance properly. Journalist George Schuyler dismissed the whole business. The current enthusiasm for authentic "Negro Art," he argued, served only to reassure "the Nordics" that the Negro was a savage, that "even when he appears to be civilized, it is only necessary to beat a tom tom or wave a rabbit's foot and he is ready to strip off his Hart Shaffner & Marx suit, grab a spear and ride off wild-eyed on the back of a crocodile."

Hughes shared the era's fascination with Africa, invoking the continent in several of his early poems. For the most part, he hewed to the prevailing neoromantic view of Africa as racial source, wellspring of a primal black vitality still carried in the "blood" of African Americans. The best example— surely not the best poem—was "Danse Africaine," written shortly after his arrival in New York City:

The low beating of the tom-toms,
The slow beating of the tom-toms,

Low . . . slow

Slow . . . low—

Stirs your blood.

Dance!

"Poem [1]," published a year later, explored similar themes. Subtitled "For the Portrait of an African Boy after the Manner of Gauguin," the poem contrasted African "soul" with the cold, hard materialism of Western civilization.

All the tom-toms of the jungles beat in my blood,

And all the wild hot moons of the jungles shine in my

soul.

I am afraid of this civilization—

So hard,

So strong,

So cold.

Like so many other African American travelers to Africa, Langston Hughes had explored the continent in his imagination long before he set sail.

The recurring image of tom-toms is worth pondering. Tom-toms were everywhere in the Harlem Renaissance, usually as symbols of racial authenticity, the thumping lifeblood of a race. Yet when viewed historically, the trope is less a symbol of authenticity than of the continuing, paradoxical engagement of African Americans with Western discourses of race. The term "tom-tom" was originally imported into the English language from Urdu during the British colonization of India, though by the late nineteenth century the term was usually used in reference to Africa. Tom-toms were ubiquitous in the work of H. M. Stanley and other Dark Continent travel writers, symbolizing savagery or imminent war. The association of tom-toms with the Negro race was reinforced at the 1893 World's Columbian Exposition, where millions of visitors were entertained by Dahomean drummers in an ersatz African village. Among those who visited the Dahomean exhibition was Hughes's literary hero, Vachel Lindsay, who incorporated drums into his celebrated 1914 poem, "The Congo." Whether Hughes ever saw Lindsay perform his blackface epic is not clear, but he certainly saw O'Neill's *The Emperor Jones*, which gave the equation of race and tom-toms an additional Freudian gloss. Throughout the play, tom-toms sound at a steady seventy-two beats per minute, the rate of a human heartbeat, growing in volume as Jones (famously portrayed by Charles Gilpin in the 1920 New York premiere) was driven into the jungle and slowly stripped of his clothing and his sanity. All of which is to say that when Hughes invoked tom-toms in his early poetry, he was participating in a long Western tradition—a tradition that would be carried into the next generation by Tarzan movies and the *Ramar of the Jungle* serial.

WHAT ULTIMATELY DISTINGUISHED Hughes from most of his contemporaries was not his stereotypical ideas about Africa but the fact that he actually went there. After an undistinguished year at Columbia, he quit school and set out to see the world, just as his literary mentors—Whitman, Twain, Lindsay, Sandburg—had done before him. After working for a time on a Staten Island produce farm, he acquired sailor's papers and secured a berth on a ship. Unfortunately, the ship onto which he signed was a derelict, moored up the Hudson along with other surplus vessels belonging to the wartime Shipping Board. Hughes spent a lonely winter on the frozen river, performing odd jobs and gambling with other sailors stranded on the ghost fleet. In his free time, he wrote poetry and read fiction, including Conrad's *Heart of Darkness*. Finally, in the early summer of 1923, he secured a berth on a real freighter, the *West Hesseltine*, bound for West Africa.

As the ship cleared the lighthouse at Sandy Hook, Hughes looked back at the American shore, aflame in the sunset, and reflected on his life. Moved by an impulse he did not fully understand, he went below and fetched a crate of books, which, in the haste of his departure, was virtually the only thing he had brought with him. Standing on the fantail, he consigned the books, one by one, to the deep, watching each flutter in the breeze and disappear in the ship's wake. (In an early draft of *The Big Sea*, though not in the final version, Hughes confessed to being unable to part with one book: Whitman's *Leaves of Grass.*) "It was like throwing a million bricks into the sea," he wrote, a symbolic jettisoning of the pain and perplexity of his childhood, the confusion of being black in a white country, the debilitating feeling of experiencing life at a distance. There would be no need of books where he was bound. Africa was the "real thing, to be touched and seen, not merely read about in a book."

In years to come, Hughes would offer different accounts of his African journey. The romantic rendering of black bodies in *The Big Sea*—"the bare, pointed breasts of women in the marketplace," "the rippling muscles of men loading palm oil and cocoa beans"—bore little relationship to the sentiments he expressed at the time. "You should see the clothes they wear here," he told his mother, in a letter written after the ship first made landfall in Dakar. "[E]verything from overcoats to nothing. I have laughed until I can't. No two people dress alike. . . . It's a scream." Both versions differed from an unpublished 1925 autobiographical fragment, "L'Histoire De Ma Vie," prepared at the behest of Carl Van Vechten, who was writing the foreword of *The Weary Blues*, Hughes's first book of poetry. "It was a gorgeous trip," he wrote, striking the pose of vagabond poet—"a ship full of young life touching the edges of a dark, living land."

The broad outlines of the trip are known. The *West Hesseltine*—in *The Big Sea*, Hughes called it the S.S. *Malone*—set out on June 13, 1923, and returned in late October, more than five months later. The forty-man crew—as drunken and dissolute a lot as ever sailed the ocean, by Hughes's account—included a few men of color, including Hughes, a pair of Puerto Rican stewards, and George, a dark-skinned, blues-singing pantryman from Kentucky, who had left his career as valet to a female impersonator to go to sea. A fat Dutch captain, a figure straight from the *Katzenjammer Kids*, presided over the motley crew. The ship also carried six passengers, including five white missionaries bound for the Congo, a timorous bunch who watched the crew's dissolution with ill-concealed horror. The final passenger was a black tailor, a follower of Marcus Garvey, bound for Lagos, where he hoped to open a school and business. While the "missionaries carried Bibles and hymnbooks," the Garveyite carried "bolts of cloth, shears, and tailoring tools." He "had long worshipped Africa from afar and . . . had a theory of civilization all his own," Hughes recalled. "He thought that if he could just teach the Africans to wear proper clothes, coats and pants, they would be brought forward a long way toward the standards of our world."

In Freetown, the ship added a hundred Kru men and boys to its complement, in keeping with local custom and still prevalent ideas about the dangers to white people of working in the African sun. The Kru worked the ship for the duration of its stay on the coast, loading and unloading cargo, swabbing decks and polishing brass, cooking and cleaning for crew and passengers. Kru men earned just two shillings per day, a fraction of what Hughes, the lowest-paid crew member, earned; Kru children, two of whom assumed the poet's messmate duties, worked for free. At the close of each workday, the Kru showered naked beneath a saltwater hose on the afterdeck, a practice that naturally horrified the missionaries. "The Africans were very polite, however—more so than the Nordics—and, respecting the missionaries, they turned their backs and hid their sex between their legs, evidently not realizing it then stuck out behind." Whatever discomfort he himself felt, Hughes got over it quickly, and several of the Kru men became good friends. For him, as for generations of Western travelers to West Africa, the Kru played the role of cultural interpreters, explaining many things he might otherwise have misunderstood or overlooked completely. It was one of the Kru men, probably his friend Tom Pey, who first explained to the disconcerted poet why Africans regarded him as a "white man."

Over the course of three months, the *West Hesseltine* visited more than thirty ports, from Dakar in French Senegal to Luanda in Portuguese Angola. Some were major coastal cities; others were flyblown outposts carved from the jungle. (At Boma, eighty miles up the Congo River, the ship tied not to a dock but to a massive baobab tree, conceivably the same tree on which missionary William Sheppard had carved his initials a generation before.) Hughes described several of the stops in "Ships, Sea and Africa," an impressionistic prose poem published in *The Crisis*. The piece was essentially a litany of exotic images: the "billowing robes" of "Muhammedans"; villages "hidden in deep cocoanut groves"; surfboats filled with "black naked paddlers, their superbly muscled bodies, damp with sea-spray, glistening in the sunshine." Most of the stops were too brief to allow exploring, and on those occasions when Hughes and his shipmates did get shore leave they made straight for bars and brothels. Describing the visit to Carl Van Vechten two years later, Hughes remembered "the vile houses of rottening women in Lagos" and the "millions of whiskey bottles" bobbing in the ship's wake, but such images did not appear in "Ships, Sea and Africa," which rendered the continent as an enchanted land.

In his two surviving letters from the journey and in most of his statements after returning, Hughes described the voyage as "a delightful trip," full of novel sights and colorful incident. "Old sailors" described the West African run as "the worst trip in the world," he told Van Vechten. "But for me it wasn't. For me it was the 'Great Adventure.'" Only rarely did he allow a glimpse of deeper emotions. In one British colony, he was befriended by a mulatto boy, Edward, the offspring of an African mother and a white merchant banker, who had since returned to England. Edward and his mother were no longer welcome in the white compound in which they had lived; at the same time, they were ostracized by other Africans. The youth took to Hughes, peppering him with questions: "Could we take him away with us? Was it true that in America the black people were friendly to the mulatto people?" Hughes had little to offer in response, besides his address and the suggestion that he write. One letter did arrive, but it went unanswered. "I have a way of not answering letters when I don't know what to say," the poet confessed. Years later, he would craft the episode into a short story, "African Morning."

Part of what made the episode so heartrending to Hughes was his sense of identification with the boy, not only as a man of mixed descent himself but also as an individual searching for a sense of identity and home. Traveling to Africa was supposed to have resolved the problem. "Africa!" he had cheered, when the "dust-green hills" of the continent first materialized on the eastern horizon. "My Africa, Motherland of the Negro peoples! And me a Negro!" But the resolution he sought eluded him. To borrow a phrase from contemporary novelist Thomas Wolfe, Hughes was discovering that "you can't go home again." He had crossed the ocean, jettisoned his books, penned poems about palm trees and tom-toms, yet he remained a stranger, unable to bridge the great historical chasm that separated him and other African Americans from Africa.

It was an unsettling predicament, at once familiar and radically new. Nineteenth-century African American visitors to Africa had obviously experienced their own feelings of dislocation and disillusionment, but they had traveled under different auspices, with different, less personal, expectations. As Tom Pey, who had seen African Americans come and go, put it, they came "mostly as missionaries, to teach us something, since they think we know nothing." Even a secular black nationalist like Martin Delany assumed the mantle of missionary in Africa, projecting a great black nation-state, enriched by modern education, science, commercial agriculture, and other "Mechanical and Industrial Occupations." Hughes, living on the other side of the great intellectual revolution of the early twentieth century, came not to share the blessings of modern civilization but to flee them, to escape the ambiguity of black life in America and reclaim a better, truer self. But Africa had rebuffed him, as it would rebuff other visitors who presumed to claim it as their own.

Innumerable African American travelers in Africa have experienced such moments of disillusionment, moments bringing them face-to-face with Africa's unfamiliarity and their own painful Americanness. Some have responded with resignation, others with rage. Hughes responded, characteristically, by translating alienation into art. Though Africans' refusal to accept him "hurt me a lot," it also suited him, placing him in the same position of loving outsider that he occupied in relation to the African American folk he had long celebrated in his poetry. Probably the best example is "Burutu Moon," an impressionistic account of a village on the Niger Delta, published in *The Crisis*. Walking amid thatched huts and mango trees under a low moon, Hughes heard the sound of drums, the thumping tom-toms he had conjured so often in his poetry. It was "the drums of Omali," his guide explained. When Hughes asked to see them he was politely but firmly rebuffed: the ceremony was not for the eyes of a "white man." "I climbed the straight ladder back to the deck of my ship," the essay concluded. "Far off, at the edge of the clearing, over against the forest, I heard the drums of Omali, the Ju-ju. Above, the moon was like a gold-ripe fruit in heaven, a gold-ripe fruit too sweet for the taste of man."

Hughes struck the same wistful tone in a quartet of short stories, written in 1926, shortly after his enrollment at Lincoln University. The stories, re-counting the experiences of the crew of the *West Ilana*, a freighter obviously based on the *West Hesseltine*, "plowed warmer, more sensual waters than he had ever sailed before," as the poet's biographer Arnold Rampersad has noted. All turned on the inability of "civilized" Westerners, white and black, ever fully to possess Africa, which Hughes personified as a luscious but elu-sive black woman. In "Bodies in the Moonlight," for example, two ship-mates, one plainly based on Hughes himself, vainly vied for the affections of a strangely enigmatic African woman, revealingly named Numina, or spirit. In "Luani of the Jungle," the bedazzled Westerner was a French poet, who had fallen under the spell of a West African student named Luani. Again and again, the Frenchman tried to leave her, but each time he returned. "I write poems about her and destroy them," he explained to the story's narrator. "I leave her and I come back. I do not know why. I'm like a madman and she's the soul of her jungles, quiet and terrible, beautiful and dangerous, fascinat-ing and death-like. I'm leaving her again, but I know I'll come back . . . I know I'll come back."

In such works Hughes expressed and resolved his conflicted feelings about Africa, fusing hurt and hope, reverence and wry resignation into art. Over the next few years, that resolution would be sorely tested, as Hughes struggled to adapt himself to the demands and expectations of a forceful new patron.

A PARK AVENUE HEIRESS, Charlotte Mason epitomized the early-twentieth-century American search for authentic experience and primitive vitalism. Her late husband, Rufus Osgood Mason, was a pioneer in the field of "psychical" research, publishing books on such topics as hypnotism, spir-itualism, and the "subliminal self." Charlotte shared his psychical interests, but she devoted most of her energy to "primitive" peoples, whom she be-lieved retained access to reservoirs of spirit and harmony lost to modern man. Prior to World War I, her interest focused chiefly on Indians: she un-derwrote the first collection of Native American music, and even lived for a time among Plains Indians herself. Initially, she disdained African Americans as too tainted by white civilization to be interesting, but in the 1920s she was swept up in the Negro vogue. Her initial plan, conveyed to her in a "mystical vision," was to establish a "Harlem Museum of African Art," a "great bridge reaching from Harlem to the heart of Africa, across which the Negro world, that our white United States had done everything to annihilate, should see the flaming pathway . . . and recover the treasure their people had had in the beginning of African life on the earth." When that plan did not materialize, she set her sights more modestly, offering herself instead as a financial patron and spiritual counselor to young Negro writers. Through the offices of Alain Locke, whom she met at a lecture on African art, she acquired two promising protégés: Langston Hughes and Zora Neale Hurston.

For historians and literary scholars, Mrs. Mason (or Godmother, as she insisted on being called) has come to symbolize all the unsettling aspects of the 1920s Negro vogue: paternalism, decadence, exoticism. According to Hurston, Mason sat in a "throne-like chair" and ate caviar and capon while her clients sat "on footstools at her feet" and regaled her with "the raucous sayings and doings of the Negroes farthest down," those who were "utterly sincere in living." Yet Mason's support clearly served Hughes. Most obvious, it gave him the financial stability he had always craved. From their first encounter in 1927 (when she graced the penniless poet with a fifty-dollar bill) to their final breakup in 1930, Hughes received a generous monthly stipend, as well as a host of perquisites—stationery, theater tickets, the services of a typist, even the use of her town car and driver. The relationship also fed Hughes emotionally. Not only did Mason confirm his belief in the soul beauty of the black race, but she also provided the kind of lavish praise and doting attention that he had never received from his own beleaguered mother, much less from his father. He was her "winged poet Child," a "shining messenger of hope for his people," a "golden star in the Firmament of Primitive Peoples," whose achievements would dazzle the heavens.

Zora Neale Hurston played Mrs. Mason as the tricksters she described in her books might have played her, offering fulsome gratitude in her presence and then ridiculing her behind her back. Hughes lacked Hurston's emotional armor. Awed by Mason's generosity and spiritual grandeur, he struggled to become the artist she envisioned. When she divined his calling to write a novel, he wrote a novel. When she dismissed a poem as lacking soul or smacking of self-consciousness, he dutifully tried again. The hard-earned perspective that he had achieved in his relationship with African American folk culture (and later with Africa) did not suit Mason at all. He must allow the spirit of his African and Native American ancestors to possess him. He must burn away all the civilized debris that cluttered his art and life.

Writing in *The Big Sea* a decade later, Hughes recounted the inevitable breakup. The precipitant was a gift that he had not adequately acknowledged, but behind the charge of ingratitude was Mason's belief that the poet was not owning his gifts, not taking full advantage of his responsibility to create a truly racial art. "She wanted me to be primitive and know and feel the intuitions of the primitive," he wrote. "But unfortunately, I did not feel the rhythms of the primitive surging through me, and so I could not live and write as though I did. I was only an American Negro—who had loved the surface of Africa and the rhythms of Africa—but I was not African. I was Chicago and Kansas City and Broadway and Harlem." The account captured the burden of the dispute, but the matter-of-fact tone could not have been more misleading. Devastated by Mason's rejection, Hughes penned abject letters, begging her forgiveness. "I love you," he wrote. "I need you very much. . . . You must not let me hurt you again. I know well that I am dull and slow, but I do not want to remain that way. I don't know what to say except that I am truly sorry that I have not changed rapidly enough into what you would have me be." Mason took him back, and even gave him $500 for a trip to Cuba, an experience that she hoped would reawaken his primitive sensibility. But the seeds of hurt and suspicion continued to sprout, and by the middle of 1930 she had permanently expelled him from her life, provoking another emotional and physical collapse.

For all her expostulations on Hughes's divine gifts, Charlotte Mason had failed to recognize his genius. She wanted him to claim his racial birthright, not realizing that he was fundamentally a poet of loss; she wanted him to be whole, never understanding the depth of his incompleteness. It was during the turmoil of 1930 that Hughes produced "Afro-American Fragment," arguably the single greatest poem he ever wrote:

So long,

So far away

Is Africa.

Not even memories alive

Save those that history books create,

Save those that songs

Beat back into the blood—

Beat out of blood with words sad-sung

In strange un-Negro tongue—

So long,

So far away

Is Africa.

Subdued and time-lost

Are the drums—and yet

Through some vast mist of race

There comes this song

I do not understand

This song of atavistic land,

Of bitter yearnings lost

Without a place—

So long,

So far away

Is Africa's

Dark face.

IN HUGHES'S ACCOUNT in *The Big Sea*, his abandonment by Mrs. Mason was of little long-term significance, since the Harlem Renaissance had already run its course. "We were no longer in vogue, anyway, we Negroes," he wrote. "Sophisticated New Yorkers turned to Noël Coward. Colored actors began to go hungry, publishers politely rejected new manuscripts, and patrons found other uses for their money." The claim, ratified by countless historians, was not in fact true. More books by black writers were published in the 1930s than in the preceding decade. Prizes and patronage remained abundant. Nonetheless, the early 1930s did mark a transforming moment in the history of the black arts movement, as the dark cloud of depression settled over the land. With Americans, white and black, standing in breadlines, with half of Harlemites unemployed, the exuberant hopes of the 1920s, the dreams of revolution through art, seemed self-indulgent and silly. "[N]o cultural advance is safe without some sound economic underpinning," admitted Alain Locke, one of the New Negro's most extravagant boosters, "and no emerging elite—artistic, professional or mercantile—can suspend itself in thin air over the abyss of a mass of unemployed stranded in an over-expensive, disease- and crime-ridden slum."

The early 1930s also marked a watershed in the career of Langston Hughes. In the aftermath of the break with Mrs. Mason, his writing veered sharply toward political radicalism. Hughes had always fancied himself a progressive, a tribune of the common man, in the tradition of Whitman and Sandburg. Like other black writers, he was touched by the radical currents coursing through Harlem in the 1920s, and occasionally published his work in socialist journals like *The Messenger* and *The Workers' Monthly*. But his radicalism had remained muted in his poetry, partly because of the influence of Mrs. Mason but also because of qualities of his temperament—his eagerness to please, his difficulty expressing anger, his gift for seeing beauty in even the bleakest circumstances. In a few poems, his anger burst forth, most obviously in "Johannesburg Mines," a mocking rejoinder to Jessie Fausett, literary editor of *The Crisis*, who had rejected one of his early Africa poems as too angry. "In the Johannesburg mines / There are 240,000 / Native Africans working," he wrote. "What kind of poem / Would you / Make out of that?" For the most part, however, Hughes eschewed overtly political themes, focusing instead on the laughter, resilience, and beauty of Negro people.

All that changed abruptly in the early 1930s. In later years, Hughes would insist that he never joined the Communist Party, but there is no doubt that he spent most of the Depression decade in party circles. He participated in the John Reed Club and the League of Struggle for Negro Rights, both C.P. fronts, and made *The New Masses* the primary outlet for his poetry. He first unveiled his new persona in "Merry Christmas," a withering attack on Western imperialism in Africa and Asia, published at the end of 1930. In "Advertisement for the Waldorf-Astoria," he turned his eyes to the United

States, juxtaposing images of diamond-draped women eating watercress in the newly opened luxury hotel with images of back-bent millions shivering beneath the tracks of the elevated train. The poem ended with a revolutionary Annunciation: "Hail Mary, Mother of God! / the new Christ child of the Revolution's about to be born. / (Kick hard, red baby, in the bitter womb of the mob.)"

For Hughes, as for so many of his contemporaries, the revolutionary road passed through Scottsboro, Alabama. In March 1931, nine young black men were hauled from a freight train and falsely accused of raping two white women. In the farcical trials that followed, eight were condemned to death, and the ninth was sentenced to life in prison. The case became a cause célèbre, especially after International Labor Defense, an arm of the Communist Party, assumed control of the defense. Hughes raised money for the case and even traveled to Scottsboro to meet the young men, from which came the book *Scottsboro Limited*, featuring a quartet of poems and a one-act play. If there were any doubts about Hughes's new political affiliation, the book erased them. In the poem "Scottsboro," he placed the eight condemned men in a tradition of martyred freedom fighters stretching from Christ to Lenin. The politics of the play were even broader, with a finale in which black and white workers joined together under a red flag to smash the electric chair, before joining the audience in singing the "Internationale."

In 1932, Hughes traveled to the Soviet Union along with a troupe of African Americans to participate in a party-sponsored film on American race relations. The venture quickly collapsed in acrimony (much to the delight of the mainstream American press), and troupe members trickled back to the United States, bearing tales of disappointment and betrayal. Hughes, however, was too seasoned a traveler—and too blithe a spirit—to succumb easily to disillusionment. "Quite truthfully, there was no toilet paper," he later wrote. "And no Jim Crow." He spent nearly a year in the Soviet Union, most of it in Central Asia, where he examined the country's policy toward its dark-skinned minorities. His observations (which Soviet officials collected and published as a short book) were glowing: after centuries of czarist oppression, the Soviet Union had abolished all forms of racial discrimination and created a genuinely equalitarian society. Other realities of Soviet life—

famine, stifling bureaucracy, brutal suppression of political dissent—were left unremarked. Hughes's reticence is especially noteworthy given that his main traveling companion was Arthur Koestler, whose 1940 novel, *Darkness at Noon*, a searing account of a political show trial, would mark an epoch in the international Left's renunciation of the Soviet Union. Hughes actually attended the Turkistan trial on which Koestler partially based his novel, but the experience left him unmoved. When Koestler tried to engage him in a discussion about the accused, he had only a flippant reply. He "looks guilty to me," he reportedly said, "of what I don't know, but he just *looks* like a rogue." For Koestler, this vapid response was almost as depressing as the trial itself.

As Hughes's politics became more revolutionary, his poetry became less so. While poems like "Goodbye Christ" and "Good Morning Revolution" still relied on vernacular language—Hughes never lost his ear for how ordinary people speak—they were written in plain style, with none of the jazz experimentation that had marked his earlier work. The sentiments were direct and didactic; the tone was angry rather than wistful. Hughes's friend Carl Van Vechten, who had helped to arrange the publication of his first volume of poetry in 1926, tried to call him back to original gifts. "The revolutionary poems seem very weak to me," he wrote in 1933. "I mean very weak on the lyric side. I think in ten years, whatever the social outcome, you will be ashamed of them." The remark would prove prophetic, but Hughes at the time had little interest in reverting to an aesthetic that he, like other leftist critics of the 1930s, had come to disdain as bourgeois. In an address "To Negro Writers," prepared for the first American Writers' Congress in 1935, he disparaged poets—presumably including his former self—who focused on black people's capacity "to laugh and sing and dance and make music." What was needed was not irresponsible bohemianism but "practical" poetry, poetry that would inspire revolutionary consciousness "on the *solid* ground" of the working class.

Hughes remained a Soviet loyalist until 1939. He joined the procession of left-wing intellectuals to Spain, extolling the heroism of Republican forces in such poems as "Letter from Spain." He defended the show trials of "the Trotskyite–Bucharinite traitors" and hailed the U.S.S.R. as a bulwark against fascism. For him, as for so many other American leftists, revelation of the

Nazi-Soviet pact was a crushing blow. At that moment, Hughes renounced his faith in Communist revolution. He also renounced revolutionary poetry. "I am laying off political poetry for a while," he wrote a friend in early 1940, affecting something of his old insouciance. "[T]he world situation, methinks, is too complicated for so simple an art. So I am going back (indeed have gone) to nature, Negroes, and love."

The Big Sea, the book that would offer the fullest account of Hughes's visit to Africa, was written in the aftermath of that declaration. As Arnold Rampersad has noted, the autobiography is best read as an act of literary self-rehabilitation. Written in a breezy, light-hearted style, the book was intended as "The Saga of a Negro Poet"—not the revolutionary poet of the 1930s, but the youthful poet of the 1920s, struggling to claim kinship with a graceful, beautiful race. (Hughes strategically ended the book with his 1930 divorce from Mrs. Mason, saying nothing about his Depression-era links to the party or his long sojourn in the Soviet Union.) The 1923 journey to Africa provided the book's centerpiece. Hughes rendered the trip as a kind of "innocents abroad," a tale of youthful adventure and racial self-discovery. He recounted jettisoning his books from the fantail of the ship. He described his colorful cabinmate, George, the hijinks of his pet monkey, Jocko, and the Garveyite tailor setting off with bolts of cloth, determined to capture Africa's vast, untapped market for pants. And he rehearsed the conversation with the Kru man who called him a "white man."

In keeping with the book's purposes, Hughes steered clear of explicitly political discussion. Yet the account was less innocent than it appeared. Threaded through the tropical sunsets and swaying palms was a devastating portrait of Western imperialism, though one rendered in poetical rather than polemical language. In one extraordinary sentence, Hughes offered a catalogue of images to describe his ship's passage down the African coast. In form and tone, the sentence hearkened back to his 1923 prose poem, "Ships, Sea and Africa," but inserted between the "singing boatmen on dark rivers" and "distant beat of obea drums in the night" was a litany of a different kind: "ten-year-old wharf rats offering nightly to take sailors to see 'my sister, two shillings,' elephantiasis and swollen bellies under palm trees, white men with guns at their belts, inns and taverns with signs up, EUROPEANS ONLY, missionary churches with the Negroes in the back seats and the whites who teach Jesus in the front rows." Hughes may have reverted to themes of "nature, Negroes, and love," but he had not forgotten what he had learned in the 1930s.

Like the Marxist he had once been, Hughes focused on questions of production and exchange. The men with glistening skin and rippling muscles were not just objects for aesthetic contemplation but workers, paid a pittance to load the bounty of Africa—"palm oil and cocoa beans and mahogany"—into the holds of alien ships. In exchange, Africans received "machinery and tools, canned goods, and Hollywood films"—the detritus of Western civilization. In such passages, Hughes revealed again the great historical gulf that separated twentieth-century African Americans from their nineteenth-century predecessors. For men like Paul Cuffe, Martin Delany, and Henry McNeil Turner, commerce was an agency of progress and civilization, but for Hughes, in contrast, commerce was a cancer, slowly devouring the continent. The *West Hesseltine* (rechristened the S.S. *Malone* in the book) became a symbol of Western fraud and rapacity. After Africans in a French colony declined to accept the crew's British money, one of Hughes's shipmates hit upon the idea of using United Cigar Store coupons, which bore a likeness to French francs. When local traders accepted the coupons as tender, the crew poured ashore and "bought up the town," steaming away before the ruse was discovered. At another port, a pair of young prostitutes rowed out to the ship, "hoping to make some money." While one of the girls was claimed by the bo'sun, the other was thrown to the floor of the crew's quarters, "stripped of her flowered cloth," and gang-raped, while thirty sailors "sat up on bunks to watch, smoked, yelled, and joked, and waited for their turn. Each time a man would rise, the little African girl on the floor would say: 'Mon-nee! Mon-nee!' But nobody had a cent . . ."

The Big Sea said little about the journey back to New York, which ended with the summary firing of the entire crew. Other hands would offload the ship's cargo, including 1,770 casks of palm oil from Nigeria, nearly 5,000 bags of cocoa beans from the Gold Coast, and 100 massive mahogany logs from the Ivory Coast, each weighing several tons. Hughes had watched in wonder as Kru men, bobbing alongside the ship, fastened chains around those floating logs so that the ship's crane could winch them into the hold. Writing about the spectacle seventeen years later, he was still impressed with the beauty and danger of the work, which he compared to the bullfights he had once watched in Mexico. But he also reflected on the forces that compelled men to cut down their ancient forests and risk being crushed to death between wood and steel hull for two shillings a day. Some of those logs would become chests of drawers. Others would be joined to ebony and ivory, also looted from Africa, and fashioned into pianos. For the author of "The Weary Blues," it made for a sobering image: an aging jazzman, wringing a melody from an instrument "made of wood and life, energy and death out of Africa."

LANGSTON HUGHES was just twenty-one when he visited Africa in 1923. By the time he returned, he was nearly sixty. Much had changed in his absence. Africa was ablaze with the promise of independence; in 1960, the year of his return, no fewer than seventeen African colonies joined the ranks of independent nations. In Kenya, Ghana, Senegal, Nigeria, even apartheid South Africa, a generation of young writers offered the world a new vision of the richness and complexity of modern African life. Many, indeed most, of these emerging African writers counted Hughes as one of their formative influences.

Over the years, Hughes had received occasional letters from aspiring African writers. He had a strong following among the Francophone writers of the Négritude movement, who found in his evocations of the soul beauty of the Negro race a keynote for their own developing aesthetic. His writing had an even greater impact in South Africa. At a time when the South African government, under the auspices of its Grand Apartheid policy, was tightening urban influx laws and forcibly removing hundreds of thousands of "redundant" Africans from cities to desiccated ethnic homelands, a generation of African and "Coloured" writers—Peter Abrahams, Bloke Modisane, Richard Rive, Can Themba, Ezekiel Mphahlele, Henry Nxumalo—found in the work of Hughes and other African American writers, musicians, and artists a precious model of black urbanity and achievement. Many of these writers were associated with *Drum* magazine, a monthly published in Sophia-town, a mixed-race slum outside Johannesburg, which had already been tar-geted for removal by the state. The very first issue of *Drum* included Countee Cullen's "Heritage"—"What is Africa to me?"—and subsequent issues fea-tured the work of other Harlem Renaissance–era poets, including Hughes.

In 1954, Henry Nxumalo, *Drum*'s editor, wrote to Hughes and asked him to serve as a judge in the magazine's annual short-story contest. The invita-tion could hardly have come at a better time for the poet, whose career was at a low point. Hughes's literary reputation had plunged in the years after World War II, as the high priests of high modernism dismissed his work as too accessible, simple, not serious literature at all. He had also endured a re-cent political humiliation, appearing in 1953 as a cooperating witness before Senator Joseph McCarthy's Permanent Sub-Committee on Investigations. In his prepared statement and in responses to questioning, Hughes acquitted himself better than most, expressing contrition for his youthful "errors" but defending the American values of free speech and open dissent. Still, there was something more than a little unseemly in the spectacle of the poet agree-ing, under McCarthy's prodding, on the need to remove his books from the shelves of overseas libraries opened by the U.S. Information Service lest they infect Africans with dangerous Communist sentiments.

The invitation from *Drum* buoyed Hughes's spirits, and he threw himself into the task, reading not just the submitted entries but as much recent African writing as he could get his hands on. By 1955, he had begun work on two books. *The First Book of Africa* was a collection of African short stories for young readers, an audience that Hughes had long cherished. *An African Treasury: Articles, Essays, Stories, Poems by Black Africans* was a more con-ventional anthology, which afforded American readers one of their first glimpses not only of the *Drum* contingent but also of such writers as Léopold Senghor, Efua Sutherland, and future Nobel laureate Wole Soyinka. During the last years of his life, Hughes would become a friend and mentor to many of the writers featured in the books, extending to them the same encourage-ment and genial companionship he had always extended to younger African American writers.

In December 1960, Hughes returned to Africa for the first time in thirty-seven years to witness the installation of his old Lincoln University class-mate, Nnamdi Azikiwe, as governor general of newly independent Nigeria. In the eighteen months that followed, he made two more visits, attending a festival of Afro-American and African arts in Nigeria in late 1961 and an African writers conference in Uganda six months after that. He had obvi-ously come up in the world since his messmate days, sleeping in first-class hotels and receiving encomiums at state dinners, yet he was much the man he had always been—unpretentious, approachable, full of enthusiasm and wonder. Everywhere he went, he was surrounded by young African writers, who, in the words of *The New York Times,* "haunted his hotel the way Amer-ican youngsters dog favorite baseball players."

As in his first visit, Hughes found the continent at once exhilarating and disillusioning. The promise of African independence thrilled him, yet he recognized the problems of poverty, corruption, and creeping authoritarian-ism. He was particularly alarmed by the violent chaos of Lagos, which he de-scribed as "a combination of the most enticing travel folders on the tropics and Dürer's impressions of Dante's *Inferno.*" He was also struck, as he had been four decades before, by moments of miscommunication between visit-ing African Americans and their African hosts. But any disappointment he felt was masked with his trademark irony and self-deprecation. "In the new African countries, honest, I thought everything was roses and sunrise and dew," he wrote. "How naïve can even an ancestor-worshipper like me be?"

During his 1962 visit to the African writers' conference in Uganda, Hughes made a side trip to Accra, Ghana, to dedicate the new U.S. Informa-tion Service library. Hughes was no naïf (though he could play the role) and he had no illusions about the reasons for the invitation. Africa had become important terrain in the global Cold War, with Americans and Soviets vying to persuade African people of the superiority of their respective social sys-tems. Not surprisingly, the Soviet campaign emphasized American racism, contrasting the debasement of black people in the United States with the U.S.S.R.'s enlightened policy toward "national minorities." To counter such efforts, the U.S. government organized a variety of exchanges and tours by prominent African Americans, including Louis Armstrong and Duke Elling-ton, both of whom toured Africa under the auspices of the State Department. Hughes's dedication of Accra's new U.S.I.S. Library was part of that effort, though it was also a distinctly ironic event, coming as it did just nine years after his books had been removed from U.S.I.S. libraries around the world. Hughes, characteristically, expressed no bitterness, offering instead a moving reflection on the relationship of African and American freedom. Perhaps mindful of his old Kru friend, Tom Pey, who had complained of African Americans who came "to teach us something, because they think we know nothing," Hughes stressed that he had come "to offer an *exchange* of knowledge (not merely to *give* in the old patronizing sense)"—an exchange that promised not only to benefit Africa, but also to reinvigorate America's own values of freedom and equality. "Black Africa today is sending rejuvenating currents of liberty over all the earth reaching even as far as Little Rock, Birmingham, and Jackson, Mississippi," he declared.

Hughes visited Africa for the last time in 1966, a year before his death, when he was appointed by President Lyndon Johnson to head the American delegation at the First World Festival of Negro Arts in Dakar, Senegal. Though cast as a celebration, the festival unfolded in grim circumstances. The wave of postindependence coups d'état that had begun with the C.I.A.-sponsored overthrow of Congo prime minister Patrice Lumumba had claimed his old friend Nnamdi Azikiwe, who was ousted by the Nigerian military in early 1966. Ghana's Kwame Nkrumah, global symbol of African independence, would fall a few months later. The situation in the United States, while less catastrophic, was also deeply distressing to Hughes. Despite the achievement of landmark civil rights and voting rights legislation, the racial situation grew increasingly polarized. The ghetto uprisings that began in the northeast in the summers of 1963 and 1964 reached a climax in the cataclysmic Watts riot of 1965, and few doubted that more "long hot summers" awaited the nation. In the realm of art, a new generation of black writers had come to the fore, led by LeRoi Jones (later Amiri Baraka), whose angry, abusive writing Hughes found depressing and distasteful. "The most talented of the young Negro writers," he warned, "have become America's prophets of doom, black ravens cawing over carrion."

Hughes delivered the keynote address to the World Festival of Negro Arts against this backdrop. If "The Negro Speaks of Rivers" represented the prolegomenon of his career, then "Black Writers in a Troubled World" was his valedictory. Addressing an audience of writers from all over the globe, Hughes reviewed the three pillars of his creed: love of humanity, faith in art, and reverence for the Negro race, that endless river of blackness that flowed in and through him. "If one may ascribe a prime function to any creative writing," he declared, "it is, I think, to affirm life, to yea-say the excitement of living in relation to the vast rhythms of the universe of which we are a part, to untie the riddles of the gutter in order to closer tie the knot between man and God. As to Negro writing and writers, one of our aims, it seems to me, should be to gather the strengths of our people in Africa and the Americas into a tapestry of words as strong as the bronzes of Benin . . . the beat of the blues, and the *Uhuru* of African freedom, and give it to the world with pride and love."

SIX

The Spell of Africa

THE EPISODE IS better suited for bad historical fiction than for history. The specific occasion has been forgotten—some dinner or public function—but W. E. B. Du Bois and Marcus Garvey once found themselves sharing an elevator. The year was probably 1923 or 1924. The two titans had spent the preceding months attacking one another in the pages of *The Crisis* and *The Negro World*, their respective newspapers. In essays such as "Back to Africa" and "A Lunatic or Traitor," Du Bois derided Garvey as a braggart and buffoon, just the latest demagogue come to defraud the credulous black masses. Garvey, taking a leaf from politics in his native Jamaica, responded by labeling Du Bois a self-hating mulatto, more in love with his Dutch and English ancestry than his Negro blood. Relations would spiral down from there, culminating with Garvey's prosecution for mail fraud and eventual deportation—a prosecution brought in part at the behest of Du Bois's N.A.A.C.P. But on that particular evening, somewhere in New York City, the two men arrived simultaneously at the doors of an elevator. Too proud to give way, they rode upstairs together, along with several other passengers, in stony silence. Witnesses later reported that the Jamaican visibly shook as the elevator ascended, while Du Bois, renowned for his icy reserve, merely arched his nostrils in disdain.

Among the other passengers on the elevator was journalist George Schuyler. Schuyler had only recently arrived in New York City, but he had already made a name for himself as the era's most savage satirist. In his monthly column in *The Messenger*, "Shafts and Darts: A Page of Calumny and Satire," he happily exposed the "imbecilities, knavery and pathological virtues" of modern American life, especially in relation to the Negro. Schuyler fully shared Du Bois's aversion to Garvey, whom he memorably called a "lampblacked Klansman," a characterization seemingly borne out (much to the columnist's delight) when the Jamaican met with leaders of the Ku Klux Klan to discuss their shared interest in racial purity. In years to come, however, Schuyler would direct most of his fire at Du Bois. While less publicized than the epic battle between Du Bois and Garvey, the duel between Du Bois and Schuyler would have an equally dramatic impact on the course of African American politics. By the time the smoke cleared in the early 1930s, Schuyler had displaced Du Bois in the inner councils of the N.A.A.C.P. and at the managing editor's desk of *The Crisis*, and the two men had been launched on diametrically opposite political trajectories. While Du Bois moved leftward, eventually becoming a member of the Communist Party, Schuyler, a youthful socialist, became an arch-reactionary, ending his life as a member of the John Birch Society.

The conflict between Garvey, Du Bois, and Schuyler reflected great gulfs in personalities and temperaments, as well as profound differences in ideas about race and racial leadership. But what is perhaps most extraordinary about the conflict is the terrain on which it was fought. While the three men lived within a few blocks of one another, the battle between them was joined half a world away, in the struggling African republic of Liberia.

GROWING UP in Great Barrington, Massachusetts, Du Bois felt little connection to Africa. His roots, he later recalled, "were not African so much as Dutch and New England. The speech was an idiomatic New England tongue, with no African dialect; the family customs were New England, and the sex mores." The "one direct cultural connection" with Africa that he could claim was a childhood lullaby, a "heathen melody" handed down from his great grandmother, the words of which had no meaning to him: "Do bana, coba, gene me, gene me! / Do bana coba, gene me, gene me! / Ben d'nuli, ben d'le." Late in his life, Du Bois would transcribe the words from memory and circulate them among African linguists in a vain attempt to establish their origin and meaning. But the song's meaning remained opaque, as if to symbolize the veil that separated him from his ancestral continent.

Thus for Du Bois, as for generations of African American intellectuals, the bond with Africa was a product not of memory or direct experience but of "later learning and reaction." Such learning did not come easily. "When I was a boy in school there was no reference in my courses or textbooks, to the History of Africa," he remembered, nor did Africa feature in any of the daily newspapers that he religiously read. Three years at Fisk University did little to remedy the omission. Students prayed for the missionaries who were bringing light and civilization to the "Dark Continent"—the main building on campus was Livingstone Hall—but they learned nothing of the Conference of Berlin, where at that very moment European statesmen were carving Africa into colonial empires. (To his later embarrassment, Du Bois dedicated his 1888 graduation address at Fisk to Otto von Bismarck, the German statesman who had convened the conference.) The situation was little better at Harvard or the University of Berlin, where neglect of African history had the force of a philosophical proposition: Africa, in Hegel's famous dictum, was the land without history, a place that had contributed nothing to human civilization. Much of Du Bois's career can be read as an effort to rebut that proposition, to illuminate Africa's history and gifts to the world.

With no formal curriculum, Du Bois was left to piece together an idea of Africa from the materials at hand. As a student at Fisk and as a young professor at Wilberforce University, an A.M.E. Church–sponsored college in Ohio, he was exposed to the arguments about African missions and emigration that roiled late-nineteenth-century black American life. He met the aging Alexander Crummell, apostle of African "redemption," at a Wilberforce commencement. (He later devoted a chapter of his masterwork, *The Souls of*

Black Folk, to Crummell.) He also met Henry McNeil Turner, though at the time he had little interest in African emigration, which he thought unrealistic and foolish. (Little could Du Bois have imagined that he would spend his own last days in Africa.) Like other literate Americans of the day, he read African explorers' accounts—not only of the celebrated Livingstone but also of Mungo Park (whom he admired) and H. M. Stanley, whose fawning tribute to King Leopold, *The Congo and the Founding of Its Free State*, appears to have been the first book on Africa that Du Bois ever read.

The Africa that emerged in the young Du Bois's mind was, perhaps predictably, impressionistic and intellectually inconsistent. In some ways, he was a conventional nineteenth-century romantic racialist, who viewed Africa as a "racial fount," the wellspring of a distinctively Negro racial temperament. In Du Bois's rendering, Negroes were creatures of the heart rather than the head, whose "rich tropical imagination" and "innate love of harmony" attuned them to beauty and sociability rather than to logic or individual gain. Yet Du Bois was also a twentieth-century social scientist, determined to rescue Africa from the fog of mythology and misprision that had long enveloped it. In 1907, he began work on an Encyclopedia Africana, intended to provide an accurate, objective compendium of all existing knowledge about the continent and its people. While he never finished the project—he was still working on it when he died in Ghana at the age of ninety-five—he did complete a half dozen books exploring Africa's history and place in the modern world. Du Bois apparently never felt the need to reconcile his romantic racialist and social scientific identities, and both would be in evidence when he first visited Africa in the 1920s.

Du Bois's interest in the continent came to a head during the First World War. In 1915, he published *The Negro*, his first scholarly book on Africa. He also wrote "The African Roots of the War," a classic essay, published in *The Atlantic Monthly* magazine, which traced the war's origins to competition for African colonies. Anticipating an argument offered two years later by Lenin, Du Bois argued that Europe had been snared in a web of its own spinning. Even as new forms of economic organization and industrial technique unleashed unprecedented economic growth, Europe clung to an irrational system of distribution, in which most people lived hand to mouth while a fortunate few enjoyed fabulous wealth. At the best of times, such a system was politically unstable; in the circumstances of the late nineteenth century, with an enfranchised and increasingly well-organized working class, it was utterly untenable. African colonialism offered a seeming solution. Profits wrung from Africa could be used, in essence, to buy off white workers, giving them a stake in the existing system and forestalling the necessity of more thoroughgoing change. Whatever qualms some workers might feel about the palpable injustices of colonialism could be managed by recourse to race, the reassuring idea that the world's darker people were fashioned for drudgery, indeed that they were scarcely people at all. The result, which hearkened back to the days of the transatlantic slave trade, was an edifice of white progress, wealth, and comfort erected upon a foundation of black backwardness, penury, and pain. In the case of colonialism, however, the system that saved the old order also ironically proved its undoing. As European states recognized the necessity of colonies, Du Bois argued, they were drawn into rivalry with one another, provoking a series of diplomatic crises and a suicidal arms race, all culminating in fratricidal war.

The argument in "The African Roots of the War" remained a cornerstone of Du Bois's politics for the rest of his life. The global economic order was not simply unjust and irrational; it was also the fundamental cause of war. Yet in that realization lay the seeds of hope. Having counted the cost of colonialism in corpses, Europeans might finally be willing to relinquish their colonial empires and to confront the fundamental irrationality of their own social systems. For the first time, it might be possible to build a rational, just economic order in which all would enjoy self-government and a share of the bounty made possible by modern industrial technique. When Du Bois declared, in 1919, that mankind had an opportunity to unleash on the African continent "a final crusade for humanity," this is what he meant.

Du Bois's instrument to bring this future to pass was the Pan-African Congress, which convened for the first time in Paris in 1919, alongside the Versailles Peace Conference. An assembly of black leaders from around the world—what Du Bois revealingly called "the thinking classes of the future Negro world"—the congress presented itself as the representative body of the darker world, whose interests were otherwise unregistered at Versailles. Its nominal head was Blaise Diagne of Senegal, one of a handful of black members of the French House of Deputies, but it was Du Bois who called the congress, organized the sessions, and wrote the resolutions. By the standards of his later politics, the demands were modest but in the context of their time they were radical indeed. On the issue of African self-government, for example, delegates resolved: "The natives of Africa must have the right to participate in the government as fast as their development permits in conformity with the principle that the government exists for the natives, and not the natives for the government. They shall at once be allowed to participate in local and tribal government according to ancient usage, and this participation shall gradually extend, as education and experience proceeds, to the higher offices of state, to the end that Africa shall be ruled by the consent of Africans."

The inaugural congress did not unfold as Du Bois had planned. Though Woodrow Wilson arrived in France intoning idealistic ideas about self-determination and the right of consent in one's government, the victorious powers assembled at Versailles had no intention of dismantling their colonial empires, and still less of taking instruction from a group of self-proclaimed black leaders. The congress itself was hamstrung by a lack of resources, which prevented the hiring of a stenographer, let alone the creation of the permanent secretariat envisioned by Du Bois. ("If the Negroes of the world could have maintained in Paris during the entire sitting of the Peace Conference a central headquarters with experts, clerks and helpers, they could have settled the future of Africa at a cost of less than $10,000," he wrote in one of his more extravagant assessments of the movement.) The congress was also dogged by tensions between the African American delegates and their French counterparts, many of whom were quite wealthy and surprisingly conservative in their politics. The differences were papered over in 1919, but they burst into the open at the second Pan-African Congress in 1921, with French delegates denouncing a Du Bois-authored resolution on restoring "the ancient common ownership of land" as "Bolshevism" and "rank communism." While Du Bois endeavored to put the best face on the dispute, the Pan-African Congress never recovered from the debacle.

Du Bois managed at the eleventh hour to organize a 1923 congress, which met in London and Lisbon in two sessions, but it was a desultory affair, with only a handful of delegates and Du Bois himself delivering most of the speeches. For all practical purposes, the 1923 meeting marked the end of the movement. But it did not end Du Bois's interest in Africa. A few days after the congress adjourned, he boarded a German steamer and embarked for Liberia, where he served as the official American representative at the inauguration of President C. D. B. King. A strange and disturbing new chapter in Du Bois's African romance had begun.

DU BOIS'S CHOICE of destination was not arbitrary: Liberia was imperiled, and he had come to save it. A century after its founding, the republic had yet to find the kind of staple crop that had enabled other settler colonial societies to survive and, in a few cases, to prosper. During the American Civil War, the republic had enjoyed a brief sugar boom, but the revival of sugar production in Louisiana and the development of a European sugar beet industry squeezed Liberians from the international market. In the 1890s, coffee seemingly promised a bounteous future, but the growth of the Brazilian industry put an end to that. In the early twentieth century, a British firm, the Liberian Development Company, proposed to make the republic a leading producer of rubber. The company cleared land and planted several thousand rubber trees, but it soon fell into bankruptcy, leaving the jungle to reclaim the venture.

With no sources of revenue, the Liberian government lurched from foreign loan to foreign loan, sinking ever further into debt and dependency. In 1871, following the collapse of the sugar boom, Liberia borrowed $500,000 from London financiers, but most of it found its way into the pockets of European middlemen and corrupt local officials. In 1906, the government borrowed another $500,000 to extinguish the earlier debt and build the roads and rail facilities required by the Liberian Development Company; when the company collapsed a year later, Liberians were left holding the bag. In 1912, the government took out its largest loan yet, for five million dollars, from a consortium of European banks, but to obtain the money it was forced to surrender control of the exchequer to a group of international "receivers"—an American, a Frenchman, an Englishman and (until 1914) a German, who ensured that all revenues went first to servicing the debt. Most years there was nothing left.

The republic's weakness made it a prey to its colonial neighbors. Under the terms of the Berlin Conference, claims to territory in the African interior required the demonstration of effective sovereignty, something that Liberia plainly did not exercise. Britain and France both used that stipulation to claim huge swaths of Liberian territory as their own. By 1900, more than a third of the country had been excised and incorporated into neighboring Sierra Leone and Ivory Coast. For a time, it appeared that France and Britain might engorge the republic entirely.

Du Bois watched Liberia's unraveling with alarm. His feelings about the republic had always been ambivalent. He had long regarded the idea of mass emigration back to Africa as utter folly, especially to a place like Liberia, "where the American Negroes die like sheep." But he also recognized the symbolic importance of the republic. In an era in which black people's capacity for self-government was everywhere disparaged and denied, the survival of the world's two black republics, Liberia and Haiti, was vital to black people everywhere. In his first two newspapers, *The Moon* and *Horizon*, Du Bois gave generous coverage to Liberian affairs, reprinting items from the *Monrovia Mail* and waxing lyrical about a 1908 visit to the United States by a Liberian delegation headed by President Arthur Barclay. (Such were the racial niceties of the period that the American government refused to receive the delegation, though President Theodore Roosevelt, pressed by Booker T. Washington, eventually consented to meet them unofficially.) In the years that followed, Du Bois's concern blossomed into full-blown panic. With the loss of Haitian independence—the island became a U.S. protectorate in 1915 under the occupation of American marines—Liberia was the last frail reed upholding the principle of black self-government. As the Versailles conference approached, Britain and France continued to meddle, complaining loudly of the republic's inability to govern the indigenous population within its claimed territory. "Unless Liberia makes a strong stand and convinces the great powers that she is able to stand alone and develop the country and civilize the natives, her territory will be dis-membered," Du Bois warned.

Liberia survived Versailles, but the crisis continued. In late 1919, Liberia's new president, C. D. B. King, traveled to the United States seeking a new five-million-dollar loan, in effect asking the Americans to buy out the British and French. After endless haggling, the two governments negotiated a loan, only to have the U.S. Senate refuse to ratify the treaty. Du Bois was devastated, seeing the rejection as a sign of American indifference and, by implication, an invitation to additional British and French depredations. His anxiety was ratcheted up even further a year later, when he learned that the American government did not intend to send a representative to the inauguration of the reelected President King. It was at this point that he hatched the idea of representing the U.S. government himself.

In the swirl of controversy following his visit, Du Bois insisted that he had not sought appointment as American envoy to Liberia; in fact, he arranged the whole thing. In September 1923, shortly before sailing to Europe for the third Pan-African Congress, he wrote to William H. Lewis, one of the country's most influential black Republicans. It was "barely possible" that he would be in Liberia for the upcoming inauguration, he wrote. "Would it not be a graceful thing if the United States could make me their special representative on that occasion?" Such an appointment, he added in a second letter, offered "a splendid opportunity to show to the Liberian Republic, that notwithstanding the failure of the five million dollar loan in Congress, yet the Government of the United States still continues to maintain a kindly, and friendly interest in that Republic." A veteran political fixer, Lewis forwarded the proposal to the White House, with the suggestion that it offered "a good chance to play a little politics, which will not cost anybody anything." Indulging Du Bois's request, he explained, could "insure the support of *The Crisis* in the upcoming presidential election," or at least "stultify it, if it should come out against us." Thus was Du Bois appointed American Envoy Extraordinaire and Minister Plenipotentiary to the Republic of Liberia. Despite the august title, the position was purely a courtesy office, with no powers, formal instructions, or salary (the State Department later begrudged even expenses). But Du Bois, characteristically, embraced it as an "epochal" honor, "the highest rank ever given by any country to a diplomatic agent in black Africa."

ON DECEMBER 22—at 3:22 P.M.—Du Bois spied Cape Mount, rising from the sea in "two low, pale semi-circles." Later that evening, in the light of a full moon, the ship anchored off Monrovia. Du Bois, still spry for a man of fifty-five, clambered into a Kru longboat for the exhilarating ride through the breakers. Thus did the self-proclaimed "ambassador of Pan-Africa," the "sixth generation in descent from my stolen forefathers," step onto African soil for the first time.

If Du Bois and his Liberian hosts shared anything, it was a love of pomp and circumstance. On January 1, 1924, he presented himself at the executive mansion in Monrovia, adorned in tails and a top hat left from his German student days; he was accompanied by an aide-de-camp and an orderly, both lent for the occasion by the Liberian government. With the entire European diplomatic corps in attendance, he delivered a short address, in which he essentially announced as fact the policy that he believed the American government should pursue toward Liberia. In "designating me as his personal representative," he began, the U.S. president "wished publicly and unmistakably to express before the world the interest and solicitude which the hundred million inhabitants of the United States have for Liberia. Liberia is a child of the United States, and a sister Republic. Its progress and success are the progress and success of democracy everywhere and for all men; and the United States would view with sorrow and alarm any misfortune that might happen to this Republic and any obstacle that was placed in her path." None of this was he authorized to say. Not surprisingly, the speech caused some consternation at the State Department, as well as among the European diplomats in attendance, who immediately wired Washington for clarification of this new, vaguely threatening American policy.

Having reoriented American foreign policy, Du Bois now set about reforming Liberia's internal affairs. Though he remained in the country less than a month, he played a central role in two historic controversies, the first involving Marcus Garvey, the second the Firestone Tire & Rubber Company. It is a measure of Liberia's perplexities that Du Bois, the great Pan-Africanist and future Communist, worked to entice Firestone into Liberia while laboring to keep Garvey out.

As with his more famous rivalry with Booker T. Washington, Du Bois's conflict with Garvey was a clash of both principle and personality, with the mantle of representative race leader as the assumed prize. The Jamaican arrived in the United States in 1915 and immediately began to gather a following. Thousands of African Americans bought five-dollar shares in his Black Star Line, a venture intended, like the earlier initiatives of Paul Cuffe and Henry McNeil Turner, to develop commerce within the black world while facilitating the emigration of African Americans back to Africa. To Du Bois, Garvey was everything that black America did not need in a race leader—a bombastic, ill-educated "demagog" with no understanding of history or the "technic of civilization," "no business sense, no flair for *real* organization." His antagonism doubtless flowed partly from jealousy; he resented Garvey's popularity, as well as the way in which he "walked onto the scene" and stole the Pan-African show. (White officials routinely conflated the Pan-African Congress and Garvey's Universal Negro Improvement Association, despite Du Bois's strenuous denial that his venture had "anything to do with the so-called Garvey movement.") But along with jealousy was genuine foreboding. The Black Star Line was a pyramid scheme, and Du Bois dreaded the damage to black people's morale and reputation when the inevitable collapse came.

Du Bois said nothing when Garvey declared himself "Provisional President of Africa," but when the Jamaican began meddling in Liberia he was stirred to action. In 1920, Garvey dispatched a U.N.I.A. delegation to the republic. Following its return, he unveiled a "constructive plan and program for the uplifting of the Negroes and the redemption of Africa." The scheme included a two-million-dollar fund for Liberia, to be used to build hospitals and schools and pay off the republic's white creditors, as well as a mass migration of African Americans to Liberia using ships of the Black Star Line. A second U.N.I.A. deputation was soon en route to Liberia, to begin laying out farms and constructing shelters for the first wave of African American settlers, an anticipated twenty thousand families in the first two years. So heady was the prospect that Garvey announced his intention to move the headquarters of the organization from Harlem to Monrovia.

In retrospect, it is obvious that Garvey's plan had no chance of fruition. The U.N.I.A.'s campaign to raise $2 million for Liberia netted just over $16,000. (While Garvey variously claimed one, two, even five million followers, total paid membership in the U.N.I.A. at the time was about forty thousand.) As for the Liberian government, there was no way that it was going to accept tens of thousands of settlers, particularly settlers professing allegiance to an outsider. The entire Americo-Liberian population in the 1920s—the community of settlers and their descendants—numbered only about fifteen thousand. At the core of that group was a small knot of intermarried families, who had long monopolized political power. Far from welcoming new arrivals, the Liberian oligarchy was distinctly hostile to them, especially to black immigrants, who were automatically qualified to vote.

None of this was clear to Du Bois, however, who saw Garvey's scheme as one more threat to Liberia's future. Even if the Jamaican did not succeed in taking control of the republic, his intemperate statements offered another pretext for British aggression. In late 1920, Du Bois wrote to President King, urging him to state formally that Liberia would not permit its territory to be used as a base for anticolonial agitation. He also penned a two-part article on Garvey in *The Crisis,* warning of the Jamaican's "very serious defects of temperament and training," including vanity, paranoia, and a lack of business acumen. The article touched off one of the most venomous exchanges in the history of African American politics. Responding in *The Negro World* a few days later, Garvey dismissed Du Bois as an "unfortunate mulatto who bewails every day the drop of Negro blood in his veins." "That is why he likes to dance with white people and dine with them and sometimes sleep with them," he added, "because from his way of seeing things all that is black is ugly, and all that is white is beautiful." Du Bois, blood boiling, lashed back, beginning one essay with a description of a "little, fat black man, ugly, but with intelligent eyes and big head," seated on a makeshift throne, adorned in "a military uniform of the gayest mid-Victorian type." "What did it all mean?" he asked rhetorically. Was it "the dress-rehearsal of a new comic opera?" The answer, of course, was that it was Marcus Garvey.

Relations between Garvey and the Liberian government were still superficially cordial in late 1923, when Du Bois sailed for Africa. A third U.N.I.A. deputation, arriving in Monrovia just a few weeks before him, had been treated to the usual round of receptions and banquets. But a fourth group, arriving a few weeks after Du Bois's visit, was summarily arrested, divested of its supplies, and deported. Given the sequence, many people blamed the reversal on Du Bois, a charge that he haughtily denied. (He and his hosts had too many important matters to discuss to bother with so trivial a topic as Garvey, he wrote.) Whatever his precise role, there was no mistaking his triumphalism on his return to the United States. The first issue of *The Crisis* after his return reprinted a press release from Monrovia, announcing a ban on immigration of anyone associated with the U.N.I.A. The next issue included "A Lunatic or Traitor," Du Bois's most vicious attack on Garvey yet.

While Du Bois's role in the Garvey affair remains opaque, his contribution to the disastrous Firestone rubber concession is crystal clear. In the generation after the Congo genocide, world demand for rubber latex had continued to skyrocket, spurred by the burgeoning automobile industry. Unfortunately for the United States, which accounted for more than three quarters of that demand, most of the world's rubber rested in British hands, chiefly in plantations in south and Southeast Asia. In 1922 the British government engineered a sharp reduction in production, in order to drive up the commodity's price. The move set off a panic in the United States, prompting both the government and private firms to embark on a search for new rubber-producing sites. The campaign, spearheaded by the Ohio-based Firestone corporation, centered initially on the Philippine Islands, but local restrictions on the size of landholdings, as well as on the importation of "coolie" labor, rendered large-scale plantation agriculture impractical. Firestone looked next to Liberia. As fate would have it, the investigator dispatched by the company, D. A. Ross, arrived in Monrovia at almost exactly the same moment as Du Bois.

How Ross and Du Bois met is not clear; they were probably introduced by American resident minister Solomon Porter Hood, who had long touted Liberia's potential as a rubber-growing area. In early January, the three men drove into the interior to inspect the rubber plantation begun by the short-lived Liberian Development Company a generation before. The visit confirmed Ross's conviction that Liberia offered the "best natural advantages" for large-scale rubber production, with ideal climate and soil, as well as an "indigenous and practically inexhaustible" labor supply. Firestone immediately began negotiations with the Liberian government for a massive, million-acre concession. Du Bois fully shared Ross's enthusiasm, hailing the plantation as an "Enchanted Forest" which would solve all of Liberia's chronic ills.

Given his long history of anticolonial activism (not to mention his later membership in the Communist Party), Du Bois's promotion of an American multinational corporation seems more than a little incongruous, but desperate times seemed to call for desperate measures. For a half century, Liberia had stumbled from loan to loan, falling deeper into debt and eventually into international receivership. Private investment seemed to Du Bois to offer a lesser evil, providing Liberians access to capital without the assumption of new debt or further affronts to national sovereignty. The Firestone agreement, he predicted, would inject more than one hundred million dollars into the Liberian economy, stimulating development of rail and harbor facilities, the erection of new schools and hospitals, and a host of other benefits. As Liberia prospered, other companies would follow. The commitment of American dollars would, in turn, compel the attention of the U.S. government, which would have no choice but to defend the republic against British and French depredations. Liberia would be saved, and with it the future of African self-government.

Du Bois elaborated the argument in the months after his visit. In magazine articles and a series of long letters to Harvey Firestone, the burly, self-made president of the rubber giant, he sketched a vision of a great corporate commonwealth, with independent black leaders and philanthropic white capitalists cooperating to produce "far-reaching reforms" in the global color line. He was not oblivious to the risks. "[I]f the Firestone Plantations Company wishes it can repeat in Liberia the hell that white imperialism has perpetrated heretofore in Africa and Asia," he conceded, a predacious order of white expatriate managers and exploited native workers. But Du Bois held out hope that the lessons of the past had been learned, that concessions to Firestone and other American companies could be drafted in ways that respected Liberia's sovereignty and the welfare of its people.

Looking back years later, Du Bois would lament his naïveté. "I had not then lost faith in the capitalist system," he wrote ruefully, "and I believed that it was possible for a great corporation, headed by a man of vision, to go into a country with something more than the mere ideal of profit." But even more than faith in capitalism, Du Bois's Firestone fantasy revealed his abiding faith in progress, his belief that increasing human knowledge and the unprecedented efficiencies of modern industrial organization could be harnessed for good, to produce dignity and sufficiency for all rather than obscene wealth for a few. He would carry that faith to his grave. Unfortunately, neither the Liberian oligarchy nor Firestone shared his creed. Firestone would indeed begin operations in Liberia, but it would neither redeem the republic nor safeguard the future of black self-government in Africa. On the contrary, it would spawn a new species of horror, hearkening at once to the forced labor scandals of the turn-of-the-century Congo and to the system of neocolonialism to come, in which private American corporations would command the politics of nominally independent third world nations. And W. E. B. Du Bois was midwife to the birth.

DU BOIS RETURNED to the United States in March 1924, "full, very full with things that must be said." For the next six months, he poured out his impressions of Africa in the columns of The Crisis, even publishing excerpts from his diary, something he did on no other occasion of his career. As David Levering Lewis has noted, Du Bois's writing often exhibited a "vertiginous" quality when he traveled, a hyper-lyricism brought on by the sheer euphoria of having slipped the surly bonds of American racism. By that standard, his account of his first African journey was virtually hypoxic. "Africa is vegetation," he wrote. "It is the riotous, unbridled bursting life of leaf and limb." It was also "star-faced palms and thatched huts," "sunlight in great gold globules," and "soft, heavy-scented heat," producing a "divine, eternal languor." Where other visitors to Monrovia saw a steamy colonial port, without electricity, paved roads, or a modern sewage system, Du Bois glimpsed a beautiful brown maiden, with hair of plaited "palm leaves and mangoes," her face half turned from the ocean in "coy African modesty." "The spell of Africa is upon me," he declared. "The ancient witchery of her medicine is burning my drowsy, dreamy blood. This is not a country, it is a world—a universe of itself and for itself, a thing Different, Immense, Menacing, Alluring. It is a great black bosom where the Spirit longs to die."

Du Bois's feminization of the continent was in keeping with an enduring tradition in Western thought, which has long imputed to Africa and Africans a host of traditionally feminine qualities—dreaminess, sensuality, emotion-

alism, fecundity, and so forth. His account also exhibited the enduring Western tendency of representing the continent in undifferentiated terms. Du
Bois had come to a particular country, Liberia, at a critical moment in its history, but that specificity was washed away in the flood of romantic general-
ization. In the thousands of words he wrote about his trip, one can literally
count on one hand the number of people mentioned by name, not one of
whom was an indigenous African. To be sure, he described innumerable
Africans, but he rendered them not as individuals, with experience and subjectivity, but rather as bearers of racial attributes, touchstones in his own
quest for identity. This essentialism was perhaps most evident in his descriptions of black bodies. Like most Western visitors, Du Bois was powerfully
affected by the sight of naked or nearly naked bodies; unlike many, he found
the sight beautiful rather than awkward or horrifying. His account teemed
with "lithe black" bodies, "black shiny bodies, perfect bodies, bodies of
sleek, unearthly poise and beauty." "I believe that the African form in color
and curve is the beautifulest thing on earth," he wrote. "[T]he face is not so
lovely—though often comely with perfect teeth and shining eyes—but the
form of the slim limbs, the muscled torso, the deep full breasts!" Obviously
such passages were intended to rebut Western notions of African ugliness,
yet there is something disconcerting in seeing Africans' humanity reduced,
as so often in history, to their physiques.

Two days after his arrival, Du Bois, wearing a pith helmet to protect him
from the tropical sun, climbed into a hammock and was hoisted onto the
shoulders of four African men, who bore him on a three-hour walk into the
bush. "I am riding on the singing heads of black boys swinging in a hammock," he wrote. "The smooth black bodies swing and sing, the necks set
square, the hips sway. Oh, lovely voices and sweet young souls of Africa."
The destination was a small African settlement, occupied by Vai people, one
of the groups that inhabited the coastal region near the capital. The village
struck him with the force of a revelation. "How can I describe it?" he asked.
"Neither London nor Paris nor New York has anything of its delicate, precious beauty. It was . . . done in cream and pale purple—still, clean, restrained, tiny, complete." At the center of a dozen huts was a well-swept
square, where the community welcomed the "wayfarers," in keeping with
cherished African values of "hospitality." "Their manners were better than

those of Park Lane or Park Avenue," he wrote of his hosts. "They showed breeding."

Du Bois spent only a few hours in the village, but he would return to it again and again in his writing, including in "Criteria of Negro Art," his 1926 intervention in the aesthetic debates of the Harlem Renaissance, in which he held the "Village of the Veys" alongside the Venus de Milo and the cathedral at Köln as illustrative of the universal principle of "Beauty." In "The Answer of Africa," also published in 1926, he offered the "Village" as one of Africa's three "gifts" to human civilization (alongside "beginnings" and "beauty"). This "little village was a mighty thing," he wrote in the latter essay, with origins reaching "back in time thousands of thousands of years," almost to "the birth of the world." While modern societies punched out soulless, mechanical men, Africans had devised a social structure that balanced the needs of liberty and order, "individuality" and "intertwined collective soul." People growing up in such a setting brooked "no monopoly, no poverty, no prostitution." Authority rested lightly on them, embodied in chiefs and headmen who served at the pleasure of the community. Children were "well-bred and courteous," with none of the "ignorance and impudence," "sniffling and whining" of children in New York. Women walked about "naked to the waist," yet there was none of the salaciousness and "sex dalliance" that he saw "daily on Fifth Avenue."

Such passages reveal again the curious abstractness of Du Bois's vision. Though brought to Africa by a specific historical crisis, the place he described was not historical at all but "timeless," "ancient," a manifestation of "the Eternal World of Black Folk." Such rhetoric was, of course, characteristic of the man; indeed, it is one of the keys to the timelessness of his prose. But such terms carry costs. The Vai village did not reach back to "the birth of the world"; the Vai had only migrated into the region in the seventeenth and eighteenth centuries. Far from living in some timeless harmony of man and nature, the Vai had borne the brunt of great historical changes, from the coming of Islam to the transatlantic slave trade (in which they played an important intermediary role). At the time of Du Bois's visit, they were living through another upheaval, as they struggled to meet the demands of an extortionate and violent colonial state.

. . .

FOCUSED AS HE WAS on the plight of a black republic in a colonial world, Du Bois never recognized, or at least never acknowledged, that Liberia was itself a settler colonial society, with two distinct black populations: a large, ethnically diverse indigenous population, numbering something between one and a half and two million people; and a tiny Americo-Liberian settler elite, concentrated in a narrow coastal enclave and numbering some fifteen thousand. Though they represented less than 1 percent of the country's total population, the settler population monopolized wealth and political power (with few exceptions, Liberian natives were ineligible to vote). Though not inscribed in law, segregation between settlers and indigenes was the norm. What intermixture there was came chiefly through concubinage, a system that was rife in the country, or through the practice of pawning, an adaptation of a traditional practice, in which African families offered up the labor of children in settlement of debts. Americo-Liberian officials typically characterized pawning as apprenticeship, a system for educating and uplifting native children, and in some cases it doubtless operated in that fashion. In many other cases, however, it was nothing more or less than a system of domestic slavery.

Relations between settlers and indigenes had always been contentious, going all the way back to the founding days of the colony. Conflict erupted anew in the early twentieth century, as the Liberian government introduced a new system of government over the hinterland, designed to demonstrate effective sovereignty and thus check the ambitions of Britain and France. The interior was divided into districts, each with its own commissioner and, after 1908, contingent of the Frontier Force, a newly created conscript army. Africans confronted a host of new exactions (each village was required to supply the state with 125 hampers of rice and several tins of palm oil per month) and ever-increasing demands for labor for road building, construction of barracks, and service on government officials' farms. The state also imposed a hut tax of one dollar for every adult male, which quickly became Liberia's single largest source of revenue. In theory, the system operated through traditional authorities, but chiefs who were judged to be insufficiently cooperative were deposed or worse. In 1912, for example, a commissioner in a rural district responded to rumbles of discontent by publicly hanging eight chiefs.

By the time Du Bois arrived, the system had devolved into semiofficial banditry. Frontier Force soldiers, their salaries years in arrears, periodically appeared at villages to demand hut taxes, food, and labor. Hostage taking became endemic, especially of women, who were claimed as wives by soldiers or simply raped. Villages were torched, traditional authorities were humiliated, and young men were conscripted into the ragtag army. (Like the Congo's Force Publique—and like the rebel armies that would ravage Liberia in the late twentieth century—the Frontier Force had an elegantly self-reproducing logic, generating through its activities a vast pool of brutalized, deracinated young men.) Demands for labor rose relentlessly, especially for road building, which, in a climate like Liberia's, was truly the labor of Sisyphus. By the early 1920s, many native Liberians were spending up to nine months per year working on the roads, for which they received no pay. Probably the closest parallel to the system was the chain gang of the American South, except that Liberian forced laborers were required to supply their own tools and food.

In 1914, the Liberian government devised yet another way to exploit African labor, signing an agreement with Spain to supply workers to the cocoa plantations on the island of Fernando Po. For each worker transported, Liberia received £9 (or $45), a third of which went to the tax collector, with the balance pocketed by state officials. In theory, these workers were contract laborers, who served for two-year terms, at the end of which they received a lump-sum payment. Yet what evolved in practice was, in most respects, a system of slave trafficking. Africans were captured, marched under guard to the coast, and confined in baracoons where they waited to be loaded into the holds of Spanish ships. In Fernando Po, they worked long hours under the lash of overseers, and slept in barracks. Various devices were employed to confiscate wages and extend sentences. Disease was rampant. In the end, something between a third and a half of the Liberians sent to Fernando Po did not make it home alive.

Africans did not tamely submit to the new regime. In the 1910s alone, the

Liberian government faced four large-scale armed insurrections, by the Grebo, the Kru, the Golubs, and the Kpelles. Each uprising was violently put down, in the Kru case with the active support of the U.S. government, which feared that the upheaval would give the British a further pretext for annexing Liberian territory. The final act of the Kru rebellion remains one of the most notorious crimes in Liberian history. In 1916, Liberian officials invited sixty chiefs to a parlay; when they arrived, they were arrested and summarily sentenced to death. A Liberian court commuted the sentences, but most of the chiefs were executed anyway. Significantly, one of the loudest voices demanding reprisals against the rebels was future president C. D. B. King, Du Bois's esteemed host, who memorably declared, "Bad sore requires hard medicine."

What is most disturbing about Du Bois's conduct is not that he "didn't know" what was happening, but that he did and chose to hold his peace. While the full dimensions of the Fernando Po traffic were not exposed until the late 1920s, other Liberian realities were known, especially to a man like Du Bois, who, in his capacity as editor of *The Crisis*, routinely read dozens of American, European, and African newspapers. The Kru, in particular, had publicized their plight, petitioning the U.S. government in 1910 and 1912 and dispatching a formal delegation in 1914—a delegation that the editor chose to ignore. On the rare occasions that he acknowledged Liberia's "native" problem, he offered pleas in mitigation: Liberian crimes were insignificant compared to the atrocities of Europeans; discontent was a tribal atavism or worse, the work of a few agitators in the pay of the French or British. Du Bois's report to the State Department after his return in 1924 was a model of disingenuousness. Liberia had "never had a revolution or internal disturbance save, in comparatively few cases, with the war-like native tribes," he declared proudly, adding that the country had recently "extended her democracy to include natives on the same terms as Liberians" (a claim both revealingly worded and untrue). When an undersecretary of state asked about reports of mistreatment of Africans, he was only briefly nonplussed. "This question a little confused him," the official reported, "but he got out of it by saying that it was absolutely necessary for the Government to take a high hand with them, in order to assure them that it really was a government; otherwise the tribal chiefs would take things into their own hands." Du Bois reportedly added that the future economic development of Liberia would likewise provoke "a good deal of what appeared exploitation of the natives, but that he was sure this would be less unfortunate than in any British or French colony, partly for the reason that the natives were inter-marrying with the original settlers from here."

Cast against this backdrop, some of the romantic effusions of Du Bois's travel account, his expostulations about "leisure" and his hosts' "grace" and "hospitality" become more than a little unsettling. The "singing . . . black boys" who bore him in a hammock during his foray to the Vai village were quite likely forced laborers. The "gay" and "thrifty" Kru who performed a charming Christmas masque for him had seen their men impressed into service, their women ravished, and their chiefs hanged. The "endless native servants" who served him Christmas dinner on the upriver plantation of a Liberian nabob were, by any meaningful definition of the word, slaves. Du Bois's account of the dinner is particularly disconcerting, reading like a blackface version of *Gone With the Wind*. While an army of Africans cooked and served, Du Bois and his Americo-Liberian hosts glutted themselves on "duck, chicken, beef, rice, plaintain and collards, cake, tea, water and Madeira wine." The "little granddaughter of the house" flounced playfully about, "a wide pink ribbon on the thick curls of her dark hair." An old "native man, gay with Christmas and a dash of gin," danced a jig for the guests' amusement. Du Bois stayed at the party late into the night, gazing at the stars, replete with "happiness and cheer."

IN YEARS TO COME, Du Bois would watch his efforts to save Liberia unravel. The marriage of Firestone and Liberia, on which the editor had pinned such hopes, quickly soured. Negotiations over the terms of the company's concession dragged on for two years, with Firestone demanding extraordinary guarantees and Liberian officials balking at what they rightly regarded as an assault on their sovereignty. Though Du Bois strove to put the best face on it, the eventual agreement represented an almost complete victory for the company, which received a generous ninety-nine-year lease on up to a million acres of land, for a cost of just six cents an acre. Significantly, the company was only required to pay for land under active production, initially a parcel of less than fifty thousand acres. The government, for its part, agreed to take out a new loan, in order to build the road, rail, and harbor facilities that Firestone needed to get its rubber to market. (Unbeknownst to the Liberians, the New York bank that extended the loan—at a substantial premium—was a wholly owned subsidiary of Firestone.) As a final indignity, Liberia was required to pay the salaries of a team of ten American administrators, whose task was to ensure that all government revenues went to servicing the loan.

To make matters even worse, the international price of rubber collapsed. By 1928, the value of raw rubber was less than a quarter of what it had been in 1924, in part because of the breaking of the British monopoly. With the onset of global depression in 1929, the price was halved again. In such circumstances, Firestone had very little incentive to develop its holdings. Liberia would eventually grow into an important rubber producer, but for the first decade total rubber revenues averaged less than $10,000 per year, a sum that did not even pay the salaries of the American administrators overseeing the fund. Far from freeing the country from the grip of foreign debt, as Du Bois had prophesied, the Firestone concession precipitated the worst fiscal crisis in Liberian history. By the late 1920s, the state and company were completely at loggerheads, with the Liberians threatening to repudiate the debt and Firestone demanding the deployment of American marines to defend its interests.

The government and the company also squabbled over labor. In his original report, D. A. Ross, the Firestone representative who had accompanied Du Bois on his visit to the "Enchanted Forest," had enthused about the country's "inexhaustible" supplies of native labor. In fact, Liberia was relatively underpopulated. There was also (to put the matter politely) intense competition for such labor as there was. Even with its limited scale of operations, Firestone had difficulty recruiting an adequate workforce. In theory, district commissioners were expected to mobilize labor for the company, but most preferred to direct workers to Fernando Po, for which they received hefty commissions. Firestone officials railed against the situation, but soon joined in, paying bribes and bounties and not scrupling over much about the origins of their workforce. They recovered the additional costs by cutting daily wages in half, from a paltry shilling a day to a pitiful sixpence.

Unfortunately for Firestone, their resort to forced labor coincided with the visit of a Harvard University research team conducting a survey on labor conditions in tropical Africa. The results, published in 1928 under the title *The Native Problem in Africa,* offered a damning account of Liberia's labor regime, highlighting in particular the role of Firestone. The book touched off an international scandal. U.S. officials had long brushed off reports about conditions in Liberia, but facing a scandal that threatened to engulf an American corporation (a corporation whose chairman, Harvey Firestone, was President Herbert Hoover's single largest campaign contributor), they stirred themselves into action. Shortly after the report's publication, the secretary of state formally accused the government of tolerating conditions "analogous to forced labor." The idea, as historian Ibrahim Sundiata has argued, was to preempt criticism of Firestone by laying the onus on Liberian authorities. By focusing on domestic slavery and the Fernando Po traffic—a traffic that seemed particularly abominable in a nation founded by former slaves—American officials hoped to present Firestone not as a culprit but as a victim, a responsible corporation whose efforts to recruit a labor force had been stymied by corrupt officials.

At American urging, the League of Nations dispatched a three-member commission to Liberia to investigate the allegations. The League commission confirmed all of the allegations against the Liberian government and issued a series of recommendations, including restoration of chiefly authority, reorganization of the Frontier Force, and an end to slavery, pawning, and the Fernando Po traffic. Firestone escaped largely unscathed; indeed, the commission's first recommendation was to open the door to American investment even wider.

The League of Nations' report inaugurated a three-year standoff between Liberia and the international community. Initially, the government made a pretense of implementing the recommendations. Domestic slavery was legally abolished and the Fernando Po traffic outlawed. President King and Vice President Yancy, both of whom were deeply involved in the traffic, were forced to resign. But beyond that, the Liberians refused to budge. King's successor, Edward Barclay, a veteran of the often bruising world of Liberian politics, played an extraordinary game of political brinksmanship, braving diplomatic isolation and endless ultimata from the League in the belief that international outrage would ebb. The strategy worked. Frustrated with Liberian intransigence, the League washed its hands of the whole affair. The Americans quietly restored diplomatic recognition. Firestone returned to the negotiating table, trading debt relief for a batch of lucrative new concessions, as well as a promise of state assistance in labor recruitment. Having weathered the scandal, the Barclay government launched a campaign of brutal reprisals, targeting especially those who had dared to testify before the League commission. Political opponents were imprisoned under terms of a draconian new sedition law. Chiefs were murdered, and scores of villages were burned to the ground. While the Fernando Po trade stopped, forced labor within Liberia continued unabated.

As the unedifying spectacle unfolded, Du Bois continued to defend the embattled republic. He initially endorsed the League's "excellent plan of reform," but as the battle lines were drawn he switched sides, urging the Liberians to "stand fast" against what he now portrayed as an international conspiracy against the republic. Many of his arguments were indisputably correct. British and French concern for the plight of Liberian natives was indeed "a piece of smug hypocrisy." (As Du Bois noted, the British had abolished domestic slavery in neighboring Sierra Leone only in 1928.) The absence of any sustained criticism of Spain, Liberia's partner in the Fernando Po traffic, surely bespoke a "double standard," as did the conduct of American officials, who condemned forced labor in Liberia while tolerating it in Mississippi. There surely were powerful interests in the West who wished to extinguish the nation's independence, and with it the idea of black self-determination. The atrocities in Liberia paled before the genocide a generation before in the Belgian Congo, yet no voices arose in its aftermath to question Belgians' capacity for self-rule.

Many of Du Bois's arguments, however, were false, even base. The scandal was not the work of a few corrupt officials. The worst offender, Vice President Yancy, was not "a native African"—his parents came from Georgia—as if that somehow extenuated his crime. There were political prisoners in Liberia. The argument that the "intermixture" of blood was fast rendering meaningless the distinction between the republic's two populations might have been advanced with equal plausibility in the Old South. The Liberian government's record of "peace, efficiency, and ability" was not "one of the most heartening efforts in human history." The depredations of the Frontier Force were not indistinguishable from "the brutalities of police everywhere," though they were certainly not unprecedented. Perhaps most disappointing was Du Bois's effort to place the onus for slavery on Africans themselves, an effort that evoked the strained logic of proslavery apologists in antebellum America. The labor regime in Liberia was not merely an extension of the traditional practice of pawning children, nor a continuation of the domestic slavery practiced "among the more primitive Liberian tribes." The "clan organization of the tribes" did not make "free labor" impossible, nor did it mean that the "labor supply for modern industry in Africa" must always "approximate slavery." This was precisely the sort of nonsense that W. E. B. Du Bois had dedicated his life to dispelling.

DU BOIS WAS NOT the only African American caught up in the Liberian crisis. The commission appointed by the League of Nations to investigate charges of slave trading included Charles Johnson, a professor of sociology at Du Bois's alma mater, Fisk University. Johnson spent several months in Liberia, traveling through the country and interviewing men and women who had endured the Liberian government's depredations (many of whom would later be victimized for having testified). In the commission's report and in his book *Bitter Canaan*, published posthumously, Johnson described many of the ills that Du Bois had contrived to ignore, including corruption, forced labor, and organized plunder. Where Du Bois described tidy villages in which Africans lived in timeless harmony with nature and one another, Johnson saw grim cities of the dead, full of burned huts and terrified people. Where Du Bois saw "well-bred and courteous children, playing happily and never sniffling and whining," Johnson saw children whose "faces were a mass of sores," whose "favorite game was 'soldiers catch men and beat them'." But Johnson was not Du Bois's chief antagonist on Liberia. That honor fell to George Schuyler.

When all his writing is assembled—his novels and essays, his pulp fiction (most of it written pseudonymously), more than two thousand weekly newspaper columns, and four decades of signed and unsigned editorials—George Schuyler may be the only African American in history to have published more than Du Bois. In his day, he was far more widely read. Yet unlike Du Bois, who has become a cottage industry among scholars, Schuyler has been consigned to obscurity. The reason is not far to seek: most scholars today find his views, or at least the views that he expressed in the last years of his life, abhorrent. A one-time editor of the socialist *Messenger*, Schuyler by the 1950s had transmogrified into a fanatic anti-Communist, a red-baiting defender of Senator Joseph McCarthy and a vocal proponent of European colonialism in Africa. He was also the leading black critic of the civil rights movement, especially of the movement's "Typhoid Mary," Martin Luther King, Jr.

Schuyler was born in 1896 in Providence, Rhode Island, and grew up in Syracuse, New York. After high school, he enlisted in the U.S. Army where, according to his 1966 autobiography, *Black and Conservative*, he received an apprenticeship in journalism, as well as valuable instruction in discipline, responsibility, and patriotism. (According to a recent biographer, Schuyler's military service also included a two-year stint in the stockade for desertion, a fact he kept hidden during his lifetime.) After his discharge in 1919, Schuyler returned to Syracuse, where he worked as a laborer and became the first black man to join the local chapter of the Socialist Party (another episode absent from his memoirs). Like tens of thousands of other young African Americans, he was drawn to New York City, where he settled permanently in 1922. He found work as a porter and dishwasher and slept in a Bowery flophouse, an experience later immortalized in "Hobohemia," one of his greatest essays. It was the custom of New Negro writers to romanticize the low-down folk, but Schuyler was one of the few who actually lived among them, and he genuinely revered their generosity, lack of pretension, and freedom from racial cant. Even as his politics moved from extreme Left to extreme Right, he retained his populist touch, as well as his disdain for what he called the snobbocracy.

Schuyler gravitated toward New York City's socialist circles, where he met union organizer and editor A. Phillip Randolph, who hired him as an office assistant at *The Messenger*. By late 1923, he was producing a column for the paper, "Shafts and Darts: A Page of Calumny and Satire." The "dominant motive" of the column, according to Schuyler and his sometime collaborator, Theophilus Lewis, was purely malicious: "[Our] intention is . . . to slur, lampoon, damn and occasionally praise anybody or anything in the known universe, not excepting the President of the immortals." The column continued until *The Messenger*'s collapse in 1928, by which time Schuyler had undertaken a second column, "Views and Reviews," which ran weekly in the *Pittsburgh Courier* for nearly four decades. Partly as a result of his popularity, the *Courier* grew into the largest-circulating black newspaper in the United States, with more than 350,000 subscribers. His work soon caught the attention of editor H. L. Mencken, self-appointed scourge of the American "boobocracy," who recognized in the caustic columnist a kindred soul. Through the 1920s and 1930s, Schuyler would appear in Mencken's *American Mercury* more frequently than any other writer, white or black.

Though he possessed little formal training, Schuyler produced some of the classic journalism of the era. "Aframerica Today," which ran in the *Courier*, was based on a tour of the American South that Schuyler undertook to set up a distribution network for the paper. Over the course of nine months, he visited every southern city or town with a substantial black population, some two hundred of which were detailed in the series. While rife with Schuyler's antic wit—he dubbed one Oklahoma town "Ku Klux Klan Uber Alles" and awarded the "pennant in the Lynching League of America" to the state of Florida—the series was a serious exploration of the diverse ways in which African Americans operated within a stupid and violent system. The tour also provided the basis for the *American Mercury* essay "Traveling Jim Crow," a brilliant examination of the elaborate (and locally diverse) etiquette of segregation in public transport.

While capable of "serious" journalism, Schuyler was at his best as a satirist, a role that relieved him of any obligation to be responsible, constructive, or even consistent. Like Mencken, with whom he was inevitably compared, he cultivated the persona of a cynical, world-weary misanthrope. He professed "no desire to assist in the rescuing of humanity," nor did he "give a whoop" who was offended or outraged by his words. Utterly catholic in his scorn, he mocked everything from Marcus Garvey (whom he variously described as "the Imperial Blizzard," "the Sable Ponzi," and "America's Greatest Buffoon") to prevailing theories of Nordic superiority. (What other civilization, he asked rhetorically, had given the world such wonders as the Rotary Club, the Ku Klux Klan, and Mutt and Jeff?) In "This Simian World," his first *Courier* column, he examined the raging debate over evolution from the perspective of a gorilla, who ruefully concluded that humanity must have "descended" from apes "because it has never shown any evidence of ascending."

Disclaiming all loyalty to race, religion, and nation, Schuyler was the definition of an iconoclast. Yet that very iconoclasm marked him, paradoxically, as a man of his times. Urbane, unsentimental, utterly unsparing, he embodied what historian Ann Douglas has called "terrible honesty," the signature sensibility of the generation of American intellectuals emerging from the wreckage of the First World War. In the parlance of the time, Schuyler was a "debunker," a term coined by William Woodward in his 1923 book *Bunk*. The debunker's calling was to expose all forms of hypocrisy, cant, and philistinism, a role that fit Schuyler to a tee. Even those who had occasionally felt the sting of his pen valued the service. As Langston Hughes remembered, readers of *The Messenger* always turned first to "Shafts and Darts," "to see who would get shafted."

Schuyler's sheer outrageousness makes it easy to overlook the depth and consistency of his vision. While he possessed none of Du Bois's formal education, he was supremely well read, not only in African American letters but also in European and American literature, classic and modern. Not surprisingly, his tastes ran toward satire. He adored Swift and Shaw, Twain and Anatole France, but he was equally at home with contemporaries like Sherwood Anderson, Sinclair Lewis, and Edgar Lee Masters (whose *Spoon River Anthology* he brilliantly lampooned in his own "Coon River Anthology"). In the 1920s, he supplemented his education by attending free lectures at the Rand School, where he was introduced to many of the era's leading social scientists. His lecturers included economist Thorstein Veblen, whose concepts of "conspicuous consumption" and "pecuniary emulation" helped him to explain not only the vulgarity of the American bourgeoisie but the desperate urge of American workers, black and white, to join it. He was also a vocal proponent of the antiracist scholarship of anthropologist Franz Boas and his students, most notably Melville Herskovits, whose research on miscegenation mocked any notion that Americans might be neatly divided into "black" and "white." As if to validate Herskovits's theories, Schuyler married a white woman (and a southerner at that), Josephine Lewis, the daughter of a prominent Texas family.

Schuyler's chief field of study, however, was not economics or anthropology but psychology, the discipline that he believed held the key to understanding America's racial madness. While contemporaries bowed to Freud, he embraced the work of Alfred Adler, whom he first heard lecture at the Rand School. Adler, who had famously broken with Freud in the 1910s, is best remembered today for coining the term "inferiority complex," a concept that became the cornerstone of Schuyler's work. Schuyler's notorious aversion to all forms of black chauvinism did not bespeak any want of pride (as some critics suggested), and still less "an urge to whiteness," but rather a belief that genuinely proud people had no need to advertise the fact. For Schuyler, Garvey's expostulations on ancient African glories or Du Bois's learned lectures on "the blackamoor's gifts to the Great Republic" smacked of overcompensation at best; at worst, they simply flattered white vanity, since the "gifts" highlighted invariably assumed white standards of civilization and achievement. As for claims that such rhetoric was necessary to educate whites about black people's achievements and innate capacity, Schuyler was dismissive: if whites had any doubts about black people's capacity to rise, he observed, they would hardly make such strenuous efforts to keep them down.

The Rand School also introduced Schuyler to John Watson, founding father of behaviorism. If the history of the human sciences is an ongoing debate over the influences of nature and nurture, Watson occupied the extreme end of the nurture camp. To him, human beings were blank slates, whose characters and capacities were shaped by their interactions with concrete social environments. Watson was naturally contemptuous of the idea of race, which he saw as a form of mysticism, just one more vestige of the bankrupt idea of innate characteristics. One can scarcely overstate Watson's influence on Schuyler. When he and Josephine had a daughter, Philippa, born in 1932, they raised her on strict behaviorist precepts, using Watson's book, *The Psychological Care of Infant and Child,* as their bible. Their object, quite explicitly, was to raise a genius, thus vindicating behaviorist theory and exposing the folly of prevailing racial ideas, including persistent notions of "mulatto" inferiority. Perhaps the most extraordinary thing about the child's upbringing (which included rigid schedules, a carefully controlled diet, and a complete absence of childish cosseting) is the extent to which it succeeded. Philippa was a genuine prodigy, a pianist and composer of such precocious talent that she was featured in *Life* magazine, which hailed her as the American Mozart. Only later did the emotional costs of her childhood become manifest.

More important than behaviorism's imprint on Schuyler's parenting was its impact on his politics, which, even as they drifted rightward, remained anchored to the belief that individuals were products of experience rather than of biological race. In his columns, he lashed out at each new manifestation of American racialism, white or black, from the passage of Virginia's 1924 Racial Integrity Act, with its notorious "one-drop rule," to African Americans' use of skin lighteners and hair straighteners, which he dubbed "The Yellow Peril." "We cannot decry the Caucasians for their prejudices when we have the same or worse prejudices rights within our group," he declared. He was equally scornful of those who touted their blackness too much, awarding monthly prizes—a "beautifully lacquered dill pickle" or a "cut glass thunder-mug" engraved with the name of Lothrop Stoddard—to the Negro leader who had uttered that month's most extravagantly racialist statement. (Du Bois, needless to say, was a multiple winner.)

Schuyler's response to the Harlem Renaissance was predictably derisive. The extravagant critical praise for the "lowly smoke" was just the flip side of American racism, he argued, offering nervous Nordics reassurance that the Negro really was a savage. In a "Shafts and Darts" column cast as advice to aspiring black authors, he outlined all the ways to exploit the vogue: learning the Charleston, larding one's texts with references to "the jungle, the plantation or the slum," cultivating a "naïve" style befitting someone "just a century or two removed from the so-called uncivilized expanses of the Dark Continent." In a more serious vein, he warned that the New Negro enthusiasm served to "salve the conscience of white America for looting and robbing black America by emphasizing that Negroes are inferior, sentimental, sensual, ignorant, irresponsible children, thus different from white folks and therefore not deserving of the same treatment and consideration as other citizens."

All these arguments came together in "The Negro Art Hokum," a 1926 essay in which Schuyler notoriously described the "Aframerican" as "merely a lampblacked Anglo-Saxon." So heretical did the essay seem to editors at *The Nation* that they refused to publish it without a rejoinder, which was eventually supplied by Langston Hughes, whose essay, "The Negro Artist and the Racial Mountain," ran a week later. Partly because of the association with Hughes's essay (with which it is routinely anthologized), "The Negro Art Hokum" is often misread as an "assimilationist" text, but it was classic Schuyler satire, with a jerry-built edifice of overstatement and ridicule erected atop a behaviorist foundation. The current enthusiasm for "Negro Art," he declared, was simply "the last stand of the old myth palmed off by Negrophobists for these many years, and recently rehashed by the saintly [President] Harding, that there are 'fundamental, eternal, and inescapable differences' between white and black Americans." In fact, "Aframerican" art, like all art, bore the impress of specific historical circumstances—of education, region, language, class background, and a thousand other circumstances not reducible to race. Leaving aside Schuyler's signature exaggerations (including the "lampblacked Anglo-Saxon" remark), there was actually little in the essay with which Hughes disagreed.

WHILE SCHOLARS OF THE HARLEM RENAISSANCE typically pit Schuyler against Hughes, his chief bugbear in the 1920s, at least after Garvey's arrest and deportation, was Du Bois. In contrast to his feelings about Garvey, whom he regarded as an ass, Schuyler's feelings about Du Bois were distinctly ambivalent; his published remarks on the man exhibited not only his characteristic derision but also expressions of genuine admiration. The two men, who lived within a stone's throw of one another in New York, were actually much of a piece. Both were confirmed urbanites, cosmopolitan to the core, with thoroughly modern views on sexuality and women's rights. Both were steeped in social science, and saw themselves as champions of reason in a world befogged by ignorance and superstition. Yet there were also profound differences between them. While Schuyler was the archetypal modern intellectual, Du Bois was a curious synthesis of twentieth-century modernist and nineteenth-century romantic. The same Du Bois who insisted that race was an unscientific superstition—a sentiment with which Schuyler was in complete agreement—could, in virtually the next sentence, launch into paeans to tropical temperament and the "message" of Negro blood— precisely the sort of "flubdubbery" that sent Schuyler around the bend. While Du Bois revered Africa, Schuyler saw the current vogue for things African as romantic nonsense, just one more manifestation of America's race mania. To these differences was added a great gulf in style and temperament. There was a self-seriousness in Du Bois, a fulsomeness of manner and expression, that Schuyler could never resist puncturing.

All of Schuyler's principles and prejudices—his love of satire, his contempt for racialism, his disdain for American piety and optimism—came crashing together in his first novel, *Black No More*, published in early 1931. The germ of the story came from a *Courier* article about a Japanese scientist who claimed to have invented a special glandular treatment to "change black skin into white." (The scientist, a Dr. Nogushi, also claimed to be able to transform dwarves into giants and habitual criminals into law-abiding citizens.) In Schuyler's version, the mad scientist was a black man, Dr. Junius Crookman, who believed that the surest way to eliminate the "Negro problem" was by eliminating Negroes. Crookman and his shady financial backers created Black-No-More, Inc., a network of sanitariums where, with an investment of fifty dollars and three days, any Negro could obtain straight hair and the "open sesame of a pork-colored skin." A series of riotous reversals followed, culminating in what is surely the only comic lynching scene in American literature.

While Schuyler's white characters—Arthur Snobbcraft, Samuel Buggerie, and the memorable Senator Kretin—were composites, the novel's black characters were thinly fictionalized versions of well-known figures. Mme. Blandish, head of a black cosmetics empire, was L'Alelia Walker, daughter of Madame C. J. Walker and a patron of the Negro Arts movement. The buffoonish Santop Licorice was obviously Marcus Garvey. Yet in terms of sheer viciousness, nothing in the book rivaled Dr. Shakespeare Agamemnon Beard. Known equally for his "haughty bearing" and chronic grandiloquence, Beard was a spokesman for the National Social Equality League and editor of *The Dilemma*, the league's monthly journal. He was also a master of the race-leader racket, producing "scholarly and biting editorials in *The Dilemma* denouncing the Caucasians whom he secretly admired and lauding the greatness of the Negroes whom he alternately pitied and despised. In limpid prose he told of the sufferings and privations of the downtrodden black workers with whose lives he was thankfully unfamiliar. Like most Negro leaders, he deified the black woman but abstained from employing aught but octoroons. He talked at white banquets of 'we of the black race' and admitted in books that he was part-French, part-Russian, part-Indian, and part-Negro. He bitterly denounced the Nordics for debauching Negro women while taking care to hire comely yellow stenographers of weak resistance."

Black No More received mostly negative reviews, with a few critics expressing admiration for the novel's courage and inventiveness but a far larger number expressing shock and horror. Even the merciless Mencken found it "uncomfortably savage." Surprisingly, it was Du Bois who rose to the book's defense. By coincidence, Du Bois had published a tribute to Schuyler in *The Crisis* in January 1931, the month the novel appeared. "There is something tremendously refreshing and hopeful about George Schuyler," he wrote. Other "young radicals" had "turned capitalist, conservative, trade-unionist, or, worse than all, they kept still," but Schuyler had refused to be bought off, insisting on saying "things that most people do not want to hear." He was "starving like a gentleman, and one has to read what he says, whether they agree with it or not." In his review of the novel two months later, Du Bois sounded the same note, hailing the book as "a rollicking, keen, good natured criticism of the Negro problem in the United States." As a satirist, Schuyler was apt to be "misunderstood by the simple," but the book was required reading for all thoughtful black Americans. "You are bound to enjoy it," he wrote, "and to follow with joyous laughter the adventures of Max Disher and Bunny, Dr. Crookman and—we say it with all reservations—Dr. Agamemnon Shakespeare Beard."

While Du Bois could forgive the affront of Dr. Beard, he never forgave what Schuyler did next. At the very moment that the editor was defending *Black No More* in *The Crisis,* Schuyler was in Liberia as a special correspondent for the *New York Evening Post* to investigate the government's response to the recent League of Nations' slavery commission. The fruits of the journey, which was undertaken in secrecy, appeared in July and August 1931, in a six-part series that ran not only in the *Post* but in major white newspapers all over the country. The series denounced the Liberian regime as "the most shiftless, untrustworthy, incompetent and grafting ruling class to be found today anywhere." While Du Bois had spent a decade defending Liberian sovereignty, Schuyler called upon the United States to "step in and straighten things up as she has in some small states nearer home"—doubtless a reference to Haiti. If he had set out deliberately to enrage Du Bois—which to some extent he probably did—he could not have done a more thorough job.

While Du Bois cast his visit to Africa as a personal pilgrimage, Schuyler traveled as a muckraking journalist, determined "to draw aside the draperies of official camouflage and expose conditions in Liberia as they are." Not surprisingly, the two men's descriptions of the country diverged sharply. Du Bois rendered Monrovia as a coy African maiden; Schuyler saw a filthy, garbage-strewn colonial port. Du Bois described Liberian officials as heroic statesmen in the manner of Washington and Lincoln; Schuyler saw a bunch of bloated scoundrels, bouncing along rutted dirt roads in imported limousines. Most important, Schuyler drew a sharp distinction between the country's indigenous people and its Americo-Liberian rulers, a distinction that Du Bois had contrived to ignore. While the series focused on allegations of slavery and slave trading (which Schuyler believed still existed, despite formal abolition), it also examined sexual exploitation of African women and the continuing exactions of forced labor and tribute from hinterland villages. The only institution spared Schuyler's wrath was the Firestone Company, which he saw as a "model" of efficient and responsible development. To enter Firestone's large rubber plantation, he wrote, was "to enter a totally different world, a picture of what this beautiful country might be under intelligent control."

Even by Schuyler's standards, the series was unsparing. The various explanations and extenuations offered on Liberia's behalf by Du Bois were all conspicuous by their absence; for Schuyler, such things smacked of racial special pleading, a contemptible refusal to hold black people up to the same standards as white people. Arguments about the sanctity of Liberian independence, about vindicating black people's capacity for self-government, were dismissed as rationalizations by the oligarchy (and its irresponsible African American supporters) to justify its continuing exploitation of indigenous Africans. The final article in the series was, by Du Bois's standards, nothing less than racial treason. Liberia, Schuyler argued, required "outside control," specifically the imposition of American colonial authority. "There are times," he wrote, "when the masses are actually better off when ruled by efficient, foreign imperialists than by their own clique who are frequently more cruel and exacting."

But Schuyler was not finished. In the months after his return to the United States, he churned out a novel, *Slaves Today: A Story of Liberia*. Published in late 1931, the book centers on a pair of Gola newlyweds, Pameta and Zo, whose lives are thrown into upheaval when a contingent of the Liberian Frontier Force arrives in their village. In the course of three hundred melodramatic pages, the young lovers experience all of the horrors Schuyler had described in his *Evening Post* exposé, climaxing in Pameta's abduction by the local district commissioner, a Scotch-swilling, syphilitic sadist named David Jackson (plainly modeled on David Carter, a notorious district commissioner and the sole Liberian prosecuted for his role in the atrocities discussed in the League of Nations' report). Zo, a man of singular courage and character, spends the remainder of the novel seeking his beloved—enduring arrest, forced labor on a road crew, and a harrowing two years on Fernando Po. The couple is finally reunited when Zo literally stumbles upon the dying Pameta in the road, where Jackson has hurled her after discovering on her body the telltale pockmarks of syphilis. She dies in his arms, after which an enraged Zo slays Jackson, sacrificing his own life in the process.

The novel ends with the appointment of an ambitious new district commissioner, leaving little doubt that the horror will continue.

Probably the biggest question about Schuyler's Liberian work is how he possibly could have written it. While the broad argument was consistent with his long-time views about race and equality—black people placed in the position of colonial overlords had behaved, unsurprisingly, exactly as whites had acted in similar circumstances—the newspaper series and novel were otherwise completely out of character. For a decade, Schuyler had loudly disclaimed any desire to make the world a better place; reform, he argued, was just another racket, a way to "extract coin" from the gullible and sentimental. How could he now plausibly present himself as the champion of Liberia's oppressed indigenous people? Where was the irreverence, the sardonic wit, that marked *Black No More?* In that novel, Schuyler had blended fantasy and allegory in the manner of Swift or Anatole France to expose the foibles of Americans across the racial and political spectrum. *Slaves Today,* in contrast, was ripe melodrama, with idealized Africans, humble children of nature, mercilessly tormented by an Americo-Liberian population exemplifying every form of human corruption. Insofar as the book had a literary model, it appears to have been Harriet Beecher Stowe's *Uncle Tom's Cabin,* precisely the kind of pious sentimentality that Schuyler loathed.

As with so much of Schuyler's curious career, we may never know his true motives. The most charitable explanation is that the things he saw in Liberia so moved him that he for once dispensed with cynicism and wrote with seriousness and sincerity. A less charitable explanation, offered by opponents at the time, is that he had been bought, that he was motivated by nothing more than the promise of a fat check from a white newspaper. While harsh, the accusation needs to be taken seriously. Unlike Du Bois, Schuyler had no income beyond what he earned from his writing, and his predicament at the time was desperate, with his wife pregnant and his salary at the struggling *Courier* cut to a paltry $15 per week. Or perhaps Schuyler simply saw an opportunity to flog Du Bois, long a favorite whipping boy, on a subject on which he was completely exposed and vulnerable.

If Schuyler's object was to provoke Du Bois, he got his wish. The editor had accepted a personal roasting in *Black No More,* but he regarded *Slaves*

Today as a threat to the entire black race. Better the book had never been written, he declared in a furious review in *The Crisis*. While conceding the substance of some of Schuyler's charges, he insisted, as he had so often over the preceding decade, on the importance of "background." He rehearsed yet again the history of Liberia's stern struggle for survival, its poverty and the endless affronts to its sovereignty. In the end, "there was only one thing that Liberia had left, and that was her native labor." In trafficking that labor to the highest bidder, Liberia "was guilty, but she was not nearly as guilty as Spain, Belgium, France and England." If Schuyler were "to study Liberian history and the economics of West Africa," he added archly, he would see the fallacies of his own book.

But Schuyler was not prepared to defer to Du Bois on Liberia, especially now that he too could speak with the authority of an eyewitness. "Right is right and wrong is wrong, Dr. Du Bois," he wrote, "regardless of the color of the individuals or groups involved, and admiring you immensely as I do . . . I am sorry that you permitted your belligerent and commendable Negrophilism to warp your vision in the case of the Liberian racketeers." Du Bois printed the letter in *The Crisis*, though he edited out a paragraph detailing the deaths of more than six hundred Africans in the Liberian government's recent punitive raids against the Kru, essentially confirming Schuyler's allegations of bias. The exchange continued in the columns of *The Crisis* right to the end of Du Bois's tenure in 1934.

LIKE SHIPS AT SEA, Du Bois and Schuyler passed within hailing distance of one another in the 1920s and early 1930s and then proceeded on their way, bound for the far shores of the Left and Right. In 1934, Du Bois resigned from the N.A.A.C.P. Though prompted by the association's refusal to endorse his controversial "black economy" plan, the resignation was also a byproduct of his rivalry with Schuyler, who had become an influential figure within the association, under the auspices of its new executive director, Walter White. (As if to pour salt in the wound, Schuyler was appointed business manager of *The Crisis* in 1935.) Though he was sixty-six years old when he resigned, Du Bois did not retire, but instead returned to Atlanta University, where he embarked on the most productive phase of his entire career. In addition to his work as a teacher, he launched a new journal, called *Phylon*, renewed work on his long-dreamed-of *Encyclopedia Africana*, and published a steady stream of articles and books, including the magisterial *Black Reconstruction in America, 1860–1880; Dusk of Dawn*, a classic autobiography; and *Black Folk, Then and Now*, a four-hundred page "essay" on the "history and sociology of the Negro race."

In 1944, Walter White invited Du Bois to return to New York as the N.A.A.C.P.'s Director of Special Research. The post was clearly intended as a sinecure, a symbolic act of atonement to an injured elder statesman before his presumably imminent passing. But White had underestimated the old man, who proved to be as energetic as ever, and just as prickly. From the moment of his return, Du Bois protested everything from the failure to include him in important decisions to the location of his office, which opened onto a noisy common area. (He waged a constant battle with Thurgood Marshall, head of the N.A.A.C.P. Legal Defense Fund, who conducted rowdy impromptu seminars with his clerks and colleagues in the main office.) More important than the clash of personalities, however, was the clash of philosophies. For leaders like White and Marshall, the N.A.A.C.P.'s first priority was the home front, the struggle of African Americans for full equality in the United States. For Du Bois, that struggle could not be separated from the injustice and irrationality of the global economic order. The conflict came to a head in the early years of the Cold War, with an increasingly marginalized Du Bois decrying the N.A.A.C.P.'s craven surrender to anti-Communist hysteria and insisting on the continuing importance of Pan-Africanism and the wider anticolonial struggle. In 1948, Du Bois was fired, after the leaking of a memo in which he accused White of aligning the association "with the reactionary, war-mongering colonial imperialism of the [Truman] administration."

Du Bois, now eighty, found a more congenial home at the Council on African Affairs, a New York–based organization founded in the 1940s as a clearinghouse for information about Africa. But the council came in for merciless Red-baiting during the McCarthy era and was forced to close in 1955. Du Bois himself was indicted for refusing to register as an agent of a foreign power, a charge related to his support for the Stockholm Appeal, a petition against the use of nuclear weapons. He was eventually acquitted, but not before the nation was treated to the image of the venerable black leader being led away in handcuffs. Even after the acquittal, the U.S. State Department continued to withhold its one-time envoy's passport, on the grounds that his traveling overseas was not in the best interests of the United States. Restored his passport by a 1958 Supreme Court decision, Du Bois set out to confirm the department's fears, embarking with his second wife, Shirley Graham Du Bois, on a triumphal tour of the Soviet Union and China. (He celebrated his ninety-first birthday with Chairman Mao.) In 1961, facing a renewed threat to his passport, he and his wife left the United States for good, resettling in Africa as the guests of Ghana's president, Kwame Nkrumah. On the day of his departure, Du Bois formally enrolled in the American Communist Party, a final gesture of defiance to a nation that had rejected his gifts.

George Schuyler's journey was, if anything, stranger than Du Bois's. By the mid-1930s, his migration to the political Right had begun, but he remained unpredictable. While he continued to attack Liberia in articles such as "The Lord's Work" and "Monrovia Mooches On," he emerged as one of the nation's most outspoken defenders of Ethiopian independence, decrying the Italian invasion of 1935 and calling on African Americans to rally in defense of their embattled brethren in Africa—precisely the sort of sentiment he had disallowed for Liberia. In one column, he expressed a desire to "machine gun" an Italian, a fantasy that he proceeded to indulge in a pair of serialized novels in the *Courier,* in which he envisioned a global uprising of the black race. Published under the name "Samuel Brooks," the books were only recently discovered to be Schuyler's work. While some scholars have found in the novels evidence of an incipient black nationalism, Schuyler himself described them as "hokum and hack work of the purest vein." "I deliberately set out to crowd as much race chauvinism and sheer improbability into it as my fertile imagination could conjure," he explained to a friend, adding that the enthusiasm with which each week's installment was greeted "vindicates my low opinion of the human race." Yet he also remained capable of producing work of great seriousness and courage. When the U.S. government began to round up Japanese Americans after Pearl Harbor, Schuyler was the only prominent newspaper columnist, black or white, to condemn the action.

The one consistent thread in Schuyler's politics was anticommunism. Even during the 1920s, when he was an avowed Socialist, he disdained the Communist Party, which he regarded as opportunistic, anti-intellectual, and utterly indifferent to individual freedom. Communists, for Schuyler, epitomized the cardinal sin of reform movements: the desire for simple solutions to complex problems. During the Scottsboro controversy of the early 1930s, he relentlessly attacked the party, which he accused of cynically risking the lives of the accused to advance its own fortunes. The Communist Party's "insane tactics," he warned, "give the murderous Southern Neanderthals the very opportunity and excuse they are looking for to commit additional homicides." On several occasions, he went even further, suggesting that the party, by recklessly enflaming "racial animosity," was risking an "actual civil war which would certainly lead to genocide." If there was a silver lining, it was that Communist appeals to black Americans appeared to fall on deaf ears. In "Negroes Reject Communism," a 1939 essay in the *American Mercury*, Schuyler pinned his hopes on the good sense of black Americans, whose "three-century struggle to avoid extermination" had endowed them with a "healthy cynicism" about "crackers" who preached revolution. "Right now, it's enough trouble being black without going Red," he concluded.

In the post–World War II period, Schuyler's anticommunism became more extreme, metastisizing into a strange kind of monomania. Long before most Americans had heard of Senator Joseph McCarthy, he warned of a vast Communist conspiracy eating away at the vitals of American society. He saw signs of the threat everywhere, from the Eisenhower administration to the Montgomery bus boycott. As his anticommunism grew, the qualities that had distinguished his work in the 1920s and 1930s—the antic spirit, the reckless honesty, the refusal to take anything (including himself) too seriously—shriveled. The Schuyler of the 1920s would have made mincemeat of Joe McCarthy, whatever his feelings about communism; the later Schuyler defended the senator as "a great American," a "well-intentioned politician who was appalled by what he learned of the Communist conspiracy against America." In 1954, Schuyler ostentatiously resigned from the Committee on Cultural Freedom—an organization later revealed to be a C.I.A. front—because of what he regarded as its tepid support of the senator.

By the late 1950s, anticommunism overshadowed everything Schuyler wrote, including his work on Africa. Between 1958 and 1961, he made several trips to the continent, visiting a half dozen newly independent countries in West Africa, as well as Mozambique and Angola, where Portuguese colonizers struggled to hold back the tide of decolonization. While most contemporary visitors saw a long-exploited continent struggling to throw off the shackles of European imperialism, Schuyler saw "hapless aggregations of people" claiming a status they were unequipped to bear, thus throwing open the door to the Soviets. (In "Krushchev's African Foothold," a 1959 *American Mercury* essay, he described Ghana's Kwame Nkrumah, Du Bois's soon-to-be host, as a card-carrying Communist and "demagogue with a Napolean complex.") The respect and sympathy that Schuyler had evinced for indigenous Africans in Liberia a generation before were nowhere in sight. Africans, he declared bluntly, were "international retardates," whose only hope for development rested on continued "European and American investment and direction."

Anticommunism also dictated Schuyler's response to the civil rights movement, whose leaders he saw as "pied pipers," taking Negroes down the garden path to communism. In 1964, he campaigned as the Conservative Party's candidate for the Harlem congressional seat of Adam Clayton Powell, Jr. He was easily outpolled by Powell, but he made a considerable stir nonetheless, railing against Reds, crime, and what he called "welfare colonialism"—a concept foreshadowing the conservative resurgence of the 1980s. The 1965 Harlem race riot was, for Schuyler, confirmation of all he had been saying about the breakdown of social order. By grimly apt coincidence, Schuyler was one of two black members of the grand jury whose refusal to indict a police officer accused of shooting an unarmed black youth precipitated the riot.

Schuyler reserved his most extravagant attacks for Martin Luther King, Jr., whom he described as a "sable Typhoid Mary, infecting the mentally disturbed with [his] perversion of Christian doctrine." He was incensed when King won the 1964 Nobel Peace Prize, memorably declaring that he more properly deserved the Order of Lenin. The claim was too much for his ever-indulgent editors at the *Pittsburgh Courier,* who for the first time in four decades refused to run a column. Undeterred, Schuyler promptly sold the piece to the archconservative *Manchester Union.* By 1966 he had cut his ties to the *Courier* completely and gone to work full-time for the *Union.* (The paper's editor and publisher, William Loeb, memorably described Schuyler as one of the "three great untwisted negro intellects" ever produced in the United States, the other two being Booker T. Washington and George Washington Carver.) He also became a regular contributor to *American Opinion* and *Review of the News,* periodicals of the John Birch Society, which he joined sometime in the early 1960s. By that time, he had lost virtually all his black readership, though he was lionized by white conservatives, who honored him with the American Legion Award and the Valley Forge Freedoms Foundation Award. The George Schuyler of the 1920s would surely have awarded himself a lacquered dill pickle for that.

· SEVEN ·

Native Son, American Daughter

DURING HIS LONG DEFENSE OF LIBERIA, W. E. B. Du Bois had regarded the republic as a bellwether. If Liberia survived and prospered, it would offer irrefutable proof of black people's capacity for self-government, thus speeding the progress of independence all over the continent. If it was extinguished, the cause of African independence would be set back for generations, perhaps for all time. Fortunately for Du Bois, decolonization did not wait for Liberia. In the thirty years after World War II, the edifice of European colonialism collapsed, and some forty-five African colonies and territories emerged as independent nations. The process was watched and analyzed by literally thousands of scholars, journalists, and pundits, including many African Americans. Among the first were Richard Wright and Era Bell Thompson.

Wright and Thompson appear never to have met, but there was some strange magnetism between them, some force that repeatedly drew them together and then prised them apart. In personality and temperament, they were as different as the Mississippi plantation and the North Dakota prairie from which they sprang, yet they both came to Chicago in 1927, determined to be-

come writers. Both recounted their upbringings in classic autobiographies—
Black Boy, published in 1945, and *American Daughter*, published a year later.
Their paths then parted. While Wright went into brooding self-exile in
France, Thompson found a home at Chicago's *Ebony* magazine, a new mass-
circulation monthly whose upbeat tone and proud Americanism matched her
temperament as thoroughly as the smoky cafés and existential angst of
Paris's Left Bank matched his. But in May 1953, compelled by interests that
were at once radically different and curiously similar, they both embarked
for Africa. Their accounts of their journeys—Wright's *Black Power: A
Record of Reactions in a Land of Pathos* and Thompson's *Africa: Land of My
Fathers*—were published in the very same week in 1954.

Not surprisingly, the books differed in most particulars, but taken together they return us to a pregnant historical moment, a moment just before
the final assaults on African colonialism and American Jim Crow. Yet they
also illuminate some of the pressing questions of our own postcolonial,
post–civil rights era—questions about the nature and limits of "racial" affiliation, the impact of a shrinking global geography on individual and collective identities, and the human capacity for empathy.

BORN ON A Mississippi plantation in 1908, Richard Wright grew up in
circumstances of utter bleakness and deprivation. He was six when his father, a sharecropper, abandoned the family; he was ten when his mother suffered a paralytic stroke. Wright spent the rest of childhood bouncing from
home to home, living in Natchez and Jackson, usually with relatives, briefly
in an orphanage. He spent several years with his maternal grandmother, a
staunch Seventh-Day Adventist who refused to allow books in her house and
regaled her grandchild with tales of the damnation awaiting him. A brief sojourn in Elaine, Arkansas, was cut short when his uncle, a successful businessman, was lynched. Wright attended school when he could, and managed
to complete the ninth grade before fleeing to Memphis, where he found a job
as a dishwasher. Few who knew this angry, alienated, fearful child could
have imagined that he would survive, let alone become one of the century's
greatest writers.

In years to come, Wright would ponder his surprising survival. "What was it that made me conscious of possibilities?" he asked. "From where in this southern darkness had I caught a sense of freedom?" His answer was books. From his earliest encounter with a dog-eared copy of *Bluebeard and His Seven Wives,* smuggled into his grandmother's house by a sympathetic boarder, he was entranced by books, by their capacity to conjure worlds beyond the stifling confines of his own. (The plot of *Bluebeard,* it should be noted, turns on the serial murder of women, a recurring theme in Wright's own work.) In a famous episode in *Black Boy,* his autobiography, he recounted how he sought out the work of H. L. Mencken after seeing the acerbic editor, who delighted in lampooning the South, denounced in a Memphis newspaper. Using a borrowed library card and a forged note—"Dear Madam: Will you please let this nigger boy have some books by H. L. Mencken?"—he obtained copies of *Prejudices* and *A Book of Prefaces* from the white public library. If the former book offered a creed—"using words as a weapon . . . as one would use a club"—the latter provided a syllabus. Through Mencken, he discovered not only Theodore Dreiser (his favorite writer) but also Mark Twain, Sherwood Anderson, Sinclair Lewis, and Joseph Conrad, whose portentous prose style he strained to imitate in his earliest stories. Like Mencken, Wright's tastes ran to contemporary naturalist writers, authors who penetrated beneath social convention to plumb "the great forces that circumscribe and condition personality." "All my life had shaped me for the realism, the naturalism of the modern novel, and I could not read enough of them," he recalled.

The idea of literacy as the gateway to self-expression and freedom is a ubiquitous theme in African American literature, from the slave narratives of Olaudah Equiano and Frederick Douglass to the *Autobiography of Malcolm X.* But few have pressed the theme further than Richard Wright. Books, he insisted, not only endowed him with a voice; they also awakened in him a capacity for "self-reflection." For Wright, it was this capacity that distinguished man from brute, that enabled a human being to rise above primal terror and the "direct, animalistic impulses" of the body to fashion a meaningful identity and destiny. He believed, moreover, that self-reflection was neither innate nor universal. Rather, it was the signal achievement of the

West, a prize wrung from Western man's slow rise from the dark "feudal" past to the light of modern individualism. When Wright lamented that most "Negroes had never been allowed to catch the full spirit of Western civilization, that they lived somehow in it but not of it," it was this capacity to which he referred.

Such sentiments may ring strangely across today's postcolonial landscape, but they are vital to understanding Richard Wright. Most obviously, they help to explain his profound commitment to individual freedom against the demands of family, church, race, or other collective loyalties. Most writers, in Wright's time and in our own, have represented the "black community" as a refuge, a haven from the West's soulless individualism, but for Wright communal bonds were impediments to freedom, vestiges of tribalism perpetuated by ignorance, illiteracy, and Jim Crow terror. And yet Wright was no unabashed worshipper of the West. He recognized that Western freedom rested on a foundation of slavery and racism, that the same civilization that celebrated the sanctity of the individual personality casually condemned millions to lives of ignorant, brutish toil. He would carry this double ambivalence with him to Africa, where the horrors of "tribal nonentity" and Western colonialism converged.

In 1927, Wright moved to Chicago, terminus of the Illinois Central Railroad and destination of tens of thousands of black Mississippians. He described his arrival in the city in the opening sentences of *American Hunger*, the sequel to *Black Boy*: "My first glimpses of the flat black stretches of Chicago depressed and dismayed me, mocked all my fantasies. Chicago seemed an unreal city whose mythical houses were built of slabs of black coal wreathed in palls of gray smoke, houses whose foundations were sinking slowly into the dank prairie." The echo of T. S. Eliot's "Unreal City" was obviously deliberate, but for Wright Chicago was anything but a wasteland. Over the next decade, he would meet many of his literary idols, including Theodore Dreiser, Carl Sandburg, and Nelson Algren. A stipend from the Federal Writers' Project enabled him to begin writing full-time. Chicago also afforded him an apprenticeship in politics. By the early 1930s, he was active in the John Reed Club, and in 1933 he formally joined the Communist Party. He spent the next nine years in the party, an experience recounted in a classic essay, "I Tried to Be a Communist." If the essay is to be believed, Wright spent most of his tenure clashing with party leaders over what he should and should not write, but the experience was clearly formative, and left an enduring imprint on his politics and his art.

Chicago was the fountainhead not only of the naturalist novel but also of American social science. Led by Robert Park and Louis Wirth, scholars at the University of Chicago had fused sociology and psychology, history and anthropology, into a new "science" of urban life. Wright's introduction to the Chicago School came through Wirth's wife, Mary, who was fortuitously assigned as his case worker by the local relief office. While the first job she secured him, as a custodian at a medical laboratory, ended disastrously— Wright recounted the experience in *Black Boy*—she was impressed with his seriousness and ambition, and continued to assist him, eventually helping him to secure a position with the Illinois Writers' Project. At about the same time, Louis Wirth delivered a lecture at the John Reed Club on the impact of ghetto life on personality development. The talk so impressed Wright that he sought Wirth out at his office and asked for a reading list, returning a few weeks later to discuss the books with the surprised sociologist. Though he never formally enrolled at the university, Wright became the Chicago School's most avid student, poring over journals, monographs, even survey data, searching for insight into his world and his own chronic fear and restlessness.

While the Chicago School embraced a range of different approaches and arguments, it rested on a set of shared problems and premises. All of the scholars in the school were concerned with the struggle between individual and collective, between the individual's quest for self-realization and the society's need for unity and conformity. More broadly, the Chicago School represented one of the first attempts to chart what later social scientists would call modernization. Drawing on Ferdinand Tönnies's germinal 1887 study, *Gemeinschaft und Gesellschaft*, the Chicagoans explored what happened to human beings as they moved from "community," associated with rural life and characterized by personal social bonds, traditional folkways, and the rhythms of nature, to "society," associated with cities and characterized by impersonality, competition, and change. Tönnies's model offered the Chicagoans a framework for understanding the predicament of the European immigrants—and, after 1914, the African American migrants—pouring into American cities. Uprooted from collapsing rural worlds, tossed into the maelstrom of modernity, these new urban migrants were human flotsam—spiritually homeless, confused, and distrustful, completely unprepared for (and usually unwelcome in) the modern American city. In the phrase of Park and his colleague, Everett Stonequist, they were "marginal men," suspended between traditional and modern worlds, belonging to neither.

As Wright's own career would show, the insights of the Chicago School could lead to a range of different conclusions. In the hands of conservatives, they gave a scientific veneer to shopworn notions of black people as simple, rural folk, unprepared for the cold, competitive rigors of northern urban life. (Before coming to Chicago, Robert Park had spent a decade at Tuskegee working as a ghostwriter for Booker T. Washington, perhaps the most famous exponent of this argument.) In more liberal hands, the arguments of the Chicago School led to racial paternalism, embodied in the host of initiatives and institutions launched by white philanthropists to help "bewildered" southern migrants "adjust" to urban life. (Wright briefly worked at one such institution, the Chicago South Side Boys' Club, before resigning in frustration.) Yet whatever its racial overtones, the Chicago School was music to Wright's ears. Here was an approach to "the Negro problem" that relied on science rather than superstition, that analyzed behavior in terms of environment and experience rather than racial inheritance. More importantly, the Chicago School offered the chronically self-conscious young writer insight into his own psychology and historical predicament. "I had fled [the South] with the dumb yearning to write, to tell my story," he later recalled. "But I did not know what my story was, and it was not until I stumbled upon science that I discovered some of the meanings of the environment that battered and taunted me."

After a decade in Chicago, Wright moved to New York City in 1937 to become the Harlem editor of the Communist Party's *Daily Worker*. He continued to read voraciously in New York, seeking concepts to enable him to tell his story in more universal, more encompassing ways. Introduced to existentialism by Ralph Ellison, he quickly devoured all the major texts. He also began to explore psychology and psychoanalysis, accumulating a library of several hundred volumes, as well as a collection of clinical case studies, assembled with the help of his friend Frederic Wertham, a controversial New York psychoanalyst best known for the book *Dark Legend*, a study of matricide. While Wright was interested in the therapeutic possibilities of psychiatry—he and Wertham opened a free clinic in Harlem in the early 1940s—he approached the field chiefly as an imaginative artist, seeking additional insights into psychopathology, the terrain he had already begun to chart in his writing. The more widely he read, the more persuaded Wright became that his story was not simply the story of black America but the experience of all humankind. It was the tale of millions of atomized human beings, uprooted from traditional societies and cast into a modern world offering few clear guides to identity and meaning.

Wright published his first book, *Uncle Tom's Children*, in 1938 but he owed his celebrity to *Native Son*, published two years later. Set in the fetid tenements of Chicago's Black Belt, *Native Son* charted the psychological universe of an inarticulate black thug, Bigger Thomas. The book declared war on existing representations of African American life in its opening scene, in which a skillet-wielding Bigger battered a rat that had invaded his family's kitchenette apartment. From that harrowing beginning, the story unfolded with a relentless, Dostoyevskian logic, through two murders and the ensuing manhunt, arrest, and trial, ending with Bigger on death row. The book became an immediate sensation, selling a quarter million copies in the first month alone. "The day *Native Son* appeared, American culture was changed forever," critic Irving Howe later wrote. "It made impossible a repetition of the old lies [and] brought out into the open, as no one ever had before, the hatred, fear and violence that have crippled and may yet destroy our culture." Even the stodgy Book-of-the-Month Club embraced *Native Son*, designating it a main selection, the first time a black-authored book had been so honored. (The club newsletter reassured nervous members that the novel "is quite as human as it is Negro.") The book's popularity, combined with the even greater success of *Black Boy* five years later, established this sharecropper's son as the representative literary voice of black America, a singularly ironic position for a soon-to-be exiled ex-Communist who consistently disavowed membership in any race, tribe, or tradition.

With its violent protagonist and unstinting portrayal of ghetto life, *Native Son* is typically held up as representative of the early, "visceral" Richard Wright, before he emigrated to Paris and was "spoiled" by alien, academic theories. Yet most of the ideas that would animate his later work, including his writing about Africa, were already on display. In the very first chapter of the book, Wright used the device of a movie double feature to highlight Bigger's status as marginal man, uprooted from the old and mocked by the new. The first film, *Trader Horn*, was a Dark Continent adventure yarn, full of throbbing "tom toms" and "naked black men and women . . . dancing against a background of barbaric jungle." The second, *The Gay Woman*, showed millionaire whites casually cuckolding one another while "lolling on beaches, swimming, and dancing in night clubs." Neither world offered any identity or meaning to Bigger, who, in the original, unexpurgated version of the text, idly masturbated in the theater.

Native Son also exhibited Wright's universalism, his abiding aversion to racial explanations of behavior. In the book, he relied on Max, Bigger's Communist attorney, to articulate the argument, but he made it in his own voice in "How Bigger Was Born," an essay published a few months after the novel and adopted as an introduction to most subsequent editions. In the essay, Wright addressed allegations that *Native Son* perpetuated racial stereotypes, a charge, he argued, that misconstrued the entire book. Conduct and consciousness were conditioned not by race but by "concrete social environment"—in Bigger's case, by the American ghetto, with its filth, overcrowding, and material deprivation, all made worse by the "teasing torture" of simultaneous exposure to and exclusion from the glittering abundance of the American city. Of course, most ghetto residents did not resort to murder. Bigger's mother represented the millions who found refuge in "hysterical" religion. Others sought the anodyne of liquor or sex, or the cheap stimulus of movies, pulp novels, and detective magazines. But all bore the scars of a blighted environment.

Finally, *Native Son* exhibited Wright's penchant for presenting black life in an utterly unsparing, even harshly negative light. His justification was simple: "Oppression oppresses." Racial oppression deformed personalities. It sapped initiative. It poisoned even the most intimate human bonds. (*Black Boy* began with the young author being beaten unconscious by his mother after torching the family's home.) Wright's celebrated grievance against the writers of the Harlem Renaissance was not simply that they lacked realism but that they refused to confront this trauma, peddling instead romantic caricatures of Negroes as saintly victims or redoubtable folk. Given the enduring influence of romantic racialism in American life, Wright's approach had much to recommend it, but it also conduced to an extremely impoverished conception of black culture, as Ralph Ellison long ago noted. In his most extreme formulations, black people had no culture at all, only a history of oppression that had persisted so long as to "become a tradition, in fact a kind of culture." In time, Wright would bring this bleak analysis to bear on the predicament of Africans emerging from colonialism.

THE CIRCUMSTANCES of Wright's exile are well-known. In 1946 he spent six months in Paris as a guest of the French government. After an unhappy return to New York, he emigrated permanently in 1947. At a time when American intellectual life withered in the chill of the early Cold War, Paris, liberated from Nazi occupation, bloomed. Though he had publicly broken with the Communist Party, Wright gravitated to the left-wing intellectuals of the Left Bank, especially the existentialists. He formed lasting friendships with Jean-Paul Sartre and Simone de Beauvoir, and had more fleeting encounters with Albert Camus and Frantz Fanon, a then obscure Martiniquan psychiatrist, whose germinal 1952 study of colonial psychopathology, *Black Skin, White Masks*, was inspired in part by *Native Son*. Just as he had met literary heroes like Dreiser and Sandburg in Chicago, in Paris Wright met André Malraux, his favorite French writer, and the new Nobel laureate, André Gide. Significantly, one of the first books he appears to have read after arriving in Paris was *Travels in the Congo*, Gide's 1927 homage to Conrad's *Heart of Darkness*. Echoes of both Conrad and Gide would reverberate through Wright's own African account.

During his years in the Communist Party, Wright had evinced no interest in Pan-Africanism, which seemed just another manifestation of racial parochialism. In France, he plunged headlong into the movement. He met René Maran, whose African novel, *Batouala*, had so inspired the writers of the Harlem Renaissance, as well as Aimé Césaire and Leopold Senghor, founders of the Négritude movement. In 1947 he joined Sartre, Camus, Gide, and other intellectual luminaries on the committee of patronage for *Presence Africaine*, a new journal celebrating the artistic and literary genius of the African race. The differences between Wright and his new comrades would soon become apparent. A committed, if conflicted, modernist, Wright had little patience with the invocations of African spirituality that were the stock-in-trade of Négritude writers; the Harlem Renaissance writers that they embraced as models, he disdained. But such differences were initially outweighed by what was shared. Like Wright, the Négritude writers were skeptical of both communism and capitalism, struggling to create a non-aligned, anticolonial movement in an increasingly bipolar world. They also shared his interest in the psychological effects of colonialism, as well as his belief in the liberating potential of art.

Wright formed a more enduring friendship with George Padmore, whom he met in London in 1947. An indefatigable fighter for the liberation of the colonial world, Padmore had organized workers' movements all over the world, from his native Trinidad to the United States, the Soviet Union (where he headed the Profintern's Negro Bureau) to Nazi Germany (where he spent time in a concentration camp). Following his break with the Communist Party, Padmore settled in London, where he founded the International African Service Bureau, intended as a kind of nerve center for the global anticolonial movement. The cluttered kitchen of Padmore's Cranleigh Street flat served as a seminar room for many of the people who would spearhead African decolonization, including Kenya's Jomo Kenyatta, Nigeria's Nnamdi Azikiwe, and the Gold Coast's Kwame Nkrumah, all future heads of state. Through his friendship with Padmore, Wright acquired not only an education in African nationalism but also a feeling—exaggerated, in retrospect—of direct participation in the movement. Increasingly, he saw himself not simply as a chronicler of black Americans' plight, but as a champion of the world's colonized peoples. So persuaded was he of this new mandate that he blocked publication of an edition of his collected works, lest it fix him in an American Negro "provincialism."

The problem, of course, was that Wright had never set foot in the colonial world. Indeed, aside from a visit to Argentina to work on the disastrous film version of *Native Son*, he had never been outside of North America and western Europe. In 1941, he volunteered his services as a foreign correspondent to the Associated Negro Press—he proposed to travel to China and India to see "how the brown, red, and yellow people are faring"—but the State Department, well aware of his Communist affiliation, refused to act on his passport application. Wright returned to the Associated Negro Press after the war. Now he wanted to visit Africa, where he believed his experience as a black southerner would give him privileged insight into the predicament of Africans living under European colonialism. Again, nothing came of the proposal, but the determination remained. "I must see Africa," he wrote in his journal in 1947. "I say here and now that I shall write the only book about Africa that will be written in my time."

By the early 1950s, Wright's interest had come to focus on the Gold Coast, where Padmore's protégé, Kwame Nkrumah, had launched an unprecedented challenge to British colonial rule. Like his mentor, Nkrumah had ranged widely across the Atlantic world. Born in the Gold Coast, he came to the United States as a student in 1935, earning degrees from Lincoln University and the University of Pennsylvania. Following World War II, he moved to England, where he and Padmore convened the fifth Pan-African Congress in Manchester, reviving the organization founded by W. E. B. Du Bois after World War I. In 1947, Nkrumah returned home to take up a position as general secretary of the United Gold Coast Convention. Frustrated by its middle class, constitutional nationalism, he broke with the group in 1949 and launched the Convention People's Party, a mass-based movement demanding immediate independence. Under the spur of the C.P.P.'s Positive Action campaign, a wave of nonviolent strikes and protests, the British were forced to concede popular elections, which swept Nkrumah from a jail cell into parliament, first as leader of government business and later as the colony's first African prime minister. In 1953, Nkrumah readied a parliamentary motion setting the Gold Coast on an irreversible path to independence.

In "How Bigger Was Born," written in 1940, against the backdrop of European fascism, Wright had speculated about the emergence of a personality or movement capable of mobilizing the Bigger Thomases of the world, of fusing all those dark, aimless human atoms into a coherent political force. Kwame Nkrumah appeared to have conceived such a movement. And who better to herald the birth than Bigger's creator, Richard Wright?

WRIGHT TRACED the classic African American migration route, following the Illinois Central Railroad up from Mississippi through Memphis to Chicago. Era Bell Thompson came to Chicago from the other direction, virtually from the other end of the universe: a homestead on the North Dakota prairie. Like Wright, Thompson was the grandchild of slaves. Her father was born on a Virginia plantation, the illegitimate issue of a house servant and the son of the manor. Pop, as she called him, moved north with his family after the Civil War before setting out on his own. A charming, chatty man, he spent the decades of Reconstruction, Redemption, and the onset of Jim Crow in the Midwest, working variously as a waiter, cook, coal miner, hotelier, storekeeper, and cloakroom attendant in the Iowa State Senate. He had acquired and lost at least two wives by the time he married Era Bell's mother, also a Virginian, who was working as a nursemaid for a wealthy white family. Era Bell, the couple's youngest child, was born in 1906 in Des Moines, but she spent most of her childhood on a North Dakota farm, where her father tried his hand at homesteading.

Growing up, Thompson and her family were the only African Americans in a fifty-mile circle, a black island in a sea of Norwegian farmers. She and her brothers caused some consternation on their first day at school, being the first "bona fide Negroes" that their classmates (and several of their teachers) had ever seen. They endured the obligatory taunts—even Norwegian immigrants learned the word "nigger"—but it passed. Era Bell's status was secured not only by her distinction in the classroom but also by her prowess on the playground. Though she never grew past five feet, she was a gifted basketball player, as well as a champion sprinter. (In her later career at North Dakota State University, where she was again the sole black student, she set several state and national intercollegiate records in track.) For

Thompson, sports became the quintessentially American arena, a world in which people were measured not by the circumstances of their births but "by the strength of their arms and the speed of their feet."

Thompson would later recount her childhood in an autobiography, *American Daughter*, published in 1946, just a year after Wright's *Black Boy*. The book was as sunny as Wright's book was dark, reading less like Dostoyevsky than an installment of the *Little House on the Prairie* series. While Wright described a world of stunted hopes and arbitrary terror, Thompson sketched a universe of blue sky, golden prairie, and unbounded horizons. What adversity the family encountered was of the natural rather than human kind—winter blizzards, summer grasshoppers, uncertain rainfall. Local folk were warm and neighborly, supplying the newcomers with food and shelter, as well as a wealth of practical advice, communicated in a mutually intelligible dialect that she dubbed "Negrowegian." Though Thompson had occasional encounters with racism—she first met Jim Crow in a Fargo movie house—she played them chiefly for comic effect in her book. In her church's annual missionary pageant, for example, she was invariably cast as Mother Africa, sparing another child the necessity of donning blackface. Soon every church in the region was asking her to play the part, but her budding theatrical career was cut short by an incident involving her torch and the feather headdress of a little girl representing Native Americans.

Ruminating on his childhood, Richard Wright traced his emotional difficulties to the fact that he had so little contact with white people while growing up, and thus never mastered the habits of submission and self-effacement essential to survival in Jim Crow Mississippi. "Perhaps I had waited too long to start working for white people," he wrote; "perhaps I should have begun earlier, when I was younger—as most of the other black boys had done—and perhaps by now the tension would have become an habitual condition, contained and controlled by reflex." Era Bell Thompson had precisely the opposite problem. As a result of her upbringing, she felt "more comfortable," even "more accepted," among whites than she did among African Americans, few of whom she had ever met. Her first glimpse of a wider black world came through the *Chicago Defender* and it terrified her. The very first issue she saw, sent home in 1919 by her brother Dick, a new migrant to the city, featured a report on the recent Chicago race riot, as well as a grisly photograph of a southern lynching. For Thompson, that hanging body "became a symbol of the South, a place to hate and fear. And Dick's civilization was a riot, where black and white Americans fought each other and died. I wanted never to leave my prairies, with white clouds of peace and clear blue heavens."

Yet Thompson too would eventually be drawn to Chicago. She first lived in the city in 1927, the same year Wright arrived, after an illness had forced her temporarily to leave college. She returned and settled permanently in 1933. Though she and Wright appear not to have met, they moved in some of the same circles. Thompson's first job was at the University of Chicago Settlement House, where the theories about urbanization and migrant adjustment developed by the university's famed sociologists were put to the test. In the years that followed, she worked in various public agencies, including the Works Progress Administration, the Department of Public Works, and the Chicago Relief Administration, mostly in clerical jobs. Like Wright, she had set her sights on becoming a writer, though her vision of that calling could scarcely have differed more from his. In her last years in North Dakota, she had begun freelancing articles for the *Chicago Defender*, eventually producing a regular column, a light-hearted rendering of "the wild and wooly West," under the nom de plume Dakota Dick. She later worked on her college newspaper, writing a humor column as well as an advice column for the lovelorn (for which she wrote both queries and responses). While working at Chicago's Public Works Department, she began to produce a single-page daily, *The Giggler*, which eventually grew into the department's in-house newspaper.

On the strength of her journalism, Thompson was offered a position with the Federal Writers' Project, but reluctantly declined it, on the grounds that it paid less than she was earning as a clerk. But she was given a second chance in 1945, when she received a fellowship from the Newberry Library to write a memoir of her childhood. Her object, as she explained in her grant application, was to put to rest the two questions that had plagued her since her arrival in Chicago: "Where is North Dakota?" and "What in the world was a nice Negro girl like you doing in that godforsaken country in the first place?" She maintained the same light-hearted tone in her book, rehearsing the travails and triumphs of her upbringing with wry humor and nary a hint of hurt or rancor. Whether Thompson intended her title, *American Daughter*, as a rejoinder to *Native Son* is uncertain, but that is how the book was read at the time. "There is nothing of Richard Wright" in the book, one critic noted. "Here is an autobiography by a Negro author that does not deal with the thwarting and distorting effects of the American race problem," wrote another. "Here is a life of a Negro girl who, for a while at least, lived and thought and acted like any other American."

Wright had fled the "southern darkness" for the promise of Chicago, only to discover new kinds of darkness, violence, and fear. Thompson, in contrast, offered a vision of America as expansive as the North Dakota prairie. While not denying the existence of racism, she regarded it as a minor impediment, a temporary aberration that would pass as Americans came to know and appreciate one another. As Wright prepared for a life of exile, Thompson concluded *American Daughter* with a paean to this color-blind future. "I know . . . that way down underneath, most Americans are fair; that my people and your people can work together and live in peace and happiness, if they but have the opportunity to know and understand each other," she wrote. "The chasm is growing narrower. When it closes, my feet will rest on a united America."

BY A STROKE OF FORTUNE, *American Daughter's* appearance coincided with the launch of *Ebony* magazine, a mass-circulation monthly dedicated to the same sunny view of African American life and prospects. Published in Chicago, Ebony was the brainchild of John H. Johnson, an ambitious, Arkansas-born entrepreneur destined to become the first African American to crack *Fortune* magazine's roster of the four hundred wealthiest Americans. How Johnson first met Thompson is unclear, but he immediately recognized her as a kindred spirit. In 1947, Thompson joined Johnson Publishing as an editor and staff writer. In 1951, she was elevated to co–managing editor, making her the first woman editor of a mass-circulation magazine in American history. She retired from her position in the 1970s, but stayed on as international editor, a title she retained until her death in 1986. In all, Thompson spent nearly forty years at *Ebony*, helping to transform it from a cash-strapped upstart into an internationally recognized brand with a global readership of more than ten million.

Johnson, who came to Chicago in 1933 to attend high school, built his publishing empire on a simple but prescient insight. Years of northward migration, particularly during the Second World War, had wrought a fundamental transformation in the character of the African American population. While a majority of black people still lived in the states of the old Confederacy, millions had settled in the urban North, where they enjoyed, if not their full portion as Americans, then at least far greater freedom and prosperity than they had ever enjoyed in the Jim Crow South. Johnson believed that these people wanted a periodical that was something more than a "protest organ," a magazine that did not harp on "negativism and advocacy" but instead set out "to chronicle in a positive, informative and entertaining way the remarkable story of Negro progress as solid citizens in all income groups." The last few words were particularly significant. Long before his contemporaries, Johnson recognized that African Americans represented a vast, virtually untapped consumer market, and he calculated that advertisers, once awakened to that market's existence, would pay handsomely to reach it.

Unfortunately, Johnson had no journalism experience. To remedy the lack, he turned to Ben Burns. An editor at the *Chicago Defender*, Burns was an ironic choice: he was not only white but also Jewish and a member of the Communist Party. In 1942, this unlikely pair launched *Negro Digest*, a low-budget knockoff of *Reader's Digest*, which reprinted, without editorial elaboration, articles about black people culled from other periodicals. Three years later, they launched *Ebony*, a glossy pictorial, whose layout, logo, and even typeface were adopted wholesale from *Life* magazine. An editorial in the inaugural issue, "The Happier Side of Negro Life," stated the *Ebony* philosophy in the breezy style that was to become the magazine's signature. "We're rather jolly folks, we *Ebony* editors. . . . We like to look at the zesty side of life. Sure we can get all hot and bothered about the race question (and don't think we don't) but not enough is said about all the swell things that Negroes do." The title alone distinguished the magazine from previous black periodicals, which carried names like *The Crisis*, *The Whip*, and *The De-*

fender. (Ironically, ebony was one of the shades not allowed on *Ebony*'s cover; according to Burns, Johnson believed that African Americans "subconsciously disliked" brown colors, identifying them as the "root cause" of their problems.)

Though only available on newsstands in a handful of northern cities, *Ebony*'s inaugural issue of 25,000 copies sold out. But with the magazine selling for only a quarter an issue, success depended on attracting advertising revenue, not only from black businesses, the lifeblood of previous African American periodicals, but also from large, white-owned corporations, whose advertising budgets ballooned in the years after the war. Johnson proved a master at attracting these accounts. Bypassing marketing departments, he set out to persuade company presidents that reaching out to the black market was both profitable and patriotic, that drawing African Americans into the consumer republic cemented black loyalty and ensured the national unity essential to winning the Cold War. Reliance on white advertisers, in turn, reinforced Johnson's own accommodationist instincts. Whatever his feelings about racial injustice—and there is evidence that he felt its sting more keenly than his public pronouncements revealed—Johnson knew that white advertisers would not tolerate anything controversial, let alone "militant." Instead, *Ebony* offered readers reassuring stories of racial progress—the first black navy pilot, the first black entertainer to headline in Miami Beach—interspersed with celebrity profiles, beauty tips, and stories of black business success. On a few occasions, Johnson veered from his own formula, most notably in 1955, when *Jet,* a sister magazine to *Ebony,* published photos of the battered body of Emmett Till, a fourteen-year-old Chicagoan who was lynched while visiting relatives in Mississippi. For the most part, however, Johnson's magazines gave politics a wide berth.

Predictably, *Ebony*'s positive, resolutely apolitical approach to African American life earned it plaudits from the white establishment. Magazines such as *Reader's Digest* and *Time,* the twin towers of postwar anticommunism, routinely cited *Ebony* stories to demonstrate Negro progress in the United States and, by implication, the superiority of American institutions. Reaction from black political leaders was, predictably, more mixed. While some praised *Ebony* for offering a vision of black achievement and normality, others condemned it for its political quietism and uncritical embrace of middle-class consumerism. Critics warned that the magazine's unalloyed emphasis on black progress played into the hands of reactionaries, suggesting that the nation's race problem was insignificant or at least well on the way to solution. Such fears were borne out in 1947, when a Thanksgiving editorial, "Time to Count Your Blessings," was used by Alabama senator John Sparkman to oppose President Truman's proposed civil rights legislation. If the "standard of living" and "civil rights" enjoyed by American Negroes were already the envy of the world, Sparkman argued, then surely there was no need for a civil rights bill.

The anomalies of *Ebony*'s position were even more starkly revealed in the magazine's ambivalent relationship with Richard Wright. Given his beliefs about "the essential bleakness of black life in America," Wright was the least likely of *Ebony* contributors. But he was also the most distinguished black writer in the United States and a former Chicagoan, precisely the kind of figure the magazine championed. And he was an old friend of Ben Burns, with whom he had once worked at *The Daily Worker*. When Wright visited Chicago in 1950, Burns invited him to submit an essay on how the city had changed since he had lived there in the 1930s. Wright responded with "The Shame of Chicago," a savage exposé of the continuing misery and hopelessness within the city's much-enlarged black ghetto. The essay contradicted the *Ebony* ethic in every particular and Johnson refused to run it. After a year of pestering by Burns, he finally relented, but only on condition that the same issue include an editorial rebutting the essay's argument. While Burns later professed to be embarrassed by the assignment, he complied, penning a "scurrilous editorial" in which he accused Wright of having become so accustomed to "striking out in blind fury" that he "failed to perceive the remarkable advances made by Negroes in Chicago since the Depression days." The average "Chicago Negro is better off than most Frenchmen," he added, in a clear dig at Wright's exile status.

The episode had an even more curious coda. In an effort to mend fences with his old friend, Burns invited Wright to submit a piece on life in Paris, a subject he assumed to be uncontroversial. But he had not reckoned with Wright. In the second essay, "I Chose Exile," Wright broadened his criticisms of Chicago to embrace the entire United States, which he accused of conducting a barbarous campaign not only against Negroes but also against the very "concept of a free person." "I tell you frankly that there is more freedom in one square block of Paris than there is in the entire United States of America!" he declared. This time Johnson refused to budge and the essay never appeared. Once again, Burns protested, but Johnson was fast losing faith in his judgment. He fired him a short time later, promoting Era Bell Thompson in his place.

IN ITS EARLY YEARS, *Ebony* had little to say about Africa. Indeed, a reader with only the magazine to go on might have been surprised to learn that Negroes had ever lived anywhere other than the United States. The whole purpose of *Ebony* was to emphasize black people's Americanness— their political loyalty, their material progress, their role in making "the United States the glorious democracy it is." Within that framework Africa represented, at best, a distraction and, at worst, an impediment, evoking all the associations of "backwardness" and "savagery" that *Ebony* was designed to expunge.

By the early 1950s, however, the burgeoning African decolonization movement made Africa impossible to ignore. As Thompson put it, "big time newspaper and magazine correspondents" were visiting the continent, producing stories about the Gold Coast's drive for independence, South African apartheid, and the Mau Mau uprising in Kenya. In early 1953, *Life* magazine published an entire special issue on Africa, "A Continent in Ferment," featuring a Masai warrior on the cover. Leaving aside a 1943 story on South African prime minister Jan Smuts and a 1950 travelogue on the valley of the Nile, it was the first time that an African had ever appeared on the cover of the nation's premier magazine. (At the time, only two African Americans had ever graced *Life*'s cover: Jackie Robinson, who appeared three years after breaking baseball's color line, and a shirtless black man driving a wagonload of watermelons for a feature on "The Watermelon Harvest.") In this context, Thompson and her publisher, John Johnson, decided that the time had come for *Ebony* to assay Africa.

By her own account, Thompson knew virtually nothing about Africa when she embarked on her journey. "[M]y knowledge of the continent, like that of most Americans, both black and white, was geared to concepts handed down by Livingstone and Stanley," she wrote. School textbooks were not much help, portraying Africa as a land of thick-lipped, thick-skulled "savages with rings in their noses . . . who boiled Englishmen in iron pots and traded tons of priceless ivory for handfuls of dime store beads." Through the writings of black scholars such as W. E. B. Du Bois, Thompson had some exposure to an alternative tradition, one that stressed Africa's cultural richness and the glories of its ancient civilizations, but she continued to view the continent with uneasiness, even distaste. "Had anyone called me an African, I would have been indignant," she confessed. "Only race fanatics flaunted their jungle ancestry or formed back-to-Africa movements." But she was also curious. How would Africans "receive a prodigal daughter who had not been home for three hundred years?" And how would she react to her "African ancestors"?

Thompson spent more than two months in Africa, visiting or at least passing through eighteen countries and colonies, starting with Liberia and ending with Egypt. In the course of her visit and in the months after her return she produced a half dozen *Ebony* features, as well as a book, *Africa: Land of My Fathers*. Over the years, many American women, black and white, had visited Africa, most under the auspices of mission societies; a few had published books about their experiences. But none had visited as many countries, or interacted with as diverse a set of interlocutors, as Thompson did. Her closest rival was probably Eslanda Robeson, whose *African Journey*, published in 1945, recounted a trip that she and her son, Paul Jr., had taken to South and East Africa in the late 1930s. But Robeson had the advantage of graduate training in anthropology, as well as a long list of friends and contacts in Africa, based on the years that she and her husband, Paul, had spent in London. Thompson, in contrast, embarked as a single woman into unknown territory, armed only with a typewriter, camera, and the same genial optimism that had guided her steps in the United States.

Thompson's magazine articles conformed to the *Ebony* formula—the first African this and the largest African that, accompanied by innumerable photo-

graphs, apparently taken by Thompson herself. "Liberia's Rubber King" pro-
filed a successful black businessman, Harry Morris, "the world's biggest Negro processor and grower of raw rubber." "Africa's Beauties" offered beauty
tips from African women, as well as a collection of photographs of "glamor
girls" from around the continent. "Is the Garden of Eden in Africa?" offered
a portrait of Ife, an ancient city in southwest Nigeria and a leading center of
Yoruba religion and art. While the subject matter occasionally necessitated
some comment on racial issues, the articles generally avoided politics or anything else likely to provoke controversy. The African slave trade, for example,
long a staple subject for visiting African Americans, was mentioned only
once, and that in a photo caption: "Once the greatest brasswork craftsmen in
West Africa, the men of Ife forsook the trade to deal in slaves in 1800s."

Probably the strangest of Thompson's articles was her first one, "World's
Top Negro Statesmen Meet," which recounted a meeting between Liberian
President William Tubman and the Gold Coast's Kwame Nkrumah. Whether
the visit represented "Africa's most momentous meeting since Stanley met
Livingstone" is debatable, but it was a historic occasion, the first ever meeting between two elected African heads of state. It was also a distinctly fraught
event, as Nkrumah, the charismatic proponent of African socialism, sought
to wrest the mantle of leadership of independent Africa from Tubman, a
staunch Cold War ally of the United States. But the complexities of the encounter were lost on Thompson, who played it as a society event. The meeting "was not all politics," she wrote. "It had its social highlights too, and in
some ways represented the biggest Negro society in our time. Arriving on
Liberia's luxurious new $1 million presidential yacht, Nkrumah was treated
to a round of banquets, balls and receptions rarely seen by Negroes anywhere in the world."

THOMPSON'S BOOK *Africa: Land of My Fathers*, was a more reflective
work, revealing political complexities absent from the *Ebony* dispatches, as
well as her own progressive disillusionment. The book began in a flush of
enthusiasm. Thompson landed first in Liberia and found it utterly enchant-
ing. Like the society set of Chicago, the Americo-Liberian elite of Monrovia

was insular, inbred, and acutely conscious of social status, and an editor of black America's premier periodical commanded a high status indeed. Thompson was immediately deluged with invitations to afternoon teas and evening dinner parties, most hand-delivered by the ubiquitous African "houseboys." "A carrier pigeon service, with houseboys as pigeons, added a personal touch to little white cards and pink note paper," she gushed, oblivious to what the system suggested about Liberian society. Aside from these "houseboys," she had virtually no contact with indigenous Africans, and those she saw left her distinctly unimpressed. "My first reaction to my aborigine brothers was negative," she confessed. "I was especially loath to accept the half-naked man with the mop of fuzzy red hair, and the bony old ladies who squatted behind foul smelling shops with their bosoms exposed." On balance, however, she had no hesitation in placing Liberia on "the positive side of the ledger."

Thompson's initial enthusiasm carried into Nigeria and the Gold Coast, soon to be renamed Ghana. She enjoyed the bustling streets of Lagos—"like a scene from a Katherine Dunham dance," she remarked—and she was positively rapturous about Ife, whose centuries-long tradition of carving and metalwork confirmed all that Du Bois and others had said about African civilization. "Here, indeed, was proof of the Africans' cultural past, priceless art finished by black hands many centuries ago," she wrote. "If these were my ancestors, I had reason to be proud." She was less impressed with the Gold Coast—Accra "lacked the robust progressiveness of Lagos"—but her disappointment was more than compensated by the opportunity to spend time with the colony's charismatic young prime minister. Nkrumah had left the United States just before *Ebony* began publication, but he certainly knew of the magazine and appreciated its usefulness in rallying international support for Ghanaian independence. He graciously sat for interviews and photographs, and even gave Thompson his private telephone number. For a besmitten Thompson, Nkrumah was the perfect symbol of the new Africa aborning— "handsome, dreamy-eyed, and wistful," yet disciplined and steely, with a "cold, calculating calmness that lay close beneath the boyish charm." In good *Ebony* fashion, she titled this chapter of her book "Gold Coast Glamor Boy."

The first month of Thompson's journey more or less conformed to the Ebony script, offering abundant evidence of Africa's past glories and future greatness. But her next destination, the Belgian Congo, presented a more perplexing picture. Whether Thompson had any knowledge of the colony's gruesome past is unclear; her text made no mention of King Leopold or of the millions who perished in his vaunted Free State. Yet she was astute enough to realize that not all was well in the Congo, that Belgian claims about enlightened colonialism needed to be taken with a pinch of salt. Claims that the colony had "no color line," for example, were dashed the first time she boarded a ferry and had to decide whether to join the Europeans in the forward cabin or the Africans in the rear. Missionaries and state officials all boasted of their liberality but warned that the Congolese were not yet ready for independence, being "hundreds of years" behind their black American counterparts. An official at a Union Miniere copper mine proudly explained how the company had planted banana trees on the grounds "to make bush people feel at home." Virtually everyone Thompson met, African and European, asked about the United States, to the point that she sometimes felt like she was "conduct[ing] a seminar" on the Negro. A group of bitter Congolese clerks asked why black Americans, with all their wealth and education, did nothing for their African brothers. A Belgian businessman momentarily stunned her by asking whether *Native Son* represented "a true picture of American life." She explained that the character of Bigger was a "composite," but conceded that such cases did exist.

The next destination, Rwanda-Urundi, was stranger still, raising questions not only about colonialism and decolonization but also about ethnic conflict between Africans. Like the Congo, the territories were Belgian possessions, having been acquired under a League of Nations mandate following Germany's defeat in World War I. The population was divided between two groups: the Hutus, who had occupied the highlands for millennia; and the Tutsis (or Watusi, as they were still called at the time), the descendants of pastoralists who had migrated into the region from the Horn of Africa in the fifteenth century. The two populations had a long history of conflict, with the far more numerous Hutus living as vassals to the dominant Tutsis. The division was exacerbated by the arrival of the Germans, who quickly decided that the Tutsis—generally taller, with fairer skin and less stereotypically negroid features—were the superior race and thus entitled to better treatment than the more primitive Hutus. The system was perpetuated by the Belgians, past masters in the colonial art of divide and rule. Under Belgian rule, all Africans were required to carry ethnic identity cards, and Tutsis were routinely employed to collect taxes and enforce colonial labor levies on the Hutus.

Thompson had little if any knowledge of this history, and she obviously had no inkling of the horrors to which it would later give rise. But she was intrigued by the division between Hutus and Tutsis and asked everyone she met about it. If her book offered no firm conclusions, it at least illuminated something of the range of contemporary discussion. A group of Catholic nuns explained how Hutu children, being more "docile," made better students. The Belgian governor argued that Tutsis, more "highly developed mentally" than the Hutus, were better equipped for the burdens of citizenship but also more prone to neurosis. The Tutsi king and his statuesque wife (the "most beautiful black woman I had ever seen," Thompson wrote) insisted that the gulf between them and the Hutus was wider than that between them and the Belgians. The Hutu king (dressed "for all the world like a Harlem businessman") essentially agreed. Such comments were a portent of genocide.

Thompson made no mention of her experiences in the Congo or Rwanda-Urundi in her *Ebony* dispatches. Indeed, the last half of her journey, which included visits to more than a dozen colonies and countries, yielded only one more article, a profile of Ethiopian emperor Haile Selassie that was published (and probably written) long after her return to the United States. The reasons for her reticence are unclear. There is some evidence that she lost her camera, which would have prevented her from taking the photographs essential for *Ebony* articles. But Thompson was also undergoing some changes herself. If she had lost some of her initial aversion to her "aborigine brothers," she had also lost much of her early enthusiasm, as she began to grapple with some of the complexities of life in colonial Africa—complexities that did not easily lend themselves to *Ebony*'s reassuring platitudes. Weeks of solitary travel and the welter of unfamiliar sights and experiences had left her emotionally frayed and homesick. Perhaps most important, she faced an escalating campaign of harassment by British colonial officials, who had somehow come to the conclusion that she and her magazine were a threat to colonial rule.

Thompson's first inkling of trouble came in the Gold Coast. She entered the country without difficulty, but after making a flying visit to Nigeria she was denied reentry by British officials. (Though Nkrumah had been installed as prime minister, the civil service, including customs, remained in British hands.) After an intervention by the American consul, she was granted a week's stay, but the problem resurfaced in the next British colony she entered, Northern Rhodesia. Traveling by train—she had missed her flight out of the Congo—she was accosted by a customs official, who not only refused to allow her off the train but also carefully copied down her itinerary, presumably to alert authorities in other colonies to her approach. The experience was repeated in Southern Rhodesia, where authorities refused to allow her to disembark. (Thompson had the rare experience of hearing but not seeing Victoria Falls, the great waterfall "discovered" by David Livingstone a century before.) In South Africa, where she had a valid entry permit, she was met at the station by authorities, who immediately bundled her onto another train bound for Portuguese Mozambique.

Mozambique offered a respite of sorts: though denied a room in the best hotels, she was at least allowed to enter and travel freely. But the harassment recommenced as soon as she reentered British colonial territory. Authorities in Zanzibar declared her a prohibited immigrant. In Uganda, she was expelled from her hotel for unexplained reasons. Kenyan authorities initially admitted her, but then tried to deny her reentry, apparently in the belief that she and her magazine were pro-Communist. As Thompson ruefully put it, the "return of this native was quickening into a rout."

The idea that *Ebony* was pro-Communist was absurd on its face, and Thompson was understandably perplexed by her treatment. Yet there was a certain historical logic to officials' actions. Just as generations of African Americans have looked to Africa for hope and inspiration, so has the figure of the black American bulked large in the imagination of Africans. Everywhere Thompson traveled, she met Africans who were anxious to learn about their Negro cousins. The origins of this interest reached back at least to the late-nineteenth-century mission movement, but it swelled over the course of the twentieth century, especially among urban Africans, whose fascination with African Americans was stoked by newspaper reports, newsreels, popular music (especially jazz), and Hollywood movies. As Thompson discovered, many Africans entertained highly exaggerated ideas about America, imagining a place in which black people enjoyed all the freedoms for which they struggled in their own lives—the right to vote, to own land, to control their own churches, businesses, and schools. Educated Africans dreamed of attending one of black America's legendary colleges; several hundred actually did so, overcoming all manner of financial and logistical obstacles in the process. The roster of African graduates of American colleges and universities included a host of men and women who would later play central roles in African nationalist movements, including three presidents of South Africa's African National Congress and three future heads of state: Nkrumah, Nnamdi Azikiwe, and Hastings Banda of Malawi.

White authorities were naturally uneasy with the transatlantic traffic. From the earliest days of the century, colonial officials warned that "the influx of the American negro with his peculiar ideas" gave the "wrong warp" to native aspirations, sharpening "racial self consciousness" and poisoning the otherwise harmonious relations prevailing between Europeans and Africans. Many feared full-blown "native uprisings," a prophecy seemingly confirmed in 1915, when an American-educated minister, John Chilembwe, led a short-lived rebellion at Livingstonia, in what was then Nyasaland. (Among the victims of the rebels was William Jervis Livingstone, a descendant of the pioneering missionary.) Official anxieties flared anew in the 1920s, with Marcus Garvey's entrance on the international stage. Even as Garvey faced prosecution and jail in the United States, his ideas spread throughout Africa, initially through *The Negro World* (copies of which were smuggled into Africa by African American and West Indian sailors) and later through word of mouth. In South Africa's Transkeian territories, rumors of returning African Americans combined with indigenous prophetic traditions to spawn a series of millenarian movements, all centered around the idea of a great black army arriving from across the sea to drive out Europeans and restore the land to its rightful owners. Such expectations were obviously misplaced, but that did not stop colonial officials from taking them seriously and responding forcefully. *The Negro World* was banned throughout British Africa. African Americans visitors faced tough new visa requirements, while

Africans wishing to study in the United States were required to post bonds and submit (white) character references. South African authorities went so far as to declare an immigration ban on all nonresident black people. (One immigration official, obviously new to the job, inquired whether the restriction on so-called foreign natives was meant to apply to the migrant workers who were the backbone of the country's mining industry.)

Thompson had wandered unwittingly into the final act of this long-running colonial farce. Even as Africa stood on the cusp of independence, criminal investigation departments across the continent continued to work overtime, trying to ferret out the sinister "agitators" responsible for South Africa's Defiance Campaign, the Mau Mau in Kenya, and swelling trade union movements all over the continent. In such a context, it is hardly surprising that white officials would view the arrival of an African American journalist with suspicion and alarm. Nor is it surprising that Thompson received the most hostile reception in South Africa. The vision of black urbanity and sophistication conjured by *Ebony* could not have been more contrary to the logic of apartheid, which rested on the notion that black people were simple rural folk, who lived in special native "reserves" and entered white cities only as temporary workers. Whether officials in other colonies were specifically aware of *Ebony* is unclear, but South African officials certainly were, and they had banned it long before Thompson's arrival.

Thompson had little if any knowledge of this history; indeed, she was only dimly aware of colonialism. "That was my first trip to Africa," she later told an interviewer. "I thought because it's a black country, I can go there. But right after leaving Liberia, going south, it [was] like going south in this country." With no context for interpreting her experience, her reaction inclined more to bemusement than to indignation. In her mind, and later in her book, official harassment became just one more sign that Africa was not her home, one more source of alienation to go with the poor accommodations and rude cab drivers, the noisome odors and maddening flies. She came to cherish her time in airplanes, where she could sit in air-conditioned comfort and enjoy the courtesy of crew members, free from anxiety and harassment. "Two months in Africa had made me feel more at home in the air than on land," she confessed. "[T]here was a peace of mind above the earth that dwarfed even the problems of Africa." By the time Thompson reached Ethiopia, a cherished symbol of independence to generations of African Americans, she could barely bring herself to leave the plane. "From high in the sky, Addis Ababa was picturesque," she wrote, "but the closer we came to its sad sod roofs, the more disappointing it became. When we taxied down a runway guarded by ugly gray vultures, I unfastened my seat belt with reluctance."

As her enthusiasm for Africa dwindled, Thompson's sense of identification with the United States swelled. She spent much of her time in Ethiopia sitting in the reading room of the U.S. Information Service library, perusing American newspapers. In Kenya, she wrote rapturously of a consular official—"a great big beautiful American with a smile on his face"—who rescued her from the clutches of immigration authorities. "Free again. Once more my country had gone to bat for me. An hour before I had felt 'like a motherless child, a long way from home,' but an American public relations officer and an American consul general had fought for my rights as an American citizen." There were compound ironies in the statement, which not only turned the sentiment of an old spiritual squarely on its head but also neglected the fact that African Americans in the United States were still systematically denied basic rights of citizenship. But the irony was lost on Thompson. "If I ever get back on American soil, I promised myself, I'll tell the world about this!"

Thompson concluded her trip in Egypt. Just two weeks before, Egypt had declared itself a republic, ending millennia of monarchical rule, but Thompson had nothing to say on the subject. "No more interviews and notes," she wrote; "no more hunting for blood brothers among Africa's aborigines. For the last three days on the continent I was going to be myself, an American—an American tourist, no less. Tomorrow was the Fourth of July." Ensconced in a comfortable hotel, she took a long bath. "Cleansed of the red dust of Africa," she stood on her balcony and "looked down upon the ancient city of the Pharaohs," thinking she would trade it all for "one good American firecracker." A maid came to turn down the bed. Thompson saw her out, and then "returned to the moonlit balcony to thank the Pharaohs for their hospitality and to thank God for the Stars and Stripes."

. . .

RICHARD WRIGHT'S *Black Power: A Record of Reactions in a Land of Pathos* was a very different book from Era Bell Thompson's *Africa: Land of My Fathers*, yet it too was a tale of disillusionment and alienation. Wright began the book with an Easter luncheon in 1953 with Dorothy Padmore, wife of his friend George Padmore. "Now that your desk is clear"—he had just published *The Outsider*, his first novel since *Native Son*—"why don't you go to Africa?" she asked. According to Wright, the suggestions awoke "a vague sense of disquiet." He had "never seen Africa," he protested, "hardly ever thought of Africa." Yet something in the word—*Africa!*—set his mind to racing. "What would my feelings be when I looked into the black face of an African, feeling that maybe his great-great-great-grandfather had sold my great-great-great-grandfather into slavery?" he wondered. "Was there something in Africa that my feelings could latch on to to make all this dark past clear and meaningful?" He retreated to his office and pulled the *Encyclopaedia Britannica* from the shelf. He read the entry for the Gold Coast and returned to the table. "I'm going," he declared.

It was a charming story, obviously intended to establish the author's freedom from prejudice and preconception. Yet it was also thoroughly misleading. Wright's journey to Africa was not only a product of long consideration; it was also a logical, even inevitable, next step in his intellectual odyssey. Far from innocent, Wright approached the continent with powerful, if sometimes contradictory, preconceptions. As a universalist social scientist, he assumed that African behavior was logical and fully explicable using the same "concepts that one would use in observing life anywhere." Yet as an imaginative artist, steeped in Conrad, he inherited an image of Africa as a dark, mysterious place, unbounded by civilization or the constraint of reason. Hostile to prevailing ideas about race, Wright nonetheless identified profoundly with the African struggle. Virulently opposed to Western colonialism, he continued to see freedom in distinctly Western terms, as the "sacred inviolability" of the individual personality against the demands of the collective. All these tensions and more bubbled beneath the surface as Wright boarded a Union Castle steamer out of Liverpool, one-time headquarters of the British slaving fleet, and embarked for the Gold Coast, soon to become the independent nation of Ghana.

By 1953 regular commercial air service linked Europe and Africa, and indeed most capitals within Africa. Era Bell Thompson flew to Africa and, aside from her bewildering train trip through southern Africa, traveled within the continent by air, finding in the chill air of an airplane cabin a respite from the heat and confusion below. Wright elected to travel to Africa by boat. He needed the time for background reading, he claimed, but there was more to the decision than that. In African travel writing, the voyage across the sea has long figured as a kind of ritual passage, a liminal period for reflection and preparation before immersion in a new reality. For African American travelers, the passage was doubly significant, inevitably evoking thoughts of the prior passage of millions of enslaved Africans. Wright's account was faithful to these conventions. As his ship bore down on the continent, his reflections became more portentous, a quality doubtless enhanced by a fever brought on by a typhoid vaccination. "The ocean seemed to possess a quiet but persistent threat of terror lurking just beneath the surface," he wrote, "and I'd not have been surprised if a vast tidal wave had thrust the ship skyward in a sudden titanic upheaval of destruction." The fact that the ship operated from Liverpool, a city whose foundations "were built of human flesh and blood," added yet another layer of significance. Africa and the West were not separate realms but parts of a single totality, one vast heart of darkness.

As the ship churned south, Wright's travel journal, begun in the days before his departure, quickly swelled past a hundred typed pages. The journal, from which he would later fashion *Black Power*, included several drafts of an address "To the People of Ghana," intended as a statement for "the African newspaper men [who] will undoubtedly be on hand" to greet him when his ship arrived. In fact, no reporters met the ship, but the address, which Wright eventually delivered to a mass meeting of Nkrumah's Convention People's Party, is worth examining, since it reveals again the elaborate preconceptions that he brought with him to Africa. Ghana had a "rendezvous with the twentieth century," Wright wrote, a "rendezvous with freedom." "Do not think that I shall find the political and social events in your country odd or strange," he added. "I've traveled widely and I've seen mankind uprooted and groping to define his future just as you fight and grope today to define yourselves. Though I do not personally know you, be assured that I know your problem in general, having seen that same drama of yours in a score of other lands and countries."

The ship's passengers included a large complement of Africans, offering Wright an opportunity to confirm his theories. They "stammer and grope," he reported in his journal, clearly unable to fathom "the meaning of what they're living through." Much of his attention was directed at a tablemate, J. J. Thomas, the first African justice on the Nigerian high court, who was returning home after attending the coronation of Queen Elizabeth. As "black as the ace of spades," Thomas was of Sierra Leonean descent, a product of the polyglot community of recaptives and returning African Americans forged in Freetown in the late-eighteenth and early-nineteenth centuries. A graduate of Fourah Bay College in Freetown, Thomas had studied law in London, where he was admitted to the bar in the mid-1920s. He returned to Africa a few years later to work as a functionary in the colonial government, an appointment sufficiently noteworthy to merit mention in "Along the Color Line," W. E. B. Du Bois's monthly column in *The Crisis*. Thomas epitomized the Western-educated elite who dominated twentieth-century nationalist politics in British West Africa, at least before the rise of Nkrumah's C.P.P.

By an unbelievable coincidence, Thomas was also a relative of Matthew Thomas, Bishop Henry Turner's cabinmate during his first visit to Africa in 1891. The comparison between Turner's portrayal of the elder Thomas and Wright's portrayal of the younger throws the two travelers' preconceptions into stark relief. For Turner, Matthew Thomas was "one of the most learned" men on the planet. Proud, articulate, fluent in a dozen modern and ancient languages, he offered living proof of African "intellectuality" and manliness. Wright, looking at J. J. Thomas six decades later, saw a changeling, an embodiment not of African promise but of the psychic violence of colonialism. Under the novelist's clinical dissection, Judge Thomas emerged as the quintessential Chicago School marginal man, torn between love and loathing for the Western world that made and rejected him. Egged on by Wright, the judge declaimed on everything from cannibalism to Kwame Nkrumah, whose efforts to forge a modern nation out of a "tribal rabble . . . running naked in the bush" he dismissed as delusional. Even the judge's diet, a regimen of wheat germ, yeast tablets, vitamins, and laxative sticks, became for Wright evidence of his inner alienation. "I struggled against an oblique sympathy that was dawning in me for the man," he wrote in *Black Power*. "How England had mangled his soul."

After a brief stop in Freetown—a "mudhole," Wright called it, "free from anything smacking of humanity"—the ship proceeded to the Gold Coast, anchoring off Takoradi. Wright cleared customs and boarded a bus for Accra, the capital, one hundred and seventy bumpy miles up the coast. Writing in his journal later that night, he rehearsed the bus ride, endowing it with a palpably Conradian air. As the bus navigated "streets clogged with black life" and entered "the jungle," he experienced something akin to panic. He saw "no order, no fences, no vast sweeps of plowed earth"—just a "profuse welling of plants in a tangled confusion stretching everywhere, seemingly with no beginning and no end." Villages, "mythical and unbelievable," materialized out of the bush and vanished. Drums throbbed in the distance, "the vibrations coming to my ears like the valved growl of a crouching beast." The air itself seemed threatening, "so hot and humid that I felt that the flesh was melting from my bones." By the time the bus reached Accra, seven hours later, Wright was drenched with sweat and exhausted. He felt an "oppressive burden of alertness . . . engendered by the strangeness of a completely different order of life," an "absolute otherness." Native son, indeed.

AFTER A DAY OF REST at a government bungalow, Wright was taken to meet Nkrumah. The prime minister had been extensively briefed about the visit by George Padmore, who predicted that the novelist's "tremendous prestige" would generate favorable publicity for the Gold Coast revolution. The two men, who had met briefly during Nkrumah's student days in the United States, spent several days together, taking a driving tour of the capital, attending a mass meeting of the C.P.P., and campaigning in a by-election in Cape Coast, in the shadow of the village's massive, moldering slave fortress. The experiences confirmed Wright's sense of the significance of Nkrumah's movement. The prime minister was greeted by "frenzied assent" and "a kind of half-Nazi salute," the signature gesture of the C.P.P. Everywhere Wright heard the same exhilarating, strangely ominous cry: "Free-dooooom! Free-dooooom!" After all of seventy-two hours in the country, he already envisioned the book he would write. Nkrumah and the C.P.P. had built a "bridge" between "tribalism and twentieth-century forms of mass political organization"; they "had moved in and filled the vacuum which the British and the missionaries had left when they had smashed the tribal culture of the people." The "teeming millions of Africa" were being ushered onto "the political stage of the twentieth century."

The vision dissolved as quickly as it appeared. It is difficult to say, at this remove, exactly what happened. In *Black Power*, Wright blamed his hosts. After their initial conversations, Nkrumah became standoffish, unwilling to admit Wright into his confidence. When the novelist requested a copy of a loyalty oath sworn by C.P.P. members at a mass meeting in Accra, he pretended not to have heard. Eventually he avoided Wright altogether. Party officials were distrustful and evasive. Often they conversed in vernacular languages rather than English, which Wright interpreted as an attempt to exclude him. Questions about factions within the C.P.P. or the operation of party discipline—issues of obvious interest to a former Communist like Wright—elicited only blank stares. "I cannot escape the feeling that my seeking information has somewhat frightened the African politicians," he wrote. "I'm completely immobilized."

In *Black Power*, Wright would weave his hosts' alleged secretiveness into an elaborate theory on the psychological damage done to Africans by colonialism. Yet reading his travel diary, one is chiefly struck by Wright's own psychological instability. He had always been volatile, but never were his mood swings more extreme and seemingly erratic than during his time in Africa, where the combination of heat and unfamiliarity appears to have produced a kind of emotional meltdown. On June 19, three days after his arrival, he stayed up late into the evening, pouring out his enthusiasm in his diary. "All my life I've asked for this," he wrote. "Tonight is a night of decision for me. If this is what I think it is, then I must be with this." He imagined an intellectual triumvirate of himself, George Padmore, and their mutual friend C. L. R. James settling in Accra to advise Nkrumah. "I can see radiating out from this land an organization devoted full time to redeeming the blacks of this world. And, for the first time in history, we have a nucleus of a leadership for it." Yet just three days later he was "enervated, listless" and seriously considering "chucking up the whole thing." "I find myself longing to take a ship and go home," he wrote.

The pattern persisted in the weeks that followed, with Wright's mood alternately soaring and plummeting, sometimes in reaction to messages from Nkrumah, sometimes for no apparent reason. On July 2, two weeks into his journey, Wright was invited to the Gold Coast Legislative Assembly to watch the tabling of the C.P.P.'s white paper on self-government. It was a historic occasion, but all he saw was a bunch of bewigged black men aping the mannerisms of their British overlords. "I lost all interest in the Gold Coast as I sat in that hushed room," he wrote in his journal. The next morning, after a "hellish" sleepless night, he tried to book a passage back to Europe, but learned that the next available departure was months away. "There's nothing here for me now," he lamented; "this is just another hot and muddy city full of scheming politicians." Yet a message from Nkrumah the following day brought a revival of his spirits and a total revision of his account. "Thinking back on the spectacle of yesterday's meeting, I'm more and more amazed at the miracle accomplished by the C.P.P.," he wrote. So striking was the reversal that Wright himself observed it. "Funny creature that I am: just a word or a lack of a word can send me to heaven or dash me down to hell."

Clearly Wright's difficulties with his hosts were as much a product of his own psychological "complex" as theirs. Yet there was more to the problem than that. Beneath the issues of personality and wounded vanity lay a profound cultural gulf. W. E. B. Du Bois misjudged many things when he visited west Africa in the 1920s, but one thing he did appreciate was Africans' respect for "manners." And nowhere has esteem for manners survived more conspicuously than in Ghana. Through all the centuries of slavery and colonialism (and ensuing decades of postcolonial upheaval), Ghanaians have preserved a rare appreciation of the ceremony of daily life, and of verbal protocol in particular. Visitors, whether strangers or old friends, are greeted with formal felicitations, often accompanied by the pouring of libations to ancestors. Conversations proceed slowly and by indirection—*akutia,* in Twi—avoiding open disagreement or anything that might impeach the dignity of the participants. Chiefs, still the primary custodians of social order, tend not to speak at all, expressing themselves instead through court linguists, whose artistry consists precisely in their gift for the oracular. Qualities that Westerners, and Americans in particular, value in communication—candor, directness, efficiency—are not simply disdained but regarded as rude and uncultured. This penchant for circumlocution reaches its apotheosis in Ghanaians' love of proverbs, their seemingly endless store of adages, many of which address the folly of those who demand unambiguous answers to life's mysteries: "A wise child is not spoken to directly but given proverbs"; and "Only a fool requires interpretation when a proverb is given."

Obviously such a bare summary cannot do justice to the complexities of verbal art in a diverse, changing society, but it does suggest some of the sources of Wright's difficulties. Indeed, it is hard to imagine a society more ill suited to his temperament. Wright himself occasionally glimpsed the problem. "I suspect that my attitude caused a lot of background talk," he wrote in *Black Power*, "for my reactions were open and direct and I could not order them otherwise. When something struck me as being strange, I erupted with questions; when something seemed funny, I laughed; and when I was curious, I dived headlong to uncover the obscurities." Yet it seems never to have occurred to him to amend his approach. Instead, he attributed the problem to his hosts, specifically to a deficiency in the "African personality." In constructing his theory, he drew liberally on Octave Mannoni's *Psychologie de la Colonisation*, one of the books he brought with him on his journey. Written by a psychoanalyst and former colonial official in Madagascar, the book explored (in Wright's words) "the fateful subjective emotional relationship" between colonizer and colonized, a perverse emotional complementarity born of a neurotic quest for dominance on the one hand and of torpid dependence on the other. Craving the approval of their conquerors, whom they identified with their own dead fathers, Mannoni's Africans enthusiastically donned the habiliments of European life, only to be traumatized when their achievements failed to win white approval.

Suspended between an unnourishing past and an unreceptive modernity, Mannoni's neurotic native bore an obvious resemblance to the Chicago School's marginal man. Like African American folk adrift in the modern city,

Wright wrote, colonized Africans were "uncertain, uneasy, nervous, split deep within themselves." "[D]istrust had become enthroned in the very processes of their thoughts," making them virtually incapable of candor or direct address. Thus did the author's difficulties communicating with his hosts become proof of their pathology. Protocol became persiflage. Africans' discretion and tolerance of ambiguity became secretiveness, a "childlike . . . mania for hiding the facts of [their] life." Even African laughter rang false to Wright, suggesting less pleasure than a desperate desire "to hide." The very qualities that scholars today cite as evidence of Ghanaians' extraordinary cultural resiliency became for Wright proof of their deracination, of the essential "pathos" of African life. "All that the African personality seemed to have gotten from the West so far was a numbed defensiveness, a chronic lack of self-confidence," he concluded. "Eroded personalities loom here for those who have psychological eyes to see."

WRIGHT HAD COME to a crossroads. Having "given up hope of getting close to the political boys here," he could not write the book he had initially intended. Yet he needed to produce a book of some sort, having already expended the three-thousand-dollar advance he had received from Harper and Brothers, his New York publisher. In a letter to George Padmore, written on July 16, a month after his arrival, he outlined a new project, focusing not on the C.P.P. but on his own reactions to African life. Instead of temporizing, waiting for Nkrumah and his lieutenants to reveal the inner workings of their movement, he would simply plunge into African life himself, recording his observations and reflections.

Wright set up operations at the Seaview Hotel, in Accra's densely settled Jamestown district. It was "the kind of hotel one read about in a Joseph Conrad novel," he wrote, dingy and flyblown, with a balcony where one could sit and listen to the "continuous and mysterious beating of drums deep in the maze of streets." With some trepidation, he descended into the streets, exploring the narrow alleyways, the Greek- and Syrian-owned shops, the wide beach, where fishermen dried the day's catch in the sun. He must have cut quite a figure, dressed all in khaki with a sun helmet atop his head—the time-honored uniform of the Dark Continent explorer. He also carried a brace of cameras around his neck, snapping hundreds of photographs, which he developed himself in a makeshift lab in his hotel room. As his confidence grew, he hired a car to carry him to outlying villages, eventually venturing as far as Kumasi, capital of the old Ashanti empire, two hundred miles in the interior. Deliberately flouting protocol, which required visitors first to present themselves to local chiefs, he entered villages alone and unannounced, talking to the people he met and freely taking photos. He knew that he would "miss a lot" traveling without a guide or interpreter, but he wanted to "catch the native African without warning," leaving him "no chance to dress up or pretend."

As he embarked on his new project, Wright continued to filter his impressions through the lens of the Chicago School. Like the bleak tenements of Chicago's Black Belt, Accra's jumbled huts housed human jetsam, "psychologically detribalized Africans living uneasily and frustratedly in two worlds and really believing in neither." Clinging "in secrecy and shame" to a "fetish-ridden past," torn between love and loathing for the colonial world that reared and rejected them, these African native sons seemed devoid of idealism and imagination, incapable of any kind of self-assertion to improve their lives. For Wright, this psychological "soddenness" was mirrored in Africans' physical surroundings, in the "mudholes" in which they lived. Writers of the Harlem Renaissance generation had valorized Africans' alleged proximity to the soil as evidence of rootedness and organic wisdom, but to Wright it connoted only ignorance and insensibility. "The over-all impression was that the black human beings had so completely merged with the dirt that one could scarcely tell where humanity ended and the earth began," he wrote. Africans "lived in and of the dirt, the flesh of bodies seeming to fuse insensibly with the soil."

Inevitably, much of Wright's attention was directed at naked black bodies. Given Western inhibitions about nudity, and the different standards prevailing in much of Africa, nudity has long been a staple subject in African travel writing. Yet few travelers, black or white, dwelled so insistently on African nudity, or invested it with such diverse significance, as Wright. Seeing naked bathers on his initial bus ride from Takoradi to Accra, he struck a romantic pose: "What innocence of instincts! What unabashed pride!" By the end of the day, his first in Africa, he had crafted a complete psychological analysis. Africans, he argued, had created a society in which "sex was so blatantly prevalent that it drove all sexuality out," and with it all the "sublimated and projected sexual symbolization" that underlay Western neuroses. Yet Wright also detected a dark side. The lack of "symbolization" bespoke not only freedom from neurosis but an incapacity for self-reflection. There was "no sighing, longing, or other romantic notions" among Africans, he reported—only obedience to a biological imperative.

Wright's ambivalence was most palpable in his descriptions of women's breasts. One does not need to be a psychoanalyst to see that Wright had a conflicted relationship with female sexuality. Women in his novels evoke not only desire but also fear and loathing, along with an acute sense of vulnerability, often culminating in homicide. In *Black Boy,* he recounted a childhood nightmare in which "huge wobbly white bags, like the full udders of cows," hung from the ceiling above him, threatening "to fall and drench me with some horrible liquid." Perhaps not surprisingly, the sight of African women's exposed breasts repulsed him. Everywhere he looked, he saw breasts "flopping loosely and grotesquely in the sun." African women's breasts were "flat and remarkably elongated," he reported, a "deformation" that he attributed to "the constant weight and pressure of babies sagging upon their backs and pulling the cloth that went across their bosoms." One woman, too busy to stop and nurse "the inevitable baby" on her back, thrust "the long, fleshy, tubelike teat" under her arm for the child to suck. Others allegedly "tossed it over their shoulder." Thirty years before, the visiting W. E. B. Du Bois had celebrated naked breasts as proof of African pride and chastity, a refreshingly frank alternative to the salaciousness of American popular culture. To Wright, on the other hand, they signified ignorance, insensibility, imprisonment in an endless, unreflective round of birth and death.

On a few occasions, Wright stepped back from his analysis, pondering whether he was actually seeing Africans at all or simply projecting his own assumptions and anxieties onto them. Maybe there was no "Africa," he wrote, just a "vast black mirror" reflecting back upon the observer himself. "What is Africa to me?" he asked rhetorically, quoting Harlem Renaissance poet Countee Cullen. After weeks on the continent, Wright was less able to answer the question than he had been when he arrived. "Either what I'm looking at is the foundation of human life and can lend a meaning to all life on this earth, or it is nothing but a mass of writhing beasts," he concluded.

The incoherence of Wright's analysis was most starkly apparent when he tried to explain Africa's predicament. Why were Africans in such sorry shape? For the most part, he blamed European colonialism, which he described as one of the most atrocious crimes in human history. Colonialism not only dispossessed Africans of their land, it also robbed them of their identity, destroying that "organic view of existence" that had once given meaning to their lives. "The gold can be replaced; the timber can grow again, but there is no power on earth that can rebuild the mental habits and restore the former vision that once gave significance to the lives of these people," he wrote. In other passages, however, Wright placed the onus not on colonialism but on traditional culture itself, which he described as "rot," "mush," "a living death." As in his writings about African Americans, he was particularly troubled by traditional religion, which he regarded as a vestige of irrationalism, a "delusion" that prevented Africans from facing "reality." *Black Power* resounded with derogatory remarks about "juju," "fetish," "ancestor worship," and "mumbo jumbo." (The term "mumbo jumbo" was more fitting than Wright knew, having been first introduced into the English language by Mungo Park, progenitor of nineteenth-century Dark Continent travel writing.) Wright was equally contemptuous of chiefs, particularly after his visit to Ashanti, the region in which traditional authority was most intact (and, not coincidentally, the region least sympathetic to Nkrumah). "The chiefs are and were, one and all, scoundrels," he declared. Surrounded by retainers and draped in "ridiculous" regalia, they used superstition and existential terror to keep their credulous subjects in a kind of "involuntary emotional slavery." Where W. E. B. Du Bois had held up chiefly society as a model of commonwealth, of order and liberty harmonized, Wright saw a "fabulous power structure," erected atop religious "mumbo jumbo" and a "barbaric" system of justice.

The thing that most infuriated Wright, however, was not the persistence of tradition nor the ravages of modernity but the promiscuous ways in which Africans combined elements of both in their daily lives. Everywhere

Wright saw signs of what scholars today call hybridity—the blending of elements from different cultures and orders of knowledge into new, syncretic forms. Depending on one's point of view, such blending might be interpreted as a sign of health, of a people's resilience and cultural inventiveness. But for Wright, it was just more proof of Africans' pathology and pathos. The idea of pouring a libation to the ancestors at a modern political rally struck him as absurd—a surrender to irrationality, and "a waste of good gin," to boot. The appropriation of European umbrellas as an emblem of chieftainship was absurd. Pidgin, a coastal language combining English with words and inflections from Twi, appalled him—"a frightful kind of baby talk," he called it. The Gold Coast was a "a halfway world," "a vast purgatorial kingdom." Everything was "all mixed up, blended."

Wright's lament reached a climax of sorts at a high-life club to which he was taken by an African acquaintance. High life was the signature sound of the postwar Gold Coast. Derived from traditional dancing and drumming, it incorporated influences from across the Atlantic world, including African American blues and jazz, Cuban mambo, and Caribbean calypso. Over the next generation, the influence of high life would reverberate through popular music all over Africa, but Wright was unmoved. "The specialty of this establishment, as with all dance spots in the Gold Coast, was a shuffling, lazy kind of somnambulistic dance step called High Life," he wrote. "I compelled myself, out of politeness to my host, to watch the dancing. Nothing could have been more boring to my temperament than such spectacles, and I sat with a fixed smile on my face, nursing a bottle of beer, wishing I was someplace else. I'd seen better and more spirited dancing among the Negroes of New York's Harlem and Chicago's South Side, but since it was expected of me to watch Africans demonstrate that they could imitate Europeans or Americans, I thought that I'd better pretend to be interested." And so he pretended, while around him the world shimmered to the rhythm of high life.

To read such passages is to be struck yet again by the power of preconception over perception. All of Wright's preliminary research told him that Africans would be shattered people, and that is what he saw. Signs of Africans adopting modern ways—Christianity, Western dress and music, canned food—offered further proof of their dependence, their desperate pursuit of white approval. When confronted with evidence of cultural persistence, Wright reversed tack, accusing Africans of clinging to an irrational past. When Africans creatively combined old and new, he threw up his hands. One might well ask what Africans could have done to persuade him that they were not shattered.

In his final days in Africa, Wright visited some of the old slave castles along the coast: the towering fortress at Elmina, built of stone hewn in Portugal and carried to Africa a decade before Columbus's first voyage to the Americas; Cape Coast, jewel in the crown of the Royal Africa Company; Christiansborg, headquarters of the British colonial administration, soon to be the official residence of Kwame Nkrumah. Between the Portuguese and the now retiring British had come Swedes, Danes, and Dutchmen, all vying to control the swelling trade in gold and humans. Unbeknownst to Wright, Era Bell Thompson had visited some of these same sites a few weeks before. Writing with unwonted seriousness, she had described her feelings as she stood in the dungeon of Christiansborg castle, looking at the portal through which enslaved Africans had passed on their way to the waiting ships: "I looked at the guide. For an instant our eyes held, and in that infinitesimal moment, we heard the chains, smelled the stench of my forefathers." Wright stood in the same dungeon, probably with the same guide, and tried to imagine the experience of his ancestors. But the only image he could conjure was of a gold- and cowrie-bedecked African chief, leading another string of prisoners down to the coast to be sold.

THE FINAL PAGES of Wright's travel journal, and later of *Black Power*, consisted of an open letter to Kwame Nkrumah, written during the voyage back to England. "Dear Kwame," he began. "My journey's done. The ship that bears me from Africa's receding shore holds a heart that fights against those soft, sentimental feelings for the sufferings of our people. The kind of thinking that must be done cannot be done by men whose hearts are swamped with emotion." Continuing in this masculinist vein, Wright called upon Nkrumah to face "hard facts," to imbue his people with "the necessary hard-

ness for the task ahead," to *"be hard!"* Yet even that overture scarcely prepared readers for the novelist's prescription: "Our people must be made to
walk, forced draft, into the twentieth century!" he declared. "AFRICAN
LIFE MUST BE MILITARIZED!"

Viewed today, in the light of the endless military coups that have plagued
postcolonial Africa, such a recommendation seems chillingly ironic. Wright,
however, was at pains to emphasize that he was "not speaking of a military dictatorship," but of a "militarization of the daily, social lives of the people,"
leading to social, psychological, and economic reconstruction. He also stressed
that the process would be temporary, a single generation of sacrifice to spare
people five hundred years in purgatory. Militarization would discipline the instincts; it would give "form, organization, direction, [and] meaning" to people
whose capacity for purposive action had been sapped by "a gummy tribalism"
and the ravages of colonialism; it would "atomize the fetish-ridden past . . .
and render impossible the continued existence of those parasitic chiefs who
have too long bled and misled a naive people." At the same time, militarization
would save independent Ghana from being caught in the coils of Western capital or Soviet domination. Only by building their own nation, with their own
will and hands, could Ghanaians become truly free.

Wright arrived back in Liverpool in early September 1953. After a stop in
London to see George and Dorothy Padmore, he proceeded to Paris to write.
By December, he had completed a four-hundred-page manuscript. As the
speed of composition suggests, most of *Black Power* was assembled by cutting
and pasting from his travel diary. While this method gave the text a certain
immediacy as a "record of reactions"—the book's eventual subtitle—it also
introduced a raft of problems, including repetition, irresolution and, in several places, blatant self-contradiction. Did Wright's status as an African
American give him special insight into the plight of African people, as he
sometimes claimed, or were African realities just as opaque to him as they
were to other Western visitors, as he also maintained? Was African culture
"completely shattered" by colonialism or "completely intact"? Wright acknowledged some of these problems, but defended the book's basic structure
and method, significantly by invoking Conrad. "By going from spot to spot,
talking to this person and that one, I had to gather this reality as it seeped into

me from the personalities of others," he explained in a letter to his editor, Paul Reynolds. "Conrad wrote all his novels in this roundabout way. It involves going back to some extent over ground already covered, but each going back reveals more and more of the things described."

With McCarthyism still rumbling through American intellectual life, Reynolds worried that *Black Power*'s critique of European colonialism might be interpreted as pro-Communist, notwithstanding Wright's highly publicized break with the party a decade before. At Reynolds's urging, Wright added a preface, "Apropos Prepossessions," in which he discussed his past involvement with the Communist Party, as well as his conviction that the Gold Coast revolution was not Communist inspired. The "current mania" of ascribing all the unrest in the colonial world to the "omniscient hand of Moscow," he wrote, overlooked not only the brutal realities of colonialism but also the powerful appeal of Western values of freedom and justice. "In fact, it can be definitely stated that Communist strength is predicated upon Western stupidity . . . the abandonment by the West of its own ideals and pretensions." Written just months before the French defeat at Dien Bien Phu and the accelerating American slide into Vietnam, "Apropos Prepossessions" stands out for its courage and prescience. Yet it loses some force in light of recent revelations that Wright, in his last days in the Gold Coast, had "voluntarily" submitted a four-page memo at the American Consulate in which he described the C.P.P. as being "conscientiously modeled . . . upon the Russian Communist Party." Party leaders' hostility to him, the memo suggested, may have reflected their fear that he, as an ex-Communist, would discern more than they wished to reveal.

Black Power appeared in September 1954, the same week as Era Bell Thompson's *Africa: Land of My Fathers*. Reviews ranged from respectful to perplexed. Wright seemed uncertain whether he was writing a "picturesque travelog" or a "weighty social and political analysis," one critic complained. Another objected that the book revealed more about "Mr. Wright's own emotional processes" than about the people and place it purported to describe. African American critic J. Saunders Redding, whose travel account of India appeared at the same time as Wright's book, linked the book's problems to Wright's own "confused orientation." "*Black Power* is almost as tortured and tortuous as *The Outsider*," Redding wrote, referring to Wright's recent novel. "[O]ne can only hope that this is a final purging of confusion, and that from now on Richard Wright can devote himself to the kind of writing that earned him his early reputation for genius." Whatever the merits of the criticism, *Black Power* sold poorly. Plans for a paperback edition were canceled, a blow to Wright's ego as well as to his increasingly precarious finances. Within Pan-African circles, the book was greeted with studied silence. W. E. B. Du Bois read the book, but aside from an angry letter to George Padmore he did not deign to discuss it. Nkrumah also refrained from comment, at least at the time. (Years later, while living in exile in Guinea, Nkrumah would cite Wright's argument about militarization to defend his regime against charges of authoritarianism.)

Though wounded by the book's reception, Wright continued to see his role as that of an independent radical intellectual, writing unsentimental, polemical nonfiction. *Pagan Spain* was another hastily assembled travel account, interspersing psychology and anthropology with Wright's own reactions to an alien culture. Echoes of *Black Power* were even more obvious in *The Color Curtain,* his account of the 1955 Afro-Asian conference at Bandung. Whether assaying Africans, Asians, or Spaniards, Wright saw nervous, bewildered people, clinging stubbornly to "irrational customs and traditions" even as they were "cast into the void" of modernity. While his sympathies for such people waxed and waned, he consistently abjured nostalgia. The future of the postcolonial world, he declared in *The Color Curtain,* resided not in some vestigial tradition, but "in the willingness of nations to take up modern ideas and live out their logic." He went even further in his address to the First Congress of Negro Artists and Writers in Paris in 1956, urging the audience, which included all the luminaries of the Négritude movement, to stop wasting time expostulating on the spiritual wonders of dead cultures. While careful not to endorse colonialism, he applauded its consequences: "I do say 'Bravo' to the consequences of western plundering, a plundering that created the conditions for the possible rise of rational societies for the greater majority of mankind."

Wright's final years were troubled ones. Paris, his one-time refuge, depressed him. He became convinced—correctly in some instances—that several recent African American émigrés were American spies, sent to infiltrate anticolonial organizations. Hounded by American authorities for his alleged

Communist sympathies, he found himself assailed by erstwhile allies on the Left for his alleged conservatism. "I'm about the only 'uncontrolled' Negro alive today and I pay for it," he complained, with that strange mixture of persecution and grandiosity that characterized his final days. All the while, his physical and mental health deteriorated, a process that his most recent biographer has traced to the effects of bismuth, a heavy metal that had been prescribed by a Paris doctor as a treatment for gastrointestinal problems. Among the reported side effects of bismuth therapy, an experimental treatment that was later discredited and banned, were sharp mood swings, depression, and paranoia. It appears from his travel journal that Wright was taking bismuth while in the Gold Coast, which may help to explain the extremity of some of his reactions to the place. Bismuth poisoning may also have been a factor in his still mysterious death in November 1960, at the age of fifty-two.

As his world unraveled, Wright dreamed of returning to Africa. He drafted a plan for a nine-month tour of French West Africa, culminating in a companion volume to *Black Power,* but his appeals for funds—from the Ford Foundation, the American Society for African Culture (later exposed as a C.I.A. front), *The New Yorker* magazine—were fruitless. Plans for a coauthored volume with his doctor (the same man who prescribed bismuth), intended as a counterpoint of "black" and "white" impressions of the continent, likewise came to naught. Using George Padmore as an intermediary, he volunteered his services as a teacher or consultant to Ghana, but Nkrumah never acknowledged the offer. He repeated the offer to Ghana's ambassador in Paris in the days after Padmore's death. Wright "wishes to know in what way Ghana would like to make use of his vast experience and nationalism so that he conforms to it," the ambassador reported. "He is prepared to come for discussions with the Party leaders." This offer too went unacknowledged.

Fate was kinder to Era Bell Thompson. Unfazed by her "African ordeal," she threw herself back into her job at *Ebony.* In her capacity as international editor, she traveled all over the world, broadening her own horizons and those of *Ebony*'s readers. She produced stories about Indians and Israelis, Australian aborigines and Pacific Islanders. Her 1965 *Ebony* essay on Brazil, "Does Racial Amalgamation Work?" became a minor classic, inspiring a generation of scholarly and journalistic investigation of the effects of inter-marriage on race relations. Her own answer to the question, predictably, was positive: amalgamation in Brazil was breaking down the artificial barriers that separated black and white people and might, by implication, do the same for people in the United States. In the dawning era of Black Power, this was not a popular position, but it was consistent with Thompson's lifelong vision of a color-blind future.

Thompson also covered Africa. During its early years, *Ebony* had avoided the continent, lest the association somehow undermine black claims to full American citizenship. That reluctance disappeared after Thompson's 1953 visit. *Ebony* gave lavish coverage to African independence celebrations, and it was the first magazine to popularize the scholarship of William Leo Hansberry, a pioneering Afrocentrist. In an era in which white media still tended to give Africa short shrift, *Ebony* emerged as a primary source of information about the continent for millions of African Americans. At the same time, the magazine became an important source of information about black America for Africans. A pilgrimage to Johnson Publishing's gleaming Chicago headquarters soon became de rigueur for touring African heads of state, including Thompson's old friend Kwame Nkrumah, who visited in 1958.

Unlike Richard Wright, who never made it back to Africa, Thompson regularly returned to the continent. She first went back in 1957, the year of Ghanaian independence. In contrast to her first visit, when she traveled alone, she was accompanied by a large contingent of *Ebony* staffers, including publisher John Johnson. She obtained a scoop of sorts when she and an *Ebony* photographer, en route to Tanganyika, found themselves stranded in the Johannesburg airport after their connecting flight was delayed. Unable to provide a satisfactory account of themselves to police and immigration authorities, they ended up spending the night in jail. Less reticent than she had been four years before, Thompson wrote about the experience for *Ebony*, even posing for photos in ersatz prison garb.

Thompson returned to Africa in 1960 to cover the independence ceremonies in Congo and the Ivory Coast, again accompanied by Johnson, who had been appointed to the official U.S. delegation by President Eisenhower.

She made another half dozen trips in the years that followed, probably the most remarkable in 1968, when she retraced the course of her 1953 visit with a documentary film crew, intent on "comparing the Africa that was colonized with the current Africa that is independent." In good *Ebony* fashion, the film was cheerful and positive, offering abundant evidence of the continent's progress. "Everybody was writing about the woes of Africa, the problems they had," Thompson later recalled, "but nobody was noting the advances that were being made."

Yet alongside these advances were many ominous developments, which even Thompson could not ignore. A decade after decolonization, ordinary Africans had seen little or no improvement in their material circumstances. A new term, "neocolonialism," was in the air, coined to describe the pattern of European (and increasingly American) economic domination that persisted after the cession of formal political authority. Ethnic conflict flared all over the continent, a legacy of the arbitrary colonial, now national, boundaries inscribed by the Berlin Conference eighty years before. In Rwanda and Burundi, long-smoldering conflict between Hutus and Tutsis sparked violence and the forced relocation of hundreds of thousands of people, with far worse to come. In Nigeria, the continent's most populous nation, an Igbo secession movement ignited a three-year civil war. In a grim harbinger of future conflicts on the continent, most of the casualties of the Biafran War were civilians, killed not by bombs and bullets but by starvation. Everywhere, dreams of democracy were dashed, as a wave of military coups engulfed the continent. Among the victims was the Gold Coast Glamor Boy himself, Kwame Nkrumah.

EIGHT

Black Star

ROBERT E. LEE met Martin Luther King, Jr., only once. Lee had recently arrived in Accra, in time to see the British Gold Coast became the independent nation of Ghana. He watched the lowering of the Union Jack and the raising of a new flag, a single black star on a field of red, yellow, and green. He stood with the throng and listened as his old schoolmate Kwame Nkrumah cried out to history and the heavens: "Freedom at last! Freedom at last!" It was March 1957 and the Lee family—Robert, Sara, and their two young sons—had come to live in Africa.

In the course of the festivities, an acquaintance stopped Lee on the street and asked him to come quickly. "He didn't know what kind of doctor I was," Lee later explained. "Told me one of my people was sick. My people." They drove to a house in Achimota, near the old golf course. A worried woman, an African American, met them and hurried them inside. "I opened the door and there laying on the bed was Martin King," Lee recalled. "So I say, 'What are you doing sick here, man'? He says 'I think I've got fever, malaria or something.' I told him, 'Well, I'm a dentist. But I'll find you a physician. You just hang in there, I'm coming back.'" They hurried back to Accra, where Lee re-cruited another African American doctor he had met, a man named Foster, in town for the independence celebration. But he turned out not to be a physician either. "Foster didn't tell me he was a psychiatrist. When I told him it was Martin King, I guess he just kept quiet because he wanted to see him."

After an inexpert examination, the dentist and the psychiatrist deter-mined that King did not have malaria, but they had little idea of what he did have. So Lee returned to Accra again and found George Padmore, one of the organizers of the independence festivities, and told him that a feverish King was stranded in Achimota. "They went and got him and put him in town somewhere. I never saw him again."

It is a homely story, but the convergence that it describes was historic. For a brief moment, three of the defining movements of twentieth-century history—the African American freedom struggle, the African independence movement, and the global anticolonial movement—flowed together, each drawing impetus and inspiration from the other. And it was the singular for-tune of Robert E. Lee, a dentist from Charleston by way of Brooklyn, now an old man in Accra, to stand at the confluence.

CONTRARY TO COMMON BELIEF, Ghana was not the first African nation to graduate from the postwar decolonization process; that honor belongs to Sudan, which became independent in 1956. Yet it was Ghana that seized African Americans' imaginations. In part, this interest reflected the country's location, on the same coast from which millions of Africans were carried into New World slavery. It also reflected the unique appeal of Ghana's charismatic young prime minister, Kwame Nkrumah. A seeming synthesis of African tra-ditionalism and Western modernity, Nkrumah was also one of black Amer-ica's own, having spent a formative decade living as a black man in the United States.

Nkrumah was just shy of twenty-six years old in 1935 when he enrolled at Lincoln University. At first glance, Lincoln seems an unlikely destination for a future revolutionary. Originally called Ashmun Institute, Lincoln was founded in the 1850s as a joint venture of the Presbyterian Church and the

Pennsylvania Colonization Society; its object was to prepare ministers for the Liberian field. With the coming of the Civil War and emancipation, colonization was discredited, and the school, renamed Lincoln University, became a more or less conventional black college. But something of its original mission persisted, and the school offered scholarship assistance to African students. More than forty Africans earned Lincoln degrees in the first four decades of the twentieth century, including another future head of state, Nnamdi Azikiwe of Nigeria. Nkrumah received his bachelor's degree in 1939 and, following two years at the University of Pennsylvania studying philosophy, returned to study in Lincoln's theological seminary.

Nkrumah read voraciously while at Lincoln, devouring everything from Marx to *Mein Kampf*. But his chief influences were black American and Caribbean writers, from whom he gained not only knowledge about the United States but also new perspectives on Africa. He read George Padmore's *How Britain Rules Africa* soon after its publication in 1936. He imbibed the works of W. E. B. Du Bois, whom he first met in New York in 1944 or 1945 and to whom he would later extend asylum in Ghana. But the work that truly inspired him—"the book that did more than any other to fire my enthusiasm"—was *Philosophy and Opinions of Marcus Garvey*. Nkrumah's regard for Garvey would later be registered in the Ghanaian flag, as well as in the new national shipping company, the Black Star Line.

During his decade in the United States, Nkrumah immersed himself in black American life. He spent several summers in Harlem, working odd jobs (he peddled fish for a time), attending lectures and conferences, and listening to the ubiquitous soapbox speakers. Among the people he met in New York was Trinidadian historian and activist C. L. R. James, who became something of a political mentor. It was James who directed him to George Padmore in London in 1945. Nkrumah was "not very bright," he warned in a now legendary letter of introduction, "but do what you can for him because he is determined to throw the Europeans out of Africa." After two years in England, Nkrumah returned to the Gold Coast and proceeded to do exactly that.

Small wonder that Nkrumah invited African American leaders to attend the independence celebration in 1957 or that so many of them agreed to come. Martin Luther King, Jr., was probably the most conspicuous member of the delegation, having recently appeared on the cover of *Time* magazine, but the roster also included veteran trade unionist A. Philip Randolph, Claude Barnett, head of the Associated Negro Press, Congressman Adam Clayton Powell, Jr., Horace Mann Bond, president of Nkrumah's alma mater, U.N. undersecretary Ralph Bunche, and *Ebony* magazine's John Johnson. The only obvious omissions were W. E. B. Du Bois, who was denied a passport by the U.S. State Department, and Richard Wright, who was not invited. (Wright considered attending anyway, but Dorothy Padmore discouraged him: the Ghanaians, she explained tactfully, lacked "appreciation of your efforts and your motives.")

Ghanaian independence was front-page news in every leading black newspaper and magazine in the United States. *Ebony* produced a lavish pictorial. The Pittsburgh *Courier* (still home to conservative columnist George Schuyler) published a thirty-two-page supplement, "Salute to Ghana." In a front-page editorial, the *Courier* underscored the special meaning that Ghana's independence had for African Americans: "Ghana's contributions, as a free nation, to peace, to art, to industry, to government, will be regarded by American Negroes as symbols of their own worth and potential. When we, American Negroes, shake hands with Ghana today, we say not only 'Welcome!' but also, 'Your opportunity to prove yourself is our opportunity to prove ourselves.'" An editorial in the Baltimore *Afro-American*, "Proudly We Can Be Africans," went even further, arguing that black people in the United States should no longer describe themselves as "Negro," "colored," or even "Afro-American," but simply as African.

Inevitably, some of the press coverage betrayed hints of an older tradition of cultural condescension. Visiting journalists described Africa—predictably— as a Dark Continent awakening from its slumber. Others contrasted Africans, in their "traditional" robes, with their more "advanced" American cousins in suits and ties. But with Ghanaians seated at the United Nations while African Americans fought for a seat on a bus, it was no longer obvious who was in advance of whom. The changing terms of the transatlantic relationship were thrown into sharp relief by an oft-repeated, perhaps apocryphal, story involving Vice President Richard Nixon, who led the official U.S. delegation to the independence ceremony. Encountering a group of black men in Accra,

Nixon asked, "How does it feel to be free?" "We wouldn't know," they answered. "We're from Alabama."

In terms of political stature, Africans had indeed leaped ahead of African Americans. But in terms of education, technical expertise, and accumulated capital, they still lagged woefully behind. No one understood this better than Nkrumah, who was compelled to retain legions of British civil servants, teachers, doctors, and engineers simply to keep the government and economy running. During his meeting with King, Nkrumah raised the possibility of recruiting hundreds, even thousands, of skilled African Americans to Ghana to lend technical assistance to the new nation. He raised the issue again a year later, during his triumphal state visit to the United States. Even as he enjoyed courtesies that African Americans could scarcely imagine—lunch at the White House, a speech before Congress—he continued to stress his nation's urgent developmental needs and the role that black Americans might play in addressing them. At the conclusion of his visit, he issued a formal invitation, offering an entry visa to any African American who wished to come and build a free Africa.

Nkrumah's appeal contained echoes not only of Marcus Garvey but also of Paul Cuffe, Martin Delany, and Henry McNeil Turner, all of whom had dreamed of an Africa remade by the skills, energy, and culture of black people from the diaspora. But this was no dream; it was an open invitation from the head of state of an independent African nation. In the months and years that followed, many people availed themselves of the offer, joining the handful of African Americans who had already settled in the Gold Coast. Determining exact numbers is impossible. No one kept a register. Julian Mayfield, a prominent member of the expatriate community, told a visiting Malcolm X in 1964 that there were three hundred black Americans living in Ghana. If one includes embassy personnel, Peace Corps volunteers, and others who passed through Ghana for short periods of time, the number may be larger. A few were famous and arrived amid great fanfare; others came unannounced, in some cases simply showing up at Accra airport without money or return tickets. Most left after the 1966 coup, but some remained through the years of the National Liberation Council and the various civilian and military regimes that followed. A few are still there today.

. . .

TO REFER TO AN EXPATRIATE COMMUNITY is in some sense a mis-
nomer, since the African Americans who found themselves in Ghana during
the Nkrumah years were a disparate group. Some fit Nkrumah's vision of
nation builders, men and women with the technical and professional skills to
help build a free Africa. Carlos Allston and Frank Robertson were electrical
contractors, whose company, All-Afra, worked on many of the grand public
buildings erected in the early days of independence. Lou Gardner, a plumbing contractor, often worked with them. Max Bond became the prime minister's personal architect. Robert and Sara Lee were dentists. (On the day they
arrived, the number of dentists in Accra increased from one to three.) Ana
Livia Cordero was a doctor, a specialist in tropical medicine. Robert Freeman, Nkrumah's classmate at Lincoln University, established Ghana's national health insurance company. Pauli Murray taught at the new Ghana
School of Law, where she produced the standard textbook on the country's
new republican constitution. (Concerned by what she regarded as an erosion
of civil liberties, Murray left after only eighteen months.) The largest single
contingent were teachers, who came to participate in the new government's
ambitious program of public education—a program that, in scope and conception, bore a more than passing resemblance to the campaign launched
among the freed people during American Reconstruction.

Others in the émigré community did not fit the nation builder profile.
Earl Grant was a photographer. Vicki Garvin was a union organizer. Jean
Bond wrote children's books. William Gardner Smith was a novelist and
journalist, living in exile in Paris, when he was recruited to work at Ghana
Television; he later directed the Institute of Journalism at the new Kwame
Nkrumah Ideological Institute at Winneba. Journalism was also the calling
of Julia Wright Hervé, the daughter of Richard Wright, who, with her Algerian husband, produced L'Étincelle—"The Spark"—a fiery left-wing
journal. (Hervé, as one veteran of the expatriate community drolly put
it, "shared none of her father's aversion to Nkrumah's one-party state.")
Julian Mayfield and Maya Angelou (known at the time by her married
name, Maya Make) were creative artists—writers, actors, and playwrights—

though in Ghana they also worked chiefly as journalists. The expatriate community even had its own art colony, featuring Ted Pontiflet, Tom Feelings, Herman Bailey, Curtis Morrow, and Earl Sweeting. Sweeting was probably the best known at the time, having been commissioned by Nkrumah to create a series of large murals in public buildings on Afrocentric themes.

The University of Ghana at Legon, flagship of the new nation's educational system, boasted a large contingent of African American professors and students, several of whom—David Levering Lewis, Nell Irvin Painter, Preston King, Sylvia Boone, Martin Kilson—went on to distinguished academic careers. The dean of the group was St. Clair Drake, who arrived at Legon in 1954, when the school was still a satellite college of the University of London, and taught there intermittently until 1966. Best known as coauthor of *Black Metropolis*, a classic work of Chicago School sociology, published when he was still a graduate student, Drake had a personal history that virtually recapitulated the history of twentieth-century Pan-Africanism. He never forgot his first encounter, when he was only six years old, with William Sheppard, the celebrated Black Livingstone, who settled in his hometown of Staunton, Virginia, following his dismissal from the Congo. In the years that followed, Drake learned about W. E. B. Du Bois (like most members of the expatriate community, he grew up reading *The Crisis*) and about Marcus Garvey's Universal Negro Improvement Association, for which his Barbados-born father worked as an organizer. Conducting dissertation research in Britain in the 1940s, he fell in with George Padmore, through whom he met many of the young lions of African independence, including Nkrumah. When the opportunity to teach in Africa presented itself, Drake seized it.

Politically, the expatriates were a diverse bunch. Almost by definition, those who came to Ghana supported Nkrumah, at least initially. All had tasted the bitterness of American racism, and the hypocrisy of the United States was a common, even compulsive, topic of conversation. But further generalizations are difficult. While emigrants clustered to the left side of the spectrum, they avowed a range of political loyalties, including communism and anti-Communist socialism, pacifism and Pan-Africanism, color-blind liberalism and Black Power. Some saw their work in Ghana as a continuation of the American civil rights struggle; others came to Ghana seeking a revolutionary alternative to an American movement that they derided as bourgeois and merely symbolic. A few evinced no interest in politics at all, asking only to live, work, and raise their children free of the blight of racism.

Several different political generations were represented. The oldest member was obviously W. E. B. Du Bois, who was ninety-three when he and his wife, Shirley Graham, arrived in 1961, bloodied but unbowed after their long battle with the U.S. government. The youngest member, leaving aside children who accompanied their parents, was probably Sylvia Boone, who was just twenty when she first came to Africa, initially to Guinea, with Operation Crossroads, a grassroots youth exchange program. In between these extremes lay a group of men and women in their thirties and forties. Differences in age inevitably produced some differences in political perspective. While the modern civil rights movement provided the political frame of reference for some of the younger members of the community, older emigrants hearkened back to the beginnings of the Cold War, to World War II, even back to the Popular Front era of the late 1930s.

Many of the expatriates had experience of political persecution. Viewed in hindsight, the 1950s and '60s appear as years of fresh hope and expanding freedom for African Americans, but they were also distinguished by Red-baiting and the ruthless repression of anyone who dared to envision a black politics that went beyond narrow questions of domestic civil rights. The classic example, of course, is Du Bois, whose efforts to uphold a radical anticolonial tradition in the early years of the Cold War led to the suspension of his passport and a federal prosecution. But Du Bois was hardly alone. Vicki Garvin, a left-wing labor organizer in New York, faced the wrath of both the House Un-American Affairs Committee and the State Department. Alphaeus Hunton, executive secretary of the Council on African Affairs, spent six months in jail for defying H.U.A.C. Julian Mayfield fled the United States in advance of a federal manhunt.

Another recurring element in expatriates' stories, at least among the men, was the U.S. Army. Many who came to Ghana were veterans. Others came to escape military service. But in either case, exposure to the American military, nominally integrated but still a distinctly southern and deeply racist institution, contributed to émigrés' alienation from the United States. Ray Kea, destined to become a leading historian of the precolonial Gold Coast, came to Ghana directly from Europe after mustering out of the army. After enduring two years of racist abuse, witnessing brutal assaults on black soldiers who dared to date European women, he had no interest in returning to the United States. (The situation became so bad that Kea and other black soldiers discussed commandeering a truck and seeking asylum in Czechoslovakia.) David Levering Lewis was in the middle of a dismal two-year hitch in Germany when he discovered a loophole for certain categories of university teachers. He leaped through and landed in Legon, where he taught "British and European History, 1200–1500." Lewis had doubts about the custom of lecturing in academic gowns, as well as about the relevance of the European Middle Ages to students living through the Ghanaian revolution, but a gown in Ghana certainly beat a uniform in Germany.

Preston King, Lewis's classmate at Fisk, did not escape the army's clutches so easily. After graduating from Fisk, King requested a deferment from his draft board in Albany, Georgia, in order to attend graduate school at the London School of Economics. He received the deferment, but made the mistake of presenting himself in person to make sure that his papers were in order. The board, which had awarded the deferment on the assumption that King was white, reversed itself and ordered him to report for induction. More galling still, the letter informing him of his new status was addressed to "Preston" rather than "Mr. King," it being the custom of southern boards not to use honorifics when corresponding with Negroes. Determined to salvage a small measure of dignity from the experience, King refused to appear for his physical until the board agreed to address him in the same manner that it addressed white draftees. He was prosecuted as a draft dodger.

King's eventual trial might, in other circumstances, have been comic, with the defendant, who had acquired something of a Mid-Atlantic accent during his time in London, quoting Thoreau's essay on civil disobedience to an all-white jury. As if that were not provocation enough, the trial coincided with the arrival in Albany of Martin Luther King, Jr., and the leaders of the Southern Christian Leadership Conference, who had selected the city as the next battleground in their escalating campaign against segregation. In such circumstances, Preston King's conviction was a foregone conclusion, and he

324 · MIDDLE PASSAGES

was sentenced to two years in prison. He returned to London while the sentence was under appeal, only to have the British government, at U.S. authorities' behest, cancel his visa. Facing deportation and incarceration, he was tossed a lifeline by the government of Ghana, which provided him with a passport and a job teaching political philosophy at the university in Legon. It would be almost forty years before he was permitted to return to the United States.

Preston King's story is obviously unusual, but so are most of the stories of the men and women who settled in Ghana during the Nkrumah years. There is obviously no way in a single chapter to do justice to all of them. But by examining a handful of journeys, it may be possible to discern the broad outlines of the expatriate community and to recapture something of its meaning and fleeting magic to those who were a part of it.

OVER THE COURSE of fifty years in Ghana, Robert E. Lee encountered many people who changed their names, from Malcolm X, born Malcolm Little, whom he met in Accra in 1964, to Kwame Toure, née Stokely Carmichael, whom he met at Kwame Nkrumah's funeral in 1972. Inevitably, some people asked why Lee, saddled with the same name as the Confederacy's favorite son, did not change his name as well. His answer was always a shrug. "It's my name. Why would I change it?"

As a descendant of Charleston's free mulatto community, Lee knew more about his surname's origins than most African Americans. According to family tradition, the Lees were already free when they arrived in South Carolina from Jamaica in the 1730s. The story of how they acquired freedom is lost, though presumably there was a white planter or two in the mix. In the still-fluid society of the Low Country, the family was able to acquire land. Growing up, Lee heard of forebears who were rice planters, and of others who owned Charleston's first hotel and first floral shop. Remarkably, the family was able to maintain its social position right through the antebellum period, even as South Carolina moved toward secession. Jon Lee, a steward at the elite Charleston Club and the family patriarch, owned real estate valued at more than $6,000 in 1860. Edward Lee, who was probably his brother, was nearly as wealthy. Both men were members of the Brown Fellowship Society, an organization representing Charleston's leading mulatto families.

By the time Robert E. Lee was born in 1920, decades of Jim Crow had stripped the family of most of its fortune and many of its social pretensions. The seventh of eleven children, Lee was born in Somerville but grew up in Charleston, where his father, Samuel, worked as a barber in a white hotel. Cutting hair—at least cutting white hair—was a high status job in those days, and Samuel Lee was a proud and respectable man, a member of the local Episcopal church and a regular reader of *The Crisis*. But these distinctions could not save his children from racist insult. A lifetime later, Robert Lee still remembered his baptism into Jim Crow, which occurred on the same day that his mother first entrusted him with the job of delivering his father's lunch.

Lee, who was about twelve at the time, reached the hotel without incident. He was momentarily perplexed when his father did not allow him into the shop—"I thought it was his barbershop," he remembers—but agreed to wait outside for the dishes. There was a lake on the other side of the street, so he crossed over and sat down on a bench beside it. "I was just waiting for them to call me to collect the dirty dishes," he explains. "A big man with red hair, he said something to me. But I didn't hear what he said. He was a man, so I stood up and said, 'Yes, sir?' That man took me and threw me in the damn water! Fortunately, I could swim, but he didn't know that. He threw me in the water and started walking away." Lee climbed out of the water and, without a further thought, ran after the man and tackled him. Shouting and spluttering, he held him on the ground as a crowd gathered. "Some of the white men in the barbershop cursed that man," he continues, "had those towels still on, they were shouting, giving that man hell." But his father did not say a word. "I looked in his eyes. And he was *frightened*. He was frightened and he was so embarrassed that I got to see him like that."

Years later, Lee would understand his father's predicament, the sickening awareness of his son's jeopardy and of his own inability to protect him. But such considerations were lost on a twelve-year-old boy. "My father was just looking. And I told him, 'I'm not coming here anymore.' And I left and I never went to the barbershop anymore, the rest of my life I never went there. Never rode the streetcar into town again. They had those electric streetcars in those days. Told him, 'No, I'm not coming.'" His father never mentioned the episode again. But a quarter century later, when Lee told him of his intention to move to Africa, he approved.

Africa did not figure in the curriculum of Charleston schools in the 1930s. Lee's introduction to the continent came in 1938, when he enrolled at Lincoln University. He befriended a classmate from the Gold Coast, K. A. B. Jones-Quartey, with whom he sang in the glee club. Through him, he met other African students, including Ebenezer Ako-Adjei, a future Ghanaian foreign minister, and Kwame (known at the time as Francis) Nkrumah, who already avowed his intention of bringing down the British Empire. While most of their classmates regarded the African students as a curiosity, Lee found himself spending evenings at Houston Hall, the theology dormitory, where most of them lived. He learned that Africa was not "all one place," that his new friends came from different backgrounds and had different political opinions. "I realized that they knew things I didn't," he explains. "They knew about the British Empire. They knew about colonialism. . . . I realized that I was living in a colonial situation too."

After leaving Lincoln, Lee entered the dental college at Nashville's Meharry Medical College, where he met his wife-to-be, Sara. A graduate of Morgan College in Baltimore, she was the only woman in her class. She was also, by all accounts, a person of great beauty and even greater determination. They graduated from Meharry together in 1945 and, now married, moved to New York City to complete their residencies. Lee was quickly drawn into New York's African community, attending lectures and meetings of the African Students Union, an organization once headed by Nkrumah. But the idea of moving to Africa had not yet crystallized. On the contrary, he and Sara set about making a life for themselves in the United States. They opened two practices, his in Brooklyn and hers in Long Island, where they bought a home. On the day he opened his Brooklyn office, she gave birth to a son, whom they called Larry. (In Ghana, he would be known by his "day name," Kojo.) A second son, Randy, was born a few years later.

No single episode prompted Lee's decision to leave the United States, but two years on a Georgia army base clearly contributed. In 1948, Harry Truman had signed an executive order desegregating the U.S armed forces, but word had not reached Camp Stewart, outside Savannah, where Lee was posted in 1950. The camp had segregated barracks and messes, but it had only one dental clinic, run by a colonel from Georgia. Lee, a captain, was the only African American dentist. For the first three months, he was assigned no chair and no patients, until the colonel himself came up with an impacted tooth and could find no one else to treat it. Like the lion in the ancient fable, the colonel was thereafter Lee's most supportive friend, even suggesting that they open a joint practice after leaving the army. When Lee declined the offer, he was genuinely hurt. "I don't understand niggers," he said, shaking his head.

But as bad as the base was, the world off base was far worse. Lee had grown up in the South, scarcely an hour away, but nothing had prepared him for Georgia—the gratuitous racism, the constant encounters with police, some of whom were restrained by his captain's uniform; some of whom were provoked. "Finally, I had enough of Georgia," he explains. "I just got tired of being on the highways. Every time you hear a police car your heart goes *boom, boom, boom*. He stops the car, he gets out. So damn rude. So *insulting*. He's got all these weapons. And you can see that this is a stupid man. And if you say the wrong thing, this man will hurt you. You're always like this, waiting for what's going to happen. You just get tired of it." By the end of his army hitch, Lee had decided to emigrate to Africa.

Listening to Lee describe his thinking a half century later, one senses that his departure from the United States was propelled not simply by hatred of white racism, but by uneasiness with the qualities he felt sprouting inside himself—fear and frustration, suspiciousness and self-doubt. As a new father, he also dreaded the impact of racism on his children, not wanting them to get "hemmed in, growing up thinking they can't do this or that because they're black." Sara Lee needed no convincing. She had not spent the last two years in Georgia, but she had spent it as the mother of two young black children on Long Island, which was enough. "She didn't like racial discrimination either," Lee notes. "You could see it coming on already on your children. Well, she didn't want to go through that. She didn't want her children to go through that."

In December 1953, Lee flew to the Gold Coast to see whether emigration was practical. He stayed three months, but he did not need that long to make up his mind. Within days of his arrival, he found himself at a conference on independence in Cape Coast, discussing Africa's future with delegates from around the region. He had a personal audience with Nkrumah, who spoke of the colony's need for doctors and dentists. The whole trip was inspiring. "You could feel, when you came here, that these people weren't kidding, that they were quite capable. They knew exactly what they were doing. . . . After that visit I went back to my wife and said, 'I think we can be happy here.'"

Lee was not naive. He observed the poverty and the vestiges of colonialism, but he also noted how comfortable he felt. "I didn't come here because I thought I was going to discover King Solomon's mine," he explains. "Nor was I so ignorant that I thought I would earn more money practicing dentistry in Accra than in New York City. . . . But I did find . . . that I was psychologically suited for living here." The feelings that had welled up inside him in the United States seemed to recede. "I didn't have any fear. Nobody on the road was threatening me, even though the road had potholes in it. . . . I didn't see any hostile people. Nobody made me nervous. No policeman came after me with a stick in his hand. . . . I felt immediately like I could be at home here."

Through 1954 and '55, as the U.S. Supreme Court struck down the doctrine of separate but equal and Rosa Parks refused to relinquish her seat on a Montgomery, Alabama, bus, Lee and his wife prepared to move to what would soon become Ghana. Their decision provoked a variety of reactions. Lee's parents, who had long feared for their headstrong son's safety, supported the decision. Others thought it reckless. W. E. B. Du Bois and George Schuyler, both of whom Lee knew on a nodding basis, had diametrically opposed reactions. Du Bois, whose home in Brooklyn was just around the corner from Lee's office, listened carefully and offered his blessing. Schuyler told him he was a fool. (Whatever else you do, Schuyler warned, do not give up your U.S. citizenship, advice that Lee was pleased to ignore.)

Organizing affairs and obtaining the necessary papers took two years. Sara actually emigrated first, settling in the Gold Coast with the children in 1956. Robert followed several months later, arriving in time to attend the independence celebration. They opened a joint practice, operating initially out of a caravan that they had outfitted and shipped from the United States. After a few years, they built an office in Osu, a poor district of Accra, not far from the old Christiansborg slave fort. The years to come would bring happiness and unfathomable heartbreak, but Robert and Sara Lee never looked back.

ON HIS INITIAL VISIT TO AFRICA in December 1953, Lee met another African American, Bill Sutherland, who had arrived just a few weeks before. Sutherland was one of the first African Americans to settle in the Gold Coast, and he traced an unusually circuitous route to get there—a route that included stops in a New Jersey ashram and a federal penitentiary, as well as an abortive bicycle trip from Paris to Moscow.

Born in 1919 in Glen Ridge, New Jersey, Sutherland is one of the rare African Americans able to trace his descent to a specific enslaved African. Scipio Vaughan (the name was obviously acquired after arrival in the United States) was about twenty years old in 1805, when he was brought from Yorubaland to South Carolina and sold to a Camden planter. Little else is known of him, though he apparently was locally renowned for his skills in carpentry and metalwork—skills he may have brought with him from Africa. He was also apparently a favorite of his owner, who made provision for his freedom in his will. Vaughan married a Cherokee woman, by whom he had thirteen children. One of those children was Bill Sutherland's great-grandmother.

By the standards of most enslaved Africans, Vaughan had fared extraordinarily well, but he never forgot his home. His final injunction to his children before his death was that they should return to Africa. Two of his son honored the request, embarking for Liberia in the early 1850s, under the auspices of the American Colonization Society. Burrel Vaughan's fate is unclear, but James, his younger brother, proceeded on to Yorubaland, where he worked as a missionary of the Southern Baptist Church. He ended up in Abeokuta, the same Egba settlement selected by Martin Delany and Robert Campbell in 1859 as the site for their planned Niger Valley colony. Though he is not mentioned in either Delany's or Campbell's accounts, it appears that Vaughan was in Abeokuta during their visit. He later moved to Lagos, where he founded the city's first Baptist church and became a successful merchant. What is perhaps most astonishing about the story is that the African and American branches of the Vaughan family remained in contact. James returned to the United States on one or two occasions, and his descendants continued to visit periodically thereafter, right through the twentieth century. If the experience of meeting his African cousins did not motivate Sutherland immediately to emigrate, it at least gave him a more sympathetic impression of the continent than that of contemporaries whose images of Africa came from *Tarzan* serials.

Sutherland came to his politics early. He grew up reading *The Crisis* and was an active member of the junior N.A.A.C.P. He was introduced to socialism by a white Congregational minister, a southerner at that; he first learned about Gandhian nonviolent direct action from an Indian nationalist who spoke at a nearby black church. By the time he finished high school, the basic elements of his political philosophy were in place. In 1942, while living in the Newark Ashram, a pacifist community founded by legendary peace activist Dave Dellinger, Sutherland refused induction into the military. He was sentenced to four years in a federal penitentiary (twice the sentence meted out to whites convicted of the same crime) and served three, one of them in a punishment block for his role in organizing a strike against segregation in the federal prison system. On his release, he recommenced organizing, helping to found the New York chapter of the Congress of Racial Equality. In 1947, CORE staged the first freedom rides, exposing illegal segregation in interstate transport.

Sutherland first became politically involved with Africa in 1951 in, of all places, Paris. He was working with an organization called Peace Mission, which was visiting major cities around the world organizing opposition to the Korean War. Speaking on street corners, members of the group were heckled by people who told them, in more or less polite fashion, to tell it to the Russians. They decided to take the suggestion. In the spring of 1951, four "peacemakers," including Dellinger and Sutherland, set out to bicycle to Moscow to "present a call to the people on the other side of the Iron Curtain to end the war." The group never reached Moscow—they were stopped at the West German border and again in Vienna—but the experience changed Sutherland's life. While organizing the venture in Paris, he met many African students whose energy and optimism about the future stood in stark contrast to the fear and beleaguerment of radicals at home. With McCarthyism at full flood, he wondered whether decolonizing Africa might offer a better base for organizing an international peace movement than America. More broadly, he began to question whether the game in the United States was worth the candle. "I got to the point where I rejected the basic values of that society—a society where there were no real connections and friendship," he later recalled. "For me to continually go to jail, get my head beaten in order to be a part of this, I just felt that it simply wasn't worth it."

For the next two years, Sutherland devoted his energies to Africa. In 1952, he organized in support of the South African Defiance Campaign against apartheid. A year later, he traveled to London to participate in a conference on Nigerian independence. His interest was encouraged by George Padmore, whom he met in London. Padmore had little interest in nonviolence and even less in Sutherland's inchoate ideas about African spirituality, but he recognized his conviction, as well as his potential value as a bridge between progressive movements in Africa, Europe, and the United States. Under Padmore's tutelage, Sutherland decided to move to Africa. His initial destination was Nigeria, but the British colonial office, well aware of his political background, denied him a visa. He then set his sights on Ghana, where, with Nkrumah already installed as prime minister, he was able to obtain the necessary papers.

As a final preparation for the journey, Padmore took him to meet Richard Wright, who was just back from the Gold Coast and working furiously on what would become *Black Power*. They met in a Paris café. Years later, Sutherland would ponder the irony of a pacifist being instructed on Gold Coast politics by a man advocating the complete militarization of the society. He also mused on the differences in temperament that enabled him to flourish in Africa while Wright floundered. Wright had come to Africa "seeking his own salvation," he warned. "One can't expect a country to solve a problem that is a personal one. If one is seeking a psychological home, then one may automatically project upon that country the home one seeks." Inevitably, the real Africa could never match the projection, setting the stage for disappointment.

Sutherland arrived in Africa in late 1953. He would spend the next fifty years on the continent, though most of it would be in Tanzania rather than Ghana. He worked initially at an experimental high school in a place called Tsito, where he met his future wife, Efua Theodora Morgue, a Ghanaian teacher and later one of the nation's most distinguished poets and playwrights. They had three children. In late 1956, Sutherland was hired as chief of staff for K. A. Gbedemah, one of Nkrumah's main lieutenants in the C.P.P. and a future minister of finance. Through Abedemah, Sutherland found himself at the heart of the Ghanaian revolution. Yet there were times when he wondered, from a purely political standpoint, whether he had made the right decision in coming to Africa. "I really misjudged the situation in America," he later noted. "I didn't foresee the bus boycott or the anti–Vietnam War movement or the women's movement or anything of that sort. I thought that the United States was in for a very bad period." As the civil rights revolution unfolded, he sometimes felt a great urge to go back and join the fight. But he consoled himself with the knowledge that he had left the United States for a reason, that the future he envisioned could never be brought to fruition by a movement dedicated solely to inclusion in the existing society.

If Sutherland sometimes felt isolated from the struggle in the United States, he also found that his location in Ghana enabled him to contribute to it in unexpected ways. It was he who assembled the list of African American invitees to the 1957 independence ceremony. And he was with Gbedemah later that year when the minister, who had come to the United States for meetings at the World Bank, was famously denied service at a Howard Johnson's restaurant in Maryland, a rebuff that became an international cause célèbre. With the Soviets broadcasting the episode around the globe, an embarrassed American government hastily invited Gbedemah to the White House for a private breakfast with President Eisenhower, a meeting that helped to secure U.S. funding for the massive Volta Dam project. The incident was the perfect illustration of the potential synergy between African and African American freedom movements—so perfect, in fact, that U.S. officials in Accra later accused Sutherland of orchestrating the whole thing. He denied the charge, though he conceded that he "knew full well" what would happen when Gbedemah entered the restaurant. "[I]t wasn't my job to take care of the U.S.'s dirty linen."

The Gbedemah episode seemingly vindicated Sutherland's decision to live in Africa, but in the months that followed he grew increasingly restless and discouraged. In 1958, Nkrumah signed the Preventive Detention Act, which empowered the government to detain those it deemed a threat to national security without the formality of a trial. Sutherland wrote a private letter to the prime minister, describing the act as unnecessary and unwise, the equivalent of using "a sledgehammer to kill a gnat." Nkrumah never replied, but he did dispatch the secretary of home affairs, who told Sutherland that anyone else writing such a letter would have been deported. The act stayed on the books. It was strengthened in 1961, empowering the state to hold suspects indefinitely.

Sutherland was also frustrated by the government's indifference to nonviolence. He had come to the Gold Coast in hopes that it might become a beacon leading the world toward peaceful methods of social change. Nkrumah initially seemed receptive to the idea. He permitted Sutherland to found local chapters of the Fellowship of Reconciliation and the War Resisters League and provided funding for an international conference on nonviolent methods of protest. He also promised to create a center for the study of nonviolence at the new ideological institute that he was building at Winneba. But the center never came to pass, and it became increasingly clear to Sutherland that Nkrumah's interest in nonviolence was, at best, tactical. Even that interest soon evaporated, as the Congo crisis and the Sharpeville massacre in South Africa illustrated the violent lengths to which white regimes would go to defend their prerogatives. By 1961, Nkrumah was creating training bases for guerrilla fighters from southern Africa and trying to organize a joint African military force to combat counterrevolutionaries in the Congo and elsewhere.

While these changes were happening, Sutherland had also come to a crossroads in his own life. His marriage was unraveling. He was without a job, having resigned his position with the Ministry of Finance in order to work on a pair of peace projects, one in the Sahara (where he and a small cadre of direct-action activists tried to stop a French nuclear test) and one in India. When he returned to Ghana in early 1961, he found himself unemployable, a result, he learned, of his association with Gbedemah, who had fallen out of favor. (Gbedemah later went into voluntary exile, taking his leave with a speech in which he accused Nkrumah of dousing "the lights of liberty" all across Ghana.)

When all these factors were added together, Sutherland knew that the time had come to go. He left Ghana in mid-1961, becoming the first prominent member of the African American expatriate community to depart. With little interest in returning to the United States, he took a short-term job with a progressive workers' organization in Israel, before finally settling in East Africa, in what would soon become the independent nation of Tanzania. He would remain there for the next forty years.

SUTHERLAND'S DEPARTURE from Ghana in 1961 coincided with the arrival of another émigré stratum, known locally as the Politicals. Though they came from different parts of the country and ranged widely in age, the Politicals—or Revolutionist Returnees, as Maya Angelou dubbed them— shared a range of experiences and considerable ideological coherence. Most had spent time in New York City, chief battleground in the postwar struggle between the liberal and radical wings of the African American freedom movement. Some, though by no means all, were members of the Communist Party. With the expulsion of leftists from the N.A.A.C.P., many migrated into organizations like the Council on African Affairs, the Civil Rights Congress, and the Committee on the Negro in the Arts, only to see those groups declared subversive and shut down. Not surprisingly, the Politicals arrived in Africa carrying deep anger toward the United States and extravagant hopes for the Ghanaian revolution.

The doyen of the Politicals was, of course, W. E. B. Du Bois. Du Bois had been prevented from attending the 1957 independence celebration, but he and his second wife, Shirley Graham Du Bois, came to Ghana in 1960 for the ceremony inaugurating the country's new republican constitution. It was his first visit to Africa since his Liberian journey of 1924. As on that occasion, he was positively rapturous about what he saw, finding in Ghana a confirmation of all his hopes and dreams for an independent Africa. Tragically, he arrived too late to see his old friend, George Padmore, whose service as Nkrumah's adviser for African affairs had ended with his death in 1959. He also saw surprisingly little of Nkrumah, whose attention was consumed by the Congo crisis, which erupted the very week that Du Bois arrived in Africa. But when they finally met, Nkrumah greeted him warmly, listening patiently as the old man laid out plans for reviving the *Encyclopedia Africana*, the definitive compendium of knowledge about Africa that he had first proposed more than half a century before.

Back in New York six months later, Du Bois received an unexpected cable from Nkrumah announcing the creation of an *Encyclopedia Africana* secretariat within the Ghanaian government and inviting him to come and launch the work. He accepted the invitation. On October 1, 1961, he left the United States for the last time, accompanied by his wife. On the day of his departure, he formally enrolled in the American Communist Party. (Shirley Graham Du Bois was already a member.) "Capitalism cannot reform itself," he declared in his letter of enrollment; "it is doomed to self-destruction."

In Accra, Du Bois received a hero's welcome. He and Shirley were soon ensconced in a comfortable house in Cantonments, the leafy suburb that had once housed the Gold Coast's colonial elite. Though he was ninety-three and in declining health, he remained lucid, energetic, and emphatically unready for retirement. He commenced another memoir—he had already written three—and tried to put in a few hours a day at the secretariat office near Flagstaff House, the compound housing the Ghanaian government. He was, as he had always been, difficult to work with, holding those around him to the same standards of efficiency to which he had always held himself. Officials at Ghana's Academy of Learning (later the Academy of Sciences), the body ostensibly in charge of the *Encyclopedia Africana* project, found him demanding and peremptory, but Nkrumah invariably stepped in before matters could escalate. Even as his own troubles mounted, Nkrumah continued to cherish Du Bois, appreciating not only his long service but also the luster that his presence conferred on Ghana.

Just as votaries had once trekked to Monticello to consult the wisdom of the aging Thomas Jefferson, so did a procession of pilgrims appear at the Du Bois residence to consult, honor, or simply gape at the old man. For the most part, he received visitors courteously, though several recall that he was defensive on the subject of Marcus Garvey, insisting that he had never opposed the Jamaican but merely tried to warn him of the disaster awaiting the ill-administered Black Star Line. He enjoyed the occasional drink and took daily drives to Tema to watch the construction of the new artificial harbor, tooling along the coast road in a chauffeured black Chaika donated by Nikita Khruschev. On February 23, 1963, his ninety-fifth birthday, he took Ghanaian citizenship. The University of Ghana presented him with an honorary degree on the same day.

W. E. B. Du Bois died on August 27, 1963, on the eve of the March on Washington. Having long prided himself on being born the week of Andrew Johnson's impeachment, the event that marked the onset of Radical Reconstruction, he would doubtless have been delighted by the timing of his departure, at the highwater mark of the civil rights movement. (That news of his death was passed to the crowd at the march by Roy Wilkins, one of the men who had driven him from the N.A.A.C.P., would have pleased him less.) A few days later, members of the African American expatriate community gathered with Nkrumah and members of the diplomatic corps for a state funeral in Accra. They laid Du Bois to rest next to George Padmore, on the grounds of Christiansborg Castle, an old slave fortress. It was a place that some of his ancestors might have recognized.

WHILE DU BOIS WAS THE DIRECTOR of the *Encyclopedia Africana* secretariat, the actual business of getting the project up and running fell to William Alphaeus Hunton, Jr. It was a characteristic role for Hunton, a gentle, unassuming man whose labors typically took place behind the scenes.

Like so many members of Ghana's African American community, Alphaeus Hunton grew up in a very political family. His father, William Alphaeus, Sr., was born in the black expatriate community in Canada, the son of a former slave and confederate of John Brown. William Sr. was the first black man appointed general secretary of the black Y.M.C.A., on whose behalf he traveled all over the world. Addie Waite Hunton, his wife, was a founding member of the National Association of Colored Women and an officer in the black Y.W.C.A., as well as a vigorous early supporter of Du Bois's Pan-African Congress movement. Alphaeus, their only child, was born in Atlanta in 1903, but grew up in Brooklyn, where his family moved following the 1906 Atlanta race riot. He earned a bachelor's degree from Howard University in 1924, followed by a master's degree from Harvard and a Ph.D. in literature from New York University. He wrote his dissertation on Tennyson and the ideology of nineteenth-century British imperialism.

Though literature was Hunton's profession, politics was his passion. He was a founding member of the National Negro Congress, established in 1936. By that time he was also, in all probability, a member of the Communist Party. In 1943, he left Howard, where he was a professor of English, to work as educational director, and later executive secretary, of the Council on African Affairs. Neither title did him justice. For twelve years, as the officers of the council battled the Cold War state and one another, Hunton single-handedly kept the organization afloat. He edited the council's publications, *New Africa* and *Spotlight on Africa*, distributed press releases on African events to a network of more than a hundred American newspapers, convened conferences (including a 1944 conference, "Africa: New Perspectives," attended by Kwame Nkrumah), and organized an endless number of demonstrations, boycotts, marches, and food drives in support of colonized people in Africa and Asia. Just as English workers in Tennyson's day had come to recognize "that their own interests lay in the overthrow of American slavery," he explained on the day he joined the council, "so today it is necessary for Americans and all the people of the anti-axis world to realize that their future security and peace must ultimately depend upon the abolition of the principle and practice of imperialism."

Such sentiments did not seem subversive in 1943. In August 1941, Franklin Roosevelt and Winston Churchill had signed the Atlantic Charter, embracing a vision of a postwar world defined by self-determination, an end to colonial spheres of influence, and disarmament. Negotiations to create a strong "United Nations," to replace the failed League of Nations, proceeded apace.

Even the N.A.A.C.P., under the cautious leadership of Walter White, embraced the anticolonial cause, passing resolutions linking African Americans' quest for citizenship to Asians' and Africans' struggle for self-determination. White and W. E. B. Du Bois served together as consultants to the U.S. delegation at the founding U.N. conference in San Francisco in 1945, and while there was no love lost between them, there was also little sense of a vast gulf between their postwar visions.

Two years later, the world looked completely different. With Eastern Europe under Soviet occupation and left-wing parties in Western Europe exhibiting growing electoral strength, American policy makers feared that all of Europe might soon fall to communism. In this context, the commitments of the Atlantic Charter simply fell away, replaced by the urgent priority of rebuilding the shattered economies of Western Europe. The centerpiece of this campaign was the Marshall Plan. Less noted (at the time and since) was the American role in the colonial world, especially in Africa. Working through agencies like the World Bank, the International Monetary Fund, and the Export-Import Bank, the U.S. channeled hundreds of millions of dollars in loans and grants to colonial Africa, modernizing electrical grids, railroads, and harbor facilities, all to ensure that the continent's bounty could be extracted as quickly and efficiently as possible, the better to rebuild Europe as a bulwark against communism. Anticolonial principles that had been matters of broad political consensus only a few years before were now seen as threats to America's global interests.

Different organizations responded differently to the shift in political winds. After enduring a season of Red-baiting in 1945–46, the N.A.A.C.P. fell into line with the Cold War consensus, retreating from the international sphere and focusing its energies narrowly on questions of domestic civil rights. Walter White joined the presidential advisory panel for the Marshall Plan. A long-maturing scheme to bring the United States before the bar of the U.N. (on the grounds that its treatment of minority populations violated the U.N. charter) was discreetly dropped, lest it embarrass the American government in the propaganda battle with the Soviets. The Council on African Affairs also went through a period of internecine conflict in the early Cold War, but that battle ended with leftists and internationalists firmly in control. The Left's triumph, however, only ensured that the council and its leaders would become targets of government harassment. Singer Paul Robeson, the council's president, lost his passport and career after suggesting in a speech in Europe that African Americans might refuse to fight in a war with the Soviet Union. Du Bois, who became the council's vice president following his ouster from the N.A.A.C.P., was prosecuted for failing to register as a foreign agent. Hunton paid the highest price, spending six months in jail for contempt of court for refusing to turn over a list of donors to a civil rights bail fund to the House Un-American Activities Committee.

The attack climaxed in 1955, when a federal grand jury in Washington, D.C., ordered the council to turn over all of its correspondence for the last decade. The ostensible focus of the grand jury's investigation was a 1946–47 South African famine campaign, essentially a canned food drive on behalf of hungry Africans. Because the council had worked with the African National Congress to coordinate the campaign, federal prosecutors maintained that it had violated the Foreign Agents Registration Act. The council, on Hunton's recommendation, dissolved itself rather than release the records.

The demise of the Council on African Affairs wiped away twelve years of Alphaeus Hunton's life. It also left him unemployed and blacklisted. Unable to find a university job, he was reduced (in his wife Dorothy's words) "to the level of taking anything he could get to keep his self-respect and sanity." He worked seasonal jobs, including a stint with the Hudson Bay Fur Company. But he also put the extra time to good use, writing *Decision in Africa: Sources of Current Conflict*, a brilliant exposition of the structure of the new imperial order in Africa and of the role of American capital, private and public, in underwriting it. Encompassing everything from harbor construction in Liberia to uranium processing plants in South Africa, *Decision in Africa* was a book that could only have been written by someone who had spent the last decade of his life collecting every scrap of available information about African politics. It was also a book that very few Americans deigned to read.

Like the proverbial prophet without honor in his own country, Hunton was feted abroad even as he was marginalized at home. In 1958, he scratched together a ticket to attend the All-African People's Conference in Accra, the opening gambit in Nkrumah's campaign for continental unity. Many of the attendees had read *Decision in Africa*, and Hunton was treated like a visiting dignitary. Nkrumah deputed an official to take him on a tour of the country. A representative of the Soviet Academy of Sciences informed Hunton that his book was being translated into Russian, and invited him to stop in the Soviet Union on his way home, an honor that Hunton happily accepted.

By the time he embarked on his 1958 trip, Hunton had decided to emigrate to Africa, and he spent much of his journey visiting possible destinations, weighing their pros and cons. To the surprise of many, he initially chose Guinea, not Ghana. Given the country's lack of development and the poor state of Hunton's French, it was a curious choice, but also a considered one. The streets of Conakry, the capital, had few cars but they also had no Coca-Cola signs. More important to Hunton, Guinea lacked the entrenched African middle class that was already threatening to derail Nkrumah's socialist revolution. "There's something else that makes me hesitate about coming to Nigeria or Ghana to settle down at the present time," he explained in a letter to his wife, written from Conakry. "With some notable exceptions here and there, those in influential positions in government or university circles tend towards being a snobbish, high-living elite class with too little real concern about the welfare and advancement of the whole nation. Liberia, of course, is the classic example of that, and Ghana and Nigeria are not as bad as Liberia by any means but they do manifest the same fatal tendencies at the present time." Given subsequent events, it was a prophetic remark, though one that probably stemmed as much from Hunton's experiences in the United States as from his insight into Ghanaian politics.

In 1960, Hunton accepted President Sékou Touré's offer of a professorship at the planned national university of Guinea. (With the university still on the drawing board, he initially taught at Conakry's Lycée Classique.) He threw himself into the new situation with characteristic enthusiasm. In addition to teaching, he produced English-language news broadcasts for Radio Conakry and began preparing an English edition of Sékou Touré's writings. He also penned a glowing article, "Guinea Strides Forward," for the inaugural issue of *Freedomways*, a new black radical journal launched by Shirley Graham Du Bois and others in 1961. But life in Guinea was far harder than he admitted. Food was scarce and consumer goods nonexistent. The Huntons managed to find a car, a Czech Skoda comically undersized for Alphaeus's six-foot-five frame, but there was no gas to run it. When a cable came from Du Bois in late 1961 asking Hunton to come to Ghana to organize the *Encyclopedia Africana* secretariat, he leaped at the opportunity, little imagining the troubles that awaited him.

AMONG THE YOUNGER POLITICALS, the acknowledged leader was Julian Mayfield. Mayfield was born in 1928 in Greer, South Carolina, but grew up in Washington, D.C. Like so many of the expatriates, his path to Ghana included stints in the U.S. Army and at Lincoln University. Though he would make his reputation as a writer, both as a journalist and a novelist, he first earned public acclaim as an actor, appearing in a Broadway hit, *Lost in the Stars,* an adaptation of Alan Paton's searing antiapartheid novel, *Cry, the Beloved Country.* In the early 1950s, he emerged as a leading member of New York City's black radical community. He was a founding member of the Harlem Writers' Guild and served as chair of the Committee for the Negro in the Arts, until it was Red-baited out of existence in 1954. Following the committee's closure, he and his wife, Ana Livia Cordero, a medical doctor, moved to Puerto Rico, where they had a son and where Mayfield finished two novels, *The Hit* and *The Long Night.* While there is no evidence that he and Cordero ever belonged to the Communist Party, they were certainly treated as subversives by the American government, which kept them under surveillance.

Mayfield and Cordero returned to New York in 1959 and were quickly gathered back into the fold of the black radical community. In 1960, Mayfield traveled to Cuba as a member of the Fair Play for Cuba Committee, a group that opposed the American embargo of the new revolutionary government. But what prompted his eventual flight from the United States was his involvement with a support committee for Robert Williams, head of a renegade N.A.A.C.P. branch in Monroe, North Carolina. A pioneer of what would become the black power movement, Williams had rejected the N.A.A.C.P.'s nonviolent posture after several much publicized skirmishes with the Ku Klux Klan. His advocacy of armed self-defense, announced in the late 1950s and subsequently elaborated in the book *Negroes with Guns,* led to his suspension from the N.A.A.C.P. It also made him a hero to black radicals, who had long accused the mainstream civil rights movement of inculcating submissiveness and passivity. Over the course of 1960, Mayfield helped to organize caravans from New York to bring food and clothing to the embattled people of Monroe. On at least one trip, he also brought guns.

Mayfield was in Monroe when events came to a head. Precisely what happened remains a subject of dispute, but it appears that a white couple inadvertently drove into a crowd of African Americans who had surrounded Williams's house in anticipation of an attack by night riders. When the crowd grew threatening, Williams sheltered the couple in his home, an act that led to a federal kidnapping charge. Mayfield drove Williams and other leaders of the movement out of Monroe that night, evading police and National Guard roadblocks. The flight marked the beginning of two remarkable global sojourns. Williams settled first in Cuba, from which he beamed a radio program, Radio Free Dixie, into the southern states; he later moved to China. Mayfield, also a fugitive, fled to Canada and then to Britain and Ghana, where Cordero had accepted a job with the Ghanaian Ministry of Health. They arrived in Accra in December 1961, settling into a house in Cantonments, within sight of the Du Bois residence.

FOR THE NEXT FOUR YEARS, the Mayfield-Cordero house remained the headquarters of the Politicals, the place where the expatriates gathered to discuss Ghanaian events or the latest evidence of American neocolonialism. When people were not there, they could usually be found at a second house, a modest bungalow inhabited by three African American women. Alice Windom, still in her mid-twenties, hailed from St. Louis. The daughter of prominent educators and civil rights activists, she arrived in Ghana with a master's degree in sociology from the University of Chicago and a fierce determination to advance the African revolution. Vicki Garvin, twenty years her senior, was a legendary figure in the New York Left, a radical trade unionist who had endured all that the Cold War state could dish out. The third resident, and the one destined to become best known, was Maya Angelou, known at the time as Maya Make. Make was separated from her husband. Garvin and Windom were single.

Even in a revolutionary society like Ghana, a single woman in Africa had a hard row to hoe. While many of the expatriate men quickly established liaisons with Ghanaian women—some with several women—Ghanaian men often disdained African American women, finding them too outspoken and independent. Ghanaians also had very little experience of seeing women in responsible professional positions, certainly not in positions where they would command men. Garvin and Windom both searched in vain for work befitting their training and experience. Windom eventually found a job as a receptionist at the embassy of Ethiopia, while Garvin taught conversational English to embassy staff from Cuba, China, and Algeria. Angelou worked as an office assistant at the Institute for African Studies at Legon. All three experienced some frustration with their circumstances, but they remained devoted to Ghana and to the global revolution that it symbolized.

Of the three, it is Angelou whose journey is best documented, thanks to a series of best-selling autobiographies. Zora Neale Hurston's famous lament—"I have been in Sorrow's kitchen and licked out all the pots"—applies equally to Angelou's early life. She was born Marguerite Johnson in 1928 in St. Louis, but spent most of her childhood in Stamps, Arkansas. At the age of eight she was raped by her mother's boyfriend, who was subsequently murdered by her uncles; for the next five years, she did not speak. At sixteen, she bore a son, Guy, out of wedlock. To keep food on the table, she worked as a fry cook, a dancer, a nightclub singer, and, briefly, as a prostitute. Her great professional break came in 1954 when she was tapped as lead dancer for a Broadway production of *Porgy and Bess* that toured Western Europe, Yugoslavia, and Egypt under the auspices of the U.S. State Department. The tour entailed a year's separation from her son—an unnerving experience for Angelou, who had often been left behind by her own mother—but it gave her a set of political and professional contacts that launched her career.

In 1959, Angelou and her son moved to Harlem. She had jettisoned her birth name some years before, but it was during the years in Harlem that the figure the world would come to know as Maya Angelou was born. She experienced success as a singer (she played the Apollo) and an actor, starring as the White Queen in Jean Genet's satirical play, *The Blacks*. She began to write in earnest, presenting her work at meetings of the Harlem Writers' Guild, where she met Julian Mayfield. The period also saw her entry into radical politics, though her politics, by her own account, were driven more by enthusiasm than ideological consistency. She worked as a fund-raiser and northern organizer for Martin Luther King, Jr.'s, Southern Christian Leadership Conference, but she was entranced by Malcolm X and the Black Muslims, who projected an image of black masculinity and defiance the likes of which she had never seen. At the same time, her involvement with the Harlem Writers' Guild drew her into radical Pan-African circles, into a group of black internationalists determined to link the black freedom struggle in the United States with the surging independence movements of Africa.

Black New York at the time was alive with excitement about Africa. Harlemites lined the streets in 1958 to catch a glimpse of the visiting Kwame Nkrumah. Patrice Lumumba had a similar reception in 1960, when he came to address the United Nations. Angelou was quickly caught up in the enthusiasm. She began to wear her hair in a "natural," the forerunner of the Afro, and to dress in African prints. She joined a group called the Cultural Association for Women of African Heritage, which later spearheaded the angry disruption of the U.N. General Assembly following Lumumba's murder. It was at this moment that she met Vusumzi Make, local representative of South Africa's banned Pan-Africanist Congress, a black nationalist offshoot of the African National Congress, also recently banned.

Make did not look the part of freedom fighter, standing several inches shorter than Angelou, with wide hips and folds of skin protruding from his expensive suits. But he took her by storm. Within a day of meeting her, he announced that he had come to America "with the intention of finding a strong beautiful black American woman, who would be a helpmate," and that he had chosen her for the role. Though engaged to another man at the time, Angelou accepted the proposal, partly because she was overwhelmed by his confidence and charisma, partly in the belief that rejecting him "might be betraying the entire struggle." They were married within a week.

It was a rash decision. Make was soon sleeping with other women, a practice that he defended as part of his prerogative as an African man. He spent
money the couple did not have, but refused to let Angelou work, lest it injure
his reputation. He patronized her in political discussions. Angelou quickly
realized her folly, but when Make was appointed P.A.C. representative in
Cairo she and Guy dutifully followed. But his transgressions continued and
she left him in 1962. Through various African contacts, she obtained a job
with the Department of Information of Liberia, a decision that got her out
of Egypt but that also suggests the still hazy outlines of her radical Pan-
Africanism. She stopped in Ghana en route to Liberia to enroll Guy, who had
reached college age, at the university in Legon.

On their third day in the country, Guy broke his neck in an automobile
accident. He eventually recovered, but there was no way that Angelou was
leaving him. She relinquished the Liberian job and settled down to live in
Ghana, moving in with Windom and Garvin. The most celebrated survivor
of the expatriate community settled in Ghana by accident.

"WHAT HAPPENED IN GHANA?" The question, the title of a 1966 pamphlet by Shirley Graham Du Bois, was on many people's lips following the
coup that toppled Nkrumah. The conventional answer, promulgated in
the coup's aftermath by U.S. officials and mainstream media, emphasized the
Nkrumah government's own failings—corruption, authoritarianism, and
irresponsible economic policies, as well as the increasing detachment and
self-grandiosity of the president himself. For Shirley Graham Du Bois, such
allegations were smokescreens to obscure a naked act of aggression by "imperialists and neo-colonialists . . . determined to halt progressive and anticolonial movements" in Africa and around the world. It was true "that there
were stresses and strains in Ghana, that there were difficulties and that the
nation was called upon to work very hard," Du Bois wrote. "But that there
was dictatorship or tyranny, that there were widespread disillusion and un-
happiness, that the people were crying out for a 'liberator'—such allegations
are lies. *Any resemblance to a revolt on the part of the people of Ghana had to be
manipulated and fabricated by skillful, directed intelligence from the outside.*"

We will likely never know the entire truth of "what happened in Ghana," but it is safe to say that it lay somewhere between these two versions. There was indeed corruption in the Ghanaian government, and if Nkrumah himself did not have his hand in the till he did precious little to bring to book those who did. There were rumblings of discontent, though they tended to emanate from the elite circles that had always opposed the C.P.P.—from chiefs, members of the British-educated professional classes, and others who rightly regarded the new regime as inimical to their own privileged positions. And there clearly was a drift toward authoritarianism. By the time of the coup, opposition parties had been banned, Nkrumah had declared himself president for life, and at least a thousand political opponents were in detention—fewer, to be sure, than were held in other countries that the United States warmly supported, but a depressing total nonetheless. On the other hand, charges of a neocolonialist conspiracy ought not to be dismissed. There were powerful forces at work, inside and outside the country, to destroy the Nkrumah government and the dream of continental unity that it symbolized. Whether American officials had any involvement with the various assassination attempts against Nkrumah is unclear, but they were certainly collaborating with his opponents. (The role of the C.I.A. in the 1961 murder of Nkrumah's friend Patrice Lumumba, prime minister of the Congo, has now been established beyond dispute.) It is likewise unclear what precise role, if any, American officials played in the 1966 coup, but they were apparently aware of it before it happened and they made little secret of their delight with the change in government.

The purpose here is neither to praise Nkrumah nor to bury him but simply to recreate the complex political landscape that African American radicals discovered when they arrived in Ghana in the early 1960s. As historian Kevin Gaines writes in his fine study of the expatriate community, the Politicals' predicament was "fraught with ambiguities." Given their own experiences and convictions, they strongly supported Nkrumah and the C.P.P., but it did not take long to realize that the reality of the revolution was far murkier than the idealized pictures they had brought with them from the United States. Not all Ghanaians, they discovered, welcomed their presence. Leaders of the opposition tended to view them as interlopers, a group of de-

racinated dreamers in thrall to Nkrumah. More disappointing, they sometimes encountered hostility from C.P.P. supporters, who resented their access to the president and the rapidity with which they gained influential
positions. The fact that some of the expatriates were women, assuming positions not normally occupied by women in Ghana, exacerbated the problem.
(Shirley Graham Du Bois, who was appointed head of Ghanaian Television
by Nkrumah following her husband's death, experienced hostility of all
three varieties.)

The wave of popular anti-Americanism that engulfed Ghana after the
first assassination attempt in 1962 complicated matters still further. Rumors
flew of African American involvement in the plot. Unfamiliar faces, obviously C.P.P. agents, appeared at the University of Ghana to monitor the
classes of African Americans, many of whom faced charges of working with
the C.I.A. There surely were C.I.A. informants within the expatriate community, but in the prevailing climate of suspicion such allegations could also
be a way to settle a personal grudge or dislodge a rival from a coveted job. At
least one African American, Wendell Jean Pierre, a professor of French at
the university, was deported on charges of spying for the C.I.A. (Whether
the accusation against Pierre originated with Ghanaians or with other members of the expatriate community remains a matter of dispute, as does the ve-
racity of the charge.)

Even when allegations could be brushed aside, they took a psychic toll.
As Leslie Lacy, a member of the African American contingent at the university, later explained, having one's legitimacy called into question could be
shattering to a political exile. "Put simply, you are there because you hated
America; given this hatred—blind and complete—coupled with the knowledge that the CIA is constantly subverting, embarrassing, confusing, dis-
rupting governments which carry out or are thought to be carrying out
policies which seriously jeopardize American interests, either in that country
or elsewhere, you want to do anything within your power to help the country you have temporarily adopted. But if you think that you are being
watched (which you are), it becomes difficult to function honestly and creatively. And you find yourself making statements, doing things—sometimes
exaggeratedly—all in the hope of proving that you are really loyal to the

revolution." Of course such reactions were inherently self-defeating, since they were precisely the actions one might expect of a spy trying to throw off suspicion.

THE EXILES' RELATIONSHIP to American politics was equally fraught. Historically, African Americans have tended to emigrate to Africa during periods of conservative retrenchment, when prospects for black citizenship seem bleakest. Those arriving in Ghana in the early 1960s, in contrast, came during a period of political resurgence. Even the most disaffected of the expatriates could not help but sympathize with the civil rights movement, and many grappled with complicated feelings of guilt and self-doubt as they saw their brothers and sisters in America facing fire hoses and police dogs. At the same time, many of the exiles, certainly those of a more radical persuasion, were deeply skeptical of the movement, which they saw as seeking mere integration rather any substantive change in the structure of American society or in the operation of U.S. foreign policy.

All the Politicals at some point during their stays wondered whether their energies could be more productively spent in the United States than in Ghana. Yet they also found, as Bill Sutherland had found, that being in Africa gave them unexpected leverage in the American struggle. As several recent historians have shown, the course and progress of the American civil rights movement was inextricably bound up with the global propaganda war waged between the United States and the Soviet Union. Whatever their private feelings about racial equality, American policy makers understood that Jim Crow undermined the U.S. internationally. It was difficult to portray America as a beacon of freedom and democracy when its darker-skinned citizens were disfranchised, segregated, and mobbed. The problem became particularly acute in the late 1950s and early 1960s, as newly independent Africa emerged as the next terrain of Cold War struggle. "Every instance of racial prejudice in this country is blown up in such a manner as to create a completely false impression of the attitudes and practices of the great majority of the American people," Vice President Nixon complained after his 1957 visit to Ghana. "The result is irreparable damage to the cause of freedom." In the years that followed, officials in U.S. consulates across the continent produced regular reports on local press coverage of American racial issues—the brutal attack on the freedom riders in 1961, the deadly riot following James Meredith's attempt to enroll at the University of Mississippi in 1962, and other events that might cast the nation in an embarrassing light. (Among those following Ghanaian press coverage of the Meredith riot was W. E. B. Du Bois, who quipped, "The only thing I can't understand about that young man . . . is why anyone would want to go to the University of Mississippi.")

The obvious solution to the conundrum was to enforce constitutional guarantees of equality, thus eliminating the embarrassing disjunction between profession and practice. The federal government made some movement in this direction. The earliest civil rights gains of the postwar period—Truman's presidential order extending the wartime Fair Employment Practices Commission, the appointment of a U.S. Civil Rights Commission, and the desegregation of the armed forces—were all taken under the spur of the Cold War. The amicus brief filed by Eisenhower's Justice Department in support of the N.A.A.C.P.'s *Brown v. Board of Education* suit explicitly linked civil rights to national security. Kennedy's dispatching of federal marshals to the University of Mississippi likewise stemmed from concerns about how the spectacle of southern intransigence (now broadcast to the world through the magic of television) was playing internationally, particularly in Africa.

For the most part, however, the American government approached the issue as a public relations problem—a matter of spin rather than substantive reform. Working through agencies like the U.S. Information Agency and the Voice of America, Washington officials sought to portray civil rights upheaval in a favorable light. As Mary Dudziak has shown, the official narrative emphasized two themes: progress (yes, Mississippi had a long way to go, but consider how far it had come since slavery); and openness (in what other nation did people enjoy such freedom to air their grievances?). This approach reached a perfection of sorts in 1963, when the U.S. Information Agency produced and distributed a film of the March on Washington. While Martin Luther King, Jr., portrayed the marchers as plaintiffs coming to collect on a bad check written a century before, the auteurs of the U.S.I.A. turned the event into a vindication of American values, a case of a proud democracy gathering its dissenters to its bosom.

An even more remarkable bit of Cold War legerdemain came in the form of government-sponsored tours of African American musicians and artists launched by the State Department in the 1950s and early 1960s, a subject illuminated by historian Penny Von Eschen. Initially directed toward Europe and the Eastern bloc—hence Maya Angelou's performing in a production of *Porgy and Bess* in Yugoslavia in 1954—the tours took on additional significance in decolonizing Africa, enabling policy makers an opportunity to showcase an America in which black people were not silenced or suppressed but hailed for their genius. Inevitably, the tours generated contradictions; many of the featured artists were themselves progressives who deeply resented American racism and refused to play the role of apologists for it. But for U.S. officials, the potential propaganda gains justified the risks, a calculus spectacularly borne out in 1956, when more than a hundred thousand Ghanaians turned out to hear a performance by Louis Armstrong and his All Stars.

The presence of a large community of disaffected black exiles in an independent African country was, to say the least, a threat to the State Department campaign. Sitting in the most conspicuous capital on the continent, the expatriates were ideally positioned to debunk U.S. claims of racial progress at home and benign intentions abroad. Julian Mayfield leaped immediately into the fray, defending Nkrumah in articles in American periodicals while contributing blistering anti-American commentary to the Ghana *Evening Press* and other pro-C.P.P. papers. He even launched a regular column, "Is This America the Beautiful?," featuring photographs of lynchings, attacks on civil rights demonstrators, and other images calculated to disabuse Africans of any residual respect for the United States.

Mayfield's most conspicuous achievement was the launching of *The African Review,* a radical journal modeled on *Freedomways* and published under the auspices of Ghana's Ministry of Information. The inaugural issue took forever to complete, but it finally appeared in May 1965 with contributions from a dozen different expatriates. The tenor of the journal was apparent from the cover, which featured a stern-visaged Nkrumah and the words

NEW HORIZONS IN MODERN PHILOSOPHY, a reference to the president's recent philosophical treatise, *Consciencism*. Tom Feelings contributed a political cartoon, a savage caricature of bourgeois Ghanaians who opposed Nkrumah. ("The Europeans and the Americans love me. I don't know what's the matter with you Africans," said the grinning figure, bedecked in morning coat, ribbons, and dollar signs.) The opening editorial, written by Mayfield, addressed the collaboration of American and Belgian forces in the Congo, an episode that revealed not only "the hypocritical savagery of Africa's enemies" but also the need for a stronger African union, presumably under Ghanaian leadership. The journal was distributed not only throughout Ghana but also across the continent.

U.S. officials in Accra and Washington watched the activities of Mayfield and other African Americans with alarm, well aware of the threat they posed to American interests in Africa. The result, as Kevin Gaines has shown, was a concerted campaign to discredit the exiles, waged in government circles as well as in the mainstream liberal media. African Americans who lived abroad were cast as delusionists and dreamers, irresponsible fanatics who had opted out of the noble civil rights cause. An item in *Newsweek*, for example, ridiculed one of the Afrocentric murals created by African American Earl Sweeting, which depicted learned Africans exchanging ideas with ancient Greeks. "If you have no history, invent one," the editors mocked. "Ghana, apparently, has taken that bit of Russian advice." Every sign of cultural miscommunication or friction between Africans and African Americans, of which there were inevitably many, was seized upon by American officials as evidence of the exiles' folly and, by implication, the folly of the radical Pan-African politics they espoused. The burden of the attack, as Gaines notes, was that African Americans had no business in Africa, that they were "really" Americans.

Though few at the time were in a position to appreciate the irony, the attack on the émigrés precisely reversed the terms of the nineteenth-century debate over African colonization. In the earlier period, black people had struggled to assert their American identity against white officials who denied their capacity for U.S. citizenship and proposed to send them back to Africa. The 1830s change in nomenclature from "African" to "Negro" grew out of this controversy. One hundred and thirty years later, black people found their claims to identity assailed anew by whites, now telling them that they were Americans after all.

THE ANOMALIES of the expatriates' position came to a point in two events that everyone in the community would forever remember: an August 1963 demonstration at the U.S. Embassy in Accra, timed to coincide with the March on Washington; and the 1964 visit of Malcolm X. Both episodes brought precious validation, mixed with anger, sadness, and regret.

Though they were aware of the approaching March on Washington, the Politicals initially chose to ignore it. But a few felt the need for some show of solidarity. After a flurry of meetings and discussions, they decided on an evening vigil, followed by a march outside the U.S. Embassy, where they would present a petition. Though organized at short notice, the event may have produced the single largest gathering of expatriates during the entire period. As the group assembled in the darkness, word spread of the death of W. E. B. Du Bois, investing the event with additional historical significance, as well as a large dose of heartache.

The group's petition had something for everyone, endorsing the major demands of the Washington event while also decrying American policy in Cuba and Vietnam, issues that the Washington marchers avoided. (Martin Luther King, Jr., featured speaker at the march, would come around to a similar position in the last years of his life, linking the nation's unjust treatment of African Americans with the injustice of the war in Vietnam.) The petition was delivered in the morning by a delegation led by Alphaeus Hunton, who made a short statement. But the protest continued all day, even as marchers in Washington, six hours behind, began to gather at the foot of the Lincoln Memorial. At sunset, two embassy guards, one of them an African American, appeared to take down the flag. Accounts of what transpired next differ, but there was some kind of confrontation, which ended with the black soldier clutching the banner to his breast and carrying it inside, amid "booing and hissing" from the demonstrators. Embassy officials were quick to decry the episode, which they took as further proof of the expatriates' disloyalty.

None seems to have stopped to ponder the pain and ambivalence encapsulated in a dispute between African Americans over an American flag. Meanwhile, marchers in Washington listened to the soaring cadences of Martin Luther King, Jr.'s, "I have a dream" speech.

BY MAY 1964, when Malcolm X first arrived, the problems in the Ghanaian revolution were becoming difficult to ignore. Political opposition had been banned, and rumors of spies and plots abounded. Leaders of the exile political community were clearly aware of what was happening. As Julian Mayfield later wrote, "The President's office was like a Plantagenet court—full of intrigue and self-seeking—and a foreigner who had the ear of the President had to have mastered many skills." Yet Mayfield and his colleagues did not—could not—avow such sentiments at the time, at least not publicly. Though the historical situations are utterly incomparable, their predicament was akin to that of supporters of the Soviet Union, who, knowing the stakes in the global struggle and having seen the American alternative at close hand, found reasons to ignore or extenuate Soviet failings. In some ways, the exiles' situation was even harder, for many had sacrificed everything, including U.S. passports and citizenship, to come to Ghana. In such circumstances, news of the imminent arrival of Malcolm X fell like rain on parched ground, nourishing spirits and reviving hope.

Malcolm visited Accra in May, on his way back to the United States from a life-altering pilgrimage to Mecca. His departure from the Nation of Islam had been announced two months before, and he was now promoting a new body, the Organization of Afro-American Unity. In his search for new political ground, he had hit upon an old idea: to bring the United States before the bar of the United Nations for its abuse of African Americans, the same idea that the N.A.A.C.P. had adopted and then dropped in the early years of the Cold War. With thirty independent African nations now sitting in the U.N., it was a piquant strategy. The Americans would obviously be able to veto any resolution in the Security Council, but simply having the debate on the floor of the General Assembly would be an excruciating embarrassment, putting the United States in the same position as apartheid South Africa. On his way back from Mecca, Malcolm visited a number of African countries hoping to find one willing to introduce the resolution.

Malcolm's itinerary in Ghana was organized by a committee of the Politicals, including Mayfield and Cordero, Alice Windom, Maya Angelou, and Vicki Garvin (who had first met Malcolm when he was still "Detroit Red," tending bar in Small's Paradise in Harlem). Anticipating that the American press would minimize the significance of the visit, "in keeping with the campaign to divide Africans and Afro-Americans," Windom produced an exhaustive record of the trip, which she mailed to correspondents in the United States. Over the course of five whirlwind days, Malcolm met the local and international press at the Ghana Press Club, spoke with legislators at Parliament House, and delivered major addresses at the University of Ghana (an event sponsored by Leslie Lacy's Marxist Study Forum) and at the Kwame Nkrumah Ideological Institute at Winneba. (The only "discordant note" at Winneba, according to Windom, came when an African American in the audience, a teacher working in a local high school, tried to defend the passive resistance techniques of the mainstream civil rights movement. He was immediately deluged with cries of "stooge" and "C.I.A.") Malcolm met the Chinese and Algerian ambassadors, and the Cuban Embassy held a reception on his behalf—events presumably arranged by Vicki Garvin, who worked with personnel at all three embassies. Alice Windom, who worked at the Ethiopian embassy, tried to organize a meeting there, but the Ethiopians, confirmed clients of the United States, wanted no part of Malcolm.

The obvious absence on the agenda was a meeting with Kwame Nkrumah. Though relations with the United States had soured, Nkrumah was anxious to avoid a complete break, especially at a time when he was in negotiations with the World Bank for a desperately needed loan. His reluctance to meet Malcolm was probably reinforced by Shirley Graham Du Bois, who, as a longtime Communist Party stalwart, had little sympathy with black nationalism. But Mayfield arranged for her to meet Malcolm at a party, and "she was absolutely captivated." The next day he got his meeting with Nkrumah, though precisely what was said between the two men remains unclear. Whether Malcolm brought up his proposed U.N. resolution is unknown, but if he did Nkrumah apparently refused to sponsor it.

On most nights, the expatriates kept their visitor up until two or three in the morning, peppering him with questions about this new Organization of Afro-American Unity. "How do you unify with Uncle Toms?" they asked. "How do we, living in another country, unify with people who are actually working with the U.S. government and who rush out to save American flags?" Malcolm answered their questions with characteristic intensity, insight, and humor. For people living in exile, grappling with doubts about the Ghanaian revolution and their own political relevance, the whole experience was utterly exhilarating. By the time Malcolm departed, the exiles had formed the first African chapter of the O.A.A.U. This was "the beginning of a new phase of our struggle," Windom wrote, and she and her comrades were back in the vanguard.

It must have seemed so close then. After decades of struggle and repression, all the pieces were finally in place for a global black revolutionary movement: a militant, charismatic African American leader with a mass political following; revolutionary governments in Africa; and a cohort of black internationalists ideally positioned to connect the two. Yet the moment had already passed. Ghana by 1964 was a frail reed upon which to stake one's revolutionary hopes. And Malcolm's position was far more tenuous than his international celebrity suggested. Not only did he confront severe government repression, but he also faced threats against his life by his erstwhile comrades in the Nation of Islam. His isolation was cruelly driven home on his last day in Ghana when he was snubbed by his old friend and protégé, Muhammad Ali, who had arrived in Accra the day before. As the expatriates stood at the airport and watched his airplane disappear, trepidation tempered their excitement.

Malcolm returned to Ghana few months later. The mood during this second visit, which included no public events, was far grimmer. Threats to his life had escalated, and he had little doubt of the fate that awaited him. Several members of the expatriate community urged him to remain in Ghana, to "let that jazz [in America] cool off." Malcolm declined the suggestion, though he expressed the hope, in a letter to Mayfield written after his return to the United States, that Ghana might shelter his wife and children in the event of his death. He was murdered on February 21, 1965.

. . .

EXACTLY ONE YEAR LATER, on February 21, 1966, Shirley Graham Du Bois headed to the airport in Accra to see off Kwame Nkrumah. The president was bound for Hanoi, on a self-proclaimed quest to broker a peace settlement between the United States and North Vietnam. It was a characteristically grandiose gesture, a final turn upon the international stage for a leader whose emergence scarcely a decade before had transfixed the world. It was also a very reckless thing to do. It was the coup season in Africa. Just a month before, the government of Nigeria had fallen in a military takeover timed to coincide with the absence of President Nnamdi Azikiwe, Nkrumah's fellow Lincoln University alumnus. Many in Nkrumah's inner circle, aware of the rumblings within the military and police, begged him not to go. Whether Shirley Graham Du Bois, a member of that ever-shrinking circle, advised him to go or stay is not clear.

Two days later, on February 23, Du Bois quietly marked what would have been her late husband's ninety-eighth birthday, unaware of a convoy of soldiers approaching from the north. She was awakened the next morning by the clatter of machine guns. The coup was all but complete. Leaders of the C.P.P. had been arrested in the night, and strategic sites had been occupied, including her offices at Ghana Television. A dawn radio broadcast announced the formation of a new military government, calling itself the National Liberation Council. "Long live Ghana," the broadcast concluded. Fighting continued through the morning, especially around Flagstaff House, the complex that housed most of the main government ministries, but by the close of the day the new regime was in firm control.

Nkrumah first heard of the coup when he landed in China, en route to Hanoi. He immediately flew back to Africa, hoping to rally loyalists, but he was unable to reenter the country. He found asylum in Guinea with Sékou Touré, who ceded to him the title of President of the Republic of Guinea, a grand, if distinctly unrepublican, gesture of Pan-African solidarity. Nkrumah spent the rest of his life in exile, spinning plans for his restoration. He died in 1972 in Romania, where he had gone to seek medical treatment.

The leaders of the National Liberation Council wasted no time erasing symbols of Nkrumahism. They banned the C.P.P., shuttered the Ideological Institute at Winneba, closed the bases for African freedom fighters, and staged a ceremonial bonfire of Nkrumah's writings, creating (in Shirley Graham Du Bois's understandably overwrought words) "a scene from Dante's *Inferno* in Accra's celebrated Black Star Square." They also signaled their intention to bring Ghana firmly within the American orbit. Privately gleeful about the coup, American officials waited what they considered a decent interval—a week—before extending diplomatic recognition to the military regime. American food aid, suspended during Nkrumah's reign, was restored. Large loans from the World Bank and I.M.F., the terms of which Nkrumah had refused to accept, followed. The alacrity with which the American government embraced the N.L.C. inevitably fueled allegations that the United States had played a role in the coup. The fact that the American ambassador in Ghana at the time, Franklin Williams, had been a Lincoln University classmate of Nkrumah's, gave the business an aspect of personal betrayal.

African American expatriates watched unfolding events with varying measures of shock, dismay, and anger—anger at an American government that most blamed for Nkrumah's fall; anger at Ghanaians who had seemingly betrayed the great trust they had been handed by history; anger at their own fecklessness. Some had already left Ghana by the time the coup occurred, and most of the rest left in the months that followed, voluntarily or involuntarily. They became the diaspora of a diaspora, scattered to the winds in a process that was, in its way, as moving as the process that brought them to Ghana in the first place.

A few refused to mourn Nkrumah's demise. The most obvious example was Pauli Murray, who had come in 1960 to train a new generation of Ghanaian lawyers and left just eighteen months later, ahead of what would surely have been a deportation order. Having warned of the danger of state encroachments on civil liberties at the time, she clearly felt a measure of vindication at the coup. (The short discussion of Ghana in her 1987 autobiography, *A Song in a Weary Throat*, closed with an image of a crowd tearing down Nkrumah's statue in a public square.) But Bill Sutherland, who left Ghana a few months before Murray and for some of the same reasons, took no pleasure in Nkrumah's fall. He spent the months after the coup arranging the affairs of refugees and displaced freedom fighters who flooded into Tanzania, now the chief vessel of Pan-African hopes.

Predictably, the coup bore hardest on the Politicals, those with the closest ties to Nkrumah and the C.P.P. Shirley Graham Du Bois was placed under house arrest and deported, without being given an opportunity to collect her and her husband's books and personal effects. She settled into angry exile in Egypt. A few years after the coup, she attempted to reenter the United States but was denied a visa—like her husband, she had taken Ghanaian citizenship—because of her association with subversive groups. She was finally allowed to make a short visit to the United States in the early 1970s. Stricken with cancer, she sought treatment in China, where she died in 1977.

William Gardner Smith, who had been recruited by Du Bois to work at Ghana Television and who later directed the Institute of Journalism at Winneba, was also detained and ordered to leave the country forthwith. He and his wife, Solange, returned to Paris. Julia Wright Hervé and her husband, whose journal had become the voice of the left wing of the C.P.P., met the same fate. Cartoonist Tom Feelings, who had supplied that barbed political cartoon to the inaugural issue of *The African Review,* was also expelled, though unlike the more prominent deportees he was required to pay for his own air ticket.

Some of the Politicals had already left the country, sparing them the indignity of deportation. Vicki Garvin had departed in late 1964, accepting a job teaching English at the Chinese Institute for Foreign Languages in Shanghai. She was gone by the time Shirley Graham Du Bois arrived in China, but her stay did overlap with that of Robert Williams, the legendary black nationalist and Klan fighter, who had once been smuggled out of Monroe, North Carolina, in the back of Julian Mayfield's car. Like Williams, Garvin eventually returned to the United States; unlike Williams, she continued her career as a radical activist, playing a particularly notable role in the international movement against South African apartheid. In the course of her work, she was occasionally reunited with her old housemate, Alice Windom. Windom also missed the coup, having moved to Ethiopia to work with the U.N. Economic Commission for Africa in late 1964. She too eventually returned to the United States, settling in St. Louis, not far from her child-hood home, where she worked as the director of a university center for so-cial change and conflict resolution.

The third resident of that extraordinary household, Maya Angelou, had perhaps the most remarkable return journey. She too left Ghana before the coup, returning to New York in early 1965 to work with Malcolm X in his new Organization of Afro-American Unity. Years later, Angelou would re-call strolling onto the plane in Accra in traditional African dress, looking at the sea of white faces (the flight was en route from South Africa to London), and actually feeling a mite of sympathy. "The passion my people would ex-hibit under Malcolm's leadership was going to help us rid our country of racism once and for all," she confidently predicted, after which they would make quick work of South African apartheid. Clearly the years under Nkrumah had not divested Angelou of her penchant for idolizing charis-matic male leaders, which made the denouement all the more shattering. Af-ter speaking with Malcolm on the telephone from the airport in New York, she proceeded to California to attend to family matters. She was there a few days later when the call came, informing her of his death.

But Angelou was nothing if not a survivor. Over the coming years, she threw herself back into the world of creative arts, earning critical acclaim as a poet, playwright, screenwriter, and actor. (She had a major role in the 1977 television miniseries *Roots,* for which she was nominated for an Emmy.) But the main basis of her fame was her own extraordinary life, which she retailed in a series of best-selling autobiographies. The series, which began in 1969 with the publication of *I Know Why the Caged Bird Sings,* currently stands at six volumes. (*All God's Children Need Traveling Shoes,* her account of the Ghana years, was the fourth volume to be published, though the fifth chronologically.) The popularity of the books transformed the once un-gainly, silent girl from Stamps, Arkansas, into the most visible black woman in the United States, save perhaps for her friend Oprah Winfrey. In 1993, An-gelou recited one of her poems, "On the Pulse of Morning," at the inaugu-ration of President Bill Clinton. Standing on the steps of the U.S. Capitol, looking across to the Lincoln Memorial, where Martin Luther King, Jr., had once stood even as she demonstrated in Accra, Angelou called upon Americans "To give birth again / To the dream." The appearance of two children of Arkansas, born on opposite sides of the Jim Crow divide, standing on the same rostrum offered an alluring vision of racial hope. It also demonstrated, yet again, the extraordinary capacity of the American political system to metabolize dissent, to find nourishment for national myths in the struggles of the very people who have been excluded from the nation's bounty.

If anyone would have appreciated the irony, it would have been Angelou's old friend, Julian Mayfield. Mayfield was also gone by the time the coup occurred, on a self-declared sabbatical in Spain, where he hoped to write a book about Nkrumah—a book that would look seriously at the problems in the Ghanaian revolution while also crediting its achievements. He continued to work on the project after the coup and apparently produced several different versions of the manuscript, none of which was ever published. In 1967, he returned to the United States to teach writing at Cornell University. Over the next few years, he wrote plays, short stories, and one screenplay. The most curious chapter of his post-Ghana career came in 1971–74, when he worked as an adviser to the prime minister of Guyana, Forbes Burnham. As Kevin Gaines notes, Mayfield's term in Guyana was a shabby reprise of his years in Ghana, another example of Marx's dictum of history repeating itself as farce. Mayfield knew that the politics of Guyana were divided between parties representing people of African and South Asian descent, who were roughly equal in numbers. He apparently did not know that Burnham, the leader of the black faction, was a client of the C.I.A., nor did he realize or remember that his opponent, Cheddi Jagan, had been an ally of Nkrumah. Mayfield left Guyana in 1974, and went back to university teaching. He died in 1984 at the age of fifty-six.

Among the Politicals, it was Alphaeus Hunton who drew the shortest straw. Arriving in Ghana in 1962, he poured himself into the *Encyclopedia Africana* secretariat, just as he had once poured himself into the work of the Council on African Affairs. He organized a staff, hammered out a list of entries, recruited contributors, and launched a monthly bulletin to keep all interested parties informed of the progress of the work. In late 1963, a few weeks after Du Bois's death, he embarked on an exhausting continental tour to organize corresponding secretariats in other decolonizing nations, part of

Nkrumah's scheme to use the encyclopedia as a vehicle of Pan-African solidarity. As always, Hunton pushed himself relentlessly, undeterred even by a heart attack in 1964. In late 1965, the secretariat board formally appointed him director of the project, an office he had exercised in all but name since the beginning, but the decision was vetoed by officials in the Ghana Academy of Sciences, who instead appointed a Ghanaian—a Latin scholar—in his place.

Three months later, the coup came. The secretariat offices, near Flagstaff House, were caught in the fighting. Doors and cabinets were forced and papers strewn everywhere; the walls were pocked with bullet holes. Hunton cleaned up and recommenced working on the project, which, to his surprise, the new government chose to continue. But he was demoted again, this time to the rank of area editor. In November 1966, he and his wife, Dorothy, were served with deportation papers. There was no appeal. They resettled in Zambia, where President Kenneth Kaunda, a supporter of Nkrumah, announced plans for a rival encyclopedia. But there was no steam left in the dynamo, and Hunton experienced, in his wife's words, a "gradual withdrawal into injured despondency." He died in Zambia in 1970.

In general, the African American faculty at the University of Ghana was spared deportation. But some had already left, particularly after the deportation of Wendell Jean Pierre, and most of the others soon followed. Leslie Lacy, who had established the Marxist Study Group at the university, stayed for six months before proceeding to Nigeria. In Nigeria, he noted cynically, the military had already taken control, eliminating any temptation to dream reckless dreams. Preston King moved to Kenya. Still facing prosecution as a draft dodger in the United States, King spent the ensuing decades teaching and living in a dozen different countries, from Canada to Cameroon. In all, he lived for almost forty years in enforced exile. He was finally able to return to the United States in 2000, after receiving a midnight pardon from the departing president, Bill Clinton. (Among those who signed the clemency petition was the ninety-seven-year-old former judge who had presided over the kangaroo court that had initially convicted and sentenced King.)

Probably the most remarkable thing about the University of Ghana contingent is the number of its members who went on to academic distinction. Indeed, one would be hard-pressed to identify a contemporary American university that produced the scholarly talent that issued from Legon. David Levering Lewis, Preston King's Fisk University classmate, earned a brace of Pulitzer Prizes for his two-volume biography of W. E. B. Du Bois. Nell Irvin Painter, who initially worked as a lecturer in French, earned a doctorate in history at Harvard. Now an emeritus professor at Princeton, she was recently elected president of the Organization of American Historians. Sociologist Martin Kilson, who first came to Ghana on a Ford Foundation graduate fellowship, was the first African American to become a fully tenured member of the faculty at Harvard. Sylvia Boone, an art historian, produced a germinal work on Mende art. In 1988, she became the first African American woman to earn tenure at Yale. St. Clair Drake, the dean of the group, founded the black studies program at Stanford. The final volume of his life work, *Black Folk Here and There*, a sweeping history of the black world from antiquity to the present, was published in 1990, the year of his death.

Of the scholars, it was Drake who knew Nkrumah best and whose leave-taking was most poignant. After teaching at Legon during the 1954–55 academic year, he returned in 1958 for a three-year stint as chair of sociology. Like his friend Bill Sutherland, Drake faced his moment of decision—the moment when you had to "decide if you wanted to play for keeps"—in 1961, when he was offered the directorship of the new Ideological Institute at Winneba. He declined the position and went back to teaching in the United States. In 1965, he returned to Ghana with his wife, Elizabeth, also a Chicago-trained social scientist, and daughter, Sandra, to conduct an anthropological study of workers at Tema. (The field notes from the project were destroyed in the coup.) By 1965, suspicion and intrigue were rampant, and Nkrumah had retreated into isolation. Drake himself faced accusations of being a C.I.A. spy, based on his role in training Peace Corps volunteers. All his efforts to secure a meeting to see his old friend were rebuffed, but one day he received a curious note. Nkrumah had always been fond of Sandra Drake, whom he had known as an infant in London and who, as a teenager in Accra, had written him a poem after the murder of Patrice Lumumba. The note, from the president's office, said nothing about a meeting, but it did say that if Sandra Drake and her parents were interested, they were welcome to tour the new zoo behind Flagstaff House. The family accepted the invitation, hoping they might see Nkrumah. He did not appear, and Drake never saw him again.

ROBERT LEE REMAINED IN GHANA. Having taken citizenship, it might have been difficult to return to the United States, but neither he nor his wife, Sara, were inclined to do so anyway. Though obviously distraught about the coup, Lee was not shattered in the way that some of the Politicals were, not having staked his own identity so closely to Nkrumah's. He was a Pan-Africanist, but he had also come to Ghana with a very personal motive: to make for himself and his family a better, saner, freer life than they could have had in the United States. And, with all the disappointments, he had done so.

Lee tried to explain his thinking to an interviewer shortly after Nkrumah's fall. Though not asked explicitly about the coup, he was asked whether he had found everything he sought when he came to Ghana. "[N]ot by a long shot," he answered. "But when I came here I wasn't a child. I was a grown man. . . . I didn't come here expecting to find all the Africans perfect." The country was "going through some difficult readjustments," he continued, but the people were no strangers to hardship, and they would not be deterred by "those who may wish that Ghana does not succeed." Lee also noted the benefits of being in Ghana for his sons, the oldest of whom, Kojo, was twenty when the coup came. "I think that my children, growing up here, are actually growing up in a freer mental environment," he said, obviously hearkening back to his own South Carolina childhood. "[H]ere in Africa a black child grows up in an environment that is not set up to make him hate himself." In that statement lay the seeds of one final tragedy.

Lee rarely shares his thoughts about his eldest son with interviewers, and Ghanaians, with their legendary reticence, tend to avoid the subject as well. Suffice to say that Kojo Lee had a difficult adolescence, running with a rough, if still relatively privileged, crowd. One of his friends was named Jerry Rawlings, the son of a Ghanaian mother and a Scotsman who had briefly lived in the Gold Coast in the 1940s. After leaving Achimota School, Rawlings and Lee entered the air force, where they both became pilots, renowned at once for their acrobatic skills and for their recklessness and disregard of authority. In 1979, Rawlings seized control of Ghana in a military coup. After briefly ceding authority to a civilian government, he staged another coup on New Year's Eve 1981. Kojo Lee had left the military by the time Rawlings took power, but he returned to the ranks after the second coup.

Robert Lee had moved to Africa to spare his children the feelings of impotence that consumed so many black people in America. He ended up facing the opposite problem: a child who felt virtually omnipotent. Kojo Lee once again became a familiar sight in the skies above Accra. He also became a familiar and increasingly menacing sight inside the city, drinking and smoking with his military comrades, guns at the ready. In 1983, he killed a man. Nothing happened initially—such was the political climate at the time that soldiers, particularly soldiers close to Rawlings, could and did get away with murder. But Lee's erratic behavior had made him a potential liability to his old friend. Some months after the episode, he was arrested, charged, and convicted. According to a detained journalist who saw him in prison, Lee was initially unconcerned, boasting of his political connections and predicting that "his current problems would soon be over." But he misjudged the situation. On September 29, 1984, Kojo Lee died before a firing squad at the Nsawam firing range.

Of all the African Americans who came to live in Ghana, Robert Lee suffered perhaps the cruelest fate. The son he came to save was lost; his wife, devastated, died a few years later. Yet in the end it was Lee who remained, living quietly, plying his trade, patiently answering the questions of the endless people who arrived at his doorstep, many of whom imagined that they could "sit down here for fifteen minutes and learn the whole thing." "Everybody thinks I should be angry, I should be this or I should be that," he muses. "I just know that living in this society, where I am living now, I feel better. I feel like a person."

NINE

Counting the Bodies

BODIES FLOATED DOWNRIVER. Bloated and discolored, they tumbled over a cascade, catching in the crags. Most were naked. Many were bound hand and foot. Others were missing limbs. Like a sluice in a slaughterhouse, the river carried bodies down from the killing fields of Rwanda.

Keith Richburg stood on a bridge above the falls and watched the procession. As East African bureau chief of *The Washington Post*, Richburg should have been in Rwanda, covering the story. But as a dark-skinned African American, he feared that he might be mistaken for a Tutsi and find himself among the floating corpses. So he had come instead to this bridge over the Kagera River, on the Tanzanian side of the border. He tried to time the flow—a body every minute or two, sometimes clumps of two or three—but soon recognized the folly of the exercise: "Because this is Africa, and they don't count the bodies in Africa."

It was not supposed to be like this. When Richburg accepted the East Africa desk in the early 1990s, the continent was awash in hope. The end of the Cold War in 1989 freed Africa from four decades of superpower meddling. In February 1990, Nelson Mandela strode triumphantly from a South

African prison, tolling the end of Africa's last white supremacist regime. Bloody, decades-long civil wars in Mozambique and Angola had come to negotiated ends (temporarily, in Angola's case). All over the continent, the dictators who had dominated African politics since decolonization, or at least since the first wave of postindependence coups—Félix Houphpouët-Boigny of Ivory Coast, Hastings K. Banda of Malawi, Kenneth Kaunda of Zambia, Mobutu Sese Seko of Zaire, Mengistu Haile Mariam of Ethiopia, Mohamed Siad Barre of Somalia—were gone or going, swept from power by a combination of old age, international pressure, and domestic insurgency. Politicians and pundits spoke of an "African Renaissance," of a dawning era of democracy and development in a beleaguered continent.

By the end of the 1990s, the wreckage of Africa's renaissance lay strewn across the land. While a handful of nations succeeded in creating democratic dispensations and functioning economies, their achievements were swallowed up in a new wave of violent upheaval and economic collapse. The annulment of a democratic election by Nigeria's military government threw Africa's most populous nation into chaos. In Somalia, a United Nations peacekeeping mission launched after President Barre's forced departure devolved into a brutal counterinsurgency war. Sierra Leone and Liberia were ravaged by rebel armies, featuring soldiers as young as ten years old. The greatest carnage, however, occurred in the heart of the continent, in a swath of Central African states stretching from Uganda in the east to Angola in the west. In Rwanda, Hutu militiamen perpetrated the most rapid genocide in human history: more than eight hundred thousand people killed in ninety days, most of them dispatched with machetes and clubs. At least three million more perished in the slow, surreal implosion of Mobutu Sese Seko's Zaire. In virtually every measure of human welfare—per capita income; infant mortality; access to clean water, education, and primary health care—Africa experienced stagnation or decline. Diseases all but eradicated in the West—cholera, tuberculosis, polio—continued to decimate Africans. Malaria alone killed more than a million people per year, most of them children. As if all this were not enough, Africa found itself the epicenter of the AIDS pandemic. In Zimbabwe, one of the nations hardest hit by the disease, average life expectancy declined from sixty-five to thirty-nine in a single decade.

As Africa's agonies multiplied, a legion of journalists descended on the continent. Though they carried satellite phones and fax machines rather than Maxim guns and Bibles, these reporters were the lineal descendants of the explorers and missionaries of the nineteenth century, the latest participants in the long tradition of Western writing about Africa. Like their pith-helmeted predecessors, they sought out the continent's most harrowing corners, creating through their daily dispatches a new Dark Continent narrative to edify and horrify readers in their comfortable homes in Europe and the United States. Several members of the journalistic corps were African Americans, three of whom—Keith Richburg and Lynne Duke of *The Washington Post* and Howard French of *The New York Times*—would later publish memoirs of their experiences. Their accounts, similar in scope yet radically different in substance and tone, offer a final meditation on Africa, America, and the tangled ties that bind them.

RICHBURG, DUKE, and French were all products of the post–civil rights era, a period of unprecedented hope and unexpected perplexity. Born within a short time of one another—Duke in 1956, Richburg and French in 1958— they came of age after the great battles over public accommodations and voting rights had been won. By the standards of their parents, let alone of more distant ancestors, they inherited a world of unimaginable opportunity. In 1960, only about 130,000 African Americans attended college, virtually all of them in segregated institutions; a generation later, the number of black matriculants had grown tenfold, to more than 1.3 million. Though still underrepresented in most professions, African Americans were a conspicuous and growing presence in law and medicine, on university faculties, and in the business world. The very fact that African Americans reported for *The New York Times* and *Washington Post* was an index of how much had changed. Despite perennial complaints about "the liberal media," newsrooms historically have ranked alongside churches and country clubs as bastions of segregation. As late as 1960, the number of African Americans writing for major metropolitan daily papers could literally be counted on one hand. A generation later, every self-respecting newspaper in the nation had at least one black reporter; many had special programs to recruit and mentor African Americans.

Yet this best of times was also, in curious ways, the worst of times. Even as the black middle class grew in size and visibility, millions of African Americans remained trapped in blighted urban ghettoes, where they bore the brunt of poverty, joblessness, inferior public services, and violent crime. The rapid deindustrialization of the American economy after 1970 had a devastating impact on African Americans, who had only recently gained access to the industrial jobs that had long provided the ladder of upward mobility for European immigrants and their descendants. Segregation, abolished in law, persisted in practice, most dramatically in public education. By the 1990s public school systems in cities such as Chicago, Philadelphia, Detroit, and Dallas were more than 90 percent black and Latino, as whites fled to the sanctuaries of suburbia or private schools. A generation after the passage of the 1964 Civil Rights Act, African Americans continued to face significant discrimination in hiring, access to housing, medical care, criminal sentencing, even the interest rates they were charged for mortgages and car loans. In contrast to the injustices of the Jim Crow era, however, such discrimination was typically not inscribed in law but rooted in the operation of ostensibly race-neutral institutions, making it much harder to document and combat.

The African American predicament was complicated further by sweeping changes in American politics. While the post–Jim Crow era produced an increase in the number of black elected officials, it also saw a dramatic erosion of racial comity, as the civil rights coalition fragmented and a new Republican majority gained control of the federal government. If the civil rights movement of the 1960s represented the second Reconstruction, as numerous historians have suggested, then the resurgent conservative movement of the 1970s and 1980s might fairly be characterized as the second Redemption, though with Republicans playing the role Democrats had played a century before. While the two periods differed sharply in levels of violence, they had a similar dynamic, with conservatives in both cases tapping into a deep reservoir of white resentment against a federal government that had allegedly been captured by black people and their irresponsible white allies. Programs associated with the racial liberalism of the 1960s—affirmative action, Job Corps, the Equal Employment Opportunity Commission, Aid to Families with Dependent Children (welfare, in common parlance)—came under withering attack. In the new conservative catechism, such programs were poisoned gifts, sapping personal responsibility and reinforcing a "culture of poverty" characterized by dependency, indolence, and family disintegration.

For the most part, proponents of the new conservative orthodoxy eschewed explicitly racial appeals, attributing the predicament of the so-called black underclass not to race per se but to cultural pathologies and the perverse incentives of the welfare state. Indeed, some of the most prominent purveyors of the analysis were themselves African American. Individuals such as Thomas Sowell, Shelby Steele, and Glenn Loury were only the most conspicuous of a cohort of black conservatives that emerged in the 1980s to denounce welfare, affirmative action, and other vestiges of 1960s-era liberalism. Like George Schuyler, the conservative gadfly of an earlier generation, they took particular delight in skewering other African American political leaders, whom they accused of betraying Martin Luther King, Jr.'s, dream of color-blind democracy in favor of special pleading and perpetual victimhood.

The end result was a world undreamed by King and other apostles of the civil rights era, a world of formal equality and persistent inequality, of increased familiarity and diminished empathy. For the first time in history, African Americans enjoyed full civil and political rights in the land of their birth. Yet they also faced the continuing wages of institutional racism, as well as a raft of daily indignities and affronts, some so subtle that one might wonder whether they were real or imagined: arbitrary traffic stops by police; taxi cabs that failed to stop; sidelong glances by coworkers, wondering whether one owed one's position to "merit" or the operation of some "racial preference." Compared to the horrors endured by black people during slavery and Jim Crow, such afflictions might seem petty, but they exacted a heavy emotional toll, breeding frustration and a kind of chronic ambivalence, a sense of living between two worlds yet belonging fully to neither. This ambivalence, paradoxically, tended to be most acute among members of the burgeoning black middle class, those seemingly enjoying the fruits of an integrated America.

· · ·

AS SO OFTEN IN THE PAST, the perplexities of black life in America would play out on the terrain of Africa. The last decades of the twentieth century witnessed a resurgence of African American interest in the continent, a renewed sense of identification expressed in everything from fashion to the names that families gave to their children. The herald of this new era was Alex Haley, whose best-selling book, *Roots: The Story of an American Family*, appeared in 1976, the year of the U.S. bicentennial. Haley retold American history through the life of his own family, whose descent he traced to an African captive from the Gambia, Kunta Kinte. The book became an immediate sensation, claiming the Pulitzer Prize and National Book Award and spawning an entire African American genealogy industry. A television version, aired over a week in January 1977, became the most watched program in American history. Though subsequent scholarship would raise serious doubts about the historical accuracy of Haley's work, there is no disputing its impact on African Americans, who glimpsed in the figure of Kunta Kinte the previously unthinkable possibility of discovering their true names.

While the genealogy fad subsided, Africa's grip on the black imagination did not. Books such as Martin Bernal's *Black Athena* and Molefi Asante's *Afrocentricity*, both published in the 1980s, proclaimed the rise of Afrocentrism, a scholarly movement emphasizing the African roots of Western civilization, as well as the essential Africanity of African American people. Kente cloth, a colorful woven fabric from Ghana, emerged as both a fashion and political statement. Thousands of families adopted Kwanzaa, a "traditional" holiday invented in the late 1960s by black nationalist Ron Karenga and marketed as an African American alternative to Christmas. Each of the seven days of the festival was dedicated to what Karenga regarded as an essentially African principal, each rendered in KiSwahili: umoja (unity); ujama (cooperative economics); kuumba (creativity), and so forth.

But the best evidence of Africa's salience in African American life was simply the term "African American" itself. Rarely heard before the 1970s, the term emerged in the 1980s as the preferred, and soon the prescribed, designation for people of African descent in the United States. As with previous changes in collective address, the shift provoked controversy. Conservative critics decried "African American" as a further sign of the nation's ethnic balkanization; others debated whether the term properly belonged to American-born black people or to new immigrants from Africa, whose numbers had grown exponentially in the years after 1965. But by the early 1990s, the new term was embedded in the style guides of U.S. newspapers and publishing houses, as well as in common parlance. Though few observed it at the time, black nomenclature had now come almost full circle, returning the nation to the 1830s, when free people of color, anxious to assert their status as American citizens in the face of the colonization movement, renounced "African" in favor of "Negro" or "Colored." A century and a half later, their descendants, having finally achieved full American citizenship, reclaimed the identity their ancestors had relinquished.

But what precisely was the identity to which African Americans laid claim? What was the substance of this new solidarity? In contrast to previous periods of African enthusiasm, the late twentieth century spawned no substantial emigration movement; for all the invocations of "home," few African Americans proposed to resettle permanently in Africa. Nor did the era engender much in the way of political solidarity, certainly nothing to compare with the radical Pan-Africanism that flowered in the springtime of Kwame Nkrumah's Ghana. The antiapartheid movement of the 1980s represents an exception, but it may be the exception that proves the rule. Not only was South African apartheid an unusual case, offering a literally black and white example of injustice, but the movement against it was also waged chiefly on the terrain of domestic politics, with activists pressuring American corporations and universities to demonstrate their commitment to racial justice at home by divesting from a racist regime abroad. South Africa aside, the period produced little sustained African American engagement with African politics, indeed little engagement with the realities of postcolonial Africa at all. In donning the mantle of African American, Americans of African descent were not claiming identity with contemporary Africans as much as reclaiming their own ancestral past—in Haley's terms, their roots.

The character of African American interest in Africa was starkly revealed in the rise of an African tourist industry. For most of history, the number of African Americans traveling to Africa in a given year has been very small, growing from mere handfuls in the early nineteenth century to a few hundred in the days of decolonization. In the 1990s, the number soared to tens of thousands per year. The roster included individuals from every walk of life, from students to diplomats to development specialists, but the lion's share were tourists making pilgrimages to their ancestral land. An entire black heritage tourism industry emerged, complete with chartered flights, air-conditioned buses, and other amenities. In some ways, this new tourism paralleled developments within white America, where expanding middle-class affluence and a yearning for ethnic identity propelled millions back to the old country, but the peculiarities of African American history gave African tourism a different valence. However desperate the circumstances of the huddled masses arriving in America from Europe, they did not come as slaves, nor did their descendants experience the continuing discrimination and degradation meted out to African Americans. For white Americans, treading the old sod was chiefly an exercise in nostalgia. For African Americans visiting Africa, the emotional palette was inevitably darker.

Black and white heritage tourism differed in one other respect. Americans of European descent generally know where their ancestors came from, if not the specific village then at least the country. African Americans do not. In the absence of such information, the heritage tourism industry quickly came to focus on a handful of representative sites, each associated with the history of the slave trade. Initially, the most popular destination was Jufurre in the Gambia, the village reputed to be the home of Haley's Kunta Kinte. By the 1990s, the traffic was centered on old slave forts, particularly Goree Island in Senegal and Cape Coast castle in Ghana, places recommended not only by their intactness but also by their proximity to international airports and Western-standard hotels. Whether a particular individual's ancestors passed through these sites is obviously impossible to know, but there is no gainsaying their impact on visiting African Americans, for whom they have acquired the character of religious shrines.

All these contradictory processes and pressures would come to a point in the experiences of Keith Richburg, Lynne Duke, and Howard French. As products of the African American middle class in the post–civil rights era, as black reporters for white-owned newspapers, and as African Americans in Africa during the bloodiest decade in the continent's history, all three faced complex questions of intepretation and identity. They would answer these questions in very different ways.

PUBLISHED IN 1997, Keith Richburg's *Out of America: A Black Man Confronts Africa* was the first of the new journalistic accounts of Africa and surely the most controversial. Based on the author's three years as *Washington Post* bureau chief in Nairobi, *Out of America* was, like Langston Hughes's *The Big Sea*, a tale of disillusionment, but one rendered not in irony or wistfulness but in an outpouring of rage and horror. Assailing what he called the myth of "Mother Africa," Richburg sketched a landscape of misery and senseless slaughter, full of people who "look like me," yet whose behavior and wretchedness he found unfathomable. By the time he left Africa, he counted himself a different man, "devoid of hope ... drained of compassion," and determinedly indifferent to the continent's never-ending sorrows.

By his own account, Richburg was an unlikely pilgrim. The son of a union official, he grew up in a solidly working class neighborhood on Detroit's west side. He did not have "a particularly 'black' childhood—just a childhood, an average American childhood." He and his brother bought candy at the corner store and escaped the summer heat in an air-conditioned movie house up the street. His parents, who had converted to Catholicism after arriving in Detroit from the South, attended weekly mass at St. Leo's, the local parish, and sent their children to St. Leo's School, alongside the children of their Irish and Polish neighbors. It was, in Richburg's rendering, an idyllic boyhood, which came to an abrupt end on July 23, 1967, with the eruption of the Detroit riot, the bloodiest of the "urban disturbances" that roiled the United States in the late 1960s. By the time the U.S. Army and National Guard had restored order five days later, forty-three people had been killed, seven thousand had been arrested, and several square miles of the city had been reduced to ashes. Richburg's father took him to see the flames. "I want you to see this," he told him. "I want you to see what black people are doing to their own neighborhood."

While *Out of America* includes only a few pages about Detroit, it is worth attending to the account, since it anticipates Richburg's later portrayal of Africa. Presented without explanation or historical context, the 1967 riot appears as unaccountable as a thunderclap, a senseless act of black self-destruction that gutted a functioning, comfortably integrated city. In fact, Detroit was one of the most segregated cities in America, with a long history of violent racial conflict. While Richburg's family appears to have been spared, most black families moving into white neighborhoods encountered intense resistance, ranging from restrictive covenants and redlining (the refusal of banks to provide mortgages to black families outside designated neighborhoods, a policy virtually mandated by federal law) to outright terrorism. More than two hundred black families in Detroit had their homes bombed in the 1940s and 1950s, and countless others endured vandalism and verbal abuse. When such tactics failed to stem the tide, whites decamped for the suburbs. By the time the riot occurred, some 40 percent of white Detroiters, more than six hundred thousand people, had already left the city.

The decades of Richburg's childhood also saw an accelerating process of deindustrialization. The auto industry, long the engine of the Detroit economy, began to shed jobs in the 1950s, initially because of a deliberate decentralization policy, later because of automation and rising international competition. Inevitably, the layoffs bore hardest on African Americans, who were not only the first fired but who possessed fewer accumulated assets with which to weather long periods of unemployment. The deepening poverty of black neighborhoods, in turn, exacerbated tensions between residents and the Detroit police force. Inevitably, the 1967 riot began with a confrontation with police, who raided a Twelfth Avenue blind pig—an after-hours drinking establishment—where neighbors had gathered to welcome home two soldiers just returned from combat tours in Vietnam. None of this context excuses looting and arson, nor is it meant to deny the momentous importance of the riot in the history of the city, and indeed the nation. But it does suggest that the riot, and the baleful consequences that followed, flowed from something more than black people's own violent irresponsibility.

Richburg's neighborhood was spared by the flames, but it did not escape the riot's aftermath. Whites fled to suburbia. Merchants shuttered their shops. St. Leo's High School closed. The riot also had an impact on Richburg's own life, catapulting him into the privileged white institutions in which he would spend the rest of his life. With the closing of St. Leo's, his parents enrolled him in a private school, University Liggett, in the posh suburb of Grosse Pointe Woods. One of a handful of black students at the school, he had mostly white friends, most of whom had only the "vaguest sense" of where he lived. Suspended between worlds, he became a master of not taking sides, insisting, in the words of Martin Luther King, Jr., that individuals should be judged "not by the color of their skin but by the content of their character." He continued to steer to that lodestar at the University of Michigan, where he retained both black and white friends and resisted what he calls "voluntary resegregation" or, more prosaically, "the dining hall test." In his early years at *The Washington Post*, he angrily rejected suggestions that he should temper criticism of local black officials in the interests of his race.

When his editors at the *Post* offered him an African assignment, Richburg hesitated. Aside from one or two undergraduate courses, he had always given the continent a wide berth. How would he respond to the poverty? What if Africans rejected him? How would it feel not to be a minority, to be just another "face in the crowd?" Above all, Richburg feared that Africa would compel him to confront his own racial identity, force him "to choose which side of the dining hall I would sit on." But in the end he accepted the offer, having been assured by various "well-meaning academics and Africa specialists" that the continent stood on the verge of an economic and political renaissance.

PREDICTIONS OF A continental renaissance were first put to the test in Somalia. In early 1991, Siad Barre, the dictator who had ruled the country for more than two decades, was toppled from power by a coalition of rebel armies. But instead of prosperity and democracy, his ouster brought a complete dissolution of civil order. As Richburg noted at the time, Somalia represented the first great challenge of post–Cold War Africa, a test case of the international community's ability to provide political and humanitarian assistance to nations still "teetering between strongman rule and violent anarchy." With the commitment of a massive U.N. peacekeeping force, spearheaded by twenty thousand American troops, the country became something grander still, a proving ground for what President George H. W. Bush called the "new world order." Basking in the glow of victory in the First Iraqi War, Bush prophesied a world "where the United Nations, freed from Cold War stalemate, is poised to fulfill the historic vision of its founders; a world in which freedom and respect for human rights find a home among all nations." Scarcely a year later, the new world order had been consigned to the historic rubbish heap, and Somalia had devolved into yet another kind of test, measuring America's capacity to sustain an urban counterinsurgency war against a determined adversary.

Somalia became Richburg's first great story and, in time, his obsession. Yet in all his dispatches and in his extended account in *Out of America,* he included virtually no mention of the country's history. Neglect of history is hardly unusual among journalists—there is only so much one can fit in a thousand-word story—but Richburg elevated this occupational hazard into something like a political principle. To him, Africans were ill served by their "backward-looking attitude," their penchant for placing the onus for their predicament on colonialism and superpower meddling rather than on their own failings. Yet if the Somali debacle of the early 1990s illustrated anything, it was that past and present are not so easily disentangled.

A union of former British and Italian colonies, Somalia obtained its independence in 1960, the so-called "Year of Africa," in which seventeen African territories achieved national independence. Among the seventeen, Somalia inherited one of the least promising legacies. Though united by a common language and a widely shared religion, Islam, Somalia possessed little in the way of economic development, infrastructure (more than 60 percent of the population was nomadic), or exploitable natural resources. Few Somalis had ever seen the inside of a school or experienced running water, much less participated in a parliamentary system of government. In retrospect, it is surprising that the government created in 1960 lasted as long as it did—until 1969, when it was overthrown in a bloodless coup led by General Siad Barre.

One asset Somalia did possess was a strategic location on the Horn of

Africa, guarding the approaches to the Red Sea, a situation that naturally ex-
cited the interest of the superpowers. In 1970, on the first anniversary of the
coup, Barre declared Somalia a Socialist state, and the country entered the
orbit of the Soviet Union. The governing ideology of the new Somalia was
what Barre called "scientific socialism," his own eccentric blend of Marxism-
Leninism and the Koran, supplemented with bits borrowed from Mussolini
and Mao. In 1977, in the midst of a border war with Ethiopia that Barre had
launched, the Somalis were betrayed by their Soviet patrons, who concluded
a new alliance with the Mengistu regime in Ethiopia, an alliance sealed by the
arrival of Soviet military advisers and ten thousand Cuban troops. The
United States stepped into the breach, and Barre became an American client,
receiving military assistance and a hundred million dollars a year in aid in exchange for basing rights for American forces. The United States continued to
support him through 1989, even as the country descended into a brutal civil
war. Determined to cut off rebel militias from popular support, Barre
launched a scorched-earth policy in the countryside, killing literally hundreds of thousands of Somali civilians. But the rebel drive to the capital continued, and Barre fled in early 1991. Richburg arrived later that year.

By the time Richburg arrived, Somalia was "a nation in meltdown." Unable to agree on a successor government, the rebels carved the country into
fiefdoms, each under the control of a clan militia. All the normal appurtenances of civil life—government, police, schools, basic public services—
collapsed. Rival militias, often little more than armed bandits, operated
unchecked, especially in Mogadishu, the capital, where more than five thousand civilians died in anarchic street battles. In the countryside, the combination of war, banditry, and stubborn drought brought food production to a
halt. With the airport and ports under regular shelling, little food aid could
enter the country, and what stores did arrive were quickly looted. More than
half of the nation's eight million people faced the imminent prospect of starvation.

Yet few in the West seemed to care. In contrast to the collapse of the former Yugoslavia, which commanded the attention of the international media
and prompted the dispatching of international peacekeepers, Somalia's slow
death scarcely merited a mention in American and European papers. Rich-

burg set out to change that. By his own account, he became "fixated" on Somalia, churning out articles on the impending famine and browbeating his
editors to give the story more coverage. Doubtless there was an element of
journalistic self-promotion here—every reporter believes that his or her
story deserves more play—but Richburg's efforts also flowed from a perverse kind of "racial pride," a conviction that the suffering of Africans
was as newsworthy as the suffering of Europeans in the former Yugoslavia.
"If ever there was a reason for being in Africa—for being a black journalist
in Africa—this seemed like one," he later wrote. "The world, and Washington policy makers specifically, may not have cared about Somalia in early
1992. But I could force them to care by rubbing their faces in it every day, by
shoving the pictures of starving kids in front of people's noses as often as I
could, in the newspaper seen daily by the White House and members of
Congress."

Richburg got his wish. In August 1992, President Bush announced an
emergency airlift of food and medical supplies, the distribution of which was
to be overseen by U.N. peacekeepers. (The fact that the U.N. was compelled
to bribe a local warlord to allow the troops to land was an index of how topsy-
turvy Somalia had become.) Four months later, with food still not finding its
way to the needy, Bush announced Operation Restore Hope, deploying
twenty thousand American troops under a U.N. mandate. Richburg hailed the
move, which he saw as an opportunity "to raise the flag for a new kind of
American interventionism, a benevolent, selfless interventionism" motivated
only by the "desire to relieve human suffering." The idea that the Somalis
would defy the military might of the United States scarcely occurred to him.
Like television viewers around the world, he had "marveled at the pinpoint
accuracy of America's high-technology weaponry" in the recent Gulf War,
and he anticipated little trouble from a bunch of ragtag bandits with rusty
weapons. Indeed, he predicted that Mogadishu's militias would "scatter in terror" at the first sight of an American helicopter or well-equipped marine.

While that assessment was too optimistic, the intervention initially
showed every sign of success. Violence abated. Food was distributed
through the country. The danger of famine passed. In May 1993, most of the
U.S. troops were withdrawn from Somalia, leaving an international peace-

keeping force representing two dozen nations, including about three thousand Americans. Mission accomplished, or so it seemed.

THOUGH RICHBURG MADE MANY VISITS to Somalia, his base of operations was not Mogadishu but Nairobi, Kenya. With its relative stability, functioning international airport, and easy proximity to various trouble spots in the region, Kenya was the chief staging area for the international community in East Africa, home to offices of the United Nations, Red Cross, and an alphabet soup of N.G.O.s and development agencies. As Richburg put it, the city offered "the perfect ringside seat on Africa's chaos." A journalist based there could grab an early morning taxi to the airport, fly to Sudan or Somalia, and be back to file before nightfall, leaving time for a shower, dinner, and drinks at the Carnivore Disco, Buffalo Bill's, or "any of the handful of sleazy bars where reporters rubbed elbows with aid workers and U.N. bureaucrats and crazy white expat pilots and assorted adventurers out here for the cold Tusker beer and the easy African women."

While shocking, the final comment perfectly captured the ambiance and attitude of the foreign press corps, the community within which Richburg lived during his years in Africa. One of the abiding truths about foreign correspondents is that they usually spend as much time talking with one another as they do with the folk whose countries they cover. Correspondents in Nairobi not only frequented the same parties and bars but most also operated out of the same building, Chester House, a grungy, two-story block where the *Post* kept its office. When a story broke elsewhere on the continent, they embarked en masse, reconvening in the bars of the Sheraton Lagos, Kinshasa's Inter-Continental, or, in the case of Mogadishu, the Al-Sahafi, a bullet-pocked high-rise with a makeshift rooftop bar and a contingent of Nigerian peacekeepers. Though competing against one another, members of the correspondents' fraternity—and most, though not all, were men—shared sources, drivers, even girlfriends. Inevitably, shared experience produced shared points of view, helping to create a kind of collective "story" about Africa, a story that privileged certain aspects of life (killing and dying preeminently) over others.

As the local correspondent of one of the world's premier papers, Richburg was quickly gathered into this motley fraternity and baptized in its distinctive rituals and beliefs. While members of the Nairobi press corps wrote about Africa's travails with insight, eloquence, and passion, they proved to be far different in person, cultivating a "rampant cynicism" that could, when lubricated with alcohol, devolve into something close to racial contempt. Correspondents argued over "Africa's dumbest country" and proposed mock titles for their memoirs. (A reporter for the London *Times*, an expert on rebel movements, offered *Baboons with Rifles*.) Inevitably, some of this sensibility rubbed off on Richburg, though he was also astute enough to see it for what it was—a way to blow off steam, a defense mechanism for people overexposed to death and suffering. "It wears you down," a reporter for Newsweek warned him, in a rare bout of seriousness. "You just keep running and running to one shithole after another. After a while, you feel like a rat on a treadmill."

The places to which members of the African press corps traveled were not simply depressing; they also tended to be extremely dangerous. The African stories that captivated Western readers in the 1990s were, almost without exception, violent—military coups, civil war, ethnic cleansing—and covering them often put journalists in harm's way. Like most of his peers, Richburg learned what it felt like to stare down the barrel of a gun. He also learned that most of the people holding the guns did not shoot journalists, deferring to their professional neutrality or perhaps simply to the color of their passports or skins. Living in such circumstances inevitably took a psychological toll, breeding not only depression and fear but also recklessness and a strange sense of immunity. To Richburg, it felt like living in a "parallel universe," which permitted reporters to observe the suffering around them yet shielded them from its consequences. "I was always on the outside looking in," he later wrote, "like a stranger who had wandered aimlessly into a movie set and ended up in the middle of the film."

The quality of surrealism was greatest in Mogadishu. The day's stories filed, reporters made their way up to the roof of the Al-Sahafi, where they drank whiskey sours (concocted with lemon Kool-Aid from the U.S. Army PX) and loudly rehashed the latest turn in the American intervention. One evening, on a lark, Richburg brought up his portable stereo and blasted

Bruce Springsteen's "Born in the U.S.A." over the darkened streets. "We all found it hilarious and played it over and over," he recalled, stopping only when a sniper in the neighborhood whistled a few rounds over their heads. No anecdote better captures the universe of the Africa correspondent or Richburg's own ambivalent relationship to his ancestral continent.

But Mogadishu was not a movie set, and neither U.N. peacekeepers nor journalists were as invulnerable as they imagined. In June 1993, Richburg made a flying visit to the city to close down the *Post*'s temporary office. Most of the U.S. troops had withdrawn the month before and the Somalia story seemed played out. Eating breakfast with a few of the reporters still in the city, he heard the sound of gunfire. Supporters of Mohammed Farah Aidid, leader of one of Mogadishu's clan militias, had ambushed a contingent of Pakistani peacekeepers, killing twenty-four, whose bodies were then mutilated. The ambush marked a watershed in Somalia's history. Exhibiting new defiance, militiamen began to fire on U.N. officials and troops, including the remaining Americans, who made easy targets as they rolled slowly through the narrow streets in unarmored vehicles. U.S. officials responded by announcing a manhunt for Aidid, complete with WANTED posters offering $25,000 for his apprehension. They also launched a half dozen special-forces raids to capture or kill him, but succeeded only in elevating his prestige. A "humanitarian mission to feed starving people" had devolved into "an embarrassing manhunt for an egotistical baldheaded warlord."

In October, U.S. forces made a seventh attempt to capture Aidid. The raid, which later became the subject of a Hollywood blockbuster, became a bloodbath. Two Blackhawk helicopters were shot down by ground fire; the relief columns dispatched to rescue the pilots were pinned down by snipers. Mogadishu became a free-fire zone. By the time the battle ended a day later, more than a thousand Somalis had been killed or wounded, including hundreds of women and children caught in the crossfire. But the figure that mattered to the American public was eighteen U.S. soldiers dead, including one whose trussed and mutilated body was captured by television cameras as it was dragged through the city. A few days later, President Bill Clinton announced plans to withdraw the remaining American troops. The U.N. followed, leaving Somalia to its own devices. Today, more than a decade later, the country still lacks a government. It is also alleged to be a major staging area for insurgents fighting American soldiers in Iraq.

While it was the Black Hawk Down debacle of October that turned the tide of American public opinion against the Somalia mission, the turning point for Richburg came earlier, in July, when U.N. forces attacked a house in which Aidid's chief lieutenants were reportedly meeting. A squadron of Cobra helicopters poured sixteen TOW missiles and more than two thousand rounds of heavy-caliber ammunition into a residential neighborhood of Mogadishu, killing at least seventy people. Four journalists, all friends of Richburg's from Nairobi, arrived at the scene a few minutes later. They were surrounded by a crowd of Somalis and beaten, stoned, and stabbed to death.

Richburg was not in Nairobi when the raid occurred, or he would likely have been with his friends. While other correspondents mourned, he "became obsessed" with the episode, hoping to "pin the blame" for the disaster, and thereby to restore his "protected little journalistic universe." He interviewed the commanders who ordered the raid, as well as leaders of Aidid's faction. He visited the scene of the killings over and over, "letting the anger roil up again." Part of his anger was directed at American officials for launching an ill-considered assassination under the U.N. flag. But most was focused on Somalis—not just on the murderers, but on Somalis in general, who, in resisting a benign American intervention, had shattered the hopes of a continent, as well as Richburg's own "reason for being a reporter in Africa—a black reporter in Africa." "And I'm hating them, the Somalis," he wrote. "Hating them because they betrayed me."

LOOKING BACK, Richburg would identify the murder of his friends as the "turning point" of his career in Africa, "the start of a bitter wake-up call that would forever alter my view of Africa and how the continent could—or could not—be saved from itself." Though he covered innumerable other stories—the collapse of Zaire; the Rwandan genocide; rebel wars in Liberia and Sierra Leone—Somalia remained his point of reference, the "prism" through which he viewed "the rest of Africa." Everywhere he traveled, he found the same themes: self-destructive violence; governments led by "buffoons and misfits"; the breakdown of all codes of "civilized behavior between human beings." Again and again, he asked himself how such things—how such people—could exist in the twentieth century.

The only nation to escape Richburg's all-pervading scorn was South Africa, the last bastion of white supremacy on the continent. Richburg had written editorials on South Africa in his college days, demanding that the University of Michigan divest itself of all ties with the apartheid regime. Fifteen years later, he came to the country hoping to recover that certainty, to cover a story that offered "moral clarity" rather than the "vexing emotional and moral dilemmas of black Africa." There certainly was much to report. Nelson Mandela and other political prisoners had been released from jail and negotiations for ending apartheid were under way, but the nature of the new dispensation was still bitterly disputed. In the meantime, the country bled. Hundreds died in urban commuter trains and rural kraals in attacks orchestrated by operatives of the military and the police. Violent crime spiraled out of control. Yet very little of this found its way into Richburg's book. What appeared instead was a place "that looked and smelled . . . like home, like America," a nation with "modern" airports and "refreshingly efficient customs and immigration procedures," "supermodern freeways," and a plethora of sleek suburban shopping malls, indistinguishable from "shopping malls everywhere from D.C. to Detroit to Dallas." Expecting to loathe white South Africans, Richburg instead found himself feeling empathy for them, as they watched the eclipse of their illusory world. "It's an illusion," he wrote, "because no matter how 'Westernized' their lives seem, they live in Africa, and I know what darkness lurks out there, beyond the fence, beyond the borders, further north, in the 'real Africa'."

Anticipating objections to his account, Richburg adopted the standard defense of the traveler: "I've been there . . . I've seen it." In his book, he frequently resorted to direct address, usually at the grimmest moments of the narrative. "Is this depressing you? Do you want to put this book down now? No, please, press on. . . . I want you to walk with me, hold my hand as we step over the rotting corpses." "I'm tired of lying," he wrote at another point in the text. "And I'm tired of all the ignorance and hypocrisy and the double standards I hear and read about Africa, much of it from people who've never been there, let alone spent three years walking around amid the corpses."

It is a compelling technique. Yet if attending to two centuries of African journeys had taught us anything, it is that seeing is not so simple a thing, that even "open-minded" travelers (as Richburg claimed to be) view the world through specific cultural and historical lenses. This is especially the case when confronting a place like Africa, which has long figured in the Western imagination as a netherworld of violence and irrationality, disease and sexual license. The fact that some travelers possess black skin does not necessarily inoculate them against this influence, though it often complicates their reactions. In Richburg's case, the combination of inherited discourse and personal disillusionment yielded statements that would fit easily in even the most lurid nineteenth-century Dark Continent travelogue. Tribalism seethed through Africa, and "the potential for a violent implosion is never far from the surface." Club-wielding Hutu genocidaires were not "fully evolved human beings" but "cavemen." Africa itself was pestilential, a "breeding ground for myriad viruses, germs, plagues, parasites, bacteria and infections that most people in the West probably never knew existed." These "unseen enemies" paved the way for AIDS, which spread rapidly through Africa because of "rampant prostitution and the Africans' free-and-easy attitude toward sex." (Sex was "almost a way of life in Africa," Richburg reported.)

So powerful were these inherited discourses that they seemingly blinded Richburg to complexities in his own account—complexities suggesting a far more nuanced picture of African life and character than the book as a whole allowed. He acknowledged Africa's dizzying geographical, cultural, and linguistic diversity, even as he indulged sweeping continental generalizations. He conceded that terms like "anarchy" and "chaos," favorite words in the African press corps' lexicon, often reflected reporters' superficiality, their failure to grasp "the norms and rules and codes of conduct" in unfamiliar circumstances. He acknowledged the "heroism, honor and dignity" of ordinary Africans, as well as the "endless little acts of kindness" he encountered everywhere he traveled in Africa. Yet ultimately the force of such insights was swallowed up in his rage and despair.

The limits of Richburg's vision came most sharply into focus when he set out to explain why Africa was in the shape it was. Was there "something in the nature of Africans that makes them more prone to corruption?" Whence came this "maddening propensity to accept all kinds of suffering while waiting for some outside deliverance"? Having rejected in advance all structural and historical explanations as "platitudes" and "excuses," Richburg had no choice but to seek his explanation in Africans' own flaws—indiscipline, promiscuity, irresponsibility, and lack of initiative. This unpromising culture was further compromised by decades on the "aid dollar dole," courtesy of the continent's supposed friends in the West.

If all this sounds familiar, it should, for it was precisely the battery of charges that was forwarded in the 1980s and 1990s to explain the poverty and pathology of America's so-called ghetto underclass. On a few occasions, Richburg made the linkage explicit, arguing, for example, that African leaders had come to view foreign aid "the same way many American blacks see government assistance programs as a kind of entitlement of birth. In both cases, you're left with black people wallowing in a safety net of dependency." The problem, in both cases, was exacerbated by the "hypocrisy" and "double standards" of guilty white liberals and "do-gooders," as well as by black leaders who habitually blamed white racism for their predicament rather than confronting the "enemy within." "Most Africans were born in independent black countries," he wrote, "but their leaders still harp about colonialism the way black America's self-described 'leaders' like to talk about slavery and Jim Crow."

Needless to say, Richburg exhibited little patience with the contemporary African vogue in African American life, with all the people who "hanker after Mother Africa, as if Africa is the answer to all the problems they face in America." And he was utterly contemptuous of the "self-anointed spokesmen" who came to Africa and pronounced on its problems from the vantage of presidential receptions. He described with telling effect a 1993 black "summit" in Libreville, Gabon, where a bevy of black American leaders heaped praise on African strongmen like Nigeria's Ibrahim Babangida, extolled by Jesse Jackson as "one of the great leader-servants of the modern world." (A few months later, Babangida annulled the results of a national election, sending Africa's most populous country into a spiral of violence and repression.) "Maybe I would have been better off if I had never come to Africa at all, except on a weeklong tourist trip, staying in five-star hotels, buying tourist souvenirs, wearing African kente cloth," Richburg mocked. "Maybe then I, too, could have spouted the same vacuous criticisms of American meddling as the sole root of all the continent's ills. I, too, could have been a fervent supporter of the land of my roots."

The emotional climax of Richburg's journey came at Goree Island in Senegal. By the standards of the transatlantic slave trade, Goree was not a major embarkation point, but its location in Dakar, Africa's most delightful city (together with the aggressive marketing of the Senegalese tourism board) has turned it into the premier pilgrimage site for African American heritage tourists. Richburg arrived "hoping to feel that same kind of spiritual connection, to find some emotional frame of reference," but nothing came. While feeling "revulsion at the horrendous crime of slavery"—he compared the site to Auschwitz—he experienced "little personal connection or pain." What bubbled up instead, "so unspeakable, so unthinkable," was thankfulness—thankfulness to the forgotten ancestor who made it out, thankfulness that he was an American and not one of the nameless, faceless bodies left behind in Africa.

Again anticipating objections, Richburg emphasized that he was "not making a defense of slavery" or suggesting that it was anything other than a monstrous crime. "But condemning slavery should not inhibit us from recognizing mankind's ability to make something good arise in the aftermath of this most horrible evil," he declared. Such distinctions, however, cut little ice in the climate of 1990s America. Published in 1997, *Out of America* became an instant touchstone in the nation's ongoing "race wars." While some conservatives commended Richburg for speaking unpopular truths, most reviewers lashed into the book, deriding him as a race traitor, a brainwashed black man whose diatribes against Africa betrayed his own self-hatred. Most offered his reflections at Goree as exhibit A. Viewed in the long context of African American history, of course, Richburg's sentiment were hardly unusual. The idea that slavery was progressive, part of an unfolding providential plan, was an axiom of African American thought for more than a century, from the era of the American Revolution to the age of Booker T. Washington. But in our own more secular age, an age schooled in cultural relativism and skeptical of Western narratives of progress, such a sentiment represents the gravest of heresies. Perhaps historical context matters after all.

Richburg's journey ended where it began—with a young, idealistic black journalist arriving in Nairobi to assume the role of *Washington Post* bureau chief. And just as the old Africa hands broke in Richburg, so did Richburg break in his successor, starting with dinner at the Carnivore Disco, followed by a flying visit to Rwanda's capital, Kigali, where most of the blood had been scrubbed from walls and stairwells. A few days later, he boarded a British Airways flight to London, leaving Africa for the last time. A BBC news program on the flight carried a story about renewed fighting on the Rwanda-Zaire border, but Richburg switched his headset over to a music station. "And why should I feel anything more?" he asked, indulging direct address one last time. "Because my skin is black? Because some ancestor of mine, four centuries ago, was wrenched from this place and carried to America, and because I now look like those others whose ancestors were left behind? Does that make me still a part of this place? Should their suffering now somehow still be mine?"

"Maybe I would care more if I had never come here and never seen what Africa is today," he added. "But I have been here, and I have seen—and frankly, I want no part of it."

RICHBURG'S BLEAK VISION OF AFRICA was challenged, in different ways, by two other African American journalists working in Africa in the 1990s, Lynne Duke and Howard French. Like Richburg, Duke was a descendant of the Great Migration, though her forebears came not to Detroit but to southern California. Her parents, both children of domestic servants, attended state universities and found careers as public sector professionals. Lynne, the youngest of four children, was born in 1956. The family initially lived in Watts, but left there just before the cataclysmic 1965 riot. They settled in a middle class, previously all-white neighborhood called Windsor Hills. Duke went to integrated schools, briefly attended U.C.L.A., and went on to take bachelor's and master's degrees from Columbia.

Though her background was as middle class as Richburg's, Duke's politics evolved differently. She was deeply influenced by the black nationalist wave that swept through southern California in the wake of the Watts riot, even though she was too young to be involved directly. With their appeals to armed self-defense and global black revolution, organizations such as the Black Panther Party and Ron Karenga's U.S. Organization attracted large followings, especially on local college campuses, where Duke's older siblings were then enrolled. "The way I grew up, issues of civil rights [and] social justice . . . always included Africa," she later recalled, especially "in terms of South Africa and the struggle against apartheid." She carried her interest in the continent with her to college, taking courses on Africa and becoming involved with activists working for the liberation of South Africa and Namibia. The Africa of Duke's imagination was not a land of "grass skirts, Tarzan, bare breasts, [and] starving people" but the front line in a global black struggle for justice and equality.

Duke's first opportunity to travel to Africa came in early 1990, a few years after she joined the staff of *The Washington Post*. Asked to provide a ground-level view of the end of apartheid, she spent nine weeks in South Africa, living in townships, squatter camps, and rural reserves, speaking with ordinary people about their experiences and aspirations. The assignment resulted in a four-part, front-page series, published to coincide with Nelson Mandela's triumphal tour of the United States. If the series offered no earth-shaking revelations, it did provide a different perspective on African life, a vision of Africans' "normality and humanity," even in circumstances of great injustice and deprivation. Many of the individuals discussed in the series were women, a fact that distinguished Duke's reporting from that of male peers like Keith Richburg (whose entire book referenced only one African woman by name). Duke would bring this same attention to quotidian life—what she dubbed "the poetry of ordinary Africa"—to her work when she was returned to the continent in 1994 as the *Post*'s Johannesburg bureau chief.

Howard French developed an even more intimate connection with Africa. Born in 1958 in Washington, D.C., French grew up "in a strong African American family, where pride and self-respect were passed on daily and in abundance—together with lots of history." In 1975, as he enrolled at the University of Massachusetts, his family moved to the Ivory Coast, where his father, a doctor, directed a World Health Organization rural clinics project. French spent summers in Ivory Coast, and moved there after his graduation. He remained six years, teaching English at the university in Abidjan and writing freelance articles for newspapers and magazines. The experience not only converted him to the profession of journalism but also instilled in him a deep affection for Africa—for the food, the music, the "beauty and unfussy grace of the people." His bond was deepened still further when he met and married an Ivorian woman.

In reflecting back on his developing relationship with Africa, French would focus in particular on a trip that he took soon after his graduation from college. Sporting "billowy Afros" and the blessed recklessness of youth, he and his younger brother set out to discover the "real Africa," something they did not find in Abidjan, with its highways and skyscrapers. French would later come "to distrust this concept of authenticity deeply," but the trip, which carried the brothers deep into the interior of Mali, left a lasting imprint. He marveled at the routine gestures of hospitality—of offers of food and lodging and other courtesies that Americans would never imagine extending to strangers. He learned local patois, as well as the elaborate protocol that was sometimes required to cross a border, hire a car, or complete other tasks that might take only minutes in the efficiency-minded West. In the process, he learned the unwestern art of "surrendering control," of drifting with events. When he returned to Abidjan some years later as bureau chief for *The New York Times,* French would see "many foreign correspondents tearing their hair out in frustration over Africa's chaos or cursing the venality or supposed incompetence they claimed to see everywhere," but he would rarely join them.

Though they settled on different corners of the continent, Duke and French both arrived determined to represent Africa differently from their journalistic peers, to render Africans as rounded human beings rather than as characters in the "theater of misery and suffering." In reporting "the kinds of stories of African people and culture that do not often get told," they hoped to plant a germ "of understanding, or at least of feeling for a continent so many others were content to damn." At the same time, both recognized the danger of the opposite fallacy, of turning Africa into the "Disneyfied cradle of civilization" beloved of some African Americans. In the course of their travels through Africa, both would meet many black tourists caught "in the emotional throes of the 'motherland'," and they would exhibit as little patience with them as Keith Richburg had. The stories they sought lay in "the space between the archetypes," stories that confronted suffering and trauma but also conveyed the resilience and dignity of real people.

In the course of their tenures, Duke and French were able to write many such stories—accounts of the opening of the first bookstore in Soweto, the sprawling black township outside Johannesburg, or of the gala premiere of the African Film Festival in Ouagadougou, the dusty capital of Burkina Faso. Duke was particularly fortunate, arriving in South Africa in the midst of its first free elections, as inspiring a story as Africa had offered since the heady days of decolonization. A long-time supporter of South Africa's liberation struggle, Duke churned out dispatches on the election and its aftermath, many of them focused on Nelson Mandela, for whom she developed an extravagant admiration. Mandela was the good shepherd, an icon of courage and integrity for "a new Africa in the making." By her own account, she came to imagine a "symbiotic relationship" between herself and South Africa's new president, akin to what Richard Wright had briefly imagined between himself and Kwame Nkrumah, with Mandela cast "as a leader destined to lead his nation out of bondage, and I as one of the key correspondents on hand to report South Africa's progress to the world."

But other, less hopeful stories beckoned, stories that had to be covered, regardless of personal preferences. In Angola, ravaged by thirty years of civil war, a painstakingly negotiated peace treaty crumbled. Nigeria spiraled ever deeper into chaos, as the regime of General Sani Abacha executed the nation's leading human rights proponent, poet Ken Saro-Wiwa, in open defiance of the international community. The simmering civil war in Liberia, which had already given the world the terrifying spectacle of drugged child soldiers, erupted anew, engulfing neighboring Sierra Leone. All the while, the AIDS pandemic ravaged the continent, as if to confirm every Dark Continent stereotype of African contagion, hypersexuality, and death.

Yet all of these horrors would pale before events in Zaire, or, as it has been known for most of its history, the Congo. The land that William Sheppard had watched bleed in the 1890s would hemorrhage anew a century later, as the phantasmagoric regime of Mobutu Sese Seko, born in a C.I.A.-sponsored coup more than thirty years before, entered its death throes. The conflict spawned by Zaire's collapse eventually engulfed a dozen nations, claiming the lives of more than three million people. This was precisely the kind of story that French and Duke had hoped to avoid writing, yet it fell to them to report it.

IN HIS BRIEF DISCUSSION OF ZAIRE, Keith Richburg refused to rehash history. He said nothing about the slave trade or King Leopold, and mentioned the coup that brought Mobutu to power only in order to dismiss it. "Of course, I know the history of the C.I.A.'s complicity in the overthrow and assassination of Zaire's independence hero, Patrice Lumumba," he wrote. "But that was thirty years ago!" It was a characteristic position, rooted not only in Richburg's own neoconservative beliefs about individual responsibility but also in deeply engrained American beliefs about freedom and the human capacity for reinvention. From the first Puritan errand into the wilderness to the *Extreme Makeover* reality television show of our own time, Americans have clung to the belief that people can be born again, that it is possible to draw a line under the past and move on. Whether that faith is America's virtue or its vice (or perhaps a bit of both) depends on one's point of view, but in any case it has little relevance to the Congo, where history is not so easily eluded.

Like Somalia, the Congo achieved independence in 1960. In terms of natural resources, it was the most blessed of new African nations, but in other respects it was the most accursed. Over the centuries of the transatlantic slave trade, something between three and four million captives were shipped from the Congo region, more than a quarter of the total number carried to the Americas; another million or more were marketed through the Indian Ocean by Arab and Swahili traders. The onset of European colonialism brought an even greater holocaust. In the thirty years following the Berlin Conference, half the inhabitants of King Leopold's Congo Free State, some ten million people in all, lost their lives. The Belgian colonial government that succeeded Leopold was less deadly but scarcely less rapacious, pursuing diamonds and copper (and later uranium) with the same reckless greed with which Leopold's minions had once pursued ivory and rubber. The lesson of this long and terrible history was not lost on the Congo's postcolonial rulers: political authority was a license to loot.

Though the coming end of colonialism was obvious by the mid-1950s, Belgian authorities made no effort to prepare the Congo for self-government. At independence, the country's population of fifteen million people included a hundred-odd high school graduates and just seventeen university graduates. There was one Congolese lawyer, a half dozen doctors, not a single engineer. The country possessed no infrastructure, save what was needed to get minerals rapidly to transshipment points in Angola and Zambia. An area equivalent in size to the United States east of the Mississippi boasted less than eight hundred miles of paved roads, less than a middling American city. The population was divided among more than 250 different ethnic groups, speaking a babel of languages. Most Congolese continued to live under some semblance of chiefly authority, but chieftaincy had long been evacuated of political meaning. The country had no tradition of parliamentary democracy or the rule of law—only a tradition of political parasitism.

In retrospect, it is hard to imagine any scenario under which the Congo would have survived, let alone prospered. Nonetheless, most Congolese greeted independence with pride and hope—emotions captured in an independence-day speech by the new prime minister, Patrice Lumumba. A child of Kasai Province, the one-time home of William Sheppard, Lumumba prophesied a Congo of "peace, prosperity, and greatness," where every citizen would enjoy "just remuneration for his labor," as well as "the fundamental liberties foreseen in the Declaration of the Rights of Man," the idealistic charter of the French Revolution. He would not be given the opportunity to bring this vision to fruition. While much about the Congo crisis remains opaque, it is clear that in the days after Lumumba's independence speech both the Belgian and American governments determined to overthrow him, the Belgians in deference to multinational mining interests, the Americans out of fears of communism. Both nations found a useful ally in an ambitious army colonel named Joseph-Désiré Mobutu. In September 1960, three months after the coming of independence and two months after a Belgian-engineered secession movement in the mineral-rich Katanga Province, the Congo government was toppled in a military coup, the first of some eighty coups in postcolonial Africa. Lumumba was apprehended by troops loyal to Mobutu, tortured, and executed by a firing squad composed of Congolese and Belgian soldiers, all with the connivance of the American C.I.A., one of whose agents reportedly stashed Lumumba's body in the trunk of his car. It was this assassination that prompted disruptive protests at the U.N. headquarters by Maya Angelou and other African Americans.

Lumumba was replaced by Joseph Kasavubu, with Mobutu, now head of the army, hovering in the shadows. In 1965, Mobutu staged a second coup and declared himself president, an office to which he was nominally reelected in 1970. He continued to enjoy the support of the United States, which twice intervened militarily to defend him against advancing rebel armies. During the Reagan presidency of the 1980s, Mobutu enjoyed his closest links with the United States, which used his country as a staging area to provide weapons and supplies to rebels opposing Angola's Marxist government. With the end of the Cold War, however, Mobutu's stock plummeted, and he was forced by the international community to accept multiparty democracy in preparation for elections. But through deft political maneuvering, he managed to cling to power until 1997, even as terminal cancer ate away at his body—an apt metaphor for the nation he ruled.

Though Mobutu would in time become the poster child for African misgovernment, he initially enjoyed considerable support in the West, not only because of his staunch Cold War support but also because of his mastery of political symbolism. As Howard French noted in one of his early dispatches (aptly entitled "An Ignorance of Africa as Vast as the Continent"), Americans, blacks as well as whites, have a history of accepting authoritarianism in Africa as long as it is cloaked in the mantle of "cultural originality." Mobutu was a master of the game. In 1971, he inaugurated his Authenticité policy, designed to purge the nation of the decadent cultural influence of the West. The Congo became Zaire. Neckties and other accoutrements of Western dress were prohibited; Mobutu himself took the lead, appearing ever after in his signature leopard-skin pillbox hat, a carved wooden scepter in his hand. Zaireans were also required to change their Christian names to African ones. Thus Joseph Mobutu became Mobutu Sese Seko Nkuku wa za Banga, which roughly translates as "Mobutu, the all-powerful warrior who, through his endurance and inflexible will, shall go from conquest to conquest, leaving fire in his wake." By that time, the once reluctant autocrat had banned all political opposition. Newspapers were prohibited from mentioning the names of any Zaireans other than Mobutu or, as he preferred to be known, the Guide.

Mobutu sealed his international reputation in 1973 by offering a then unprecedented ten-million-dollar purse to stage a heavyweight championship match between Muhammad Ali and George Foreman. (The inimitable Ali dubbed the fight the Rumble in the Jungle.) For two memorable months, Zaire and Mobutu basked in the international limelight as symbols of African culture and pride. Few Americans, black or white, troubled to ask where the ten million dollars had come from. Fewer still reflected on the irony that the man providing the purse, the apostle of Authenticité, was the same man who, just thirteen years before, had been denounced by protestors at the U.N. as the murderer of Patrice Lumumba.

In the long run, however, there was no disguising the nature of Mobutu's regime. The term "kleptocrat" was virtually invented to describe the man, who during his tenure accumulated one of the world's great fortunes, including palaces and luxury yachts, a collection of European chateaux, and Swiss bank accounts running to billions of dollars. Over the same period, Zaire's gross domestic product fell by more than two thirds, while per capita income plummeted to less than $150 per year. The local currency, the zaire, pegged at two to the dollar when it was introduced in 1967, was trading at more than two million to the dollar by early 1993. By then, fiscal policy, such as it was, was dictated less by the state than by "Wall Street"—the name given to female currency traders in Kinshasa's main market, who determined what notes to accept and how to value them. (When the government introduced a new currency in 1997, the women refused to accept it, dubbing the notes prostates, in reference to Mobutu's terminal cancer.) Unable to pay his soldiers, Mobutu ordered them to "live off the land," igniting two sustained looting sprees, known locally as *les pillages.*

By the time Howard French and Lynne Duke arrived, the Zairean treasury was empty, civil authority was nonexistent, and daily life had devolved into what Zaireans called *debrouillez-vous* or simply système D—essentially, fend for yourself. Every interaction became an occasion for extortion, especially when foreigners with hard currency were involved. Passengers flying into Kinshasa were greeted by *le protocole*, fast-talking fixers who, for a fee, negotiated the necessary bribes with customs officials, baggage handlers, cab drivers, and so forth. Policemen and soldiers set up arbitrary roadblocks, shaking down anyone unfortunate enough to drive by, though with fuel supplies exhausted there were few cars on the road. Schoolteachers, paid irregularly if at all, demanded bribes before accepting children into their classrooms. Surely the most enterprising practitioner of *débrouillez-vous* was the Zairean ambassador to Japan, who sold the country's embassy in Tokyo and pocketed the proceeds.

French and Duke both entered Zaire in suitably surreal circumstances. French first came in May 1995, to report on an outbreak of the Ebola virus. For weeks, Zairean doctors in the Kikwit district had appealed in vain for international assistance in containing a mysterious virus that was killing local people. When the virus was identified as Ebola, a contagion with no known cure, the world suddenly took interest. Doctors from a dozen different international agencies flooded into Kikwit, looking like some kind of alien invaders in their respirators and decontamination suits. A horde of journalists followed, many of whom were "getting their first taste of Africa." It was exactly the sort of story that French had hoped to avoid, "yet here I was, just like everyone else, rushing toward another lurid African mess that, thanks to the magic of television, had become the global story of the week."

For French, the visit to Kikwit offered an opportunity to assay not only the state of Zaire, but also the operation of the foreign press corps. He outlined his conclusions in a blistering Sunday *Week in Review* essay, provocatively entitled "Sure, Ebola Is Bad. Africa Has Worse." In the essay, French posed a series of troubling questions about the latest "celebrity virus." Why did Ebola attract journalists' attention when nearby outbreaks of polio, cholera, and sleeping sickness, all easily preventable diseases, went unreported? Why did the ravages of a preventable disease like malaria, which killed ten times more Africans *per day* than the total number of people who died in the Kikwit outbreak, provoke not "a flicker on the screen of the world's conscience?" Was it simply the possibility that the virus might spread to Europe and America? (Ebola, a British reporter opined, was just one of the "savage African diseases ready to break out anywhere at any time.") Or had Western audiences become so jaded that they needed "cinematically compelling" fare like Ebola, with its "massive hemorrhaging and projectile vomiting," to keep them stimulated? What did it say about Africa's place in the global imagination that it required Ebola, the Rwandan genocide, or some other extreme of "human catastrophe or primordial exoticism" for Westerners to pay attention? In the course of his subsequent travels through Zaire, French would have many occasions to revisit these questions.

Lynne Duke had an equally bizarre introduction to Zaire. In January 1996, an Antonov cargo plane taking off from a military airport in Kinshasa crashed on takeoff, plowing into a crowded market, killing at least three hundred people. Duke caught a flight to Kinshasa the next day and, after running the gauntlet of bribe-seeking officials at the airport, proceeded to the scene. Expecting an American-style crash site, with a police cordon and a team of investigators combing the wreckage for clues, she was astonished to find no authorities in sight, just a swarm of people, picking through the debris for scrap metal and other useful tidbits, occasionally turning up a human head severed by the plane's propellers. To use Keith Richburg's phrase, Zaire was clearly a place where they no longer counted the bodies. Yet there was a broader story behind the crash, which became clear in the ensuing months. The plane and airfield were part of a system created by Mobutu and the United States to ferry arms to antigovernment rebels in neighboring Angola. With the end of the Cold War, the United States had cut off support for the rebels, who agreed to lay down their arms under a U.N.-brokered peace agreement. But as the Antonov crash revealed, the arms traffic continued, no longer financed by the C.I.A. but by the trade in conflict diamonds, a burgeoning contraband traffic that linked war-ravaged countries like Zaire, Angola, and Sierra Leone with cities like Antwerp, Brussels, and New York. Zaire may have been a circus, but not all the ringmasters were in Kinshasa.

By the mid-1990s, Mobutu Sese Seko's Zaire was an empty shell of a nation. An invasion from Rwanda would shatter it.

· · ·

MEDIA ACCOUNTS OF THE 1994 Rwandan genocide portrayed it as a singular event, a paroxysm of unfathomable horror and savagery. It was certainly all of that, but it was also the culmination of a long history of violent ethnic conflict between Hutus and Tutsis reaching back all the way to the fifteenth century, when Tutsi pastoralists first migrated into the region. The division was exploited and exacerbated by German and Belgian colonizers, both of whom discriminated in favor of the minority Tutsis, whom they regarded as a superior "Nilotic" racial stock. In 1959, shortly before independence, the Hutus rose against their African overlords, sending more than a million Tutsis into exile in Uganda, Burundi, and the eastern Congo. The years that followed brought persistent ethnic conflict and several local exercises in ethnic cleansing, culminating in the genocide of 1994.

The timing of the genocide would prove critical. At the moment the killings began, there were virtually no Western journalists in the country, the entire international press corps having gone to South Africa to cover the election there. More important, the genocide began just one month after the final withdrawal of American troops from Somalia. Determined to avoid further African entanglements, the Clinton administration deliberately turned a blind eye to Rwanda. U.S. officials ignored a mountain of evidence of the planned killings; they refused to jam radio broadcasts inciting the genocidaires; they vetoed proposals to deploy peacekeepers. (Indeed, the United States sponsored a U.N. Security Council resolution to withdraw the peacekeepers that were already in the country.) As the scale of the killing became apparent, administration officials carefully avoided the word "genocide," a term that would have entailed an obligation to act under prevailing international treaties, as well as potential political complications. Susan Rice, an African American member of the National Security Council (later promoted to undersecretary of state for African Affairs), betrayed the administration's priorities at an interagency meeting when she asked, "If we use the word 'genocide' and are seen as doing nothing, what will be the effect on the November election?" In the end, the killings stopped not because of international action but because of the Rwandan Patriotic Front, a Tutsi army that entered from neighboring Uganda and wrested control of the country from the Hutus.

The R.P.F. victory ended the genocide but it did not resolve the underlying conflict. Fearing retribution, more than two million Hutus fled Rwanda, most into eastern Zaire, where they found refuge in some forty massive U.N. refugee camps. Determining who in the camps were genocidaires was an impossible task. While many refugees were women and children, others were clearly veterans of the Interahamwe, the Hutu militia that had taken the lead in the killing. Shielded by the large civilian population and the flag of the U.N., the Interahamwe regrouped and rearmed. By 1996, the U.N. camps had become staging areas for raids into Rwanda, as well as for attacks on the ethnic Tutsi population in eastern Zaire, known locally as the Banyamulenge. Mobutu, a past master at exploiting ethnic instability in neighboring countries to advance his own interests, supported the Hutus, whom he saw as a counterweight to the increasingly powerful Rwanda-Uganda axis. Initially, he was content to ship arms to the Hutu camps, but in November 1996, he went a step further, ordering all Tutsis to leave Zaire.

Mobutu had finally overplayed his hand. The Banyamulenge rebelled. Their uprising provided the government of Rwanda with a pretext to address the threat of the Hutu refugee camps. In a carefully planned campaign, the Rwandan Defence Force, backed by units from Uganda, swept into eastern Zaire, overrunning the U.N. camps and sending hundreds of thousands of refugees spilling into the forest. With the remnants of the Zairean army melting before them, the Rwandans continued to drive westward, transforming the incursion into an outright invasion. It made for an extraordinary spectacle: one of the smallest nations on the continent, still reeling from a gruesome genocide, overrunning one of the largest. The Rwandans were supported by a phalanx of states in the region—not only Uganda, but also Burundi, Tanzania, Zambia, and Angola, all of which had scores to settle with Mobutu.

Recognizing that the international community would never ratify the outright conquest of a neighboring state, the Rwandans portrayed their force as an indigenous insurgency against Mobutu rather than as an invading army. They found an unlikely fig leaf in the figure of Laurent-Désiré Kabila, a figure as garish in his way as Mobutu. A one-time supporter of Patrice Lumumba, Kabila had fought against Mobutu in the so-called Simba rebellion of 1964. After the Simba rebellion was crushed (with the help of the C.I.A., which supplied Mobutu with aircraft and Cuban exile pilots left over from the Bay of Pigs fiasco), Kabila retreated with a few followers to a remote region in eastern Congo to continue the fight. He was briefly joined by Che Guevara and a contingent of Cuban revolutionaries, but they soon left in disgust, convinced that Kabila was more interested in drinking and womanizing than revolution. In 1967, Kabila cast his lot with the People's Republic of China, refashioning himself as a Maoist and declaring his small fief an independent nation. In practice, he was little more than a local warlord, living off illegal diamond and ivory trading and, in one case, kidnapping and holding for ransom a group of American university students. By the late 1980s, most observers assumed he was dead, but the Rwandans found him in Tanzania, dusted him off, and presented him to the world as leader of "the Alliance of Democratic Forces for the Liberation of Congo-Zaire."

If the Rwandan invasion exposed the inadequacies of the Zairean army, it also revealed the limitations of the international press corps. Even veteran journalists had no idea who Kabila was, and most had never heard of the Banyamulenge. The Western diplomats and relief agency officials to whom they habitually turned for answers were no better informed. Recounting the early days of the invasion in his book, French was scathing of journalists' performance, including his own. "The scramble to do some rudimentary ethnic detective work brought to mind just how normal it was for reporters to operate in nearly perfect ignorance of their surroundings on this continent," he wrote. "[F]or many of us an assignment here involved little more preparation than thumbing through a Lonely Planet guide. Anywhere else in the world we would have been judged incompetent, but in Africa being able to get somewhere quickly and write colorful stories was qualification enough." To add to the bewilderment, the Rwandan invasion flew in the face of the prevailing "story line," in which Mobutu was a villain, the Hutus were genocidaires, and the Tutsis were outraged victims. Such preconceptions made it possible for many reporters to overlook the atrocities perpetrated against Hutu refugees by the invading army, or at best to accept them with "a journalistic shrug."

The situation was complicated still further by Washington's not-so-subtle support of the Rwandans—support that French and Duke both worked to expose. As French noted at the time, acceding to the invasion became a kind of perverse "penance" for Washington, a way to atone for American inaction during the Rwandan genocide and for decades of support of Mobutu Sese Seko. At the same time, the invasion was consistent with American geopolitical interests in the region, which, with memories of the Cold War fading, increasingly focused on international terrorism and the "failed states" that allegedly bred it. The new hope for American policy makers was a cohort of strong African leaders emerging in a belt of states across central Africa: Uganda's Yoweri Museveni, Zambia's Frederick Chiluba, Angola's José Eduardo dos Santos, and Rwanda's Paul Kagame. None were democrats in any meaningful sense of the word, but all were pro-Western and committed to market economies, political stability, and at least a semblance of good government. Not coincidentally, all were involved in the invasion of Zaire. And so the United States endorsed the invasion, accepting the fiction that Kabila was the leader of an indigenous movement. As for reports of mass killings of Hutu refugees by Kabila's forces, American officials consistently downplayed them, arguing that refugee numbers were exaggerated or that most of the refugees were genocidaries anyway, and hence beyond the world's concern. "They are the bad guys," the U.S. ambassador to Zaire replied when French pressed him on the refugee issue.

Duke and French were among a small number of journalists who refused to accept the administration orthodoxy. With American officials declaring the refugee crisis substantially over, both set out for eastern Zaire to see for themselves. French accompanied the U.N. High Commissioner for Refugees to a place called Tingi Tingi, a makeshift camp housing some 150,000 displaced refugees, including many children who had been separated from their parents in the trek through the forest. A few days later, many of those people were dead, killed by the advancing rebels and buried in hastily dug mass graves. Duke took a more reckless approach. She and four other Johannesburg-based correspondents somehow persuaded the director of Air Zaire to lend them a plane to fly to Kisangani, the erstwhile Stanleyville, at the great bend of the Congo River. The plan was to rent a small plane to look for refugees in the forest below, though Duke later confessed that she also coveted a Kisangani dateline, to feed her "swashbuckling self-image" as a foreign correspondent. What she and her companions found was a city overrun with retreating Zairean troops, from which they were lucky to escape with their lives.

Duke tried again a short time later, this time driving into the war zone with a few colleagues in a hired Land Cruiser. They soon came upon a group of Hutu refugees, about seventy people in all, including children and women, at least one of whom was heavily pregnant. A man named Jean, a former postal worker, stepped forward to speak, brushing the dirt and twigs from his incongruous double-breasted blazer. Jean explained how the group had been on the road for a month, herded along by Hutu militiamen as human shields against the advancing Rwandans. Those who refused to go were shot. During the last battle, Jean and his group had slipped into the forest and escaped the main column, but now they found themselves stranded between the two forces, sick and starving. "There are many bodies in the mountains," he said. "Can you tell people that we need help? We need something to eat. We are very tired. And medicine, we need." Duke passed along the request in her next dispatch, probably the most poignant story she wrote during her years in Africa. Yet she also knew the story would make no difference, for Jean and his companions had been sacrificed long before.

AS THEY CHRONICLED Zaire's slow implosion, Duke and French experienced fury, frustration, and all the other emotions that had consumed Keith Richburg during his years in Africa. Richburg eventually took refuge in indifference, repudiating any sense of fellow feeling for Africans. Given their different temperaments and politics, neither Duke nor French sought that resort, but they often struggled against despair and hopelessness. Duke confessed to spending many nights crying in her hotel room; tears became her "private release," though one she never indulged "in public, and certainly never around a male colleague." She also found solace in South Africa, where she could still bask in a vision of hope and possibility, of an independent Africa that was prosperous and democratic. She recognized some of the problems of the "New South Africa" and did not shy away from reporting them—the escalating violent crime rate; the rightward turn in economic policy; the government's criminally slow response to the AIDS crisis—but as long as Nelson Mandela remained in office, her hope endured. Mandela, father to his country, also became a reassuring father figure to her, her "personal talisman." "[W]hen I felt especially hopeless about Africa's fate," she later recalled, "I needed only to remember one of its most remarkable sons."

French had a different, though equally personal, response. The continent he had come to love in the 1980s "had now settled into a spiral of bloody traumas and chronic disorder. I needed to understand why." Clearly part of the answer lay in the venality and brutality of Africa's own "woeful leaders," as Keith Richburg had insisted, but part of it lay beyond the continent, in recurring "patterns of treachery and betrayal of Africa by a wealthy and powerful West." Both lines of explanation converged in Zaire. For his last two years in Africa, French wrote incessantly about the country, delving deeply into its past, exposing the long history of Western, and particularly American, support for Mobutu. In his memoir of his years in Africa, he would trace the story even further back, all the way to the late 1400s, when the first Portuguese ships arrived at the mouth of the Congo River. More than five centuries later, the pattern continued, as Western officials opportunistically embraced another authoritarian despot, Laurent Kabila, leaving the Congolese to bear the consequences.

Mobutu Sese Seko fled Zaire in May 1997, ending a thirty-two-year reign. Soldiers of the Rwandan "Alliance" arrived in Kinshasa a few days later. Under President Kabila, the name of the country reverted back to the Democratic Republic of the Congo, but little else changed. Political parties were banned and opposition leaders jailed. Soldiers continued to rule the streets of the capital, a fact made more galling to residents by the fact that most of the soldiers were ethnic Tutsis, who spoke no Congolese languages. Still the United States endeavored to put the best face on things. In December 1997, Secretary of State Madeleine Albright embarked on a seven-nation tour of Africa, intended to solidify the emerging alliance of pro-Western African leaders—what some were already calling the African Renaissance club—in advance of an upcoming visit by President Clinton. Albright included the Congo on her itinerary, essentially inducting Kabila into membership. At a bizarre joint press conference, covered by both French and Duke, the secretary stressed the importance of "open markets, honest government, and the rule of law," praising Kabila, who was standing at her side, for making "a strong start toward these goals." Kabila, however, strayed from the script. Asked by journalists about the arrest of a political opponent, he suggested that the man might soon have company in prison, ending the tirade with a sarcastic: "Long live democracy. Ha-ha-ha."

The alliance of African leaders acclaimed by Albright did not last long. In 1998 a border dispute between Ethiopia and Eritrea, two charter members of the club, escalated into full-scale war. At the same time, Kabila and his Rwandan patrons fell out spectacularly. Anxious to demonstrate his independence from his patrons, Kabila ordered all Tutsis to leave Zaire, the same order that had led to Mobutu's downfall. Rwanda responded by launching another attack, again supported by Uganda and Burundi. For the second time in two years, a Rwandan army rolled west across the Congo. This time, however, the Rwandans were stopped, after the governments of Angola and Zimbabwe, both of which had supported the original invasion, intervened on the side of Kabila. By the time Duke and French left Africa in late 1998, ten nations were embroiled in the war. Kabila himself would soon depart the scene. Struck down by an assassin in 2000, he was succeeded by his son Joseph.

Given the nature of the conflict, it is virtually impossible to determine how many people died in what some have dubbed Africa's First World War. French estimated the death toll between 1996 and 2002 at 3.3 million. Others put the total higher. By any measure, the war represented the deadliest conflict in the world since World War II, a distinction made even more remarkable by the fact that few in the West have any idea that it even occurred. While an international war crimes tribunal continues to examine the 1994 Rwandan genocide, the more recent and far bloodier conflict in the Congo has been virtually forgotten by the world community, like so many previous horrors in that beleaguered land.

Meanwhile, there are profits to be made. The coveted commodity today is not ivory or rubber or copper or uranium or cobalt but columbite-tantalite— coltan—a heat-resistant metal harvested from muddy streambeds deep in the Congo forest. Coltan is an essential component in the manufacture of cellphone circuit boards. Just as previous generations of Americans tickled ivory piano keys and pedaled about on rubber bicycle tires, so do we today carry in our pockets traces of a commodity gathered by hand by hungry Congolese workers.

There is much to ponder in all this. A century ago, a single African American missionary, armed with a portable Kodak camera, aroused the moral conscience of the West. Today, when satellites beam words and images instantaneously around the globe, the death of millions in the same country passes virtually unnoticed. Perhaps the problem lay in the absence of white actors; part of what made the atrocities in King Leopold's Congo so shocking to Americans and Europeans was the fact that the perpetrators were themselves white. Perhaps it is the lack of a clear story line, of easily identifiable villains and victims, especially after the departure of the cartoonish Mobutu. Or perhaps the problem is simply boredom, a kind of moral fatigue that comes from having seen too much mass death, particularly of the African kind. As Howard French put it, "Serving up atrocities is a business of diminishing returns."

The Language We Cry In

On November 8, 1755, a ship called the *Hare* cleared Newport, Rhode Island, bound for West Africa. Nothing unusual in that: Rhode Islanders dominated the North American portion of the transatlantic slave trade, mounting over a thousand "Guinea" voyages in the century before the congressional ban of 1807 (and scores more illegal voyages thereafter). The *Hare* was owned by William and Samuel Vernon, wealthy merchants who would later earn a place in the history books by financing the creation of the United States Navy. The Vernons were no strangers to the slave trade: between 1735 and 1797, they sponsored more than thirty African voyages. The ship's captain, Caleb Godfrey, was also an old Guinea hand, indeed something of a legend in the trade, having on previous voyages survived a mauling by a leopard and a lightning strike on his ship. (Godfrey and the crew escaped on the burning ship's longboat, leaving the enslaved Africans in the hold to their fate.) With the *Hare* fitted out and the crew aboard, the Vernons sent Godfrey a standard letter of instructions, ordering him to take the first favorable wind and proceed to the Windward Coast of Africa, to acquire a cargo of slaves with "quick Dispatch," and to accompany them to "Charles-Town in South Carolina." "Keep a watchful Eye over 'em, and give them no Opportunity of making an Insurrection," the owners warned, "and let them have a sufficiency of good Diet, as you are Sensible your Voyage depends upon their Health." For his services, Godfrey was offered a "Privilege" of six Africans to sell on his own account, as well as the standard commission of "four on a hundred & four."

The transatlantic voyage was uneventful and the *Hare* set to coasting, working its way along from the northern reaches of what is today Guinea down to Bunce Island, the large British slave fortress on the Sierra Leone River. On April 8, 1756, Godfrey wrote from Bunce Island, informing the Vernons of his imminent departure, with the ship in "Good order" and a full cargo of captives. But ill winds and weather beset the ship on the return trip, which dragged on for ten weeks. Reporting his arrival in Charleston, the captain was less optimistic. Of the eighty-four Africans he had purchased, thirteen had died in the hold and another three had perished in the Sullivan's Island pest house, where all captives entering Charleston harbor endured a mandatory period of quarantine. The survivors were in "But porr order," having received "damage a Laying" during the long voyage, thus reducing their value at auction. One can only imagine the horrors that underlay this matter-of-fact report, but whatever remorse Godfrey felt was directed not toward the enslaved Africans but toward the Vernons, who stood to earn little or no return on their investment. "I thought by my Purchass I Should have made you a good Voiage but fear the Low market and Mortality Shall miss of my Expectation," he wrote apologetically.

The survivors from the *Hare* were consigned to Henry Laurens, the Vernons' local agent. Laurens ran the largest slave-trading firm in North America; in the 1750s alone, he handled the sale of nearly eight thousand Africans, many of them from Bunce Island. (Captives from the region around Sierra Leone were much prized by South Carolina planters because of their expertise in growing rice, the staple crop of the Low Country.) Like the Vernons, Laurens would find his way into the historical record. In 1777, he was elected president of the Continental Congress, succeeding John Hancock. Six years later, he served with Benjamin Franklin in the American delegation that negotiated the Treaty of Paris, ending the Revolutionary War and securing British recognition for American independence. Though you will not find it in any textbook, the treaty was facilitated by the fact that two of the negotiators were business partners: Richard Oswald, head of the British delegation, was the proprietor of Bunce Island, and Laurens was his Charleston agent.

Laurens shared Caleb Godfrey's assessment of the *Hare*'s captives. "[R]eally they are a wretched cargo," he wrote. "They are a most scabby flock, all of them full of the Crocheraws"—a reference to yaws, a contagious bacterial infection producing eruptions on the skin and painful inflammation of the joints. Yaws was common on slave ships, particularly afflicting children; traders sometimes tried to disguise its effects by oiling slaves prior to selling them. Laurens's assessment did not deter him from placing an advertisement in the *South Carolina Gazette* announcing the sale of "a Cargo of Likely and Healthy Slaves," just arrived "directly from Sierra Leone." Planters who came to the auction complained of being offered "refuse slaves," but they bought the lot. The most active bidder was Elias Ball, a Cooper River rice planter and Laurens's nephew. Ball bought five African children off the *Hare*, three boys and two girls, for £460. He recorded the expenditure in his account book, including the estimated age of each child and the names he had assigned them. One was a girl of about ten years, whom he named Priscilla.

We will never know Priscilla's real name, nor many of the elementary facts of her life—her birthplace, her ethnic identity, the circumstances of her capture. What she carried in her heart as she lay in the hold of the *Hare* during its long passage across the Atlantic is, mercifully, beyond our ken. But thanks to the meticulous business records of Elias Ball and his descendants, and the more recent efforts of two historians, we know something of what became of her. We know that Priscilla lived another fifty-five years, until 1811, and that she bore ten children, half of whom survived into adulthood. Through those children, she had at least thirty grandchildren. The facts of demography being what they are, there are today literally thousands of Americans who carry in their veins a trace of this little girl's blood.

Thomalind Martin Polite is one such person. A speech therapist in the Charleston public school system, Ms. Polite is Priscilla's great-great-great-

great-great-granddaughter. In May 2005 she traveled to Sierra Leone as a guest of the government for what was billed as Priscilla's Homecoming. Through an unlikely set of connections, I was one of a small group invited to accompany her. I have spent the better part of my adult life reflecting on the meaning of such journeys, and being presented with an opportunity to witness one firsthand seemed, well, providential. I had no intention of writing about the trip when I embarked, but the experience brought together so many of the themes discussed in this book that I would be remiss not to include it. For those readers who share my distaste for history written in the first person, I can only beg your pardon.

OF THE TWELVE MILLION or so Africans who survived the Middle Passage, about a half million were imported into the territory of what is now the United States. Their descendants today number well over thirty million. Yet one could count the number of African Americans who can trace their origins back to an individual African, let alone specify the moment that he or she arrived. (The example that obviously springs to mind is Kunta Kinte, the protagonist of Alex Haley's book *Roots*, but it now appears that he was a composite, if not an outright fiction.) Thomalind Polite's ability to trace her lineage back to Africa is a gift from a historian, Edward Ball. Ball has an interesting lineage of his own: he is the great-great-great-great-grandson of Elias Ball, Priscilla's purchaser.

Because Ball attended Brown University, where I teach, I have had occasion to meet him. At first glance, he seems the least southern of South Carolinians. He speaks with no discernible accent. Tall and angular, he has a reserved, even austere, manner, suggestive more of New England, where he now lives, than of his natal region. But his South Carolina roots run deep. The Balls were a Low Country dynasty, rulers of an empire that included, at its peak, some twenty rice plantations and well over a thousand slaves. Virtually all of that fortune had evaporated by the time Edward came along, but it is still a prepossessing legacy. In the United States today there are between 75,000 and 100,000 people whose ancestors were once owned as chattel property by Ball's ancestors.

Though aware of the family's slaveholding past, few of Ball's relatives discussed the topic. "There are five things we don't talk about in the Ball family," Edward's father used to joke. "Religion, sex, death, money, and the Negroes." But an invitation to a family reunion in the early 1990s launched Edward on a journey of self-discovery, from which came the prize-winning book *Slaves in the Family*, published in 1998. Drawing on the records kept by Elias and his descendants—ten thousand manuscript pages that somehow avoided the fires, floods, and spring cleanings that consume most historical documents—Ball reconstructed his family's plantation empire, focusing not only on the white lords of the manor but also on their black (and, inevitably, brown) vassals. But *Slaves in the Family* is more than a work of history. It is also a meditation on memory, on the ways in which Americans today confront—or choose not to confront—their racial past. Every schoolchild knows of the arrivals hall at Ellis Island, through which passed about 40 percent of the European immigrants who came to America during the golden age of immigration, but how many know of the pest house on Sullivan's Island, through which passed about 40 percent of the enslaved Africans imported into mainland North America? Tourists flock to Fort Sumter at the mouth of Charleston harbor, but Sullivan's Island, on the far shore, did not boast so much as a plaque until Ball himself arranged to have one installed. *Slaves in the Family* is an attempt to understand this evasion and, in a small way, to remedy it.

In the course of his research, Ball spoke with others whose ancestry traced back to his family's plantations. Not surprisingly, not everyone welcomed his inquiries. Many of his relatives refused to cooperate, denouncing the exercise as misguided, divisive, even disloyal. And many African Americans were nonplussed by the appearance of a white stranger professing to be descended of people who had once owned their forebears. But some people, black and white, consented to talk, and it is these conversations and reflections that give *Slaves in the Family* its power, turning what might otherwise be an exercise in lugubriousness into a testament of hope. Among those most eager to talk was Thomas Martin, a retired school principal and Thomalind Polite's father. Probably the most moving moment in *Slaves in the Family* is the day that Ball walked into Martin's home and carefully unfolded a family tree connecting him to a ten-year-old African girl.

· · ·

WHILE IT WAS EDWARD BALL who redeemed Priscilla from historical obscurity, it was another historian, Joseph Opala, who organized Priscilla's Homecoming. A professor at James Madison University, Opala is Ball's opposite: short and stocky, with a round, cherubic face and an ebullient manner. And no subject animates him more than Sierra Leone, his home for most of the last thirty years. By his own account, Opala could scarcely have found Sierra Leone on a map when he arrived as a Peace Corps volunteer in 1974 with the title of rice extension officer to the village of Bumbuna. The idea that an American could teach Sierra Leoneans anything about rice was ludicrous, as Opala ruefully admits, but his hosts welcomed him into their world and he, in turn, grew to admire and love them. He remained in Sierra Leone an extra two years following his Peace Corps term and, after a stint in graduate school in the United States, came back to teach history and anthropology at Freetown's Fourah Bay College. He remained in Freetown until 1997, when he was forced to flee, along with most of the city's residents, to escape the advancing rebels of the Revolutionary United Front.

Opala's scholarly research focuses on Bunce Island, but his real specialty is homecomings. In addition to the Priscilla venture, he has organized two major African American homecomings, both of which resulted in popular documentary films. *Families Across the Sea,* released in 1989, records a visit to Sierra Leone by a deputation of Gullah people—African Americans from the Sea Islands of South Carolina and Georgia, whose language and culture still contain many elements that can be traced back to Sierra Leone. *The Language You Cry In,* released a few years later, focuses on a five-line African song, first recorded in the Georgia Sea Islands in the 1930s by a pioneering African American linguist, Lorenzo Turner. Like the "heathen melody" crooned to the young W. E. B. Du Bois by his great-grandmother, the song was handed down through the generations, ending with a Gullah woman named Amelia Dawley, who sang it to Turner. Unlike Du Bois, Turner was able to identify the language of the song as Mende, one of the languages of Sierra Leone. Armed with that knowledge and a copy of the original recording, Opala and two colleagues, Cynthia Schmidt and Tazieff Koroma, set out to find the song's exact origin. After fruitless visits to scores of villages, they came to Senehum Ngola, where an old woman immediately began to sing along with the tape. The woman, whose name was Baindu Jabati, explained that the song had died out in the nineteenth century, with the spread of Christianity and Islam, but that her grandmother had insisted that she learn and remember it, for it was the song with which their people buried their dead—a song to help the dead cross the water to the land of the ancestors.

Everyone come together;
Let us work hard;
The grave is not yet finished.

For Opala, the next step was obvious: to reconnect the song's two branches. He located Amelia Dawley's daughter, Mary Moran, who still remembered the song that her mother had taught her. Getting Moran to Sierra Leone proved a difficult task, as the country was engulfed in civil war. But during a ceasefire in 1997, Moran traveled to Senehum Ngola, where she and Baindu Jabati performed the song together in a graveside ceremony. In the course of the festivities, Opala asked the wizened old chief of the village why an African living in America would have troubled to preserve a song. The question surprised the chief, for whom the answer was obvious. The song bound her to her ancestors, he explained, and thus assured her of who she was. He underscored his point with a Mende proverb: "You know who people really are by the language they cry in."

When Opala encountered the story of Priscilla in Edward Ball's book, he saw an opportunity for a third homecoming, one that would give an even more intimate face to the transatlantic connection. By the time he assembled a film team, Thomas Martin had passed away, but his daughter, Thomalind Polite, agreed to travel as his—and Priscilla's—representative. She embarked in May 2005, accompanied by her husband, Antawn; the film crew; and another twenty or so assorted hangers-on—a motley crew representing a cross section of different professions, including actor, author, businessman, diplomat, educator, journalist, musician, poet, and storyteller. At some point during the weeklong festivities, it struck me that aside from the missing mis-

sionary, the group included virtually all the different sorts of travelers represented in this book.

PRISCILLA'S HOMECOMING was the quintessential "back-to-Africa"
journey. We had come to honor an ancestor, to return the spirit of a little girl
to the home from which she had been torn two and a half centuries before.
But we were not time travelers; our destination was not the Sierra Leone of
1756 but of 2005. And make no mistake: the Sierra Leone of 2005 was a very
disturbing place. I do not mean to be patronizing or ethnocentric here. I
understand that there are different ways of defining human welfare, that
Africans (as W. E. B. Du Bois, among others, insisted) live lives that are in
many respects richer, more fulfilling, and yes, more civilized than the mad-
cap lives we in the United States have come to regard as normal. Yet cultural
relativism is not a license for moral indifference. Sierra Leone today ranks
dead last among the nations of the world—174th out of 174—in the U.N. development index. Average life expectancy in the country is thirty-four years.
Infant mortality is 181 per 1,000 live births. (The comparable U.S. figure is
about 6.5.) Overall, about one in three Sierra Leonean children die before
reaching age five, most of easily preventable diseases. Annual per capita income is $490—by an unnerving coincidence, exactly the sum I paid for seven
nights in my international hotel. Atop it all, the country is just emerging
from a gruesome eleven-year civil war. Yes, Sierra Leoneans today laugh
and love and do every other thing that human beings do, but they have also
drunk the dregs of human misery.

How did Sierra Leone come to be in such terrible shape? We have already had occasion to review the country's origins: the arrival of the "Black
Poor of London" in 1787 and of subsequent groups of settlers from Nova
Scotia and Jamaica; the imposition of British colonial rule in 1807, the same
year that Parliament abolished the transatlantic slave trade; the designation
of Freetown as the main depository for so-called recaptives, Africans liberated from slave ships captured by the Royal Navy's Anti-Slavery Squadron.
The result is a nation unlike any other in Africa. While the vast majority of
the population was and is indigenous to the country, Sierra Leone includes

people whose ancestry traces to every corner of the continent. (A linguist visiting Freetown in the 1930s was able to document more than two hundred languages still being spoken in the city.) The country also includes a small but conspicuous Krio population that traces its ancestry back to the colony's original African American settlers. The distinctive creolized English that these settlers developed, also called Krio, remains Sierra Leone's lingua franca.

Sierra Leone achieved national independence in 1961. By the standards of decolonizing Africa, it seemed almost uniquely promising. The country boasted a substantial professional class, including doctors, lawyers, merchants, and civil servants. Its educational system, while humble by American standards, was the envy of West Africa. Generations of students in Nigeria, the Gold Coast, and other British colonies were taught by teachers trained at Freetown's Fourah Bay College, the oldest university in sub-Saharan Africa. (Fourah Bay's first graduate was Samuel Ajayi Crowther, the linguist and missionary who aided Martin Delany during his expedition to Yorubaland in 1859.) By African standards, Sierra Leone's gross national product was quite high, indeed higher than in many decolonizing nations in Asia, including Singapore and Malaysia. As in other African nations, GNP was a somewhat deceptive measure, since much of the country's economy focused on mineral extraction, the revenues from which accrued chiefly to foreign companies rather than to local people. Still, few people present at the seeding time of independence could have imagined that Sierra Leoneans would reap such a bitter harvest.

Sierra Leone's prime minister at independence was Sir Milton Margai, a British-trained medical doctor and founder of the Sierra Leonean People's Party. Margai is still remembered with reverence by his countrymen; his brother Albert, who succeeded him after his death in 1964, is not. In 1967, Albert Margai's bid for reelection was opposed by Siaka Stevens, leader of the opposition and mayor of Freetown, provoking a constitutional crisis and a series of rapid-fire coups. Civilian authority was restored in 1968 and Siaka Stevens assumed office, but hopes for a return to good government were quickly dashed. Sierra Leoneans today refer to Stevens's reign, which lasted until 1985, as the plague of the seventeen-year locusts. Ruling as the head of a one-party state, Stevens deliberately and systematically destroyed every institution that might challenge his authority, including the judiciary, press, civil service, universities, even the military, whose soldiers, allotted just one bullet per year for training, became national laughingstocks. Through such tactics, he secured that rarest of blessings for an African dictator: a peaceful retirement under the auspices of his handpicked successor, Joseph Momoh.

Momoh's rule lasted until 1992, when he was overthrown by a group of junior military officers led by twenty-seven-year-old Valentine Strasser. Joseph Opala remembers the day of the coup vividly because Strasser had him brought to the president's office. Opala feared the worst. He was publicly associated with Momoh, who had hosted the original Gullah homecoming. He had also worked with the president's office in preparing a popular history text, *Sierra Leonean Heroes: Fifty Men and Women Who Helped to Build Our Nation*. The heroes book provides a useful backdrop to the story of Priscilla, whom Opala clearly hopes to elevate into the national pantheon, offering beleaguered Sierra Leoneans another model of resilience and survival alongside such figures as Sengbe Pieh, the Mende captive who led the 1839 revolt on the slave ship *Amistad*, or Bai Bureh, leader of the 1898 Temne rebellion against British rule. But on the day of the 1992 coup, he wondered whether the book might be his death warrant. In the event, the coup plotters merely needed a translator. Anxious to secure American recognition, they had contacted the U.S. Embassy, but the ambassador was unable to understand their Krio or they his American English. "His English is too big for me," Strasser told Opala, who spent the next several days shuttling between the presidential office and the U.S. Embassy.

Like a large majority of Sierra Leoneans, Opala was initially supportive of the new government, which called itself the National Provisional Ruling Council. Though they had come to power by force, Strasser and his colleagues pledged to root out corruption and return the country to democratic rule. Freetowners celebrated in the streets; murals appeared overnight, many of them featuring images from *Sierra Leonean Heroes*. But the honeymoon proved brief. As N.P.R.C. leaders descended into cocaine-addled confusion, their professions about democracy and good government fell by the wayside. The economy crumbled. (At one point, the government found itself in the ex-

traordinary position of lacking the money to print more money.) Most ominously, a rebel army calling itself the Revolutionary United Front gathered
strength in the countryside. After decades in purgatory, Sierra Leoneans were
about to enter hell.

THE CIVIL WAR that ravaged Sierra Leone began in neighboring Liberia.
When last we saw that country, following the visits by W. E. B. Du Bois and
George Schuyler, it was awash in scandal, as a League of Nations' commission exposed the mistreatment of Africans by the ruling Americo-Liberian
oligarchy. Though battered, the oligarchy weathered the scandal. It also survived the winds of decolonization that swept through the rest of sub-Saharan
Africa, in part by recasting itself as a staunch Cold War ally of the United
States. But all things must pass, and Americo-Liberian rule passed on April
12, 1980, when a group of African soldiers broke into the presidential palace
in Monrovia, dragged President William Tolbert from his bed, and eviscerated him. Calling themselves the People's Redemption Council, the soldiers
then rounded up Tolbert's cabinet ministers, drove them to a nearby beach,
and machine-gunned them, sparing the one minister of indigenous rather
than Americo-Liberian descent. Liberia, Africa's first republic and one of its
last settler colonies, had finally achieved home rule.

One might imagine that overthrowing an ardent American ally would
provoke the ire of the U.S. government, but the opposite was more nearly the
case. The leader of the new government, Master Sergeant Samuel Doe, became Washington's man in Africa. A new C.I.A. listening post, a forest of
antennae and satellite dishes called Omega, sprouted outside Monrovia. U.S.
planes supplying the rebel UNITA movement in Angola refueled at a massive American-built airfield, and the Voice of America broadcast from Liberian soil. When Doe consolidated his power by rigging a presidential election
in 1985, Secretary of State George Shultz flew to Monrovia to certify the result. Doe was later invited to the White House to meet President Ronald
Reagan, who, in one of his more endearing malapropisms, addressed his
guest as Chairman Moe.

But Doe's days were numbered. On Christmas Eve 1989, a rebel army entered Liberia from the Ivory Coast. At the head of the group, which called itself the National Patriotic Front of Liberia, stood a charming, garrulous, murderous warlord named Charles Taylor. Taylor bestrode the great divide of Liberian politics: his father, a judge and Baptist lay preacher, was Americo-Liberian; his mother, originally a servant woman, was Golah. After studying at Bentley College in Massachusetts, he returned to Liberia in 1980, becoming a minor official in the Doe government. In 1983, he fled to the United States to evade embezzlement charges. Arrested in Massachusetts, he was bound over for extradition but escaped from jail in circumstances that remain unexplained. He ended up in Libya, at one of Mu'ammar Gadhafis terrorist training camps.

Taylor's forces advanced rapidly on Monrovia, but by the time they reached the capital he had fallen out with one of his own lieutenants, Prince Johnson. It was Johnson who eventually succeeded in taking the capital and installing himself as president. (Johnson and his men also had the pleasure of capturing Samuel Doe and slowly dismembering him, an ordeal videotaped for posterity.) Deprived of the prize he thought rightfully his, Taylor declared himself president of the Republic of Greater Liberia and retreated back to the countryside. Operating from a series of different headquarters— he lived for a time in the old manager's mansion at the Firestone rubber plantation—he and his rebel army laid waste to the nation. Between 1989 and 1996, a large majority of Liberians were uprooted from their homes. More than a quarter million were murdered and countless others were raped or maimed. Many of the worst atrocities were committed by children, some as young as ten or eleven, who were impressed into service by Taylor's army and inured to killing with massive doses of marijuana, crack cocaine, and brown brown—a mixture of heroin and gunpowder. In 1997, Taylor finally achieved his dream, winning the presidency in a hastily organized election. While his victory was certified by the international community as free and fair, it is clear that many Liberians voted in the belief that any other outcome would lead to renewed civil war. Taylor's supporters encouraged that impression, employing machete-wielding children as election canvassers and coining such campaign slogans as "He killed my ma, he killed my pa, but I'm going to vote for him anyway."

Once installed in office, Taylor set about repackaging himself from war-lord to responsible statesman, relying on his formidable charm, as well as his sophisticated knowledge of the American political system. He hired a leading Washington lobbyist, Herman Cohen, former assistant secretary of state for Africa under George H. W. Bush, to promote his interests on Capitol Hill. He completely seduced former president Jimmy Carter, a fellow Baptist and leader of the international monitoring team that certified the 1997 election re-sult. (Taylor was "a family man, a man of God," Carter assured reporters, adding that it was "inconceivable" that his election would lead to further vio-lence.) He also actively courted African American political leadership, pre-senting himself, the child of an Americo-Liberian father and African mother, as the embodiment of the historical relationship between Africa and the United States. Taylor was the ideal bridge between African Americans and the "motherland," opined New Jersey congressman Donald Payne, chair of the Congressional Black Caucus, "because he's intelligent, he knows what sells here, and he's from over there. He has the knowledge of both worlds."

Taylor found his most valuable ally in the Reverend Jesse Jackson, who served under President Bill Clinton as U.S. special envoy for Africa. It was precisely the same honorary office that W. E. B. Du Bois had held during his 1924 visit to Liberia, and Clinton appointed Jackson to it for precisely the same reason that Calvin Coolidge had appointed Du Bois—to "play a little politics" with the black vote, while avoiding any serious entanglement with African problems. Jackson reprised Du Bois's role unerringly, if unwittingly, insisting on the importance of America's historical relationship with Liberia while dismissing allegations of government-sponsored atrocities as exagger-ated or politically inspired. As the evidence against the regime mounted, he changed tack, touting Taylor as the key to any enduring peace settlement in the region. It was Jackson who prevailed on Clinton to call the Liberian pres-ident from Air Force One during the 1998 presidential visit to Africa, a move decried by other West African leaders. He later invited Taylor to address by video link a special Liberian Reconciliation Conference organized by his Operation Push in Chicago.

There is more to be said about Charles Taylor, but the significant point for present purposes is his decision to export his war. In 1991, a rebel army, the Revolutionary United Front, crossed into Sierra Leone from Liberia. Its leader was Foday Sankoh, a one-time wedding photographer who first met Taylor in a Libyan terrorist camp. The incursion was an utterly characteristic move for Taylor, rooted in a perverse calculation that the more violently chaotic the region became, the more essential he became to any political settlement. But he also coveted eastern Sierra Leone's alluvial diamond fields, which offered a virtually inexhaustible revenue stream for financing mayhem. Taylor and his supporters were already stripping Liberia's gold and timber supplies, and they had also branched out into drug running, but these activities paled before blood diamonds, which at that time were still easily traded on international markets. By the mid-1990s, Liberia was exporting hundreds of millions of dollars of diamonds per year, a remarkable distinction for a nation with few substantial diamond deposits of its own.

Despite its name, the Revolutionary United Front made no pretense of ideology or revolutionary discipline; its business was banditry, pure and simple. Indeed, Sankoh dubbed the initial invasion Operation Pay Yourself, inviting his soldiers to live by looting. Over the course of the next decade, nearly half the population of Sierra Leone would be driven from their homes, and nearly a quarter million would die. The R.U.F. became notorious for two tactics, both borrowed from Taylor's forces, though they hearkened back further, to the Force Publique of King Leopold's Congo. The first was the use of amputation as a terror tactic. The transcripts of Sierra Leone's Truth and Reconciliation Commission, convened in 2002, are replete with stories of individuals whose hands, feet, ears, noses, even lips were hacked off by R.U.F. soldiers. More horrifying still was the R.U.F.'s policy of abducting children—girls for use as sex slaves and boys as fighters. Like Taylor, Sankoh and his lieutenants developed a keen understanding of the psychological process by which children could be converted into remorseless killers. New conscripts were forced to participate in burning their own villages, sometimes even in killing loved ones, thus severing any connection with their former identities. They were also plied with drugs, generously supplied by the R.U.F.'s Liberian allies. An entire generation of children was deliberately bestialized. Needless to say, the question of resocializing and reintegrating child combatants is one of the most urgent priorities in Sierra Leone today.

During their 1992 coup, Valentine Strasser and his colleagues in the N.P.R.C. made much of the previous government's ineffectiveness in combatting the R.U.F. invasion, but they proved equally feckless. In effect, they simply ceded control of the countryside to the R.U.F., while retaining control of Freetown. By the mid-1990s, fighters from the two sides were actively collaborating with each other to plunder the country. There was a glimmer of hope in 1996, as the N.P.R.C. fell and civilian rule was restored. But with the economy in chaos and the army in disarray, the new government, led by President Ahmed Kabbah, was foredoomed. In May 1997, another group of junior soldiers, this one calling itself the Armed Forces Revolutionary Council, seized control. Under the A.F.R.C., the de facto alliance that had existed between the rebels and the Sierra Leone army became official, as the council invited the R.U.F. into a governing partnership called the Junta. Sankoh and his soldiers marched triumphantly into Freetown, which they proceeded to pillage.

The first rebel occupation of Freetown lasted until March 1998, finally ending after a military intervention from Nigeria, operating under the mandate of the Economic Community of West African States. But the rebels continued to control the countryside, and in early 1999 they retook Freetown, holding it for six weeks before being expelled again by the Nigerians. The second rebel invasion, which Sankoh dubbed Operation No Living Thing, produced thousands of deaths and some of the worst atrocities of the war. On the day that the rebels were driven out of Freetown for the last time, Junior Lion, the nom de guerre of the leader of an R.U.F. splinter group called the West Side Boys, ordered his troops to perform two hundred amputations and then to burn the city.

How are we—how is anyone—to understand all this? The question obviously hearkens back to the problems of responsibility and complicity raised by Keith Richburg, Howard French, and other journalists who covered Africa in the 1990s. Surely the people most to blame are those who ordered and perpetrated the atrocities (though that judgment becomes complicated in the case of child combatants). Yet some responsibility must also accrue to the West, particularly to the U.S. government, whose response to events partook equally of cynicism, ignorance, and indifference. Still suffering the effects of Somalia Syndrome, the Clinton administration declined to become involved in Sierra Leone, an approach rationalized under the rubric of "African solutions to African problems." With the administration turning a blind eye to the crisis, control of policy devolved onto secondary actors like Jesse Jackson and Congressman Payne, who vigorously opposed any American peacekeeping role, insisting that peace in the region required accommodating the interests of Charles Taylor and his Sierra Leonean client, Foday Sankoh. Under pressure from the United States, President Kabbah signed a peace treaty with the R.U.F. in 1996, promoting rebels to office and offering amnesty for atrocities against civilians. The R.U.F. immediately violated the accord. Following his restoration to office by the Nigerians, Kabbah was once again pressured by the United States to reach out to the rebels. Another cease-fire was negotiated and again violated by the rebels, who proceeded to invade Freetown for the second time.

The story gets worse. Having twice driven the rebels out of Freetown, the Nigerian government announced in early 1999 that it was no longer prepared to shoulder the costs of peacekeeping alone; unless Western governments agreed to make a financial contribution, Nigeria would withdraw its troops. The government of Great Britain made an immediate pledge, but the U.S. government refused, insisting instead on the need to negotiate with Taylor and Sankoh. At the time, Sankoh was in jail facing charges of treason, but Special Envoy Jesse Jackson demanded that he be released unconditionally. (In one memorable statement, the envoy compared the rebel head to another African jailed for his political beliefs, Nelson Mandela.) In July 1999, Jackson brokered the so-called Lome Accord, creating a power-sharing arrangement between the Kabbah government and the R.U.F. Foday Sankoh, pardoned of all crimes, was installed as vice president and chairman of the Strategic Mineral Reserve Council, the body in charge of Sierra Leone's diamond reserves.

The ink was scarcely dry on the Lome Accord when Sankoh and his troops spectacularly violated it, making hostages of five hundred U.N. soldiers sent out to oversee the demobilization process. At last, the scales fell from American eyes. U.S. officials renounced the Lome Accord, Jackson was quietly dismissed from his position as presidential envoy, and Washington called for a war-crimes tribunal, akin to the courts established after genocides in Rwanda and Bosnia. The fighting raged on, finally drawing to a close in 2002, with the R.U.F.'s defeat by an unlikely coalition of Nigerians, British special forces, and an indigenous militia movement called the Kamajors. Foday Sankoh was arrested and bound over for prosecution, but suffered a stroke and died before coming to trial. Charles Taylor, driven from power in Liberia in 2003, has also been indicted for war crimes, though he has thus far evaded prosecution. As for the people of Sierra Leone, there is little for them to do but to try to rebuild, to pick up the pieces from a war of which all but a few Americans are blissfully unaware.

The object here is not to rehash another African horror story nor to indict the United States for another act of reckless cynicism, but simply to establish the setting in which Priscilla's Homecoming unfolded. The "home" to which we were returning the spirit of Priscilla was a grievously wounded land. For reasons that are perhaps understandable, the facts of Sierra Leone's current predicament went largely unmentioned during the homecoming, but for me, and I'm sure for my traveling companions, it was impossible to think about Priscilla outside this context. Only gradually did I realize that the same was true for Sierra Leoneans, that they too viewed the homecoming through the prism of the present and understood its significance in surprisingly contemporary ways.

AMONG THE CURIOUS CONTINUITIES in postindependence Africa are airplane routes. If you fly to a former colony of Britain, France, or Belgium, chances are that you will fly from London, Paris, or Brussels. But British Airways does not fly to Freetown. By the end of the 1990s, the only European connections to the country were through Holland and Belgium, Europe's two chief markets for raw diamonds. It is an early indication that Sierra Leone is something other than just another struggling postindependence African country. Others await us inside the country: convoys of blue-helmeted U.N. peacekeepers; the multitude of people missing limbs and others whose limbs are shriveled by polio or grotesquely swollen by elephantiasis. Perhaps the weirdest sight is a squadron of Russian-made Mikoyan helicopters at Lungi Airport. The helicopters were brought to Sierra Leone by Executive Outcomes, a South African–based mercenary army hired by the government in 1995 to drive the rebels from the Kono diamond fields. After the war ended, the machines stayed behind, along with their Ukranian pilots, who won the concession to ferry arriving passengers from the airport across the estuary to the capital. It is a strange way to enter a country.

And yet our reception could scarcely be more warm or generous. Led by Thomalind Polite, we descend from our plane into a throng of drummers and dancers. A local chief pours a libation on the tarmac in honor of the ancestors. A government minister presents Thomalind with a basket of cola nuts, a traditional gesture of welcome. Though our party includes no dignitaries, our visit is accorded the status of a state visit, ensuring all manner of courtesies. President Kabbah receives us, listening to the Priscilla story with obvious interest and emotion. The mayor and town councilors of Freetown, after the obligatory speeches, burst spontaneously into a Krio hymn of thanksgiving, which they insist on teaching to us. Students at Fourah Bay College perform an original play based on the Priscilla story. The Freetown Players, a distinguished local a cappella group, have prepared an original song: "Rush with the news / Priscilla is coming home."

Listening to that song, it struck me that the transatlantic encounter I was witnessing was different from the others described in this book. Typically it is Africans who are cast in the role of "ancestors," the keepers of the racial past. In Priscilla's Homecoming, the ancestral presence was embodied by an African American. To an American reader, this reversal of roles may not seem that significant, but it was clearly of great moment to our hosts. One needs to be careful of overgeneralization here, but it is safe to say that most Africans regard ancestors with a seriousness that is lost on Americans, black and white. Even in countries like Sierra Leone, where Islam and Christianity have made substantial inroads, public events routinely begin with the pouring of libations to the ancestors, just one of many rituals employed by Africans to bridge this world and the next. ("A waste of good gin," Richard Wright huffed during his visit to Ghana in 1953.) This is not to say, as some nineteenth-century missionaries alleged, that Africans indulge in "ancestor worship," but simply to suggest that many Africans today continue to feel the presence of their ancestors in their lives, and to regard the maintenance of a correct relationship with them as essential to individual and collective health.

The importance that Africans attach to ancestors is most evident in the rituals surrounding death and burial. Many Africans today would regard mortuary practices in the United States as barbarous; for them, preparing a loved one for his or her passage into the world of the shades is one of the most intimate and profound of human obligations, not a task to be handed to a hireling. (The struggle of public-health workers to stop the spread of the Ebola virus in Zaire in the 1990s stemmed in part from family members' insistence on washing the bodies of their dead.) Many Africans would be equally aghast at the American custom of interring people wherever they happened to reside at the time of death. In Africa, the dead come home for burial, back to their own communities, where they can commune with the other dead and see to the welfare of the living. This practice persists even in today's age of labor migration and rapid urbanization, thanks in part to the operation of burial societies—cooperative schemes, ubiquitous across sub-Saharan Africa, in which members pay a small monthly subscription to ensure that their bodies are returned to their ancestral homes. Again, we are talking in very broad generalizations here, but most Africans, including most Sierra Leoneans, regard a proper burial as essential to the well-being of the deceased spirit and of the community of which he or she remains a part.

Understanding African ideas about ancestry, and the matrix of ideas about place, time, and identity that underlay them, casts the transatlantic slave trade in a fresh and horrifying light. The trade represented not only a physical but also a spiritual holocaust, a rupture in the relationship between past, present, and future. Communities were bereft not only of their living but also of their dead, and of the protection that their presence might have afforded. The rupture must have been even more devastating for captives themselves, who were ripped from the ancestral train, cut off from both past and future. No doubt many struggled to maintain some connection with the spiritual universe that they left behind, a task that was perhaps easier in places where many Africans from the same area were concentrated. Yet time did its work even there. Consider again that Mende burial song—a song to guide the dead on their journey—handed down through the generations on the Georgia Sea Islands, preserved in form yet slowly leached of meaning, like a piece of petrified wood.

Understanding Africans' ideas about ancestry also helps to explain the significance that Sierra Leoneans attached to Priscilla's Homecoming. This was not simply an African American visiting Africa; this was an ancestor coming home. Betrayed and lost for centuries, Priscilla had found her way back across the water. And in her return lay a glimmer of hope, the possibility that harmony might be restored and that the misfortunes that had engulfed the land might finally end.

Only later did it occur to me how strange this must have been to Thomalind Polite. In contrast to most of the people discussed in this book, she had not spent years dreaming of traveling to Africa; she seems scarcely to have considered Africa at all, until the day that Joseph Opala knocked on her door carrying a written invitation from the Sierra Leonean government. Insofar as she had a personal motive in accepting that invitation, I suspect it had less to do with pursuing her African roots than with keeping faith with her late father, whose final years had been brightened by the discovery of Priscilla. She surely did not foresee herself feted by national leaders, her every reaction recorded on film. Sierra Leoneans, who had been alerted to the homecoming by newspaper, radio, and television coverage, strained to catch a glimpse of her, invariably addressing her as Priscilla rather than as Thomalind. But if she felt any discomfort with her role, she never betrayed it in public. She seemed intuitively to understand the significance that Sierra Leoneans attached to her presence, and bore the attention with grace and patience, assuring all and sundry that Priscilla was home and at peace.

LIKE MANY OLD IMPERIAL OUTPOSTS, Freetown has its share of unlikely locales. One of them is the Sierra Leone Yacht Club. It does not contain many boats anymore, if it ever did, but it does boast a pair of U.S. Embassy speedboats, for emergency evacuations of embassy personnel. The boats were used during the rebel invasion of Freetown in 1997, but on this morning they have a different assignment: to carry Thomalind Polite and her entourage to the old British fort on Bunce Island, the final stop of the slave ship *Hare* before its departure for South Carolina in 1756.

Out on the water, it is possible to imagine how this place appeared to Captain Caleb Godfrey and his crew two hundred and fifty years ago: the broad estuary, eight miles wide at the mouth; the thin coastal plain; the green massif rearing up behind. Portuguese explorers first mapped the river mouth in the 1460s; the first slave traders, also Portuguese, arrived in the early 1500s. By the time Godfrey arrived, Africans had been carried from Sierra Leone to the Americas for well over two centuries. Freetown was grafted onto this unlikely landscape. As we move upriver, we pass Fourah Bay College, the first university in West Africa, built on the site of an old Portuguese slave trading post. Some of the towering figures of modern African history studied or taught at Fourah Bay—Samuel Crowther, James Africanus Horton, Edward Blyden—in a stately brick building whose roof was constructed from the timbers of captured slave ships. The building remained after the college relocated to the hills above the city in the 1960s. When the rebels abandoned Freetown for the last time in 1999, they torched it. Only the brick walls survive, visible from the river.

The Sierra Leone River is navigable for only about twenty miles, at which point it dissipates into swamps and creeks, passable only by canoe. Bunce Island sits at the head of navigation. At first glance, it is indistinguishable from the other islands that dot the river—a low green tangle of trees and vines, perhaps five hundred yards long and a hundred yards wide at the waist. There is no sign of the old fortress, nothing to indicate that we are approaching what was once the most important slave factory on the Windward Coast. In Caleb Godfrey's day, there would have been no missing the fort, with its rectilinear lines and whitewashed walls, crowned by a massive Union Jack. There were no trees then, the whole island having been clear-cut to eliminate the decaying vegetation and miasmas which were believed to cause Africa's mortal fevers. Had Godfrey been so inclined, he could even have joined his merchant hosts, several of whom were Scotsmen, for a round of golf on the island's two-hole links, a course that predated the introduction of the game to England, let alone America. (W. E. B. Du Bois briefly stopped over in Freetown during his first visit to Africa in 1924 and was incensed to discover a golf course, which to him symbolized the worst of colonial decadence. One can only imagine what he would have said had he known of the course on Bunce Island.)

The original fort on Bunce Island was erected in 1670 by the Company of Gambia Adventurers, a syndicate of London merchants. In 1684, the Gambia Adventurers were superceded by the Royal Africa Company, which ran the facility until 1728, when the company was chased out by Afro-Portuguese rivals. The island reopened in 1744, under the auspices of a private London firm, and it continued to supply enslaved Africans right up until the abolition of the British trade in 1807. In the course of its history, the fort was attacked and razed six times, twice by pirates and four times by the French, the last time in 1794, when Freetown also came under attack. The ruins on the island today date back to 1795, when the fort was rebuilt for the last time, ironically by African American settlers, who had taken refuge on the island after their expulsion from Freetown. How many Africans were trafficked out of Bunce Island is difficult to say: certainly fifty thousand, probably more. Several of the captives on the *Hare* were acquired on Bunce, though it is impossible to know whether the girl who became Priscilla was one of them.

Visiting Bunce Island is a very different experience from visiting Goree Island, Cape Coast castle, or any of the other heavily touristed slave-trade sites along the West African coast. Located near large settlements, many of those sites were converted to other uses after the abolition of the slave trade and thus preserved. (Accra's Christiansborg Castle, built by the Danes in 1661, is today the seat of the Ghanaian government.) Bunce Island, by contrast, was abandoned shortly after the 1807 parliamentary act abolishing the slave trade. Neglected by Europeans and avoided by Africans (who continue to regard it as an unholy place), the island has been reclaimed by the forest. Forgive the image, but it seems a place straight from *The Jungle Book*, all crumbling walls and collapsed arches, filigreed with thick vines that, having toppled half the place, now appear to be holding up the other half. But with the help of Joe Opala, we begin to recognize features: the crumbling jetty from which captives were loaded onto the waiting ships; the old battlement, still lined with a row of rusty cannons, their wooden carriages long since rotted away; two graveyards, one for white merchants (whose average life expectancy on the island was less than a year) and one for Gramettos, the free African workers who staffed the facility. We also see the remnants of two large holding pens, one for women and children, the other, far larger, for men. In her memoirs, Mary Falconbridge, wife of an early governor of the Sierra Leone colony and a frequent visitor to the island, described standing on a second floor balcony in the proprietor's residence and looking out over more than two hundred naked men, chained together in circles, eating from troughs of rice. The sight was disturbing enough that she thereafter frequented only the front portion of the house, though not sufficient to cause her to question the slave trade. Three weeks after her husband's death, she married one of the merchants on the island and sailed with him to the Caribbean on a slave ship.

To say that Opala is devoted to Bunce Island would be to do him a disservice; the place is his passion. He has explored every inch of the site, and dedicated decades of his life to ensuring that it is properly preserved. His long-term goal is to see Bunce Island become an important pilgrimage site for African Americans, thus generating visibility and desperately needed foreign exchange for Sierra Leone. It pains him to see tourists flock to places like Goree Island (a relatively minor site in the transatlantic trade) and Jufurre (home of Alex Haley's reputed ancestor, Kunta Kinte), while Sierra Leone, the ancestral home of millions of African Americans, is virtually ignored. He certainly has a point, but it is hard to imagine tourists flocking to Bunce Island anytime soon, certainly not as long as Freetown remains in its current shape. In effect, Sierra Leoneans face the African version of catch-22, needing tourist revenue for reconstruction and reconstruction to attract tourists.

Bunce Island is also handicapped in the tourism stakes by the absence of an ocean view. I do not say that facetiously. Proximity to the sea is always an asset for a tourist site, but it is particularly important in African American heritage tourism. Standing on the edge of the Atlantic, gazing westward toward the Americas, one can imagine oneself standing at ground zero of African American history, the geometric point of origin from which African people radiated out into the Atlantic world. Tourists at Goree and Cape Coast are invited to reenact that originary moment, marching from the dark, dank dungeons in which captives were held through the "door of no return," the portal through which enslaved Africans passed en route to the waiting ships. The experience, suggestive at once of birth and death, overwhelms many visitors; if the guest books at such sites are any guide, many African

Americans feel their kinship with Africa more keenly in that instant than at any other moment in their lives. Yet paradoxically, it is also an experience rooted in a distinctly African American rather than African perspective. Viewed from the standpoint of the Americas, such places may indeed mark the beginning of the journey, but they would likely not have seemed so to the captives who passed through them. For them, these coastal fortresses were not starting points but way stations, transit points in journeys that had begun days, even weeks or months before, sometimes hundreds of miles in the interior.

Bunce Island, more than any other slave trade site that I have visited, evokes that neglected African perspective. Perhaps it is the island's unusual location, in the middle of a river twenty miles from the sea; perhaps it is the view from the back of the island, where nameless creeks meander off into the forest. But standing on Bunce Island, looking both west and east, one can scarcely help but reflect on the travail that brought captives to this place as well as the one that awaited them in the Atlantic world. It is an unsettling prospect, raising questions that at least some tourists would prefer not to broach.

THE FORTRESS ON BUNCE ISLAND is not the only ruin on the upper reaches of the Sierra Leone River. A mile downstream, at a place called Pepel, two vast steel conveyors project out over the water. In the 1940s, the Sierra Leone Development Company, DELCO, carved a ninety-kilometer trunk line through the forest to connect Pepel to the newly discovered iron fields at Marampa. Where European and American ships had once filled their holds with slaves, they could now take on loads of iron ore. In the 1970s, a combination of circumstances—falling world prices, a decline in the grade of ore, political chaos in the country—rendered the Marampa fields uneconomic, and the whole operation was left to rust.

Like so much of Africa, Sierra Leone possesses great mineral wealth. Minerals are at once the country's hope and its bane, holding out a promise of economic revival but also making the country a prey for looters, of both the rebel and multinational kind. The current hope is rutile (titanium oxide), a lightweight, heat-resistant metal used in manufacturing everything from jet engines to golf clubs. During our group's visit to President Kabbah, I chanced to look at a bulletin board in the waiting room, which displayed photos of the president's recent visit to a rutile mine, where he signed a concession agreement with Jean-Raymond Boulle. The name rang a bell, so I did a bit of research. A French-speaking, Mauritian-born British citizen, currently residing in Monaco, Boulle was for many years chief diamond buyer for De Beers, the South African firm that controls the international diamond cartel. In the 1980s, he established his own firm, American Mineral Fields, based in—of all places—Hope, Arkansas, hometown of the state's governor (and future American president), Bill Clinton. With Governor Clinton's support, Boulle secured special legislation allowing him to mine diamonds on state-owned land, but he kept his eye on Africa. In 1997, as the rebels of Laurent Kabila seized control of Mobutu Sese Seko's Zaire, American Mineral Fields, with reported capitalization of thirty-odd million dollars, paid Kabila one billion dollars for the right to exploit the country's cobalt and zinc resources, outbidding such giants as De Beers and Anglo-American. (As part of the arrangement, Kabila was given use of Boulle's private jet.) It is hard to imagine much good coming of Sierra Leone's association with Jean-Raymond Boulle, but the country is hardly in a position to choose its suitors.

Sierra Leone's chief foreign exchange earner remains diamonds, most of which are produced from alluvial fields in the Kono District, near the Liberian border. Sierra Leonean diamonds are abundant and of exceptionally fine quality. They are also deposited in surface gravel, making them extremely inexpensive to produce. These qualities ensured that the Kono District would become a major battlefield during the civil war, as rebels and government troops (aided, for a time, by South African mercenaries) vied to control an industry worth hundreds of millions of dollars per year. Sierra Leonean stones were eventually banned from the global market, as part of the international campaign against contraband or blood diamonds, but the industry is now recovering. International capital has begun to flow to Kono, not only from Europe and America but also from China, which is bidding to expand its influence in Africa. Tens of thousands of destitute Sierra Leoneans have also arrived, hoping to make their fortunes. The diamond fields are one of the sites where the country's future will be determined.

On the boat ride back from Bunce Island, I discuss Kono's prospects with another member of the Priscilla party, Joe James. James is president and chief executive officer of the Corporation for Economic Opportunity, a non-profit economic development agency based in Columbia, South Carolina. He has spent more than three decades working in the community development field, under both private and public sector auspices, to encourage entrepreneurship and sustained growth in economically distressed communities. While James has worked chiefly with African American communities, he recently launched a Sierra Leonean venture, Kono's Hope, LLC. Working in collaboration with the Peace Diamond Alliance and the U.S. Agency for International Development, Kono's Hope has created several small cooperatives on the diamond fields, offering local miners start-up capital as well as facilities for direct marketing of gems. James hopes that the venture will stimulate the flow of African American capital to Africa, offering black American investors an opportunity to help rebuild their ancestral continent while earning reasonable rates of return for themselves.

Whether he realizes it or not, James is part of a long tradition in African American history. From the commercial ventures of Paul Cuffe to the flood of African American entrepreneurs into postapartheid South Africa, Africa has long beckoned as a place to do well while doing good, a place where one can serve the cause of racial uplift and make money in the process. Few of these schemes have realized the dreams of proponents, and it is easy to deride them as naive or opportunistic. (Recall Langston Hughes's story of the Garveyite tailor embarking for Africa with scissors and bolts of cloth, hoping to make a killing by teaching Africans to wear pants.) Yet Joe James is neither a naïf nor an opportunist. He is a serious and successful businessman, with a passionate commitment to helping Sierra Leoneans escape the cycle of poverty and dependency in which they have long been locked. Under the cooperative arrangements established by Kono's Hope, 90 percent of the revenues generated from diamond sales are plowed back into the local community, underwriting food production, housing, and health care, with the remaining 10 percent going to James and his fellow investors. It is, by any measure, a better arrangement than what currently prevails in Kono, where diggers, many of them children, labor for the equivalent of a dollar or two a day without shelter, schools, hospitals, or clean water.

But significant obstacles remain. James ticks them off: smuggling, corruption, competition from large-scale international investors more interested in profits than the welfare of local people. The Sierra Leonean government is clearly supportive of the cooperative idea, but whether it has the power to influence events remains to be seen. The day before our talk, James had gone to the government ministries building to deliver a copy of a form, only to find himself stymied because none of the offices could afford paper for the photocopier. As the name of his company suggests, Joe James is a hopeful man. One suspects that he will need all the hope he can muster.

TWO DAYS LATER, we are back on the water, taking a battered, rusty ferry across the estuary to the Bullom shore. Though only a few miles separate it from Freetown, the Bullom shore looks far more like what Africa is "supposed" to look like, which suits the filmmakers, who want to film Thomalind Polite in a more traditional setting. The village they have selected, Kafu Bullom, could not be more perfect: a ribbon of palm-frond huts strung along a beautiful white beach, with the endless Atlantic stretching west to the horizon. Yet it is also a deeply ironic choice. During Priscilla's day, the chief of the Bullom shore controlled the slave trade out of the Sierra Leone River; indeed, he was the landlord of Bunce Island. Given that chiefs rarely if ever sold children from their own villages, the one thing that we can say about Priscilla's origins with relative certainty is that she did not come from Kafu Bullom.

The role of the Bullom shore chief in the transatlantic slave is well documented. The merchants of Bunce Island paid him an annual tribute, as well as a duty on every African sold through the fort. (The diary of a clerk who worked at the island around the time of Priscilla's departure described the chief once arriving for the annual rent collection in a kilt, in deference to his Scottish hosts.) As insurance against fraud, the chief required the merchants to send one of his sons to Britain for education and further stipulated that all merchants at Bunce take local women as wives, creating, in essence, a network of informants on the island. The Bullom chief's dominance of the local slave trade continued even after the closure of the Bunce Island operation. In 1810, Paul Cuffe took a canoe across the estuary to meet with King George, the chief at the time, to implore him to desist from slave trading. The king listened patiently to Cuffe's appeal but declined the suggestion. If the Bullom people gave up the trade, he explained, it would make "them poor and they could not git things as they used to git when they traded in slaves."

All of which makes the staging of a homecoming ceremony at Kafu Bullom more than a little ironic. But I bite my tongue, reminding myself that the people we will be meeting are not responsible for selling Priscilla, any more than I, a resident of Caleb Godfrey's Rhode Island, am responsible for buying her. And the ceremony itself is genuinely moving. Whether prompted by the national tourism board or by their own sense of the occasion, our hosts have rolled out the proverbial red carpet. Musicians and dancers perform. Dignitaries speak, including the current chief, who thanks Thomalind for returning the spirit of Priscilla to her home. The children of the village, dressed in tidy green school uniforms and green berets, sing for us, beaming as only children presented with an unexpected holiday from school can beam. Arrayed in two long lines, they sing a marching song, swinging their arms, feet shuffling in place. It takes me a minute or two to catch the words:

Home again, home again
When shall I see my home?
When shall I see my native land?
I shall never forget my home.

It is obviously an English song. It could not have been sung by Priscilla, who did not, in any case, come from here. Yet the children conjure her presence.

ONE MORNING, as the Priscilla party prepares for another round of receptions, I slip away with a journalist friend to the U.N. compound on Pademba Road. A city block square, the compound is a hive of trailers and prefabricated buildings, surrounded by a high steel fence, topped with razor wire and studded with sentry towers. Sitting incongruously in the center is a large modernist building, fashioned from concrete and wood in a shape intended to suggest the scales of justice. The building houses the Special Court for

Sierra Leone, an international tribunal that is prosecuting crimes against humanity committed during the recent civil war.

The S.C.S.L. has a curious history. It exists largely at the behest of the international community, particularly the United States, which, after twice compelling President Kabbah in the 1990s to grant amnesty to rebel fighters, suddenly reversed course and insisted that individuals responsible for human rights violations be prosecuted as war criminals. In contrast to the tribunals for Rwanda and Bosnia, the Special Court is not strictly a U.N. enterprise but a product of a treaty between the U.N. and the Sierra Leonean government. It is also unique in that it is being convened inside the country in which the offenses occurred. This would seem a risky approach in a society still reeling from civil war, but the risks were outweighed (at least as far as international officials were concerned) by the opportunity of using the Special Court to help rebuild Sierra Leone's shattered judicial system. Whatever the wisdom of that decision, the court has clearly been handicapped by its hybrid character. Unlike the Bosnian and Rwandan courts, the S.C.S.L. cannot compel nations to hand over defendants. Thus Charles Taylor, the most conspicuous of the nine men indicted by the court, will never appear unless or until the government of Nigeria chooses to deliver him, which it has thus far declined to do. The Special Court is also not guaranteed U.N. funding, as the Rwandan and Bosnian tribunals are, but instead subsists on voluntary contributions from member states. Not surprisingly, donations have dwindled as global interest in Sierra Leone has faded. In early 2005, the Special Court was forced to hire a private fund-raiser, based in New York, to scratch together a few million dollars to allow it to finish its work.

As for Sierra Leoneans themselves, most seem to view the exercise with something between indifference and hostility. Obviously I am working from a very small sample, but virtually every individual I spoke to expressed reservations about the court. Many contrasted it to the recently completed Sierra Leone Truth and Reconciliation Commission, a separate tribunal, which focused on atonement and forgiveness rather than prosecution. It is tempting to attribute Sierra Leoneans' preference for reconciliation to their forgiving natures, but it probably has more to do with their realism, their awareness of the fragility of the current government and of the risks of

434 · MIDDLE PASSAGES

prosecuting men who still command considerable popular loyalty. Sierra Leoneans have also been perplexed by the Special Court's decisions about whom to prosecute. Few would dispute the indictments of Charles Taylor and Foday Sankoh, and fewer still the indictment of Johnny Paul Koroma, the leader of the A.F.R.C., or Junta, that overthrew the Kabbah government in 1997 and twice put Freetown under the harrow. But many were baffled by the court's decision to prosecute the leaders of the Kamajors, the local militias who fought against the rebels to restore the authority of the elected government. Presumably the Special Court was attempting to demonstrate its even-handedness, but the inclusion of the Kamajors, widely regarded today as heroes, provoked outrage. Sierra Leoneans were especially bewildered by the prosecution of Sam Hinga Norman, a Kamajor commander who, until his indictment and arrest, served as minister of defence in President Kabbah's cabinet. To make matters worse, Foday Sankoh and Johnny Paul Koroma both had the bad grace to die before their trials began, while Charles Taylor has yet to be handed over by Nigeria, thus leaving Norman as the most conspicuous defendant.

Some years ago, I had the opportunity to attend some hearings of the South African Truth and Reconciliation Commission, and entering the Special Court transports me immediately back to those days. As the testimony unfolds, however, I find myself mostly thinking about William Sheppard. Sheppard was virtually unique among nineteenth-century missionaries, white or black, in his respect for African culture, yet one custom he could never abide was witchcraft accusation. Like other premodern people, the BaKete and BaKuba among whom he worked responded to premature death or other seemingly inexplicable misfortunes by turning the matter over to religious adepts—whites called them witch doctors—whose task it was to "smell out" the culprits and bring them to justice, thus restoring social order. Sheppard regarded such practices as irrational and barbarous, and on several occasions risked his life to try to save the accused. Sitting in that courtroom, it strikes me that war-crimes tribunals may be the Western equivalent. Confronted with a massive social breakdown, the Special Court has identified nine witches. Of course, the forensic techniques are different; there is no poison ordeal. The judges appear in black robes and scarlet collars rather than leopard skin and cowrie shells. Yet the purpose seems much the same: to explain the inexplicable; to vindicate social order; to make it possible for all of us to sleep at night.

There is another reason I think of William Sheppard. The defendants before the court are Kamajors, and the atrocities of which they are accused are eerily similar to those he described in the Congo a century ago. The term "Kamajor" refers to a traditional Mende hunting society, whose members were renowned for both their physical courage and their mastery of certain supernatural techniques. As the rebels advanced through the countryside in the early 1990s, the Kamajors were recast as local militias to defend their villages. With the regular troops of the Sierra Leonean army having joined the rebels in looting the country, the militias, under Sam Hinga Norman's leadership, came to bear the brunt of the war. In an extraordinary blending of traditional belief and modern military science, initiates into the Kamajors learned small-arms use, as well as how to prepare traditional medicines and charms to enhance their courage and render them impervious to the bullets of their foes. Only initiates would know precisely how to prepare these medicines, but it is clear that they often employed body parts harvested from enemies, which were variously smeared on the body, worn as amulets, or eaten.

The witness in court today discusses something more mundane: the murder of her brother. The Kamajors came to her village in 1998 and accused her and several others of being rebels. In her case, at least, the charge was not entirely unfounded: abducted by rebels as a child, she had spent several years as a sex slave. The accused were taken into the forest, where the men were beaten and killed—in one case, disemboweled. The witness describes how her brother was tied to the ground while a gasoline-soaked tire burned above him, dripping melted rubber onto his bare skin. He was then covered with palm fronds, which peeled away his flesh when lifted. "He kept crying out our mother's name," she says quietly. "He continued to cry out our mother's name until he died." She testifies in Mende. I presume that this is also the language in which her brother cried.

LATER THAT EVENING, I sit in the hotel bar and talk with Charles Black, another member of the Priscilla party. Black is a movie actor—you would recognize his face—with a beautiful baritone voice that will provide the homecoming film's narration. He is traveling with his wife, Alice, who is covering the event for a black travel magazine. The Blacks are exceptionally gracious and thoughtful people. Aside from a trip to Egypt, neither has visited Africa before. The trip clearly means a great deal to them, particularly to Charles, who has just learned that his own ancestors came from Sierra Leone.

Black discovered his Sierra Leonean roots through a DNA test. For a few hundred dollars, a Washington-based firm called African Ancestry will take a sample of your DNA (painlessly collected by swabbing the inside of your mouth), compare it with samples from its trademarked African Lineage Database, and trace your origins to a particular group or area. On first hearing, it sounds like the latest in the long history of back-to-Africa scams, but the science is sound. Because of the preservation of certain genetic signatures across generations—in the Y chromosome of the paternal line and the mitochondrial DNA of the maternal line—it is indeed possible to trace lines of descent across hundreds, even thousands, of years. To be sure, the tests are not foolproof. African Ancestry's database is not only extremely small but it is also organized around current ethnic or "tribal" labels, some of which say more about colonial classificatory schemes than about actual lines of historical descent. The problem is further complicated by the substantial infusion of European and Native American blood after Africans arrived in the Americas. Nonetheless, for the vast majority of African Americans, who lack the documented lineage of Thomalind Polite, DNA testing offers the best tool yet for establishing one's specific African roots. As fate would have it, Charles Black's report, which arrived just as he embarked on his journey, linked him to the Mende and Temne people, the two largest ethnic groups in Sierra Leone. "So I guess you could say I'm home," he says.

But the home to which he has returned is a far harder place than he, or indeed any of us, anticipated, and his emotions are not following the expected script. He did not break down on Bunce Island, as he anticipated he might, but a few nights later, as he sat in his hotel room and reflected on the things he had seen in the streets of Freetown, he found himself sobbing uncontrollably. "I just couldn't stop crying," he says. I fumble for a response. Only later does it occur to me what I ought to have said: it is when the tears stop that we really need to start worrying.

In official homecoming events, however, the tone is much more upbeat. Sierra Leone's current predicament is rarely mentioned. Partly this reflects the efforts of Joe Opala, who is not only intent on keeping the spotlight on Priscilla but also determined to cast the homecoming as a celebration, a story of resilience and redemption rather than suffering and loss. But it also reflects deference to our hosts, who are anxious to project a positive image of their country and who clearly find the subject of the civil war and its aftermath awkward. Yet there are times that the subject cannot be avoided. The national power grid was crippled by the war, and Freetown is still subject to frequent blackouts, one of which occurs in the middle of a state dinner. As luck would have it, I am sitting next to the minister of energy. What exactly do you say to a minister of energy when the capital city of his country, including the room in which you are sitting, has just been plunged into darkness? Part of my mind is immediately rehearsing the comic possibilities of the episode, but another part grieves. When the lights return, five or ten minutes later, the minister looks shrunken. "We talk about health and education," he says, "but I don't see how we can begin to move forward without energy."

The following day brings an even more striking collision of past and present. It is another day of celebrations, including a ceremony at the national museum, at which Thomalind Polite presents an original painting depicting Priscilla. The painting, created by South Carolina artist Dana Coleman from childhood photographs of Thomalind, shows a little girl in a slave coffle, her hands bound, a rope around her neck. It is a harrowing image, yet there is a quality in the face—the focus of the eyes, the upraised chin—that leaves no doubt that this child will survive. The ceremony unfolds according to the script, until a local man steps out of the crowd and presents Thomalind with a picture of his own, depicting a rebel soldier. This is what happened here, he explains, but now that you are home things will be better.

I HAVE A PILGRIMAGE of my own to make. All historians have favorite historical figures—not heroes exactly, but individuals whose lives we find compelling. One such person for me is Daniel Coker, whose 1820 journey to

Africa is recounted in the first chapter of this book. Born of a white mother but consigned to a life of slavery; educated at the insistence of his white half brother, whose name he later adopted as his own; fugitive slave and pioneering antislavery pamphleteer; founder of the African Methodist Episcopal Church, America's first black independent denomination; leader of the first contingent of American Colonization Society settlers to what would become Liberia: Coker led a most peculiar life in the shadow of a most peculiar institution.

Coker believed that Providence guided human affairs. It was this conviction that enabled him to brave the opposition of other free black leaders and embrace the cause of African colonization. But the journey did not go as he imagined. By the time his ship, the *Elizabeth*, reached Freetown, the settlers had fallen out with the society's white agents. They soon rejected Coker as well. When the surviving colonists moved down the coast to what would become Liberia, Coker remained behind in Sierra Leone. He spent the last decades of his life working as a teacher and minister at a place called Hastings, a satellite village outside Freetown, built for the recaptive Africans liberated from slave ships by the Royal Navy's Anti-Slavery Squadron. On the final day of Priscilla's Homecoming, I hire a driver and head to Hastings to see if I can find any trace of him.

We climb east out of Freetown, over the escarpment, toward the base of the peninsula. It is a relief to be out of the city, passing through forests and small villages. These are the old recaptive villages, whose names—Regents, Grafton, Bathhurst—reflect their colonial origins. Many of the houses are built in the old Krio style, with wooden walls and shutters and tin roofs. But the serenity is deceptive. The rebels twice passed along this road on their way to Freetown, raping, murdering, and burning as they went. Interspersed among the villages are refugee camps, identifiable from the tattered tents bearing the logo of the U.N. High Commission of Refugees. I read the signs as we rattle along. REPENTANCE DRIVE. BE PROUD TO BE A SIERRA LEONEAN. REHABILITATION VILLAGE FOR WAR WOUNDED AND AMPUTEES. A passing taxi sports a legend on its back bumper: EVEN THE DEAD NEED PEACE.

We reach Hastings and seek out the village headman, who, after the requisite exchange of courtesies, consents to speak with us. His name is

J. M. Douglas. As the name suggests, he is of Krio descent. With rain clouds spilling in from the west, we take refuge on his porch, where he unfolds the history of the village, raising his voice to be heard over the rain beating on the tin roof. After being deposited at Freetown, he explains, liberated Africans began to sort themselves out by ethnic and language groups. Most of those who settled Hastings were Yoruba speakers—Aku, in local parlance—who congregated around a spring they called Doctor Water. Coker lived near the spring. No Cokers remain in the village today, he tells me, but "that particular Daniel" has many descendants, most of them in Freetown. In returning to the land of his ancestors, Daniel Coker became an ancestor himself.

I ask how Hastings fared during the civil war, though I have already seen enough to know the answer. In 1997, the village spent seven months under rebel occupation. Residents had only begun to rebuild their lives when the rebels returned. By the time they left the second time, in early 1999, three quarters of the village had been reduced to ashes. Many residents lost their lives. Many more lost their children. So many lost children.

The rain ceases as quickly as it began. Mr. Douglas asks if we would like to see where Daniel Coker is buried. We drive to a graveyard down by the main road. He conducts us through waist high grass to the far corner of the cemetery, near a crumbling stone wall. There is no marker, but he seems certain of the spot. He removes his hat, bends at the waist, and pours a libation on the ground.

· NOTES ·

Introduction: What Is Africa to Me?

xiv "One of the Kru men from Liberia": *Langston Hughes, The Big Sea: An Autobiography* (New York: Thunder's Mouth Press, 1986, orig. pub. 1940), p. 103.

xiv "comedy of misrecognition": Kenneth Warren, "Appeals for (Mis)recognition: Theorizing the Diaspora," in Amy Kaplan and Donald E. Pease, eds., *Cultures of United States Imperialism* (Durham, N.C.: Duke University Press), pp. 393–94.

Prologue: Ayuba's Journey

1 "twenty Negars . . . Dutch manne o war": John Smith, *The Generall Historie of Virginia, Newe England, and the Summer Isles* [. . .] (London, 1624), quoted in Engel Sluiter, "New Light on the '20. and Odd Negroes' Arriving in Virginia, August, 1619," *William and Mary Quarterly* 54:2 (1997), p. 395.

3 "to make them appear like Slaves": Thomas Bluett, *Some Memoirs of the Life of Job, the Son of Solomon, the High Priest of Boonda in Africa* [. . .] (London, 1734), in Philip Curtin, ed., *Africa Remembered: Narratives by West Africans from the Era of the Slave Trade* (Madison: University of Wisconsin Press, 1967), p. 40.

3 "leave to redeem . . . his man": Bluett, *Life of Job*, p. 40.

4 "was no common slave": Bluett, *Life of Job*, p. 42.

4 "affable carriage" and "easy composure": Bluett, *Life of Job*, p. 42.

5 "acquainting him with his misfortunes": Bluett, *Life of Job*, p. 43.

5 "strove who should oftenest invite him": Douglas Grant, *The Fortunate Slave: An Illustration of African Slavery in the Early Eighteenth Century* (New York: Oxford University Press, 1968), p. vi.

6 "he had proper clothes to go in": Bluett, *Life of Job*, p. 46.

7   "with the greatest Respect": Grant, *The Fortunate Slave*, p. 112.

7   "upon paying two other good Slaves for one": Grant, *The Fortunate Slave*, p. 110.

8   "make so good an understanding between": Francis Moore, *Travels into the Inland Parts of Africa* (London, 1738), in Curtin, ed., *Africa Remembered*, p. 59.

8   "a great deal of the horror of the Pholeys": Moore, *Travels into the Inland Parts*, p. 57.

8   "imagined that all who were sold": Moore, *Travels into the Inland Parts*, p. 57.

8   "a woman-slave and two horses": Moore, *Travels into the Inland Parts*, p. 57.

12   "By the eve of the American Revolution": David B. Davis, *The Problem of Slavery in the Age of Revolution, 1770–1823* (Ithaca: Cornell University Press, 1975), p. 48.

Chapter One: Windward Coast

17   "leave the province . . . *fellow-men* to enslave them": Herbert Aptheker, *A Documentary History of the Negro People in the United States*, vol. 1 (Secaucus, N.J.: The Citadel Press, 1951), pp. 7–8.

18   "The inhabitants of Rhode Island": *Providence Gazette*, October 13, 1787.

18   "spread the light of the gospel": John Saillant, *Black Puritan, Black Republican: The Life and Thought of Lemuel Haynes, 1753–1833* (New York: Oxford University Press, 2003), p. 98.

18   "in the case of Joseph being sold a slave": Saillant, *Black Puritan*, p. 98.

19   "'Twas mercy brought me from my Pagan land": John C. Shields, ed., *The Collected Works of Phillis Wheatley* (New York: Oxford University Press, 1988), p. 18.

19   "Did Fear and Danger so perplex": *Newport Mercury*, December 21, 1767, in Shields, ed., *Collected Works of Phillis Wheatley*, p. 133.

19   "to promote this laudable design": Phillis Wheatley to Samuel Hopkins, February 9, 1774, in Shields, ed., *Collected Works of Phillis Wheatley*, p. 176.

20   "earnest desire of returning to Affrica": William H. Robinson, ed., *The Proceedings of the Free African Union Society and the African Benevolent Society, Newport, Rhode Island, 1780–1824* (Providence: The Urban League of Rhode Island, 1976), p. 16.

21   "He is a discerning, judicious, steady": George Champlin, ed., *Mason's Reminiscences of Newport* (Newport: Charles E. Hammett, 1884), p. 157.

21   "natural abilities . . . acquaintance as to letters": Lamin Sanneh, *Abolitionists Abroad: American Blacks and the Making of Modern West Africa* (Cambridge: Harvard University Press, 1999), p. 46.

23   "stain and contamination . . . more dangerous": Mavis C. Campbell, *Back to Africa: George Ross and the Maroons: From Nova Scotia to Sierra Leone* (Trenton, N.J.: Africa World Press, 1993), p. iii.

25   "terrestrial Elysium . . . comfortable situation": Adam Hochschild, *Bury the Chains: Prophets and Rebels in the Fight to Free an Empire's Slaves* (Boston: Houghton Mifflin, 2005), pp. 145, 148–49.

25   "I could not have conceived that men": Hochschild, *Bury the Chains*, pp. 176–77.

26   "very peculiar emotions": Ellen Gibson Wilson, *The Loyal Blacks* (New York: G.P. Putnam and Sons, 1976), p. 242.

27 "Your thoughts were evil": Wilson, *The Loyal Blacks*, p. 242.

28 "to return to Africa, our native country": Sidney Kaplan and Emma Nogrady Kaplan, *The Black Presence in the Era of the American Revolution* (Amherst: University of Massachusetts Press, 1989), pp. 207–9.

28 "mutual intercourse and profitable commerce": Kaplan and Kaplan, *Black Presence*, p. 208.

28 "We are waiting and longing": Robinson, ed., *Proceedings of the Free African Union Society*, p. 18.

29 "lands proper and sufficient to settle": Robinson, ed., *Proceedings of the Free African Union Society*, p. 16.

29 "warm climate . . . more agreeable": Kaplan and Kaplan, *Black Presence*, p. 208.

29 "inlightening and civilizing those nations": Kaplan and Kaplan, *Black Presence*, p. 208.

29 "calamitous state . . . wicked as to sell one another": Robinson, ed., *Proceedings of the Free African Union Society*, p. 19.

30 "simplicity, innocence, and contentment": Peter Williams, "An Oration on the Abolition of the Slave Trade [. . .] January 1, 1808," in Dorothy Porter, ed., *Early Negro Writing* (Boston: Beacon Press, 1971), p. 346.

30 "imposters and bloodsuckers": Daniel Coker, quoted in Floyd J. Miller, *The Search for Black Nationality: Black Emigration and Coloniation, 1787–1863* (Urbana: University of Illinois Press, 1975), p. 67.

30 "strangers and outcasts in a strange land": Robinson, ed., *Proceedings of the Free African Union Society*, p. 19.

30 "good and proper title . . . Heirs or children": Robinson, ed., *Proceedings of the Free African Union Society*, p. 16.

30 "civil society united by a political constitution": Kaplan and Kaplan, *Black Presence*, p. 208.

32 "poor Dispised miserable" . . . "the white peopel do": Aptheker, ed., *Documentary History*, vol. 1, pp. 14–16.

32 "[W]hen Mr. Clarkson's History of the Abolition": Sheldon H. Harris, ed., *Paul Cuffe: Black America and the Africa Return* (New York: Simon & Schuster, 1972), p. 52.

32 "from which may issue the seeds of reformation": Thomas Clarkson, *The History of the Rise, Progress, and Accomplishment of the Abolition of the African Slave-trade by the British Parliament*, vol. 2 (London: Longman, 1808), pp. 344–45.

33 "rise to be a people": Harris, ed., *Paul Cuffe*, p. 208.

33 "useful arts" . . . "Rice, Indigo, Cotton or Tobacco": Harris, ed., *Paul Cuffe*, p. 177.

34 "as to Poor me i feel very feeble": Rosalind Cobb Wiggins, ed., *Captain Paul Cuffe's Logs and Letters, 1808–1817* (Washington, D.C.: Howard University Press, 1996), p. 78.

34 "dust of Africa": Wiggins, ed., *Captain Paul Cuffe's Logs*, p. 104.

34 "mental endowments": Lamont Thomas, *Rise to Be a People: A Biography of Paul Cuffe* (Urbana: University of Illinois Press, 1986), p. 61.

35 "a letter of advice . . . the nations of Africa": Wiggins, ed., *Captain Paul Cuffe's Logs*, p. 108.

35 "gave the king a Testament and several other books": Paul Cuffe, *A Brief Account of the Settlement and Present Situation of the Colony of Sierra Leone in Africa* (Nendeln, Liechtenstein: Kraus Reprints, 1970, orig. pub. 1812), p. 7.

36 "acknowledge by words the existence": Cuffe, *A Brief Account*, p. 7.

36 "them poor and they could not git things": Wiggins, ed., *Captain Paul Cuffe's Logs*, p. 342.

36 "So accustomed are they to wars and slavery": Cuffe, *A Brief Account*, p. 7.

36 "It must have been a strange and animating spectacle": Harris, ed., *Paul Cuffe*, p. 53.

36 "Clarkson and I are both of the mind": William Allen, *Life of William Allen, With Selections from His Correspondence*, vol. 1 (Philadelphia: Henry Longstreth, 1847), p. 103.

36 "few knew what to do with them": Wiggins, ed., *Captain Paul Cuffe's Logs*, p. 173.

37 "forefathers out of the Egyptian bondage": Cuffe, *A Brief Account*, p. 10.

37–38 "such of the native productions . . . into a state of slavery": Cuffe, "Memorial Petition, June 16, 1813," in Wiggins, ed., *Captain Paul Cuffe's Logs*, pp. 252–253.

38 "invite the emigration of free blacks": Thomas, *Rise to Be a People*, p. 90.

38 "so much acquainted with treatment": Harris, ed., *Paul Cuffe*, p. 187.

39 "[I]t is to be lamented to see & hear": Harris, ed., *Paul Cuffe*, p. 194.

39 "far greater than the number taken in": Harris, ed., *Paul Cuffe*, p. 194.

39 "the many obstructions thrown in the way": Harris, ed., *Paul Cuffe*, p. 234.

39 "[S]hould it appear that there could be no more view": Harris, ed., *Paul Cuffe*, p. 215.

39 "motions of insurrection . . . tranquility of the world": Harris, ed., *Paul Cuffe*, pp. 202, 206, 215, ff.

40 "The whole commerce between master and slave": Thomas Jefferson, *Notes on the State of Virginia* (Boston, Mass.: Bedford, 2002), p. 195.

40 "inferior in the faculties of reason and imagination": Jefferson, *Notes*, p. 180.

41 "Deep rooted prejudices entertained by the whites": Jefferson, *Notes*, pp. 175–76.

41 "[W]e have a wolf by the ear": Jefferson to John Holmes, April 22, 1820, in Ford Paul Leicester, ed., *The Works of Thomas Jefferson*, vol. 12 (New York: G.P. Putnam, 1905), p. 159.

41–42 "breeders . . . swallowing a camel": John Saillant, "The American Enlightenment in Africa: Jefferson's Colonizationism and Black Virginians' Migration to Liberia, 1776–1840," *Eighteenth-Century Studies* 31:3 (1998), p. 275.

42 "a powerful means . . . civilization and Christianity to Africa": Harris, ed., *Paul Cuffe*, p. 232.

42 "rise to that condition . . . this scheme is from God": Philip J. Staudenraus, *The African Colonization Movement, 1816–1865* (New York: Columbia University Press, 1961), pp. 17–18.

43 "other situation in Africa": Harris, ed., *Paul Cuffe*, p. 232.

44 "materially tend to secure" . . . "discontent": Staudenraus, *African Colonization Movement*, p. 29.

44 "Can there be a nobler cause": Staudenraus, *African Colonization Movement*, p. 28.

44 "unmerited stigma" . . . "blood and sweat": Aptheker, *Documentary History*, vol. 1, p. 71.

44 "[W]e will never separate ourselves voluntarily": Aptheker, *Documentary History*, vol. 1, p. 71.

44 "will never become a people": Kaplan and Kaplan, *Black Presence*, p. 162.

45 "the more enlightened they were": Staudenraus, *African Colonization Movement*, p. 33.

45 "[L]et no purpose be assisted which will stay": Staudenraus, *African Colonization Movement*, p. 33.

45 "banana, orange, lime, and plantain trees": Sanneh, *Abolitionists Abroad*, p. 196.

45 "a land stored with the choicest minerals": Miller, *Search for Black Nationality*, p. 56.

45 "a second Paul Cuffe": Amos J. Beyan, *The American Colonization Society and the Creation of the Liberian State: A Historical Perspective, 1822–1900* (Lanham, Md.: University Press of America, 1991), p. 57.

46 "[I]f the people [prove] troublesome": Staudenraus, *African Colonization Movement*, pp. 46–47.

47 "interpositions of providence": "Diary of Daniel Coker, April 21–September 21, 1821," Peter Force Collection, Library of Congress, series 8D, reel 32, entry for April 29, 1821.

48 "[H]e being nearly white, the people said": David Smith, *Biography of Rev. David Smith of the A.M.E. Church* (Xenia, Ohio: Xenia Gazette, 1881), p. 33.

48 "clearing and cultivating the land": Ralph Randolph Gurley, *Life of Jehudi Ashmun, Late Colonial Agent in Liberia* (New York: Negro Universities Press, 1969, orig. pub. 1835), p. 75.

49 "led his chosen armies through": Daniel Coker, *Journal of Daniel Coker, A Descendant of Africa [. . .] on a Voyage to Sherbro, in Africa* (Nendeln, Liechtenstein: Kraus Reprints, 1970, orig. pub. 1820), p. 15.

49 "poring over our plan" . . . "Surely something great": Coker, *Journal*, p. 14.

49 "Oh! My dears, what darkness has covered": Coker, *Journal*, pp. 43–44.

50 "from intercourse with slave-traders": Coker, *Journal*, p. 42.

50 "Such is their conduct that any one who loves": Coker, *Journal*, p. 44.

50 "natives sit[ting] naked" . . . "children of nature . . . all nearly naked": Coker, *Journal*, pp. 21–22.

50 "gross darkness": Coker, *Journal*, p. 34.

50 "[T]he water at the place is not good or plenty": Coker, *Journal*, p. 34.

51 "first impressions on heathens are to be made": Coker, *Journal*, p. 24.

51 "[T]hey well know, if we get foot hold": Coker, *Journal*, p. 36.

51 "I have no doubt that we shall succeed": Coker, *Journal*, p. 37.

51 "[W]e must not get discouraged": Coker, *Journal*, p. 38.

51 "the King & the head men . . . will not let a *white*": Miller, *Search for Black Nationality*, p. 65.

52 "[W]hite blood is good, and black blood is good": Miller, *Search for Black Nationality*, p. 66.

52 "O bigotry, thou art no friend": Coker, "Diary," May 27, 1821.

52–53 "late trials . . . well suited to my case": Coker, "Diary," July 21, 1821; August 4, 1821.

53 "Moses was I think permitted to see": Coker, "Diary," May 3, 1821.

53 "bleeding, groaning, dark, benighted Africa": Coker, *Journal*, p. 44.

55 "I go to set an example to the youth": Champlin, *Mason's Reminiscences of Newport*, p. 159.

55 "composed by Dea[con] Newport Gardner": Charles A. Battle, *Negroes on the Island of Rhode Island* (Newport, R.I.: Newport Black Museum, 1971, orig. pub. 1932), p. 28.

55 "and she said, Truth, Lord: yet the dogs eat of the crumbs": Matthew 15: 27–28.

56 "Hear the words of the Lord, O ye African race": Battle, *Negroes on the Island*, p. 28.

Chapter Two: Representing the Race

57 "the said Commissioners, on behalf of the African race": Martin Delany, *Official Report of the Niger Valley Exploring Party*, in Howard H. Bell, ed., *Search for a Place: Black Separatism and Africa, 1860* (Ann Arbor: University of Michigan Press, 1969, orig. pub. 1861), pp. 77–78.

58 "black as jet": Robert S. Levine, *Martin Delany, Frederick Douglass, and the Politics of Representative Identity* (Chapel Hill: University of North Carolina Press, 1997), p. 20.

60 "We see [slavery] now in its true light": Fergus M. Bordewich, *Bound for Canaan: The Underground Railroad and the War for the Soul of America* (New York: Amistad, 2005), p. 305.

60 "I have for several years been striving to reconcile": *Freedom's Journal* 1:34 (November 2, 1827), p. 2.

60 "We wish to plead our own cause": *Freedom's Journal* 1:1 (March 16, 1827), p. 1.

60 "In the discussion of political subjects": *Freedom's Journal* 1:1 (March 16, 1827), p. 4.

60 "Born in this Republican country": *Freedom's Journal* 1:2 (March 23, 1827), p. 2.

61 "moral, religious, civil and literary improvement": *Freedom's Journal* 1:1 (March 16, 1827), p. 4.

61 "We are unvarying in our opinion": *Freedom's Journal* 1:13 (June 8, 1827), p. 2.

61 "[E]verything that relates to Africa shall find": *Freedom's Journal* 1:1 (March 16, 1827), p. 1.

61 "progress of geographic discovery": *Freedom's Journal* 1:3 (March 30, 1827), p. 3.

62 "We are all going on with some elegant improvements": Julie Winch, *A Gentleman of Color: The Life of James Forten* (New York: Oxford University Press, 2002), p. 202.

63 "Let us and our friends unite, in baptizing the term": *The Colored American*, March 4, 1837, p. 1.

64 "to remove the title of African": "Minutes of the Fifth Annual Convention for the Improvement of the Free People of Color in the United States [. . .] 1835," in Howard H. Bell, *Minutes of the Proceedings of the National Negro Congress, 1830–1864* (New York: Arno, 1969), pp. 14–15.

64 "HEREDITARY BONDSMEN! KNOW YE NOT": Robert S. Levine, ed., *Martin R. Delany: A Documentary Reader* (Chapel Hill: University of North Carolina Press, 2003), p. 27.

65 "abolition of complexional distinctions": Floyd J. Miller, *The Search for Black Nationality: Black Emigration and Colonization, 1787–1863* (Urbana: University of Illinois Press, 1975), p. 102.

65 "has gone about the same length in favor": Levine, ed., *Delany: Documentary Reader*, p. 3.

65 "physiological condition . . . transmitted to the offspring": Delany, *The Condition, Elevation, Emigration and Destiny of the Colored People of the United States, Politically Considered* (1852), in Levine, ed., *Delany: Documentary Reader*, pp. 215–16.

65 "a conclave of upstart colored hirelings": Delany, "Introduction" to William Nesbit, *Four Months in Liberia, or African Colonization Exposed* (1855), in Wilson Jeremiah Moses, ed., *Liberian Dreams: Back-to-Africa Narratives from the 1850s* (University Park: Pennsylvania State University Press, 1998), p. 83.

66 "learned in all the ways of the Egyptians": Delany, "Origins and Objects of Ancient Freemasonry" (1853), in Levine, ed., *Delany: Documentary Reader*, p. 53.

67 "say that his talents emanate": Delany, *North Star*, July 7, 1848, in Levine, ed., *Delany: Documentary Reader*, p. 101.

67 "the *most* African of all the black men": Delany, *Christian Recorder*, July 21, 1866, in Levine, ed., *Delany: Documentary Reader*, p. 463.

68 "the late Martin R. Delany, who was an unadulterated": Anna Julia Cooper, *A Voice from the South* (New York: Oxford University Press, 1988, orig. pub. 1892), p. 30.

69 "We are slaves in the midst of freedom": Delany, *Condition*, in Levine, ed., *Delany: Documentary Reader*, p. 201.

69 "the nominally free states": Delany, *North Star*, July 28, 1848, in Levine, ed., *Delany: Documentary Reader*, p. 115.

69 "beings of an inferior order, and altogether unfit": *Dred Scott v. Sanford*, 60 U.S. (19 How.) (1857), pp. 393, 408.

69–70 "the harp-like strains that whisper freedom": Miller, *Search for Black Nationality*, p. 188.

70 "My mind of late has greatly changed": Miller, *Search for Black Nationality*, p. 190.

70 "I have found all my best friends among the white": Daniel Peterson, *The Looking Glass: Being a True Report and Narrative of the Life, Travels, and Labors of the Rev. Daniel H. Peterson* (1854), in Moses, ed., *Liberian Dreams*, p. 10.

70 "I must say that I never saw a more attractive": Peterson, *The Looking Glass*, p. 47.

70 "lands want ploughing up and sowing": Peterson, *The Looking Glass*, p. 60.

70 "On stepping ashore, I found that we had been": Nesbit, *Four Months in Liberia*, p. 88.

70–71 "The whole country presents the most woe begone": Nesbit, *Four Months in Liberia*, p. 88.

71 "violent and appalling storms" . . . "destroying insects": Nesbit, *Four Months in Liberia*, pp. 94, 96, 101.

71 "cod-fish aristocracy": Nesbit, *Four Months in Liberia*, p. 90.

71 "filthy and disgusting . . . lazy, rude, and ignorant": Nesbit, *Four Months in Liberia*, p. 111.

71 "fast retrograding": Nesbit, *Four Months*, p. 92.

71 "Let the colonist himself be barefoot": Nesbit, *Four Months*, p. 103.

72 "aliens to the laws and political privileges": Delany, *Condition*, in Levine, ed., *Delany: Documentary Reader*, p. 202.

72 "degrading, expatriating, insolent, slaveholding scheme": Delany, *North Star*, March 2, 1849, in Levine, ed., *Delany: Documentary Reader*, p. 144.

72 "the admission of blacks to the medical Lectures": Ronald Takaki, "Aesculapius Was a White Man: Antebellum Racism and Male Chauvinism at Harvard Medical School," *Phylon* 39:2 (1978), pp. 128–30, 132.

73 "nation within a nation": Delany, *Condition*, in Levine, ed., *Delany: Documentary Reader*, p. 202.

73 "the ruling element": Delany, *Political Destiny of the Colored Race on the American Continent* (1854), in Levine, ed., *Delany: Documentary Reader*, pp. 247, 250.

73   "incontrovertibly shown" . . . "Where shall we go": Delany, *Condition*, in Levine, ed., *Delany: Documentary Reader*, p. 203.

73   "Liberia is not an Independent Republic": Delany, *Condition*, in Levine, ed., *Delany: Documentary Reader*, p. 204.

73   "the qualifications of physician, botanist, chemist": Delany, "A Project for an Expedition of Adventure, to the Eastern Coast of Africa" (1852), in Levine, ed., *Delany: Documentary Reader*, p. 321.

74   "The land is ours; there it lies": Delany, "A Project for an Expedition," in Levine, ed., *Delany: Documentary Reader*, p. 323.

74   "We must not leave this continent": Delany, *Condition*, in Levine, ed., *Delany: Documentary Reader*, p. 206.

74   "who would introduce the subject": Aptheker, *Documentary History*, vol. 1, p. 363.

74   "[O]ur object and determination are to consider": Aptheker, *Documentary History*, vol. 1, pp. 363–64.

75   "We must have a position, independently": Delany, *Frederick Douglass' Paper*, July 1852, in Levine, ed., *Delany: Documentary Reader*, pp. 222–23.

75   "seemed to know no other purpose for living": Delany, *Provincial Freeman*, July, 12, 1856, in Levine, ed., *Delany: Documentary Reader*, p. 293.

75   "not having as yet read Uncle Tom's cabin": Delany, *Frederick Douglass' Paper*, April 1853, in Levine, ed., *Delany: Documentary Reader*, p. 231.

76   "knows nothing about us": Delany, *Frederick Douglass' Paper*, April 1853, in Levine, ed., *Delany: Documentary Reader*, p. 225.

78   "an efficient corps of scientific men of color": Miller, *Search for Black Nationality*, p. 176.

79   "Scientific Corps . . . Examination of the [Niger] Valley": Delany, *Official Report*, pp. 39–40.

80   "an Enlightened and Christian Nationality": Delany to Henry Ward Beecher, June 17, 1858, in Levine, ed., *Delany: Documentary Reader*, p. 183.

80   "that most pernicious and impudent of all schemes": Delany, "Introduction" to Nesbit, *Four Months in Liberia*, p. 81.

80   "the grandest prospect for the regeneration": Delany, *Official Report*, pp. 102, 122.

83   "the light of the gospel" . . . "in darkness": J. F. Ade Ajayi, *Christian Missions in Nigeria, 1841–1891: The Making of a New Elite* (Evanston: Northwestern University Press, 1965), pp. 27–28.

84   "a household word among the readers": Ajayi, *Christian Missions*, p. 40.

85   "benefit your countrymen whilest you make": Miller, *Search for Black Nationality*, pp. 176–77, n. 8.

86   "a fawning servilian of the negro-hating Colonizationists": Delany, *North Star*, March 2, 1849, in Levine, ed., *Delany: Documentary Reader*, p. 146.

86   "propogated in consequence of writers": Robert Campbell, *A Pilgrimage to My Motherland: An Account of a Journey Among the Egbas and Yorubas of Central Africa in 1859–60*, in Howard H. Bell, ed., *Search for a Place*, p. 151.

87   "history of the project": Delany, *Official Report*, p. 32.

87   "on behalf of the African race in America": Delany, *Official Report*, p. 77.

88   "sanitary means": Delany, *Official Report*, p. 98.

88 "black rascals" . . . "stand deliberately and watch": Delany, *Official Report*, p. 100.

88 "in which case . . . subdue the whites whenever they meet": Delany, *Official Report*, p. 100.

89 "morbid affliction of the mind" . . . "most ardent and abiding": Delany, *Official Report*, p. 64.

89 "a dense, heavy-wooded, primitive forest": Delany, *Official Report*, p. 87.

89 "natural remedy for the permanent decrease": Delany, *Official Report*, p. 66.

90 "the well-regulated pursuits of civilized life": Delany, *Official Report*, p. 110.

90 "habits, manners, and customs": Delany, *Official Report*, p. 109.

90 *"descendants of Africa"* . . . "claims, sentiments, and sympathies": Delany, *Official Report*, p. 110.

90 *"Africa for the African race, and black men":* Delany, *Official Report*, p. 121.

91 "the Commissioners, on behalf of the African": Delany, *Official Report*, pp. 77–78. (See also Campbell, *Pilgrimage*, pp. 248–50, which offers a slightly different version of the treaty.)

91 "the learned Oriental traveler": Delany, *Official Report*, p. 135.

92 "open new cotton fields for the supply": Delany, *Official Report*, p. 131.

92 "countries that may offer a suitable field": Delany, *Official Report*, p. 135.

93 "the Americans Mr Campbell and Dr Delany": Ajayi, *Christian Missions*, p. 191.

93 "common property; every individual enjoys": Campbell, *Pilgrimage*, pp. 174–75.

94 "[M]y destiny is fixed in Africa": Delany, *Weekly Anglo-African*, October 5, 1861, in Levine, ed., *Delany: Documentary Reader*, p. 369.

95 "explorations in certain portions of Africa": Frank A. Rollin, *Life and Public Services of Martin R. Delany* (New York: Arno, 1969, orig. pub. 1868), p. 84.

96 "triple alliance": Rollin, *Life and Public Services*, pp. 242–43.

96 "neither disheartened" . . . "see his salvation": Rollin, *Life and Public Services*, pp. 282–83.

96 "under the rallying-cry of acting for": Delany to Frederick Douglass, August 14, 1871, in Levine, ed., *Delany: Documentary Reader*, p. 439.

97 "carpet-baggers" . . . "Southern men": *New York Daily Tribune*, March 6, 1875, in Levine, ed., *Delany: Documentary Reader*, p. 451.

97 "de dam nigger dimocrat": *News and Courier*, October 16, 1876, in Levine, ed., *Delany: Documentary Reader*, p. 456.

98 "government favors": Levine, ed., *Delany: Documentary Reader*, p. 484.

Chapter Three: Emigration or Extermination

100–1 "Adventurers swarmed" . . . "to protect the Southern country": The quotation is culled from Woodrow Wilson, *A History of the American People*, vol. 5: (New York: Harper and Brothers, 1903), pp. 38, 46, 49, 58, 60.

104 "owing to some British statute": Stephen Ward Angell, *Bishop Henry McNeal Turner and African American Religion in the South* (Knoxville: University of Tennessee Press, 1992), p. 7.

105 "We have, as far as possible, closed": Fergus M. Bordewich, *Bound for Canaan: The Underground Railroad and the War for the Soul of America* (New York: Amistad, 2005), p. 106.

106 "fought, bled and died here": Edwin S. Redkey, ed., *Respect Black: The Writings and Speeches of Henry McNeal Turner* (New York: Arno Press, 1971), pp. 34–35.

107 "chin deep" . . . "if they were a set of varmints": David Blight, *Race and Reunion: The Civil War in American Memory* (Cambridge, Mass.: Harvard University Press, 2001), p. 147.

107 "thronged the windows" . . . "'we are your masters'": Blight, *Race and Reunion*, p. 147.

108 "old things will be forgotten": Redkey, ed., *Respect Black*, p. 9.

108 "I became a convert to emigration": Redkey, ed., *Respect Black*, pp. 13–14.

108 "cowardice" . . . "pusillanimity": Redkey, ed., *Respect Black*, p. 15.

109 "resting place for the Negro's feet": Angell, *Bishop Henry McNeal Turner*, p. 119.

109 "There is no more doubt in my mind": Redkey, ed., *Respect Black*, p. 42.

110 "a load of humanity" . . . "broad African continent": Walter L. Williams, *Black Americans and the Evangelization of Africa, 1877–1930* (Madison: University of Wisconsin Press, 1982), p. 39.

111 "We hold these truths to be self-evident": "First Convention of the Liberia Exodus Arkansas Colony[. . .]1886," in *Annual Report of the New York State Colonization Society for the Year Ending May 1, 1886* (New York: 1886).

112 "wealth and refinement" . . . "millions to Christ": Kenneth C. Barnes, *Journey of Hope: The Back-to-Africa Movement in Arkansas in the Late 1800s* (Chapel Hill: University of North Carolina Press, 2004), p. 18.

112 "pianos and organs, carpets, pictures": Barnes, *Journey of Hope*, p. 18.

113 "remarkable achievements" . . . "unprecedented advance": For the progressive school of postbellum black politics, see William J. Simmons, *Men of Mark: Eminent, Progressive and Rising* (New York: Arno Press, 1968, orig. pub. 1887) and H. F. Kletzing and W. H. Crogman, *Progress of a Race or, the Remarkable Advancement of the Afro-American* (New York: Negro Universities Press, 1969, orig. pub. 1897).

113 "All this native land talk": Frederick Douglass, "The Lessons of the Hour: Address by the Honorable Frederick Douglass in the Metropolitan A.M.E. Church, Washington, D.C., January 9, 1894."

114 "What one thoughtful man among us": Edwin S. Redkey, *Black Exodus: Black Nationalist and Back-to-Africa Movements, 1890–1910* (New Haven, Conn.: Yale University Press, 1969), p. 33.

114 "aimless, objectless, selfless, little-souled": Redkey, ed., *Respect Black*, p. 57.

114 "I would like to take yearly those who are sent": Redkey, ed., *Respect Black*, p. 56.

114 "barbarous decision" . . . "absolves the negro's allegiance": Redkey, ed., *Respect Black*, p. 60.

115 "If the decision is correct, the United States Constitution": Redkey, ed., *Respect Black*, p. 63.

115 "But just so long as we are a people within a people": Redkey, ed., *Respect Black*, p. 43.

115 "Washington's policy is not worth a cent": Gayraud Wilmore, *Black Religion and Black Radicalism* (Garden City, N.Y.: Doubleday, 1972), p. 187.

115 "standard of beauty" . . . "hair-straighteners and skin-bleachers": Redkey, ed., *Respect Black*, p. 179.

116   "The whole tendency of our ignoble status": Redkey, ed., *Respect Black,* p. 57.

116   "the large size of the negro's penis": George Fredrickson, *The Black Image in the White Mind: The Debate on Afro-American Character and Destiny, 1817–1914* (New York: Harper and Row, 1971), p. 279.

118   "high offices, dignitaries, artisans, mechanics": Redkey, ed., *Respect Black,* p. 59.

118   "United States of Africa": Redkey, ed., *Respect Black,* p. 44.

119   "the world's future paradise": "The Letters of Henry M. Turner," *The A.M.E. Church Review* 8:4 (1892), p. 446.

119   "the Crew tribe seems to be a superior class": Turner, "Letters," p. 453.

119–20   "a regular African" . . . "Talk about the African being ignorant": Turner, "Letters," p. 455.

120   "Things are gloomy here" . . . "I am crazy with delight": Turner, "Letters," p. 467.

120   "Great heavens, how white people": Turner, "Letters," p. 475.

120   "paradisical spot" . . . "easiest place to make a living": Turner, "Letters," p. 481.

120   "could hibernate six months annually": Turner, "Letters," p. 481.

120   "in mountain heaps" . . . "the finest wood on earth": Turner, "Letters," p. 472.

120   "would be worth millions in a few years": Turner, "Letters," p. 483.

120   "True, there is an acclimating change": Turner, "Letters," p. 481.

120   "I thought it was a second-class portion": Turner, "Letters," p. 483.

120   "inestimable—enough to run the machinery of the world": Turner, "Letters," p. 482.

121   "all the mere common labor": Turner, "Letters," p. 496.

121   "twenty-five cents per day or five dollars per month": Turner, "Letters," p. 482.

121   "I never wanted to be a young man so badly": Turner, "Letters," p. 496.

121   "beautiful ginger-cake-colored": Turner, "Letters," p. 473.

121   "the equal of any man on earth": Turner, "Letters," p. 476.

122   "said to be 108 years old" . . . "sold to America": Turner, "Letters," p. 488.

122   "those who think the receding forehead, the flat nose": Turner, "Letters," p. 488.

122   "take intelligent possession": Turner, "Letters," p. 494.

123   "the most susceptible heathen" . . . "an easy matter": Turner, "Letters," p. 484.

123   "There is no reason under heaven": Turner, "Letters," p. 483.

124   "to leave Georgia and go to their own country": Clarence A. Bacote, "Negro Proscriptions: Protests and Proposed Solutions in Georgia, 1880–1908," in Charles E. Wynes, ed., *The Negro in the South Since 1865: Selected Essays in American Negro History* (Tuscaloosa: University of Alabama Press, 1965), p. 107.

125   "the oiled advocate of a white man's corporation": Redkey, *Black Exodus,* p. 124.

126   "man in the moon": Redkey, ed., *Respect Black,* p. 137.

126   "possession of the gold, silver, tin, lead, iron": Redkey, ed., *Respect Black,* p. 139.

128   "when Providence opens to us a door" . . . "freedom in Canaan": Alfred Lee Ridgel, *Africa and African Methodism* (Atlanta, Ga.: Franklin Publishing, 1896), pp. 90–91.

128   "to leave the haunts of American slavery": Ridgel, *Africa and African Methodism,* p. 39.

128   "powerful tendencies toward white men absorbtion": Ridgel, *Africa and African Methodism,* p. 45.

128   "despise Africa" . . . "extol negro-hating America": Ridgel, *Africa and African Methodism,* pp. 43–44.

128 "to my mind the negro in foreign lands": Ridgel, *Africa and African Methodism*, p. 45.

128 "Awful! Awful! Awful!" "the gospel is needed here": Williams, *Black Americans and the Evangelization of Africa*, p. 111.

128 "We regard the British government as a godsend": Ridgel, *Africa and African Methodism*, pp. 40–41.

129 "the morning-star to the pure sun of Christianity": Turner, "Letters," p. 495.

129 "laid down the Bible for the Koran": Ridgel, *Voice of Missions*, February, 1896.

129 "colorphobia" . . . "blood, death and ruin" . . . "higher senses": Ridgel, *Africa and African Methodism*, pp. 67, 69, 72–72.

130 "Africa doesn't need me one-thousandth part as much": Smith, quoted in Ridgel, *Africa and African Methodism*, p. 52.

130 "tropical outfit" . . . "red silk cummer-band": Charles Spencer Smith, *Glimpses of Africa: West and Southwest Coast (Containing the Author's Impressions and Observations during a Voyage of Six Thousand Miles from Sierra Leone to St. Paul de Loanda and Return)* (Nashville, Tenn.: A.M.E. Sunday School Union, 1895), pp. 156–57.

131 "very unattractive ": Smith, *Glimpses of Africa*, p. 185.

131 " their persons disgustingly filthy by besmearing": Smith, *Glimpses of Africa*, p. 164.

131 "They were never enslaved and are evidently": Smith, *Glimpses of Africa*, p. 164.

131 "surpasses all other low-grade varieties of man": Smith, *Glimpses of Africa*, pp. 82–83.

132 "would be a wilderness were it not for European": Smith, *Glimpses of Africa*, p. 77.

132 "a degenerate and retrogressive": Smith, *Glimpses of Africa*, p. 60.

132 "to redeem West Africa from the grasp of barbarism": Smith, *Glimpses of Africa*, p. 54.

132 "the bright flames of the heated furnace": Smith, *Glimpses of Africa*, p. 213.

133 "the advent of Europeans" . . . "fierce growl of untamed beasts": James T. Campbell, *Songs of Zion: The African Methodist Episcopal Church in the United States and South Africa* (New York: Oxford University Press, 1995), p. 240.

133 "back to the Thames": Carol Page, "Colonial Reactions to A.M.E. Missionaries in South Africa, 1898–1910," in Sylvia Jacobs, ed., *Black Americans and the Missionary Movement in Africa* (Westport, Conn.: Greenwood Press, 1982), pp. 187–88.

133 "We have as much right biblically and otherwise": Redkey, *Respect Black*, pp. 176–77.

135 "the last of his clan" . . . "spiritual progeny of African chieftains": W. E. B. Du Bois, *The Crisis*, July 1915.

Chapter Four: Mundele Ndom

136 "one of those African trees famous for their short": Charles Spencer Smith, *Glimpses of Africa: West and Southwest Coast (Containing the Author's Impressions and Observations during a Voyage of Six Thousand Miles from Sierra Leone to St. Paul de Loanda and Return)* (Nashville, Tenn.: A.M.E. Sunday School Union, 1895), p. 218.

138 "slice of this magnificent African cake": Adam Hochschild, *King Leopold's Ghost: A Story of Greed, Terror, and Heroism in Colonial Africa* (Boston: Houghton Mifflin, 1998), p. 58.

139 "We have attacked and destroyed 28 large towns": Hochschild, *King Leopold's Ghost*, p. 49.

139 "of valuable service in helping civilisation": Hochschild, *King Leopold's Ghost*, p. 97.

140 "African savages brought to act the monkey": Donald L. Miller, "The White City," *American Heritage Magazine* 44:4 (July/August, 1993), p. 70.

142 "adaptation" . . . "tropical fitness": J. W. E. Bowen, ed., *Africa and the American Negro: Addresses and Proceedings of the Congress on Africa*[. . .]*1895* (Atlanta: Gammon Theological Seminary, 1896), pp. 137–148, ff.

142 "hearken to your message where the white messengers": H. B. Parks, "The Redemption of Africa the American Negro's Burden," *Voice of Missions,* March 1899.

143 "the obligation of the American Negro to missionary work": Bowen, ed., *Africa and the American Negro,* p. 10.

144 "How can we remain contented / in illuminated": Walter L. Williams, *Black Americans and the Evangelization of Africa, 1877–1930* (Madison: University of Wisconsin, 1982), p. 42.

144 "kindred o'er the sea": Levi J. Coppin, "The Negro's Part in the Redemption of Africa," *A.M.E. Church Review* 19:2 (1902), p. 511.

144–45 "The white people were always very kind": William H. Sheppard, *Presbyterian Poneers in Congo* (Richmond, Va.: Presbyterian Committee of Publication, 1917), p. 15.

145 "Before and directly after the war, when all the best": W. E. B. Du Bois, *The Souls of Black Folk* (Boston: Bedford, 1997, orig. pub. 1903), p. 144.

145 "hard core remnant of old family retainers": Stanley Shaloff, *Reform in Leopold's Congo* (Richmond, Va.: John Knox Press, 1970), p. 14.

145 "I loved my new home, for Dr. Henkel and his wife": Sheppard, *Presbyterian Pioneers,* p. 16.

146 "it was on the whole better for them": Donald Spivey, *Schooling for the New Slavery: Black Industrial Education, 1868–1917* (Westport, Conn.: Greenwood Press, 1978), p. 7.

147 "every advantage" . . . "a great, tender-hearted father": Sheppard, *Presbyterian Pioneers,* p. 17.

149 "kind" . . . "bright and gentle" . . . "good king": William E. Phipps, *William Sheppard: Congo's African Livingstone* (Louisville, Ky.: Geneva Press, 2002), pp. 17–18.

149 "thronged with half clad natives": Sheppard, *Presbyterian Pioneers,* p. 21.

150 "[J]ust like our own darkies": Pagan Kennedy, *Black Livingstone: A True Tale of Adventure in the Nineteenth-Century Congo* (New York: Viking, 2002), p. 30.

151 "foreigners" . . . "trials and triumphs": Sheppard, *Presbyterian Pioneers,* p. 29.

151 "no good here for Sierra Leone man": Kennedy, *Black Livingstone,* p. 37.

151 "These imported workmen raise a question": Kennedy, *Black Livingstone,* p. 37.

151 "sun-bleached skeletons of native carriers": Sheppard, *Presbyterian Pioneers,* p. 28.

151 "If a party of white men approaches": Phipps, *William Sheppard,* p. 29.

152 "Your Majesty's Government is engaged in the slave-trade": Hochschild, *King Leopold's Ghost,* p. 111.

152 "Russian" . . . "a handle I hope to use on him": Hochschild, *King Leopold's Ghost,* p. 154.

152 "I found many of them afraid I was a State man": Phipps, *William Sheppard,* p. 45.

153 "human head they brought him during the course": Hochschild, *King Leopold's Ghost*, p. 196.

153 "Going up that river was like traveling back": Joseph Conrad, *Heart of Darkness*, Paul B. Armstrong, ed., Norton Critical Edition, fourth edition (New York: W.W. Norton, 2006), pp. 33–34.

153 "It makes a terrible mark where it strikes": Kennedy, *Black Livingstone*, p. 56.

154 "sensible" . . . "in accord with their traditions and sentiments": Phipps, *William Sheppard*, p. 147.

154 "Sheppard is a most handy fellow": Phipps, *William Sheppard*, p. 39.

155 "Brother Sheppard has the constitution needed": Phipps, *William Sheppard*, p. 40.

155 "carefully and tenderly": Sheppard, *Presbyterian Pioneers*, p. 81.

155 "broadest and best smiles": Sheppard, *Presbyterian Pioneers*, p. 62.

156 "You can trust them as far as you can see them": Sheppard, "Into the Heart of Africa," *Southern Workman*, December 1893, p. 182.

156 "superiority in physique, manners, dress and dialect": Sheppard, *Presbyterian Pioneers*, p. 81.

157 "with low verandah" . . . "in old Virginia again": Kennedy, *Black Livingstone*, p. 121.

158 "aboriginal vigor" . . . "for the seed of the Word": H. A. C. Cairns, *Prelude to Imperialism: British Reactions to Central African Society, 1840–1890* (London: Routledge and Keegan Paul, 1965), p. 241.

158 "mounds of triumphant martyrs": Sheppard, *Presbyterian Pioneers*, p. 25.

158 "weeping and wailing" . . . "grief to Almighty God": Sheppard, *Presbyterian Pioneers*, p. 84.

158 "desired so much to journey into that land": Sheppard, *Presbyterian Pioneers*, p. 87.

159 "If the king hears you are here all our heads": Sheppard, "Into the Heart of Africa," p. 184.

159 "We may possibly escape the King's wrath": Sheppard, "Into the Heart of Africa," p. 184.

159 "These people are not to blame": Sheppard, "Into the Heart of Africa," p. 185.

159 "Well, that is very strange": Sheppard, "Into the Heart of Africa," p. 185.

159 "They knew me better than I knew myself": Sheppard, *Presbyterian Pioneers*, p. 101.

160 "made the forest look like a beautifully painted": Sheppard, *Presbyterian Pioneers*, p. 102.

160 "perfect blocks" . . . "a checker board": Sheppard, "Into the Heart of Africa," p. 185.

160 "what had once been white linen": Sheppard, *Presbyterian Pioneers*, p. 106.

160 "I want to acknowledge to you that I am not": Sheppard, *Presbyterian Pioneers*, p. 107.

161 "had their judges, jurors, lawyers and officers": Sheppard, *Presbyterian Pioneers*, p. 72.

161 "Many times in Central Africa foreigners": Sheppard, *Presbyterian Pioneers*, pp. 39–40.

161 "prying into the king's customs": Sheppard, *Presbyterian Pioneers*, p. 131.

161 "knowledge of weaving, embroidery, wood carving": Sheppard, *Presbyterian Pioneers*, p. 137.

161 "trying to find out what they were thinking about": Sheppard, *Presbyterian Pioneers*, p. 127.

161 "highly civilized": Sheppard, *Presbyterian Pioneers*, p. 137.

161 "enlightened but in darkness": Sheppard, *Presbyterian Pioneers*, p. 132.

162 "In the native mind no one dies a natural death": Sheppard, *Presbyterian Pioneers*, p. 121.

162 "wicked custom": Sheppard, *Presbyterian Pioneers*, p. 130.

162 "I tried to prove to him that the poisonous cup": Sheppard, *Presbyterian Pioneers*, p. 131.

162 "If a person is innocent he can never die": Sheppard, *Presbyterian Pioneers*, p. 131.

162 "They serve us here and then go with us": Sheppard, *Presbyterian Pioneers*, p. 131.

162 "conspicuous consumption": Jan Vansina, *The Children of Woot: A History of the Kuba People* (Madison: University of Wisconsin, 1978), p. 181.

163 "in the strongest language I could command": Sheppard, *Presbyterian Pioneers*, p. 131.

163 "burying the living with the dead": Sheppard, *Presbyterian Pioneers*, p. 131.

163 "Seeing these awful customs practiced by these people": Sheppard, *Presbyterian Pioneers*, pp. 131–32.

163 "indifferent, stony-hearted, and superstitious": Sheppard, "The Bakuba Mission," *Southern Workman*, July 1904, p. 408.

163 "well organized, independent, and exceedingly industrious": Sheppard, "The Bakuba Mission," p. 408.

163 "culture, mode of living, and intelligence": Sheppard, "The Bakuba Mission," p. 408.

164 "a Virginia Negro, through the power": Phipps, *William Sheppard*, p. 125.

164 "has been speaking to crowded houses": Phipps, *William Sheppard*, p. 98.

164 "Will you lend a helping hand": Sheppard, "Into the Heart of Africa," p. 186.

165 "has thrown open its doors, given up the keys": Kennedy, *Black Livingstone*, pp. 119–20.

166 "a howling mob of jabbering idiots": Robert Benedetto, ed., *Presbyterian Reformers in Central Africa: A Documentary Account of the American Presbyterian Congo Mission and the Human Rights Struggle in the Congo, 1890–1918* (London: E. J. Brill, 1996), p. 104.

166 "never were enslaved": Sheppard, "Into the Heart of Africa," p. 187.

166 "the Baluba are by far the most numerous": Phipps, *William Sheppard*, p. 63.

168 "There is no man in all this country": Benedetto, ed., *Presbyterian Reformers*, p. 116.

169 "both the lever and the fulcrum for uplifting": Anna Julia Cooper, *A Voice from the South* (New York: Oxford University Press, 1988, orig. pub. 1892), p. 45.

169 "When I saw the first native woman in her strip": Sylvia Jacobs, "Their Special Mission: Afro-American Women as Missionaries to the Congo, 1894–1937," in Jacobs, ed., *Black Americans and the Missionary Movement in Africa* (Westport, Conn.: Greenwood Press, 1982), p. 164.

170 "Christian ideals of womanhood": Jacobs, "Their Special Mission," p. 167.

170 "Christian mothers of Christian families": Jacobs, "Their Special Mission," p. 170.

170 "little home missionaries": Jacobs, "Their Special Mission," p. 158.

170 "totally depraved and degraded state": Jacobs, "Their Special Mission," p. 167.

170 "demonstration and practice center": Jacobs, "Their Special Mission," p. 163.

170–71 "making of a Christian home was part": Jacobs, "Their Special Mission," p. 163.

171 "I called it my *Ladies' Home Journal* home": Kennedy, *Black Livingstone*, p. 116.

173 "a small forest is as profitable as a gold mine": Phipps, *William Sheppard*, p. 134.

173 "refuse obstinately to work" . . . "take hostages": Phipps, *William Sheppard*, p. 133.

173 "I have the honour to inform you that from": Phipps, *William Sheppard*, p. 140.

174 "It is just as if I were to take a rope and go out": Sheppard, "Light in Darkest Africa," *Southern Workman*, April 1905, p. 220.

174 "We hear of atrocities being committed": Sheppard, "Light in Darkest Africa," p. 220.

174 "These were orders. I had to go": Sheppard, "Light in Darkest Africa," p. 221.

174 "Sheppard! Sheppard": Sheppard, "Light in Darkest Africa," p. 223.

175 "I don't like to fight, but the state": Benedetto, ed., *Presbyterian Reformers*, p. 122.

175 "We are going to kill them all": Benedetto, ed., *Presbyterian Reformers*, p. 122.

175 "conducted us to a framework of sticks": Benedetto, ed., *Presbyterian Reformers*, p. 124.

176 "The whole country is pillaged": Phipps, *William Sheppard*, pp. 143–44.

176 "You have sent me to do this": Sheppard, "Light in Darkest Africa," p. 225.

176 "Shepete! Shepete!": Benedetto ed., *Presbyterian Reformers*, p. 154.

177 "turned out to be a gigantic slave": Phipps, *William Sheppard*, p. 144.

177 "We have heard reports for years past of the terrible": Phipps, *William Sheppard*, p. 144.

177 "We can hardly think it necessary" . . . "non-political character": Benedetto, ed., *Presbyterian Reformers*, p. 127.

178 "to expose and destroy what I knew": Hochschild, *King Leopold's Ghost*, p. 186.

178 "the incorruptible Kodak": Mark Twain, *King Leopold's Lament: A Defense of His Congo Rule*, second edition (London: Unwin, 1907), p. 40.

178 "highly improbable" . . . "grossly overstated": Benedetto, ed., *Presbyterian Reformers*, p. 127.

179 "the greatest Negro of his generation": Phipps, *William Sheppard*, p. 125.

179 "tool in the hands of Morrison": Kennedy, *Black Livingstone*, p. 157.

179 "when Sheppard arrived, things were at top notch": Kennedy, *Black Livingstone*, p. 161.

179 "Being a colored man, I would not be understood": Kennedy, *Black Livingstone*, p. 161.

181 "We are not now suffering from the old forms": Kennedy, *Black Livingstone*, p. 168.

182 "one of the most prosperous and intelligent": Benedetto, ed., *Presbyterian Reformers*, pp. 281–82.

182 "any calumny against a Congo state official": Phipps, *William Sheppard*, pp. 164–65.

182 "the entire abolition of the Company": Wilfred G. Thesinger, "Report of a Journey into Kasai District," in Benedetto, ed., *Presbyterian Reformers*, pp. 310–16.

183 "invincible logic" . . . "burning sarcasm": Hochschild, *King Leopold's Ghost*, p. 264.

183 "Throw up your hat! Sheppard & I": Benedetto, ed., *Presbyterian Reformers*, p. 417.

183 "AMERICAN NEGRO HERO OF CONGO": Hochschild, *King Leopold's Ghost*, p. 264.

183 "some family matters which I believe": Phipps, *William Sheppard*, p. 176.

184 "was guilty of the sin of adultery": Kennedy, *Black Livingstone*, p. 190.

185 "I am sorry you feel that I have talked too freely": Benedetto, ed., *Presbyterian Reformers*, p. 38.

185 "In view of all the experiences of the past few years": Benedetto, ed., *Presbyterian Reformers*, p. 33.

185 "being waited on": Kennedy, *Black Livingstone*, p. 199.

186 "He was such a good darky": Kennedy, *Black Livingstone*, p. 152.

186 "extravaganza of African artifacts, curios": Phipps, *William Sheppard*, p. 187.

Chapter Five: So Long, So Far Away

188 "the States, where you have to live like a nigger": Langston Hughes, *The Big Sea: An Autobiography* (New York: Thunder's Mouth Press, 1986, orig. pub. 1940), p. 62.

188 "My father hated Negroes": Hughes, *Big Sea*, p. 40.

188 "Look at the niggers": Hughes, *Big Sea*, p. 41.

189 "I've known rivers": Hughes, "The Negro Speaks of Rivers," in Arnold Rampersad, ed., *The Collected Poems of Langston Hughes* (New York: Knopf, 1994), p. 23.

191 "I just begun to feel like a man": Emmett J. Scott, ed., "Additional Letters of Negro Migrants of 1916–1918," *Journal of Negro History* 4:4 (1919), p. 459.

191 "the Negro race was found almost entirely": E. T. H. Shaffer, "A New South—the Negro Migration," *Atlantic Monthly*, September 1923, p. 403.

192 "the period when the Negro was in vogue": Hughes, *Big Sea*, p. 228.

195 "What American literature decidedly needs": Carl Van Doren, "The Younger Generation of Negro Writers," *Opportunity*, May 1924, p. 145.

195 "the great desideratum of modern art": Ann Douglas, *Terrible Honesty: Mongrel Manhattan in the 1920s* (New York: The Noonday Press, 1995), p. 93.

195–96 "The white man in the mass cannot compete" . . . "working alliance": Albert C. Barnes, "Negro Art and America," in Alain Locke, ed., *The New Negro* (New York: Albert and Charles Boni, 1925), pp. 20, 25.

197 "Mecca of the New Negro": "Harlem: Mecca of the New Negro," Special issue of *Survey Graphic* 6:6 (March 1925).

199 "believed in books more than in people": Hughes, *Big Sea*, p. 26.

199 "earliest memories of written words": Arnold Rampersad, *The Life of Langston Hughes (volume 1: 1902–1941): I, Too, Sing America* (New York: Oxford University Press, 1986), p. 19.

200 "You are in the final analysis the most consarned": Rampersad, *Life of Langston Hughes*, vol. 1, p. 133.

200 "He fended off every attempt to probe": Wallace Thurman, *Infants of the Spring* (New York: Macauley, 1932), p. 232.

200 "the thunderclaps of their laughter": Hughes, *Big Sea*, p. 54.

201 "to catch a glimmer of their own beauty": Hughes, "The Negro Artist and the Racial Mountain," *The Nation*, June 23, 1926, p. 694.

201 "Night-dark girl of the swaying hips": Hughes, "Nude Young Dancer," in Rampersad, ed., *Collected Poems*, p. 61.

201 "poet low-rate": *Chicago Whip*, February 26, 1927.

201 "I am a negro": Hughes, "Negro," in Rampersad, ed., *Collected Poems*, p. 24.

202 "brown faced child to her bosom": Hughes, "Aunt Sue's Stories," in Rampersad, ed., *Collected Poems*, pp. 23–24.

203 "swan-song" . . . "song-lit race of slaves": Jean Toomer, *Cane* (New York: W. W. Norton, 1988, orig. pub. 1923), pp. 14, 156.

203 "I had a swell time while it lasted": Hughes, *Big Sea*, p. 228.

204 "What is Africa to me?": Countee Cullen, "Heritage," *Color* (New York: Harper and Brothers, 1925), pp. 36–41.

204 "Does Jazz Put the Sin in Syncopation": Anne Shaw Faulkner, "Does Jazz Put the Sin in Syncopation?" *Ladies' Home Journal,* August 1921, p. 16.

204 "the Dixie Pike has grown from a goat path in Africa": Toomer, *Cane,* p. 12.

205 "[T]hree hundred years of America passed": Robert E. Hemenway, *Zora Neale Hurston: A Literary Biography* (Urbana: University of Illinois Press, 1980), pp. 74–75.

205 "had more to gain from the rich background": Countee Cullen, "Foreword" to Cullen, ed., *Caroling Dusk: An Anthology of Verse by Negro Poets* (New York: Harper and Brothers, 1927), p. xi.

205 "so complex" . . . "one had almost as well be civilized": Rampersad, *Life of Langston Hughes,* vol. 1, p. 160.

205 "even when he appears to be civilized": George Schuyler, "Black Genesis," *The Modern Quarterly* 5:4 (Spring 1929), pp. 571–72.

205–6 "The low beating of the tom-toms": Hughes, "Danse Africaine," in Rampersad, ed., *Collected Poems,* p. 28.

206 "All the tom-toms of the jungles": Hughes, "Poem [1] for the Portrait of an African Boy after the Manner of Gauguin," in Rampersad, ed., *Collected Poems,* p. 32.

208 "It was like throwing a million bricks into the sea": Hughes, *Big Sea,* p. 3.

208 "real thing, to be touched and seen": Hughes, *Big Sea,* p. 10.

208 "the bare, pointed breasts" . . . "the rippling muscles": Hughes, *Big Sea,* p. 102.

208 "You should see the clothes they wear": Rampersad, *Life of Langston Hughes,* vol. 1, pp. 73–74.

208 "It was a gorgeous trip": Hughes, "L'Histoire De Ma Vie," Langston Hughes Papers, Beinecke Library, Yale University, box 303, folder 4982, p. 3.

208 "missionaries carried Bibles" . . . "bolts of cloth": Hughes, *Big Sea,* p. 8.

209 "The Africans were very polite, however": Hughes, *Big Sea,* p. 111.

209 "billowing robes . . . glistening in the sunshine": Hughes, "Ships, Sea and Africa," *The Crisis,* December 1923, pp. 69–71.

210 "the vile houses of rottening women": Hughes, "L'Histoire De Ma Vie," p. 3.

210 "a delightful trip": Hughes to Carrie Hughes, July 21, 1923, Langston Hughes Papers, Beinecke Library, Yale University, box 260, folder 4156.

210 "Old sailors" . . . "the worst trip in the world": Hughes, "L'Histoire De Ma Vie," p. 2.

210 "Could we take him away with us?": Hughes, *Big Sea,* p. 105.

210 "I have a way of not answering letters": Hughes, *Big Sea,* p. 105.

210 "Africa!" . . . "And me a Negro": Hughes, *Big Sea,* p. 10.

211 "mostly as missionaries, to teach us": Hughes, *Big Sea,* p. 103.

211 "hurt me a lot": Hughes, *Big Sea,* p. 11.

211 "the drums of Omali" . . . "too sweet for the taste of man": Hughes, "Burutu Moon," *The Crisis,* June 1925, pp. 64–65.

212 "plowed warmer, more sensual waters": Rampersad, *Life of Langston Hughes,* vol. 1, p. 139.

212 "I write poems about her and destroy them": Hughes, "Luani of the Jungle," in

R. Baxter Miller, ed., *The Collected Works of Langston Hughes, Volume 15, The Short Stories* (Columbia: University of Missouri Press, 2002), p. 425.

213 "mystical vision" . . . "African life on the earth": Rampersad, *Life of Langston Hughes,* vol. 1, pp. 147–48.

213 "throne-like chair" . . . "utterly sincere in living": Hemenway, *Zora Neale Hurston,* pp. 106–7.

213 "winged poet Child" . . . "shining messenger of hope": Rampersad, *Life of Langston Hughes,* vol. 1, p. 149.

213 "golden star in the Firmament of Primitive Peoples": Rampersad, *Life of Langston Hughes,* vol. 1, p. 159.

214 "She wanted me to be primitive and know and feel": Hughes, *Big Sea,* p. 325.

214 "I love you" . . . "I need you very much": Rampersad, *Life of Langston Hughes,* vol. 1, pp. 168–69.

215 "So long / So far away": Hughes, "Afro-American Fragment," in Rampersad, ed., *Collected Poems,* p. 129.

215 "We were no longer in vogue, anyway": Hughes, *Big Sea,* p. 334.

216 "[N]o cultural advance is safe without some sound economic": Alain Locke, "Harlem: Dark Weather-Vane," *Survey Graphic,* August 1936, p. 457.

216 "In the Johannesburg mines": Hughes, "Johannesburg Mines," in Rampersad, ed., *Collected Poems,* p. 43.

217 "Hail Mary, Mother of God! / the new Christ child": Hughes, "Advertisement for the Waldorf Astoria," in Rampersad, ed., *Collected Poems,* pp. 143–46.

217 "Quite truthfully, there was no toilet paper": Rampersad, *Life of Langston Hughes,* vol. 1, p. 246.

218 "looks guilty to me": Rampersad, *Life of Langston Hughes,* vol. 1, p. 259.

218 "The revolutionary poems seem very weak to me": Rampersad, *Life of Langston Hughes,* vol. 1, p. 266.

218 "to laugh and sing and dance and make music": Hughes, "To Negro Writers," in Henry Hart, ed., *American Writers' Congress* (New York: International Publishers, 1935), pp. 139–40.

219 "I am laying off political poetry for a while": Rampersad, *Life of Langston Hughes,* vol. 1, p. 375.

219–20 "singing boatmen on dark rivers" . . . "Jesus in the front rows": Hughes, *Big Sea,* p. 106.

220 "palm oil and cocoa beans" . . . "Hollywood films": Hughes, *Big Sea,* p. 102.

220 "bought up the town": Hughes, *Big Sea,* p. 109.

220 "hoping to make some money" . . . "nobody had a cent": Hughes, *Big Sea,* p. 108.

221 "made of wood and life, energy and death out of Africa": Hughes, *Big Sea,* p. 112.

223 "haunted his hotel the way American youngsters": Arnold Rampersad, *The Life of Langston Hughes (Volume II: 1941–1967): I Dream a World,* second edition (New York: Oxford University Press, 2002), p. 400.

223 "a combination of the most enticing travel folders": Rampersad, *Life of Langston Hughes,* vol. 2, p. 349.

223 "In the new African countries, honest, I thought": Rampersad, *Life of Langston Hughes,* vol. 2, p. 348.

224   "to teach us something": Hughes, *Big Sea*, p. 103.

224   "to offer an *exchange* of knowledge": Rampersad, *Life of Langston Hughes*, vol. 2, p. 355.

224   "The most talented of the young Negro writers": Hughes, "Black Writers in a Troubled World," in Christopher C. De Santis, ed., *The Collected Works of Langston Hughes, Volume 9, Essays on Art, Race, Politics and World Affairs* (Columbia: University of Missouri Press, 2002), p. 475.

225   "If one may ascribe a prime function to any creative writing": Hughes, "Black Writers in a Troubled World," p. 478.

Chapter Six: The Spell of Africa

227   "imbecilities, knavery and pathological virtues": George Schuyler and Theophilus Lewis, "American Foibles," *The Messenger*, April 1924, p. 108.

227   "were not African so much as Dutch and New England": W. E. B. Du Bois, *Dusk of Dawn: Toward an Autobiography of a Race Concept* (New York: Harcourt, Brace and Co., 1940), p. 115.

228   "one direct cultural connection": Du Bois, *Dusk of Dawn*, p. 114. (See also W. E. B. Du Bois, *The Souls of Black Folk* (Boston: Bedford, 1997, orig. pub. 1903), p. 187.

228   "later learning and reaction": Du Bois, *Dusk of Dawn*, p. 115.

229   "racial fount": "Letters from Dr. Du Bois," *The Crisis*, February 1919, p. 166.

229   "rich tropical imagination" . . . "innate love of harmony": Du Bois, *Souls of Black Folk*, pp. 39, 153.

230   "a final crusade for humanity": Du Bois, "The Future of Africa," *Advocate of Peace*, January 1919, p. 13.

230   "the thinking classes of the future Negro world": Du Bois, "The Future of Africa," p. 12.

231   "the natives of Africa must have the right to participate": Du Bois, "The Pan-African Congress," *The Crisis*, April 1919, pp. 273–74.

231   "if the Negroes of the world could have maintained": Du Bois, "My Mission," *The Crisis*, May 1919, pp. 8–9.

231   "ancient common ownership of land": Du Bois, "To the World: Manifesto of the Second Pan-African Congress," *The Crisis*, November 1921, pp. 9–10.

231   "Bolshevism" . . . "rank communism": Du Bois, "A Second Journey to Pan-Africa," *The New Republic*, December 7, 1921, pp. 40–41.

233   "where the American Negroes die like sheep": Du Bois to William Pickett, January 16, 1907, Papers of W. E. B. Du Bois, reel 2/1190-1191.

233   "unless Liberia makes a strong stand": Du Bois to Ernest Lyons, April 15, 1919, papers of W. E. B. Du Bois, Reel 7/1066.

234   "Would it not be a graceful thing if the United States": Du Bois to William H. Lewis, September 20, 1923, Papers of W. E. B. Du Bois, reel 11/214. (See also 11/1217.)

234   "a good chance to play a little politics": Frank Chalk, "Du Bois and Garvey Confront Liberia: Two Incidents of the Coolidge Years," *Canadian Journal of African Studies* 1:2 (November 1963), p. 137.

234   "the highest rank ever given by any country": Du Bois, "Africa," *The Crisis*, April 1924, p. 250.

234   "3:22 p.m." . . . "two low, pale semi-circles": Du Bois, "Africa," p. 248.

235   "ambassador of Pan-Africa": Du Bois, "Pan-Africa in Portugal," *The Crisis*, February 1924, p. 170.

235   "sixth generation in descent from my stolen forefathers": Du Bois, "Africa," p. 248.

235   "designating me as his personal representative": Du Bois, "Africa," p. 251. (See also Papers of W.E.B. Du Bois, Reel 13/927-928.)

236   "technic of civilization": Du Bois, "Back to Africa," *Century Magazine*, February 1923, p. 541.

236   "no business sense, no flair for *real* organization": Du Bois, "Marcus Garvey," *The Crisis*, December 1920, p. 60.

236   "anything to do with the so-called Garvey movement": David Levering Lewis, *W.E.B. Du Bois: The Fight for Equality and the American Century, 1919–1963* (New York: Henry Holt & Co., 2000), p. 69.

236   "constructive plan and program for uplifting": Du Bois, "Marcus Garvey," p. 59.

237   "very serious defects of temperament and training": Du Bois, "Marcus Garvey," pp. 59–60.

237   "unfortunate mulatto who bewails every day": Lewis, *Du Bois: The Fight for Equality*, p. 82.

237   "That is why he likes to dance with white people": Lewis, *Du Bois: The Fight for Equality*, p. 82.

237   "little, fat black man, ugly": Du Bois, "Back to Africa," p. 539.

238   "best natural advantages . . . practically inexhaustible": Ibrahim K. Sundiata, *Black Scandal: America and the Liberian Labor Crisis, 1929–1936* (Philadelphia: Institute for the Study of Human Issues, 1980), p. 19.

239   "far-reaching reform": Du Bois to Harvey Firestone, October 25, 1925, Papers of W. E. B. Du Bois, reel 15/311-312.

239   "[I]f the Firestone Plantations Company wishes it can repeat": Du Bois, "Liberia and Rubber," *The New Republic*, November 18, 1925, p. 329.

239   "I had not then lost faith in the capitalist system": Du Bois, "Liberia, the League and the United States," *Foreign Affairs*, July 1933, p. 684.

240   "full, very full with things that must be said": Du Bois, "Africa," p. 247.

240   "Africa is vegetation. It is the riotous": Du Bois, "Little Portraits of Africa," *The Crisis*, April 1924, p. 273.

240   "star-faced palms and thatched huts": Du Bois, "The Primitive Black Man," *The Nation*, December 17, 1924, p. 675.

240   "palm leaves and mangoes" . . . "coy African modesty": Du Bois, "Little Portraits of Africa," pp. 273–74.

240   "The spell of Africa is upon me. The ancient witchery": Du Bois, "Little Portraits of Africa," p. 274.

241   "black shiny bodies, perfect bodies": Du Bois, "Little Portraits of Africa," p. 273.

241 "I believe that the African form in color and curve": Du Bois, "Little Portraits of Africa," p. 273.

241 "I am riding on the singing heads of black boys": Du Bois, "Little Portraits of Africa," p. 273.

241 "How can I describe it? Neither London nor Paris": Du Bois, "Primitive Black Man," p. 675.

241–42 "Their manners were better than those of Park Lane": Du Bois, "Primitive Black Man," p. 675.

242 "little village was a mighty thing": Du Bois, "The Answer of Africa," in Maurice Maeterlinck et al., *What Is Civilization?* (New York: Duffield, 1926), pp. 45–46.

242 "intertwined collective soul": Du Bois, "Primitive Black Man," p. 676.

242 "no monopoly, no poverty, no prostitution": Du Bois, "Answer of Africa," p. 50.

242 "well-bred and courteous" . . . "sniffling and whining": Du Bois, "Primitive Black Man," p. 675.

242 "naked to the waist" . . . "sex dalliance": Du Bois, "Primitive Black Man," pp. 675–76.

242 "the Eternal World of Black Folk": Du Bois, "Sketches from Abroad: Le Grand Voyage," *The Crisis*, March 1924, p. 203.

245 "Bad sore requires hard medicine": Sundiata, *Black Scandal*, p. 19.

245 "never had a revolution or internal disturbance": Du Bois to Secretary of State Charles E. Hughes, March 24, 1924, Papers of the U.S. State Department, National Archives, record group 59, 882.000/739. (See also Papers of W.E.B. Du Bois, reel 14/258-260.)

245 "This question a little confused him": William R. Castle, Memorandum of Conversation with W. E. B. Du Bois, March 26, 1924, National Archives, RG 59, 882.000/742.

246 "a good deal of what appeared exploitation": Castle, Memorandum of Conversation, National Archives, RG 59, 882.000/742.

246 "endless native servants" . . . "happiness and cheer": Du Bois, "Africa," p. 250.

248 "analogous to those of forced labor": Sundiata, *Black Scandal*, p. 44.

249 "excellent plan of reform": Du Bois, *The Crisis*, November 1932, p. 362.

249 "stand fast": Du Bois, *The Crisis*, November 1933, pp. 260–61.

249 "a piece of smug hypocrisy": Sundiata, *Black Scandal*, p. 22.

249 "a native African": Du Bois, *The Crisis*, March 1931, p. 102.

250 "peace, efficiency, and ability" . . . "human history": Du Bois, "Liberia, the League and the United States," pp. 682–83.

250 "the brutalities of police everywhere": Du Bois, *The Crisis*, December 1932, pp. 387-388.

250 "among the more primitive Liberian tribes" . . . "approximate slavery": Du Bois, "Liberia, the League and the United States," pp. 686–88.

250 "well-bred and courteous children": Du Bois, *Dusk of Dawn*, p. 127.

250 "faces were a mass of sores": Charles Johnson, *Bitter Canaan: The Story of the Negro Republic* (New Brunswick: Transaction Publishers, 1987), p. 216.

252 "to slur, lampoon, damn and occasionally praise": Schuyler and Lewis, "American Foibles," *The Messenger*, April 1924, p. 108.

252 "Ku Klux Klan Uber Alles" . . . "pennant in the Lynching League": Andrew Buni,

Robert Vann of the Pittsburgh Courier: *Politics and Black Journalism* (Pittsburgh: University of Pittsburgh Press, 1974), pp. 137–38.

253 "no desire to assist in the rescuing of humanity": Schuyler, *Pittsburgh Courier,* December 16, 1924, p. 8.

253 "give a whoop": Harry McKinley Williams, "When Black Is Right: The Life and Writings of George S. Schuyler," Ph.D. dissertation, Brown University, 1988, p. 92.

253 "because it has never shown any evidence": Schuyler, *Pittsburgh Courier,* November 22, 1924, p. 16.

253 "to see who would get shafted": Jeffrey B. Ferguson, "The Newest Negro: George Schuyler's Intellectual Quest in the 1920s and Beyond," Ph.D. dissertation, Harvard University, 1998, p. 37.

254 "urge to whiteness": Robert A. Bone, *The Negro Novel in America,* revised edition (New Haven: Yale University Press, 1965), p. 89.

254 "the blackamoor's gifts to the Great Republic": Schuyler, "Our Greatest Gift to America," in V. F. Calverton, ed., *Anthology of American Negro Literature* (New York: The Modern Library, 1929), p. 121.

255 "We cannot decry the Caucasions for their prejudices": Schuyler, *The Messenger,* February 1925, p. 91.

255 "a beautifully lacquered dill pickle": Schuyler, *The Messenger,* January 1924, p. 8.

255 "cut glass thunder-mug": Schuyler, *The Messenger,* March 1925, p. 129.

255–56 "the jungle, plantation or the slum": Schuyler, *The Messenger,* January 1925, p. 9.

256 "salve the conscience of white America for looting": Schuyler, *Pittsburgh Courier,* August 30, 1930, p. 10.

256 "merely a lampblacked Anglo-Saxon": Schuyler, "The Negro Art Hokum," *The Nation,* June 16, 1926, p. 662.

256 "last stand of the old myth palmed off by Negrophobists": Schuyler, "The Negro Art Hokum," p. 663.

257 "open sesame of a pork-colored skin": George S. Schuyler, *Black No More* (New York: The Modern Library, 1999, orig. pub. 1931), p. 19.

258 "scholarly and biting editorials in *The Dilemma*": Schuyler, *Black No More,* p. 65.

258 "uncomfortably savage": Williams, "When Black Is Right," pp. 209–10.

258 "There is something tremendously refreshing and hopeful": Du Bois, *The Crisis,* January 1931, p. 16.

258 "a rollicking, keen, good natured criticism": Du Bois, *The Crisis,* March 1931, p. 100.

259 "the most shiftless, untrustworthy, incompetent": Schuyler, "Slavery in Liberia (Part 5): Missionaries Silent on Liberian Outrages," *Washington Post,* July 3, 1931.

259 "step in and straighten things up": Schuyler, "Slavery in Liberia (Part 6): Reforms are Blocked by Political Influence," *Washington Post,* July 4, 1931.

259 "draw aside the draperies of official camouflage": Schuyler, "Slavery in Liberia (Part 1): Reports on Liberian Slavery Discovered to be Well Founded," *Washington Post,* June 29, 1931.

260 "to enter a totally different world": Schuyler, "Slavery in Liberia (Part 4): Firestone Plantations Found Like America," *Washington Post,* July 2, 1931.

260 "There are times when the masses are actually": Williams, "When Black Is Right," p. 239.
262 "there was only one thing that Liberia had left": Du Bois, *The Crisis*, February 1932, pp. 68–69.
262 "Right is right and wrong is wrong, Dr. Du Bois": Schuyler to Du Bois, January 27, 1932, Papers of W. E. B. Du Bois, reel 39/138. (See also *The Crisis*, March 1932, p. 92.)
263 "with the reactionary, war-mongering": Penny Von Eschen, *Race Against Empire: Black Americans and Anticolonialism, 1937–1957* (Ithaca: Cornell University Press, 1997), p. 117.
264 "machine gun": Williams, "When Black Is Right," p. 317.
264 "hokum and hack work of the purest vein": Ferguson, "The Newest Negro," p. 72.
265 "insane tactics give the murderous Southern": George S. Schuyler, *Black and Conservative: The Autobiography of George S. Schuyler* (New Rochelle: Arlington House Publishers, 1966), p. 192. (The column originally appeared in the *Pittsburgh Courier*, August 15, 1931.)
265 "actual civil war which would certainly lead to genocide": Schuyler, *Black and Conservative*, p. 344.
265 "three-century struggle to avoid extermination": Schuyler, "Negroes Reject Communism," *American Mercury*, June 1939, pp. 176–77, 181.
265 "well-intentioned politician who was appalled": Schuyler, *Black and Conservative*, p. 330.
266 "hapless aggregations of people": Schuyler, *Black and Conservative*, p. 337.
266 "demagogue with a Napolean complex": Schuyler, "Kruschchev's African Foothold," *American Mercury*, March 1959, p. 59.
266 "international retardates" . . . "investment and direction": Schuyler, *Black and Conservative*, p. 338.
266 "welfare colonialism": Ferguson, "The Newest Negro," p. 10.
266 "sable Typhoid Mary, infecting the mentally disturbed": Schuyler, *Manchester Union Leader*, November 10, 1964, p. 1.
267 "three great untwisted negro intellects": Williams, "When Black Is Right," p. 351.

Chapter Seven: Native Son, American Daughter

270 "What was it that made me conscious": Richard Wright, *Black Boy (American Hunger): A Record of Childhood and Youth*, restored text (New York: HarperPerennial, 1993, orig. pub. 1945), p. 494.
270 "Dear Madam: Will you please let this nigger": Wright, *Black Boy*, p. 291.
270 "great forces that circumscribe and condition personality": H. L. Mencken, quoted in Hazel Rowley, *Richard Wright: The Life and Times* (New York: Henry Holt, 2001), p 46.
270 "All my life had shaped me for the realism": Wright, *Black Boy*, p. 295.
271 "Negroes had never been allowed to catch the full spirit": Wright, *Black Boy*, p. 43.
271 "My first glimpses of the flat black stretches": Wright, *Black Boy (American Hunger)*, p. 307.
273 "I had fled [the South] with the dumb yearning to write": Richard Wright, "Introduc-

tion" to St. Clair Drake and Horace R. Cayton, *Black Metropolis: A Study of Negro Life in a Northern City* (New York: Harper and Row, 1962, orig. pub. 1945), volume 1, p. xvii.

274   "the day *Native Son* appeared": Irving Howe, "Black Boys and Native Sons," *Dissent* 10:4 (Autumn 1963), p. 355.

274   "quite as human as it is Negro": Quoted in Paul Gilroy, *The Black Atlantic: Modernity and Double Consciousness* (Cambridge, Mass.: Harvard University Press, 1993), p. 153.

275   "naked black men and women": Richard Wright, *Native Son* (New York: HarperPerennial, 1993, orig. pub. 1940), pp. 36–37.

276   "Oppression oppresses": Richard Wright, Foreword to George Padmore, *Pan-Africanism or Communism: The Coming Struggle for Africa* (New York: Roy Publishers, 1956), p. 12.

276   "become a tradition, in fact a kind of culture": Wright, Foreword to *Pan-Africanism or Communism*, p. 13.

278   "how the brown, red, and yellow people are faring": Rowley, *Richard Wright*, pp. 235–36.

278   "I must see Africa": Rowley, *Richard Wright*, p. 417.

280   "by the strength of their arms": Era Bell Thompson, *American Daughter* (St. Paul: Minnesota Historical Society Press, 1986, orig. pub. 1946), p. 173.

280   "Perhaps I had waited too long": Wright, *Black Boy*, p. 176.

280   "more comfortable" . . . "more accepted": Interview with Era Bell Thompson in Ruth Edmonds Hill, ed., *The Black Women Oral History Project* (Westport: Meckler Publishing, 1978), vol. 9, p. 453.

281   "became a symbol of the South": Thompson, *American Daughter*, p. 113.

281   "Where is North Dakota?": Era Bell Thompson, "What's a Nice Girl Like You Doing in a Place Like That?" *North Dakota Horizons* 3:1 (Spring 1973), p. 26.

282   "There is nothing of Richard Wright": Louise H. Elder, "Minority Saga," *Phylon* 7:3 (Fall 1946), p. 307.

282   "Here is an autobiography by a Negro": Arthur P. Davis, "Current Literature on Negro Education," *Journal of Negro Education* 15:4 (Autumn 1946), p. 647.

282   "I know . . . that way down underneath": Thompson, *American Daughter*, p. 296.

283   "negativism and advocacy": Ben Burns, *Nitty Gritty: A White Editor in Black Journalism* (Jackson: University Press of Mississippi, 1996), p. 88.

283   "to chronicle in a positive, informative and entertaining": Burns, *Nitty Gritty*, p. 126.

283   "We're rather jolly folks": Burns, *Nitty Gritty*, pp. 88–89.

284   "subconsciously disliked" . . . "root cause": Burns, *Nitty Gritty*, p. 118.

285   "standard of living" . . . "civil rights": Burns, *Nitty Gritty*, pp. 106, 137.

285   "the essential bleakness of black life": Wright, *Black Boy*, p. 43.

285   "striking out in blind fury": Burns, *Nitty Gritty*, pp. 169–70.

286   "I tell you frankly that there is more freedom": Burns, *Nitty Gritty*, p. 171.

286   "the United States the glorious democracy it is": Burns, *Nitty Gritty*, p. 126.

286   "big time newspapers and magazine correspondents": Era Bell Thompson, *Africa, Land of My Fathers* (Garden City, N.Y.: Doubleday & Co., 1954), p. 18.

287   "[M]y knowledge of the continent": Thompson, *Land of My Fathers*, p. 16.

287   "savages with rings in their noses": Thompson, *American Daughter*, p. 245.

287   "had anyone called me an African": Thompson, *Land of My Fathers*, p. 16.

287 "receive a prodigal daughter": Thompson, *Land of My Fathers*, pp. 10–11.

287 "the world's biggest Negro processor and grower": *Ebony*, December, 1953, p. 73.

288 "Once the greatest brasswork craftsmen": *Ebony*, September 1953, p. 75.

288 "Africa's most momentous meeting since": *Ebony*, June 1953, p. 15.

288 "It had its social highlights too": *Ebony*, June 1953, p. 15.

289 "A carrier pigeon service, with houseboys": Thompson, *Land of My Fathers*, p. 24.

289 "My first reaction to my aborigine brothers": Thompson, *Land of My Fathers*, p. 20.

289 "the positive side of the ledger": Thompson, *Land of My Fathers*, p. 23.

289 "like a scene from a Katherine Dunham dance": Thompson, *Land of My Fathers*, p. 52.

289 "Here, indeed, was proof": Thompson, *Land of My Fathers*, pp. 53–54.

289 "lacked the robust progressiveness of Lagos": Thompson, *Land of My Fathers*, p. 69.

289 "handsome, dreamy-eyed, and wistful": Thompson, *Land of My Fathers*, pp. 44–45.

289 "cold, calculating calmness": Thompson, *Land of My Fathers*, p. 76.

290 "to make bush people feel at home": Thompson, *Land of My Fathers*, p. 146.

290 "conduct[ing] a seminar": Thompson, *Land of My Fathers*, p. 113.

290 "a true picture of American life": Thompson, *Land of My Fathers*, p. 162.

291 "highly developed mentally": Thompson, *Land of My Fathers*, p. 142.

291 "most beautiful black woman I had ever seen": Thompson, *Land of My Fathers*, p. 134.

291 "for all the world like a Harlem businessman": Thompson, *Land of My Fathers*, p. 137.

292 "return of this native was quickening": Thompson, *Land of My Fathers*, p. 204.

293 "the influx of the American negro": James T. Campbell, *Songs of Zion: The African Methodist Episcopal Church in the United States and South Africa* (New York: Oxford University Press, 1995), pp. 139–40.

294 "That was my first trip to Africa": Hill, ed., *Black Women Oral History Project*, vol. 9, p. 460.

294 "Two months in Africa had made me feel": Thompson, *Land of My Fathers*, p. 188.

295 "From high in the sky, Addis Ababa": Thompson, *Land of My Fathers*, p. 252.

295 "a great big beautiful American": Thompson, *Land of My Fathers*, p. 243.

295 "Free again. Once more my country": Thompson, *Land of My Fathers*, p. 243.

295 "No more interviews and notes": Thompson, *Land of My Fathers*, p. 271.

295 "Cleansed of the red dust of Africa": Thompson, *Land of My Fathers*, p. 272.

295 "one good American firecracker": Thompson, *Land of My Fathers*, p. 276.

295 "returned to the moonlit balcony": Thompson, *Land of My Fathers*, p. 272.

296 "Now that your desk is clear": Richard Wright, *Black Power: A Record of Reactions in a Land of Pathos* (New York: Harper and Brothers, 1954), p. 3.

296 "vague sense of disquiet": Wright, *Black Power*, p. 6.

296 "What would my feelings be when I looked": Wright, *Black Power*, p. 4.

296 "I'm going": Wright, *Black Power*, p. 7.

296 "concepts that one would use in observing": Wright, *Black Power*, pp. xiv–xv.

297 "The ocean seemed to possess a quiet": Wright, *Black Power*, pp. 20–21.

297 "were built of human flesh and blood": Wright, *Black Power*, p. 11.

297 "the African newspaper men": Richard Wright, unpublished Gold Coast journal, Pa-

pers of Richard Wright, Beinecke Library, Yale University, box 22, folders 337-347 (hereafter Wright journal), June 5, 1953.

297 "rendezvous with the twentieth century": Wright journal, June 5.

298 "stammer and grope": Wright journal, June 7.

298 "black as the ace of spades": Wright journal, June 3.

298–99 "tribal rabble . . . running naked in the bush": Wright, *Black Power*, p. 15–16.

299 "I struggled against an oblique sympathy": Wright, *Black Power*, p. 27.

299 "mudhole . . . free from anything smacking of humanity": Wright journal, June 13.

299 "streets clogged with black life": Wright, *Black Power*, pp. 36–40, 46, ff.

299 "tremendous prestige": George Padmore to Kwame Nkrumah, April 14, 1953, Michel Fabre Papers, Emory University.

299–300 "frenzied assent" . . . "filled the vacuum" . . . "teeming millions": Wright, *Black Power*, pp. 53–54, 60, 65, 77, ff.

300 "I cannot escape the feeling": Wright, *Black Power*, pp. 136–37.

300 "All my life I've asked for this": Wright journal, June 19.

301 "enervated, listless" . . . "chucking up the whole thing": Wright journal, June 23–24.

301 "I lost all interest in the Gold Coast": Wright journal, July 2.

301 "There's nothing here for me now": Wright journal, July 2.

301 "Thinking back on the spectacle": Wright journal, July 3.

301 "Funny creature that I am": Wright journal, July 3.

302 "I suspect that my attitude caused": Wright, *Black Power*, p. 137.

302 "the fateful subjective emotional relationship": Richard Wright, "The Neuroses of Conquest," *The Nation*, October 20, 1956, pp. 330–31.

303 "[D]istrust had become enthroned": Wright, *Black Power*, p. 101.

303 "childlike . . . mania for hiding the facts": Wright, *Black Power*, p. 106.

303 "All that the African personality seemed": Wright, *Black Power*, p. 104.

303 "Eroded personalities loom here": Wright, *Black Power*, p. 153.

303 "given up hope of getting close to the political boys": Wright journal, July 14.

303 "the kind of hotel one read about": Wright, *Black Power*, pp. 80–81.

304 "miss a lot" . . . "no time to dress up": Wright, *Black Power*, pp. 140–41.

304 "psychologically detribalized Africans living": Wright, *Black Power*, p. 69.

304 "in secrecy and shame": Wright, *Black Power*, p. 65.

304 "fetish-ridden past": Wright, *Black Power*, p. 170.

304 "The over-all impression was that black": Wright, *Black Power*, p. 67.

304 "What innocence of instincts": Wright, *Black Power*, p. 39.

305 "sex was so blatantly prevalent": Wright, *Black Power*, p. 39.

305 "no sighing, longing or other romantic notions": Wright, *Black Power*, p. 116.

305 "huge wobbly white bags, like the full udders": Wright, *Black Boy*, pp. 7–8.

305 "flopping loosely and grotesquely in the sun": Wright, *Black Power*, p. 129.

305 "flat and remarkably" . . . "pressure of babies": Wright, *Black Power*, p. 38.

305 "inevitable baby" . . . "tossed it over their shoulder": Wright, *Black Power*, pp. 39, 48.

305 "vast black mirror" . . . "what is Africa to me": Wright journal, June 30.

306 "Either what I'm looking at": Wright journal, June 30.

306 "The gold can be replaced": Wright, *Black Power*, p. 153.

306 "The chiefs are and were, one and all": Wright, *Black Power*, pp. 307–8.

306 "involuntary emotional slavery" . . . "fabulous power structure": Wright, *Black Power*, p. 284.

307 "a waste of good gin": Wright journal, June 3.

307 "a frightful kind of baby talk": Wright, *Black Power*, pp. 191–92.

307 "a vast purgatorial kingdom": Wright, *Black Power*, p. 283.

307 "all mixed up, blended": Wright, *Black Power*, pp. 151–52.

307 "The specialty of this establishment": Wright, *Black Power*, pp. 107–8.

308 "I looked at the guide": Thompson, *Land of My Fathers*, p. 98.

308 "Dear Kwame" . . . "My journey's done": Wright, *Black Power*, p. 342.

308–9 "the necessary hardness for the task": Wright, *Black Power*, p. 343.

309 "AFRICAN LIFE MUST BE MILITARIZED": Wright, *Black Power*, p. 347.

309 "not speaking of a military dictatorship": Wright, *Black Power*, p. 347.

309 "atomize the fetish-ridden past": Wright, *Black Power*, p. 348.

309 "By going from spot to spot": Michel Fabre, *The Unfinished Quest of Richard Wright*, second edition (Urbana: University of Illinois Press, 1993), p. 403.

310 "omniscient hand of Moscow": Wright, *Black Power*, p. xiv.

310 "In fact, it can be definitely stated": Wright, *Black Power*, p. xii.

310 "conscientiously modeled" . . . "upon the Russian": Rowley, *Richard Wright*, pp. 436–37.

310 "picturesque travelog" . . . "weighty social": John Reilly, ed., *Richard Wright: The Critical Reception* (New York: Burt Franklin & Co., 1978), p. 262.

310 "Mr. Wright's own emotional processes": Reilly, ed., *Richard Wright: The Critical Reception*, p. 242.

310 "*Black Power* is almost as tortured and tortuous": Reilly, ed., *Richard Wright: The Critical Reception*, p. 259.

311 "in the willingness of nations to take up modern ideas": Richard Wright, *The Color Curtain: A Report on the Bandung Conference* (New York: World Publishing, 1956), p. 199.

311 "I do say 'Bravo' to the consequences": Amrit Singh, "Introduction to the Harper-Perennial Edition," *Black Power* (New York: HarperPerennial, 1995), p. xxvi.

312 "I'm about the only 'uncontrolled' Negro alive": Fabre, *Unfinished Quest*, p. 500.

312 "wishes to know in what way Ghana would like": Fabre, *Unfinished Quest*, pp. 496, 617–18.

314 "comparing the Africa that was colonized": Hill, ed., *Black Women Oral History Project*, vol. 9, p. 461.

Chapter Eight: Black Star

315 "He didn't know what kind of doctor I was": Robert Lee, interview with author, August 1993.

317 "the book that did more than any other": Kwame Nkrumah, *Ghana: The Autobiography of Kwame Nkrumah* (New York: International Publishers, 1971, orig. pub. 1957), p. 45.

317 "not very bright": C. L. R. James, ""Kwame Nkrumah: Founder of African Emancipation," in James, *At the Rendezvous of Victory: Selected Writings* (London: Allison and
Busby, 1984), p. 258.

318 "appreciation of your efforts": Kevin Gaines, *American Africans in Ghana: Black Expatriates and the Civil Rights Era* (Chapel Hill, University of North Carolina Press, 2006),
p. 67.

318 "Ghana's contributions, as a free nation": James H. Meriwether, *Proudly We Can Be
Africans: Black Americans and Africa, 1935–1961* (Chapel Hill: University of North
Carolina Press, 2002), p. 162.

318 "Proudly We Can Be Africans": Meriwether, *Proudly We Can Be Africans*, p. 163.

319 "How does it feel to be free?": Gaines, *American Africans in Ghana*, p. 5.

320 "shared none of her father's aversions": David Levering Lewis, "Ghana, 1963: A
Memoir," *The American Scholar* 68:1 (Winter 1999), p. 47.

324 "It's my name": Lee, interview with author, August 1993.

325 "I thought it was his barbershop": Lee, interview with author, August 1993.

326 "I realized that they knew things": Lee, interview with author, August 1993.

327 "I don't understand niggers": Lee, interview with author, December 1994.

327 "Finally, I had enough of Georgia": Lee, interview with author, December 1994.

327 "hemmed in, growing up thinking": Lee, interview with author, December 1994.

327 "She didn't like racial discrimination either": Lee, interview with author, August 1993.

328 "You could feel, when you came here": Lee, quoted in Ernest Dunbar, ed., *The Black
Expatriates: A Study of American Negroes in Exile* (New York: E.P. Dutton & Co.,
1968), p. 75.

328 "I didn't come here because": Lee, interview with author, August 1993.

331 "I got to the point where I rejected": Bill Sutherland, quoted in Dunbar, ed., *The Black
Expatriates*, p. 91.

331 "seeking his own salvation": Sutherland, quoted in Dunbar, ed., *The Black Expatriates*,
p. 109.

332 "I really misjudged the situation": Sutherland, interview with author, May 2003.

333 "[I]t wasn't my job to take care of": Bill Sutherland and Matt Meyer, *Guns and Gandhi
in Africa: Pan-African Insights on Nonviolence, Armed Struggle, and Liberation* (Trenton,
N.J.: Africa World Press, 2000), p. 43.

333 "a sledgehammer to kill a gnat": Sutherland, interview with author, May 2003.

334 "the lights of liberty": Sutherland and Meyer, *Guns and Gandhi*, p. 46.

335 "Capitalism cannot reform itself": David Levering Lewis, *W.E.B. Du Bois: The Fight
for Equality and the American Century, 1919–1963* (New York: Henry Holt & Co., 2000),
p. 567.

337 "their own interests lay in the overthrow": Dorothy Hunton, *Alphaeus Hunton: The
Unsung Valiant* (New York: D. K. Hunton, 1986), p. 56.

339 "to the level of taking anything": Hunton, *Alphaeus Hunton*, p. 94.

340 "There's something else that makes me hesitate": Hunton, *Alphaeus Hunton*, p. 101.

343 "I have been in Sorrow's kitchen": Zora Neale Hurston, *Dust Tracks on a Road: An Autobiography* (Urbana: University of Illinois Press, 1984, orig. pub. 1942), p. 280.

344 "with the intention of finding a strong": Maya Angelou, *The Heart of a Woman* (New York: Random House, 1981), p. 138.

344 "might be betraying the entire struggle": Angelou, *The Heart of a Woman*, p. 140.

345 "imperialists and neo-colonialists": Shirley Graham Du Bois, *What Happened in Ghana: The Inside Story* (New York: Freedomways, 1966), p. 203.

345 "there were stresses and strains": Shirley Du Bois, *What Happened in Ghana*, pp. 218–19.

346 "fraught with ambiguities": Gaines, *American Africans in Ghana*, p. 143.

347 "you are there because you hated America": Leslie Alexander Lacy, *The Rise and Fall of a Proper Negro* (New York: Macmillan, 1970), p. 161.

348 "Every instance of racial prejudice": Meriwether, *Proudly We Can Be Africans*, p. 167.

349 "The only thing I can't understand": Gaines, *American Africans in Ghana*, p. 150.

350 "Is This America the Beautiful": Gaines, *American Africans in Ghana*, p. 166.

351 "The Europeans and the Americans love me": *The African Review* 1:1 (May 1965), p. 7.

351 "hypocritical savagery of Africa's enemies": *The African Review* 1:1 (May 1965), p. 6.

351 "If you have no history, invent one": *Newsweek*, October 31, 1960, cited in Gaines, *American Africans in Ghana*, p. 126.

352 "booing and hissing": Alice Windom, remarks at a conference on "Malcolm X: Radical Tradition and a Legacy of Struggle," New York, November 1990. (Audio recording at http://www.brothermalcolm.net/sections/malcolm/contents.html.)

353 "The President's office was like": LeRoy S. Hodges, Jr., *Portrait of an Expatriate: William Gardner Smith, Writer* (Westport, Conn.: Greenwood Press, 1985), p. 79.

354 "Detroit Red": Vicki Garvin, remarks at a conference on "Malcolm X: Radical Tradition and a Legacy of Struggle," New York, November 1990. (Audio recording at http://www.brothermalcolm.net/sections/malcolm/contents.html.)

354 "stooge" . . . "C.I.A.": Windom, "Malcolm X: Radical Tradition."

354 "she was absolutely captivated": Windom, "Malcolm X: Radical Tradition."

355 "How do you unify with Uncle Toms": Windom: "Malcolm X: Radical Tradition."

355 "the beginning of a new phase": Windom, "Malcolm X: Radical Tradition."

355 "let that jazz [in America] cool off": Hodges, *Portrait of an Expatriate*, p. 78.

356 "Long live Ghana": Du Bois, *What Happened in Ghana*, p. 213.

357 "a scene from Dante's *Inferno*": Shirley Du Bois, *What Happened in Ghana*, p. 219.

359 "The passion my people would exhibit": Maya Angelou, *A Song Flung Up To Heaven* (New York: Random House, 2002), pp. 7–8.

361 "gradual withdrawal into injured despondency": Hunton, *Alphaeus Hunton*, pp. 169–70.

362 "decide if you wanted to play for keeps": "Conversations with St. Clair Drake" (video recording), October 1980, Northwestern University Library, reel 4.

363 "[N]ot by a long shot": Lee, quoted in Dunbar, ed., *The Black Expatriates*, pp. 84–85.

363 "I think that my children": Lee, quoted in Dunbar, ed., *The Black Expatriates*, p. 81.

364 "his current problems would soon be over": Mike Adjei, *Death and Pain: Rawling's Ghana, the Inside Story* (London: Black Line, 1994), p. 82.

364 "everybody thinks I should be angry": Lee, interview with author, August, 1993.

Chapter Nine: Counting the Bodies

365   "Because this is Africa, and they don't count": Keith B. Richburg, *Out of America: A Black Man Confronts Africa* (New York: Basic Books, 1997), p. 100.

373   "look like me": Richburg, *Out of America*, p. xi.

373   "devoid of hope . . . drained of compassion": Richburg, *Out of America*, p. 27.

373   "a particularly 'black' childhood": Richburg, *Out of America*, p. 10.

373   "I want you to see this": Richburg, *Out of America*, p. 12.

375   "voluntary resegregation" . . . "the dining hall test": Richburg, *Out of America*, pp. 17–18.

375   "face in the crowd": Richburg, *Out of America*, p. 21.

375   "to choose which side of the dining hall": Richburg, *Out of America*, p. 20.

375   "well-meaning academics and Africa specialists": Richburg, *Out of America*, p. 238.

376   "teetering between strongman rule and violent": Richburg, *Out of America*, p. 53.

376   "where the United Nations, freed from Cold War": "After the War: Transcript of President Bush's Address on the End of the Gulf War," *New York Times*, March 7, 1991.

376   "backward-looking attitude": Richburg, *Out of America*, p. 180.

377   "a nation in meltdown": Richburg, *Out of America*, p. 51.

378   "If ever there was a reason for being in Africa": Richburg, *Out of America*, p. 52.

378   "The world, and Washington policy makers specifically": Richburg, *Out of America*, p. 52.

378   "to raise the flag for a new kind of American": Richburg, *Out of America*, p. 59.

378   "desire to relieve human suffering": Richburg, *Out of America*, p. 59.

378   "marveled at the pinpoint accuracy" . . . "scatter in terror": Richburg, *Out of America*, p. 59.

379   "the perfect ringside seat on Africa's chaos": Richburg, *Out of America*, p. 9.

379   "any of the handful of sleazy bars": Richburg, *Out of America*, p. 9.

380   "rampant cynicism": Richburg, *Out of America*, p. 39.

380   "Africa's dumbest country": Richburg, *Out of America*, p. 38.

380   *"Baboons with Rifles"*: Richburg, *Out of America*, p. 31.

380   "It wears you down" . . . "on a treadmill": Richburg, *Out of America*, p. 39.

380   "I was always on the outside looking in": Richburg, *Out of America*, p. 55.

381   "We all found it hilarious and played it": Richburg, *Out of America*, p. 71.

381   "humanitarian mission" . . . "egotistical baldheaded warlord": Richburg, *Out of America*, p. 74.

382   "protected little journalistic universe": Richburg, *Out of America*, p. 83.

382   "letting the anger roil up again": Richburg, *Out of America*, p. 83.

382   "reason for being a reporter in Africa": Richburg, *Out of America*, pp. 88–89.

382   "and I'm hating them, the Somalis": Richburg, *Out of America*, p. 89.

382   "the start of a bitter wake-up call": Richburg, *Out of America*, p. 64.

382–83   "prism" . . . "the rest of Africa": Richburg, *Out of America*, p. 53.

383   "buffoons and misfits": Richburg, *Out of America*, p. 220.

383   "civilized behavior between human beings": Richburg, *Out of America*, p. 41.

383   "moral clarity" . . . "vexing emotional and moral": Richburg, *Out of America*, p. 21.

383 "that looked and smelled" . . . "supermodern freeways . . . shopping malls": Richburg, *Out of America*, pp. 195–96.

383 "It's an illusion, because no matter how": Richburg, *Out of America*, p. 210.

383 "I've been there" . . . "I've seen it": Richburg, *Out of America*, p. 169.

383 "Is this depressing you?" . . . "rotting corpses": Richburg, *Out of America*, pp. x–xi.

383–84 "I'm tired of lying . . . around amid the corpses": Richburg, *Out of America*, p. xii.

384 "the potential for a violent implosion": Richburg, *Out of America*, p. 104.

384 "fully evolved human beings": Richburg, *Out of America*, p. 90.

384 "breeding ground for myriad viruses": Richburg, *Out of America*, p. 127.

384 "rampant prostitution and the Africans' free": Richburg, *Out of America*, p. 123.

384 "the norms and rules and codes of conduct": Richburg, *Out of America*, p. 49.

384 "heroism, honor and dignity": Richburg, *Out of America*, p. xiv.

384 "endless little acts of kindness": Richburg, *Out of America*, p. 32.

385 "something in the nature of Africans": Richburg, *Out of America*, p. 175.

385 "maddening propensity to accept all kinds of suffering": Richburg, *Out of America*, p. 181.

385 "aid dollar dole": Richburg, *Out of America*, p. 178.

385 "the same way many American blacks see": Richburg, *Out of America*, p. 180.

385 "most Africans were born in independent": Richburg, *Out of America*, p. 180.

385 "hanker after Mother Africa, as if ": Richburg, *Out of America*, p. 158.

385 "self-anointed spokesmen": Richburg, *Out of America*, p. 180.

385 "one of the great leader-servants": Richburg, *Out of America*, p. 138.

386 "Maybe I would have been better off ": Richburg, *Out of America*, p. 153.

386 "hoping to feel that same kind of spiritual": Richburg, *Out of America*, p. 161.

386 "revulsion at the horrendous crime of slavery": Richburg, *Out of America*, p. 161.

386 "little personal connection" . . . "so unspeakable, so unthinkable": Richburg, *Out of America*, p. 162.

386 "not making a defense of slavery" . . . "should not inhibit us": Richburg, *Out of America*, p. xiii.

387 "And why should I feel anything more": Richburg, *Out of America*, p. 247.

387 "Maybe I would care more if I had never come": Richburg, *Out of America*, p. 247.

388 "The way I grew up, issues of civil rights": Lynne Duke, interview with author, July 2005.

388 "grass skirts, Tarzan, bare breasts, [and] starving people": Lynne Duke, interview with author, July 2005.

388 "normality and humanity": Lynne Duke, *Mandela, Mobutu, and Me: A Newswoman's African Journey* (New York: Doubleday 2003), p. 176.

388 "the poetry of ordinary Africa": Duke, *Mandela, Mobutu, and Me*, p. 176.

388 "in a strong African American family": Howard French, *A Continent for the Taking: The Tragedy and Hope of Africa* (New York: Knopf, 2004), p. 5.

389 "beauty and unfussy grace of the people": French, *Continent for the Taking*, p. 239.

389 "to distrust this concept of authenticity": French, *Continent for the Taking*, p. 6.

389 "many foreign correspondents tearing their hair out": French, *Continent for the Taking*, p. 82.

389 "theater of misery and suffering": French, *Continent for the Taking*, p. 202.

389 "the kinds of stories of African people and culture": French, *Continent for the Taking*, p. 239.

389 "of understanding, or at least of feeling": French, *Continent for the Taking*, p. 82.

390 "Disney-fied cradle of civilization": French, "An Ignorance of Africa as Vast as the Continent," *New York Times*, November 20, 1994.

390 "in the emotional throes of the 'motherland'": Duke, *Mandela, Mobutu, and Me*, p. 255.

390 "the space between the archetypes": Duke, *Mandela, Mobutu, and Me*, p. 9.

390 "a new Africa in the making": Duke, *Mandela, Mobutu, and Me*, p. 35.

390 "symbiotic relationship" . . . "South Africa's progress to the world": Duke, *Mandela, Mobutu, and Me*, p. 30.

391 "Of course, I know the history of the C.I.A.'s complicity": Richburg, *Out of America*, p. 102.

392 "peace, prosperity, and greatness" . . . "Rights of Man": Patrice Lumumba, speech on Independence Day, June 30, 1960.

393 "cultural originality": French, "An Ignorance of Africa."

395 "getting their first taste of Africa": French, *Continent for the Taking*, p. 50.

395 "yet here I was, just like everyone else": French, *Continent for the Taking*, p. 59.

396 "a flicker on the screen of the world's conscience": French, "Sure, Ebola Is Bad. Africa Has Worse," *New York Times*, June 11, 1995.

396 "savage African diseases ready to break out": British *Sunday Telegraph*, quoted in French, "Sure, Ebola Is Bad."

396 "cinematically compelling" . . . "projectile vomiting": French, *Continent for the Taking*, p. 58.

396 "human catastrophe or primordial exoticism": French, "Sure, Ebola is Bad."

397 "If we use the word 'genocide' and are seen as doing nothing": Susan Rice, quoted in French, *Continent for the Taking*, p. 127.

399 "the scramble to do some rudimentary ethnic": French, *Continent for the Taking*, p. 128.

399 "[F]or many of us on assignment here": French, *Continent for the Taking*, p. 128.

400 "They are the bad guys": French, *Continent for the Taking*, p. 142.

401 "swashbuckling self-image": Duke, *Mandela, Mobutu, and Me*, p. 125.

401 "There are many bodies in the mountains": Duke, *Mandela, Mobutu, and Me*, pp. 139–40. (See also Duke, "Size, Scope of Hutu Crisis Hotly Debated; Refugees Caught in Eastern Zaire Crisis," *Washington Post*, November 24, 1996.)

401 "private release" . . . "around a male colleague": Duke, *Mandela, Mobutu, and Me*, p. 60.

402 "personal talisman" . . . "most remarkable sons": Duke, *Mandela, Mobutu, and Me*, p. 274.

402 "had now settled into a spiral of bloody traumas": French, *Continent for the Taking*, p. 50.

402 "patterns of treachery and betrayal": French, *Continent for the Taking*, p. xv.

403 "open markets, honest government, and the rule of law": French, "On Visit to Congo, Albright Praises the New Leader," *New York Times*, December 13, 1997; see also French, "Albright in Africa: The Embraceable Regimes?" *New York Times*, December 16, 1997.

403 "Long live democracy. Ha-ha-ha": French, *Continent for the Taking*, p. 248.

404 "Serving up atrocities is a business": French, *Continent for the Taking*, p. 254.

Epilogue: The Language We Cry In

406 "quick Dispatch" . . . "your Voyage depends on their health": Samuel and William Vernon to Caleb Gardner, November 8, 1755, Vernon Papers, New York Historical Society, box 1.

406 "Good order": Caleb Gardner to Samuel and William Vernon, April 8, 1756, Vernon Papers, New York Historical Society, box 1.

406 "But porr order" . . . "Shall miss of my Expectation": Caleb Godfrey to Samuel and William Vernon, June 25, 1756, Vernon Papers, New York Historical Society, box 1.

407 "[R]eally they are a wretched cargo": Henry Laurens to Samuel and William Vernon, July 5, 1756, *The Papers of Henry Laurens*, volume 2 (Columbia: South Carolina Historical Society, 1968), pp. 238–39.

407 "a Cargo of Likely and Healthy Slaves": *South Carolina Gazette*, June 17, 1756.

408 "There are five things we don't talk about": Edward Ball, *Slaves in the Family* (New York: Ballantine, 1998), p. 7.

416 "He killed my ma, he killed ma pa": Helene Cooper, "The Other Election: This Month, All Eyes Turn to Liberia," *New York Times*, October 17, 2005.

417 "a family man, a man of God": Tom Kamara, "Diamonds, War and State Collapse in Liberia and Sierra Leone," http://www.theperspective.org/statecollapse.

417 "because he's intelligent, he knows what sells here": Jon Lee Anderson, "The Devil They Know," *The New Yorker*, July 27, 1998.

432 "them poor and they could not git things": Rosalind Cobb Wiggins, ed., *Captain Paul Cuffe's Logs and Letters, 1808–1817* (Washington, D.C.: Howard University Press, 1996), p. 342.

· BIBLIOGRAPHIC ESSAY ·

A book that ranges across three centuries inevitably intersects with a wide range of scholarly questions and debates. For the most part, I have tried to address such issues implicitly, so as not to divert attention from the experiences of the historical actors themselves. The purpose of this essay is to make some of these issues explicit, and to identify a few of the sources that I have found useful in thinking about them.

As originally conceived, *Middle Passages* was to be a study of **travel writing**. Specifically, I was interested in what happened when a literary form as suffused with racial and imperial ideologies as the nineteenth-century African travelers' account was appropriated by writers who were themselves African or of African descent. The book's focus changed considerably in the course of writing, but something of this original conception survives. My interest in travel writing was first piqued by Mary Louise Pratt, *Imperial Eyes: Travel Writing and Trans-culturation* (New York: Routledge, 1992) and Johannes Fabian, *Time and the Other: How Anthropology Makes Its Object* (New York: Columbia University Press, 1983). For a thorough, if somewhat uncritical, introduction to the "Dark Continent" tradition, see Christopher Hibbert, *Africa Explored: Europeans in the Dark Continent, 1769–1889* (London: Allen Lane, 1982). In the course of researching this book, I was astonished by how often African American travelers referenced the canonical works of this tradition, most notably the works of Mungo Park, David Livingstone, and, above all, H. M. Stanley.

There is less work that focuses explicitly on **African American travel writing**, but Farah Griffin's edited anthology, *A Stranger in the Village: Two Centuries of African-American Travel Writing* (Boston: Beacon, 1998) offers a host of useful suggestions. I also had the good fortune of participating in a 2004 workshop at the University of Maryland on "African American Identity Travels," organized by Elsa Barkley Brown and Mary Helen Washington, where I had the opportunity to engage with other scholars working on African American travel writing. I would like particularly to acknowledge presentations by Julius Scott ("Travel and the Origins of the Black Atlantic"), Sandra Gunning ("Imperial Subjectivity, Gender and Nineteenth-Century West Indian Emigration to Africa: The Case of Robert

Campbell's *A Pilgrimage to My Motherland*"), Penny Von Eschen ("Goodwill Ambassador: Duke Ellington and Black Worldliness"), and Maureen Mahon ("Eslanda Goode Robeson's *African Journey* and the Diasporic Politics of Identification").

Scarcely a week went by when I did not stumble on another **African American travel account of Africa,** few of which I was ultimately able to include in the book. Individuals interested in pursuing the topic further would do well to consult Marita Golden, *Migrations of the Heart* (New York: Ballantine Books, 1987); Eddy L. Harris, *Native Stranger: A Black American's Journey into the Heart of Africa* (New York: Simon & Schuster, 1992); Alexander Camphor, *Missionary Story Sketches, Folk-tales from Africa* (Cincinnati: Jennings and Graham, 1909); William Henry Heard, *The Bright Side of African Life* (New York: Negro Universities Press, 1969, orig. pub. 1898); C. C. Boone, *Liberia As I Know It* (New York: Negro Universities Press, 1970, orig. pub. 1929); Amanda Smith, *An Autobiography: The Story of the Lord's Dealings with Mrs. Amanda Smith, the Colored Evangelist*[. . .](Chicago: Meyer, 1893); and Henry Louis Gates, Jr., *Wonders of the African World* (New York: Knopf, 1999), a companion volume to a P.B.S. television documentary of the same name.

An entire book could be written simply on **African American encounters with South Africa,** drawing on such works as Levi J. Coppin, *Observations of Persons and Things in South Africa, 1900–1904* (Philadelphia: A.M.E. Book Concern, 1905); Fanny Jackson Coppin, *Reminiscences of School Life, and Hints on Teaching* (Philadelphia: A.M.E. Book Concern, 1913); Harry Dean, *The Pedro Gorino: The Adventures of a Negro Sea-Captain in Africa and on the Seven Seas in His Attempt to Found an Ethiopian Empire* (Boston: Houghton-Mifflin, 1929); Amos J. and Luella G. White, *Dawn in Bantuland, an African Expedition*[. . .] (Boston: Christopher Publishing House, 1953); Charlotte Crogman Wright, *Beneath the Southern Cross: An American Bishop's Wife in South Africa* (New York: Exposition Press, 1955); and Robert Edgar (ed.), *An African-American in South Africa: The Travel Notes of Ralph J. Bunche* [. . .] *1937–1938* (Athens: Ohio University Press, 1992).

These travel accounts represent a subset of a wider **tradition of African American writing about Africa.** If this book demonstrates nothing else I hope that it establishes the abiding presence of Africa in the imaginative and intellectual life of African Americans, as well as some of the ways in which the meaning of the continent has changed over time. My own thinking on this theme has been shaped by the work of Wilson Jeremiah Moses, especially his *Afrotopia: The Roots of African American Popular History* (New York: Cambridge, 1998) and *The Golden Age of Black Nationalism, 1850–1925* (Hamden: Archon Books, 1978). See also Adelaide Cromwell and Martin Kilson (eds.), *Apropos of Africa: Sentiments of Negro American Leaders on Africa from the 1800s to the 1950s* (London: Cass, 1969); Adelaide Cromwell, *Dynamics of the African/Afro-American Connection: From Dependency to Self-Reliance* (Washington: Howard University Press, 1987); Sidney J. Lemelle and Robin D. G. Kelley, *Imagining Home: Class, Culture and Nationalism in the African Diaspora* (New York: Verso, 1994); John Cullen Gruesser, *Black on Black: Twentieth-Century African American Writing About Africa* (Lexington: University of Kentucky Press, 2000); John A. Davis (ed.), *Africa Seen by American Negroes* (Paris: Presence Africaine, 1958); and Paul Gilroy, *The Black Atlantic: Modernity and Double Consciousness* (Cambridge, Mass.: Harvard University Press, 1993).

I first learned of **Ayuba Suleiman Diallo,** the subject of the prologue, in Philip Curtin (ed.), *Africa Remembered: Narratives by West Africans from the Era of the Slave Trade* (Madison: University of Wisconsin Press, 1967), which includes excerpts of two contemporary accounts of Job: Thomas Bluett's 1734 *Some Memoirs of the Life of Job, the Son of Solomon the High Priest of Boonda in Africa*[...] and Francis Moore's *Travels into the Inland Parts of Africa*, published in 1738. Ayuba is also the subject of a fine book by Douglas Grant, *The Fortunate Slave: An Illustration of African Slavery in the Early Eighteenth Century* (New York: Oxford University Press, 1968).

Ayuba's strange journey casts light on three of the central themes of this book: the slave trade, race, and antislavery. On the **transatlantic slave trade,** in which Ayuba was both victim and participant, see Philip Curtin, *The Atlantic Slave Trade: A Census* (Madison: University of Wisconsin Press, 1969); Joseph Miller, *Way of Death: Merchant Capitalism and the Angolan Slave Trade, 1730–1830* (Madison: University of Wisconsin Press, 1988); Herbert Klein, *The Atlantic Slave Trade* (New York: Cambridge University Press, 1999); David Eltis, *The Rise of African Slavery in the Americas* (New York: Cambridge University Press, 2000); and Hugh Thomas, *The Slave Trade: The Story of the Atlantic Slave Trade, 1440–1870* (London: Picador, 1997). Research on the trade has been immeasurably enriched by the publication of *The Trans-Atlantic Slave Trade: A Database on CD-ROM* (New York: Cambridge University Press, 1999). A central clearinghouse for all known information about slave voyages, the database includes references to more than 27,000 specific voyages.

The emergence of the transatlantic slave trade had a profound impact on indigenous systems of slavery within Africa, giving rise, in some cases, to new states dedicated to slave raiding. On this process, and on the vexed question of **African participation in the slave trade,** see John Thornton, *Africa and Africans in the Making of the Atlantic World, 1400–1680* (New York: Cambridge, 1992); Ray A. Kea, *Settlements, Trade, and Polities in the Seventeenth-Century Gold Coast* (Baltimore: John Hopkins University Press, 1982); Robin Law, *The Slave Coast of West Africa, 1550–1750: The Impact of the Atlantic Slave Trade on an African Society* (Oxford: Clarendon Press, 1991); and Law, *The Oyo Empire, c. 1600–c. 1836: A West African Imperialism in the Era of the Atlantic Slave Trade* (Oxford: Clarendon Press, 1977).

Ayuba's experience also highlights the emergence of **the idea of race,** a concept that would play a central role in subsequent debates over African repatriation and the prospects for full black citizenship in the United States. As is clear from the text, I continue to hew to the view, now much contested, that our modern conception of biological race is an artifact of the eighteenth century. The classic exposition of this process is Winthrop Jordan, *White Over Black: American Attitudes Toward the Negro, 1550–1812* (Chapel Hill: University of North Carolina, 1968), while the classic example is Thomas Jefferson's *Notes on the State of Virginia* (Boston: Bedford Books, 2002). See also George Fredrickson, *The Black Image in the White Mind: The Debate on Afro-American Character and Destiny, 1817–1914* (New York: Harper and Row, 1970) and Fredrickson, *Racism: A Short History* (Princeton: Princeton University Press, 2002).

If the idea of race represents one of the most momentous developments of the eighteenth century, the rise of **the Anglo-American antislavery movement** represents another. On the American side, the most influential figure in the movement was certainly Anthony Benezet, a French-born convert to Quakerism, who became a one-man antislavery society. Benezet's *Some Historical Account of Guinea: Its Situation, Produce, and the General Disposition of Its Inhabitants* (Philadelphia: Joseph Cruckshank, 1771) had an enduring impact on popular representations of Africa, at least among those opposed to the slave trade. Benezet's counterpart in England was Thomas Clarkson, whose career as an antislavery leader began with a prize-winning student essay at Cambridge University. See *An Essay on the Slavery and Commerce of the Human Species* (London: J. Phillips, 1786) and *History of the Rise, Progress and Accomplishment of the African Slave-trade, by the British Parliament* (London: Longman, 1808). Paul Cuffe carried a copy of the latter book with him when he first traveled to Africa; he later met Clarkson in London.

Adam Hochschild's recent *Bury the Chains: Prophets and Rebels in the Fight to Free an Empire's Slaves* (Boston: Houghton Mifflin, 2005) offers a sweeping narrative history of the abolition movement within the British Empire. It joins a rich historical literature, much of it focused on the historical relationship between antislavery and capitalism. See David B. Davis, *The Problem of Slavery in the Age of Revolution, 1770–1823* (Ithaca: Cornell University Press, 1775), and the rejoinders in Thomas Bender (ed.), *The Antislavery Debate: Capitalism and Antislavery as a Problem in Historical Interpretation* (Berkeley: University of California Press, 1992). See also David Eltis, *Economic Growth and the Ending of the Transatlantic Slave Trade* (New York: Oxford University Press, 1987), Seymour Drescher, *Capitalism and Antislavery: British Mobilization in Comparative Perspective* (New York: Oxford University Press, 1987), and Drescher, *From Slavery to Freedom: Comparative Studies in the Rise and Fall of Atlantic Slavery* (Basingstoke: Macmillan, 1999).

Africans, African Americans, and Afro-Britons all played central roles in the movement to end slavery and the slave trade, a fact that historians have generally been slow to recognize. On blacks and the antislavery movement, see Olaudah Equiano, *The Interesting Narrative and Other Writings* (New York: Penguin, 1995), Ottobah Cugoano, *Thoughts and Sentiments on the Evil and Wicked Traffic of the Slavery and Commerce of the Human Species and Other Writings* (New York: Penguin, 1999), and Ignatius Sancho, *Letters of the Late Ignatius Sancho, an African* (New York: Penguin, 1998). No scholar has done more to recover this long-neglected tradition than Vincent Carretta, though Carretta has also generated fierce controversy through his suggestion that Equiano was not, in fact, African born, as he claimed in his narrative, and thus did not write about the middle passage from personal experience. See Carretta, "Olaudah Equiano or Gustavus Vassa? New Light on an Eighteenth-Century Question of Identity," *Slavery and Abolition* 20:3 (December 1999), pp. 96–105 and Carretta, *Equiano, the African: Biography of a Self-Made Man* (Athens: University of Georgia Press, 2005). Equiano played a central role in the Sierra Leone settlement venture, but withdrew in a dispute with white promoters before the expedition sailed.

The first African emigration initiatives in the United States emerged in New England, particularly in Rhode Island and southeast Massachusetts. Valuable primary sources can be found in William H. Robinson (ed.), *The Proceedings of the Free African Union Society and the African Benevolent Society, Newport, Rhode Island, 1780–1824* (Providence: The Urban League of Rhode Island, 1976), Sidney Kaplan and Emma Nogrady Kaplan, *The Black Presence in the Era of the American Revolution* (Amherst: University of Massachusetts Press, 1989), and *The Works of Samuel Hopkins* (Boston: Doctrinal Tract and Book Society, 1853). *Freedom's Journal*, America's first black newspaper, is now freely available online, courtesy of the Wisconsin Historical Society.

There is a large (and growing) historical literature on **slavery and race in New England** in the colonial and early national periods. Lorenzo Greene, *The Negro in Colonial New England, 1620–1776* (New York: Atheneum, 1968) remains essential, though I have also profited from Joanne Melish, *Disowning Slavery: Gradual Emancipation and "Race" in New England, 1780–1860* (Ithaca: Cornell University Press, 1998); John Saillant, *Black Puritan, Black Republican: The Life and Thought of Lemuel Haynes, 1753–1833* (New York: Oxford University Press, 2003); and John Wood Sweet, *Bodies Politic: Negotiating Race in the American North, 1730–1830* (Baltimore: Johns Hopkins University Press, 2003). On the wider history of free people of color in the antebellum north, see James O. and Lois E. Horton, *In Hope of Liberty: Culture, Community and Protest Among Northern Free Blacks, 1700–1860* (New York: Oxford University Press, 1997) and Patrick Rael, *Black Identity and Protest in the Antebellum North* (Chapel Hill: University of North Carolina Press, 2002).

On **Paul Cuffe,** see Lamont Thomas, *Rise to Be a People: A Biography of Paul Cuffe* (Urbana: University of Illinois Press, 1986). Cuffe's writings are collected in Sheldon H. Harris (ed.), *Paul Cuffe: Black America and the Africa Return* (New York: Simon & Schuster, 1972) (which corrects and modernizes his spelling and punctuation) and Rosalind Cobb Wiggins (ed.), *Captain Paul Cuffe's Logs and Letters, 1808–1817* (Washington: Howard University Press, 1996).

The standard work on the **founding of Sierra Leone** is still Christopher Fyfe, *A History of Sierra Leone* (New York: Oxford University Press, 1962). See also Fyfe (ed.), *'Our Children Free and Happy': Letters from Black Settlers in Africa in the 1790s* (Edinburgh: Edinburgh University Press, 1991) and Lamin Sanneh, *Abolitionists Abroad: American Blacks and the Making of Modern West Africa* (Cambridge: Harvard University Press, 1999). On subsequent waves of settlers from Nova Scotia and Jamaica, see Ellen Gibson Wilson, *The Loyal Blacks* (New York: G. P. Putnam and Sons, 1976) and Mavis C. Campbell, *Back to Africa: George Ross and the Maroons from Nova Scotia to Sierra Leone* (Trenton: Africa World Press, 1993).

For the **history of antebellum African emigration and colonization efforts,** Floyd J. Miller, *The Search for Black Nationality: Black Emigration and Colonization, 1787–1863* (Urbana: University of Illinois Press, 1975) remains the essential work. See also Philip J. Staudenraus, *The African Colonization Movement, 1816–1865* (New York: Columbia University Press, 1961), which offers the best overview of the founding and evolution of the American Colonization Society. The papers of the A.C.S. are deposited at the Library of Congress. Its periodical, *The African Repository,* is widely available on microfilm.

The **founding and settlement of Liberia** has produced a raft of books, starting with Ralph Randolph Gurley, *Life of Jehudi Ashmun, Late Colonial Agent in Liberia* (New York: Negro Universities Press, 1969, orig. pub. 1835). Recent works include Tom Schick, *Behold the Promised Land: A History of Afro-American Settler Society in Nineteenth-Century Liberia* (Baltimore: Johns Hopkins University Press, 1980); Amos J. Beyan, *The American Colonization Society and the Creation of the Liberian State: A Historical Perspective, 1822–1900* (Lanham, Md.: University Press of America, 1991); Catherine Reef, *This Is Our Country: The American Settlers of Liberia* (New York: Clarion Books, 2002); Claude A. Clegg, III, *The Price of Liberty: African Americans and the Making of Liberia* (Chapel Hill: University of North Carolina Press, 2004); and Alan Huffman, *Mississippi in Africa: The Saga of the Slaves of Prospect Hill Plantation and Their Legacy in Liberia Today* (New York: Gotham Books, 2005).

Much about the life of Daniel Coker remains uncertain. This account draws chiefly on Daniel A. Payne, *History of the African Methodist Episcopal Church* (Nashville: A.M.E. Sunday School Union, 1891), David Smith, *Biography of the Rev. David Smith* (Freeport: Books for Libraries Press, 1971, orig. pub. 1881), and Christopher Phillips, *Freedom's Port: The African American Community of Baltimore, 1790–1860* (Urbana: University of Illinois Press, 1997). See also James T. Campbell, *Songs of Zion: The African Methodist Episcopal Church in the United States and South Africa* (New York: Oxford University Press, 1995). In addition to the African journals discussed in chapter one, Coker left a handful of essays and sermons, including *A Dialogue Between a Virginian and an African Minister* [. . .] *1810,* in Dorothy Porter (ed.), *Negro Protest Pamphlets* (New York: Arno Press, 1969), and "Sermon Delivered Extempore in the African Bethel Church in the City of Baltimore[. . .]", in Herbert Aptheker (ed.), *A Documentary History of the Negro People in the United States,* volume 1 (Secaucus, N.J.: The Citadel Press, 1951).

Martin Robison Delany enjoyed a brief scholarly vogue in the 1960s, when he was hailed as the founding father of black nationalism, but he has yet to receive the attention he deserves, particularly compared to his contemporary and rival, Frederick Douglass, who has spawned an academic cottage industry. With the recent publication of a volume of his collected works, that may change. See Robert S. Levine (ed.), *Martin R. Delany: A Documentary Reader* (Chapel Hill: University of North Carolina Press, 2003), as well as Levine, *Martin Delany, Frederick Douglass, and the Politics of Representative Identity* (Chapel Hill: University of North Carolina Press, 1997). There is also much useful material in Dorothy Sterling, *The Making of an Afro-American: Martin Robison Delany, 1812–1885* (Garden City N.Y.: Doubleday, 1971), and Nell Irvin Painter, "Martin R. Delany: Elitism and Black Nationalism," in Leon Litwack and August Meier (eds.), *Black Leaders of the Nineteenth Century* (Urbana: University of Illinois Press, 1988). Delany himself actively collaborated in the production of his first biography, Frank A. Rollins, *Life and Public Services of Martin R. Delany* (New York: Kraus Reprint, 1969, orig. pub. 1868). The book is not always reliable about his antebellum career, but it is wonderfully revealing of his efforts to reposition himself politically in the early years of Reconstruction.

Delany was only one of a group of antebellum black leaders advocating African emigration. While in Liberia, he met two of the most celebrated: Alexander Crummell and Edward Blyden. On Crummell, see Wilson Jeremiah Moses, *Alexander Crummell: A Study of Civilization and Discontent* (New York: Oxford University Press, 1989) and Moses (ed.), *Destiny and Race: Selected Writings of Alexander Crummell, 1840–1898* (Amherst: University of Massachusetts Press, 1992). On Blyden, see Hollis R. Lynch, *Edward Wilmot Blyden: Pan-Negro Patriot, 1832–1912* (New York: Oxford University Press, 1967) and Lynch, *Black Spokesman: Selected Published Writings of Edward Wilmot Blyden* (New York: Humanities Press, 1971). Blyden's thinking about Africa and African culture changed dramatically over the course of more than a half century on the continent. Compare his *Liberia's Offering: The Call of Providence to the Descendants of Africa in America* (New York: John A. Gray, 1862) with his *African Life and Customs* (London: C.M. Phillips, 1908).

In the antebellum period in particular, the path to Africa for African Americans often ran through England. On the English reception of Africans and African Americans, see Richard

Blackett, "In Search of International Support for African Colonization: Martin R. Delany's Visit to England, 1860," *Canadian Journal of History* 10:3 (1975), pp. 307–24; and Blackett, *Building an Antislavery Wall: Black Americans in the Atlantic Abolition Movement, 1830–1860* (Baton Rouge: Lousiana State University Press, 1983). Blackett has also produced the only scholarly account of Robert Campbell, Delany's less celebrated traveling companion; see *Beating Against the Barriers: Biographical Essays in Nineteenth-Century Afro-American History* (Baton Rouge: Louisiana State University Press, 1986).

On the life of Henry Turner, see Stephen Ward Angell, *Bishop Henry McNeal Turner and African American Religion in the South* (Knoxville: University of Tennessee Press, 1992) and John Dittmer, "The Education of Henry McNeal Turner," in Litwack and Meier (eds.), *Black Leaders of the Nineteenth Century*. Turner's writings are collected in Edwin S. Redkey (ed.), *Respect Black: The Writings and Speeches of Henry McNeal Turner* (New York: Arno Press, 1971). See also *Voice of Missions* (1893–1901) and *The Voice of the People* (1901–1903), both of which served as broadsheets for Turner's views.

The standard work on the postbellum back-to-Africa movement is still Edwin S. Redkey, *Black Exodus: Black Nationalist and Back-to-Africa Movements, 1890–1910* (New Haven: Yale University Press, 1969). I have also relied on Kenneth C. Barnes, *Journey of Hope: The Back-to-Africa Movement in Arkansas in the Late 1800s* (Chapel Hill: University of North Carolina Press, 2004), which examines the state that produced the largest number of would-be emigrants. On the African American church during Reconstruction, see Clarence Walker, *A Rock in a Weary Land: The African Methodist Episcopal Church During the Civil War and Reconstruction* (Baton Rouge: Louisiana State University Press, 1982), William G. Montgomery, *Under Their Own Vine and Fig Tree: The African-American Church in the South, 1865–1900* (Baton Rouge: Louisiana State University Press, 1993), and Paul Harvey, *Redeeming the South: Religious Cultures and Racial Identities Among Southern Baptists, 1865–1925* (Chapel Hill: University of North Carolina Press, 1997).

The best sources on the nineteenth-century African American mission movement are the accounts of the missionaries themselves, including not only published memoirs but the endless letters and solicitations that appeared in the newspapers and magazines of churches and mission societies. The ideology of the movement is limpidly displayed in L. G. Jordan, *Up the Ladder in Foreign Missions* (Nashville: National Baptist Publishing Board, 1903) and J. W. E. Bowen (ed.), *Africa and the American Negro: Addresses and Proceedings of the Congress on Africa* [. . .] *1895* (Atlanta: Gammon Theological Seminary, 1896). See also Walter L. Williams, *Black Americans and the Evangelization of Africa, 1877–1930* (Madison: University of Wisconsin Press, 1982) and Sylvia Jacobs (ed.), *Black Americans and the Missionary Movement in Africa* (Westport: Greenwood Press, 1982). On the role of women in the mission movement, see Jacobs, "Their Special Mission: Afro-American Women as Missionaries to the Congo, 1894–1937," in *Black Americans and the Missionary Movement in Africa* and Jacobs, "Say African When You Pray: The Activities of Early Black Baptist Women Missionaries Among Liberian Women and Children," in Darlene Clark Hine (ed.), *Black Women in American History: The Twentieth Century*, volume 3 (Brooklyn: Carlson Publishing, 1993).

Much of what is known about genocide in King Leopold's Congo Free State comes from sources from the period, many of them produced by E. D. Morel, one of the guiding forces of the Congo Reform Association. See his *Black Man's Burden* (New York: B. W. Huebsch, 1920), *Red Rubber: The Story of the Rubber Slave Trade Flourishing on the Congo in the Year of Grace 1906* (New York: Negro Universities Press, 1969, orig. pub. 1906), and *King Leopold's Rule in Africa* (London: W. Heinemann, 1904), as well as weekly issues of the *African Mail*, which he edited from 1907 to 1916. See also Roger Casement, *Correspondence and Report of His Majesty's Counsel at Boma Regarding the Administration of the Independent State of the Congo* (London: Heinemann, 1904), Wilfred Gilbert Thesiger, *The Enslavement and Destruction of the Bakuba, by the "Kasai Trust"* [...] *1909* (London: The Congo Reform Association, 1909), and Mark Twain's satirical *King Leopold's Soliloquy: A Defense of His Congo Rule* (London: Unwin, 1907).

The history of the **international movement to halt the atrocities in the Congo** is revealed in Adam Hochschild, *King Leopold's Ghost: A Story of Greed, Terror, and Heroism in Colonial Africa* (Boston: Houghton Mifflin, 1998) and Stanley Shaloff, *Reform in Leopold's Congo* (Richmond: John Knox Press, 1970). On the BaKuba people "discovered" by William Sheppard, see Jan Vansina, *The Children of Woot: A History of the Kuba People* (Madison: University of Wisconsin, 1978). John Hope Franklin's *George Washington Williams: A Biography* (Chicago: University of Chicago Press, 1985) recounts the career of another African American who exposed atrocities in Leopold's Congo, a man whose career was in some ways even more unlikely than that of William Sheppard. Phillips Verner Bradford and Harvey Blume, *Ota Benga: The Pygmy in the Zoo* (New York: St. Martin's Press, 1992) recounts the relationship of the ill-fated Batwa man with Sheppard's one-time colleague, Samuel Verner.

After decades in historical obscurity, **William Sheppard** is experiencing something of a revival. Featured in Hochschild's *King Leopold's Ghost,* he is also the subject of two recent biographies, William E. Phipps, *William Sheppard: Congo's African Livingstone* (Louisville: Geneva Press, 2002) and Pagan Kennedy, *Black Livingstone: A True Tale of Adventure in the Nineteenth-Century Congo* (New York: Viking, 2002). He also features prominently in Robert Benedetto (ed.), *Presbyterian Reformers in Central Africa: A Documentary Account of the American Presbyterian Congo Mission and the Human Rights Struggle in the Congo, 1890–1918* (London: E. J. Brill, 1996). For Sheppard's own account of his career, see his *Presbyterian Pioneers in Congo* (Richmond: Presbyterian Committee of Publication, 1917). I have also relied on articles and speeches by Sheppard and his colleagues in *The Southern Workman,* which was published at his alma mater, Hampton Institute.

African American history has been shaped by three massive demographic movements: the transatlantic slave trade; the interstate slave trade (a phenomenon fully as disruptive of black family life as the more studied transatlantic traffic); and the Great Migration of the twentieth century. The process of northern migration, urbanization, and ghettoization has attracted a large scholarly literature, much of it focused on Chicago and New York, the premier destinations for southern migrants. See, for example, Gilbert Osofsky, *Harlem: The Making of a Ghetto* (New York: Harper and Row, 1966), Allan Spear, *Black Chicago: The Making of a Negro Ghetto, 1890–1920* (Chicago: University of Chicago Press, 1969), and James R. Grossman, *Land of Hope: Chicago, Black Southerners, and the Great Migration* (Chicago: University of Chicago Press, 1989). Joe Trotter (ed.), *The Great Migration: New Dimensions of Race, Class and Gender* (Bloomington: Indiana University Press, 1991) includes essays on a number of other northern destinations. Inevitably, migration set in train new political solidarities and struggles; see Eric Arneson (ed.), *Black Protest and the Great Migration* (Boston: Bedford, 2003).

The Harlem Renaissance has had a curious scholarly history. During the heyday of the black arts movement of the 1960s, the literature of the Renaissance era was widely disdained as inauthentic, but more recently it has experienced a renaissance of its own. Nathan Huggins, *Harlem Renaissance* (New York: Oxford University Press, 1971) and David Levering Lewis, *When Harlem Was in Vogue* (New York: Random House, 1981) remain essential. More recent studies include Houston A. Baker, *Modernism and the Harlem Renaissance* (Chicago: University of Chicago Press, 1987); Cary D. Wintz, *Black Culture and the Harlem Renaissance* (Houston: Rice University Press, 1988); James De Jongh, *Vicious Modernism: Black Harlem and the Literary Imagination* (New York: Cambridge University Press, 1990); J. Martin Favor, *Authentic Blackness: The Folk in the New Negro Renaissance* (Durham: Duke University Press, 1999); and Martha Nadell, *Enter the New Negro: Images of Race in American Culture* (Cambridge: Harvard University Press, 2004).

Several recent books have tried, in different ways, to situate the New Negro movement in the context of wider transformations in American intellectual, cultural, and literary life in the post–World War I era. I have drawn on three in particular: Ann Douglas, *Terrible Honesty: Mongrel Manhattan in the 1920s* (New York: Farrar, Straus and Giroux, 1995); George Hutchinson, *The Harlem Renaissance in Black and White* (Cambridge: Harvard University Press, 1995); and Matthew Guterl, *The Color of Race in America, 1900–1940* (Cambridge: Harvard University Press, 2001).

On **changing understandings of race** in the early twentieth century see George Stocking, *Race, Culture and Evolution: Essays in the History of Anthropology* (New York: The Free Press, 1968) and Lee D. Baker, *From Savage to Negro: Anthropology and the Construction of Race, 1896–1954* (Berkeley: University of California, 1998). Franz Boas, *Race and Democratic Society* (New York: Biblo and Tannen, 1969, orig. pub. 1945) provides a compilation of Boas's writings on race, compiled by his son. Vernon Williams, *Rethinking Race: Franz Boas and His Contemporaries* (Lexington: University of Kentucky Press, 1996) explores Boas's impact on African American intellectuals, while also revealing his failure to break completely with older traditions of racial anthropometry.

My account of **Langston Hughes** rests chiefly on the poet's own writings, particularly his two-volume autobiography, *The Big Sea: An Autobiography* (New York: Thunder's Mouth Press, 1986, orig. pub. 1940) and *I Wonder As I Wander* (New York: Thunder's Mouth Press, 1986, orig. pub. 1956). Excerpts from poems are taken from Arnold Rampersad (ed.), *The Collected Poems of Langston Hughes* (New York: Knopf, 1994). I have also relied on Rampersad's extraordinary biography, as close to a definitive account of the poet's life as we are ever likely to have. See Arnold Rampersad, *The Life of Langston Hughes (Volume I: 1902–1941): I, Too, Sing America* (New York: Oxford University Press, 1986) and Rampersad, *The Life of Langston Hughes (Volume II: 1941–1967): I Dream a World*, second edition (New York: Oxford University Press, 2002). Emily Bernard (ed.), *Remember Me to Harlem: The Letters of Langston Hughes and Carl Van Vechten, 1925–1964* (New York: Knopf, 2001) illuminates one of the century's most curious and enduring friendships.

The chief source on the life of W. E. B. Du Bois is Du Bois himself, who published two full-length autobiographies: *Dusk of Dawn: Toward an Autobiography of a Race Concept* (New York: Harcourt, Brace and Co., 1940) and *The Autobiography of W.E.B. Du Bois: A Soliloquy on Viewing My Life from the Last Decade of Its First Century* (New York: International Publishers, 1968). Several other books contain autobiographical information, including *The Souls of Black Folk* (Boston: Bedford, 1997, orig. pub. 1903); *Darkwater: Voices from Within the Veil* (New York: Harcourt, Brace and Howe, 1920); and *In Battle for Peace: The Story of My 83rd Birthday* (New York: Masses and Mainstream, 1952). To these are added literally thousands of essays, articles, and speeches, and nearly a hundred microfilm reels of personal papers, almost a quarter million pages in all.

Given the sheer volume of the record, one can say with confidence that no one, living or dead, has read everything that Du Bois wrote, but two people have come close: Herbert Aptheker, his literary executor and editor of his published works, and David Levering Lewis, his biographer. See Lewis, *W.E.B. Du Bois: Biography of a Race, 1868–1919* (New York: Henry Holt and Co., 1993) and *W.E.B. Du Bois: The Fight for Equality and the American Century, 1919–1963* (New York: Henry Holt and Co., 2000). I have relied extensively on both volumes of the biography, though my account of Du Bois's visit to Liberia rests chiefly on the articles and letters that he wrote at the time.

George S. Schuyler may be the only African American in history whose total literary output rivals that of Du Bois. The account of him here rests chiefly on his published writings, including his syndicated six-part series on "Slavery in Liberia," published in the New York *Evening Post* and other newspapers in 1931; various columns and articles in *The Messenger, American Mercury,* and *The Pittsburgh Courier;* and two published novels, *Black No More* (New York: The Modern Library, 1999, orig. pub. 1931) and *Slaves Today: A Story of Liberia* (New York: Brewer, Warren, and Putnam, 1931). Schuyler also authored several serialized novels under the pseudonym Samuel Brooks, which have only recently been revealed to be his work; see *Black Empire* (Boston: Northeastern University Press, 1991) and *Ethiopian Stories* (Boston: Northeastern University Press, 1994).

My account of Schuyler also draws on a trio of biographies, the most important of which is Jeffrey B. Ferguson, "The Newest Negro: George Schuyler's Intellectual Quest in the 1920s and Beyond," Ph.D. dissertation, Harvard University, 1998. A revised version of the dissertation has recently been published, but unfortunately it appeared too late for me to consult; see Ferguson, *The Sage of Sugar Hill: George S. Schuyler and the Harlem Renaissance* (New Haven: Yale University Press, 2005.) There is also much useful information and interpretation in Harry McKinley Williams, "When Black Is Right: The Life and Writings of George S. Schuyler," Ph.D. dissertation, Brown University, 1988 and Michael W. Peplow, *George S. Schuyler* (Boston: Twayne, 1980).

Schuyler's own autobiography, *Black and Conservative: The Autobiography of George S. Schuyler* (New Rochelle: Arlington House Publishers, 1966) is a lively read but it is also distinctly unreliable, essentially rendering his entire life as an exemplary tale of sensible conservatism. See also Kathryn Talalay, *Composition in Black and White: The Life of Philippa Schuyler* (New York: Oxford University Press, 1995), which recounts the strange and disturbing story of Schuyler's only child.

Historian Ibrahim Sundiata has produced two fine books reconstructing the **Liberian labor scandal** and the wider context from which it emerged; see *Black Scandal: America and the Liberian Labor Crisis, 1929–1936* (Philadelphia: Institute for the Study of Human Issues, 1980) and *Brothers and Strangers: Black Zion, Black Slavery, 1914–1940* (Durham, N.C.: Duke University Press, 2003). See also Charles Johnson, *Bitter Canaan: The Story of the Negro Republic* (New Brunswick: Transaction Publishers, 1987), which recounts Johnson's experience as a member of the League of Nations' commission investigating the charges against Liberia.

Though his literary reputation has waned a bit in the last decade or two, **Richard Wright** remains one of most widely read and highly regarded American writers of the twentieth century. In preparing my account of Wright, I have drawn not only on his own autobiography *Black Boy: A Record of Childhood and Youth*, restored text (New York: HarperPerennial, 1993, orig. pub. 1945) but also on several fine biographies, including: Hazel Rowley, *Richard Wright: The Life and Times* (New York: Henry Holt, 2001); Michel Fabre, *The Unfinished Quest of Richard Wright*, second edition (Urbana: University of Illinois Press, 1993); Margaret Walker, *Richard Wright: Daemonic Genius* (New York: Warner Books, 1988); and Constance Webb, *Richard Wright: A Biography* (New York: Putnam, 1968).

The best introduction to **the Chicago School of sociology** is Louis Wirth's "Urbanism as a Way of Life," which originally appeared in the *American Journal of Sociology* in 1938 and is reprinted in Richard T. LeGates and Frederic Stout (eds.), *The City Reader*, second edition (New York: Routledge, 2000). See also Wirth, *The Ghetto* (Chicago: University of Chicago Press, 1928) and Robert Park, Ernst W. Burgess, and Roderick McKenzie, *The City* (Chicago: Chicago University Press, 1925). On the marginal man concept, see Everett V. Stonequist, *The Marginal Man: A Study in Personality and Culture Conflict* (New York: Scribner's, 1937). Wright carried a copy of Stonequist's book with him to the Gold Coast and it clearly shaped his reactions to what he saw.

Wright's debt to the Chicago School is most palpable in his book *Twelve Million Black Voices* (New York: Viking, 1941). The book was based, in part, on sociological data collected by St. Clair Drake and Horace Cayton for their classic *Black Metropolis: A Study of Negro Life in a Northern City*, two volumes (New York: Harcourt Brace and Co., 1945). Wright wrote the introduction for *Black Metropolis*, in which he discussed his debt to the Chicago School. See also Carla Cappetti, "Sociology of an Existence: Wright and the Chicago School," in Henry Louis Gates, Jr., and K. Anthony Appiah, *Richard Wright: Critical Perspectives, Past and Present* (New York: Amistad, 1993).

On Wright's visit to the Gold Coast, see *Black Power: A Record of Reactions in a Land of Pathos* (New York: Harper and Brothers, 1954). See also his unpublished Gold Coast journal, papers of Richard Wright, Beinecke Library, Yale University, box 22, folders 337–347. Compared to works like *Native Son* and *Black Boy*, *Black Power* has received relatively little critical attention. Among the works that I found helpful were: Jack B. Moore, "Black Power Revisited: In Search of Richard Wright," *Mississippi Quarterly* 38:2 (1988), pp. 168–86; K. Anthony Appiah, "A Long Way From Home: Wright in the Gold Coast," in Arnold Rampersad (ed.), *Richard Wright: A Collection of Critical Essays* (Englewood Cliffs: Prentice Hall, 1995); and Paul Gilroy, *The Black Atlantic: Modernity and Double Consciousness* (Cambridge: Harvard University Press, 1993).

Much less has been written about **Era Bell Thompson**. The account here is based chiefly on four sources: Thompson, *American Daughter* (St. Paul: Minnesota Historical Society Press, 1986, orig. pub. 1946), a memoir of her upbringing in North Dakota; Thompson, *Africa: Land of My Fathers* (Garden City: Doubleday & Co., 1954); "Interview with Era Bell Thompson," in Edmonds Hill (ed.), *The Black Women Oral History Project* (Westport: Meckler Publishing, 1978), volume 9; and Thompson's many stories in *Ebony* magazine, where she worked for nearly forty years. On the **origins and character of** *Ebony*, see Ben Burns, *Nitty Gritty: A White Editor in Black Journalism* (Jackson: University Press of Mississippi, 1996) and John H. Johnson and Lerone Bennett, *Succeeding Against the Odds* (New York: Warner Books, 1989). See also Robert E. Weems, *Desegregating the Dollar: African American Consumerism in the Twentieth Century* (New York: New York University Press, 1998).

All discussions of **the African American expatriate community in Nkrumah's Ghana** will henceforth begin with Kevin Gaines, *American Africans in Ghana: Black Expatriates and the Civil Rights Era* (Chapel Hill: University of North Carolina Press, 2006). I am deeply grateful to Professor Gaines for permitting me to read and reference the book while it was still in manuscript.

Several **members of the expatriate community** have published memoirs of their days in Ghana. See David Levering Lewis, "Ghana, 1963: A Memoir," *The American Scholar* 68:1 (Winter, 1999); Maya Angelou, *All God's Children Need Traveling Shoes* (New York: Random House, 1986); Leslie Alexander Lacy, *The Rise and Fall of a Proper Negro* (New York: Macmillan, 1970); and Bill Sutherland and Matt Meyer, *Guns and Gandhi in Africa: Pan-African Insights on Nonviolence, Armed Struggle, and Liberation* (Trenton: Africa World Press, 2000). (For the story of Sutherland's African ancestor, Scipio Vaughan, see Era Bell Thompson, "The Vaughan Family: A Tale of Two Continents," *Ebony*, February 1975, pp. 53–64.) Julian Mayfield did not publish a memoir, but he did write a thinly fictionalized short story about some of his experiences in Ghana; see "Black on Black: A Political Love Story," in Mayfield (ed.), *Ten Times Black: Stories from the Black Experience* (New York: Bantam Books, 1972).

I had the privilege of interviewing a few members of the expatriate community about their experiences. I am grateful to Robert Lee, Bill Sutherland, Ray Kea, and the late St. Clair Drake for their generosity and patience. I have also relied on Ernest Dunbar (ed.), *The Black Expatriates: A Study of American Negroes in Exile* (New York: E. P. Dutton & Co., 1968), which includes transcripts of interviews of several expatriates; and on "Conversations with St. Clair Drake," a videorecording of more than ten hours of interviews with St. Clair Drake, conducted in October 1980. The recording is deposited in the Media Center of the Northwestern University Library.

The most celebrated member of the expatriate community was, of course, W. E. B. Du Bois. Du Bois's experience in Ghana is discussed in the final chapter of David Levering Lewis's biography; see also Leslie Lacy, *Cheer the Lonesome Traveler: The Life of W.E.B. Du Bois* (New York: Dial, 1970) and Shirley Graham Du Bois, *His Day Is Marching On: A Memoir of W.E.B. Du Bois* (Philadelphia: Lippincott, 1971). On Alphaeus Hunton, see Dorothy Hunton, *Alphaeus Hunton: The Unsung Valiant* (New York: D. K. Hunton, 1986). Hunton's own *Decision in Africa: Sources of Current Conflict* (New York: International Publishers, 1957) is an extraordinary piece of scholarship, which, like its author, has been all but forgotten today.

BIBLIOGRAPHIC ESSAY · 487

The neglect of **George Padmore,** one of the towering figures of black history, is even more egregious. There is one biography, James R. Hooker's *Black Revolutionary: George Padmore's Path From Communism to Pan-Africanism* (New York: Praeger, 1967), as well as C. L. R. James's unpublished "Notes on the Life of George Padmore" (n.p., n.d., unpublished typescript, Northwestern University Library), but further research is urgently needed. Padmore's own books still reward reading. See Padmore, *How Britain Rules Africa* (London: Wishart Books, 1936); Padmore, *Gold Coast Revolution: The Struggle of an African People from Slavery to Freedom* (London: D. Dobson, 1953); and Padmore, *Pan-Africanism or Communism: The Coming Struggle for Africa* (London: D. Dobson, 1956). It is not fashionable these days to emphasize the historical significance of so-called great men, but events in Ghana might have unfolded quite differently had Padmore survived longer.

Kwame Nkrumah's rise and fall is examined in a host of books, some written by scholars, others by individuals who worked alongside him. For a sampling of this wide-ranging literature, see Geoffrey Bing, *Reap the Whirlwind: An Account of Kwame Nkrumah's Ghana from 1950 to 1966* (London: MacGibbon and Kee, 1968); Basil Davidson, *Black Star: A View of the Life and Times of Kwame Nkrumah* (New York: Praeger, 1974); C. L. R. James, *Nkrumah and the Gold Coast Revolution* (London: Allison and Busby, 1977); Jean Allman, *The Quills of the Porcupine: Asante Nationalism in an Emergent Ghana* (Madison: University of Wisconsin Press, 1993); and Richard Rathbone, *Nkrumah and the Chiefs: The Politics of Chieftaincy in Ghana, 1951–1960* (Athens: Ohio University Press, 2000). Nkrumah himself wrote extensively on the subject; see *Ghana: The Autobiography of Kwame Nkrumah* (New York: International Publishers, 1971, orig. pub. 1957) and *Dark Days in Ghana* (London: Panaf, 1976), which was written in exile in Conakry and published posthumously.

Several recent books examine the relationship of **the African American freedom struggle and the Cold War,** an intersection of fundamental significance to the experience of African American expatriates in Ghana. Among the most important are Penny Von Eschen, *Race Against Empire: Black Americans and Anticolonialism, 1937–1957* (Ithaca: Cornell University Press, 1997); Mary Dudziak, *Cold War Civil Rights: Race and the Image of American Democracy* (Princeton: Princeton University Press, 2000); Brenda Gayle Plummer, *Rising Wind: Black Americans and U.S. Foreign Affairs* (Chapel Hill: University of North Carolina Press, 1996); James H. Meriwether, *Proudly We Can Be Africans: Black Americans and Africa, 1935–1961* (Chapel Hill: University of North Carolina Press, 2002); and Thomas Borstelmann, *The Cold War and the Color Line: American Race Relations in the Global Arena* (Cambridge: Harvard University Press, 2001).

Chapter nine is based chiefly on the memoirs of the three journalists who covered Africa in the 1990s: see Keith B. Richburg, *Out of America: A Black Man Confronts Africa* (New York: Basic Books, 1997); Lynne Duke, *Mandela, Mobutu, and Me: A Newswoman's African Journey* (New York: Doubleday, 2003); and Howard French, *A Continent for the Taking: The Tragedy and Hope of Africa* (New York: Knopf, 2004). I have also profited from the growing scholarly literature on the **collapse of postcolonial African states,** including Jeffrey Herbst, *States and Power in Africa: Comparative Lessons in Authority and Control* (Princeton: Princeton University Press, 2000); William Reno, *Warlord Politics and African States* (London: Lynne Rienner Publishers, 1998); Jean-Francois Bayart, *The Criminalization of the State in Africa*

(Bloomington: Indiana University Press, 1999); and Mark Beissinger and Crawford Young (eds.), *Beyond State Crisis? Postcolonial Africa and Post-Soviet Eurasia in Comparative Perspective* (Baltimore: Johns Hopkins University Press, 2002).

Several works have helped to contextualize what Richburg, Duke, and French saw in the specific countries that they covered. On **Congo/Zaire**, see Crawford Young, *Politics in the Congo: Decolonization and Independence* (Princeton: Princeton University Press, 1965) and Crawford Young and Thomas Turner, *The Rise and Decline of the Zairian State* (Madison: University of Wisconsin Press, 1985). On **Somalia**, see Walter Clarke and Jeffrey Herbst (eds.), *Learning from Somalia: The Lessons of Armed Humanitarian Intervention* (Boulder: Westview Press, 1997). On **Rwanda**, see Peter Uvin, *Aiding Violence: The Development Enterprise in Rwanda* (West Hartford: Kumarian Press, 1998) and Philip Gourevitch, *We Wish to Inform You That Tomorrow We Will Be Killed with Our Families* (New York: Farrar, Straus and Giroux, 1998). Howard French is extremely critical of Gourevitch's book, or at least of the uses to which it was put by American policy makers, who routinely cited it to justify their inaction in the face of the growing Hutu refugee crisis following the Rwandan invasion of Zaire.

The careers of Richburg, Duke, and French also symbolize the rapid growth of the African American middle class in the late twentieth century, a process whose long-term significance for American politics has not yet been fully determined. The ambiguities of this group's position are explored in Mary Pattillo-McCoy, *Black Picket Fences: Privilege and Peril Among the Black Middle Class* (Chicago: University of Chicago Press, 1999). The obverse side of the process of black middle class formation, of course, is deindustrialization, which has ravaged the black working class, nowhere more dramatically than in Keith Richburg's Detroit; see Thomas Sugrue, *The Origins of the Urban Crisis: Race and Inequality in Postwar Detroit* (Princeton: Princeton University Press, 1996). All these processes—the end of legal Jim Crow and the extension of voting rights to African Americans; deindustrialization; and the emergence of a black middle class—have had a dramatic impact on contemporary African American politics; see Adolph Reed, *Stirrings in the Jug: Black Politics in the Post-Segregation Era* (Minneapolis: University of Minnesota Press, 1999).

The implications of middle class formation for African Americans' relationship with Africa are most apparent in the rise of the black heritage tourism industry. Several recent works examine this phenomenon, including Edward M. Bruner, "Tourism in Ghana: The Representation of Slavery and the Return of the Black Diaspora," *American Anthropologist* 92:2 (1996), pp. 290–304; Theresa A. Singleton, "The Slave Trade Remembered on the Former Gold and Slave Coasts," *Slavery and Abolition* 20:1 (1999), pp. 150–69; Paulla Ebron, "Tourists as Pilgrims: Commercial Fashioning of Transatlantic Politics," *American Ethnologist* 26:4 (2000), pp. 910–32; and J. Martin Favor, "What's a Million Dollars to Michael Jackson? Authentic Culture and Commercial Tourism," *Souls*, Spring 2001, pp. 28–37.

The story of Priscilla and the slave ship *Hare* was unearthed by Edward Ball; see his *Slaves in the Family* (New York: Ballantine Books, 1998). The Rhode Island roots of the tale are recounted in Paul Davis, "Priscilla: A Slave Story," *Providence Journal*, February 13–15, 2005. On Priscilla's homecoming, see Herb Frazier, "Sierra Leoneans Welcome Home Priscilla's Spirit: North Charleston Woman Walks Ground of Ancestor's Homeland,"

Charleston Post and Courier, May 29, 2005. The film of Priscilla's homecoming is still in production. For films of previous homecomings, see *Family Across the Sea* (San Francisco: California Newsreel, 1990) and *The Language You Cry In* (San Francisco: California Newsreel, 1999).

Several other works have proved helpful in making sense of present-day Sierra Leone. On the creation of a nationalist pantheon, see A. K. Turay et al., *Sierra Leonean Heroes: Thirty Great Men and Women Who Helped to Build Our Nation* (Freetown, n.p., 1987). On the Kamajors, see Daniel Bergner, *In the Land of Magic Soldiers: A Story of Black and White in Africa* (New York: Farrar, Straus and Giroux, 2003). The destruction of Sierra Leone's capital is hauntingly told in the film *Cry Freetown* (London: Insight News Television, 2000).

· INDEX ·

· PERMISSIONS ·